SLAVERY IN THE LAT

AD 27$

Capitalizing on the rich historical record of late antiquity, and employing sophisticated methodologies from social and economic history, this book re-interprets the end of Roman slavery. Kyle Harper challenges traditional interpretations of a transition from antiquity to the middle ages, arguing instead that a deep divide runs through "late antiquity," separating the Roman slave system from its early medieval successors. In the process, he covers the economic, social, and institutional dimensions of ancient slavery and presents the most comprehensive analytical treatment of a pre-modern slave system now available. By scouring the late antique record, he has uncovered a wealth of new material, providing fresh insights into the ancient slave system, including slavery's role in agriculture and textile production, its relation to sexual exploitation, and the dynamics of social honor. By demonstrating the vitality of slavery into the later Roman empire, the author shows that Christianity triumphed amidst a genuine slave society.

KYLE HARPER is Assistant Professor in the Department of Classics and Letters at the University of Oklahoma, where he teaches a range of courses on Greek and Roman civilization and the rise of Christianity. He has published articles on social and institutional aspects of later Roman history in the *Journal of Roman Studies*, *Classical Quarterly*, and *Historia*.

SLAVERY IN THE LATE ROMAN WORLD,

AD 275–425

KYLE HARPER

CAMBRIDGE
UNIVERSITY PRESS

CAMBRIDGE
UNIVERSITY PRESS

University Printing House, Cambridge CB2 8BS, United Kingdom

Cambridge University Press is part of the University of Cambridge.

It furthers the University's mission by disseminating knowledge in the pursuit of education, learning and research at the highest international levels of excellence.

www.cambridge.org
Information on this title: www.cambridge.org/9781107640818

© Kyle Harper 2011

First published 2011
First paperback edition 2015

A catalogue record for this publication is available from the British Library

Library of Congress Cataloguing in Publication data
Harper, Kyle, 1979–
Slavery in the late Roman world, AD 275–425 / Kyle Harper.
p. cm.
Includes bibliographical references and index.
ISBN 978-0-521-19861-5
1. Slavery – Rome. 2. Social structure – Rome. 3. Rome – Social conditions.
4. Rome – Economic conditions. I. Title.
HT863.H36 2011
306.3′620937 – dc22 2011001066

ISBN 978-0-521-19861-5 Hardback
ISBN 978-1-107-64081-8 Paperback

For Michelle,
Mom, and the
whole family

And the merchants of the earth shall weep and mourn over her; for no man buyeth their merchandise any more: The merchandise of gold, and silver, and precious stones, and of pearls, and fine linen . . . and wine, and oil, and fine flour, and wheat, and beasts, and sheep, and horses, and chariots, and slaves, and souls of men . . .

(John of Patmos, imagining the fall of Rome, Revelation 18
(Authorized Version))

Lest anymore Africa be drained of its own people, and in herds and columns, like an endless river, such a great multitude of both men and women lose their freedom in something even worse than barbarian captivity . . .

(Augustine of Hippo, watching the fall of Rome, New Letters 10)

Contents

Tables

Acknowledgments

This book is a heavily revised version of my 2007 doctoral thesis. Over the years spent working on this project, I have accrued more debts than I can mention, much less ever repay. First on this list are the readers of the dissertation, who have helped me develop the argument and presentation from a very early stage. Brent Shaw was kind enough to serve on an extramural dissertation committee, and then he was generous enough to provide comments whose detail and insight exceeded any call of duty. My supervisors at Harvard deserve special recognition. Christopher Jones was patient beyond measure with a thesis whose virtues never included brevity. I have learned much from his guidance and been inspired by his example as a meticulous scholar. I am grateful for his constant support and friendship. Michael McCormick has been an influential mentor, a generous patron, and a great friend. His enthusiasm is contagious, and I hope I can reflect, even a little bit, his commitment to a rigorous but enterprising brand of scholarship.

I am grateful to the entire team at Cambridge, and I owe special thanks to Michael Sharp, not only for his kind and efficient management of the publication process, but also for selecting such conscientious reviewers for the manuscript. Peter Garnsey is the greatest living authority on ancient slavery, and his generous and gentle suggestions have improved the final product considerably. Noel Lenski is a scholar-saint. He too is working on a study of late antique slavery, and the thoughtful report he gave on my manuscript was truly extraordinary. In innumerable ways, this book is better because Noel combines uncommon erudition with uncommon generosity.

Anyone who has finished graduate school knows how important friends are to survival. Jeff Webb has been a close comrade for many years and has read this manuscript in various forms numerous times. Jonathan Conant was assigned as my "mentor" in my first year of graduate school, and he has helped me ever since. Andrew Kinney made me smarter and provided cynical relief that kept me sane. Daniel Sargent has been my *arbiter elegentiae* in all matters of composition; he repeatedly read large chunks of the manuscript. Greg Smith and Scott Johnson have been trusted advisors throughout, and they remain my closest co-conspirators in the study of the late antique world.

I have been fortunate to have received such strong institutional support while working on this project. Dumbarton Oaks is the greatest scholarly sanctuary in the world, and the bulk of the research for this book was completed during a year as a Junior Fellow there. I thank Alice-Mary Talbot for her patience and support, and I will be eternally grateful to Deb Stewart, whose sharp eye brought to my attention the publication of a certain inscription from Thera. I thank William Harris for organizing the Economics Workshop for Ancient Historians, which fortuitously came just as I was making final revisions. I learned from all of the participants there, but I should single out the help of Ronald Findlay, Walter Scheidel (who has given me valuable advice on many occasions), and Peter Temin, who generously and carefully read parts of the manuscript. I thank the organizers of the Oxford Summer Epigraphy School, especially John Bodel. I am in the debt of Cam Grey, who has read parts of the manuscript and has always shared his ideas and his work. I thank Joachim Henning for teaching me so much about early medieval archaeology in general and slave shackles in particular. I am grateful for the thoughtful guidance of Daniel Smail. I thank Domenico Vera for sharing his work and for thought-provoking correspondence; I have learned much about late Roman slavery from him. I have received hospitality and generous help from both the Mainz Academy and the Groupe International de Recherche sur l'Esclavage dans l'Antiquité in Besançon. I am grateful for the support and friendship of my colleagues at the University of Oklahoma. I became a Roman historian because of Rufus Fears, and I am thankful that I can walk and talk about history with someone who knows so much about the ancient world. Ellen Greene is a great colleague, and she has provided invaluable help as I developed my argument in part II. I am deeply grateful for the support of the Department Chairman, Samuel Huskey. At crucial junctures, Ronald Schleifer has proven a valuable advisor. Thanks are due to the library staff at at the University of Oklahoma, especially for the patience of the interlibrary loan department and the indulgence of the circulation team. I thank the Honors College for funding through its research assistant program, and Jordan Shuart for her careful help with the bibliography. The office of the Vice-President for Research has provided indispensable material support, as has the College of Arts and Sciences. Last but not least, I am so grateful for the friendship and patronage of President David Boren.

Any book, but especially a first book, is the result not just of the author's effort, but of the family whose support makes such effort possible. I am infinitely thankful for my family, whose love, support, and sacrifice made possible college, graduate school, and now the long hours that go into writing. I wish my grandparents, Kenneth and Maxine Hayes, were here to hold the book, because I know how much they would have enjoyed that. Their support meant everything. I dedicate the book to my whole family, to my mom Kay, to my daughter Sylvie, and especially to my wife Michelle, whose love, care, and home cooking sustain me.

PART I

The economy of slavery

Introduction

CONQUEST AND CAPITAL: THE PROBLEM OF SLAVERY IN ROMAN HISTORY

The Roman empire was home to the most extensive and enduring slave system in pre-modern history. Slavery has been virtually ubiquitous in human civilization, but the Romans created one of the few "genuine slave societies" in the western experience.[1] The other example of classical antiquity, the slave society of Greece, was fleeting and diminutive by comparison.[2] Stretching across half a millennium and sprawling over a vast tract of space, Roman slavery existed on a different order of magnitude. Five centuries, three continents, tens of millions of souls: Roman slavery stands as the true ancient predecessor to the systems of mass-scale slavery in the New World. We cannot explain the Roman slave system as the spoils of imperial conquest. Roman slavery was a lasting feature of an entire historical epoch, implicated in the very forces that made the Roman Mediterranean historically exceptional. Military hegemony, the rule of law, the privatization of property, urbanism, the accumulation of capital, an enormous market economy – the circulation of human chattel developed in step with these other characteristic elements of Roman civilization.

This book is a study of slavery in the late Roman empire, over the long fourth century, AD 275–425.[3] Throughout this period, slavery remained

---

[1] Finley 1998 (orig. 1980), 135–60, and 1968. For the usefulness, and limits, of the concept, see chapter 1. For slavery in human history: Davis 2006 and 1966; Hernæs and Iversen 2002; Turley 2000; Patterson 1982.

[2] For Greek slavery: Cartledge 2001 and 1985; Osborne 1995; Fisher 1993; Garlan 1988; Westermann 1955, 1–46.

[3] A selective list of essential contributions to the study of late Roman slavery: Grey forthcoming; Lenski forthcoming, 2009, 2008, and 2006a; Vera 2007, 1999, 1998, and 1995; Wickham 2005a and 1984; Rotman 2004; McCormick 2002 and 2001; Klein 2000 and 1988; Melluso 2000; Nathan 2000, 169–84; Giliberti 1999; Shaw 1998; Grieser 1997; Bagnall 1993; Kontoulis 1993; Samson 1989; De Martino 1988a and 1988b; MacMullen 1987; Whittaker 1987; Finley 1998 (orig. 1980), 191–217; Brockmeyer 1979, 198–235; Dockès 1979; Fikhman 1974 and 1973; Nehlsen 1972; Shtaerman 1964; Seyfarth 1963;

a vigorous institution. The primary spokesmen of the age provide vivid testimony to the importance of slavery. Augustine, bishop of Hippo on the coast of North Africa, could claim that "nearly all households" owned slaves.[4] Eastern church fathers and social critics like John Chrysostom assumed that commercial agriculture, based on slave labor, was the road to riches.[5] Their contemporaries spoke of Roman senators with thousands of slaves toiling in the countryside.[6] The laws, papyri, and inscriptions of the age bear out these claims. An inscription, recently uncovered, lists the names and ages of 152 slaves belonging to a single land-owner in the Aegean.[7] There is not a more concrete, irrefutable artefact of large-scale rural slavery from the entire Roman era. And hundreds of more humble testimonies – a receipt for a Gallic slave boy sold in the east, a reading exercise teaching young boys how to dominate their slaves, a report of a slave who broke down watching his wife being flogged – add historical plausibility and human drama to the story of late Roman slavery.

When and why did the Roman slave system come to an end? These are classic questions, central in the effort to construct grand narratives of transition from antiquity to the middle ages. Did the end of imperial expansion generate a critical deficit of bodies on the slave market, leading inexorably to the decline of the system? Did the contradictions of slave labor force an inevitable crisis in the slave mode of production, ushering in the age of feudalism? This book will answer "no" to both of these traditional propositions. The abundant and credible evidence for slavery in the fourth century sits poorly with any narrative which posits a structural decline or transformation of the slave system before this period. And yet, somehow the slave system of the later Roman empire has always regarded as a system in decline or transition, separate from the age when Roman society was a genuine slave society, when the slave mode of production was dominant in the heartland of the empire. To understand this enduring tension between the evidence and the story of decline, we must appreciate the way that the grand narratives of ancient slavery were formed, and the assumptions their creators made about the nature of slavery, its causes and dynamics.

Verlinden 1955–77; Westermann 1955; Bloch 1975 (orig. 1947); Ciccotti 1899. See Bellen and Heinen 2003, vol. 1, 254–8, for more bibliography.

[4] Aug. Psal. 124.7 (CC 40: 1840–1): *prope omnes domus*. All Greek and Latin translations are my own, unless noted; for Syriac, Hebrew, and Coptic, I signal the translations I have used.
[5] Ioh. Chrys. In Mt. 24.11 (PG 57: 319); Ioh. Chrys. In act. Apost. 32.2 (PG 60: 237).
[6] Ger. Vit. Mel. (lat.) 18.3 (Laurence: 188–90); Pall. H. Laus. 61 (Butler vol. 2: 156); Ioh. Chrys. In Mt. 63.4 (PG 58: 608); Bas. (dub.) Is. 2.89 (PG 30: 264); SHA, Quadr. Tyr. 12.1–2 (Hohl vol. 2: 230).
[7] Harper 2008; Geroussi-Bendermacher 2005.

Let us, as a thought experiment, imagine two versions of the rise and fall of Roman slavery. The first is organized around the role of *conquest*. Having emerged victorious from the Second Punic War, the Romans looked outward and embarked on a campaign for Mediterranean hegemony that lasted two centuries. In the wake of conquest came slaves, the ultimate spoils of empire. Millions of captives flowed into Italy, chained into gangs and forced to work the plantations of the senatorial aristocracy. The small farmer, the backbone of the citizen army, was forced to take part in ever longer campaigns and found himself gradually displaced by slave-based estates. The countryside was overrun with plantations, a process which triggered spasms of servile unrest in Sicily and then the mainland. When the empire reached its boundaries, the expansion of slavery too had reached its limits. The system gradually folded in upon itself. Natural reproduction stalled the decline but also modified the nature of the slave system, as masters allowed slaves to have families, installed them on plots of their own, and treated them more leniently. By the late empire an alternative form of dependent labor was required, and the state complied in the institution of the colonate, a fiscal system tying rural laborers to the land.

Our second model of Roman slavery is organized around *capital* – shorthand for the networks of property and exchange created by Roman law and the Roman economy. In this account, the Roman conquest of the Mediterranean was a hostile takeover of the world system that Greek and Punic empires had prepared. In the crucial second century, the Romans began to create an economy on an unprecedented scale. Roman roads criss-crossed the landmass from Spain to Syria; the sea lanes were cleared of pirates; the populations on the northern shores of the Mediterranean consumed grain from the fertile fields of Africa and Egypt; cities flourished as never before. Wine became the first of history's great cash crops. Urban markets fostered trade and specialized production. Roman slavery matured not because captives of war glutted the western Mediterranean with cheap bodies for sale, but because this new economy created the ability to consume and exploit slave labor on an unprecedented scale. Far from being decadent by the second century AD, the slave system peaked in the *pax Romana*. In this model, the decline of the slave system is not encoded in its very genesis and is thus harder to explain.

These two outlines are caricatures, and if this book will favor the second interpretation, any ancient historian would admit that there is an element of truth in both accounts. The caricatures are useful, though, because they can help us understand the formation of the consensus that Roman slavery was on its downward slope by the time of the late empire. The first version of Roman slavery, the conquest thesis, took shape in an era when economic history lay in the future, when legal, military, and moral themes dominated historical investigation.[8] This narrative of Roman slavery would provide the pattern of rise and fall, the default position. Even as the second, economic model has gained a progressively larger place in the way historians think about ancient slavery, the basic trajectory of rise and fall has scarcely changed. So not only is there a tension between the extensive evidence for slavery in the late empire and the thesis of decline, there is a deeper disjuncture between the thesis of decline and the structural dynamics within which historians describe the trajectory of the Roman slave system. In other words, if capital rather than conquest was a motive force in the Roman slave system, then why has the story of decline been written almost exclusively as though the system were a product of martial expansion?

This tension goes back to the nineteenth century, when the plotline of Roman slavery's rise and fall would be recast in economic terms.[9] Max Weber was the axial figure in this turn. In 1896 he offered the classic formulation of the conquest thesis. In Weber's account, the rise of the Roman empire created a system of slave labor which was a direct outgrowth of imperial conquest. Even the control of slave labor was a continuation of war, organized on plantations that were run as army barracks, with celibate male slaves chained together. The end of conquest, then, was nothing less than "the turning point" of ancient civilization.[10] The end of military expansion catalyzed a process in which the slave supply withered, and consequently the price of labor rose. In turn, the slave system began to mutate internally, as slave-owners allowed slaves to form families, and slaves dissolved into the undifferentiated mass of rural dependents. These changes, in step with the development of the colonate, led to the gradual emergence of medieval serfdom. In his article, Weber compassed nearly every argument which would be made for the decline of slavery over the next century, and its influence would be impossible to overstate.[11] His model takes its reading of the evidence, its assumptions of rise and fall, from a pre-existing mold. And Weber's account suggests that conquest moves capital, creating a "political capitalism" that temporarily displaced

---

[8] Finley 1998 (orig. 1980), 79–134, for the early historiography. Wallon 1847; Biot 1840.

[9] Meyer 1924 (orig. 1898); Weber 1896; Ciccotti 1899. Allard rewrote his work (orig. 1876) specifically to counter the argument that the decline of Roman slavery had economic causes. Specifically the fifth edn., issued in 1914. Mazza 1977, xlii, on this debate between idealism and materialism.

[10] Weber 1896; cf. Meyer 1924 (orig. 1898), 209, when conquest ended, slavery came to a "Stillstand" and then receded.

[11] Mazzarino 1966, 140. Banaji 2001, 24–31, a critical assessment.

the natural, *oikos*-based society; slavery was the core feature of this political capitalism.[12]

In the same period, a detailed Marxist interpretation of ancient slavery was taking shape. Most of Marx's own work on pre-capitalist societies, including Roman history, was embryonic or unpublished; the details were left to Engels and the heirs of the Marxist tradition.[13] The Marxist framework that developed in the late nineteenth century would place Roman slavery within an evolutionary model of development organized around modes of production. The late Roman empire straddled the threshold between ancient slavery and medieval feudalism. Ciccotti, who provided the first full-scale treatment of ancient slavery from a Marxist perspective, identified the putative inefficiency of slave labor as the motor of class conflict which led to the crisis of the slave system.[14] This dogma would remain central in *orthodox* Marxist scholarship on Roman slavery, particularly in the Soviet bloc.[15] In fact it was only within Communist circles that the study of ancient slavery was very active for the first three-quarters of the twentieth century.[16] An enormous body of literature accumulated, little of it edifying, seeking ever finer analysis of the "crisis of the slave-holding order" in Roman history. In this tradition, conquest created slavery; internal contradictions undermined it.

It was only in the 1970s that serious reconsideration of Roman slavery began, informed by new approaches to economic history but also armed with piles of emerging archaeological data. These influences, in conjunction, would allow the first overt discussion of the relative importance of conquest and capital, of politics and economics, in the rise and fall of Roman slavery. This conversation would be caught, cross-wise, in the middle of a broader debate over the relative merits of "primitivist" and "modernist" views of the Roman economy. Finley described the rise of Roman slavery as the result of a structural shortage of labor created by the mass military mobilization of the Italian peasantry and the institutional protections that prevented land-owners from enslaving free citizens.[17] Hopkins gave

---

[12] Lo Cascio 2009, 331–4, for an insightful analysis.
[13] Hobsbawm 1964. See *The German Ideology* in Tucker 1978, 152, for the adaptation of the conquest thesis by Marx himself, although not published until 1932.
[14] Ciccotti 1899, 305. See Mazza 1977, L–LI.
[15] Criticized already by Finley 1998 (orig. 1980), 206–7. Brockmeyer 1979, 45.
[16] This scholarship is invaluably described in German in Seyfarth 1963, 1–78, and Brockmeyer 1979, 49–66. Shtaerman 1984 and 1964 is the finest product of the Soviet scholarship. Günther 1984; Held 1971. In the west Westermann's positivist *omnium gatherum* appeared in 1955. De Ste. Croix 1981 (endorsing Weber's model at p. 231) and Anderson 1974, for western Marxist approaches.
[17] Finley 1998 (orig. 1980).

the finest statement of this model in a monograph with the revealing title, *Conquerors and Slaves.*[18] Finley was too perceptive an empirical historian to believe that the decline of slavery was a foregone conclusion. He stressed the endurance of the Roman slave system and scrupulously admitted that the study of later Roman slavery remained problematic.[19]

In these same years, scholars in France and Italy began to analyze Roman slavery with the categories of class and capital, but without the dogmatism that had paralyzed Marxist historiography in the Communist bloc.[20] In diametric opposition to orthodox Marxism, the neo-Marxist school situated Roman slavery within the modern, advanced sector of the ancient economy.[21] Slavery was a profitable institution embedded in circuits of exchange-oriented production. This shift, influenced by the contemporary work on the economics of American slavery, has been a sort of Copernican revolution in the study of Roman slavery. Equally fatefully, the neo-Marxist school advanced the debate by making use of archaeological evidence. The most obvious example is the excavation of the villa at Settefinestre, which connected a specific site, and by extension an entire settlement pattern, to the economic forms described by the Roman agricultural writers.[22] The archaeology of trade played a complementary role: the slave mode of production was correlated with the extraordinary distribution of containers which carried Italian wine throughout the Mediterranean in the late republic and early empire.[23] Here it is not just military conquest, but more crucially the conquest of markets which fueled the slave system.

By the 1980s the case for emphasizing capital in the causal framework of slavery was gaining momentum. The death knell for the conquest thesis quickly followed, as for the first time research turned to ask the primary question of whether or not conquest even *could* have produced a slave system on the Roman scale.[24] The answer has been a resounding "no," which continues to echo throughout the discussion. Scheidel has shown that natural reproduction rather than military conquest was the principal source of the slave supply.[25] This research has kindled a serious discussion about the number of Roman slaves; only in recent years have credible figures

[18] Hopkins 1978.
[19] Whittaker 1987 also argued persuasively for the long endurance of the slave system.
[20] Mazza 1986, 1977, and 1975; re-edn. of Ciccotti 1899 in 1977. Carandini 1989b, 1988, 1986, and 1979. Crowned by *Società romana e produzione schiavistica* in 1981. The Besançon colloquia began in the early 1970s, and the study of ancient slavery in France has remained vigorous ever since.
[21] See the synthesis of Schiavone 2000; Carandini 1983; Kolendo 1980.
[22] Carandini 1989b and 1986.   [23] Panella 1989, 1986, and 1981.
[24] Harris 1980, was seminal. Roth 2007; Scheidel 2005a, 1999, and 1997; Bradley 2004 and 1987a; Harris 1999.
[25] See chapter 2.

for the dimensions of the Roman slave system been proposed. Based on little evidence, Beloch, Brunt, and Hopkins had produced estimates of the slave population that were fantastically overblown.[26] Downsizing the Roman slave population does nothing to mitigate slavery's significance; rather, it clarifies slavery's role in transforming an ancient economy. The new insights into the scale and supply of the Roman slave population have a dramatic effect on the way we understand the mechanics of the Roman slave system – including the significance of females, families, child labor, etc.[27] And cutting down the slave population to realistic size also reconfigures the way we understand the trajectory of Roman slavery's rise and fall, the measure of decline.

The current wisdom on the Roman slave system might be something like this. The Roman conquest in the second century BC catalyzed an economic transformation of Italy. Conquest augmented a slave supply that was diverse and even in its early phases relied profoundly on natural reproduction as a source of new bodies. The growth of urban markets, the rise of wine as a cash crop, the influx of capital, and heavy demands on the free peasantry created demand for agricultural slave labor in Italy, a need for estate labor which had no precedent on this scale. Within this revisionist narrative of slavery's *rise*, the destiny of Roman slavery has remained vague. As the colonate, at least in its older form as an intermediate stage between slavery and feudalism, has been exposed for the convenient historian's myth that it always was, it is less clear than ever what happened to Roman slavery in the late empire.[28] Old stories die hard. Many propose that Roman slavery was gradually resorbed into an economy where more traditional forms of labor, especially tenancy, dominated. Common is the idea that slaves were allowed families and used like tenants on extensive estates, *latifundia*, as part of a transition from ancient slavery to medieval serfdom.[29] The shades of Marx and Weber still stalk this corner of the past, and the history of late Roman slavery has never broken free of the intellectual coils first imposed by the conquest thesis.

Building on the work that has so profoundly renovated our understanding of Roman slavery's expansionary period, this book tries to re-frame the last phases of Roman slavery. Such a venture requires us to suspend

---

[26] Hopkins 1978, 8; Brunt 1971, esp. 124; Beloch 1886, 413–16.   [27] Esp. Roth 2007.

[28] Which is not to imply that there are not important open questions in the study of the colonate, nor that the fiscal rules bearing upon *coloni* were insignificant in the labor market (see chapter 4). Carrié 1983 and 1982 have been seminal. In general, Sirks 2008; Grey 2007a; Kehoe 2007; Scheidel 2000; the essays in Lo Cascio 1997; Marcone 1988; Eibach 1980.

[29] The significant improvement made to this narrative by Wickham 2005a (a "peasant mode of production," with little extraction of surplus, intervened ca. 400–700, before the re-emergence of a feudal mode) will be discussed below and in chapter 4.

some deep-seated assumptions about the nature and trajectory of ancient slavery, and it is worth identifying at the outset some of the principal turns introduced by this account of late Roman slavery.

(1) We should abandon the presuppositions about slavery's rise and fall planted by the conquest thesis, especially as these assumptions have been quietly embedded in the influential narratives outlined by Marx and Weber. A complete, critical reappraisal of the evidence for slavery is imperative. (2) The slave supply and the relative efficiency of slave labor were important determinants of the slave system, but they were hardly the only ones, and neither was as simple or uni-directional as has often been supposed. What is needed is a comprehensive model based on supply *and* demand, with specific focus on the occupational and demographic structures of the slave system and the institutional properties of slave labor. (3) The pattern of change is not to be described by "transition." With little basis in the evidence, and less conceptual support, evolutionary models of change have dominated the study of late Roman slavery. But Roman slavery did not become medieval serfdom, and late antiquity was not an intermediate stage between antiquity and the middle ages. This book will suggest that a deep rupture runs down the middle of the period known as late antiquity. Mediterranean society remained a genuine slave society into the early fifth century, when finally the underlying structures of demand began to disintegrate in a way that brought an end to the epoch of ancient slavery.

"THE RICH MAN DANCES IN THE SAND!": THE MEDITERRANEAN ECONOMY IN THE LATE EMPIRE

This book is a study of slavery in the territories surrounding the Mediterranean, from AD 275 to 425. At the beginning of this period, the Roman empire was emerging from a half-century of political crisis and monetary chaos – a succession of ill-starred claimants to the throne, constant civil war, and continuous debasement of the currency. But emerge the empire did. The administrative foundations of bureaucratic monarchy were reinvigorated under Diocletian; Constantine added a new capital, a new religion, and a new currency, the gold *solidus*.[30] Historians no longer speak of a suffocating oriental "Dominate," and in fact the late Roman state is now seen as a rather approachable and even responsible, if always severe, public authority.[31] A single empire, under a single civil law, held sway from

---

[30] On Diocletian, Corcoran 2000. On Constantine, Lenski 2006b. For the currency, Hendy 1985.
[31] Selectively: Kelly 2004; Frakes 2001; Harries 1999; Carrié 1994; Brown 1992; McCormick 1987.

northern Britain to the southern frontiers of Egypt, from Syria to Spain. And yet, a century-and-a-half later, at the end of our period, a new and more fundamental age of crisis would begin in the west.[32] Rome was sacked, and over the next two centuries the western territories of the empire would be parceled up among Germanic successor kingdoms. The eastern empire would remain intact longer, until it too in the seventh century was dismembered by conquerors out of Arabia.

Over the last generation, these pivotal centuries of the human past have been rescued from the pall of "decline" which had hung over them since before the time of Gibbon.[33] The idea of late antiquity, of a vital period between the age of Marcus Aurelius and Mohammed, has cleared the path to reconsider the survival and eventual demise of Roman slavery. It is no longer reflexive to view events and processes of this period as part of a transition from the bright classical past to the dark medieval future. At the same time it must be noted that the creation of an intellectual space for late antiquity has not, thus far, led to a broad reconsideration of slavery. This is understandable, not only because the notion of a mechanistic transition from slavery to feudalism is so alien to the re-conception of the age, but also because the coherence of late antiquity as a period rests on religious and cultural foundations.[34] And yet it is increasingly possible to describe massive structural changes in the material foundations of late antique societies – changes that ultimately shaped the destiny of the slave system.

Slavery is an economic phenomenon, and a history of slavery must be situated within the economic history of the ancient world. Yet anyone who would try to describe the economic foundations of slavery in the fourth century will quickly become aware that the period straddles two distinct but overlapping traditions in the discipline of ancient history. The economic historiography of the high Roman empire has turned on debates about structure and scale; in the late Roman empire the themes of continuity and change dominate.[35] A tradition of inquiry running through Weber and Rostovtzeff asks what kind of economy the Roman empire created. Historians of the late Roman period, from Dopsch and Pirenne onward, have looked to measure the extent of change in late antiquity: how long the east–west trade routes remained open, when a certain city or landscape declined. These traditions have not always been in dialogue, yet a history

---

[32] Heather 2005; Ward-Perkins 2005.   [33] Esp. Brown 1971. cf. Giardina 1997c.
[34] Though see Brown 1974, for the contribution of Pirenne.
[35] Scheidel, Morris, and Saller 2007b; Pleket 1990. It is symptomatic that late antiquity is missing from the excellent collection of essays on ancient economic structures, Morris and Manning 2005. Late antique discussion about structure is often limited to questioning the "role of the state" or the reversion to "natural economy." Banaji 2001 is illuminating.

of slavery in the fourth century squarely intersects them both. We must ask, what kind of economy nurtured the Roman slave system, and how far had it changed in the late empire?

The Roman economy was preponderantly agricultural. Wheat and barley, wine, oil, and textiles were its main products. Most of the output was consumed directly by its producers, while only a fraction of it entered the realm of exchange. Yet, the Roman economy was far more dynamic than a subsistence economy, as evidenced by a now-familiar litany of proxies: cities, shipwrecks, ceramics, coins, pollutants, and so on.[36] Commerce and urbanism expanded dramatically under Roman rule.[37] The basket of goods consumed by some fairly ordinary Romans suggests high levels of commercialization.[38] The Roman empire brought with it relative peace, a stable currency, transportation infrastructure, property rights – in short, the institutional conditions for trade and even growth.[39] But how much trade and growth existed, and how are we to describe their transformative potential in the Roman world?[40] This is where consensus ends as the frontiers of knowledge are briskly expanding.[41] The Roman economy was apparently the most successful first-millennium economy.[42] It attained levels of complexity which were only equaled in a handful of pre-industrial "efflorescences."[43] The Roman economy was exceptional.

Economic growth in the Roman empire was ultimately restricted by low levels of technology, limited specialization, and diminishing returns on the land, but what matters more for us is complexity, the rise of thick networks of exchange. Urbanism, bulk commercial exchange, and the creation of a large middling element of society were the inter-related features of this exceptionalism.[44] Complexity and integration were limited by the much larger backdrop of technologically primitive, near-subsistence production, but they were decisive for the Roman slave system.[45] Slavery has been ubiquitous in human history, but in pre-industrial societies, it was usually dominated by elite ownership of female domestics. Roman slavery

[36] Scheidel 2009b; de Callataÿ 2005; Wilson 2002; McCormick 2001.
[37] Hopkins 2000 and 1980, for an influential model emphasizing the state (see Bang 2008, 48–9).
[38] Greene 2008; Silver 2007, 206; Hitchner 2005, 218; Ward-Perkins 2005.
[39] Lo Cascio 2009 and 2006; Harris 2008a; Frier and Kehoe 2007; Silver 2007; Saller 2005.
[40] Saller 2005; Jongman 2000b; Harris 1993.
[41] Bowman and Wilson 2009; Scheidel and Friesen 2009.
[42] Allen 2009, for a suggestive approach, using fourth-century data. Maddison 2007; Hitchner 2005; Temin 2005.
[43] Morris and Manning 2005, 24; Goldstone 2002; Grantham 1999.
[44] Carandini 1989a, for bulk demand. Erdkamp 2001, for urban demand. For Roman urbanism, Parkins 1997.
[45] Schiavone 2000, 53–69, offers a synthesis of Roman slavery in these terms.

is exceptional on two counts: slave-ownership was widespread within the sizeable middling classes, and slave labor played an important role in commercialized, agricultural production on elite land.[46] The nexus of towns and trade not only marked the Roman economy as exceptional, they are the key to understanding Roman slavery.

As we move into the late Roman empire, questions of continuity and change overtake questions of structure and scale. The problems are interdependent, and the early imperial economy is often an implicit benchmark. *Given* that the Roman imperial economy was exceptional, and that trade and urbanism were markers of its complexity, how does the late Roman economy compare? Archaeology has been of paramount importance, for it offers an especially tangible index of stability and loss.[47] In recent years, moreover, a wave of synthetic work has produced some consensus on the patterns of production and exchange in late antiquity.[48] Archaeology has demonstrated the breadth and scale of the fourth-century recovery. The traces of exchange networks and settlement patterns, unsurprisingly, register the effects of the third-century crisis which, like a pulse felt across the empire, disrupted the economy. But the basic skeleton of the imperial economy perdured. The recovery was uneven, as parts of the empire, notably Italy, never recaptured their former glory. But the fourth century was the age of the provinces. Britain, southern Gaul, coastal Spain, and North Africa flourished. In the east it is possible to speak without qualification of the beginnings of an extraordinary phase of expansion. Greece and Asia Minor prospered, and the provinces of the Levant would experience their economic peak in the centuries of late antiquity.[49]

The fourth-century economy was characterized by exchange, integration, and commercialized production. It was a world built around money: "The use of money welds together our entire existence, and it lies at the

---

[46] These claims are defended at greater length in chapter 1.

[47] Archaeology is particularly difficult to use as economic evidence, particularly for scale/performance (cf. Morris 2005), deepening the dependence of late antique scholarship on conceptualization of the earlier economy.

[48] Esp. Brogiolo, Chavarría Arnau, and Valenti 2005; Ward-Perkins 2005; Wickham 2005a; Bowden, Lavan, and Machado 2004; Chavarría and Lewit 2004; Francovich and Hodges 2003; McCormick 2001; Brogiolo, Gauthier, and Christie 2000; Brogiolo 1996b.

[49] Overviews: Brogiolo and Chavarría Arnau 2005; Chavarría and Lewit 2004; Lewit 2004; Ripoll and Arce 2000; Sodini 1993. Britain: Dark 2004 and 1996; Scott 1993. Africa: Leone and Mattingly 2004; de Vos 2000; Dietz *et al.* 1995; Mattingly and Hitchner 1995; Mattingly 1994; Hitchner 1990. Sicily: Wilson 1990. Greece: Dunn 2004; Rautman 2000; Mee and Forbes 1997; Jameson *et al.* 1994; Alcock 1993. Asia Minor: Vanhaverbeke and Waelkens 2003; Foss 1994. Syria: Decker 2001; Foss 1997; Tate 1992; Sodini *et al.* 1980; Tchalenko 1953–8. Palestine: Kingsley 2001; Dauphin 1998; Hirschfeld 1997; Dar 1986.

foundation of all our affairs, and if something is to be bought, or something is to be sold, we do it all with money."⁵⁰ The cities were a hallmark
of the system. Around 400, "golden Rome, first among cities, home of
the gods," was still home to some half a million hungry inhabitants, with
Constantinople catching up, and Carthage, Alexandria, and Antioch also
thriving.⁵¹ Urbanization may have remained in the realm of 15 percent.⁵²
The lynchpin of the economy remained the politically guaranteed transfer
of food from the southern to the northern rim of the Mediterranean, but
only a part of this trade was subsidized by the state.⁵³ By no means was
the commercial system of the fourth century an administered economy.⁵⁴
The *Expositio totius mundi*, a fourth-century tract written by a merchant,
provides us with a trader's eye view of the Roman world.⁵⁵ This "practical guide to the best buys of the fourth-century empire's different shores"
presents a Mediterranean economy integrated by well-informed merchants
who paid careful attention to circuits of production and consumption.⁵⁶
The author knew where to find good cheese, wine, oils, grain, textiles, and
slaves. The Mediterranean market created by the Roman empire was still
intact.⁵⁷

While the third-century crisis did not undermine the essential framework of the Roman economy, events in the fifth century did, by contrast,
re-orient the Roman economy towards its demise – in the west.⁵⁸ This fact
makes it problematic to speak of late antiquity as a unified period.⁵⁹ The
fragmentation of the state, and the disruption of markets, progressively
eroded the conditions which had fostered the complexity of the Roman
economy.⁶⁰ There was never total depopulation or total collapse. There

⁵⁰ Ioh. Chrys. In princ. Act. 2 (PG 51: 99): τῶν ἀργυρίων ἡ χρῆσις πᾶσαν ἡμῶν συγκροτεῖ τὴν
   ζωήν, καὶ συμβολαίων ἁπάντων ὑπόθεσις γίνεται, κἂν ἀγοράσαι τι, κἂν πωλῆσαι δέη, διὰ
   τούτων ἅπαντα πράττομεν.
⁵¹ Auson. Ord. nob. urb. 1 (Green: 169): *prima urbes inter, divum domus, aurea Roma*. See esp. Morrison
   and Sodini 2002, 172–4; Lo Cascio 2001, 184–5; Bavant 1989, 473; Hermansen 1978, esp. 167–8;
   Jones 1964, 1040; Jacoby 1961. Mango 1985 and Dagron 1974 for Constantinople. Liebescheutz 1972,
   93–4 for Antioch. On the food supply, esp. McCormick 2001, 87–92. Also Wickham 2005a, 72;
   Sirks 1991; Durliat 1990; Garnsey 1988b. On the hinterland of Rome, Marazzi 2004. Purcell 1999, a
   pessimistic but evocative reconstruction.
⁵² See chapter 1. Quantification is miserably lacking in the study of the fourth century. For urban
   continuity in Egypt, see Alston 2001. The essays in Lavan 2001; Brogiolo and Ward-Perkins 1999;
   Rich 1992.
⁵³ Loseby 2007; McCormick 1998; Sirks 1991.   ⁵⁴ Lo Cascio 2006, 227.
⁵⁵ Expos. tot. mund. (SC 124).   ⁵⁶ McCormick forthcoming and 2001, 85.
⁵⁷ McCormick forthcoming, updates the famous shipwreck graph of Parker 1992.
⁵⁸ Ward-Perkins 2005.
⁵⁹ Hence this book covers the "late Roman" period, the long fourth century (275–425), but not
   the post-Roman west or early Byzantine east, which are part of "late antiquity" as it is generally
   conceived.
⁶⁰ Ward-Perkins 2005; Marazzi 2004; Patterson and Rovelli 2004.

remained local markets, regional exchange. What was lost was complexity – bulk exchange, middling consumers, the integration of markets, currencies, and laws. Urbanism is a stark index. The population of Rome fell, from some half a million in AD 400 to perhaps 50,000, perhaps even less, by AD 700.[61] There was great regional variation in the timing and extent of decline, but the direction was general and remarkably prolonged, until a universal nadir in the seventh century.[62] The Roman pattern of dispersed settlement remained the dominant system in the western countryside, but within that pattern the villas died out in a "slow agony" that only in the eighth century was reversed by a settlement system oriented around the nucleated villages which had been gestating amidst the ruins of the old landscape.[63] Exchange and connectivity slowly dwindled, until there was one pitiful line of trade running east and west across the Mediterranean.[64] Only in the Carolingian period did a long and arduous turnaround begin, based on new systems of settlement, exploitation, and trade.[65]

In the east, and in Africa, the tempo of change was altogether different. The commercial economy thrived deep into late antiquity. "O how lovely the beach looks when it's filled with merchandise and it bustles with businessmen! Bundles of different clothing are pulled from the ships, countless people delight at the sailors' cheerful singing, and the rich man dances in the sand!"[66] In Africa, the fourth and fifth centuries were a peak, the sixth and seventh centuries a phase of gradual recession.[67] In the east expansion continued throughout the fifth century. We will follow the intensification of slave labor along the edges of this great eastern migration of wealth. There is considerable debate over when this expansion slowed or involuted. In the Aegean, Asia Minor, and Egypt, there is a good case for permanent reverse in the sixth century, in the wake of catastrophes like plague and earthquake.[68] Certainly the end of *annona* shipments in AD 618 fractured a great trading spine.[69] But in the Levant expansion continued at least into the seventh century, into the Islamic period.[70] The Carolingians would find in the Caliphate a desirable and much wealthier trading partner

---

[61] Christie 2006, 55–6; Lo Cascio 2001.
[62] Whittow 2009; Christie 2006, 10; Valenti 2005, 193–5 and 2004; Alston 2001, on the eastern cities.
[63] Brogiolo 1996a, 109: "un periodo di lenta agonia." Costambeys 2009; Bowes 2006; Valenti 2004; Francovich and Hodges 2003.
[64] McCormick 2001, 566.   [65] McCormick 2002, trade; Verhulst 1966, agriculture.
[66] Ps.-Fulg. Serm. 38 (PL 65: 901–2): *Quam pulchrum apparet littus, dum repletur mercibus, et trepidat mercatoribus! Exponuntur de navibus sarcinae vestium diversarum, laetantur innumeri cantantium in iucunditate nautarum, et dives sinus tripudiat arenarum.* This felicitous translation is from McCormick 2001, 84.
[67] Leone and Mattingly 2004, lucid on the regional variations; Chavarría and Lewit 2004, 21–2.
[68] Vanhaverbeke and Waelkens 2003; Morrison and Sodini 2002, 190–1; Foss 1994.
[69] McCormick 2001, 111.   [70] Magness 2003.

whose goods they coveted, and yet they were able to maintain a balance of payments only by exporting that commodity of last resort among underdeveloped economies, their people, slaves.[71] By the end of late antiquity, the changes which began in the fifth century had come full circle, and western Europe had become a supplier of the slave trade rather than a consumer.

There are areas of debate and uncertainty, inevitably, but more striking are the outlines of consensus which make it possible to frame the history of slavery within broader structures of production and exchange.[72] The economy of the long fourth century, even if high imperial levels were never re-attained, belongs to the Roman efflorescence. It was an economy that allowed middling consumption on a mass scale and that fueled strong demand for farm labor in the commercialized sectors of the countryside. The fourth century was still home to a complex system of production and consumption, while the fundamental shocks to that economic nexus, in the fifth and seventh centuries, provide an explanation for the end of ancient slavery that is not only consistent with the evidence but also coherent in terms of its analytical architecture. By the sixth or seventh centuries, patterns of consumption and production for the market had declined, and with them the slave system. The demand curve for slaves collapsed, as both the consumption power of the middling classes and the elite's ability to control market-oriented production were eroded in an early medieval world in which there was simply far less exchange. So a history of slavery in the long fourth century is not a history of slavery in late antiquity. It is, rather, a history of slavery during the last phase of a politically and economically united Mediterranean. Roman slavery did not become serfdom; it receded, out of existence, as the Roman economy was pulled back by the tides into the sea of subsistence that engulfed all pre-industrial economies.

RECOVERING THE LATE ROMAN SLAVE SYSTEM: EVIDENCE AND MODELS

This book is organized into three parts, exploring in turn the material, social, and institutional foundations of slavery. Methodologically, it is inspired by two paradoxical convictions. First, that a new study of late Roman slavery should be founded on a fresh and thorough investigation of the late antique sources. Second, that we must operate on the skeptical assumption that the surviving evidence is inadequate. On the one hand, this book is written in the belief that there is considerable evidence for

---

[71] McCormick 2002.   [72] Loseby 2007.

late Roman slavery which has never entered the discussion and which, if presented, is sufficient to demand a revision of the dominant paradigms. Exhaustive research is the beginning of revision. On the other hand, the study of Roman slavery in the earlier periods has shown that the evidence has limits, that systematic gaps in the record fundamentally obstruct the search for a complete understanding of ancient slavery. Consequently our own assumptions – implicitly or explicitly – inevitably fill out the picture. This book thus hopes to improve our understanding of the late Roman slave system by working simultaneously on empirical and conceptual fronts.[73]

A primary goal of the book is to return *ad fontes* and to recover the world of late antique slavery. Throughout these pages it will become obvious that one objective is simply to present the abundant record on late Roman slavery in order to enrich the material available for the ongoing conversation on late Roman society. Much of the evidence for slavery in late antiquity remains unfamiliar. Cato the Elder and Spartacus dependably appear in general histories of slavery, but there is no objective reason why these cases should be more well known to the history of slavery than any of the comparable late antique examples. This book is, in one sense, an unabashed experiment in organized impressionism, trying to balance decades or more of the subtle influence which comes from greater collective knowledge of the earlier sources by putting on a canvas the thousands of small brushstrokes which can be restored from the late antique record.

The findings draw opportunistically upon the inscriptions and papyri of the period. Unfortunately, neither the papyri nor the inscriptions offer a stable data set which allows us to evaluate what is typical and what is exceptional, or to track change over time. Nevertheless, there are enough papyri from the fourth century to form an impression of household slave-ownership and estate-based slavery.[74] The fourth century cannot boast as many papyri as the early centuries of the Roman empire, but the record is superior to that of the fifth century, which is bleak.[75] The epigraphic evidence is relatively sparse compared to earlier centuries but still provides insights.[76] Above all, a set of fragmentary census inscriptions from the fourth century provides our only objective, quantitative data on the use of slaves in agriculture and on the demographics of a rural slave

---

[73] This book is not aimed at comprehensiveness. In some cases, excellent studies already exist (particularly regarding Christianity). In others, further study will remain needed. Moreover, the book's bibliography is both unwieldy and inevitably incomplete; slavery touched on virtually every aspect of late ancient civilization, so there is no upper limit on the secondary literature which could be cited (not to mention that the arguments here often engage with scholarship on the early empire). Forced to eschew full doxographies, I try to cite essential, up-to-date scholarship.

[74] Bagnall 1993.   [75] Bagnall and Worp 1980.   [76] E.g. Petsas *et al.* 2000. See chapter 9.

population.[77] Consequently, these documents will surface throughout the book. The legal record also presents a rich if highly particular source of information, and this book tries to make systematic use of the *Theodosian Code*.[78] But the laws require special handling, and part III is entirely devoted to an exploration of the legal sources.

If papyri, inscriptions, and laws are used whenever possible, at the heart of this book lies the exhaustive use of the literary sources from late antiquity. The reliance on written sources is a strategy born of necessity. It is no simple task to write the history of slavery from the texts. Imagine trying to write the history of slavery in the early Roman empire without the great sixth volume of the *Corpus Inscriptionum Latinarum*, the agricultural manuals, or the *Digest*; add a thicket of stubborn, ill-founded pre-judgments derived from nineteenth-century historiography. Those are the obstacles in writing the history of late Roman slavery. And yet, the literary evidence is extensive and vivid. The fourth century has left behind a truly extraordinary amount of material, and in exploring it we are aided by research tools which were inconceivable even in the recent past. Electronic databases of Greek and Latin texts make it possible to create instant lexical indices.[79] John Chrysostom mentioned slaves over 5,000 times in his surviving corpus. A generation ago, it took several years and a monograph to outline what he said about slavery.[80] Using the *Thesaurus Linguae Graecae* (TLG), it takes a few seconds to locate every reference to slavery in the works of this most vocal Christian warrior, and he is one of our primary informants.[81]

These tools re-configure what it is possible to do with the literary record. The databases make it immediately apparent how pervasive slavery was in late Roman society. Culling for references to the principal words for "slave" (and there are many), the computers turned up 100,000 instances from the fourth to sixth centuries in Greek and Latin.[82] The vast majority of these were of no great interest – biblical quotations, trite figures of speech, and so on. But amongst the chaff there is a bumper crop of original and interesting

---

[77] Harper 2008.   [78] Sirks 2007; Matthews 2000; Harries 1999; Honoré 1998; Archi 1976.

[79] Esp. the *Thesaurus Linguae Graecae*, TLG (Irvine, 1972-), www.tlg.irvine.edu, and the *Cetedoc Library of Christian Latin Texts*, CLCLT-5 (Turnhout, 2002-).

[80] Jaeger 1974.

[81] Maxwell 2006 and Mayer 2000, for the sermons of Chrysostom as a source of social history.

[82] Even this number does not reflect a comprehensive search. I was unfortunately unable to include some ambiguous and common words, notably *puer, liber,* σῶμα, and παῖς, in the database search, thus missing some references to slavery (though picking up many of them the old-fashioned way). The words included in my search: serv-, ancill-, mancipi-, verna-, concubina-, emptici-, manumit-, manumiss-, libert-, lupanar-, mango-, meretri-, spado-, eunuch-, semivir-, famul-, domestic-, scort-, servit-, servul-, venalici-, δουλ-, ανδραποδ-, οικετ-, παιδαρ-, παιδισκ-, ευνουχ-, δραπετ-, θεραπαιν-, δμω-, κορασι-, πορν-, οικογεν-, ελευθερ-, θρεπτ-.

evidence, much of it "new." Though some of these clues are mere flecks of insight, in conjunction they become rather significant. Often the insights are hiding in little-used texts: Asterius of Amasea will tell us about slave-girls on the auction block, Cyril of Alexandria will explain that prostitutes are forced into slavery by their masters, while Libanius and Theodoret of Cyrrhus tell us how slaves spend moments of nocturnal privacy.[83] Even the pages of old favorites, Augustine or Chrysostom, still have insights to yield.

A source base as rich and diverse as the late antique literary record still cannot necessarily provide a complete or objective account of the slave system. Certain forces have systematically shaped the literary record and make it a particular sort of lens on the past. The late antique writings which make the electronic tools such an amazing resource come largely from the process of Christianization. This process, with its theological, ascetic, and pastoral dimensions, at times takes the historian close to the dense web of human relations that constituted social life.[84] The Christians who left behind their thoughts often recapitulated the extreme upper-class bias in the ancient material. What is Jerome, with his clique of glamorous senatorial ascetics, if not another chapter in the overrepresentation of the rich and famous? But not all Christians were Jerome. In late antiquity, there was an unmistakable shift in the literary record towards mainstream Mediterranean households. The rich came to church, certainly, but Augustine or Chrysostom were in dialogue with a cross-section of society more diverse than Cicero or Pliny.[85] The overrepresentation of the urban realm at the expense of the countryside, however, is an abiding and, at times, insuperable challenge.

It is equally important to be conscious of *how* we use the literary sources. Often the written evidence will be a reliable source precisely because the literature is used obliquely. The sermons of Augustine or Chrysostom, for example, were not written in order to describe the economy, but in passing they reveal casual assumptions about who owned slaves.[86] This is not an excuse to let down our critical guard, and it will be advisable to consider key sources, like the *Life of Melania the Younger*, with a surfeit of scrutiny. But the problems with the literary evidence become more subtle in part II, which explores the role of slavery in social relations. Here, we are so richly informed by the Christian authors precisely because we are nearer

---

[83] Ast. Am. 5.7 (Datema: 49); Cyr. Ador. 14 (PG 68: 905); Thdt. Provid. 1.568C (PG 83: 568); Lib. Or. 25.66–7 (Foerster vol. 2: 569–70).
[84] For methodological cautions, Garnsey 1998a, 471–3.   [85] See chapter 1.
[86] On homiletics, Harper forthcoming d; Mayer 2008; Cunningham and Allen 1998; Kinzig 1997; Sachot 1994; Allen and Mayer 1993; Olivar 1991.

to the heart of their project. The Christian leadership of late antiquity had the idea of Christianizing society. It prompted a direct engagement with the habits of ancient society, and reformers will sometimes put words in the mouth of the average man. "You are telling me I can't have sex with my slave-woman?" "Are you telling me not to beat my slave?" These discursive moments give privileged insights into ancient society, precisely because of their critical stance.[87] But we must be aware of the possible distortions or exaggerations which were encouraged by the stance of the bishops, and part II tries to make careful, critical use of the literary evidence.

A more dangerous distortion of the evidence lies in its chronological distribution. The generations between 375 and 425 are densely represented. Those very generations lived through a critical turning point. The church found itself vaulted from a triumphal survivor to become a newly dominant religion. At the same time, the collapse of imperial institutions in the west became irreversible, and the indices of material prosperity would follow a downward trajectory for the next two centuries. In the east the retrenchment of the state permitted a longer cycle of prosperity. During the pivotal period, old and new existed side by side in ways they never would again. In his last years, Augustine could write a letter that would have traveled to Rome aboard ships carrying food to the old capital. In the letter, he would seek out the legal guidance of a trained lawyer so that, as bishop of Hippo, he could adjudicate cases of slave status according to the complex rules of Roman civil law.[88] Augustine's classical education, the imperial scale of his connections, even the infrastructure of travel which carried his letters, belonged to a world that he saw crumbling around him.

The rich picture of social life as it existed around 400 thus represents a challenge. Using the abundant material from those years, it is just possible to catch the importance of slavery in the structure of antique society. We can glimpse where slaves physically are, what they were doing, how they lived, how their masters felt about them and used their bodies and their labor. But it is a picture that is evanescent. The sources thereafter begin to dwindle in quantity and in vividness. This decline is both exaggerated and real, a product of random factors in source preservation and a phenomenon linked to the slow, steady abatement of a way of life. It is just a fact that the late sixth century remains obscure in comparison to the late fourth century, and it is correspondingly more difficult to say with confidence what the slave system looks like. But in this gathering darkness of the fifth and sixth

---

[87] Olivar 1991, 589–640. cf. Uthemann 1998 for influence from diatribe.
[88] Aug. Ep. 24* (CSEL 88: 126–7). Lepelley 1983.

centuries, the modern historian of slavery has an indispensable ally in the archaeologist. If we are able to link slavery with patterns of production and consumption, urbanism and rural settlement, then archaeology can furnish new insights into the processes which contributed to the end of ancient slavery. Stones and sherds will never tell us directly about slaves, but they do tell us about the end of a way of life in which slavery was central.

So far can the evidence take us. We cannot, however, simply rewrite the last chapters of Westermann's *The Slave Systems of Greek and Roman Antiquity* and hope to find enough evidence to set aside his claims for decline. This book, therefore, is not positivist in design. It is not a guide to the sources, nor is it framed by the sources. The book is framed by problems, often the most difficult problems, in the belief that what is needed is an effort to describe the system, how it worked, and where its center of gravity lay. The sources are used to answer, not to generate, the questions we ask, and there is no guarantee that they are sufficient to that purpose. Some of the best analyses of the social and economic dimensions of Roman slavery have been guided by the methodological premise that because the evidence is insufficient, modeling must be used to control the assumptions we deploy to fill in the inadequate data.[89] It is impossible not to "model" – in the sense of mentally filling out an inadequate record – from the moment that we ask questions of the system itself. We have already highlighted the cluster of ideas, the conquest thesis, which long steered the way historians thought about Roman slavery. The conquest thesis seriously distorted the burden of proof in the study of Roman slavery, shaping the way that the limited and hopelessly imperfect evidence is read. In this subtle way, the ghost of the conquest thesis continues to haunt the study of Roman slavery. Sublimated into other narratives, it is never very far from the surface.[90]

The ambition of this book is to construct, from the ground up, a model of the slave system in the long fourth century.[91] This exercise will make us continually aware of the limits of our evidence. The book begins by outlining the scale and distribution of the slave population. This reconstruction

---

[89] Roth 2007; Scheidel 2005a and 1997; Jongman 2003. Hopkins 1978 was foundational.

[90] Pervasive in standard histories: Westermann 1955, 57–63, 101–2; Brockmeyer 1979; Phillips 1985, 36. Still very much alive: Lo Cascio 2009, 61, 130; Laes 2008, 246; Clark 2007, 222; Frier and Kehoe 2007, 138; Giardina 2007, 756, and 1997b, 253; Morel 2007, 505; Hezser 2005, 1, 85, 221–2; Wickham 2005a, 277; Turley 2000, 31, 78; Giliberti 1999, 47, 75; Cantarella 1996, 130.

[91] Such modeling entails: 1. Considering how representative the evidence is and rigorously assessing its value. 2. Thinking of slavery as a system whose component elements (supply, distribution, demand, etc.) must be structurally compatible. 3. Specifying causal interrelationships. 4. Quantifying, for heuristic purposes, as a way of improving on vague qualitative criteria.

is the most heavily modeled part of the inquiry. Chapter 2 sets the system
in motion, considering first its sources of supply, its demographic profile,
and its mechanisms of circulation. These, in turn, should be consistent
with the occupational structure of the slave population. This proposed
material framework of the slave system must then inform our investigation
of the social fabric and institutional foundations of Roman slavery. There
is a practical check on this method: comparison. This book is not in any
strong sense a comparative work, but it aspires to be informed by the great
strides in the study of world slavery. This body of research should make us
aware of the gaps and weaknesses of the traditional historiography of our
own period. The neglect of slave-women, the constrictive view of plantation labor, the misguided idea that Christianity was incompatible with
slavery, become all the more glaring in the panorama of world slavery. The
diversity uncovered within the experience of modern slavery, even within
times and places not far apart, should make us wary when we speak of
"Roman slavery" (as we must inevitably do).[92]

Even as we scour every corner of the late antique record for the residues of
the slave system, we should remain conscious of the limits of the evidence.
One overarching deficiency cannot be stressed enough. We have not a single
slave's voice. We can and must listen to the master's words as though they
are only one side of a conversation whose other side is irretrievably lost.
When we hear a master call his slaves "lazy," we must imagine the invisible
field of tension over work conditions underneath the stereotype.[93] When
we hear that a slave's only consolation was "to invent rumors," we must
imagine the feeble leverage slaves gained from their intimate household
knowledge in a face-to-face society with a strong sense of honor.[94] We
must look proactively for the small traces of the slaves' agency within and
against the system that sought systematically to dehumanize them. This
problem is by no means unique to late antiquity, for it plagues the study of
ancient slavery in general. If anything, the late antique record is slightly less
hopelessly inadequate. The triumph of Christianity prompted a perceptible
change of inflection in the master's voice. "How many obols have you paid
for the image of God?"[95] This quiver of doubt we will try to interpret in
part II.

The book's second epigraph evokes just such a brief and unexpected
moment of candor. It is inspired by a desperate letter of Saint Augustine,

---

[92] Morris 1998, 983.   [93] Joshel and Murnaghan 1998, 15.
[94] Hier. Ep. 117.8 (CSEL 55: 431); Ioh. Chrys. Subintr. 10.10 (Dumortier: 79). See chapter 8.
[95] Gr. Nyss. Hom. in Eccl. 4.1 (SC 416: 228): πόσοις ὀβολοῖς τὴν εἰκόνα τοῦ θεοῦ ἀντεστάθμησας;... The only extant statement of opposition to slavery from antiquity: Garnsey 1996 and
part II of this book.

written in his last years as he watched the empire fold in around him. Roman slave-traders, displaced from their old haunts, had swept through his province, carrying inside the empire the terror they were accustomed to visit on those beyond the frontiers. The bishop described the columns of slaves marched to the harbor, "like an endless river."⁹⁶ There on the docks of Hippo they were boarded onto ships that would ferry them towards the social death of enslavement. That metaphor, of perpetual movement and elemental brutality, is one of our most arresting descriptions of Roman slavery. Stripped of ideology and convention, it is a glimpse of the Roman slave system as it appeared to an observer momentarily startled by its violence. How the violence and displacement were experienced by those whose bodies were stolen and sold it takes enormous will even to imagine. But the slave system has left its traces throughout the dense record of late antiquity. With enough patience and some cautious imagination, we can recover the remnants from this neglected corner of the past, often passed through in sweeping narratives of transition from antiquity to the middle ages, rarely searched with the care it deserves.

THE END OF ANCIENT SLAVERY: FROM MODES OF PRODUCTION TO SUPPLY AND DEMAND

The fourth-century Mediterranean was a vast space connected by an empire sitting on the sea. This space was home to some 50 million inhabitants, living under a single civil law, but in a society, or rather aggregation of societies, that enjoyed divergent levels of material advancement and natural resources. Over 80 percent of these inhabitants lived in the countryside, their existence absorbed in the interminable rhythms of subsistence and reproduction.⁹⁷ At the same time, this society was a volatile mixture of traditional and modern elements. Its teeming polyglot cities were nodes in an imperial network, home to a precociously large class of consumers, hustlers, slave-owners. Trade was a source of massive wealth. "Wheat becomes gold for you, wine congeals into gold for you, wool turns into gold in your hands!"⁹⁸ Grain was eaten by mouths living hundreds of miles from the fields where it was grown. Wine, the dominant psychotropic commodity, was manically consumed, a staple of nutrition.⁹⁹ High-quality lamps,

---

[96] Aug. Ep. 10*.5 (CSEL 88: 49): *perpetuo quasi fluvio*. See chapter 2.
[97] Overviews of the early empire, Scheidel 2007; Frier 2000. An estimate in the range of 50 million is comparable to the population of the Augustan empire, lower than the second-century peak, at around 60–70 million.
[98] Bas. Dest. horr. 5 (Courtonne: 25–6): Ὁ σῖτος χρυσός σοι γίνεται, ὁ οἶνος εἰς χρυσὸν μεταπήγνυται, τὰ ἔριά σοι ἀποχρυσοῦται.
[99] Erdkamp 2002. Wine trade: Pieri 2005; Kingsley 2002 and 2001.

table-wares, and rooftiles were made in bulk and circulated far from their
point of manufacture and, most remarkably, penetrated well beyond the
highest tier of society into peasant households. When the sea opened each
spring, ships loaded with wheat, wine, oil, sauce, lumber, ceramics, textiles ... and slaves criss-crossed the waters in a commerce whose volume
and velocity had almost no precedent.

The fourth-century empire needs to be conceived first as a space interconnected by webs of production and exchange. A danger lurks in thinking
of the fourth-century empire in terms of its place in time. The temptation
is too great to imagine fourth-century society, and the fourth-century slave
system, on an arc between antiquity and the middle ages. The idea of a
transition from ancient slavery to medieval serfdom has endured for so
long, cut a groove so deep, that it has created an almost inescapable course
of intellectual path dependence. Yet it is essential, if we are to understand
the slave system of the fourth century, that we scrape away these encrus-
tations of thought. The story of transition is not rooted in the sources of
the period. The slave population was not a stable group of humans capable
of undergoing a step-by-step metamorphosis. The story of transition is a
wholly inadequate way to approach the realities of a slave system in which
some 5 million souls were reduced to the status of a commodity. This
book is an attempt to spend time *among* the slaves of late antiquity and to
consider how they fit *within* the structures of empire in the fourth century
rather than *between* the ancient world and the middle ages.

Chapter 1 outlines the scale and distribution of the slave population.[100]
This is a hazardous endeavor, to be sure, but it is, at a minimum, preferable to working uncritically with qualitative labels like "dominant" and
"important." We should imagine four categories of slave-holders: Illustrious, Elite, Bourgeois, and Agricultural. Illustrious households comprised
the wealthiest 500–600 families in Roman society, the core of the senatorial order, who controlled staggering amounts of landed property and, on
average, hundreds of slaves. Elite households included the next wealthiest
1–1.5 percent of society, and they too were large-scale slave-owners. These
strata of Roman society owned half of all slaves, some 2.5 million souls.
At the same time, Bourgeois slave-holders constituted some 20 percent of
the urban population, owning on average two slaves; likewise, the top tier
of agricultural households held small numbers of slaves. These middling
orders comprised 10 percent of the Roman population, and they owned the
other half of the slave population. The Roman slave system was thus both

---

[100] What follows is a brief summary of the main arguments; citations are found in relevant chapters.

intensive and extensive. Slaves produced the commodities which underwrote Illustrious and Elite wealth, and they were embedded in the social dynamics of the broad middling strata. The top 1–1.5 percent of Roman society owned the bottom 5 percent, and the top 10 percent of Roman society owned property in humans. In a pre-industrial society, on an imperial scale, these are remarkable figures.

Chapter 2 describes the supply side of the Roman slave system, Chapters 3 and 4 the demand side. A slave population on the order of 5 million souls would have required hundreds of thousands of new bodies per annum to maintain replacement levels. Natural reproduction was the main source of new slaves, but child exposure, self-sale, kidnapping, and cross-border importation were major supplements. The supply system, in short, was diverse and decentralized. Chapter 3 analyzes the demand for household slaves. Domestic slavery is not to be equated with consumption, if that implies lack of productivity. Slave labor at the household level was economically significant. In large households, slavery allowed the family to operate as a firm, absorbing roles in education and commerce. In all slave-owning households, slave labor had an intimate relationship with textile production. The interface between the family, its labor supply, and the textile industry is one of the keys to understanding the Roman slave system. The economies of textile production encouraged the integration of slave labor within the household. Moreover, slave labor within agricultural households played a decisive part in the social stratification among village elites and wealthy peasants.

Chapter 4 offers a model of agricultural slavery organized around the interaction of four determinants: the slave supply, the total demand for labor, formal institutions, and the dynamics of estate management. Slave labor remained instrumental in agricultural production on elite land in the fourth century. Large land-owners held on the order of 30–40 percent of the land; they exploited it with a mix of tenants, slaves, and wage laborers. The labor market of the fourth century was complex. Tenancy was quantitatively predominant, but slavery played a vital role in elite control over commercialized production. Demand for slave labor was a function not only of prevailing wages and transaction costs, but also of the demand for commodities, especially wheat, wine, oil, and textiles. The markets for these goods incentivized elite control over production on a massive scale. There was no form of estate organization that was uniquely expressive of slave labor. Slave labor was adaptive to a variety of crops and work regimes; slaves can be found on stock ranches in upper Egypt, on olive factories on Lesbos, on the wineries of Thera, on vast arable *latifundia* in Italy, and in the hills of North Africa herding their master's flocks. Even though rural slaves accounted for something like 6 percent of the total rural population, they were over 20 percent of the total labor force on elite estates, a percentage that would have been higher in core regions of market-oriented production, lower in peripheral areas. Slave labor was decisive in the profitable, cash-crop enterprises that rewarded control over production.

Part II moves towards the human experience of the Roman slave system. Chapter 5 uses an incentive model to explore the aims and techniques of domination; the extraction of labor was the end of the master–slave relationship, and the nature of the labor performed by slaves was a primary influence on their exposure to violence and their prospects for reward. Chapter 6 then turns to an even murkier side of Roman slavery, the world of the slave underneath the veil of violence and vulnerability. The slave's options – to shirk or steal, to fight or flee, to form families and communities – are measured. While rural slaves enjoyed latitude to pursue family relationships, life for urban slaves was more varied, opened by the inherent anarchy of the city but lived along the razor's edge of the free family's life cycle. Chapter 7 argues that Roman slavery bore a peculiar relationship to sexual exploitation. Sexual exploitation has received only cursory attention, although it was a core feature of Roman slavery. Late marriage for men, the lack of any strong concept of male virginity, strict public and private surveillance of free women: the abuse of the slave's body was built into Roman society. In other societies, race, religion or honor deterred, however ineffectually, the sexual use of slaves; in Roman society, it was tolerated, even encouraged. Chapter 8 focuses on the circulation of social honor. Slaves made the wealth that underwrote the honor of the elite, and the middling classes built their honor on the ownership of slaves, even in small numbers.

Part III explores the institutional fabric of Roman slavery. A slave system of such magnitude and complexity would have been inconceivable without the active complicity of the state, especially in the absence of that sinister marker of status, race. Slavery was a relationship fraught with tension and a legal status whose boundaries required constant, active definition. Late Roman laws have often been read as reactionary measures against deepening status confusion. This book will stake out a position which is diametrically opposed to the idea of a progressive breakdown of the legal basis of slavery. The fourth century was an age of universal citizenship, when practically all inhabitants of the empire were subject to Roman civil law. Conflict was inherent in the system, and in the fourth century such conflict was more likely than ever to end up in Roman jurisdiction. We can identify three arenas in which the edges of status required vigilant regulation: illicit enslavement, sex, and manumission. We need to imagine the constant human struggles behind these pressure points in the law of slavery. These were centrifugal forces within a complex slave system, constantly threatening to fray the edges of legal status. The active regulation of the Roman state provided the opposite, centripetal force, holding together the property rights of slave-owners over their human chattel. In the fourth century we see an imperial state that was energetically committed to the project of ruling a slave society.

The material, social, and institutional foundations of slavery remained solid in the fourth century. The evidence will give us no reason to believe that, around AD 400, the Roman slave system was on a downward slope. The abundant evidence for late Roman slavery has often been noticed, of course, but it has proven harder to *explain* this vitality. The most enduring response to this impasse has been to argue that slaves, while still numerous, were already deployed in a feudal mode of production, managed as tenants rather than slaves. This neo-Marxist narrative is conscious of the evidence for slavery, but ultimately it represents a maneuver which Shaw has described with mordant precision: an attempt "to save appearances by endlessly re-tooling the utility of social and economic classes, modes of production, the special status of the Western city, and the origins of so-called feudalism . . . "[101] The argument that late Roman slaves were effectively serfs or organized in a feudal mode of production does little justice to the sources of the period. Moreover, it lacks a robust explanation for change, relying on a just-so narrative in which ever-larger properties made direct management unworkable. There is, simply, not an account of late Roman slavery that is both responsible to the evidence and analytically compelling.

What is really at stake in the perennial debate about the "end" of Roman slavery is the way we conceive of pre-industrial economies. Both Marx and Weber viewed Roman slavery as an exceptional interlude whose end was predestined.[102] For Marx, Roman slavery was a variant of the community economy, fundamentally tied to war; for Weber, Roman slavery was an episode of war capitalism, a temporary exception to the *oikos*-based society which typified pre-modern, pre-rational market economies.[103] The driving force of the slave system was political, exogenous to the economic system:

---

[101] Shaw 2008, 113. So too Morris and Manning 2005, 8, on the grip of eighteenth- and nineteenth-century models.
[102] Hobsbawm 1964, esp. 17. Morley 1996, 15, on Marx among the primitivists.
[103] Capogrossi Colognesi 1997, 28.

conquest moved capital. When the neo-Marxist account of Roman slavery broke away from the orthodox models and began to admit that slavery could be inherently profitable and productive, there was a revealing moment of indecision over when and why the "crisis" of Roman slavery occurred. Having admitted that slave labor was efficient, the source of crisis was no longer apparent. Some historians found in Rostovtzeff an explanation ready to hand: provincial producers arrived to wrest market share away from the slave-based estates of Italy.[104] For others, Weber's causal sequence, organized around diminishing supply, has seemed the best way to salvage the narrative of decline and transition.[105] The ghost of class struggle quietly vanished, but the machinery looks the same.

The root of the problem lies in the belief that Roman slavery was somehow a basic exception to the mechanics of pre-industrial society and that pre-industrial societies cannot really be shaped by movements of capital. The Roman economy was the most complex and successful economy of the first millennium, by some measures unmatched until the late middle ages. Even though the market was relatively limited in scope, it exerted a tremendous influence in the Roman empire. The dynamics of Roman slavery were not determined by primitive, pre-capitalist styles of exchange. Even if the Roman economy never achieved the breakthrough to continuous intensive growth, it can be analyzed in terms of capital and markets, in terms of demography, commerce, and institutions. The refinements introduced over the last generation by historical demography, institutional economics, and comparative history allow the basic toolbox of neo-classical economics to be applied with more subtlety to the Roman empire.[106] These insights open up a middle ground that does not require us to elide important differences between ancient and modern in the manner of Rostovtzeff, nor to accord them privileged status in the tradition of Bücher, Weber, and Finley. The rise of Roman slavery is increasingly appreciated in these terms, but the later phases of the slave system are still locked in older, deterministic interpretive frameworks.

Instead of looking exclusively for "the" culprit in slavery's decline, we should retreat and work with a general model of what causes slavery in the first place. Slavery was the outcome of the supply of slaves and the demand for their labor. The fundamentals of supply and demand provide a simple, core model, and that model lies behind the organization

[104] This is truly a *deus ex machina*: Giardina 1997b is an acute analysis. For more general criticisms, Tchernia 2006 and Morley 1996.
[105] Vera 2007, 494; Giardina 1997b.   [106] Lo Cascio 2009, 5–16.

of the book. The Roman slave supply was diverse, decentralized, and stable. Demand was a complex and sensitive variable, determined by the ability of elites to capitalize on production *and* the capacity of middling households to consume and exploit slaves. This model does not assume that labor relations are the substructure of change, but rather it places them within broader material, social, and institutional structures. It allows us to admit the diversity of Roman productive systems. It allows us to see intensive rural slavery and extensive household slavery as part of the same system, restoring to household slaves and female slaves a real berth in the story.[107] This model allows us to see the long fourth century for what it was: the last phase of a deep cycle of intensification and integration that lasted from the late republic until the early fifth century AD. But this cycle of Mediterranean development was not an Antiquity that mutated into the Middle Ages, and ancient slavery did not become medieval feudalism.

Even as we abandon the unwieldy terms of class struggle and modes of production, our approach will allow us to restore a credible account of human exploitation to the story of the Roman economy. The Roman economy was not an abstract wheat machine, mobilizing surpluses here and there with bloodless efficiency. The study of slavery asks us to peer inside the black box of production and to ask how the chain of commercialization and intensification worked. We will search for the fierce, little battles over time and effort, repeated on a human scale but across the Roman world, to dig trenches, to manure fields, to trim vines, to muster livestock. And it was not only the rich man who turned the slave's labor into wealth and status; we must be sensitive to the millions of small-scale slave-owners whose possession of a slave's body was a precious marker of respectability. To be a slave-owner was a manifest symbol of honor. "According to the common opinion, where there is no slave, there is no master."[108] But this was not a disembodied symbol. The ownership of slaves, even on a petty scale, brought with it the need to capitalize on their labor. Within the humble household we must imagine the constant struggle to produce, and the use of violence, deprivation, and reward to discipline slaves to their daily of quotas of work. So even if we discard the language of class struggle, the actual material relations remain integral to the story, as we try to understand how the systems of exchange in the Roman world made it

---

[107] See Roth 2007; Saller 2003; López and Pérez 2000; Joshel and Murnaghan 1998; Treggiari 1979a.
[108] Hilar. Pict. Trin. 11.13 (CC 62A: 542): *et secundum commune iudicium, ubi non est servus, neque dominus est.*

worthwhile to create wealth and honor through the domination of human chattel.

This model permits a degree of narrative freedom in the way we describe change. The argument in this book is not that the fourth-century slave system was *as* extensive as before. But reduction does not have to be construed as decline nor to bear the burden of a great historical transition from one mode of production to another. The fourth-century slave system changed in quantity from the earlier centuries of Roman slavery, but it was still essentially *Roman* slavery. The slave system of the fourth century was a mature system. Slave labor was widespread not because slaves were cheap – in fact, they were dear – but because slave labor was deployed in roles where it was highly suitable. Slavery was used when the logic of capital investment rewarded tight control over labor; it was used when effort-intensive work could be physically extracted from unfree bodies; it was used when the dynamics of human capital, legal agency, and positive incentives encouraged long-term control; it was used when the values of honor and shame inhibited the development of a free market; it was used when the domestic sphere provided a venue for the supervision of unskilled labor. The late Roman slave system was structurally stable, operating at a high equilibrium. Change would come from *without*, not from an internal crisis in the system, not from a long-term reduction in supply, not from the new-found dominance of provincial producers, but from the collapse of the material and institutional structures that drove the use of slave labor.

The fall of the Roman empire was an important rupture in the history of slavery. The language of rupture is deliberate. Terms like "transition" and "transformation" suggest seamless change and constant direction, but the period of late antiquity was not monolithic, and the history of slavery was not defined by a single trajectory. The history of slavery in late antiquity needs to be divided into two phases, before and after the fifth century, and geographically into east and west. Slavery had a different destiny in each of these times and places. In the west the salient factor was the material breakdown of the Roman economy – and with it, urbanism, bulk exchange, and elite control over production. Between the fifth and seventh centuries, the Roman system gradually unraveled in the western empire. There were always slaves in western regions. Indeed, our model would predict as much, since slavery is the outcome of both supply and demand. But the vital energy of the slave system was gradually sapped. Endemic warfare would flood the market with captives, even as that very instability washed out the foundations of the economy which had held together the demand for slaves. There was a caesura in the history of labor relations in the early medieval west. Medieval norms of power and dependency would owe virtually nothing to Roman slavery, as serfdom arose out of completely different material and institutional contexts. Roman slavery receded, and the legacy of Roman slavery to later ages of western Europe hardly extended beyond a half-forgotten vocabulary of status.[109]

In the east, change was gradual. The expansion of slavery seems to have been slowly reversed, not because demand collapsed, but because demographic growth, the availability of wage labor, and the fiscal system of the eastern empire created alternatives for estate labor.[110] Slavery would continue to play a role in Byzantine households, however, throughout late antiquity and beyond.[111] The Caliphate, inheritor of the most vibrant parts of the late antique world, would become the vortex of the medieval slave trade.[112] In this post-Roman Mediterranean, religious affiliation would overlay civic identity in new and fateful ways.[113] By the eighth century, when intensification and commercialization began a long, slow ascent in western Europe, the Christian empire of the Carolingians would look on the Islamic world from the vantage of an underdeveloped economy onto a more advanced one. The slave shackles which had once appeared on the farms of late Roman Gaul could now be found only in the trading posts out of which the Carolingians shipped slaves towards the richer markets of the Levant.[114] The European countryside was a landscape without slave labor, even as the kingdoms of the west became crucial suppliers of human chattel. By the ninth century, this very traffic in humans along the frontiers of the Carolingian world would attach a new name – *sclavus*, slave – to those men, women, and children who were truly seen as property, as commodities to be bought and sold, and not simply as dependent laborers.[115] The substitution of "slave" for "*servus*" was a belated recognition of a change that had begun with the fall of Rome.

Late Roman slavery belonged to a world that was lost when the empire fell. Roman slavery exists on its own, as the only vast and enduring slave system of the ancient world, one of history's only pre-modern slave societies. There would always be slavery in the Mediterranean, but the fall of the Roman empire meant the end of a slave society and its replacement, for the next thousand years of Mediterranean history, by a succession of societies

[109] Carolingian labor systems were not successors to the late Roman heritage: Wickham 2005a; Renard 2000; Vera 1998.
[110] Sarris 2006; Banaji 2001 and 1997.
[111] Rotman 2004; Lefort 2002, 241, highly exiguous evidence for rural slavery.
[112] Gilly-Elway 2000; Phillips 1985, 66–87.   [113] Fynn-Paul 2009.   [114] Henning 2008.
[115] See esp. McCormick 2002 and 2001; Kahane and Kahane 1962, 353; Verlinden 1943.

with slaves.[116] The role of slavery in agricultural production, and the long reach of middling slave-ownership, were not lasting. In the post-Roman centuries, female slaves came to command a higher price within a slave trade that would serve the domestic needs of a narrow elite.[117] Only with the rise of sugar, and the virulent expansion of the plantation complex out of the Mediterranean and into the Atlantic, would male slaves once again consistently draw higher prices on the market. Only in the New World would capital find such a vast unending frontier that the expansion of slavery would pass the limits it had known in the age of the Romans. But this book is about what happened in the first civilization that fostered thick commercial exchange, secure property rights, broad middling classes and extensive market-oriented production on a large scale over a long run. Roman slavery, sustained over half a millennium, and touching three continents, and taking millions of souls, was part of the unique mix of ancient and modern which the Romans created and, finally, lost.

[116] cf. Horden and Purcell 2000, 388–91, who stress continuity.   [117] See Harper 2010.

CHAPTER I

Among slave systems: a profile
of late Roman slavery

DEFINING SLAVERY AND SLAVE SOCIETIES

In late Roman Antioch, a Christian preacher named John Chrysostom found himself trying to explain the origins of slavery to his congregation, a problem which he knew "many" were "eager to understand."[1] If his audience hoped for a theoretical disquisition, they got instead a stern lecture.[2] The theme gave Chrysostom the occasion to criticize the everyday hypocrisy of the members of his flock, who dragged an army of slaves behind them into the baths or the theater, but never into church. The slave-owner, he implored, should be the steward of the slave's soul. To illustrate the network of obligations between master and slave, the preacher turned to a familiar political metaphor. "Each house is like a city, and every man is the ruler in his own house. This is obviously true among the rich households, in which there are farms and overseers, and rulers over the rulers. But I say that even the household of the poor man is like a city. For in it there are also rulers. For instance, the man rules his wife, the wife rules the slaves, the slaves rule their own wives, and again the men and women rule the children."[3]

Chrysostom's sermon is a glimpse of Mediterranean society in the late Roman empire. The baths and theaters, where masters flaunted their wealth

---

[1] Ioh. Chrys. In Ephes. 22.2 (PG 62: 157): πολλούς . . . καὶ μαθεῖν βουλομένους. The careful work of Mayer 2005 has demonstrated the uncertain basis of the traditional assignments of dates and places to Chrysostom's sermons. The homilies on Ephesians have been assigned to Antioch (p. 258), but this is now less than definite (p. 471). Maxwell 2006, 94, on Chrysostom's responsiveness to his audience.

[2] Klein 2000 and 1988; Kontoulis 1993; Jaeger 1974, esp. on theological and metaphorical aspects of slavery in the late antique fathers.

[3] Ioh. Chrys. In Ephes. 22.2 (PG 62: 158): Πόλις ἐστὶν ἡ ἑκάστου οἰκία, ἄρχων ἐστὶν ἕκαστος τῆς ἑαυτοῦ οἰκίας. Καὶ ὅτι μὲν τοιαύτη ἡ τῶν πλουτούντων, εὔδηλον, ἔνθα καὶ ἀγροὶ καὶ ἐπίτροποι καὶ ἄρχοντες ἐπὶ ἄρχουσιν. ἐγὼ δὲ καὶ τὴν τῶν πενήτων οἰκίαν φημὶ πόλιν εἶναι. Καὶ γὰρ καὶ ἐνταῦθά εἰσιν ἀρχαί. οἷον, κρατεῖ τῆς γυναικὸς ὁ ἀνήρ, ἡ γυνὴ τῶν οἰκετῶν, οἱ οἰκέται τῶν ἰδίων γυναικῶν. πάλιν αἱ γυναῖκες καὶ οἱ ἄνδρες τῶν παίδων. cf. Nagle 2006 and Hasegawa 2005, for these metaphors. Holman 2001, 1–6, for πένης. Mayer 2006. Other "poor" slave-owners: Ioh. Chrys. In Philip. 2.5 (PG 62: 197); Ioh. Chrys. In Coloss. 1.4 (PG 62: 304).

in slaves, were the façade of an exuberant urban culture, poised carefully amidst the much vaster world of agrarian society.[4] Although urban in its cultural orientation, the late Roman aristocracy was, to an exceptional degree, a market-oriented aristocracy whose power derived from the ability to capitalize on land and labor.[5] Wealth was earned by selling wine, grain, oil, and textiles in the markets created by town populations. Yet, as the sermon shows, late antique society was a traditional society, and the household remained the fundamental unit of property and labor, production and reproduction. For Chrysostom, the rich household was an agro-commercial enterprise, just as the "poor" household was a way of organizing life's material burdens. The household and the city, the rich and the poor, the urban and the rural: as Chrysostom saw, it was a world unthinkable without slaves.

A history of late Roman slavery should begin by confronting the question which Chrysostom managed to dance around: what is slavery? The Roman jurists defined slavery as "an institution of the law of nations, by which one person is subjected against nature to the *dominium* of another." Florentinus, the lawyer who authored the definition, then indulged in some speculative philology. "The name 'slave' (*servus*) derives from the fact that commanders sell captives and by this custom 'save' (*servare*) them rather than kill them."[6] The ideology of conquest retained great purchase in the late empire, but we need not take these statements at face value.[7] With extreme economy, the Roman legal description of slavery moved from myth to reality. Slavery was conceived of and justified as the outcome of military victory, allowing masters across the empire to participate in the superiority of Roman arms over the barbarian chaos.[8] The Romans had a remarkable capacity to imagine their world in militaristic terms.[9] The folk etymology of the "slave" as the spared war captive, the living dead, symbolized the master's claim to the slave's entire existence, body and soul.[10] But ultimately, even this loaded ideological definition could not avoid the fact that the spared

---

[4] Urbanism, Lavan 2001; Liebeschuetz 2001; Brogiolo and Ward-Perkins 1999; Rich 1992; Lepelley 1981a. For a quantitative approach, Alston 2001. Jongman 2003, explores the relationship between slavery and urbanism.

[5] Wickham 2005a, esp. 155–6.

[6] Dig. 1.5.4–5: *servitus est constitutio iuris gentium, qua quis dominio alieno contra naturam subicitur. servi ex eo appellati sunt, quod imperatores captivos vendere ac per hoc servare nec occidere solent.* cf. Dig. 50.16.239.1; Inst. 1.3.3. The etymology was fictitious: Wieling 1999, 4, 42.

[7] E.g. Ambrosiast. Comm. Coloss. 4.1–3 (CSEL 81.2: 202); Aug. Civ. 19.15 (CC 48: 682–3).

[8] Household objects such as lamps celebrated the control of barbarian slaves: Lenski 2008, 84.

[9] McCormick 1987.   [10] cf. Dig. 50.17.209.

victim of Roman conquest was *sold*. For, in the marketplace, master and slave truly met, and the ideology of conquest was fleshed out in the form of human bodies for sale.

The essential characteristic of slavery, distinguishing it from all other human relationships, is the commodification of the human being, the reduction of the human body to a piece of property.[11] In late antiquity the experience of slavery was diverse, because circumstances and masters and slaves were diverse. But the essential core of the slave experience, shared by slaves of all stripes, was the fact that the slave was human property. The slave was the one whose body had a price, who might someday know what it was like to sit on the auction block and watch "the bidder lifting his finger."[12] The Roman slave system was a vast and interconnected market in human bodies. This fact often lies uneasily beneath the surface, because our sources tell us so little about the workings of commerce or about the actual experience of slavery. But the Roman slave system was a market that could move bodies from Gaul to Egypt, from Mauretania to Anatolia.[13] It was a system in which sale, in which the conversion of the slave from individual to chattel, could be effected at a moment's notice. Some masters were alive to this threat and wielded it against their slaves: "There are slaves who fear this utterly, more than the penalty of incarceration or chains."[14] The commercial networks of the Roman empire were an existential reality for Roman slaves. Slaves were chattel in the Roman empire, a material, legal, philosophical and existential fact.

The existence of the slave in the market, the need to subject the slave to complete ownership, determined those inescapable symptoms of slavery: deracination from family and community alliance, lack of social honor, subjection to brutal domination, and exploitation of the slave's body, its productive and reproductive capacity. In the words of Libanius, "The slave is one who will at some point belong to someone else, whose body can be sold. And what could be more humiliating, than to have money taken

---

[11] Andreau and Descat 2006, 18; Weiler 2003, 53–4; Finley 1998 (orig. 1980), 145; Shaw 1998, 12; Garnsey 1996, 1; Harrill 1995, 14–18; Brockmeyer 1979, 3. Property is a way of constructing and systematizing power (the absolute power to use and to transfer). cf. Patterson 1982, 13, for a comparative approach which can encompass less complex societies where slave status was not articulated through a property system; Rotman 2004, 25–51; Miers and Kopytoff 1977, 11. But definitions which identify the commodification of the human person as the essence of slavery are more persuasive: Davis 2006, 30–2; Lovejoy 2003, 1; Johnson 1999; Watson 1980a, 8.

[12] Ambr. Ep. 7.17 (CSEL 82: 51): *licitatorem . . . tollentem digitum.*   [13] See chapter 2.

[14] Ambr. Tob. 8.31 (CSEL 32.2: 535): *habent servi quod amplius quam carceris poenas et vincula reformident.*

by the old, given by the new master? For indeed, has not this body been mutilated, and the soul utterly destroyed?"[15] The sale was the essence of slavery, systematic humiliation its inevitable consequence. The inevitable dehumanizing qualities of slavery are revealed in a range of late antique documents. Most immediately, a number of tracts remain, by preachers, popular orators, and philosophers, purporting to define the "true" nature of slavery by subverting its actual meaning in the late Roman world.[16] These speeches represent the self-assurance of the master class and a taste for ticklish rhetorical inversions. Yet, in purporting to describe an esoteric "true" slavery, they often put up as straw men the very presumptions they wanted to invert: the audience's mundane understanding of slavery. These speeches reveal a society familiar with slavery as a matter not only of commodification, but also of dishonor and domination.

Libanius, for instance, wanted to prove that everyone from the butcher and the baker to the philosopher was, in some way, a "slave." To do so, he had to dispel from the mind of his audience the idea that slavery was a matter of dishonor. Dishonor, for an oratorical master who had the pulse of his listeners, was the most immediately felt attribute of the slave. "Whenever someone is offended, if he is a free man he will complain vociferously. But, if a man outrages a slave, and then should be accused of it, he becomes riled and says that he is allowed to strike the slave – just as though the slave were a piece of stone."[17] Such a mundane encounter summoned for Libanius a welter of deeply felt emotions activated by the dynamics of power and social recognition. The social correlate of being a piece of chattel was a complete lack of honor. Female slaves lacked the formal power and network of relationships to protect their bodies, the measure of feminine honor; male slaves were denied access to the normal symbols of masculine dignity, right down to their name. Slaves were *outside* the system of social recognition, the game of honor.

To overturn their audience's expectations, late antique rhetors also had to argue that slavery was *not* a system of interlocking violence and fear. For those surrounded by the institution, it was all too obvious that "nothing

---

[15] Lib. Or. 25.71 (Foerster vol. 2: 571): ὁ δοῦλος ἄλλοτε ἄλλου γίνεται καὶ ἔστι πρᾶσις τοῦ σώματος. καὶ τί ταύτῃ γε ἐκεῖνος ἀθλιώτερος, εἰ ἀργύριον ὁ μὲν ἔλαβεν, ὁ δὲ ἔδωκεν; οὐ γὰρ δὴ τὸ σῶμά γε αὐτῷ τοῦτο ἐπήρωσεν οὐδ᾽ αὖ τὴν ψυχὴν διέφθειρεν . . .

[16] Garnsey 1996, 16–19, on this class of discourse.

[17] Lib. Or. 25.1 (Foerster vol. 2: 539): καὶ ὅταν δὲ προπηλακίζηταί τις, μᾶλλόν τι δεινολογεῖται τῷ ἐλεύθερος εἶναι, καὶ ἄν γε εἰς δοῦλον ὑβρίζῃ, πάλιν, εἰ ἐγκαλεῖ τις, ποιεῖται δεινὸν ἐξεῖναι λέγων τύπτειν, ὥσπερ τοὺς λίθους.

is more particular to slavery than the permanent fear."[18] Slavery was a power relationship sanctioned by violent domination and attendant fear. In a discourse on slavery, the emperor Julian would say that "he is truly a slave who has another man as a master who forces him to do whatever the master wants, and, if the slave does not obey, punishes him, and in the words of the poet, 'visits grievous pain upon him'... though, even the harshest of masters do not treat all their slaves in such a way, while often a word or a threat will suffice."[19] The arsenal of the master was as subtle as it was sinister. As Julian recognized, slavery was a relationship of exploitation achieved by domination, whether its mechanics be physical or psychological.

Slavery was such a charged metaphor because it was an exceptionally important component of the Roman social edifice. Slavery has been a virtually universal feature of human societies, but it is highly unusual for slavery to become a central rather than peripheral institution.[20] Societies with slaves are common, but slave societies are exceedingly rare. The notion of a "slave society," although it has a long pedigree, was most influentially formulated by Finley to describe societies where slaves are present in large numbers, where slave labor is instrumental in central productive processes, and where the domination of slaves has deep cultural consequences.[21] It is immediately apparent that no clear threshold guards any of these criteria. And like any tool of analysis, the idea of a "slave society" can be used and abused. There were already problems in the way that Finley used it. Writing before the great strides in non-western historiography, he underemphasized the breadth of world slavery. Writing before realistic estimates of the ancient slave population, he overstated the quantitative dimensions of Roman slavery. The categories of the slave society and the society with slaves, moreover, should be seen as types, admitting of shades and variations, and not as binary alternatives. But Finley's notion of a slave society is worth salvaging.

---

[18] Ambr. Ios. 4.20 (CSEL 32.2: 87): *nihil enim tam speciale servitutis est quam semper timere.* See chapter 5.

[19] Iul. Imp. Or. 9.15 (Rochefort vol. 2.1: 163–4): ἀλλ' ἐκεῖνός ἐστιν ὡς ἀληθῶς δοῦλος, οὗ κύριός ἐστιν ἕτερος προσαναγκάσαι πράττειν ὅτι ἂν κελεύῃ, καὶ μὴ βουλόμενον κόλασαι καί, τὸ λεγόμενον ὑπὸ τοῦ ποιητοῦ, "κακαῖς ὀδύνῃσι πελάζειν..." Καίτοι γε τοιοῦτον οὐδὲ οἱ τραχύτατοι τῶν δεσποτῶν ἐπὶ πάντων ποιοῦσι τῶν οἰκετῶν, ἀλλὰ καὶ λόγος ἀρκεῖ πολλάκις καὶ ἀπειλή.

[20] Garnsey 1996, 2.

[21] Finley 1998 (orig. 1980), 135–60. cf. Weiler 2003, 55–72; Turley 2000, 62–100; Berlin 1998; Oakes 1990, 36–9. For its origins, Higman 2001.

This book is an extended comment on the claim that Roman imperial society of the fourth century was a slave society. This chapter outlines the dimensions of the slave population; chapters 2–4 describe the material impact of slavery; the remainder of the book characterizes the social and institutional ramifications of the slave system. Throughout the discussion our most important guides will be those who witnessed the Roman slave system first-hand, for they have left behind ample indication that they lived in a slave society. They will tell us, in their own words, that slavery was central in the construction of honor.[22] They will tell us that primary social roles, such as the *pater familias*, were indelibly shaped by the presence of slaves.[23] They will tell us that the institutionalized sexual exploitation of slaves was an integral part of their society.[24] They paraded slaves through the streets in their most sacred political rites.[25] They claimed that slaves were the symbol of wealth. Most importantly, they recognized that slave labor was a primary means of accumulating wealth.[26] Not in all societies do so many contemporaries insist in so many ways that slavery was so important. The evidence of the long fourth century points to that convergence of forces, that distinct momentum, which makes slavery more than a peripheral institution. The late Roman empire was inhabited by a slave society.

TOWARDS A CENSUS OF LATE ROMAN SLAVERY

Grand narratives like "conquest" and "transition" have a special influence in ancient history for an insidious reason: our evidence is limited and a good story tends to stick. The prefabricated story of rise and fall, loosely following the fortunes of the army, has subtly influenced evidentiary standards in the study of ancient slavery. Decline was always a thing to be *explained* rather than *demonstrated* – two very different projects.[27] Scheidel has justly ridiculed the canonical estimates of the number of slaves in the late republic and early empire. They are, bluntly, "devoid of any evidentiary foundation," and yet they managed to usurp the status of received fact.[28] Scheidel's persuasive demolition of these figures clears the way for serious discussion. But it is notable that his arguments take the form of establishing plausible limits on the number of slaves. By working *down* from the absurdly overblown numbers, he reconstructs a plausible model

---

[22] See chapter 8.   [23] Lact. Inst. 4.3 (CSEL 19.1: 280–1).
[24] Hier. Ep. 77.3 (CSEL 55: 39).   [25] The consular manumission ritual: see part III.
[26] See chapter 4.   [27] McKeown 2007, 52–76.   [28] Scheidel 2008, 106; 2005a, 1999, and 1997.

of the slave population.[29] The historian of the late Roman slave population does not have the same luxury.

The sources, as in all periods of antiquity, are emphatically insufficient. If anything, the late Roman evidence presents more of a challenge, simply because the balance of documentary to literary material is tipped further towards the latter than in previous eras. However foolhardy this endeavor may seem, it remains absolutely necessary, because the problems do not simply disappear once we admit that numbers are hard or impossible to find. Even if we formally eschew "the numbers game," silent conjectures about the number and distribution of slaves are likely to operate, if only in the back of our minds. If one quietly assumes that Melania with her thousands of slaves was representative of the wealthiest 1 percent of the Roman aristocracy, or that the "poor" slave-owner of John Chrysostom was below the average level of wealth, then strange, indefensible images of Roman society emerge. It is more dangerous *not* to ask questions like how many slaves there were, or how representative a given source is, even when the answers to such questions are inevitably tentative and imprecise.

How, then, can we bring some order to the chaos of the evidence? Finley, aware that the estimates of the slave population rested on thin empirical foundations, urged historians to identify the social "location" of slavery. Scheidel has shown how this might be pursued even more robustly with what he calls a "bottom-up" approach, in place of the undisciplined "top-down" attempts to guess how many slaves there were. This is surely the right way to proceed. The method involves three steps, each of which entails margins of error: (1) identify *types* of slave-holders, (2) gather all the evidence for slave-ownership of each type in order to establish a plausible *range* of the number of slaves an owner could have owned, and, finally, (3) plug these figures into the most reasonable *models* of Roman society available. Steps (1) and (2) are of most immediate concern here, since we can rely on existing scholarship to provide us with a model of Roman social structure. Perhaps better organization of the data, more critical use of the sources, or new knowledge about Roman society as a whole will allow us to improve the numbers. In the meantime, some quantitative discipline is better than none.

The late Roman source material presents a kaleidoscope of fragmentary insights into the patterns of slave-owning in the fourth century. To bring order to this anarchy, the first step is to establish workable categories of slave-ownership. These categories are imposed, a simplified version of

[29] Scheidel 2005a.

reality, but they are justified if they improve our ability to sift and weigh the evidence. We can identify four distinct types of slave-ownership, roughly in descending order of wealth: (1) Illustrious, (2) Elite, (3) Bourgeois, and (4) Agricultural.[30] These divisions are based on multiple criteria: the scale of wealth, the labor performed by the household, and the physical location of the household. The lines between the types are not hard and fast, but when we apply the categories to the evidence, they do help us trace distinctive patterns in the structures of slave-ownership.[31]

Illustrious and Elite slave-owners sat atop the Roman social pyramid, representing the wealthiest 1 or 1.5 percent of Roman society (see p. 46); they were by far the largest scale slave-owners. Because wealth was extremely stratified even within the very top tier of Roman society, it is helpful to distinguish them as separate groups. The label Illustrious takes its inspiration from the title *illustris*, standardized in the later fourth century for the highest tier of the senatorial order.[32] We use it to refer to those 500 or 600 families who controlled the largest individual portfolios of property, the core of the senatorial order, most of whom lived in the west, in Rome. These households enjoyed staggering amounts of wealth, and they could own hundreds, even thousands of slaves, but they represented only the top five-thousandths of 1 percent of the Roman population.

Elite slave-owners included the bulk of the senatorial order (*spectabiles* and *clarissimi*), the remnants of the equestrian order, decurions, and other members of Roman society with roughly equivalent wealth – the rest of the top 1 or 1.5 percent of the aristocracy. It is especially fitting to group these individuals together in the fourth century, for during this period the senatorial order expanded from some 600 members to something like 6,000, effectively extinguishing the equestrian order and siphoning off the top layers of the curial class.[33] This process, so painful for the functioning of the town councils, makes no real difference for our reconstruction. There was, of course, tremendous stratification within this category – just imagine the difference between the lower tiers of the curial class in, say, Thagaste and a principal member of the Alexandrian town council. We will argue that slave-holding within this category varied accordingly, from half-a-dozen to possibly scores of slaves.

Illustrious and Elite households share important features that distinguish them from Bourgeois and Agricultural slave-holders. Only within

[30] Throughout the book, the capitalized use of these terms refers back to this taxonomy.
[31] These categories are not exhaustive (e.g. public slaves are omitted, see Grey forthcoming; Lenski 2006a), but in material terms, households and estates were the vital players.
[32] Jones 1964, 528–30.   [33] Heather 1998; Lepelley 1986.

wealthier households did any distinction between the *familiae urbanae* and *familiae rusticae* hold. When late antique authors spoke of them as discrete categories, it signaled households where function or location could distinguish between different sorts of slaves.[34] Moreover, the composition of the *familiae urbanae* in Illustrious and Elite households followed distinctive patterns. Historians of servitude in the high middle ages have described a crucial difference in the organization of service in aristocratic and bourgeois households.[35] Truly large aristocratic households, with staffs ranging from half-a-dozen to hundreds, exhibited structural features that distinguished them from smaller slave-holding households. Large households employed a higher ratio of male slaves than female slaves. This imbalance was an effect of the greater diversity of specializations typed as male labor.[36] Middling households, on the other hand, with few slaves, were more likely to employ a balanced number of male and female slaves – if not *more* females, who performed unskilled domestic and textile labor, to say nothing of sexual exploitation.[37] By all appearances, an analogous distinction between large and medium households, our Illustrious/Elite and Bourgeois/Agricultural, also held in antiquity.

Bourgeois and Agricultural slave-holders were distinguished from Illustrious and Elite households by the smaller scale of their wealth, and they were distinguished from each other by the type of labor they performed. The label "Bourgeois" is patently anachronistic, but there is no good terminology for that wide category of Mediterranean society under Roman rule, inferior to the highest echelon but nevertheless enjoying a lifestyle safely above subsistence, status conscious, consumerist in its economic habits. It has sometimes been called a "middle class," and the harmless if dull label "middling" is enjoying a renaissance.[38] "Petty bourgeois" is closer to what we mean, but cumbersome. The word forces us to confront the sheer size of this social element in the Roman world, so we might be forgiven for dropping the inverted commas. This group constitutes the visible element of town society beneath the curial order, stretching into the professions and trades, into the artisanal and petty mercantile families that can be found owning slaves in late antiquity. As we will see below, sub-elite slave-ownership in the Roman world was frequently noted by contemporaries,

[34] The line was still often fluid: Dig. 32.99.pr.   [35] Romano 1996, 106–17.
[36] Saller 2007a, 105; Hasegawa 2005, 30–41; Joshel 1992; Treggiari 1979b and 1975a.
[37] cf. fifteenth-century Genoa, where 97 percent of slaves were female: Gioffré 1971, and more on p. 62.
[38] "Middling," e.g. Scheidel and Friesen 2009. "Middle class," Hirschfeld 2001, 258. Goody 2004, esp. 137–8, on the rise of the bourgeois in early modern period. Morley 2006, 29, on the rhetorical strategy of such labels.

and recognizing this group will enrich our understanding of the literary evidence.

Slave-owning in the Bourgeois style is characterized by the relatively smaller number of slaves in the household, under a half-dozen slaves and frequently only two or three. In this type of household, the sex ratio among the slaves was likely to be balanced or tilted towards females. The Bourgeois household is one in which the family is largely independent from agricultural labor, even though some Bourgeois households owned land. These households were located in the city. Bourgeois slave-ownership can be found at various times and places across Mediterranean history, and it became prominent in the late medieval and early modern periods, when levels of consumption and urbanism once again expanded.[39] The intense urbanization of the Roman world was driven, in no small measure, by this style of slave-ownership. Bourgeois households were a key characteristic of the Roman city and thus of Roman society.[40]

The final type of household slave-ownership in the Roman empire is the Agricultural household, what we might call the rich peasant or the elite villager. Over 80 percent of the population lived outside the city, and the importance of slavery among well-to-do rural households cannot be ignored. In the east, rural habitation was organized around village life, and slavery appears to have been prominent among the top tier of village families.[41] In the west, rural settlement was dispersed; the countryside was dotted with peasant households, middling farmsteads, and estate centers.[42] The existence of slavery on the family farm in the west is a crucial but poorly studied phenomenon. Even in the supposed heyday of the slave villa, the archaeology of the countryside points to a diverse settlement pattern, heavily populated with small- and middle-sized structures.[43] Likewise, even village society in the east knew its small-scale stratification. The well-to-do rural household, while not Elite in scale, and not Bourgeois in habitation, was a player in the Roman slave system and must therefore find recognition in our model.

This rough, working typology can help us make sense of the fragmentary data for late antique slavery. The evidence is relentlessly impressionistic, and the ancient authors, of course, have used their terms rather than ours. In what follows, we gather evidence which provides clues about the social

[39] E.g. Stuard 1983; Goitein 1967–93, vol. 1, 130–47; Origo 1955.
[40] Jongman 2003, earlier period. MacMullen 1987; Hahn 1976 and 1961, for late antiquity.
[41] Bagnall 1996, 125.   [42] Wickham 2005a, 442.
[43] Jongman 2003, 111; Dyson 1981, 82; Potter 1979. Medium-sized rural sites: Lewit 1991, 22–4. Rathbone 2008 is esp. valuable, for the late republic.

location of slavery. There are contemporary observations on the extent of slave-ownership and, occasionally, comments on different tiers of slave-holding. These last are truly precious, for they validate and enrich our attempt to categorize different scales of slave-holding in the late empire. There are also surviving census documents, which are records that must be located, geographically and socially, no less than the literary evidence. Imperfect though they are, they remain invaluable. Finally, we sometimes know the social profile of specific, individual slave-holders whom we can place within our categories. Individually, none of these sets of information would be satisfying, but in conjunction they begin to gain some credibility, and they can help us establish plausible ranges of slave-ownership within each of our categories.

(1) *Illustrious slave-holders in the late Roman empire.* At the beginning of the fourth century, the top 500–600 families constituted the senatorial order. By the end of the fourth century, the senatorial order had expanded to include thousands of members, but the old core remained, so that the emperors were forced to recognize three distinctions within the order, *illustres, spectabiles*, and *clarissimi*.[44] The *illustres* were the top of the top, holding the highest offices of state such as the consulate and the praetorian prefecture. We do not know precisely how many enjoyed this official rank, but for our purposes we can work with a figure on the order of the scale of the old senate, some 500–600 families, the wealthiest 0.0048 percent of the empire.[45] Wealth, primarily in land, was extraordinarily stratified in late Roman society, but perhaps not radically more so than in the high empire; narratives of constant, linear accumulation rest on little evidence.[46] Although their land-holdings were scattered across Italy, Sicily, and Africa, the wealthiest senators of the fourth century still resided in Rome and formed a distinctly important socio-political bloc. Their extreme wealth is known to us, in the famous income figures reported by Olympiodorus and through the examples of Symmachus and Melania. They have left traces, archaeologically, through their grand *domus* in the City as well as their palatial villas in the countryside.[47]

The domestic establishments of Illustrious households could contain dozens, scores, possibly hundreds of slaves. Ammianus vividly described the opulent showmanship of the rich Roman household, literally parading its slaves through the street in marching order under the command of

---

[44] Jones 1964, 528–30.
[45] All calculations employ an average of four persons per household (cf. Scheidel and Friesen 2009, n. 73) and a total population of 50 million.
[46] See chapter 4.   [47] In general, Wickham 2005a, 162–63.

the *praepositus*, the head slave, like an army divided into divisions: those in front carrying the master's carriage, then the weavers, then the kitchen crew, then the rest of the slaves indiscriminately, with a contingent of eunuchs, ranked oldest to youngest, bringing up the rear. The rich Roman, he said, also took fifty slaves to the bath, an exaggeration surely, but a suggestive one.[48] In the *Historia Augusta*, the senator Tacitus was represented manumitting one hundred of his urban slaves – he supposedly had more.[49] The seventy-five slave-girls and eunuchs that Melania took with her *after* her renunciation of the material world were only a fraction of her once-great Roman household.[50] Jerome, always ready with unsolicited advice for the wealthiest women of the Roman senate, imagined a massive center of textile production within the rich household.[51] The property of the senator Symmachus helps us to visualize how a small army of male agents might be employed in a large senatorial household.[52] Within these households the degree of specialization and level of investment in human capital was greatest; the Illustrious household was a conglomerate agro-firm.[53]

The question of how many rural slaves the typical Illustrious household owned is a particularly important and intractable problem that will be discussed below, in conjunction with the related question of how many rural slaves we should imagine on the land of Elite households. For now it is worth eliciting a few immediate indications of the scale of agricultural slavery on the land of Illustrious slave-holders. The best-known case is the property of Melania the Younger, whose wealth is described in some detail by multiple sources. One witness claimed that she owned well over 8,000 slaves; her biography depicts a single estate complex with 2,400 slaves and claims, in a cautiously worded passage, that she freed thousands of her slaves.[54] John Chrysostom, in a fiesty harangue against the rich, accused eastern aristocrats of owning "so and so many acres of land, ten or twenty estates or more, and just as many baths, a thousand slaves, or two thousand, litters covered with silver and spangled with gold."[55] We should

---

[48] Amm. 14.6.16–17 (Seyfarth vol. 1: 15) and Amm. 28.4.8–9 (Seyfarth vol. 2: 78). cf. Pedanius Secundus with his 400 slaves, cited *ad infinitum* in discussions of Roman slavery.
[49] SHA, Tacit. 10.7 (Hohl vol. 2: 194).
[50] Pall. H. Laus. 61 (Butler vol. 2: 156). Olympias took fifty *cubicularii* into ascetic retirement. Ioh. Chrys. Ep. Olymp. (SC 13: 418).
[51] Hier. Ep. 130.1 (CSEL 56: 176); Hier. Vig. 6 (PL 23: 345).
[52] See chapter 4; Vera 1986b.   [53] See chapter 3.
[54] Ger. Vit. Mel. (lat.) 18.3 (Laurence: 188–90); Pall. H. Laus. 61 (Butler vol. 2: 156). See chapter 4.
[55] Ioh. Chrys. In Mt. 63.4 (PG 58: 608): πλέθρων γῆς τόσων καὶ τόσων μέμνησαι, καὶ οἰκιῶν δέκα καὶ εἴκοσιν, ἢ καὶ πλειόνων, καὶ βαλανείων τοσούτων, καὶ ἀνδραπόδων χιλίων, ἢ δὶς τοσούτων, καὶ ὀχημάτων ἀργυρενδέτων καὶ χρυσοπάστων. Schiavone 2000, 112, has believed Chrysostom's claim, while MacMullen 1987, 364, is skeptical. De Ste. Croix 1981, 242 and Liebeschuetz 1972, 47, emphasize the rhetorical character of the passage.

note too that when Chrysostom wished to say "countless" slaves (which he often did), he used the Greek "myriads."[56] In the linguistic register of Chrysostom, the use of *thousands* is deliberate. It is possible that the 152 slaves belonging to a single owner on Thera were part of an Illustrious portfolio. Parallel evidence reinforces these impressions. The slaves who appear in senatorial property disputes, the private armies of slaves raised by senators, the lingering fears of slave rebellions, the desperate debates over whether to enlist slaves in the army – if hard to quantify, these testimonies are at least consistent with the hypothesis that masses of slaves labored on the land of the Illustrious.[57]

Given their prominence in the sources which survive, we must actively remember just how thin the Illustrious crust truly was, 0.0048 percent of society. Despite the traces they have left in the literature and in the soil it is, as always, hard to establish any reliable averages. Within that very tiny elite who sat atop the precipitously steep social hierarchy, the evidence suggests a range of slave-ownership in the hundreds or even thousands of slaves.[58]

(2) *Elite slave-holders in the late Roman empire.* When we speak of Elite slave-holders, we are still within the very highest echelons of Roman society, the top 1–1.5 percent. We include here *spectabiles* and *clarissimi*, the remnants of the equestrian order, as well as decurions and other wealthy members of Roman society. Over the fourth century, the senatorial order expanded by a factor of ten, drawing principally from the top tiers of the town councils; the famous "crisis" of the town councils was first and foremost an administrative adjustment.[59] We do not know either the number of town councils, nor the average number of councilors in each city, but some reasonable orders of magnitude have been suggested.[60] Total estimates range from 100,000 to 360,000.[61] We can conservatively accept the lowest figure, 100,000, although it may exclude from our reconstruction some of the more modest councilors from lesser towns whose slave-holding patterns will thus fall into the Bourgeois pattern.[62] There were also wealthy

[56] Ioh. Chrys. Salut. Prisc. 1.4 (PG 51: 193); Ioh. Chrys. In Mt. 12.5 (PG 57: 207); Ioh. Chrys. In act. Apost. 13.4 (PG 60: 110); Ioh. Chrys. In Coloss. 7.5 (PG 62: 350).

[57] See chapter 4 and esp. Lenski 2009.

[58] Given the stratification within each group, the median will always be well below the mean; the number of slaves per slave-holder is higher than the number of slaves of the middle slave-holder.

[59] Heather 1998; Zuckerman 1998; Whittow 1990.

[60] Tacoma 2006, 132–40; Laniado 2002, 5–7; Nichols 1988, demonstrated that there was no universal size.

[61] Scheidel and Friesen 2009 (130,000); Jongman 2006 and 1988, 193; Alföldy 1986, 127 (100,000–150,000). See Duncan-Jones 1982, 283–7. Maddison 2007; Goldsmith 1984.

[62] Augustine's *Confessions* show slaves in and around his family, a modest curial family (not a poor family – see Shaw 1987a) from a third-rate town.

inhabitants of late Roman society who did not boast, or suffer, senatorial or curial rank, and they can be found owning slaves in the Elite style during the fourth century.[63] Again it is impossible to know how many there were, but informed guesses have put them between 65,000 and 130,000 in the high empire, so let us assume the lowest figure for the fourth century.[64] Excluding the Illustrious, the sum of 5,500 senators, 100,000 decurions, and 65,000 independently wealthy individuals yields 170,500 Elite households. In a population of 50 million, our Elite households would represent the top 1.36 percent of society.[65]

Elite slave-ownership, falling beneath the Illustrious tier, but above the Bourgeois level, ranged from a half-a-dozen to scores of slaves. It is reasonable to posit that when our fourth-century sources, especially outside of Rome, speak of the "rich man" with his slaves, they are describing slaveholders that fall into our Elite category. Extensive levels of slave-ownership are well attested among this class, in both household and agricultural contexts, from distant parts of the empire. Cyril of Alexandria spoke of rich households with an immoderate abundance of specialized slaves.[66] The Cappadocian fathers were concerned by this sort of opulent household, with its "cooks, bakers, winepourers, hunters, sculptors, painters, and those who serve every pleasure."[67] Basil, likewise, presumed that the rich man would have innumerable agricultural slaves, overseers, industrial workers, in addition to an extravagant contingent of household slaves.[68] Basil knew a greedy official who had amassed "an abundance of land, farms and estates, herds and slaves."[69] No large property could be mentioned without its servile component.[70] Late antique authors regularly assumed that the "rich man" not only owned slaves, but owned "multitudes," "droves," "herds," "swarms," "armies," or simply "innumerable" slaves.[71]

---

[63] CT 12.1.96 (AD 383). The evidence for land-holding from Egypt (Bagnall 1992) and Asia Minor (Harper 2008) also allows for Elite-level wealth outside the curial order. See also chapter 3 for merchants, without official rank, who owned slaves.

[64] Scheidel and Friesen 2009 (65,000–130,000).

[65] Below the estimates of Friesen 2004, 340, and towards the lower end of Scheidel and Friesen 2009.

[66] Cyr. Hom. Pasch. 11.4 (PG 77: 648).

[67] Bas. Hom. Div. 2.2 (Courtonne: 46–7): μάγειροι, σιτοποιοί, οἰνοχόοι, θηρευταί, πλάσται, ζωγράφοι, ἡδονῆς παντοίας δημιουργοί. Reflected in late Roman art: Dunbabin 2003b, 156.

[68] Bas. Hom. Div. 2.2 (Courtonne: 46–7).

[69] Bas. Hom. Mart. Iulit. 1 (PG 31: col 237): γῆς τε πλῆθος ἀποτεμόμενος, καὶ ἀγροὺς καὶ κώμας, καὶ βοσκήματα καὶ οἰκέτας.

[70] Ps.-Ath. Virg. 91 (CSCO 593: 34); Ioh. Chrys. Thdr. 2.18.17 (SC 117: 192); Ioh. Chrys. Psalm. 49.1 (PG 55: 239); Ioh. Chrys. Hoc scit. (PG 56: 275); Lib. Or. 8.1 (Foerster vol. 1: 385); Aug. Conf. 1.19.30 (CC 27: 16–7).

[71] Multitudes: Petr. Alex. Div. 55 (Pearson and Vivian: 119); Ioh. Chrys. Subintr. 9.27 (Dumortier: 76–7); Ioh. Chrys. Ad pop. Ant. 2.5 (PG 49: 40); Gr. Naz. Or. 16.19 (PG 35: 961); Cyr. Hom. Pasch.

The letters and speeches of Libanius cast light on the slave-holding patterns of Elite households. He described the rise of a man named Heliodorus, a *garum* merchant who made money, invested it in land and slaves, and then decided to pursue a legal education. He eventually served the emperor, and as a reward he was given "many farms in Macedonia, still more in Aitolia and Akarnania, gold, silver, an abundance of slaves, and herds of horses and cattle."[72] Thalassius, a man Libanius wished to nominate for the senate, had a knife factory in his household staffed with slave labor.[73] Aristophanes, a decurion of Corinth, owned estates with slaves in his native town.[74] Perhaps most revealing, Libanius praised a retired military commander for being virtuous but *not* wealthy. "This man for a long time commanded many soldiers, but he was barely able to buy one farm, and even it was nothing to praise. He had eleven slaves, twelve mules, three horses, four Laconian dogs, but he terrified the souls of the barbarians."[75] It says something that a military officer in late antiquity could retire, buy a modest farm, staff it with nearly a dozen slaves, and still be the first example of someone distinctly not wealthy. From the perspective of an Antiochene councilor, the ownership of eleven slaves was unremarkable.

The documentary evidence, incomplete though it is, adds confirmation that it is reasonable to associate curial and other wealthy households with slave-ownership of some scale. A large curial-scale property in Hermonthis included fifteen field slaves, and there were clearly numerous others in the central management unit and domestic sphere.[76] A third-century will describing the property of a wealthy Alexandrian family mentioned some twenty-two slaves.[77] A third-century land-owner, not apparently of any status, left his wife seven slaves.[78] In 289 an Oxyrhynchite man pled poverty,

11.5 (PG 77: 648). Droves: Choric. Or. 32.7 (Foerster and Richtsteig: 346). Army: Ioh. Chrys. Psalm. 49.1 (PG 55: 239). Herds: Ioh. Chrys. In 1 Cor. 40.5 (PG 61: 353); Hier. Ep. 22.16 (CSEL 54: 163–4). Swarms: Ioh. Chrys. In 1 Cor. 40.5 (PG 61: 354). Innumerable: Bas. Hom. Div. 2.2 (Courtonne: 46–7); Bas. Attend. 5 (Rudberg: 31); Bas. (dub.) Is. 2.89 (PG 30: 264); Ioh. Chrys. Salut. Prisc. 1.4 (PG 51: 193); Ioh. Chrys. In Mt. 12.5 (PG 57: 207); Ioh. Chrys. In act. Apost. 13.4 (PG 60: 110); Ioh. Chrys. In. Coloss. 7.5 (PG 62: 350).

72 Lib. Or. 62.46–8 (Foerster vol. 4: 370): πολλαὶ μὲν ἐν Μακεδονίᾳ γεωργίαι, πλείους δὲ ἐν Αἰτωλίᾳ καὶ Ἀκαρνανίᾳ, χρυσός, ἄργυρος, πλῆθος ἀνδραπόδων, ἵππων ἀγέλαι καὶ βοῶν. PLRE 1: Heliodorus 2, 411.

73 Lib. Or. 42.21 (Foerster vol. 3: 317); PLRE 1: Thalassius 4, 888.

74 Lib. Or. 14.45 (Foerster vol. 2: 103); PLRE 1: Aristophanes, 106.

75 Lib. Or. 47.28 (Foerster vol. 3: 417–18): ὧν ὁ πλεῖστον μὲν χρόνον, πλείστων δὲ ἡγησάμενος στρατιωτῶν ἕνα μὲν μόλις ἀγρὸν ἐπρίατο, ἔτι δὲ τῶν οὐκ ἐπαινουμένων, οἰκέτας δὲ εἶχεν ἕνδεκα, ἡμιόνους δώδεκα, τρεῖς δὲ ἵππους, κύνας δὲ Λακαίνας τέτταρας, ἀλλ᾽ ὅμως δέος μὲν αὐτοῦ ταῖς τῶν βαρβάρων ἐνῴκει ψυχαῖς.

76 P. Lips. 97 (AD 338). Chapter 4.   77 P. Flor. 1.50 (AD 268). Banaji 2001, 110–11; Kehoe 1997, 130–1.

78 P. Oxy. 2474 (third century, possibly late).

but he clearly had slaves on the land.[79] A receipt from 355 or later included the names of thirty-eight slaves belonging to one owner.[80] Other late Roman documents which record the rations for slaves also point to the importance of slave-ownership on some scale.[81] A papyrus of AD 402 reflects the slaves belonging to a ship-captain, precisely our sort of Elite slave-holder without senatorial or curial status.[82]

Any tally of the slave population will depend enormously on how extensively we believe slaves were employed in agriculture on Illustrious and Elite land. Precisely because this question is at once so fundamental and so difficult, the main discussion is deferred to chapter 4 where the problem is treated at length. Here we can only signal some of the key evidence and conclusions. At the center of any attempt to quantify rural slavery should be a series of fortuitously preserved census inscriptions. Precious few fragments of any ancient census have survived outside of Egypt, yet those that have come down are uniquely valuable. A series of fourth-century census records inscribed on stone has been recovered from eleven cities scattered across the Aegean islands and coastal Asia Minor. They record the tax liabilities owed by *urban* landowners on their *rural* properties. The census inscriptions are a glimpse of the way that the land-holding elite in the central regions of the eastern Mediterranean exploited their holdings in the countryside. They offer the only quantitative insights into the extent of slavery on agricultural estates in a late Roman landscape.[83]

The Greek census records provide a small and fragmentary sample. The inscriptions confirm the abundant literary evidence for rural slavery among not only Illustrious but also Elite households. What they mean, at the least, is that slavery was prominent in the repertoire of labor strategies used by the aristocracy in the eastern empire. The Greek census inscriptions show slaves used in groups of 2, 4, 8, 16, 21, 22, and 152. Chapter 4 will argue that these documents descend from a region where slavery was relatively important – we would not find such extensive numbers of slaves in peripheral regions of the empire. The census inscriptions nevertheless dissolve some old assumptions about the way slave labor fit into the countryside. The Greek census inscriptions quickly belie the claim that ancient landscapes can be labeled in terms of a mode of production. The confinement of a

---

[79] P. Hamb. 268 (AD 289). cf. PSI 10.1102 (late third century, Oxyrhynchus?); P. Rain. Cent. 85 (AD 364–6).

[80] SPP 20.106. Bagnall 1996, 126, n. 78.

[81] BGU 1.34 = P. Charite 36 (AD 322); P. Duk. Inv. 553 v (after AD 252); P. Bad. 4.95.

[82] P. Haun. 3.68.

[83] Harper 2008; Thonemann 2007; Duncan-Jones 1990, 199–210; Jones 1953. Scheidel forthcoming: "the best evidence."

"dominant slave mode of production" to a small space asks us to write off a great deal of evidence for the use of slaves in far stretches of the empire. Melania claimed to own slaves in Spain, Italy, Apulia, Campania, Sicily, Africa, Numidia, and Britain. The census inscriptions demonstrate, incontrovertibly, the use of slave labor in the Aegean and coastal Asia Minor. Papyri provide documentary proof of the penetration of slave labor into the far stretches of Egypt. A law of AD 383 allowed the town councils in Thrace to recruit from among the local plebs those "abounding in the wealth of slaves" who had avoided curial service through "the obscurity of a low name."[84] There is simply too much evidence to revert to the story that slave labor was "marginal" in all parts of the empire except Italy, at least in the fourth century.

Our quantitative problem remains: how extensively was slave labor employed on Illustrious and Elite landholdings? Virtually everyone who has spent time with the late Roman evidence has concluded that rural slaves appear as numerous in the sources as before.[85] The census inscriptions will be the only hope for meaningful quantitative impressions. Even within the small sample, they show apparent variation, with higher levels of slavery on Thera and Lesbos, lower levels at inland Tralles. Variation was both inter- and intra-regional. We would imagine that Libanius' "not wealthy" slaveholder with eleven slaves might appear quite well-to-do in large parts of the empire. Perhaps it is advisable to subdivide the Elite category into two broader groups, core and periphery, graded on the level of wealth, the proximity to markets, and the influence of commercialization. In the core regions, we might propose an average Elite slave-holding of twenty slaves, imagining some of them to be domestic slaves and the rest in the fields. In the periphery, we will propose a conservative average of six slaves per Elite household.[86] The precision of these figures is not meant to lay any claim to certainty; we are only trying to provide disciplined estimates that accord with the evidence we have as we make the challenging transition from qualitative to quantitative description.

(3) *Bourgeois slave-holders in the late Roman empire.* In the category of Bourgeois slave-ownership we include all urban households that owned less than half a dozen slaves; these were often modest households who owned

---

[84] CT 12.1.96 (AD 383): *famulantium facultate locupletes . . . obscuritate nominis vilioris.* Laniado 2002, 15.

[85] Vera 2007 and 1986a, 407; Wickham 2005a, 262; Giliberti 1999, 52; MacMullen 1987; all in different ways.

[86] The party of Theophanes, a lawyer from Hermopolis, included ca. five slaves to serve him and his two or so free assistants *on a travelling mission* undertaken for speed, not tourism: Matthews 2006, 43 and 165, and Bagnall 2007.

a handful of domestic slaves, especially slave-women. This chapter opened with John Chrysostom's claim that even the "poor" household owned whole families of slaves.[87] The literary sources, and scattered documentary evidence, strongly insist on extensive levels of sub-elite slave-ownership in the fourth century. This pattern is an important comment on the structure of Roman society and urges us to believe in a hierarchy of wealth that included a significant middling stratum between Elites and the majority hovering around subsistence. But what could an author like Chrysostom have meant by a "poor" slave-owning household?

First, we should note that the late Roman sources are unambiguous about sub-elite slave-ownership. In a sermon of the early fifth century, from the port town of Hippo, Augustine claimed that "the primary and everyday instance of man's power over man is the master's power over his slave. Nearly all households have this type of power."[88] *Prope omnes domus.*[89] "All households" was not a phrase we commonly find in Augustine's corpus. "Nearly all" is fairly common in his personal idiom, and when he used it, he meant it. He could say, for instance, that "nearly all lamps in Italy" burned on oil – as they surely did.[90] His claim that every household had slaves was not a throw-away line, and it suggests that many households in the orbit of a mid-sized late Roman town could have owned slaves.[91]

In his speech *On Kingship*, written in Constantinople around 397–8, Synesius of Cyrene made the striking claim that "every household, even one which prospers only a little, has a Scythian slave."[92] The Scythians here are the Goths, and this part of the speech was meant to stir up anxiety about the threat posed by the large number of barbarian slaves in Roman society. The speech was rhetorical and xenophobic. But it is still noteworthy that Synesius could assert that households "which prosper only a little" had not just a slave, but a Gothic one. For what it is worth, his fears proved justified, as desertion and rebellion, laced with ethnic tension, would plague the empire over the next generation.[93]

---

[87] Ioh. Chrys. In Ephes. 22.2 (PG 62: 158).

[88] Aug. Psalm. 124.7 (CC 40: 1840–1): *prima et quotidiana potestas hominis in hominem domini est in servum. prope omnes domus habent huiusmodi potestatem.*

[89] Shaw 1987a, 12–15, for *domus.*   [90] Aug. Mor. eccl. 2.42 (PL 32: 1363): *prope omnes Italas lucernas.*

[91] The sermon is distinctly *not* a lecture to the rich. The sermon was parochial and expository, not a flamboyant speech delivered before a grand audience. MacMullen 1986a, 325, is right that social filters determined who was included in Augustine's claim of "every," but by arguing that Augustine meant simply "we who are rich," he does not account for the way that Augustine addresses his audience as a group other than the rich.

[92] Syn. Regn. 20 (Terzaghi: 46–8): ἅπας γὰρ οἶκος ὁ καὶ κατὰ μικρὸν εὖ πράττων Σκυθικὸν ἔχει τὸν δοῦλον. Syn. Calv. enc. 13 (Terzaghi: 214). Cameron and Long 1993, 109–21, esp. 111.

[93] See chapter 6.

The assumption among late antique authors was that owning slaves was simply a standard element of adult life.[94] Slaves were a common form of property listed among the belongings of a household.[95] Managing slaves was a normal part of life, an everyday routine.[96] The normal audience of a Christian sermon, from Antioch to Hippo to Amasea, understood slave-ownership as an ordinary feature of existence.[97] The universal presumption of slave-ownership in the sources of the late fourth and early fifth centuries may lead to the argument that the sources only tell us about the upper strata of society. In some banal sense this is obvious, but it prompts the question: Who inhabited these strata? While the upper classes are overrepresented in the surviving sources, the shift towards mainstream households in the late antique literature is unmistakable. The sermons of preachers like Augustine or Chrysostom were part of a politically triumphant, mass-scale religious movement that put them in dialogue with a wide cross-section of society.[98] The argument that the bishop's audience was composed exclusively of the rich centers on one circular argument: the audience included slave-owners.[99] But to assume that only the wealthy owned slaves is not only a fragile assumption – it disregards the social register of these sources.

When Chrysostom openly addressed the rich directly during his sermons, he encouraged them not to own herds, armies, or multitudes of slaves. Chrysostom thought that a "philosophical" Christian would own one, rather than a *phalanx*, of slaves: "for I am talking here not about the highest form of philosophy, but one that is accessible to many."[100] Chrysostom operated with the standard that a Christian should only own what he "needed." "Even if we only have two slaves, we can live. How can we have an excuse if two are not enough, since there are some who live without any slaves? We can have a brick house with three rooms... and if you want, two slaves."[101] Chrysostom had a rough-and-ready approach to the limits involved in proper Christian slave-owning:

---

94 Bas. Ep. 2.2 (Courtonne vol. 1: 6); Eus. P.E. 4.19.2 (SC 262: 202); Ioh. Chrys. Oppug. 3.21 (PG 47: 385); Ioh. Chrys. Thdr. 2.5.2 (SC 117: 70); Sed. Op. 1.26 (CSEL 10: 190).

95 E.g. Ps.-Mac. Hom. spir. 27.2 (Dörries, Klostermann, and Krüger: 219–20).

96 Ioh. Chrys. In 2 Tim. 3.3 (PG 62: 616); Ioh. Chrys. Virg. 67 (SC 125: 336–7); Lib. Or. 45.5 (Foerster vol. 3: 361).

97 See especially part II.   98 Maxwell 2006, esp. 65–87; Mayer 2000.

99 E.g. the seminal discussion of MacMullen 1989.

100 Ioh. Chrys. Oppug. 3.9 (PG 47: 363): οὔπω γὰρ τὴν ἄκραν τίθημι φιλοσοφίαν, ἀλλὰ τὴν πολλοῖς ἐφικτήν.

101 Ioh. Chrys. In Hebr. 28.4 (PG 63: 198): Κἂν δύο μόνους ἔχωμεν οἰκέτας, δυνάμεθα ζῆν. ὅπου γάρ εἰσί τινες χωρὶς οἰκετῶν ζῶντες, ποίαν ἡμεῖς ἔχομεν ἀπολογίαν, τοῖς δύο οὐκ ἀρκούμενοι; Δυνάμεθα καὶ ἐκ πλίνθων ἔχειν οἰκίαν τριῶν οἰκημάτων... εἰ βούλει, καὶ παῖδες δύο.

Why do you have so many slaves? Just as with clothing or dining, it is right to live according to our needs, so also with slaves. What need is there for them? There's none at all. For one master should need only one slave, or really two or three masters, one slave. If this is hard to bear, think about those who don't even have one... but you, if you don't lead around a herd of slaves, think it is shameful, not realizing that this *thought* in fact is what shames you... It is not from need that slaves are owned. If it were a necessity, one slave would suffice, or at most two. What does he want with this swarm of slaves? The rich go around to the baths, to the market, as though they were shepherds or slave-dealers. But I won't be too harsh: have a second slave.[102]

It was the ownership of "herds" and "swarms" of slaves by the wealthy that irked Chrysostom. We might say that he found the Elite style of slave-ownership offensive, the Bourgeois style an inescapable necessity. A highly descriptive and socially conscious author of the late fourth century insisted that there was extensive, sub-elite slavery in his panorama.

The sources sometimes provide unexpectedly detailed information about who was expected to own slaves in late Roman society. John Chrysostom, for instance, anticipated that the Christian priest would own at least one slave.[103] Urban professionals, such as doctors or painters, were presumed to have slaves as a matter of course.[104] Less savory urban characters, such as popular prostitutes, owned slaves.[105] Petty military officers might be expected to have a slave.[106] A metal collar of the Constantinian era was worn by the slave of a linen-worker.[107] It was said that "many slaves" even owned slaves, out of their *peculium*.[108] In Gaza, it was claimed that respectable stage performers could own "droves" of slaves.[109] Humble urban households, innkeepers or families who sold grapes or figs in the marketplace, might own slaves.[110] The assistant rhetors working under Libanius at the municipal

---

[102] Ioh. Chrys. In 1 Cor. 40.5 (PG 61: 353–4): Διὰ τί γὰρ πολλοὺς ἔχει οἰκέτας; Ὥσπερ γὰρ ἐν ἱματίοις τὴν χρείαν διώκειν δεῖ μόνον, καὶ ἐν τραπέζῃ, οὕτω καὶ ἐν οἰκέταις. Τίς οὖν ἡ χρεία; Οὐκ ἔστιν οὐδεμία. Καὶ γὰρ ἑνὶ τὸν ἕνα χρῆσθαι δεσπότην οἰκέτῃ μόνον ἐχρῆν. μᾶλλον δὲ καὶ δύο καὶ τρεῖς δεσπότας ἑνὶ οἰκέτῃ. Εἰ δὲ βαρὺ τοῦτο, ἐννόησον τοὺς οὐδὲ ἕνα ἔχοντας... σὺ δὲ, εἰ μὴ πολλὰς περιφέρεις ἀνδραπόδων ἀγέλας, αἰσχρὸν εἶναι νομίζεις, οὐκ εἰδὼς ὅτι τοῦτο μὲν οὖν μάλιστά ἐστι τὸ καταισχῦνόν σε... Ὥστε οὐκ ἀναγκαῖον τὸ δοῦλον ἔχειν. εἰ δὲ καὶ ἀναγκαῖον, ἕνα που μόνον, ἢ τὸ πολὺ δεύτερον. Τί βούλεται τὰ σμήνη τῶν οἰκετῶν; Καθάπερ γὰρ οἱ προβατοπῶλαι καὶ οἱ σωματοκάπηλοι, οὕτως ἐν βαλανείῳ, οὕτως ἐν ἀγορᾷ περιίασιν οἱ πλουτοῦντες. Πλὴν ἀλλ' οὐδὲν ἀκριβολογοῦμαι. ἔστω σοι καὶ δεύτερος οἰκέτης.
[103] Ioh. Chrys. In Philip. 9.4 (PG 62: 251). Rabbis: Hezser 2003, 401.
[104] Aug. Tract. Io. 3.14 (CC 36: 26–7); Eun. Vit. 8.2 (Giangrande: 58). CT 13.4.4 (AD 374).
[105] Ioh. Chrys. In. Io. 78.5 (PG 59: 432).   [106] CT 7.22.2 (AD 326).
[107] CIL 15.7184; CIL 15.7175. Thurmond 1994, 468–9.
[108] Ioh. Chrys. In Mt. 59.4 (PG 58: 571); Aug. Serm. 21.5 (Dolbeau: 275). See chapter 3.
[109] Choric. Or. 32.7 (Foerster and Richtsteig: 346). Actors buy a slave in Pall. H. Laus. 37 (Butler vol. 2: 109–10).
[110] Thdt. H. E. 2.9 (GCS 5: 120); Ioh. Chrys. Laz. 2.3 (PG 48: 986). A smith: P. Lond. 3.983 (4C). Carpenter: P. Kellis 8 (AD 362).

school in Antioch rented, rather than owned, a home, "like shoe cobblers." They were so poor that one of them had three slaves, another two slaves, and another not even that many.[111] In other words, the adjunct professor of the late fourth century, living in a rented apartment, would own a handful of slaves.

Clearly, the ownership of a few slaves was unremarkable. Libanius claimed that the "owner of a little," with a "meager household" and "not much money," had three, maybe four, slaves.[112] A deacon at Hippo, whom Augustine claimed was a "poor man," had bought several slaves with the money he earned before becoming a cleric.[113] If the rich had multitudes of slaves that necessitated complex managerial hierarchies, and small households had multiple slaves, it was a mark of *severe* poverty to have no slaves. It was terrible to be without a single slave in one's service.[114] Libanius knew a man who had become so impoverished, he had "no hand, no foot, no slave."[115] Basil asked that a poor man he knew receive a fair tax rating, since "he was reduced to the most extreme poverty, with barely enough for his daily sustenance, having not one slave."[116] The destitute man would have "not a male, not a female slave – and maybe not even a wife."[117] Heroes of the apostolic age, like Peter, led lives of such simple poverty that they had not a single slave.[118] Everyone except "the lowest" had some slaves.[119] Fourth-century ascetics had to be counseled not to buy slaves.[120] Legal evidence points in the same direction: in a law of 365, a runaway slave was considered a trifling legal matter, even for an official like the municipal *defensor*.[121] The fourth-century visual evidence amply and convincingly confirms the impression of extensive sub-elite slave-ownership.[122]

There are few periods of Mediterranean history when contemporaries have insisted with such regularity that slave-ownership was so widespread. How can we begin to quantify these claims of sub-elite slave-ownership? Certainly the most important measure of sub-elite slave-ownership lies in extant census papyri. The papyri of Roman Egypt include a relatively large

---

[111] Lib. Or. 31.11 (Foerster vol. 3: 129).
[112] Lib. Prog. 4.1.11 (Foerster vol. 8: 110): μικρῶν γάρ, οἶμαι, κύριος, οἰκιδίου φαύλου καὶ τριῶν ἢ τεττάρων ἀνδραπόδων καὶ δραχμῶν οὐ πολλῶν.
[113] Aug. Serm. 356.6 (Lambot vol. 1: 136): *homo pauper*.
[114] Ioh. Chrys. In act. Apost. 24.4 (PG 60: 189).
[115] Lib. Ep. 1503 (Foerster vol. 11: 512): οὐ χεῖρες, οὐ πόδες, οὐκ οἰκέτης.
[116] Bas. Ep. 309.1 (Courtonne vol. 3: 185): εἰς τὴν ἐσχάτην πενίαν περιετράπη, ὡς μόλις μὲν καὶ τῆς ἐφ᾽ ἡμέραν τροφῆς εὐπορεῖν, ἀνδραπόδου δὲ μηδὲ ἑνὸς κατάρχειν.
[117] Thdt. Prov. 6.664C (PG 83: 664): οὐκ οἰκέτης, οὐ θεράπαινα, τυχὸν δὲ οὐδὲ γυνὴ σύνευνος.
[118] Gr. Nyss. Ep. 17.14 (SC 363: 224); Bas. (dub.) Is. 1.89 (PG 30: 264).
[119] Lib. Decl. 1.129 (Foerster vol. 5: 86–7): τοὺς ταπεινοτάτους.
[120] Evag. Pont. Rer. Mon. 5 (PG 40: 1256).
[121] CT 1.29.2 (AD 365). Frakes 2001, 105–8. cf. CT 2.1.8 (AD 395).   [122] Dunbabin 2003a, 464.

number of household census returns, but unfortunately they descend only from the first three centuries of the empire. Yet they deserve a prominent place in any attempt to quantify the extent of Roman slavery, and they at least provide us with a benchmark for judging how prominent slavery could be among Bourgeois and Agricultural households. The meticulous study of the census papyri by Bagnall and Frier shows that one-sixth of all households owned slaves.[123] In the cities, 21 percent of households had slaves, and slaves constituted 13 percent of the urban population. In the villages, 12 percent of households included slaves, and slaves made up almost 9 percent of the rural population.[124] None of the census returns are from Alexandria, where slavery may have been practiced on an equal or greater scale. The Egyptian data show that household slave-ownership in a Mediterranean province under the Roman empire – excluding its largest city and without any estate-scale holdings – accounted for over one-tenth of the population and touched one-sixth of households.

The standard analysis of the census records calls the extent of slavery in Egypt "unexpectedly high."[125] The significance of the Egyptian data can hardly be overstated. The data show just what we would expect of Bourgeois slavery: a large number of families owned slaves in small groups, with more female slaves than male slaves. For urban household slavery in the empire, the census documents of Egypt are the best available evidence. Do the Egyptian census records of the imperial period provide any kind of a basis for characterizing late Roman slavery? Lactantius bitterly described the scene of a late Roman census, with the city streets swelled by unfamiliar faces, as all waited to be registered: "Every single man was present, with his children and his slaves."[126] Unfortunately, no census returns survive from fourth- or fifth-century Egypt. But the papyri of the fourth century do not give the impression of drastic change, and slaves continue to appear prominently.[127] More importantly, the census records add depth to the abundant literary evidence. It is not easy to measure the urban Egyptian data, which show that one-fifth of urban households owned slaves, against the statements of Augustine, Synesius, Chrysostom, and others which qualitatively suggest high levels of slave-ownership. But the census records

---

[123] Bagnall and Frier 1994, 70.
[124] P. Oxy. 984 from a town in upper Egypt of AD 89/90 shows that 14 percent of complete households owned slaves, who were 7 percent of the population, but there are ambiguities with this data: Bagnall, Frier, and Rutherford 1997, 98, n. 30.
[125] Bagnall and Frier 1994, 48.
[126] Lact. Mort. 23.2 (Creed: 36): *unus quisque cum liberis, cum servis aderant.*
[127] Bagnall forthcoming and 1993 are most important statements, sensitive to the distribution of document-types. *Contra*, Fikhman 1997, 1974, and 1973.

at least reassure us that our informants were not collectively hallucinating when they reported a social landscape with extensive slavery. The essential message of the Egyptian papyri is that Bourgeois slave-holding, with large numbers of female slaves, was an integral component of the Roman slave system.

Late Roman authors assumed that to be "rich" was to own numerous slaves, to be ordinary was to own a few, and to be poor was to own one or none. This assumption broadly validates our distinction between Illustrious/Elite and Bourgeois/Agricultural slave-holding, and it helps us to understand how even the "poor" could own slaves. "Poor" is a relative term, and in late antiquity it was being stretched to new uses by the leaders of the Christian movement.[128] At times our authors seem to provide tantalizing clues to what they meant: in an exceptionally precise passage, Chrysostom claimed that the lowest 10 percent of society were poor.[129] Christian bishops did not discuss the poor altogether recklessly: Chrysostom spoke of the beggar who struggled to find adequate clothing, others of the huddled masses seeking shelter from the elements against the fire-pits of the ancient baths.[130] But there is no conceivable way to project slave-ownership among these "poor," and we must accept that the word could have various registers even within the corpus of a single author like Chrysostom.[131] To be a "poor" slave-owner was to be in the lower tiers of the Bourgeois, clinging to respectability, and in danger of falling off into that mute, tired mass of the populace struggling to subsist, who were so poor they "owned not one slave."[132] But where do we draw that line? How many Bourgeois households were there in the late empire?

A recent reconstruction of Roman imperial society identifies three broad tiers of wealth and income: elite, middling, and subsistence.[133] In this account, elites included senators, equestrians, decurions, and a number of wealthy households without official status, so that the category comprised 1.2–1.7 percent of the population and claimed roughly 20 percent of the empire's annual gross income: our Illustrious and Elite households. Middling households enjoyed modest, comfortable levels of existence, but not extreme wealth, and amounted to some 6–12 percent of the population. They formed a highly visible segment who consumed

---

[128] See the essays in Holman 2008; Osborne 2006, 11; Brown 2002; Holman 2001. Woolf 2006, on the construction of poverty in the earlier period.
[129] Ioh. Chrys. In Mt. 66.3 (PG 58: 630). See Mayer 2006, 467–8.
[130] Ioh. Chrys. In 1 Cor. 31.1 (PG 61: 258); Ast. Am. Hom. 3.12 (Datema: 35).
[131] Lunn-Rockliffe 2006, 126.   [132] Esp. Brown 2002, 14–15; Mayer 2006, 480–1.
[133] Scheidel and Friesen 2009; Friesen 2008. See already Harris 1988 for a similar line.

another 20 percent of the empire's annual production: our Bourgeois and
Agricultural households.[134] The remaining 86–93 percent of the population
lived around subsistence, a stark reminder how much of the Roman population was vulnerable to severe impoverishment and how many "Romans"
lie beyond our field of vision. This reconstruction is a starting place for
imagining the structure of wealth in the fourth-century empire. A middling
range of 6–12 percent is highly useful, for it is hard to imagine numbers
which are much higher or lower. There are reasons to believe that reality
may have fallen towards the upper end of that range, even in the fourth
century.[135] Certainly, the archaeology of domestic architecture is consistent
with the hypothesis of a significant middling stratum, and perhaps more
significantly, the Egyptian census papyri of the first three centuries show
that 21 percent of urban households included slaves.[136]

If we assume a fourth-century imperial population on the order of 50
million, with a 15 percent rate of urbanization (in towns of over 5,000),
then there were 1.875 million urban households in the late empire.[137] It
would be plausible to assume that one-fifth of these urban households were
"middling": that would account for 30 percent of all middling households,
leaving 70 percent of middling households in the countryside. This is to be
expected, since urban populations in antiquity were wealthier in aggregate
than the rural populace: it means 20 percent of the urban populace was
middling, whereas just over 8 percent of the rural population attained
this level of relative comfort. Many Bourgeois households owned multiple
slaves, and one is a minimum to qualify in our taxonomy. To own no
slaves was a mark of destitution, of social irrelevance – a sign that the
household had fallen out of the middling ranks, into that 88 percent of the
population who lived near subsistence. This reconstruction helps us make
sense of the abundant literary record for sub-elite slave-ownership, and it
helps us understand how the "poor" household – let us now say modest or
vulnerable Bourgeois family – could own a handful of slaves in the towns
of the late Roman empire.

(4) *Agricultural slavery in the late empire.* By this label we mean not
the estate-based slavery on the land of Illustrious and Elite households,
but the slaves owned and exploited within middling rural households, in

[134] For documentary evidence for the distribution of wealth, see esp. Bagnall 1992 for Egypt and Harper 2008 for Asia Minor.
[135] The estimates of Scheidel and Friesen 2009 cohere with the levels of slave-ownership in the Egyptian census records (which suggest a middling population towards the very upper end of their spectrum).
[136] Hirschfeld 2001, for a substantial middle class.   [137] For population, see Introduction.

other words, rich peasants or village elites.[138] The urban bias of our literary evidence is unyielding; the countryside, when it is mentioned at all, is described only insofar as it affected tax collection or elite land-ownership. In other words, rural householders are largely beyond the blinkers of our sources. It is all the more striking, then, that vivid, credible, and geographically dispersed evidence attests slave-holding within this category.[139] Theodoret of Cyrrhus spoke of a small farmer with one field and just enough to pay the taxes and feed his family and slaves.[140] A law of 373 assumed that a "peasant" in Illyricum might well own a slave.[141] Valentinian and Valens jealously guarded the tax exemption of military veterans, shielding them from dues on the slaves they brought "to the farm."[142]

Documents from late Roman Egypt confirm that slaves were owned by specific, small-scale rural households. In a will from a village outside Oxyrhynchus, a man left property to his two households – a total of seven free adults, four slaves, and at most 10 to 15 arouras of land.[143] The inheritance of two women in late Roman Karanis had included 61 sheep, 40 goats, 1 grinding mill, 3 talents of silver, 2 artabas of wheat, 2 slaves, and around 22 arouras of arable land – a "very middle-range holding for a villager of moderate means."[144] An early fourth-century papyrus records the estate of a man with four slaves, two of them farmers and one a weaver.[145] The papyri show that in late Roman rural Egypt "the ownership of a small number of slaves – one to four – was not remarkable. The economic importance of slavery in such households was not marginal."[146] This pattern of slavery probably held in other villages of the Roman east, where the documentation is more exiguous. A substantial series of manumission inscriptions from a village of southern Macedonia, mostly of the third century, re-confirms that slavery was important in some rather humble environments.[147] It is harder to know if this sort of household slavery among the upper tier of village families was common in Syria and Palestine, though there are certainly tantalizing hints.[148]

The only quantitative evidence we have once again comes from the Egyptian census records. In the villages, 12 percent of households included slaves, who made up almost 9 percent of the rural population.[149] If we

---

[138] Comparatively, Turley 2000, 77.   [139] Vera 2007, 503.
[140] Thdt. H. rel. 8.14 (SC 234: 400).   [141] CT 11.11.1 (AD 373): *rusticano...*
[142] CT 7.20.8 (AD 364): *... ad agrum.* Also CT 11.1.12 and Nov. Val. 13.13.
[143] P. Oxy. 14.1638 (AD 282), with the comments of Bagnall 1996, 123–4.
[144] P. Cair. Isid. 64 (AD 298). Bagnall 1996, 124.   [145] P. Lips. 26 (4C). Bagnall 1993, 229.
[146] Bagnall 1996, 125.   [147] Petsas *et al.* 2000. See chapter 9.
[148] Tchalenko 1953–8, vol. I, 410–11. Syria: IGLS nos. 1409–11. Palestine: P. Nessana 31, line 43.
[149] Bagnall and Frier 1994, 71.

follow our assumptions, outlined above, that 10 percent of the population enjoyed middling levels of wealth, that up to 15 percent of the population lived in towns, and that one-fifth of urban households were Bourgeois households, then we would conclude that 8.2 percent of the rural population was middling. In a population of 50 million, this would give us 875,000 households of such means that we might expect them to be slave-owners. This estimate is below the levels of rural slave-ownership attested in imperial Egypt, a fact that reassures us we are not wildly overstating the possible extent of small-scale slave-owning. It is also interesting to note that among village households in Egypt, slave-ownership tended to follow the Bourgeois pattern in preferring female slaves to male slaves.[150] Chapter 2 will add further plausibility to this reconstruction, arguing for a decentralized slave supply inherently embedded in demographic practices such as child exposure, and Chapter 3 will explore the economic dynamics of these households. For now let us assume, conservatively, that the top 7–8 percent of rural householders entered the ranks of slave-ownership.

The aim of this exercise has been to gather the available data, to suggest an analytical way of organizing it, and to propose how the apparent patterns fit into a reconstruction of Roman society as a whole. Not a single ancient author has deigned to leave a believable report about the number of slaves in any given space or sector of Roman society; efforts to import figures from the modern world (along the crude reasoning that slavery was important in both the United States and Rome) are grossly misplaced. The only way to quantify the dimensions of the Roman slave system is through the prism of slave-ownership. If this type of investigation induces feelings of squeamishness, any analysis which describes Roman slavery as "important" or "dominant," without critically examining what those labels mean, should make us even more uncomfortable. This approach exploits three types of data, including contemporary social observation, census records, and profiles of individual slave-owners; these three types of data have been basically convergent, and we have not found ourselves in the uncomfortable position of having to marginalize the evidence which does survive in order to fit our model.

Our reconstruction allows us to imagine ranges of possibility, different scenarios within those ranges, and hypothetical averages. These ranges operate within the assumption that our background model of the structure of wealth in late Roman society is broadly accurate. If we took the lowest

---

[150] Bagnall and Frier 1994, 97–8. Although there is cause to suspect that male slaves are underreported, for a very good reason: tax evasion. Compare Harper 2008.

Table 1.1 *Quantifying the number of slaves in the late Roman empire*

Category	% of population	Range of slave-holdings	Average no. of slaves	No. of households	Total no. of slaves
Illustrious	0.0048	100s–1,000s	250	600	150,000
Elite	1.36	6 to 20s	20 (core)	85,000	1,700,000
			6 (periphery)	85,000	510,000
Bourgeois	3.0	1 to 5	2	375,000	750,000
Agricultural	7.0	1 to 5	2	875,000	1,750,000

end of the slave-owning range for each category (100, 6, 1, 1) and the highest end (1,000, 20, 5, 5) we emerge with a realistic floor and ceiling of the late Roman slave population: 2.33 million to 9.65 million slaves, 4.6 to 19.3 percent of the population.[151] Then, within these upper and lower limits, we could imagine multiple scenarios. Perhaps some would insist that Illustrious households owned slaves at higher levels, or that there were fewer Agricultural households than we have proposed. The suggestion of averages will involve the greatest margin of error. But under duress, and forced to abandon the disciplinary caution of the ancient historian, we could endorse a working reconstruction along these lines: a moderate estimate for Illustrious households (250 on average), a high number for Elites in core regions (20 on average), a low number for Elites in more peripheral regions (6 on average), and a modest average for middling households, Bourgeois and Agricultural alike (2).[152] With a population of 50,000,000 and an urbanization rate of 15 percent, this yields the totals in table 1.1.

Every figure in this matrix is contestable, but this reconstruction produces a slave population of 4,860,000 souls, just under 10 percent of the imperial population. The (hypothetical) distribution is revealing. The wealthiest 1.365 percent of Roman society owned 49 percent of slaves, a level of stratification that is remarkable but not at all incompatible with our knowledge of Roman social structure nor out of line with comparative evidence. The top 1.365 percent of Roman society thus owned the

---

[151] Note that the ceiling of 1,000 on the range of Illustrious slaveholdings is notional; some holdings were larger, but these were surely exceedingly few in number.

[152] cf. Scheidel 2005a, 66: 5 *household* slaves per decurion throughout the empire, 20 per equestrian, 80 per senator, all "best regarded as minima." 67: "The average senator could easily have owned hundreds of slaves, and the average knight, dozens." My analysis divides the Elite population into core and peripheral groups based on economic and geographic criteria (see p. 49). The "core" was defined as regions under the influence of urban markets or commercial networks; here it is assumed (conservatively) that half of elites were in this group.

bottom 5 percent of Roman society. Equally noteworthy is the extensive side of Roman slavery, the long tail of slave-ownership. The historically broad middling strata of Roman society participated in the slave system, a fact which helps us appreciate why slave-ownership was such an important element of social definition. Moreover, this distribution tells us that half of all slaves were owned in small groups, half within larger proprietary formations. These basic distributional hypotheses will be essential as we consider the evidence, in future chapters, for the exploitation of slave labor, the life conditions of slavery, the opportunities for familial relationships, and so on.

An estimate of the slave population near 5 million souls and at 10 percent of the total population compares with the best attempts to quantify the slave system of the early Roman empire.[153] It is slightly lower than the estimates of the high imperial slave population, as we might expect, but here we sense an important difference in perspective. Recent work on the extent of early Roman slavery has taken the form of trying to ascertain the *upper limits* of the slave population. This is an interventionist approach aimed to correct long-standing but baseless estimates that overstated the number of slaves in the Roman empire. A strong case has been made that the slave population could not have exceeded 10–15 percent of the imperial population; any greater estimate would require implausible levels of transformation in a pre-modern context.[154] Our reconstruction of slavery in the fourth-century empire is consistent with these models of early imperial slavery. Subsequent chapters will make a case that our reconstruction is consistent with the supply patterns, occupational structure, social impact, and institutional framework of the late Roman slave system. If, throughout the rest of the book, we proceed to speak without too much hedging and hesitation of a late Roman slave population on the order of 5 million slaves, it is implicit that this estimate entails all the uncertainty we have encountered in our attempt to reconstruct the scale of Roman slavery; even if the signals of epistemological humility are muted, readers are referred back to this discussion, where hypotheticals and equivocations are plentiful.

LATE ROMAN SLAVERY IN HISTORICAL CONTEXT

Roman society in the fourth century was a slave society.[155] Slaves existed in large numbers, they played a crucial role in agricultural production, and

---

[153] It also resembles the conclusions of MacMullen 1987.
[154] Scheidel 2005a, 67–8, 1999, and 1997; Jongman 1988.
[155] Andreau and Descat 2006, 255: "au IVe siècle ap. J-C., la société romaine mérite encore, à notre sens, d'être qualifiée d'esclavagiste."

their presence deeply stamped social relationships and cultural values. We have already made allusion to the essential fact that not all slave societies are alike, so it is fitting to conclude this chapter by trying to place the late Roman slave system along the spectrum of history's slave societies and to consider its distinctive traits. It should be remarked straightaway that, if the slave system remained so important in the fourth century, then Roman slavery is noteworthy for its sheer longevity and breadth. It underlines our claim that Roman slavery should not be written within the frame of a national story, tied intimately with military conquest. Roman slavery was a distinctive phase of Mediterranean history, when a convergence of forces acted to intensify both the supply and demand for slaves over an extended arc of time. Roman slavery, as a category, is like Atlantic slavery, a big, complex backdrop against which a particularly tragic chapter in the long history of human enslavement played out.

Another feature of the Roman slave system is immediately striking: the overall weight of male slaves within the system. Caution is in order here, for chapter 2 will argue that the Roman slave population enjoyed a balanced sex ratio. The significance of male slaves in the Roman system has often been overstated, but in comparative terms, even our reconstruction proposes an unusually large complement of male labor within the system. Female slaves, especially in domestic contexts, are historically far more common than male slaves. In most slave systems, female slaves greatly outnumber male slaves, because slavery is limited in extent, principally associated with domestic or sexual labor, and largely confined to wealthy households.[156] Certainly this has been true for most of later Mediterranean history. Rome, however, combined extensive levels of household slavery with a strong component of slave-based agricultural production. There is a simple but elegant way to demonstrate this pattern: the price schedule of Roman slaves. The Price Edict of Diocletian reproduces what the imperial bureaucracy considered the fair maximum market value of slaves of different sexes and at different ages (table 1.2).[157]

The higher price of male slaves is a crucial fact, and the empirical data bear out the evidence of the Price Edict.[158] Slave prices reflect aggregate supply and demand for slaves on the market. Demand, in turn, is a function of the marginal value of slave labor and the consumption preferences of those with market power. The price schedule of Diocletian's Edict supplies indirect proof that late Roman slavery was still a system with

[156] See p. 162.
[157] *Edictum de pretiis rerum venalium*, 29 (Giacchero: 208). See now, on the text, Salway 2010. Prices are in *denarii*. Harper 2010; Scheidel 1996b. cf. Arnaud 2007, 334.
[158] Saller 2003, 185–6; Scheidel 1996b. See Harper 2010, for the empirical data.

Table 1.2 *Maximum prices for slaves in Diocletian's Price Edict*

Age (years)	Male	Female	% of male price
0 to 8	15,000	10,000	67
8 to 16	20,000	20,000	100
16 to 40	30,000	25,000	83
40 to 60	25,000	20,000	80
60+	15,000	10,000	67

a strong demand for male slaves, and thus with a strong component of agricultural production. This pattern is the historical aberration. In most slave systems, not only do female slaves outnumber their male counterparts, they command higher prices on the market. After antiquity, the price of female slaves would remain higher than the price of male slaves up until the opening of the Atlantic, when once again need for slave labor in agriculture outstripped the force of demand for female slaves.[159] The middle ages were bounded on either end by Roman and New World slavery, two exceptional phases when slavery was a vital force in agricultural production.[160] The evidence of slave prices suggests that the tectonic shift which would create the patterns of medieval Mediterranean slavery had not yet occurred in the fourth century.

The temporal longevity and price schedule point to another salient fact of the Roman slave system: the role of natural reproduction. As female

[159] Campbell, Miers, and Miller 2006, 163; Goody 1980, 37–40. Is it significant that already by AD 530, a detailed administrative price schedule (CJ 7.7.1) did not differentiate between the price of male and female slaves? McCormick 2001, 248, higher prices for female slaves in the medieval period. In the early tenth century Raffelstetten Toll, female slaves were charged a higher premium: *Inquisitio de theloneis Raffelstettensis*, no. 253.6, 251. Prominence of female slaves in middle ages: Goitein 1967–93, vol. 1, 147; Ragib 2002, vol. 2, 45–7, for medieval Egypt. Origo 1955, 336, females ten times as numerous as males and more expensive in fourteenth- and fifteenth-century Tuscany. Epstein 1999; Stuard 1983, 161–3; Phillips 1985, 103–5; Balard 1968, 649–50, females 63 percent of slaves in thirteenth-century Genoa, and 659 for prime (females always higher). Gioffré 1971, 137, fifteenth-century Genoa. Romano 1996, 108 (servants, sixteenth-century Venice, nearly twice as many females). Budak 2000, 751. In the New World, the price of prime-age female slaves was regularly in the range of 80–95 percent of the price of a male slave, except when urban slavery was predominant over rural slavery: see Fraginals, Klein, and Engerman 1983, esp. 1209–13. Verlinden 1955, 800–1, and 1977, 29: empirical evidence that male prices higher when used in agriculture and industry, female prices higher when domestic and urban slavery predominate. Lovejoy and Richardson 1995. Watson 1980b reports higher prices for boys in China, but explains that it was because they were purchased for the purpose of adoption.

[160] The Islamic middle ages were a notable period of slaving, and while most slaves were female domestics, there were important phases where plantation slavery developed, notably leading up to the Zanj rebellion. See in general Gilly-Elway 2000, 139.

slaves began to enter reproductive maturity, their price equaled that of male slaves; this pattern reflects their reproductive value. Chapter 2 argues that natural reproduction was the most important source of new slaves. In most slave systems, radical imbalances in the sex ratio, brutal mortality regimes, or high rates of manumission prevent slave populations from coming anywhere close to achieving levels of reproductive success that would perpetuate the system in the long run. The apparent longevity and scale of the Roman slave system, and its manifest dependence on births to slave-women, suggest that this was a society in which the slave population achieved a large measure of reproductive success. This in turn implies that the sex ratio was sufficiently balanced, that the mortality schedule was sufficiently normal, that the rate of manumission (at least of females) was sufficiently low, to allow the slave population to endure on a massive scale over centuries. The crucial variable militating against the reproductive success of modern slave populations was sugar; Roman slavery was organized around the production of the standard Mediterranean crops, which exposed the slave population to no extraordinary patterns of mortality or sex imbalances.[161] To be sure, alternative sources such as exposed children and imported barbarians were vital supplements in the Roman slave supply, but in comparative terms we must reckon with one of the few large slave populations in history that was shaped and stabilized by the processes of natural reproduction.

Even if exceptional by historical standards, the productive element of Roman slavery does not compare with the deployment of slave labor in the context of the New World. In the New World, slaves represented a high percentage of the overall population and in some regions and economic sectors constituted the primary force of productive labor. The uniqueness of New World slavery lay its dependence on cash crops, its integration with trans-Atlantic markets, and its relationship to a frontier environment, where super-abundant land and perennially insufficient labor combined to push slavery outwards along with the expansion of European settlement.[162] Voracious demand for sugar, tobacco, indigo, rice, and eventually cotton pushed against the supply curves for these goods, until eventually some 11 or 12 million slaves were taken from Africa to the western hemisphere. In the Roman world, it is true that wine became one of the first great cash crops, produced and marketed on a mass scale. Consumption habits changed massively under Roman rule. As an addictive, psychotropic product that provided a precious source of energy, in a world, moreover, without

---

[161] See chapter 2.   [162] Findlay 1989; Fogel 1989, 22; Solow 1985.

caffeine, tobacco, or other stimulants, wine already possessed many of the characteristics of the tropical groceries that drove New World slavery. But ancient wine production was typically pursued within polycultural strategies, and Roman slavery was adaptive not only to the production of wine, but also of wheat, oil, meat, and textiles.[163]

Historians should perhaps set aside comparisons between Roman slavery and the more intensive regions of modern slavery, the frontiers of cash-crop production that come to mind when we think of New World slavery – the coffee plantation in Brazil, the sugar plantation in the Caribbean, the cotton plantation in the Deep South. Instead we should search for parallels in the peripheral regions of slavery's great westward advance.[164] It is easy to forget that modern slavery flourished in a strikingly broad range of contexts – from the wheat and tobacco lands of the Virginia Piedmont and Chesapeake to the urban centers of the eighteenth-century North, such as New York.[165] Roman slavery finds closer parallels in regions of the New World where slaves were on the order of 10 percent of the population, and where mixed agriculture dominated the economy, with strong elements of wheat cultivation, animal husbandry, and small-scale craft production. In these regions, as in the Roman world, alternatives such as tenancy competed with slavery in a complex labor market. In these regions, as in the Roman world, slavery did not always radically transform the productive process. The uniqueness of Roman slavery is that, without the domineering influence of a frontier or a nascent world market, a vast and enduring pre-modern slave system became so intertwined in agricultural production. Even if slave labor in the Roman Mediterranean was always a limited input to the total labor supply, Roman slavery allowed a market-oriented aristocracy to control agricultural resources and to capitalize on market forces.

A slave population on the order of 10 percent, many of whom were employed in urban and domestic settings, is below what was once imagined in the context of the ancient slave systems. But reducing the scale of the Roman slave system to realistic levels does not undermine its significance. We now have a much clearer understanding of the limited potential of pre-industrial societies and underdeveloped economies. The Roman empire, in the long view, remains an exceptional place, one of the most notable efflorescences of the pre-modern world; it was perhaps the largest, longest

---

[163] See chapters 4 (on agriculture) and 5 (on management).   [164] Roth 2007.
[165] For the former, see the essays of Koons and Hofstra 2000; Inscoe 1995; Lepore 2005, eighteenth-century New York.

Table 1.3 *A profile of Roman slavery: structural features of a slave society*

Ownership	Labor	Supply	Incentives	Sexuality	Ideology	Institutions
Both upper and middling	Agriculture, textiles, and specialized	Natural reproduction, importation, and enslavement	Extremes of both pain and positive incentives	Late male marriage, pre-Christian honor–shame	Civic ideology of conquest	Roman law of property and status

phase of complexity before the second millennium. Slavery was an intimate part of that complexity. Rather than trying to salvage the uniqueness of Roman slavery by identifying a dominant slave mode of production, limited in space and time, we should see slavery as an integral component of the Roman imperial system. Slaves were often a thin presence within a given space, but this does not vitiate the claim to significance. The Roman empire was the interconnection of these zones of thin modernization, flung across a vast territory. Seen against the background of the giant, slow-moving world of subsistence and reproduction, the Roman slave system will appear small; seen, appropriately, within the vibrant, fast-moving world of capital floating atop the Mediterranean empire, Roman slavery takes on its true measure.[166] The extent of Bourgeois and Agricultural slave-ownership, and the significance of slave labor on the land of Illustrious and Elite households, made Roman society that truly rare organism, a slave society.

In subsequent chapters we will identify other distinctive features of Roman slavery, including its incentive structure (an exceptionally broad spectrum from physical torture to manumission with citizenship), its deep relation to sexual exploitation (where late male marriage and strong norms of female honor exposed slave-women to extraordinary abuse), and its institutional foundations (rooted in the Roman law of status and property). In many of these arenas, the practices and structures of Roman slavery resemble other historical slave societies, but Roman slavery was the convergence of these features in a unique system of slavery, the most extensive and enduring slave system before the discovery of the New World (table 1.3).

The present chapter has concentrated on a certain kind of evidence – anything touching on the extent, numbers, significance, role, or social location of slavery. This cull is only a small part of the harvest. The next eleven chapters add testimony, including thousands of references to the

---

[166] Compare Schiavone 2000, for the earlier period.

ancient authorities, which further substantiate the claim that Roman society in the long fourth century was a genuine slave society. The idea of a slave society will prove useful in the book's conclusion, too, when we briefly look into the decisive changes that occurred over the fifth to seventh centuries. There was always slavery in the Mediterranean. The history of slavery is continuous, in a qualified sense. As the Roman imperial system unraveled, slavery became less prominent in precisely the two sectors that made Roman slavery exceptional: sub-elite households and agricultural estates. In the centuries of the post-Roman kingdoms and the early Byzantine empire, a slave society was replaced by a series of societies with slaves. By the late sixth century, it would be hard to find an urban crowd, pressing together in the basilica, demanding from their priest an account of the peculiar institution of slavery. It is even harder to find a preacher casually and earnestly claiming that the "rich" household was an elaborate pyramid of slaves, while the "poor" household included families of slaves. This book is therefore an account of the Mediterranean slave system, in the last period during which the Roman empire was home to a slave society.

CHAPTER 2

The endless river: the supply and trade of slaves

STUDYING THE ROMAN SLAVE SUPPLY

The definition of slavery in Roman law and ideology blended the imaginary order in which slavery was the rightful outcome of Roman conquest and the mundane, material fact of the slave trade.[1] It is important, analytically, not to conflate the two. The Roman slave system was not in any simple sense the product of wars of conquest, and the slave supply was not a direct function of military expansion.[2] Over the last generation, there has been a new recognition that it is necessary to account for the extraordinary movement of human bodies that was the Roman slave trade, without the easy, ideological explanation of mass warfare.[3] In retrospect, the theory of conquest has never been able to offer a very detailed story of how millions of captives could be filtered through an infrastructure of trade, or how a massive sudden influx of slaves would be absorbed in society – consumed, managed, and exploited.[4] More importantly, if war was instrumental in the generation of Roman slavery, it does not perforce follow that the end of conquest reversed the trajectory of the slave system, leading inevitably to a reduction in supply, a rise in prices, and overall decline.

The revisionist work on the slave supply has been paradigm-shifting. It is thus remarkable just how simple and elegant the revisionist argument is. In a few concise articles, Scheidel demonstrated that – in any plausible demographic regime – a slave population on the order of 5 million slaves would require an annual input of ca. 200,000–300,000 new slaves per

---

[1] Dig. 1.5.4–5. See chapter 1.
[2] For captives in the earlier period, Welwei 2000; Boese 1973. Bradley 2004 and Gonzales 2002 for the high empire. Lenski 2008 for late antiquity.
[3] Scheidel forthcoming and 1997; Harris 1999 and 1980; Bradley 1994, 31–56, and 1987a; Finley 1998 (orig. 1980), 151–4; Bieżuńska-Małowist 1974–7 vol. 2, 13.
[4] cf. Scheidel forthcoming, "despite the huge scale and frequent occurrence of war-time enslavements, the sources allude only sketchily to the logistics of these transactions."

annum.[5] With that math, there is hardly room left for debate over where
the majority of new slaves came from. One of the largest recorded hauls
of the legions was the 150,000 Epirote captives brought in on a purposeful
slaving expedition in 167 BC. The Roman slave supply required twice that
number – *annually*. Sources such as cross-border importation and child
exposure were surely significant inputs, but when we consider the likely
population figures of human groups bordering the empire, and compare
the relative extent of the Atlantic slave trade, the conclusion becomes ever
more inexorable.[6] The Roman slave population was sustained, above all,
by natural reproduction.[7]

The purpose of this chapter is to consider the supply and circulation
of slaves in the fourth century. As always the evidence is fragmentary
and uncertain, but we can at least test whether and how it might be
consistent with a proposed slave population of 5 million souls. At the
same time, the testimony of the late empire deserves to be brought into
the broader discussion over the Roman slave supply. The longevity of
the slave system is in itself a serious argument for viewing the supply
system as the convergence of several processes rather than a sequence
of military events. Moreover, the sources of the fourth century are rich
and contribute new insights into the ancient slave supply. Finally, the
categories of slave-ownership outlined in chapter 1 prove essential in the
effort to understand the supply system. Knowing where slaves are, and
in what kinds of groups they were owned, illuminates some of the key
questions which arise from demographic modeling of the slave population.
Mortality, manumission, sex ratios, and familial opportunity have rightly
become central considerations in the study of the ancient slave population,
and our model of the fourth-century slave system helps us organize the
imperfect evidence which does survive.

This chapter first considers the contribution of natural reproduction,
internal enslavement, and trans-frontier importation to the maintenance of
the slave population. The second half of this chapter tries to reconstruct the
slave trade. Once again, we lack evidence which we can confidently consider
representative. Nevertheless, there are glimpses of a vast, sophisticated, and
interlinked commerce in slaves which acted to connect the supply of slaves
to demand. It will be argued that the evidence is at least consistent with a
view of the slave trade that posits intense, vibrant patterns of local slave-
trading and larger, interregional systems of exchange. The evidence for

---

[5] Scheidel 1997, 164.   [6] Scheidel 1997, 159–64.
[7] See now Roth 2008 and 2007. Not all have agreed: Bradley 2004; Herrmann-Otto 2002; Lo Cascio
2002; Harris 1999.

slave-traders and for the network of markets behind the trade is assembled. This analysis offers a new reading of Augustine's dramatic *Letter 10**, in which the elderly bishop pleaded for imperial help as he watched Roman slave-traders invade his province. This letter is not simply a symptom of growing disorder. It is a snapshot of the moment when the Vandals took control of the southwestern Mediterranean, and the Roman slave trade, ever so briefly, began to mutilate a Roman province. A final point, too rarely considered, is that the slave trade was the essence of the slave experience. The lack of first-person slave narratives from antiquity is a devastating blind spot. This chapter does not hope to reconstruct that experience. But by trying to envision the dimensions of the trade, we may recognize the extent of our ignorance about the experience of ancient slavery.

REPRODUCTION AND REPLACEMENT OF THE SLAVE POPULATION

The argument that the Roman slave supply was dominated by natural reproduction, it must be said, has always relied on parametric modeling, not on the accumulation of explicit evidence for slave fertility. Whether the reproductive performance of the slave population was high or low, it is striking that the concept of slave reproduction is muted in the surviving source material. This indicates, above all, a silence amounting to repression about one of the structural features of the slave system. The reproduction of the slave population fell outside the discussion of polite mastery, perhaps for the chilling reason that it was exploitative beyond repair. Of course, explicit discussion of "breeding" or natural reproduction was relatively rare in a slave system like that in the US South.[8] In fact, careful study of the US slave system – with abundant quantitative evidence – has revealed some important patterns for the discussion here. The reproductive success of the American slave population was not the result of conscious manipulation so much as the natural outcome of decent conditions: a balanced sex ratio, a normal mortality pattern, low levels of manumission (which only matters in the case of females), and *relative* opportunity to forge stable and semi-private familial bonds.[9]

Because there is so little quantitative evidence for the Roman slave supply, one approach is to ask, as a test of plausibility, whether the prerequisites of reproductive success were in place. Our inquiry should thus begin by considering the determinants of slave reproductive success: sex ratios,

[8] See Sutch 1975, 175.   [9] Fogel 1989, 114–53.

mortality, manumission, and familial opportunity.[10] It has sometimes been argued that the sex ratio of the Roman slave population was heavily skewed towards males.[11] This objection certainly does not apply to the late empire and seems unlikely even in the earlier period. If natural reproduction was the main source of new slaves, then human biology would have acted quickly, within a generation, to level out any disproportion in the sex ratio. It cannot be demonstrated that males were more often taken captive, exposed as infants, or imported across the frontiers. In the absence of input mechanisms which were highly biased towards male slaves, biology would have inexorably prevailed. No such input mechanisms have been adduced, and if anything the impression is that capture and exposure favored female entrance into slavery.[12] The supposition of a male-dominated slave system in the earlier stages of Roman history relies on two sorts of evidence, neither of which will bear scrutiny: the agricultural writers and the inscriptional testimony for large, urban *familiae*.

The agricultural writers, it is true, display at times only a limited awareness of the existence and labor of female slaves.[13] Their objective was to describe profitable agricultural strategies, including the management of a slave labor workforce. It is far from clear how dominant the pure agrofirms they describe actually were.[14] Roth has now shown, moreover, that the selective concerns of Cato and Varro have filtered females out of their discussion, but this does not mean that there were not large numbers of female slaves in the countryside in the late republic.[15] Here absence of evidence is not compelling. The stray remark of Columella that he rewarded slave-women for reproduction is an important comment.[16] Moreover, by good fortune, the most objective evidence for the sex ratio on an agricultural estate comes from late antiquity, the inscription from Thera. In the available sample, female slaves were unequivocally a major constituent of the rural population.

The tomb inscriptions of senatorial families at Rome, where far more male slaves were commemorated, also might suggest an imbalanced sex ratio.[17] The male-dominated staff of the great families reflects an important

---

[10] cf. Steckel 1982, for the United States.
[11] Lo Cascio 2002 and Harris 1999. Both are focused on the earlier period, and while their arguments might be contested, in my view, even for the late republic or early empire, neither position commits them to disagreeing with the claim that the sex ratio of the *late imperial* slave population was balanced.
[12] Scheidel 2005a, 72. Exposure: Bagnall 1997b.
[13] Harris 1999, 66. Though cf. Palladius, discussed in chapter 4.
[14] E.g. Jongman 1988, 97–154.   [15] Roth 2008, 2007.
[16] Scheidel 1994a.   [17] Harris 1999, 69.

social niche, but certainly not a representative one. Here the analytical distinction between Illustrious and Elite households, on the one hand, and Bourgeois and Agricultural families, on the other, is crucial. Enormous households, such as those characteristic among Illustrious and larger Elite households, were most likely to employ a *predominantly* male workforce. Compact households, with only a few slaves, were more likely to employ females. This distinction appears to have held in the Roman world. Both social niches were important in the Roman slave system, but it would be a grave error to read the senatorial slave staff as a comment on the sex ratio of the slave population as a whole. Moreover, commemoration practices are not a direct reflection of demographic reality, and certain filters may have acted to select which slaves were memorialized.[18] In sum, the evidence for a significantly skewed sex ratio in the Roman slave system is flimsy, while the arguments and evidence for a relatively balanced sex ratio are much more powerful.

Along with sex ratios, mortality patterns were the strongest determinants of reproductive success in New World slavery. The devastating mortality regimes which accompanied the production of crops like sugar undermined the demographic stability of the slave population and necessitated constant external replenishment.[19] In the United States, the only place where a large-scale slave population experienced increase, the success of biological reproduction is attributable to the moderate mortality patterns associated with crops like tobacco and cotton. In the Roman world, which experienced high and unpredictable mortality in general, differential patterns of slave mortality are impossible to discern.[20] Nutrition and location were probably the most important determinants.[21] Slaves, as valuable investments, may have been more effectively guaranteed their (surely unappealing) flow of minimum calories than many of the poorest elements of Roman society.[22] Location, however, was a double-edged sword. If ancient cities were mortality traps, then urban slaves would have been disproportionately exposed to urban disease environments, whereas rural slaves lived in the relatively healthy country air. Because the slave population was probably more urbanized than the free population, differential urban mortality would have probably translated to a slightly higher slave mortality.

The incidence of manumission is equally complex. Clearly many Roman slaves were manumitted, but volume and frequency are decisively different

---

[18] Scheidel 2005a, 73 and Hasegawa 2005, 65, suggest distortion.
[19] Follett 2003; Tadman 2000.   [20] Scheidel 2001a, 29.
[21] Harper 2008.   [22] Frier 2000, 794–5.

things. Estimates of manumission rates in the Roman slave system have, rightly, come down over the last generation.[23] Chapters 5 and 12 will argue for modest rates of manumission in the fourth century. The slaves most likely to be manumitted were those in positions which required trust and responsibility.[24] Manumission was used as a positive incentive for male slaves in positions of trust, responsibility, or skill.[25] But slave children followed the status of their mother, and for reproductive purposes all that matters is the rate of manumission among pre-menopausal females. The Egyptian papyri make it perfectly clear that these rates were practically negligible.[26] The inscription from Thera (discussed on p. 75) is another compelling piece of evidence that slave-women were not manumitted when they could still bear children. On the other hand, females in sexual relationships with their masters might be manumitted, and they could represent a drain on the slave population and its reproductive potential.[27]

The question of family life among Roman slaves is a more complex problem. The slave family is discussed at more length in chapter 6. There it is argued that although Roman law preserved the master's absolute legal claim over the slave's private life, in reality slave families were relatively common.[28] We must be wary of considering any individual piece of ancient evidence representative. In the United States, the incidence of family formation varied according to the region, the crops being cultivated, the size of the plantation, and so on.[29] In Illustrious and Elite households, marriages could have existed within the family, although there would have been a surplus of available men. Ammianus mentioned a slave in a noble household at Rome who retaliated against his master for flogging his wife.[30] In the *Historia Augusta*, Aurelian was represented ruling over the private lives of his slaves, putting to death a slave-woman who committed "adultery" on her slave-husband.[31] If there was a surfeit of unmarried men in these households, then perhaps they would have sought wives from other households or even among poor women of free status. This would explain one of the most prominent dynamics in the slave family of the Caesars. Slaves of the emperor were highly successful at attracting relationships with free women, and perhaps the deficit of female co-slaves in the aristocratic household is an underappreciated part of this phenomenon.[32]

[23] Wiedemann 1985 is still fundamental.
[24] Scheidel 2008; Temin 2004, for high rates of manumission. See chapter 5.
[25] Harper 2008, arguing that some rural male slaves were manumitted.
[26] Bagnall and Frier 1994, 158.   [27] Weiler 2001; cf. Sweet 2002, for Brazil.
[28] Ulp. Reg. 5.5. Roth 2007; Martin 2003. See chapter 6.   [29] Fogel 1989, 150–2.
[30] Amm. 28.1.49 (Seyfarth vol. 2: 69).   [31] SHA, Aurel. 49.3–5 (Hohl vol. 2: 185).
[32] Harper forthcoming b; Weaver 1972.

Slaves living in smaller households would have suffered more vulnerability in their private life, given the claustrophobic environment of domestic slavery and the volatility of the family life cycle. Still, there is impressionistic evidence for extensive family formation in these sorts of households. John Chrysostom claimed that "rich" households were enormous, with stacked pyramids of authority, while the "poor" household contained the husband and wife, the slave men and their wives, and the children.[33] An abundance of inscriptions from these sorts of households in Asia Minor points to frequent and diverse forms of family life, even if such documents firmly resist quantification.[34] If reproduction was common among small households, then it follows that many households would have been involved in petty transfers of slaves as the need for slaves fluctuated with the life cycle of the household. Indeed, this is precisely what the extant slave sales preserved in the papyri reflect.[35] Virtually all of the sales were transfers of one or a few slaves by private owners; slave-traders are only dimly visible in these papyri. The papyri are a good reminder that the Roman slave trade was, in addition to massive movements of people across borders, a feverish world of tiny exchanges.[36] Houseborn slaves figure prominently in these sales, proof that even the intimacy of being born in the household was little impediment to sale if the need arose.[37]

In smaller households, more than elsewhere, reproduction would not necessarily have depended on marriages between male and female slaves. Illegitimate children followed the status of their mother. Chapter 7 gathers extensive evidence for the sexual exploitation of female slaves. Certainly some slave offspring born from the master were killed or exposed in the interest of "harmony" or patrimonial planning.[38] A late Roman joke exploited the tension between a man who wanted to keep his illegitimate progeny and the stern grandfather, who wanted nothing to do with the child.[39] But discretion usually sufficed: Paulinus of Pella proclaimed that he had never met his illegitimate offspring.[40] The considerable amount of case law preserved from late antiquity dealing with illegitimate slave children hints at significant dimensions for mixed-status reproduction.[41] Of course, some urban slave-women were prevented from having sex, and the fertility of urban slaves would have been further depressed by their importance as wet-nurses.[42] It remains impossible to assign numbers to these

[33] Ioh. Chrys. In Ephes. 22.2 (PG 62: 157).
[34] Martin 2003, with further discussion in chapter 6.   [35] Straus 2004.   [36] Bradley 1978.
[37] Bradley 1987a.   [38] Herrmann-Otto 2002, 121.   [39] Philogel. 57 (Thierfelder: 50).
[40] P. Pell. Euch. lines 165–72 (SC 209: 68–70).   [41] See chapter 11.
[42] On wet-nursing, see chapter 3. cf. Bagnall 1997b, 135, for wet-nursing to increase slave fertility. Gould 1997, for a comparison from New Orleans.

patterns – even for the intrepid quantifier – and we can only say that in small settings, slave families were vulnerable. This did not necessarily translate into lack of reproduction.

In short, as far as the evidence allows us to see, sex ratios, mortality patterns, rates of manumission, and opportunities for private life were compatible with a large element of natural reproduction. The reproductive success of the ancient slave population ultimately hinges on the countryside, where females were plentiful, disease was less menacing, manumission was infrequent, and privacy was greater. The profile of late Roman slavery outlined in chapter 1 would predict that half or more of all slaves lived in rural environments. Unfortunately, the ancient sources are far more vocal about life in the city than life in the country. There is so little evidence that much of the debate has turned on the single remark of Columella that he rewarded slave-women for bearing and raising three children.[43] There is at least similar, impressionistic evidence for reproduction from the late empire. Caesarius of Arles could say, as a matter of common knowledge, that "everyone wants slaves to be born to them who will serve them. A slave-woman, however many children she conceives, will either raise them or hand them to others to be raised."[44] Comments like this provide insight into expectations but not necessarily realities.

A new document of the fourth century, however, now provides our best opportunity to recover objective, random data on the demographics of rural slavery: the census inscription from Thera. The inscription is a tax record listing the slaves belonging to a single landowner. Covering two stones, the inscription is headed with the title, "And Slaves on the Farms," followed by the names and ages of 152 slaves.[45] Although the investigation is of course hazardous, the stone provides invaluable demographic data.[46] The number of slaves in this inscription is greater than the number recovered from *three centuries* of Egyptian census returns ($n = 118$).[47] It represents a documentary source for a social environment of ancient slavery that has proven absolutely inaccessible to empirical investigation.

The two stones are damaged. Of the 152 names, 87 lines retain legible data on the slave's age, and the age data are the most straightforward.[48] Only

[43] Scheidel 1994a.
[44] Caes. Arel. Serm. 44.2 (CC 103: 196): *unaquaeque vult ut sibi nascantur mancipia, quae illi serviant, ita et illa, quantoscumque conceperit, aut ipsa nutriat, aut nutriendos aliis tradat.* cf. Dig. 5.3.27.pr, with Roth 2008, 576–7; Herrmann-Otto 1994, 271.
[45] Geroussi-Bendermacher 2005, 340: καὶ δούλους ἐπὶ τῆς χώρας.
[46] This account is reliant on the presentation of Harper 2008.
[47] Bagnall and Frier 1994, 342–3.
[48] The second digit in the age of one male in his 20s is illegible, so he has been distributed equally between the 20–24 and 25–29 bracket.

Table 2.1 *Demographics of the slave population on Thera*

Age	Male	Female	Sex unknown	Total
0 to 4	4	4	0	8
5 to 9	5	9	2	16
10 to 14	3	4	0	7
15 to 19	1	2	1	4
20 to 24	.5	5	1	6.5
25 to 29	3.5	1	2	6.5
30 to 34	1	5	0	6
35 to 39	1	2	0	3
40 to 44	3	4	4	11
45 to 49	1	1	1	3
50 to 54	2	4	0	6
55 to 59	1	4	0	5
60 ±	3	2	0	5
Total	29	47	11	87 slaves

119 names can be assigned a sex, most of these with a degree of certainty. There are 76 lines with both sex and age data. The inscription provides invaluable data about the sex ratio of an actual rural slave population. In the 119 names that provide information, there were 63 females and 56 males. The balance is striking and supports the view that in late antiquity the sex ratio of the slave population was not heavily tilted towards males, even in the countryside (table 2.1).

The number of children is immediately striking. Only one slave child under three was recorded, though ages under ten are well represented. Infant mortality is not reflected in the graph.[49] The number of males, especially young adult males, may be understated – probably a form of tax evasion. On the other hand, the number of elderly slaves, particularly slaves in their forties, seems to have been overstated – probably because of age rounding.[50]

The age structure of this population is revealing. First, it would seem to show that the mortality patterns among this population of rural slaves were not unusually devastating. The slaves of Thera did not experience the brutal sort of mortality which was common in the islands of the western hemisphere. Secondly, the age structure shows that there may be reason to suspect the manumission of adult male slaves. The sex ratio becomes more tilted towards females among slaves over the age of thirty. This could

[49] cf. Hasegawa 2005, 65–6, on the invisibility of infants in the *columbaria* inscriptions.
[50] Harper 2008.

be an aberration, or it could imply that male slaves experienced higher mortality. But if manumission is the underlying cause of the pattern, it provides an important parallel to the Egyptian census data, which show that female slaves were rarely manumitted while they were still capable of bearing children – an important clue that the fertility of slaves was highly valued.[51]

There are several signs that natural reproduction through slave families was important among the slaves on Thera. The first is simply the number of children. Of course it is possible that the slave children were imported at a young age or that they were exposed infants who had been collected and enslaved. But the most obvious explanation would be that the young slaves were the children of the adult slaves in this population. As the editor has noticed, the slaves in the inscription are grouped "manifestement par familles, chaque famille commençant par le membre le plus âgé."[52] Moreover, the patterns in which the names are recorded strengthens the case for family life among these slaves. The sequences in which the names are recorded show an especially strong link between the adult females and the children.[53]

A plausible intepretation of the data from Thera would envision a population shaped by natural reproduction, family life, and some adult male manumission. This reconstruction is intrinsically plausible, because stable family life would both account for the large number of children and is consistent with a model of domination in which positive incentives, such as manumission and privacy, played an important role. The presence of females and children immediately shows that this estate did not follow the radical model of plantation labor which some have hypothesized for the Italian wine villa, and it is also worth noting that one of the best excavations of a late Roman villa, at the *Villa Magna* in Italy, has recently uncovered a massive residential complex, which the excavators interpret, very plausibly, as large-scale barracks that accommodated slave families working on the estate.[54] Even if our interpretation of the inscription from Thera is uncertain, it is undeniably striking that the only documentary source for a large, rural slave estate exhibits precisely the demographic profile which has been deduced as necessary to sustain a large slave population over a long stretch of time.

We should even ask if a construction cautiously built around the verb "sustain" is rooted in argument or pre-judgment. There is nothing to

---

[51] Bagnall and Frier 1994, 71, 156–8.   [52] Geroussi-Bendermacher 2005, 345.
[53] Harper 2008.   [54] Fentress, Goodson, and Maiuro 2009.

preclude the possibility that the rural slave population was the demo-graphic dynamo of the supply system. Before the intervention of Scheidel, the belief in the limited scope of natural reproduction was based on the vaguest of equations – Roman slavery was bad, so it must have been tough to reproduce. The single instance of a self-reproducing slave population could easily enough be considered an aberration. The trebling of the US slave population was the outcome of a unique set of circumstances – the abolition of slave imports, the high value of cotton, a paternalist regime, etc. But it is now clearer that this was not the case. In a brilliant study, Tadman demonstrated there was one, overwhelming variable in the repro-ductive performance of modern slave populations: sugar. Where there was sugar, demographic decline; where there was not, demographic stability or increase.[55] Roman slavery was one of the few pre-modern slave systems with a large element of rural slavery and agricultural production over a long timescale; it was organized around the production of the standard Mediter-ranean triad of wine, oil, and grain. Roman slaves did not suffer from an abnormal reproductive ecology. It is certainly plausible that the rural slave population replaced itself successfully, and nothing excludes the possibility that it was even capable of producing extra bodies to be consumed in urban settings where higher mortality and lower familial opportunity depressed the levels of reproduction.

A final insight into the aggregate value of reproduction in the Roman slave system may exist in the form of slave prices.[56] The maximum prices for slaves in Diocletian's Price Edict show that only during adolescence was the price of a female slave equivalent to her male counterpart (figure 2.1).

The demand for female slaves was the composite of three forces: the demand for female labor (which was itself productive), the demand for female slaves as consumption items, in particular their sexual value, and the demand for the reproductive potential of female slaves. It is impossible to disaggregate the variables, and certainly they were not always independent in the mind of the buyer – Libanius spoke of female slaves who were valued for their looks and their capacity for textile work.[57] But the high value of nubile female slaves implies, surely, that reproductive capacity carried a premium in the marketplace.

The case for a naturally reproducing slave population has been based on demographic modeling. Ultimately, this consists of simply juxtaposing the number of new slaves needed per annum with the implausibility of

---

[55] Follett 2003; Tadman 2000.   [56] *Edictum de pretiis rerum venalium*, 29 (Giacchero: 208).
[57] Lib. Decl. 6.35 (Foerster vol. 5: 395).

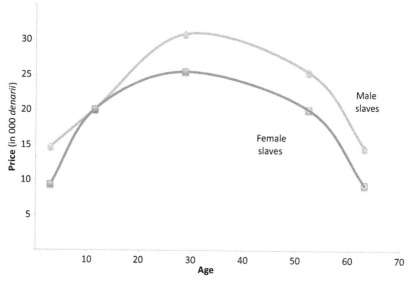

Figure 2.1 Slave prices, by age

finding anywhere close to this number from war, importation, or internal enslavement. There is little or no positive evidence which could estimate the actual number of slaves born to slaves in the Roman empire, while the arguments against the reproductive model have focused on the sex ratio and the lack of familial opportunity. The late antique evidence strongly supports the reproductive model. The sheer longevity of the system implies highly stable input mechanisms, which are most likely to be found in demographic patterns, not events. The late Roman sources undermine the assertions of an imbalanced sex ratio and a lack of familial opportunity. The one random, objective source of data reveals a demographic structure that is perfectly consistent with a high degree of natural reproduction. Biological reproduction was the main engine of the Roman slave supply.

CANNIBALIZING THE MEDITERRANEAN: INTERNAL SOURCES OF THE SLAVE SUPPLY

The slave trade in the Mediterranean, from the piracy of the Homeric age down to the sex trafficking of the present day, has victimized the populations of the Mediterranean itself, with different levels of regularity

and different modes of extraction. The Roman slave trade was no exception
and almost certainly marked a peak of efficiency in pulling bodies from the
territories around the sea and feeding them into the commerce in slaves.
The strong force of demand for slaves, the sophisticated organization of
the slave trade, the demographic regime of the ancient world, and – so
chapter 10 argues – the collusion of the legal system all made the "internal"
sources of the Roman slave trade structurally significant. If just as difficult
to quantify, internal sources were a major input to the Roman slave supply,
a fact with repercussions for the overall complexion of the slave system.

At least four different means of enslavement contributed to the internal
supply: self-sale, the sale of children, abduction, and child exposure. Their
relative importance can only be sketched from the extant sources. The sale
of oneself into slavery is not widely documented in the sources.[58] But it
was certainly well known in the high empire: Dio Chrysostom spoke of
"countless" free men who sold themselves into slavery.[59] Precisely because
it was a black-market practice, self-sale was beyond the social blinkers of
our sources.[60] The phenomenon is thus more amply attested in the laws
than in the literary sources. Roman law contained loopholes denying those
who sold themselves into slavery the right to re-claim their freedom if they
had shared in the price.[61] Against the threat of crushing poverty, some
found the specialized niches of slavery more appealing than life among the
free.[62]

The sale of children into slavery is widely attested in antiquity, although
again the evidence is murky precisely because the practice was not legally
recognized.[63] Much of the evidence which turns up is literary and plainly
guilty of stereotyping: the practice was first reported by Herodotus in
his discussion of Thracians.[64] It was thereafter repeated by Caesar of the
Gauls and Tacitus of the Germans.[65] None of these reports are illuminating. Moreover, it has been assumed that the practice of selling children
was widespread among the eastern peoples of the empire.[66] Philostratus reported the sale of children as a Phrygian custom. He contrasted

---

[58] Bieżuńska-Małowist 1974–7, vol. 2, 16; Taubenschlag 1944, 52, 56.
[59] Dio Chrys. Or. 15.22–23 (Arnim vol. 2: 238): μυρίοι. cf. Sen. Benef. 4.13.3 (Hermes vol. 1: 96–7) with Ramin and Veyne 1981, 472.
[60] Ramin and Veyne 1981, 472–3.
[61] See esp. Dig. 40.12.7; Dig. 40.12.14; Dig. 40.13.1. Söllner 2000, 86–8, 90.
[62] Ramin and Veyne 1981, 492–7. Aug. Ep. 24*.2 (CSEL 88: 127).
[63] Esp. Vuolanto 2003, 170. cf. Mommsen 1905; Mitteis 1891, 358–64.
[64] Hdt. 5.6 (Rosén vol. 2: 3–4).
[65] Caes. Gall. 6.13.2 (Hering: 184); Tac. Germ. 24 (Koestermann vol. 2.2: 19); Tac. Ann. 4.72 (Heubner: 174).
[66] Cameron 1939a, 51: "inveterate in the eastern provinces."

barbarians, who "do not consider slavery a disgrace," with the Greeks, who loved freedom.[67] Despite the ideological veneer, the importance of slaves imported from Asia Minor, especially in the imperial period, is undeniable. The prevalence of slave markets along the southeastern rim of Asia Minor is compelling testimony that, somehow, slaves were being extracted from the region on a significant scale.[68] But the evidence, as a whole, does not point to any particular region as the sole source of enslaved children.

Conspicuously, the sale of children is known largely from literary reports on *peoples* who practiced it, not from specific cases. The sale of free children has left virtually no documentary trace as a source of slavery in Ptolemaic or Roman Egypt.[69] But it is plausible that a practice considered lower-class or even barbaric has simply failed to produce receipts. Roman rescripts, at least, show that the sale of children did produce court cases.[70] The sale of children, to take the literary sources at face value, was part of a frontier dynamic, whether that frontiers was the imperial *limes* or the more complex political and economic fissures inside the empire. In late antiquity, with a more balanced view of provincial life and a new Christian concern for the poor, we begin to see specific testimony about the sale of children by Mediterranean parents, not barbarians. Roman law in the late empire, in an age of universal citizenship, struggled to find stable norms permitting the sale of infants into slavery, while confining the sale of older children to a form of labor "rental."[71]

Abduction, too, marked a systematic input to the slave supply. Roman lawyers knew that free men were sometimes captured by pirates and bandits.[72] In spatial terms, the Roman state never established perfect order in parts of the empire.[73] The literary documents of late antiquity were deeply anxious about the danger posed by "kidnappers," a word semantically equivalent in Greek to slave-trader.[74] Chrysostom knew that slave-catchers would "often hold out candies or cakes or dice or other things to little children to bait them."[75] Others reported very similar tricks.[76] Athanasius said that they would wait until the parents were gone and then snatch the child away.[77] Fathers had to worry constantly about slave-catchers.[78] Augustine was aware of the danger that a child, angrily

[67] Philostr. Vit. A. 8.7.37 (Jones vol. 2: 367): οὔπω τὸ δουλεύειν αἰσχρὸν ἡγοῦνται. Jones' translation.
[68] Harris 1999, 75.   [69] Bieżuńska-Małowist 1974–7, vol. 1, 28; 1974–7, vol. 2, 16.
[70] See chapter 9 and appendix 2.   [71] See chapter 10.
[72] E.g. Dig. 49.15.19.2; Dig. 28.1.13.pr.   [73] Shaw 1984. cf. Lenski 1999.   [74] See p. 95.
[75] Ioh. Chrys. Adv. Iud. 1.7 (PG 48: 855): τραγήματα καὶ πλακοῦντας καὶ ἀστραγάλους καὶ ἕτερά τινα τοιαῦτα πολλάκις τοῖς μικροῖς προτεινόμενοι παιδίοις καὶ δελεάζοντες.
[76] Bas. (dub.) Is. 10.245 (PG 30: 249).   [77] Ath. Ep. Aeg. Lib. 1 (PG 25: 540).
[78] Ioh. Chrys. In act. Apost. 6.3 (PG 60: 60).

running away from a parent, would fall into the hands of slave-traders.[79] Chrysostom imagined a pedagogue disciplined to keep a constant eye on the child going to school.[80] These writers had the city in mind. If slave-catchers worked the streets of Antioch, the problem must have been rife in the more vulnerable rural spaces of the empire. These warnings are proverbial, but not in every society does parental paranoia focus on the slave trade.

The trade in kidnapped children could be a delicate operation. Libanius claimed that slave-traders lived in perpetual fear because they were worried about punishment.[81] Chrysostom assumed that a kidnapped child would be sold on distant shores, a strategic but cruel way to minimize the chances of being discovered.[82] The trade itself, the physical distance, was part of the deracination enforced by the internal slave trade. The most honest assessment of the practice came from Cyril of Alexandria, who was the only author candid enough to criticize not just the slave-catchers, but the buyers who colluded with the system. Slave-owners who bought enslaved children knew that the children were born free, but the masters feigned ignorance about their slaves' true origins.[83]

If the sale of children occurred along the edges of civilization, and the abduction of children was a disturbing but real disruption of late antique society, the exposure of infants was woven into the very fabric of the classical world.[84] By some estimates, child exposure in the ancient Mediterranean attained grievously high levels. Harris has argued, in fact, that exposure ranks as one of the most important sources of the Roman slave supply. He has entertained the possibility that levels of exposure could have reached 20 percent of all newborns, and historical *comparanda* show that such rates were possible in certain times and places.[85] Unfortunately there are no quantitative data which could provide hard, satisfying information about the demographic scope of the practice. Perhaps such high levels were possible during famines or other catastrophic episodes, if not permanently.[86]

The evidence for widespread child exposure is insistent. Child exposure played a prominent role in the mythological and literary imagination of Mediterranean antiquity.[87] Greek and Latin authors reported surprise if

---

[79] Aug. Ep. Io. 7 (PL 25: 2033).
[80] Ioh. Chrys. Ad pop. Ant. 16.4 (PG 49: 168).   [81] Lib. Or. 25.41 (Foerster vol. 2: 556).
[82] Ioh. Chrys. Mut. Nom. 1.1 (PG 51: 115).   [83] Cyr. Ador. 8 (PG 68: 537f).
[84] Corbier 2001; Bagnall 1997b; Harris 1994; Boswell 1988; Weiss 1921; Glotz 1877.
[85] Harris 1999, 74, and 1994, 1. cf. Scheidel 1997, 164; Gavitt 1994, early modern Tuscany; Corsini 1976, for seventeenth–nineteenth centuries.
[86] CT 11.27.1 (AD 315, *contra* Seeck); CT 11.27.2 (AD 322).
[87] Harris 1994, 3; Boswell 1988, 95–100.

a people did *not* practice exposure.[88] Plutarch claimed, bluntly, that the poor did not raise their children.[89] Some casual clues are truly striking: in a Roman will from Cappadocia, the decedent enjoined his freedmen not to expose infants, as though it were one of the few things worth saying in a last testament.[90] Late Roman laws – in an effort to suppress pastoral banditry – prohibited exposing infants to be collected by shepherds.[91] In a revealing document, a letter of Pliny during his term as governor of Bithynia described legal suits involving foundlings as a "great issue and one that affects the whole province."[92] The systemic effects of exposure have also been detected in the papyri.[93]

The motivations for child exposure were complex and diverse.[94] Poverty must rank as the absolute leading cause. Lactantius urged the poor to abstain from sex with their wives if they could not afford children.[95] Family planning – patrimonial planning would be a better term – could impel parents, in a world of partible inheritance, to expose children in the name of unifying the family's property.[96] Gender, controversially, was likely a factor, putting girls at a higher risk of exposure.[97] Illegitimacy must have been another cause, and never should the blinding force of sexual shame be underestimated: Ambrose spoke of girls who were able to hide pregnancies carried to term, though they then killed or exposed the infant.[98]

The survival rate of exposed infants is likewise controversial.[99] Infant mortality was excruciatingly high in the ancient world, surely more so for the cast-outs. And yet it is apparent that exposed infants ended up, in large numbers, on the slave market. The documentary evidence is unambiguous.[100] Lactantius imagined that exposed children ended up in slavery or the brothel – and in antiquity there was a close link between those two destinations.[101] Wet-nursing was common in antiquity, and some contracts imply a sophisticated slave trade which harvested bodies for sale.[102] The process could also be informal: in a papyrus from the village of Kellis,

---

[88] Diod. Sic. Bibl. (Bertrac and Vernière: 151–2). Pomeroy 1986, 159–60.
[89] Plut. Am. Prol. 5 (Pohlenz: 497). Harris 1994, 6. cf. Philo Spec. Leg. 3.110 (Mosès vol. 25: 130).
[90] Jones 2004.   [91] CT 9.31.1 (AD 409). Russi 1986.
[92] Plin. Ep. 10.65 (Mynors: 323–4): *magna et ad totam provinciam pertinens quaestio.* See chapter 10.
[93] Bagnall 1997b.   [94] Harris 1994, 11–15; Boswell 1988, 109. cf. Gavitt 1994; Corsini 1976.
[95] Lact. Inst. 6.20.25 (CSEL 19.1: 560).   [96] Bas. Hex. 8.6 (SC 26²: 460). Harris 1994, 7.
[97] Bagnall 1997b.   [98] Ambr. Ep. 56.14 (CSEL 82: 171). cf. Corsini 1976, 998.
[99] Optimistic: Boswell 1988, 131. Pessimistic: Harris 1994, 1. Intermediate: Harris 1999, 74.
[100] Taubenschlag 1944, 55; Cameron 1939a. P. Kellis 8 (AD 362); P. Athen. 20 (3C). Bagnall 1997b.
[101] Lact. Inst. 6.20.22 (CSEL 19.1: 559). cf. Tert. Apol. 9.18 (CC 1: 105); Clem. Paed. 3.21.5 (SC 158: 50). See chapter 7.
[102] Manca Masciadri and Montevecchi 1982; Bagnall 1997b, 129.

in the year 362, the carpenter bought a little slave-girl whom a local woman had "raised from the ground" and reared with her own milk.[103]

The exposure of newborns was endemic and geographically diffused. It was a stable and integral component of the slave supply.[104] While the late antique evidence will not resolve the debate over the quantitative significance of exposure, it can add a new perspective: the legal angle. Of course, legal enactments are not a reliable proxy for the social importance of a phenomenon; a single case can generate a response from the government. But a long trail of complex, earnest, and pragmatic legal reform *can* suggest a significant and recurring problem. The late Roman legal codes show that, just as Pliny was confounded by what to do about exposed infants who were enslaved, the late Roman state struggled to find a workable middle ground. Several laws claimed, explicitly, that lawsuits concerning foundlings were a nuisance, which allows us to infer a relatively significant dimension for the practice.[105]

The Roman slave supply drew heavily from the peoples of the Mediterranean. Harris and others have placed appropriate emphasis on the patent cannibalism of the Roman slave system in the high empire, and the evidence from late antiquity emphatically confirms this image. The Romans conquered the Mediterranean, but before, during, and after their rule, the empire was made up of a vast patchwork of distinct microregions. Economic inequalities and demographic instabilities created the conditions for internal enslavement. Self-sale, child sale, abduction, and child exposure all constituted regular practices which could have accounted for significant passages into slavery. The internal sources may defy quantification, but the Romans knew that amongst their slaves lurked many who had not been captured in war or born to slave mothers, but who rightfully belonged by birth among the free peoples of the Mediterranean.[106]

TRANS-FRONTIER TRADING AND RAIDING: EXTERNAL
SOURCES OF SLAVERY

For late antique men and women, the slave trade was the image of the strange, populous world beyond the frontier. Augustine could conjure the outside world for his congregation by pointing to the slave population of his port city. "There are in Africa innumerable barbarian peoples, who do not yet know the gospel, who are led here as captives and joined to the

---

[103] P. Kellis 8: δούλην χαμαίρετον. Bagnall 1997b, 121–3.
[104] Harris 1999, 74; Bagnall 1997b; Motomura 1988.   [105] See chapter 10.   [106] Dig. 41.3.44.

slavery of the Romans, as we can see every day before our own eyes."[107] Chrysostom told his Christians not to gawk at exotic barbarian slaves in the marketplace of Antioch.[108] A Gallic courtier could fawn over his white, Germanic slave-girl or mock a drunken black one.[109] A xenophobic tract claimed that every household had a Gothic slave.[110] From Gaul to Egypt, barbarian slaves were a conspicuous element of Roman society.[111] A law of AD 374, trying to staunch the flow of gold out of the empire to the barbarians, found slaves the only import worth mentioning.[112] The forced, inward migration brought Romans face to face with the enormity of the uncivilized world which surrounded them.

The late antique testimony emphasizes the regularity and volume of cross-border importation. The Roman army, as always, scored periodic victories which could flood the market.[113] But more important was the steady operation of professional slave-traders. The frontier slave trade becomes visible in the late antique record because it happened to intersect with *histoire événementielle*. After Julian fortified the Thracian border against the Goths, for instance, he said "that the Galatian merchants were a match for the Goths, by whom they are sold everywhere without any regard for their condition."[114] "Galatian merchants" were specialized slave-dealers and, from Julian's remark, they handled both the procurement and mercantile sides of the trade. The co-operation of the Roman state with slave-traders was policy, if it sometimes made for an uneasy alliance. In 372, an officer of Valentinian was on a reconnoitering mission across the Rhine, when his squad crossed paths with slave-traders. "And because he did not trust the guards he happened to find there leading slaves to sale, who might quickly leave to report what they had seen, he, having seized their merchandise, slaughtered them all."[115] The slave-traders had to work both sides of the border, and their loyalty was too suspect for a sensitive

---

[107] Aug. Ep. 199.12 (CSEL 57: 284): *hoc est in Africa barbarae innumerabiles gentes, in quibus nondum esse predicatum evangelium ex his, qui ducuntur inde captivi et romanorum servitiis iam miscentur, cotidie nobis addiscere in promptu est.*

[108] Ioh. Chrys. In Rom. 4.4 (PG 60: 421). cf. Ioh. Chrys. In Io. 78.5 (PG 59: 432); Ioh. Chrys. Subintr. 9.27 (Dumortier: 76–7).

[109] Auson. Biss. 5 (Green: 132); Auson. Epig. 21 (Green: 72), if the latter in fact is about a real slave.

[110] Syn. Regn. 20 (Terzaghi: 46–8).

[111] Sulp. Sev. Dial. 3.15 (CSEL 1: 213); Cyr. Rom. 7.18 (Pusey vol. 3: 207).

[112] CJ 4.63.2 (AD 374). Also CT 3.4.1 (AD 386) for barbarian imports.

[113] Lenski 2008. For the high empire, Bradley 2004; Gonzales 2002.

[114] Amm. 22.7.8 (Seyfarth vol. 1: 259): *illis enim sufficere mercatores Galatas, per quos ubique sine condicionis discrimine venundantur.*

[115] Amm. 29.4.4 (Seyfarth vol. 2: 113): *et quia suspicabatur venalia ducentes mancipia scurras casu illic repertos id, quod viderant, excursu celeri nuntiare, cunctos mercibus direptis occidit.*

mission. Other motives might be suspected, too: having killed the dealers, the officer kept the slaves.

The triangulation of power between the Roman state, slave-traders, and the enemy was an enduring problem. Shortly after Julian's decision to leave the Goths to the Galatian slave-traders, war erupted. Only with difficulty did Valens impose "peace" on the region. In a celebration of this treaty, Themistius delivered a panegyric before the senate and the emperor. The control over commerce along the Danube was a principal theme, and though Themistius refrained from saying as much, the truce sounded like a trade concession:

Taking pity on the barbarians, [Valens] allowed them to hold, now with official sanction, the markets and trading centers which under the previous peace they had conducted wherever they wanted without any fear. Even though the profits which arose from the exchange of agreements benefited both peoples in common, he established as trading centers only two of the cities founded along the river . . . The Goths could see that our fort commanders and garrison leaders were actually merchants and slave-dealers, since this was essentially their only occupation, to buy and to sell as much as they could.[116]

The entire framework of Romano-Gothic relations was colored by the importance of the slave trade. The commerce reached its pitch on the eve of the battle of Adrianople, when a famine ignited the tinderbox that Valens had created. "When the barbarians were so worn down by want of food that they came into the empire, the most hateful generals conceived a filthy deal. In their greed they gathered as many dogs as they could from everywhere. They traded the Goths, one dog for one slave, taking even some of their nobles into slavery."[117]

Surely it is noteworthy that the slave trade was the proximate cause of one of the most significant battles in Roman history. Ammianus had unbounded contempt for the Roman generals, but his outrage stemmed from the callous abuse of the Goths' hunger and the inclusion of well-born

[116] Them. Or. 10.135c–6b (Downey and Schenkl vol. 1: 207): ἀλλὰ φεισάμενος τῶν βαρβάρων, ὥστε οὐδὲ τὰς ἐμπορίας αὐτοῖς οὐδὲ τὰς ἀγοράς, ἃς ἐπὶ τῆς προτέρας εἰρήνης ἐπ' ἀδείας εἶχον ὅποι βούλοιντο ποιεῖσθαι, νῦν ἐπ' ἐξουσίας ἔχειν ἀφῆκεν. Ἀλλὰ καίτοι τοῦ κέρδους ὑπάρχοντος κοινοῦ τοῖς ἔθνεσιν ἀμφοτέροις ἐκ τῆς ἀμοιβῆς τῶν ἐν χρείᾳ συναλλαγμάτων, δύο μόνας πόλεις τῶν ποταμῷ προσῳκισμένων ἐμπόρια κατεσκευάσατο . . . ὁρῶντες . . . φρουράρχας δὲ καὶ ταξιάρχας ἐμπόρους μᾶλλον καὶ τῶν ἀνδραπόδων καπήλους, οἷς τοῦτο μόνον ἔργον προσέκειτο, πλεῖστα μὲν ὠνήσασθαι, πλεῖστα δὲ καὶ ἀπεμπολῆσαι·

[117] Amm. 31.4.11 (Seyfarth vol. 2: 170): *cum traducti barbari victus inopia vexarentur, turpe commercium duces invisissimi cogitarunt et, quantos undique insatiabilitas colligere potuit canes, pro singulis dederant mancipiis, inter quae quidam ducti sunt optimatum.* For echoes of Tacitus, see Vuolanto 2003, 172. cf. Eun. Fr. 42 (Blockley 60).

Goths among the slaves. The trade *per se* was normal. The Romans, of course, found their comeuppance. Just as Synesius would predict, Gothic slaves joined their free kinsmen *en masse*, starting at Adrianople and culminating a generation later with the defection of barbarian slaves after the sack of Rome.[118] From 407 onward, the northern *limes* was porous and indistinct; it was hardly the safe, organized line of *emporia*, buffered by the Roman army, that it had been a generation before. In the later phases of our period, the Roman state progressively lost its ability to dictate the terms of slave trafficking in the west.

A prime literary witness to the fourth-century economy confirms the significance of the cross-border trade. The tract, written by a merchant who was probably from Syria, carried the humble title, "A Description of the Whole World and its Nations."[119] The author claimed that Mauretania and Pannonia were especially remunerative sources of slaves.[120] The *Expositio* preceded the collapse of the northern frontier and thus demonstrates that the northern supply lines were reliable conduits of the slave trade into the late fourth century. This categorical statement by a well-informed merchant argues that the impressionistic testimony of Ammianus and Themistius was reflective of a larger phenomenon. The *Expositio* also suggests that southern sources of the supply were well established in late antiquity. Three distinct trunk routes of African supply are visible in the late antique documents: Mauretanian, Saharan, and Nilotic.[121] The *Expositio* claimed that the inhabitants of Mauretania "have the life and culture of barbarians, though they are subject to the Romans."[122] Mauretania encompassed both Mauretania Caesarea and Mauretania Tingitana, the thinly Romanized strip of land across from Spain along the straits of Gibraltar, cut off from the east by the Atlas mountains. It was a region long garrisoned by the army far out of proportion to its Roman population.[123] The lowland Roman population lived in an uneasy truce with the tribes inhabiting higher altitudes, who were led by their own potentates with dubious loyalties. The social geography would have made it a plausible supply line for the slave trade.

Mauretania Caesarea was more Romanized, with numerous coastal cities and a countryside dominated by Roman-style farm structures.[124] But the

---

[118] Zos. 5.42.3 (Paschoud vol. 3: 63–4).
[119] McCormick 2001, 85 and forthcoming on the value of the *Expositio*.
[120] Expos. tot. mund. 57 (Pannonia) and 60 (Mauretania) (SC 124: 196, 200).
[121] For the earlier period, Garrido-Hory 1996.
[122] Expos. tot. mund. 60 (SC 124: 200): *homines qui inhabitant barbarorum vitam et mores habent, tamen Romanis subditi.* Lepelley 1981b, 49–57.
[123] Shaw 1995, 68–9. Kulikowski 2004, 71–82, for the Diocletianic reorganization.
[124] Leveau 1984.

giant hinterland of Mauretania included many non-Romans in its midst. As the author of the *Verona List* claimed, Mauretania included whole tribes within its borders, entire "barbarian nations who have thrived under the rule of the emperors."[125] An inscription from the late third century commemorated a governor for having subdued one of these tribes and, significantly, "carried off all their booty and slaves."[126] Roman Mauretania was, in terms of human geography, a tide-wall set up against the vast and populous world between the Mediterranean and the Sahara. The Berber tribes of the semi-desert were a giant reservoir of human bodies, tapped by the Roman slave trade. A third-century inscription lists the imposts on goods traded across a vital mountain pass between the nomadic tribes of the semi-desert and northern, Romanized markets. Slaves were, ominously, the first commodity listed.[127] Augustine witnessed this trade and feigned incomprehension at the fact that a "Getulian" dragged into the pleasant orchards of the north would flee back to his dry native land.[128]

Mauretanian slaves washed up on shores all over the Mediterranean. Ambrose knew of girls from Mauretania whose families were *in vinculis*, but who had maintained their virginity.[129] An epitaph in Alexandria commemorated the fate of a Mauretanian slave-girl.[130] In an interesting and neglected document of the Roman slave trade, a man named Aurelius Quintus from Caesarea sold a Moorish slave-girl at an auction held by or in conjunction with the state bank of Rhodes.[131] The transaction suggests a sophisticated financial arrangement in which buyers and sellers had accounts at the bank which could be credited or charged as needed. The papyrus, and presumably the slave, ended up in Oxyrhynchus. The most plausible explanation is that Quintus was a slave-dealer from Mauretanian Caesarea, Rhodes an entrepôt of the slave trade, and the buyer another merchant who sold the girl in Egypt.

The evidence for the trans-Saharan slave trade in antiquity is scattered though suggestive. Archaeologists have uncovered an extraordinary civilization centered in the Fazzān, the Garamantian kingdom, which managed to achieve a high level of material culture based on irrigated agriculture and trans-Saharan commerce.[132] The Garamantians also served as middle-men in the slave trade.[133] Already at the end of the first century, a Roman named

[125] Later. Veron. 13–14 (Seeck: 251–2): *gentes barbarae, quae pullulaverunt sub imperatoribus.* Shaw 1995, 82.
[126] CIL 8.21486 (late third century) from Zucchabar: *praedasque omnes ac familias eorum abductas.*
[127] CIL 8.4508 (AD 202), from Zarai.   [128] Aug. Psalm. 148.10 (CC 40: 2173).
[129] Ambr. Virg. 1.9.59 (Gori: 158).   [130] CIL 3.6618 (third century). Straus 2004, 281.
[131] P. Oxy. 50.3593 (AD 238–44). Fraser 1972; Oates 1969.   [132] Mattingly 2003.
[133] Mattingly 2003, 287.

Julius Maternus visited the king of the Garamantians, whom he accompanied on what seems to be a "hunting" raid against Ethiopians.[134] The Garamantians consumed Roman commodities, which they had to pay for with something. Slaves seem to be one obvious candidate to explain the balance in trade between the Mediterranean and the Fazzān.

The *chalcidicum* at Leptis Magna has been proposed as a plausible slave market, one end point of the trans-Saharan land route which slaves would have trudged in their coffles.[135] The ostraca at Bu Djem, a Roman fort south of Leptis along one of the major arteries leading to the coast, indeed show the presence of Garamantian traders and black slaves along this axis of the trans-Saharan trade.[136] Another branch of the trans-Saharan trade may have headed to the west, towards Carthage. A third-century inscription from coastal Hadrumentum preserved a vicious invective against the presence of black slaves, brought explicitly by the Garamantians:

The scum of the Garamantes comes into our world, and the dark slave is proud of his black body. If not for the human voice issuing from his lips, this demon with his awful face would horrify men. Hadrumentum, let the furies of hell take your monster for themselves! The house of the underworld should have this one for its guardsman.[137]

This trade explains, for instance, the presence of black slaves at Carthage in the fifth century who were "Ethiopian by color, brought from the farthest reaches of the barbarian regions where the dried parts of the human are blackened by the fire of the sun."[138] There is also visual evidence for black slaves in Roman antiquity, including the mosaics at Piazza Armerina.[139]

A third African route, running down the Nile, was especially active in late antiquity. The traffic of slaves across the frontiers of Egypt from the Red Sea and from Ethiopia was evident as early as the *Periplus* of the Red Sea.[140] The importation of slaves from the southeast seems to have

---

[134] Mattingly 2003, 85.   [135] Braconi 1995.

[136] Marichal 1992. Garamantes mentioned in 28, 71, 72, 147. Black slaves explicitly attested in number 90, with comments on 109. The mosaics at Zliten likely show Garamantians in Roman *venationes*: Aurigemma 1926, 137, Table D.

[137] Anth. Lat. 1.183 (Buecheler and Riese: 155–6): *faex Garamantarum nostrum processit ad axem, et piceo gaudet corpore verna niger, quem nisi vox hominem labris emissa sonaret, terreret visu horrida larva viros, dira, Hadrumeta, tuum rapiant sibi Tartara monstrum; custodem hunc Ditis debet habere domus.*

[138] Ferrand. Ep. 11.2 (CC 91: 360): *colore aethiops, ex ultimis credo barbarae provinciae partibus, ubi sicca hominum membra solis ignei calore fuscantur.* Snowden 1970, 212, and generally Thompson 1989, 57–85.

[139] Dunbabin 2003b, 149, 156; George 2003. Also the fourth-century mosaic of the Maison d'Isguntus at Hippo Regius. See Dunbabin 1978, plate XIV, lower right panel.

[140] Peripl. M. R. (Casson).

Table 2.2 *Origins of slaves sold in papyri AD 300–600*

Papyrus	Date	Origin
P. Ryl. 4.709	Early 4th century	Homeborn
P. Herm. Rees 18	323	Arabian littoral
P. Neph. 30/33	329	Fragmentary
P. Lond. 3.977	330	Fragmentary
P. Köln 5.232	330–7	Homeborn
P. Sijp. 46a–c	332	Fragmentary
P. Abinn. 64	337–50	Homeborn
SB 5.8007	330–50	via Berenike
P. Ammon 2.48	after 348	Homeborn
BGU 1.316	359	Gallic
P. Kellis 8	362	Exposed infant
P. Princeton 2.85	Fifth century	Fragmentary
P. Vindob. G 39761	500	"Black"
SB 18.13173	Late sixth–early seventh century	"Alodian"

intensified, fatefully, in late antiquity, perhaps due to a combination of strong demand in the eastern Mediterranean and political changes beyond the southern borders of the empire.[141] There is considerable documentary evidence for the influx of slaves along the Red Sea and the Nile. In a papyrus of the late third century, a slave on a large property was called an Ethiopian.[142] The documents of sale are the most revealing. A slave sold in fourth-century Hermopolis claimed to be from "Rescupum," plausibly an Arabic place name along the Red Sea.[143] Another slave sold at Hermopolis in the fourth century was imported through Berenike, an entrepôt of the Red Sea trade.[144] In a slave sale of the late sixth or early seventh century from Hermopolis, two men bought a black slave-girl from a woman who had recently purchased her "from other slave-dealers of Ethiopians," implying an organized trade in Ethiopians.[145] In fact, among ten well-preserved slave sales in the late antique papyri, we detect one western slave, four sales involving homeborn slaves, one exposed infant, and four slaves from beyond the southeastern frontiers. The sample is small, but these data are highly suggestive (table 2.2).

The impression from the documentary evidence is strikingly confirmed in late antique literature.[146] Ethiopian slaves populate the monastic tales of

[141] Thompson 1969.   [142] P. Flor. 1.50 (AD 268).
[143] P. Herm. Rees 18 (AD 323): see Introduction to part III.   [144] SB 5.8007 (AD 340–60).
[145] SB 18.13173. Pierce 1995.   [146] Brakke 2001; Frost 1991; Mayerson 1978.

late antiquity.[147] The well-known ascetic, Ethiopian Moses, had been a slave of a Roman official.[148] One monk was sexually tormented by the lasting image of an Ethiopian girl he had seen during the harvest time in the days of his youth.[149] In the early fifth century, a heretical religious zealot in Egypt gathered a sizeable mob of Ethiopian slaves to attack orthodox monks and clerics at the site of Nitria: true or not, it was assumed by a fifth-century author that a gang of slaves in northern Egypt could be Ethiopian.[150] John Philoponus assumed that Ethiopians were slaves.[151] Most importantly, the Alexandrian trader and traveler, Cosmas Indicopleustes, claimed that "most slaves" imported to the empire came from Ethiopia.[152]

There was a reality behind the prominence of Ethiopian slaves in the literary imagination: a major trading vector of human bodies connected the south, down the river, to the empire. Some of these slaves passed into the Mediterranean, as evidenced by the Syriac and Palestinian authors who were aware of black slaves in the late Roman empire.[153] Other Ethiopians would have been absorbed by consumers along the Nile before making it into the Mediterranean market. It is often assumed that Egypt, with its dense settlement pattern and large free population, had little need for slavery, but the census papyri show extensive levels of household slave-ownership, and the documents of the fourth century reveal slaves on agricultural estates. The demand for slaves in Egypt and in the eastern Mediterranean during the prosperous days of late antiquity fueled the supply lines emanating from the southeast axis of the empire.

When the Arabs conquered the Levant and North Africa in the seventh century, it has been noticed that they wasted little time in establishing a massive slave trade that victimized the interior of Africa.[154] From the evidence at hand, however, it would be a mistake to see the Arab slave trade as something fundamentally new. The Romans had already established the routes and the means of supply from Africa, which survived into the Islamic period. Even the ominous mental linkage between the curse of Ham, black Africans, and slavery was taking shape in the *fourth and fifth* centuries.[155] This was due in part to the nascent social hegemony of the

---

[147] Apopth. Patr. Arsenius 32 (PG 65: 100).   [148] Pall. H. Laus. 19.1 (Butler vol. 2: 58).
[149] Pall. H. Laus. 23.5 (Butler vol. 2: 76): αἰθιόπισσαν κόρην, which is ambiguous, but her ethnicity surely provides strong grounds for inferring her status.
[150] Pall. Vit. Chrys. 7.34 (SC 341: 144).   [151] Ioh. Philop. Epit. Diait. 12 (Sanda: 96).
[152] Cosm. Ind. Top. 2.64 (SC 141: 379): Τὰ γὰρ πλεῖστα τῶν ἀνδραπόδων.
[153] Goldenberg 2003, 99–100, 134–5.
[154] E.g. Osman 2005; Pétré-Grenouilleau 2004; Goldenberg 2003; Gilly-Elway 2000, 118; Hunwick 1992, 5; Lewis 1990.
[155] Goldenberg 2003, 99–100, 134–5, though he stresses the novelty of early Islamic slavery.

Christian religion, as bishops like John Chrysostom were pestered by their congregations to explain, to justify, terrestrial social institutions like slavery. The ascent of the church coincided with the great burst of economic activity in the east, an expansion that brought with it an intensification of slavery. The slave trade out of Africa, and the ideological ingredients of a race-based justification for slavery, existed already in the late Roman empire.[156] The Roman Mediterranean was a voracious consumer of human bodies, and it obviously relied on its frontiers, north and south, to supply a meaningful portion of its victims.

THE SLAVE TRADE: MERCHANTS AND MARKETS

The commerce in humans carried an eclectic mix of barbarians and home-born slaves, exposed infants, and kidnapped children. A commerce that was capable of moving millions of bodies across continents, despite all the heavy costs and obstacles to movement in the pre-modern world, has left only erratic traces in the historical record. The evidence for the trade is impressionistic, a set of discrete points that map a trade capable of moving bodies enormous distances. These points tell us far too little about the scale or structure of the trade. What was the Roman slave trade like? How was it organized, and what mechanisms acted to integrate supply and demand? Who sold slaves, and in what kinds of markets? Unfortunately we have no log book from a slave trader, no register of sales from a market. Valiant attempts to recover the workings of the slave trade for the earlier period have yielded modest returns. The slave trade lies largely hidden from view, but the fragments of information which survive from late antiquity are at least suggestive. Like a paleontologist measuring an extinct creature from the curvature of a few bone fragments, the historian of the slave trade must infer its physiognomy from a desperately inadequate record.

The slave trade has not figured prominently in the debates over the extent and nature of Roman trade in general, but the lessons of that broader discussion provide insights into consideration of the slave trade. As the debate over Roman trade has oscillated between maximalists and minimalists, the barriers to exchange have become more clearly defined.[157] The chief obstacles to trade were institutional factors, especially poor information and high transportation costs. These forces kept the Roman Mediterranean

---

[156] Bradley 2004, 312.
[157] Morley 2007b for a brief overview; McCormick forthcoming and 2001, for late antiquity.

from being a perfectly integrated market, where prices moved in co-ordination and supply flowed directly to demand. This is true across history, though, and the challenge quickly becomes how best to describe the rela-tive efficiency of Roman markets, between the antipodes of "integrated" and "imperfect."[158] To judge the level of sophistication in the Roman slave trade, we should look for signs of organization and interlinkage. In other words, how were merchants involved in the slave trade organized, and through what kinds of markets were slaves moved? There are compelling signs in the late Roman sources that the slave trade was operated by highly organized merchants through a complex hierarchy of markets acting to move slaves towards demand.[159]

The most vivid testimony about the organization of the Roman slave trade to have survived – from any period of ancient history – is a letter of Augustine found only a generation ago. The letter is a desperate message written by Augustine very near the end of his life to his comrade Alypius. Alypius was on an embassy to the imperial court, and Augustine implored him to seek imperial help. "There is in Africa such a multitude of those who are commonly called 'slavers' (*mangones*) that they are draining the greater part of the human race and exporting what they sell into trans-marine provinces – and almost all of these are free persons."[160] These slave-traders were comprised of two separate groups, catchers and merchants. The slave-catchers had begun to roam throughout Numidia, not only buying men, women, and children, but violently seizing them in planned attacks. Augustine vividly described a number of well-orchestrated slave-catching raids. "In screaming herds with the terrible aspect of either military or barbarian guise, the predators are said to invade certain rural places where there are few men and to abduct violently those they sell to these very merchants."[161] Augustine relayed a rumor that in one *villula*, all the men were killed and the women and children carried off. The bishop himself interviewed a little girl whose house had been attacked in the night. These organized slave-raiding bands are reminiscent of nothing so much as early modern slaving practices in West Africa, and Augustine's

---

[158] Temin 2001 (integration) and Bang 2008 (imperfection).

[159] Harris 1980 is still basic. Bodel 2005; Fentress 2005; Garrido-Hory 2002; Harrill 1999. On Roman markets, Rosenfeld and Menirav 2005; Lo Cascio 2000; de Ligt 1993.

[160] Aug. Ep. 10*.2 (CSEL 88: 46–7): *tanta est eorum qui vulgo mangones vocantur in Africa multitudo, ut eam ex magna parte humano genere exhauriant transferendo quos mercantur in provincias transmarinas et paene omnes liberos.*

[161] Aug. Ep. 10*.2 (CSEL 88: 47): *ita ut gregatim ululantes habitu terribili vel militari vel barbaro remota [et] agrestia quaedam loca, in quibus pauci sunt homines, perhibeantur invadere et quos istis mercatoribus vendant violenter abducere.*

letter is perhaps our only account of ancient slaving methods.[162] Romans were being dragged out of Numidia "in columns, like an endless river."[163]

Augustine insisted that the catchers were distinct from the merchants but that the two groups were interdependent. "Four months ago, from various lands, especially from Numidia, people gathered by Galatian merchants (for these alone or to a special degree throw themselves into this business), were brought to be transferred from the shores of Hippo."[164] The merchants were the *sine qua non* of the trade, and they clearly organized the mayhem infecting the province. "Then from this crowd of merchants the multitude of those who seduce and seize has grown . . . If it were not for the merchants, these depredations would not happen."[165] The sub-specialization in the slave trade indicated by Augustine's letter is significant. The slave merchants were a specialized group – Galatians, colloquially known as *mangones* – but they were able to orchestrate slave-catching in the hinterland of Mediterranean commerce while insulating themselves from the primal criminality and violence of the slave raids.

Augustine's letter has been read as a sign of crisis in late antique Africa. The decline of imperial order, it is said, prompted the appearance of slave-traders in Numidia, who facilitated a recrudescence of slavery.[166] We can sense here the lingering influence of a supply-side explanation of Roman slavery, in which a supply of cheap slaves is the driving force behind the expansion of slavery. But the background to Augustine's call for help is more complex and more specific than a simple breakdown of Roman order or a re-birth of the slave system. There is no indication that such an organized and intricate system of slave-trading was anything new. The slave-merchants who appeared in Hippo were, clearly, Roman slave-traders. Galatian merchants, specialized slave-dealers, had long worked the frontiers of imperial power as supply lines for human chattel. But in the early fifth century, right as Augustine saw the slave trade pass through the port at Hippo, those frontiers were folding in upon the Roman Mediterranean.

Augustine's letter has been re-dated to 428, a fact with dramatic and unrecognized consequences.[167] This puts the events of his letter squarely in the context of a disruption of the old slave trade. In his *Chronicle*, Hydatius reported that Vandals pillaged the Balearic Islands and sacked

---

[162] cf. Diptee 2006, 183.   [163] Aug. Ep. 10*.5 (CSEL 88: 49): *catervatim perpetuo quasi fluvio.*

[164] Aug. Ep. 10*.7 (CSEL 88: 50): *ante quattuor fere menses . . . de diversis terris et maxime de numidia congregati a galatis mercatoribus – hi enim vel soli vel maxime his quaestibus inhianter incumbunt – ut a litore hipponiensi transportarentur, adducti sunt.*

[165] Aug. Ep. 10*.2–3 (CSEL 88: 47): *porro ex hac multitudine mercatorum ita insolevit seducentium et depraedantium multitudo . . . mercatores autem si non essent, illa non fierent.*

[166] Gebbia 1987; Humbert 1983; Rougé 1983; Lepelley 1981b.   [167] Berrouard 1985.

the southern coast of Spain in 425. Then, after they plundered Spain, the Vandals invaded Mauretania.[168] The Vandals were the first of the fifth-century invaders to take to the sea. The events which Augustine describes could be connected with a disruption of the shipping lanes which carried slaves out of the southwest Mediterranean. The spectacular discovery of fourteen sunken ships of the fifth century, off Sardinia, hypothesized as the work of the Vandals, vividly illustrates why Roman traders may have adjusted their routes.[169] In the midst of the Vandal invasion, Roman slave-traders edged eastwards from their usual Mauretanian haunts and started shipping out of Numidian ports like Hippo. Augustine's letter was written at a moment when one of the supply lines of the Roman slave trade was forced to cannibalize upon the empire rather than its usual victims.

There is another decisive clue that the slave merchants witnessed by Augustine were not mere opportunists who suddenly sprouted from the soil of fifth-century disorder. Augustine recognized that the merchants were a powerful political force with protection at high levels. The church at Hippo, distraught at the enslavement of free Romans, organized a vigilante raid and freed 120 slaves (while Augustine was away, he added rather unheroically). The maneuver left the bishop in a delicate position. His letter was more than a complaint about the situation in Africa; it was an urgent appeal on behalf of his flock. "As I write, the Galatians have already begun to harass us. Although letters came in from a power they should have feared, they nevertheless do not cease trying to re-claim their slaves."[170] He tried to threaten them with a law against selling freeborn persons into trans-marine provinces, but he was uneasy about seeking the virtual death penalty – scourging with leaden whips – which its enforcement entailed.[171] Augustine sought imperial help for his embattled flock, hardly a sign of the state's irrelevance or weakness, and his petition was firmly grounded in the complaint that *free Romans* were being abducted.[172] The real problem was that the slave-traders were powerful and protected – "the slave-traders do not lack for patrons."[173] Far from a side effect of the times, the Galatians were an established clique with protection in high places.

---

[168] Hyd. Chron. ann. 425 (Burgess: 88).

[169] McCormick forthcoming; D'Oriano and Riccardi 2004.

[170] The text is damaged but this is the sense. Aug. Ep. 10*.8 (CSEL 88: 51): *iam perturbare coeperunt quando ista dictavimus, [et] si litteris a potestate quam timere poterant supervenientibus . . . , nec tamen omnimodo ab ista repetitione cessarunt.*

[171] Aug. Ep. 10*.3–4 (CSEL 88: 47–8). Szidat 1985. For these restrictions, see chapter 10.

[172] Melluso 2002, 353; Frend 1993, 63. Aug. Ep. 10*.5 (CSEL 88: 49).

[173] Aug. Ep. 10*.8 (CSEL 88: 51): *non enim desunt patroni Galatis.*

The letter of Augustine is invaluable for the flashes of insight it provides into the organization of the ancient slave trade. Slave-traders rarely came in for description by ancient authors because they were exiled beyond the pale of polite society. Yet, they walked in its shadows. A younger Augustine, in calmer times, once noted that "drunks, moneylenders, and slave-dealers," passed through the very doors of his church.[174] Roman jurists regarded slave-traders as venal and crooked.[175] In Latin, the colloquial word for slave trader, *mango*, came from a Greek root, "to deceive, to doctor."[176] In Greek, the word for slave trader and kidnapper were the same.[177] This was the nature of the business. The slave market has always been a place of asymmetrical information, where deceit and performance squared off against careful inspection and buyer's caution to inscribe a value on a human body.[178] Thus, Roman law had an elaborate legal regime regulating consumer rights and vendor liability in the slave market.[179] The state required slave-merchants to declare physical and psychical defects in their wares, theoretically ensuring that the buyer was provided with pertinent information about his prospective property. The prosecution of vendor liability was complicated by the fact that "most" slave-dealers were part of business societies, pooling resources and responsibility.[180] The prevalence of business societies, not to mention the powerful "patrons" behind Augustine's merchants, suggest that the capital circuits involved in the slave trade might have run, discreetly, through some rather illustrious quarters, even if Roman elites insulated themselves and their reputations from the sordid business of the trade itself.[181]

There are other signs that the Roman slave trade was organized, at least in part, by specialized merchants. A sixth-century writer from Gaza described a woman who wanted to buy a young slave-girl. She waited for the "ship of slaves" to come in – a small sign that the slave trade was not simply marginal to the deeper movements of Roman commerce.[182] Clement of Alexandria claimed that Mediterranean merchants delivered boatloads of slave prostitutes wholesale, like wine or grain, while local dealers bought the girls and re-sold them, retail.[183] From Alexandria Clement was well positioned to observe this juncture between the Mediterranean and Nilotic

---

[174] Aug. Psalm. 127.11 (CC 40: 1875): *ebriosi, feneratores, mangones* . . . cf. Aug. Ep. Io. 3 (PL 25: 2002).
[175] Dig. 21.1.44.1.
[176] *mango* = from μαγγανεύω. LSJ: to use charms or philtres, to play tricks.
[177] ἀνδραποδιστής. LSJ: a slave-dealer, kidnapper. See Harrill 1999.
[178] Harrill 1999, 105; Kudlien 1986.   [179] Frier and Kehoe 2007, 120.   [180] Dig. 21.1.44.1.
[181] Serrao 2000.   [182] Dor. Doct. 6.73 (SC 92: 274–6): Πλοῖον ἀνδραπόδων.
[183] Clem. Paed. 3.22.1 (SC 158: 52).

trade. The sixth-century papyrus mentioned above referred to specialized dealers in Ethiopian slaves.[184]

The occasional glimpses of large, mercantile specialists behind the slave trade stand in apparent contrast to the apparent data offered by the papyri. A careful study of Roman slave sales found no signs of specialized slave merchants.[185] The prevalence of private sales points to the importance of natural reproduction and the consequent involvement of average slave-owners in the trade. In fact this pattern is to be expected, given the supply mechanisms of the Roman slave trade, and it demonstrates that extensive low-level trading existed underneath the larger currents of Mediterranean commerce. Yet slave-traders are not totally invisible in the papyri.[186] Clearly, slaves from Crete and Pontus, Ethiopia, Mauretania, and Gaul, were brought to Egypt by merchants.[187] It seems plausible that specialized dealers operated in the Mediterranean and sold their wares to local merchants in Alexandria, who worked the trade up the Nile. And, perhaps, some of the civic notables who are so prominent in the slave sales were speculating in slaves – buying from merchants, re-selling locally. One papyrus from the late third century points to a multi-tiered slave trade, with a long-distance commerce integrated into local markets by regional elites. In the summer of 293, Aurelius Castor, a councilor of Antinoopolis, bought a Cretan slave-woman from an Alexandrian. Only a few months later, he sold the slave to a couple from Hermopolis. Both of these acts were carried out by an agent of Aurelius Castor, and the payment was made through an exchange of credit at the local bank. Every aspect of the transaction points to a sophisticated market in slaves with local big-shots leading the speculation in human merchandise.[188]

In fact it is worth pondering how slaves from so many corners of the empire ended up in Egypt, a region hardly considered the primary destination of the slave trade. Unless the slave trade was so inconceivably vast that these distant movements were simply the froth of deeper currents, accidentally splashed here and there by the pull of the trade, a simpler answer lies in the possibility that unspecialized merchants also participated regularly in the slave trade. In a papyrus from the village of Nessana which records the accounts of a petty, itinerant trading company, slaves were among the motley wares in which they dealt.[189] Not only were there "ships of slaves"

---

[184] SB 18.13173. Pierce 1995.   [185] Straus 2004, 301–13.
[186] Social opprobrium too could have discouraged explicit declaration of occupation.
[187] Straus 2004, 280–1.
[188] P. Lips. 4 + P. Lips. 5 = M. Chr. 171 + P. Strasb. VI 594 (AD 293). Re-ed. by Straus 2004, 330.
[189] P. Nessana 89 (sixth century).

afloat on the late Roman Mediterranean, slaves were boarded as extra cargo on vessels carrying other goods. Slaves represented one more form of hedging by Mediterranean merchants who often preferred to have various types of inventory.[190] Slaves could have provided grain merchants, returning to Egypt, with a commodity to carry home – profitable ballast. In the middle of the third century, an Alexandrian, Marcus Aurelius Marcianus, registered a slave he was selling in Oxyrhynchus. The slave was a seventeen-year-old girl, Balsamea, from Osrhoenian Mesopotamia.[191] Marcus had bought her in Phoenician Tripolis the year before and brought her into Egypt on the boat of Marcus Aurelius Dioscorus: he even listed the model and ensign of the ship. Quite plausibly, this Alexandrian working in Oxyrhynchus was a merchant working between the Phoenician coast and the Nile.[192]

We see slaves from distant corners of the empire in Egypt because of the papyrological record; we might expect to find the mirror image if we had similar information from Gaul or Greece.[193] Whatever its precise causes, this dispersal of human chattel tells us that the Roman slave trade was capable of moving bodies across continents. These movements, in turn, suggest that the slave trade not only linked supply with consumer markets, but was served by intermediate markets where prices could be co-ordinated and supply linked more efficiently with demand.[194] In the late republic, Delos was the most famous of these entrepôts. The slave auction on Rhodes where a Mauretanian girl was sold from one dealer to another suggests such an intermediate point of contact. So too does the knowledge evinced by the *Expositio* of the prime sources of the slave supply, as does the claim that Alexandria acted as a transition point in the slave trade. The efforts of the Roman state to forestall the exportation of slaves registered in the census from one province to another – whether effective or not – implies that slave prices exerted a powerful pull even on the internal slave trade.[195] If we do not have the data to describe the commerce in slaves as an integrated market, we at least have the grounds to conclude that the Roman slave trade was a complex system of linked markets.[196]

Certainly the slave trade flowed through the most local conduits of exchange, and end consumers could find slaves in a variety of markets.

---

[190] McCormick forthcoming.
[191] For slaves in the Mesopotamian caravan routes, P. Euphr. 8 and 9 (AD 251, 252).
[192] P. Oxy. 42.3053 (AD 251/2).
[193] E.g. the black slaves of the villa at Piazza Armerina, the black woman mentioned by Ausonius (see p. 84), or the black girls (*puellae*) mentioned by Ennod. Ep. 7.21 (CSEL 6: 246).
[194] Gonzalez 2002, 77; more generally, Rosenfeld and Menirav 2005, 53, 59.
[195] CT 11.3.2 (AD 327); CJ 11.48.7 (AD 371).   [196] Harper 2010, on slave prices.

Slaves were on sale at festivals.[197] A Christian master might remember where he purchased a good slave. "I picked up such-and-such a slave at this festival."[198] In the sixth century, the rural Leukothea festival in southern Italy was turned from a celebration of a nymph into a feast of St. Cyprian. It still included a slave market.[199] Cities of course marked the main coordinates of the slave trade. In describing the Leukothea festival, Cassiodorus claimed that the countryside became *like* a city, precisely because of the boys and girls of all ages for sale.[200] The city was the natural haunt of the slave trade. A civic tariff of the fifth or sixth century from Anazarbus in Cilicia taxed slaves brought into the city for sale, listing them right above cattle.[201] The documentation of slave sales by public officials in Egypt is itself a sign of the regular traffic in bodies through rather humble cities. A town in the Great Oasis, Motis, which is otherwise practically unknown, had two officials in charge of the interrogation of slaves for sale.[202] Slaves were "interrogated" upon their first sale in Egypt to verify their status, and even a small town had officials whose specific competency included such hearings.[203] The hearings also prove that the legal technology of the late empire was linked with commercial life at a local level in obscure corners of the empire.

It seems that larger cities had regular slave markets. In his speech against Eutropius, Claudian imagined the eunuch's sordid experience as part of the slave trade:

How many times was he stripped while the doctor advised the buyer lest damage lay hidden in some unseen flaw! Still everyone regretted what they paid and brought him back to the block so long as he could be sold . . . He was dragged through the markets on the shores of Syria. Then led by the Galatian merchants he frequented the public marketplaces and moved from home to home. Who could follow all his many names?[204]

This was nasty political invective, but its intelligibility depended on the assumption that the eastern Mediterranean was pocked with slave

---

[197] Const. Ap. 2.62 (SC 320: 336). This passage may refer to redemption ("to save a soul"), but it is also possible that the distinction was not so clear in the mind of the purchaser. Parallels in the Talmud Yerushalmi, *Abodah Zarah* 1.1.2. tr. Neusner 1982, 13.

[198] Ioh. Chrys. Ad pop. Ant. 6.6 (PG 49: 90): Τὸν οἰκέτην τὸν δεῖνα τῇδε ἐκτησάμην τῇ ἑορτῇ . . .

[199] Cass. Var. 8.33 (CSEL 96: 341). cf. Thdt. Ep. 70 (SC 98: 155).

[200] Cass. Var. 8.33 (CSEL 96: 341). Horden and Purcell 2000, 432–3, with map 448.

[201] *Inscriptions de Cilicie*, no. 108.   [202] P. Oxy. 55.3784 (AD 227/8 or 281/2).

[203] Straus 2004, 62–71.

[204] Claud. In Eutrop. lines 35–41, 58–61 (Hall: 144–5): *nudatus quotiens, medicum dum consulit emptor, ne qua per occultum lateat iactura dolorem! omnes paenituit pretii venumque redibat, dum vendi potuit . . . Inde per Assyriae trahitur commercia ripae; hinc fora venalis Galata ductore frequentat permutatque domos varias. quis nomina possit tanta sequi?* Long 1996, 113–14.

markets.[205] In revenge for his past, the former slave Eutropius was said to put entire cities up for auction, *sub hasta*. Ambrose spoke of slave sales being written in the *tabulae auctionales* and poignantly described the slave watching his own sale.[206] The slave market lived in the consciousness of late antique men and women who knew that, somewhere in the city, human property was for sale. The bishop of Amasea could use a striking simile to evoke the idea of complete silence: "she kept quiet like a slave-girl in the market."[207] Basil of Caesarea begged an imperial official not to let the census become oppressive, "like a slave market."[208] Traders marching through the street with coffles of slaves were a familiar sight. "Why do the rich want such a swarm of slaves? They tromp around the baths or the markets like a dealer of sheep or a merchant of slaves."[209]

Festivals, markets, auctions, banks, beaches, peddlers: where buyer and seller met, slaves were traded. The Roman empire was criss-crossed by a hierarchy of interregional and local markets through which slaves were traded in the last century of a politically and economically united Mediterranean. The slave trade is largely hidden from view, but the markets and merchants which made up the trade have cast shadows that hint at the machine circulating slaves around the empire. The trade was the vascular system of Roman slavery, connecting diverse modes of supply into an integrated system. Slave merchants were organized, capitalized, politically protected, and capable of inflicting horrific violence. The trade was a multitude of complex and layered markets, with intermediate hubs connecting bulk supply to local demand. These markets created innumerable points of contact between society and the slave trade. Perhaps to a slave, it would have seemed like the market was omnipresent: "Slaves can have no rest in their souls because of the uncertainty about future masters."[210] The thing we know least about the Roman slave trade is what it was like to be on the inside.

---

[205] Fentress 2005, for the earlier period.   [206] Ambr. Ep. 7.13 (CSEL 82: 49–51).

[207] Ast. Am. 5.7 (Datema: 49): ἐσιώπησεν ὡς δούλη τῶν ἐκ πωλητηρίου.

[208] Bas. Ep. 299.1 (Courtonne vol. 3: 174): ὥσπερ ἐν ἀνδραπόδων ἀγορᾷ.

[209] Ioh. Chrys. In 1 Cor. 40.5 (PG 61: 353–4): Τί βούλεται τὰ σμήνη τῶν οἰκετῶν; Καθάπερ γὰρ οἱ προβατοπῶλαι καὶ οἱ σωματοκάπηλοι, οὕτως ἐν βαλανείῳ, οὕτως ἐν ἀγορᾷ περιίασιν οἱ πλουτοῦντες. cf. Ioh. Chrys. In Hebr. 28.4 (PG 63: 198).

[210] Ioh. Chrys. Virg. 57.2 (SC 125: 308): Ὥσπερ δὲ ἐπὶ τῶν ἀνδραπόδων ἡ τῶν ἐσομένων ἀδηλία δεσποτῶν οὐκ ἀφίησιν ἠρεμῆσαι τὴν ἐκείνων ψυχήν.

CHAPTER 3

Oikonomia: *households, consumption, and production*

THE ECONOMY OF THE ROMAN HOUSEHOLD

Contemplating ascetic withdrawal from the material world, Basil of Cae-sarea reflected on the burdens of ordinary adulthood: "Once a man is united by marriage, he takes on another welter of cares: if he does not have children, the desire for progeny. If children are born to him, anxiety about their upbringing, the surveillance of his wife, the care of the house, the management of the slaves, suits over contracts, fights with the neighbors, the complications of the law courts, the risks of business, and the tiring work of farming."[1] For Basil, care of the slaves was a standard element of household life, on the indistinct border between the human and proprietary sides of the family. The letter of Basil is a reminder that Roman slavery was essentially economic, in the root, semantic sense of *oikonomia*, household management.[2] Basil's ascetic letter described, in an unusually pessimistic tone, the typical worries of that class of "gentlemen landowners," who had been the target audience of economic discourse for nearly a millennium.[3] But conversations about sound and efficient housecraft resonated widely across the social scale – and Basil's householder, we should note, knew the exhausting work of farm labor.

Hundreds of miles to the south of Cappadocia, two Egyptian women known through a papyrus were absorbed with precisely the sort of worries enumerated by Basil – slaves, contracts, agriculture, lawsuits. The women were Taësis and Kyrillous, daughters of Kopres, who lived in the village of Karanis.[4] Their father had died, leaving his property to them, but their

---

[1] Bas. Ep. 2.2 (Courtonne: 6): τὸν δὲ ἤδη συγκατειργμένον ὁμοζύγῳ ἕτερος θόρυβος τῶν φρον-τίδων ἐκδέχεται. ἐν ἀπαιδίᾳ, παίδων ἐπιθυμία. ἐν τῇ κτήσει τῶν παίδων, παιδοτροφίας μέριμνα, γυναικὸς φυλακή, οἴκου ἐπιμέλεια, οἰκετῶν προστασίαι, αἱ κατὰ τὰ συμβόλαια βλάβαι, οἱ πρὸς τοὺς γείτονας διαπληκτισμοί, αἱ ἐν τοῖς δικαστηρίοις συμπλοκαί, τῆς ἐμπορίας οἱ κίνδυνοι, αἱ τῆς γεωργίας διαπονήσεις.
[2] cf. Pomeroy 1994, esp. 213–15.   [3] Finley 1999 (orig. 1973), 17.
[4] P. Cair. Isid. 64 (AD 298). Bagnall 1993, 228.

uncle had seized the estate and remitted to the women only a few acres of arable land, for which they could not even afford the public taxes. The women were embroiled in a legal dispute to claim back the moveable goods – which they listed as 61 sheep, 40 goats, 1 grinding mill, 3 talents of silver, 2 artabas of wheat, and 2 slaves (1 of whom was female). They implored the *strategos* to take action against their uncle. Taësis and Kyrillous hardly seem like the leisured consumers of an economics manual, but they, with their village household, land, and livestock, were practicing economics. Surely the two slaves were simply vital to their establishment, not to mention their lifestyle. As a datum of economic history, their case requires the historian to open a wide lens, geographically and analytically.

It would be difficult to overstate the importance of households in the Roman slave system. The household was the "basic unit of production as well as consumption" in the Roman world.[5] Yet the role of the household as a medium for slavery in the late Roman empire has been lost amidst the larger efforts to characterize entire periods of antiquity with sweeping categories like "mode of production." Even in the American South, half of all slaves were owned by smaller farms, not plantations.[6] The economic significance of slavery in small units should be manifest, especially in a traditional society where the family dominated the organization of repro-duction, wealth, and labor. The family was the basic particle of ancient society, and without understanding some of the essential dynamics of the family as an economic unit, the material functions of ancient slavery are bound to remain impervious to analytical treatment.[7]

There is an immediate danger lurking down this path of inquiry: the notion of "domestic" slavery. The category of domestic slavery has not had a constructive influence on the study of Roman slavery. It immediately threatens to trivialize the practice of exploiting household slaves by oppos-ing domestic to agricultural or industrial slavery, which are by implication more important.[8] The label "domestic slavery" is also reductive, insinu-ating that slaves in households were mostly sweeping floors or pouring drinks. This conceals the variety of tasks and economic functions fulfilled by slaves within Roman households. Moreover, the category of domestic slavery tends to choke off discussion of the properly economic dimension of household slavery: there were forces at work in household slavery, beyond

---

[5] Saller 2007a, 87.   [6] Genovese 1974, 7; see also Roth 2007, 139.
[7] Aug. Civ. 19.16 (CC 48: 383–4). Becker 1981 and 1965, seminal for the household as an economic unit. See too Pollak 1985.
[8] cf. Jones 1956, 185.

the master's desire for comfort, that need to be identified and, insofar as possible, measured.

This chapter explores the economic dynamics of household slavery. The method of this chapter is, for lack of a better option, taxonomical. The primordial question: what were household slaves doing? We will identify four broad types of labor performed by household slaves: unskilled domestic work, skilled labor, textile production, and agricultural labor. In each case we must ask a second question: why slaves? The choice to use slave labor was always complex, determined by the availability of market alternatives, the advantages of investing in human capital, the institutional forms of agency, the advantages of slave labor in various forms of work, the costs of supervision, and the imbalances between labor and property in the family life cycle. With a closer understanding of *what* slaves were doing, and the reasons *why* slave labor was chosen, we can begin to project the real significance of household slavery in the late Roman economy.

Across all households, one important law holds true: scale and specialization were correlated. In Illustrious and Elite households service would be more specialized, in Bourgeois and Agricultural households, with only a few slaves, much less so. The well-known funerary inscriptions of the high empire witness the variety of specialized roles assigned to individual slaves in large households.[9] The late antique epigraphy is not as revealing, but observers witnessed the same madness for specialization in rich houses. Gregory of Nazianzus described the aristocrat served by a corps of slaves that included hunters, trackers, charioteers, couch keepers, doormen, summoners, bed watchers, flowerbearers, fragrance managers, dish keepers, tasters, shade managers, slaves assigned to watch for the master's signal, bathers, ones who mixed drinks at the lift of the master's finger, and maiden girls who were a pleasure to the eye.[10] The degree of specialization on a slave staff was directly correlated with the overall size of the household.[11] Only large, aristocratic households would have required the fine-tuned specialization ridiculed by Gregory. The Bourgeois or Agricultural household would have coped with a more flexible, day-to-day orchestration of tasks.[12] The smaller the household, the wider variety of work assigned to the individual slave, down to the single slave, the factotum.

In the fourth century, slavery remained elemental in the making of the Roman family. The Roman family was a historically unique organism. It

---

[9] Bodel forthcoming; Hasegawa 2005, 30–41; Treggiari 1975a and 1975b.
[10] Gr. Naz. Carm. 1.2.8 lines 144 ff. (PG 37: 659).
[11] Saller 2007a, 107.   [12] E.g. Ast. Am. 3.11 (Datema: 34).

combined an agnatic inheritance system with a strong legal tradition of individual property rights, a patriarchal structure tempered by affective monogamy and nuclear sentimentality, and a volatile mixture of high mortality and high fertility.[13] The habits of family life in the fourth-century Mediterranean maintained many features of the "Big House" style, in which the absorption of non-kin bodies in the household was fundamental.[14] Later chapters of the book will explore the human consequences of the fact that slaves were embedded in the very tissue of the family. Here we must try to understand the material dynamics of slavery within the family, the circulation of capital through the most basic unit of society. The focus on slavery will bring needed attention to the diverse strategies of social reproduction in a highly stratified society, as we examine how Illustrious, Elite, Bourgeois, and Agricultural households strove to maintain their wealth and status in a world where slaves were ubiquitous.

UNSKILLED DOMESTIC LABOR

The category of unskilled domestic labor includes all the menial work done by slaves. This work was oriented to the comfort, domestic solvency, and even biological well-being of the family – the success of the household *qua* household. The term "domestic service," used here in distinction to skilled labor, textile production, and farm labor, covers a vast amount of the labor performed by household slaves in antiquity. Such work often produced goods which we could only consider luxury items for the master – entertainment, comfort, leisure, and so on. But we should not underestimate the energy requirements of running an ancient household, nor understate the fragility of the lifestyle enjoyed by the middle ranks of Roman society. Moreover, domestic service was often not the only role of household slaves, and one of the principal economic rationalities of domestic service is the fact that it could be a way of utilizing the extra time and labor of otherwise productive slaves.[15] Slaves are in essence fixed capital, and the owner has the incentive to use their exploitable labor maximally.[16]

The economy of domestic service in the Roman empire was peculiar. Notions of honor and shame were a decisive influence in the labor market for domestic service. Certain types of labor, especially personal maintenance, menial chores, or biological service like wet-nursing, were

---

[13] See Harper forthcoming a.
[14] cf. the evocative essay of Wallace-Hadrill 1991, for the early empire. Shaw 1987a, for late antiquity.
[15] For classical Greece, Garlan 1988, 62–3.   [16] Anderson and Gallman 1977.

Table 3.1 *The spectrum of domestic labor*

Comfort/Pleasure	Personal service	Domestic	Biological
Entertainers	Pages	Food preparation	Wet-nursing
Luxury slaves	Assistants	Water, Sewage	Child-care

fundamentally dishonorable.[17] Honor became an economic fact, in that it cordoned off a sector of labor as dishonorable, servile, the sort of work that the free poor could not or would not – and apparently did not – perform.[18] We should recognize just how peculiar this was. In late medieval and early modern societies, the service economy, especially the temporary service of young females in wealthy households, was a crucial outlet for the poor and often a means of saving for a dowry.[19] In the Roman Mediterranean, a market for free servants never seems to have developed.[20] Not only did the free poor not perform this work, but masters valued the honor they accrued from having slaves.[21] Honor and shame were formidable obstacles to entry into the market for domestic work, on both the demand and supply sides. Nor should we discount the advantages of permanence, familiarity, and the ability to exploit slaves intensively in the performance of unskilled and easily supervised tasks. As always the image provided by the sources could be a mirage, but authors overwhelmingly assumed that domestic service was essentially the reserve of chattel slavery.

Domestic service was an almost automatic function of household slaves in Illustrious, Elite, Bourgeois, and Agricultural households alike. But within the category of domestic service, there was significant variety in the nature and productivity of the work performed. The varieties of domestic labor can be broken down and placed along a spectrum which grades, roughly, their contribution to the family (table 3.1). The spectrum runs from the truly non-productive luxury slaves to the integral biological labor performed by wet-nurses.

The aristocratic household, with its tasters and flowerbearers, shade managers and bed watchers, might be stocked with superfluous slaves devoted to nothing but the comfort or pleasure of the masters. One slave in Gaza was

---

[17] See pp. 107 and 112. Ioh. Chrys. In Philip. 9.4 (PG 62: 251); Aug. Psalm. 80.10 (CC 39: 1125); Ast. Am. 3.13 (Datema: 36); Ps.-Chrys. In Psalm. 50 (PG 55: 572).
[18] Though see appendix 1 and Jones 1964, 855.
[19] Wiesner 1986; Herlihy 1985, 153. Fairchilds 1983; Maza 1983; McBride 1976.
[20] See, for instance, CJ 7.16.16 (AD 293), where a freeborn woman who entered domestic service was subsequently given away in a dowry as though she had become a slave! cf. CJ 7.14.11 (AD 294).
[21] See chapter 8.

appointed to run inside a hydraulic wheel in a garden, like a hamster in a cage.[22] Midgets, mutes, jesters, jugglers, and other servants who specialized in entertainment might be the most purely unproductive slaves, though it is hard to imagine them just stowed in the cabinet until their services were needed.[23] Female slaves who specialized in music or other means of diverting their masters might also be unproductive – though some surely knew the loom *and* the lyre.[24] Sexual exploitation was an intrinsic feature of domestic slavery in the Roman empire, but the wealthy Roman household was more like a bustling sweatshop than a languorous harem. Many unproductive activities were supplements to the more arduous, productive labor expected of slaves, particularly in smaller households.[25]

Next to such egregiously unproductive slaves, the personal servants who saturated late antique society must also be classified largely as consumption items. Slaves dedicated to the attendance and assistance of a master were common. The master's daily routine was facilitated at every step by the contribution of slave labor. Slaves woke the master in the morning.[26] Washed his face.[27] Put on his clothes, brought him water, and prepared the room for morning prayer.[28] Slaves put on his shoes (a slave who put on the left shoe first was thought to have jinxed the master).[29] When the master left the house, slaves followed. In the hostile words of Chrysostom, "He dares not go out into the forum, the bath, or the fields without a slave... he thinks himself laughable" if he does not have a slave with him.[30] The phenomenon is widely attested. There was a specific word for this sort of slave: *pedisequus*, "foot follower."[31] If he strayed from the master, vicious punishment awaited.[32] Slaves were an accessory of the master's public persona.

Late antique bathing habits bring this out clearly. Slaves carried the implements, covered the master's body with oil, scrubbed him, scraped off the oil with a strigil, and wiped him down with a towel.[33] Ammianus

---

[22] Aen. Ep. 25 (Positano: 53). With Loenertz 1958.

[23] Gr. Nyss. Ben. 105–6 (van Heck: 105–6); Amm. 24.4.26 (Seyfarth vol. 1: 340–1); Aug. Peccat. merit. 1.66 (CSEL 60: 66).

[24] Bas. (dub.) Is. 5.158 (PG 30: 376–7).   [25] Petr. Chrys. Serm. 161.3 (CC 24B: 996–7). See p. 141.

[26] E.g. Dionisotti 1982. cf. Ioh. Chrys. In 1 Tim. 14.3 (PG 62: 575); Lib. Ep. 1446 (Foerster vol. 11: 483–4).

[27] Eun. Vit. 6.4 (Giangrande: 24).   [28] Auson. Eph. 2–4 (Green: 7–11).

[29] Ioh. Chrys. In act. Apost. 10.5 (PG 60: 92–3); Ioh. Chrys. In Ephes. 12.2 (PG 62: 92).

[30] Ioh. Chrys. In Io. 79.3 (PG 59: 436): δοῦλος, χωρὶς ἐκείνων οὐκ εἰς ἀγορὰν ἐμβαλεῖν τολμῶν. οὐκ εἰς βαλανεῖον, οὐκ εἰς ἀγρόν... καταγέλαστον ἑαυτὸν εἶναι νομίζει.

[31] Ioh. Chrys. In Rom. 21.3 (PG 60: 606); Synes. Ep. 79 (Garzya: 139); Hier. Ep. 22.32 (CSEL 54: 194).

[32] Ioh. Chrys. In Rom. 4.4 (PG 60: 494).

[33] Dionisotti 1982, sections 59–64, 116. Lib. Or. 25.28 (Foerster vol. 2: 550–1); Thdt. H.E. 4.15 (GCS 5: 235); Ps.-Bas. Sel. Vit. Thecl. 2.19 (Dagron: 342); Procopius of Gaza, Kunstuhr Gaza, 313 (Diels: 38).

criticized the Roman elite "who each take fifty slave attendants into the bath – and still yell menacingly, 'where, where is my help?'"[34] When a rich man went to the baths, he looked like a shepherd or slave-dealer because of all his slaves.[35] A rabbi, we learn incidentally, had two slaves with him at the bath.[36] Chatty women gossiped if they saw someone at the baths without slaves.[37] Some conscientious Christian virgins would not bathe with the help of eunuchs.[38] But a fourth-century mosaic from Sicily celebrated the life of a woman with a scene of her going to bathe, two male slaves (eunuchs?) and two slave-girls in train behind her.[39]

Women and children enjoyed personal service too. Slaves slept near the mistress and stood ready to help her when she woke.[40] Chrysostom evoked the scene of a rich woman at her toilet with slave-girls working to prepare the perfume, weighing and mixing the ingredients, powdering her face and so on.[41] In the summer, eunuchs or slave-girls were there to fan her.[42] Women were carried around in litters by their slaves.[43] A young girl might only go out with her slave maiden.[44] Some women were followed by troops of eunuchs and slave-girls.[45] A North African preacher imagined a woman stumbling home from a martyr's festival, drunk, propped up by her *pedisequa*.[46]

It is astonishing how often a slave will unexpectedly appear in a late antique scene. A young man who tried to rob the silversmiths of Carthage . . . had done it with his *pedisequus* at his side.[47] A slave was the shadow, the body-double, of the master. This style of service, personal attendance, was of the complete and degrading sort that was necessarily servile. In a revealing comment, Chrysostom said that even a priest might have a slave, "so that he would not have to perform *shameful* labor

---

[34] Amm. 28.4.8–9 (Seyfarth vol. 2: 78): *comitantibus singulos quinquaginta ministris tholos introierint balnearum, "ubi ubi sunt nostrae?" minaciter clamant.*

[35] Ioh. Chrys. In 1 Cor. 40.5 (PG 61: 353–4); Ioh. Chrys. In Ephes. 22.2 (PG 62: 157).

[36] Talmud Bavli, *Kethub* 62a. cf. Philogel. 23 (Thierfelder: 36).

[37] Lib. Decl. 26.19 (Foerster vol. 6: 523).

[38] Hier. Ep. 107.11 (CSEL 55: 302). cf. Claud. In Eutr. 1 lines 105–9 (Hall: 147); Mirac. Steph. 2.7 (PL 41: 847).

[39] Dunbabin 2003a, 460; Fagan 1999, 29; Balty 1982, 304–5.

[40] Ps.-Bas. Sel. Vit. Thecl. 1.10 (Dagron: 208); Hier. Ep. 108.27 (CSEL 55: 346).

[41] Ioh. Chrys. Stel. Compunct. 2.1 (PG 47: 412).

[42] Claud. In Eutr. 1 lines 105–9 (Hall: 147); Hier. Ep. 108.27 (CSEL 55: 346); Thdt. Provid. 664A (PG 83: 664).

[43] Eun. Vit. 6.7–9 (Giangrande: 31–5); Lib. Ep. 615 (Foerster vol. 10: 566–7); Hier. Ep. 22.16 (CSEL 54: 163–4); Hier. Ep. 66.13 (CSEL 54: 664).

[44] Aristaen. Ep. 4 (Mazal: 12); Ioh. Chrys. Ad pop. Ant. 16.4 (PG 49: 168); Dionisotti 1982, 15, 98; Lib. Or. 23.23 (Foerster vol. 2: 505); Aug. Serm. 5.5 (CC 41: 56).

[45] Hier. Vit. Hil. 8.1 (Bastiaensen: 88).

[46] Ps.-Aug. Sobr. (PL 40: 1110).   [47] Aug. Conf. 6.9.14–15 (CC 27: 84).

himself."[48] The system of honor and shame colored certain types of labor, especially personal hygiene and maintenance. Finely tuned and powerfully felt codes governed who touched what, who saw what, and who did what, so that the free poor faced severe obstacles to entry in a market dominated by servile labor.

Within the category of personal service, different modes of deploying slave labor can be distinguished. Slaves could belong to a large household in which personal attendance on the master was a rotating job. The master would appoint a trustworthy slave as house overseer to manage the eating and sleeping...and to decide who "will go around with the master."[49] The group of slaves was a single labor organism, and in such contexts attendance on the master was only one part of their work. Attendance on the mistress surely entailed much of what should be included as productive female labor, such as textile work.[50] At the other extreme, a single slave might constitute the totality of a man's possessions. St. Martin, while he was a soldier, had one slave who was always with him.[51] The different forms of personal service become significant when the category is considered as an economic product. In a large household, personal servants added marginally to the ability of the house to sustain a luxurious lifestyle. The benefits of attendance – in security, efficiency, communication, and hygiene – were certainly part of the "good life" under Roman rule, but they did not add up to much social good. In a small setting, however, down to a single slave, the comforts of service were only part of the product. In a papyrus, a soldier in rural Egypt bought a slave to help with his tasks, which included organizing food distribution.[52] In such situations, a slave might be a personal servant *and* expand the capacity of the master to do other jobs. That was the essence of slave labor: the combination of flexibility and complete control.

Most domestic service was of the third type, directed towards the operation and maintenance of the household. This class of slave labor would have consumed immense sums of human energy. It is difficult to imagine the amount of work required to maintain a pre-modern household, without the benefit of basic technologies. The lack of running water, for instance, meant that slaves were regularly assigned water-fetching, or sewage work.[53] Slaves *were* the ancient equivalent of domestic appliances. From laundry

[48] Ioh. Chrys. In Philip. 9.4 (PG 62: 251): . . . ἵνα μὴ ἀναγκάζηται αὐτὸς ἀσχημονεῖν.
[49] Bars. Resp. 60 (SC 426: 296): μετὰ τίνος διάγειν . . .   [50] For which, see pp. 128f.
[51] Sulp. Sev. Mart. 2.2 (SC 133: 254–6).   [52] P. Köln 5.232 (330–7).
[53] Aug. Psalm. 103.4.10 (CC 40: 1530); Aug. Lib. 3.9.27 (CC 29: 291); Ast. Am. 3.13 (Datema: 36); Aristaen. Ep. 2.4 (Mazal: 71).

chores to watch duty, slaves made the household a more comfortable and efficient place for the master to live.

Food preparation was by far the most consuming domestic chore. Food was among the first examples of slave service in the mind of Libanius.[54] "Carrying the pots, trying the broth, bringing the bowls, breaking the bread, holding out morsels, and washing the plates, plus all the other work," was "customarily" done by slaves and slave-women.[55] Again, in larger households roles were specialized. The master would give the cook his daily instructions before leaving the house.[56] Cooks feared violence if the master disliked the plate.[57] It was a tiring job.[58] Though a cook might be a petty possession – "not like gold or silver, but a cook or a slave-girl, or perhaps a horse or a coat" – the master might be highly fond of him and his services.[59] It is notable how often the job of "the cook" was a specialized occupation in large late antique households.[60] Food service roles, too, became increasingly specialized in the iconography of late Roman art.[61]

The gourmet kitchens of the ultra-rich certainly belong to the category of luxury consumption. Even in ordinary homes, the convenience of having culinary chores delegated to slaves must have been a considerable comfort. But food preparation also began to shade into the realm of labor which contributed to the survival of the family. Food work, to a certain degree, was necessary for the maintenance of the household. Kitchen work was not field work, but it is important to imagine any unit of human organization, especially in agricultural societies, as a group dependent on a large set of urgent tasks to provide shelter and sustenance – to survive. Farm work is only one, albeit the most consuming, set of tasks. In traditional agricultural societies, gender is the nearly universal, if highly fluid, method of dividing labor in order to redistribute a maximum of male time and male labor to

---

[54] Lib. Or. 25.28 (Foerster vol. 2: 550–1).

[55] Thdt. H.E. 5.19 (GCS 5: 314): αὐτὴ καὶ χύτρας ἁπτομένη καὶ ζωμοῦ γευομένη καὶ τρύβλιον προσφέρουσα καὶ ἄρτον κλῶσα καὶ ψωμοὺς ὀρέγουσα καὶ κύλικα ἀποκλύζουσα καὶ τὰ ἄλλα πάντα ἐργαζομένη ὅσα οἰκετῶν καὶ θεραπαινίδων ἔργα νενόμισται.

[56] Auson. Eph. 4 (Green: 11).

[57] Ioh. Chrys. Virg. 69.1 (SC 125: 342).   [58] Bas. Jej. 1.7 (PG 31: 176).

[59] Them. Or. 32.362a (Downey and Schenkl: 201): οὐδὲ τὸ ἀργύριον οὐδὲ τὸ χρυσίον, ἀλλὰ καὶ ὁ μάγειρος καὶ ἡ θεράπαινα, τυχὸν δὲ καὶ ὁ ἵππος καὶ τὸ χιτώνιον.

[60] E.g. Ioh. Chrys. In act. Apost. 50.3 (PG 60: 349); Them. Or. 21.249a (Downey and Schenkl: 25–6); Gr. Naz. Or. 43.63 (SC 384: 264); Gr. Naz. Carm. 1.2.8 lines 144 ff. (PG 37: 659); Sulp. Sev. Mart. 17.5 (SC 133: 290); Aug. Serm. 36.8 (CC 41: 440); Synes. Regn. 20 (Terzaghi: 46–8); Bas. Hom. Div. 2.2 (Courtonne: 46–7); Auson. Eph. 6 (Green: 11). Cyr. Hom. Pasch. 11.4 (PG 77: 648); Amm. 14.6.16 (Seyfarth vol. 1: 15).

[61] Dunbabin 2003b, 151.

agricultural work.[62] But late antique society also deployed slave labor to accomplish many of its primary domestic tasks.

John Chrysostom could say that slaves labor "their whole lives," "all day," so that their masters could have leisure.[63] But that was not the whole story. In some households, slave labor was directed at organic functions like food preparation that allowed a more efficient distribution of all labor. A small village homestead, like that of Taësis and Kyrillous, might rely utterly on this sort of distribution. Augustine was correct to say, "if you think that your slave needs you because you provide his bread, you also need your slave, to help with your labors. Both master and slave need each other... "[64] Late antique society was built on the multiplication of these relationships of petty, intimate dependence.

Finally, slaves did work that we might call biological labor. The ancient family was a unit organized around reproductive imperatives. In this sense, the property and labor of the household were embedded in a social form whose primary purpose was fertility. It is significant, then, in both a social and economic sense, that slaves were insinuated into even the biological work of the family, in particular wet-nursing and child-rearing.[65] What may seem like the most spontaneous division of labor within the nuclear family, assigning mothers to nurse and rear young children, was very often parceled off in antiquity and delegated to unfree women. The extensive evidence for servile wet-nursing, and not just among the very highest social stratum, is a remarkable indicator that the late Roman family continued to be a complex entity in which slaves were elemental.

The defining task of the nurse was breastfeeding. Chrysostom would speak of the crying "child, torn away from breast, nurse, and milk."[66] Intricate care was taken to assure that the nurse offered a reliable supply of healthy milk.[67] The nurse was to be of medium build, not too large or too small, and preferably around the same age as the real mother, as well as clean, calm, and sober.[68] Her diet was strictly controlled to ensure the infant

---

[62] White, Burton, and Brudner 1977. In *plough*-based agricultural societies, it would be more accurate to say. See Patterson 2008, 38–9.

[63] Ioh. Chrys. In 1 Tim. 16.2 (PG 62: 589): πᾶσαν τὴν ζωὴν . . . πᾶσαν τὴν ἡμέραν.

[64] Aug. Psalm. 69.7 (CC 39: 938): *si autem putas egere tui servum tuum, ut des panem, eges et tu servi tui, ut adiuvet labores tuos: uterque vestrum altero vestrum indiget.*

[65] Bradley 1991 and Joshel 1986 are fundamental. Fildes 1988 offers a broad survey. Schulze 1998, visual evidence.

[66] Ioh. Chrys. In 2 Tim. 1.1 (PG 62: 602): παιδίον τοῦ μαστοῦ καὶ τῆς τίτθης ἀποσπώμενον καὶ γάλακτος.

[67] Ps.-Mac. Hom. spir. 45 line 122 (Dörries, Klostermann, and Krüger: 301).

[68] Orib. Coll. med. 31.4 (CMG 6.1.1: 122).

received proper nutrition.[69] If breastfeeding was the *sine qua non* of nursing, the job also entailed subsequent child-care and attendance.[70] The nurse was in charge of raising a child through its second or third year, when infancy ended and childhood began.[71] Conversely, this was when the interaction between biological parents and their children was supposed to become more intense.[72] But nurses continued to guide a child's acculturation to society and might be more strict than the natural parents.[73] Nurses were simply instrumental in much of what we call parenting. A late ancient child had three functional authority figures: father, mother, nurse.[74]

Nurses were especially prominent in the continued service of their female wards. A woman's "nurse" was with her through marriage and might follow her into the new family as part of the dowry.[75] Nurses were the elite guard in the massive project of protecting the sexual honor of free females.[76] They were on intimate terms with their young mistresses, the first to know if she lost her virginity, and the one to tell her how to cover up her indiscretions.[77] In Constantine's important law on abduction marriage, nurses were expected to act as a bulwark against elopement; at the same time, the nurse's encouragement was recognized as a source of danger, and if the nurse were complicit in arranging a clandestine union, the emperor decreed she should have molten lead poured down her throat.[78]

The job of nursing was usually filled by women of servile status. Inscriptions of the early empire show that slaves, freedwomen, and even sometimes the free poor were enrolled as nurses.[79] The reality was probably the same in late antiquity, although the evidence for free nurses is harder to come by. Jerome listed the nurse in a group of household slaves.[80] Manuals that taught reading spoke of nurses among the *familia*.[81] A nurse in Augustine's family was charged to watch *her master's* children.[82] But Constantine's law imagined that nurses could be free or slave, and we should suspect that poor free women, without other resources or familial ties, might find few economic opportunities and be willing to work as nurses.

Slave nurses were a commodity that could be bought, sold, and re-sold. Libanius described a period of economic turmoil as one in which

---

[69] Aet. Iatr. 4.6 (CMG 8.1: 362–3).
[70] Cyril Is. 5.62.5 (PG 70: 1372). Ioh. Chrys. In 1 Cor. 12.7 (PG 61: 106); Orib. Coll. med. 38.1 (CMG 6.1.1: 136).
[71] Orib. Coll. med. 30 (CMG 6.1.1: 121). Fildes 1988, 7–12.
[72] Ioh. Chrys. In 2 Thess. 2.4 (PG 62: 478).
[73] Aug. Conf. 9.8.17 (CC 27: 143); Ioh. Chrys. In act. Apost. 54.3 (PG 60: 378).
[74] Aug. Conf. 9.8.18 (CC 27: 144); Lib. Or. 58.10 (Foerster vol. 4: 186).
[75] Synes. Ep. 3 (Garzya: 7).   [76] Ioh. Chrys. Sac. 3.13 (SC 272: 214).
[77] Hist. Apoll. Reg. Tyr. 2 (Kortekaas: 280); Aristaen. Ep. 1.6 (Mazal: 15–16).
[78] CT 9.24.1.1 (AD 326). Evans Grubbs 1995, 183–93.   [79] Bradley 1991.
[80] Hier. Iov. 1.47 (PL 23: 289).   [81] Dionisotti 1982, 17, 98.   [82] Aug. Conf. 9.8.18 (CC 27: 144).

even the nurse was sold.[83] In another context, curial tax collectors were so squeezed for cash, they had to sell the sons of their nurses.[84] Multiple generations of slaves might be intertwined with an ancient family: a slave on a farm of Theodoret, the grandson of his own nurse, was possessed by a demon.[85] Jerome imagined a nurse urging her master not to convert to the ascetic life, since it brought such uncertainty upon the slave household.[86] These passages point to the peculiar emotional dynamic of nursing.[87] By fulfilling the most intimate jobs in a household, nurses earned an informal favoritism, but they remained human chattel who could be sold off at the master's whim or convenience. Surely in many sub-elite households, the purchase and re-sale of a nurse was timed by the family life cycle, while keeping a nurse for decades was an indulgence.

The use of slave nurses is extraordinarily prominent in the sources.[88] "Mother and nurse" was a common figure of speech. Ausonius pointed out that his slave girlfriend had no mother, no nurse.[89] Unexpected facts are the most casually revealing: over and over, we hear that ancient men and women got their first exposure to the world through the fables told by their nurses.[90] The geographic spread of evidence for slave nurses is equally impressive: from a Jewish family in the Balearic isles to a Roman soldier's daughter in the northern reaches of Pontus.[91] Naturally the use of slave nurses was more common among wealthy families. "A poor woman becomes a slave and a servant, for she bears a child and then becomes herself the mother *and* the nurse. Among the wealthy it is not so, but they bear a child and give it out, and this vanity cuts off parental love."[92] The rough categories of "rich" and "poor" are inexact. What is striking is the underlying concept that operated among the respectable classes in late antiquity: to rear your own child made you a little like a slave.

It is not obvious, at a distance of a millennium and a half, why antiquity employed nurses on such a scale. High mortality, among mothers and infants alike, may partly explain the phenomenon. There is also a correlation between the practices of child exposure and wet-nursing, so that the

---

[83] Lib. Or. 18.289 (Foerster vol. 2: 363).   [84] Lib. Or. 47.8 (Foerster vol. 3: 408).

[85] Thdt. H. rel. 9.10 (SC 234: 424). cf. Bas. Ep. 37 (Courtonne: 80).

[86] Hier. Ep. 14.3 (CSEL 54: 47–8).   [87] See Grey 2008; Joshel 1986.

[88] Ioh. Chrys. In Mt. 83.5 (PG 58: 744); Ioh. Chrys. In Coloss. 4.4 (PG 62: 330).

[89] Auson. Biss. 3 (Green: 131).

[90] Eus. P.E. 12.5.4 (SC 307: 46); Iul. Imp. Or. 7.21 (Rochefort: 74); Bas. Hom. temp. fam. (PG 31: 328); Ioh. Philop. Proc. 640 (Rabe: 640, line 20).

[91] Balearic: Sev. Minor. Epistula de Iudaeis 24 (Bradbury: 116). Pontus: Gr. Nyss. Vit. Macr. 38 (SC 178: 262).

[92] Ps.-Chrys. In Psalm. 50 (PG 55: 572): ἐπὶ δὲ τῶν πενήτων ἡ γυνὴ ὑπηρέτις γίνεται καὶ διάκονος, καὶ τίκτει παιδίον, καὶ γίνεται αὐτὴ καὶ μήτηρ καὶ τροφός. Ἐπὶ δὲ τῶν πλουτούντων οὐχ οὕτως ἀλλὰ τίκτει παιδίον, καὶ δίδωσιν αὐτὸ ἔξω, καὶ τὴν φιλοστοργίαν διατέμνει ὁ τῦφος.

latter is common in societies which practice the former.[93] The cultural perception of infancy and childhood could be a powerful force in separating the very earliest years of life, already so uncertain, to a nether realm in which survival preceded more emotional domains of the parent–child relationship. The sexual and reproductive control over slaves offers a further explanation for the prevalence of nursing. Ancient beliefs about the female body dictated a strict regimen of abstinence for nurses, in order to ensure salubrious lactation. "I urge that women who are nursing children abstain from sex completely. The monthly *katharseis* of women who mix with men are irritated. The milk does not stay sweet, and some become pregnant, and nothing is more harmful for a nursing infant."[94] Slave-women could be forcibly kept from sex. At the same time, free females, who might be under pressure to reproduce, experienced less urgency to lactate.

A final, uncanny, factor was at work in the economics of nursing. The woman who nursed her own children was likened to a slave: "it is *shameful* for the one who is a mother to be a nurse."[95] The forces of honor and shame were at play in the job of nursing and could impact even a devoted Christian like Gregory of Nyssa. His sister Macrina had a nurse to rear her, of course, but their mother "did the nursing with her own hands," implying a *very* odd arrangement that squared his assertion of exceptional maternal care with the sensibilities of his age.[96] If some combination of mortality, convenience, and reproductive ideology made nursing pragmatic, the economy of honor created hard rules which demanded that respectable women have nurses to rear their children. The job of nursing escapes any attempt to classify its productivity. The significance of late antique nursing is that it demonstrates the importance of slaves in the biological matrix of family life. The late antique family was a peculiar survival machine, and slaves were deployed in some of its most private offices.

SKILLED LABOR AND HOUSEHOLD SLAVERY

Slaves not only contributed to the routine labor of the household, they were some of the most educated and highly trained laborers in the empire.

---

[93] Fildes 1988, 4.
[94] Orib. Coll. med. 33 (CMG 6.1.1: 126–7): ἀφροδισίων δὲ παντάπασι κελεύω ἀπέχεσθαι τὰς θηλαζούσας παιδία γυναῖκας. αἵ τε γὰρ ἐπιμήνιοι καθάρσεις αὐταῖς ἐρεθίζονται μιγνυμέναις ἀνδρί, καὶ οὐκ εὐῶδες μένει τὸ γάλα, καί τινες αὐτῶν ἐν γαστρὶ λαμβάνουσιν. οὗ βλαβερώτερον οὐδὲν ἂν εἴη γάλακτι τρεφομένῳ παιδίῳ.
[95] Ps.-Chrys. In Psalm. 50 (PG 55: 572): Αἰσχύνεται γὰρ γενέσθαι τροφὸς ἡ γενομένη μήτηρ.
[96] Gr. Nyss. Vit. Macr. 3 (SC 178: 148): ἐν ταῖς χερσὶ ταῖς ἰδίαις.

Skilled slave labor was located primarily in Illustrious and Elite house-holds, where specialization and investment in human capital were most likely, although we should not exclude that some larger Bourgeois and Agricultural households might have possessed skilled slaves. As we move from unskilled to skilled labor, the nature of the product changes in a fundamental way. Skilled slaves added to the household laterally. Slavery expanded the functions that the household was able to perform beyond its minimal role as a unit of reproduction and subsistence. The Roman household was called upon to discharge a variety of functions that were inescapably conditioned by the existence of slavery. For example, ancient health care was frequently embedded in the wealthy household in the form of servile doctors.[97] Julian spoke of both free and slave doctors.[98] In med-ical situations, it was noticeably odd to see the master obeying his slave's advice.[99] A master could apprentice his slave to a skilled doctor in order to learn the trade.[100] We might suspect that the small size of the market lim-ited the development of the health care sector and that expensive training acted as a barrier to entry. But clearly slavery was one way of responding to the lack of a market in health services.

Skilled household slaves were truly instrumental in two sectors of the Roman economy, and it is important to consider the distinct mechanics of each. The culture industry, on the one hand, and business administration, on the other, were inextricably linked to the slave system. The ancient household was both a school and a business firm, two functions it could fulfill only through the services of slaves. In both cases, we should imagine that slavery was a structural fit because a sufficient private market failed to develop. Moreover, in fields like education or business, long-term relation-ships are advantageous, and slavery is in this sense like a (coerced) lifetime contract. Skilled jobs required investment in human capital, which may have not only deterred the genesis of a market for skilled labor but also rewarded the long-term opportunities of exploiting slaves. The institutions of agency in Roman society were a compounding factor. For all its sophis-tication, Roman law had rather limited and crude concepts of agency, so that sons, slaves, and freedmen were prominent as business agents.[101] Or rather, because sons, slaves, and freedmen were effective as agents, Roman

---

[97] Aug. Civ. 22.8 (CC 48: 816); Ambr. Ep. 56.6 (CSEL 82: 87). For the earlier period, Forbes 1955, 343–53. Physical trainers: Synes. Ep. 45 (Garzya: 84–5).

[98] Iul. Imp. Or. 7.3 (Rochefort: 49).

[99] Ioh. Chrys. Scand. 8.13 (SC 79²: 140). Free doctors also had slaves in their employ: Aug. Tract. Io. 3.14 (CC 36: 26–7).

[100] Aen. Ep. 19 (Positano: 49).   [101] Frier and Kehoe 2007, 130; Kirschenbaum 1987.

law had no need to develop more sophisticated rules of agency. For a variety of convergent reasons, then, slave labor was instrumental in education and business.

Slaves were especially prominent in the lower levels of ancient education. Not an insignificant number of slaves were literate. As pedagogues they were employed to teach the rudiments of learning to the young and later to reinforce the lessons learned from the high-status professors.[102] Pedagogues doubled as both tutors and guardians.[103] A punctilious pedagogue was admired by the father for his close care over the child, while the child might fear or loathe the exacting regimen imposed by his tutor.[104] As an adult, Julian lauded his severe pedagogue, Mardonius, a eunuch and a Scythian who had also served as tutor to his mother and was presumably of slave origins.[105] There is ample indication that many pedagogues were slaves or freedmen. Men controlled pedagogues through the exercise or threat of physical violence.[106] Pedagogues were traded around as valuable property. Seleucus, a friend of Libanius, gave him a pedagogue as a gift. Libanius made him the pedagogue of his illegitimate son: "We even now call him 'the one of Seleucus.'"[107] The pedagogue was both a part of the educational system and "an extension of the family."[108] "Everyone discerns the way of life of a young man from that of his pedagogue . . . It is the role of the father to render the money, but the rest of the concerns, without exception, belong to the pedagogue. Thus, thrashing and throttling and torturing, and all the things which the masters use against their slaves, are also deemed fitting for those who are set over their sons."[109]

Because of their skill, teachers and pedagogues could enjoy an informal sort of esteem. Ausonius composed an honorific epigram for two freedmen teachers, Crispus and Urbicus, Latin and Greek instructors, one of whom taught unskilled boys the rudiments of reading, the other, Greek.[110] A speech of Libanius provides our best information about the ranks of

---

[102] In general, Cribiore 2001, 47–50. Them. Or. 32.361a (Downey and Schenkl: 200).

[103] Ioh. Chrys. Ad pop. Ant. 16.4 (PG 49: 168); Dionisotti 1982, 15, 98. See Young 1990. P. Oxy 2190 (first century) for a revealing document, from the earlier period.

[104] Hier. Ruf. 1.24 (CC 79: 24); Lib. Or. 9.11 (Foerster vol. 1: 395–6).

[105] Iul. Imp. Mis. 22 (Lacombrade: 176). PLRE 1: Mardonius 1, 558.

[106] Ioh. Chrys. Ad pop. Ant. 16.4 (PG 49: 168).

[107] Lib. Ep. 734.3 (Foerster vol. 10: 660): ἔτι καὶ νῦν ὁ Σελεύκου καλεῖται.   [108] Cribiore 2001, 50.

[109] Lib. Prog. 3.2.8–9 (Foerster vol. 8: 76–7): τῶν γὰρ ἀνθρώπων ἕκαστος τῷ τοῦ παιδαγωγοῦ τρόπῳ τεκμαίρεται τὸν τοῦ νέου . . . τοῦ μὲν πατρὸς ἀργύριον δοῦναι, τοῦ δὲ παιδαγωγοῦ τῶν λοιπῶν φροντίσαι μηδὲν ὑποστελλόμενον. διὰ τοῦτο γὰρ καὶ παίειν καὶ ἄγχειν καὶ στρεβλοῦν καὶ ἃ τῶν δεσποτῶν πρὸς τοὺς οἰκέτας, ταῦτα καὶ τῶν υἱέων τοῖς ἐφεστῶσιν ἀξιοῦσιν ὑπάρχειν.

[110] Auson. Prof. 21 (Green: 56): *liberti ambo genus . . .*

educational workers in late antiquity and shows how closely pedagogues worked with high-status professors.[111] Libanius found himself speaking out in defense of the pedagogues against the abuses they suffered from the students of Antioch:

These things did not happen to them [pedagogues] in my youth, but they were held in honor right after the professors, and the young men imitated their professors in holding them in worthy and just esteem. For indeed, the things they do for students are truly great, enforcing the discipline of study and, what is even more splendid, self-control... [But these days the students] grasp a carpet along its sides, stretched out on the ground, sometimes many of them, sometimes fewer, according to the measure of the carpet. Then, putting the one who is to suffer humiliation on the middle of it, they throw him as high as possible – and it is very high – amidst their laughter... Now, by the gods, this practice which did not exist has arisen, and against whom? Not against the slaves by whom the books are carried, but against those in a respectable calling who are necessary to the labors of the professor... The practice is so full of shame that the one who has been carpeted is ridiculed not just when he is seen, but even when he is mentioned to those who have heard of the thing and etched it in their memory...[112]

The speech was the sincere expression of a professor who wished for the educational staff around him, slave and free, to be treated with dignity. But it was also the grousing of a fussy old man against what he perceived as the wildness of "kids these days." Surely the root cause of the shocking behavior he described – the "carpeting" which had come to Antioch – was not so much generational change as a predictable abuse of the power dynamic between gangs of free boys and their vulnerable tutors. On a

---

[111] On the schools, Cribiore 2007, esp. 118–20.
[112] Lib. Or. 58.7–20 (Foerster vol. 4: 184–191): Ἦν δὲ οὐ ταῦτα αὐτοῖς, ἡνίκα ἐφοίτων ἐγώ, ἀλλ' ἐν τιμαῖς οὗτοι μετὰ τοὺς διδασκάλους μιμουμένων τῶν νέων τοὺς διδασκάλους, παρ' ὧν καὶ αὐτῶν ὑπῆρχον τιμαὶ τοῖς παιδαγωγοῖς τὸ δίκαιον ἔχουσαι. μεγάλα γάρ, ὡς ἀληθῶς μεγάλα τὰ παρὰ τούτων εἰς τοὺς νέους, ἀνάγκαι τε ὧν τὸ μανθάνειν δεῖται καὶ τὸ πολὺ κάλλιον, ἡ σωφροσύνη ... τάπητα τεταμένον ἐπὶ γῆς ἔχουσι ταῖς χερσὶ κατὰ πλευρὰν ἑκάστην νῦν μὲν πλείους, νῦν δὲ ἐλάττους, ὡς ἂν εἰσηγῆται τοῦ τάπητος τὸ μέτρον. θέντες οὖν κατὰ μέσον αὐτὸν τὸν τὰ αἴσχιστα πεισόμενον ἀναρρίπτουσιν εἰς ὅσον οἷόν τε, πολὺ δὲ τοῦτο ἐστι, σὺν γέλωτι ... νῦν δ', ὦ θεοί, οὐκ οὖσα γεγένηται καὶ κατὰ τίνων; οὐ τῶν οἰκετῶν δι' ὧν ἔπεται τὰ βιβλία, ἀλλὰ κατὰ τῶν ἐν σεμνῇ προσηγορίᾳ καὶ ὧν δεῖ τοῖς τῶν διδασκάλων πόνοις ... οὕτω γὰρ αἰσχύνης ἐστὶ τὸ πρᾶγμα μεστόν, ὥστ' οὐχ ὁρώμενος ὁ τῷ τάπητι περιπεσὼν καταγελᾶται μόνον, ἀλλὰ κἂν εἰς οὓς ἀφίκηται γραφόντων ἐν τῇ διανοίᾳ τῶν ἀκουόντων τὸ πραττόμενον. Libanius evokes the "ideal pedagogue" (Norman 2000, 170) and does not explicitly reveal the status of the pedagogues being carpeted, who may well have included slaves, freedmen, or even free pedagogues. But the construction of the passage ("not the slaves by whom the books are carried, but those who ... " though Norman renders it "not against the slaves who follow you with your books, but against members of an honourable profession") at least suggests their slave status, and other sources demonstrate that pedagogues were not rarely slaves or freedmen attached to the household.

separate occasion when a pedagogue criticized Libanius, it prompted a vicious rebuttal with the barbed conclusion that the man should "know the difference between a professor and a pedagogue."[113]

One of the greatest, silent testimonials to the work of slaves in the ancient world is the volume of recorded writing. Slavery stands along with monasticism and the printing press as one of the principal ways that Mediterranean culture has shouldered the monumental labor of recording words.[114] Trained, literate slaves were employed as scribes and highly valued as such.[115] Even female slaves might be trained.[116] Scribes took dictation for letters and personal documents, and masters might be dependent on their trust or vulnerable to their intimate knowledge of household affairs.[117] Ancient literary texts began as a scratch in wax made by slaves. Jerome bragged of dictating through the night by the light of a lamp, but more than once complained that his scribe could not keep pace.[118] It was hard work. A scribe of Ausonius tried to flee.[119] Libanius saw a friend's slave who "looked quite pale, so I asked him if he was sick. He said no, but that the endless work was to blame. He had shut himself away for writing. I praised him for this and am delighted for you, that your slave is not lazy!"[120]

It is not clear how slaves were trained to be tutors and scribes, though some were obviously apprenticed, and it has been suspected that there were slaves alongside free children in the earlier stages of school.[121] That would give extra meaning to an extant school exercise, written in the simplest Latin, in which a free boy confronts a slave and threatens to have him crucified for insolence.[122] We should also not rule out the agency of slaves in making themselves literate, for they may have recognized the advantages of education. Augustine had it on good report that a barbarian slave, who supposedly received no training, had miraculously obtained

[113] Lib. Or. 34.31 (Foerster vol. 3: 206): ἀλλ' εἰδώς, τί μέν ἐστιν ὁ διδάσκαλος, τί δὲ ὁ παιδαγωγός.
[114] Teitler 1985, 27–37, who also notes that (free) imperial *notarii* gained in importance and that ecclesiastical institutions developed a distinctive scribal culture with a long future. The evidence gathered here shows that the servile element remained large in the fourth century, especially in the private sphere.
[115] CJ 7.7.1 (AD 530).   [116] Amm. 18.3.2 (Seyfarth vol. 1: 138). With Teitler 1985, 31.
[117] Sulp. Sev. Ep. 3.2 (CSEL 1: 146).
[118] Hier. Ep. 117.12 (CSEL 55: 434); Hier. Ep. 118.1 (CSEL 55: 435).
[119] Auson. Epig. 16–17 (Green: 70). Fitzgerald 2000, 17.
[120] Lib. Ep. 131 (Foerster vol. 10: 132): Ἰδὼν τὸν Δοσίθεον καὶ ὠχριῶντα ἠρόμην, εἰ νόσῳ γένοιτο τοιοῦτος. ἔπειτ' ἤκουον, ὡς ἐκείνῃ μὲν οὔ, συνεχείᾳ δὲ ἔργου. γράφειν γὰρ ἔφασκε καθείρξας αὐτόν. ἐκεῖνόν τε οὖν ἐπήνεσα καὶ σοὶ συνήσθην, ὅτι σοι μηδὲ ὁ οἰκέτης ἀργός. Cribiore 2007, 305, believes Dositheus was a pedagogue, which would obviously not be mutually exclusive with scribal work.
[121] Booth 1979; Forbes 1955. P. Oxy. 4.724 (AD 155) apprenticeship.
[122] Chapter 8. Colloq. Harl. 18 (CGL vol. 3: 642).

the skill of reading through praying for it.[123] Other explanations are conceivable.

It is worth pausing to reflect on the fact that the education and culture industries of antiquity were organized through the structures of the household. A metropolis like Antioch kept professors on the public payroll, and the imperial bureaucracy employed its own class of free scribes for official business.[124] But private slave labor was the foundation of literacy as well as the physical side of cultural production, such as transcription. The institutional basis of ancient culture never broke free of the household to gain traction in a separate social form such as the university, and only around 400 did the church begin to develop into an institution which could stand as a fully-fledged alternative to the household as the material basis for cultural production.[125] The ancient school existed in a symbiotic relationship with the elite household and its servile workers. The cultural output of the late ancient world stands as an impressive artifact of coercive exploitation.

The centrality of the household was likewise apparent in business administration: management, finance, commerce, and communications.[126] The economy of the fourth century is still too often underestimated. Like the high imperial economy, it was characterized by sophisticated systems of production and exchange.[127] The volume of goods traded was exceptionally high for a first-millennium economy. Trade was not confined to high-end luxuries; a bulk trade in ordinary consumer goods – foodstuffs, textiles, and manufactured items – flourished. Specialized production and trade were underwritten with investment capital in a society that continued to nurture advanced financial institutions and instruments.[128] "You will often see a man with riches and gold who has not a coin in his household. His hopes lie in papers, his substance is in contracts. He holds nothing but owns everything."[129] Commercial and maritime loans, and their secure institutional framework, promoted the circulation of capital into productive uses.[130] Preachers criticized the uses of money by evoking the risks of

[123] Aug. Doct. chr. pr.4 (CC 32: 3).
[124] Schools, Cribiore 2007; Kaster 1988. Government, Teitler 1985.
[125] Clerics were still widely using slave scribes in the late fourth century. See the will of Gregory of Nazianzus (in chapter 12). cf. Iul. Imp. Ep. 106 (Bidez: 184).
[126] Lintott 2002; Andreau 1999; Carlsen 1995; Aubert 1994; Kirschenbaum 1987; Di Porto 1984; D'Arms 1981; Garnsey 1981; Juglar 1894.
[127] For bibliography, see Introduction.
[128] Andreau 1986, pessimistic. cf. Barnish 1985; Roueché 1995, for suggestive epigraphic evidence.
[129] Gr. Nyss. Usur. 198 (Gebhardt: 198): βλέπεις γοῦν τὸν πλούσιον καὶ πολύχρυσον πολλάκις μηδὲ ἓν νόμισμα ἔχοντα ἐπὶ τῆς οἰκίας, ἀλλ᾽ ἐν χάρταις τὰς ἐλπίδας, ἐν ὁμολογίαις τὴν ὑπόστασιν, μηδὲν ἔχοντα καὶ πάντα κατέχοντα.
[130] Rathbone 2003, on the earlier period. McCambley 1991.

lending. "If it should be a maritime loan, he will sit on the seashore with worry about the movements of the wind, asking continuously about boats putting into port, in case a shipwreck should be heard of anywhere or those sailing come into dangers... "[131] But such complaints are only comprehensible in a society where capital can be multiplied by investments in production and exchange.

The household *qua* firm, and its slave laborers, remained instrumental in the thriving business sectors of the late Roman economy. Here we should distinguish between two tiers, or types, of commercial involvement: professional and patrimonial.[132] At one end of the spectrum, trade and finance required professional men – merchants, ship-captains, bankers, etc. These were *hommes d'affaires* whose day-to-day life was occupied in business and whose primary resources were invested in commercial activity: "It is great to sail and to be a trader, to know many provinces, to turn profits everywhere, not to be bound in the city to some powerful person, always to travel, to nurture the soul in various trades and lands, and to return a wealthy man enriched by profits!"[133] At the other end of the spectrum were the rich families whose principal resources were in land and capital and whose business interests were mediated through agents and investments. Not only was the management of a large patrimony and the marketing of its products a significant operation in itself, the use of slaves and freedmen as agents allowed wealthy Romans to invest in commercial activities without directly involving themselves in the mundane affairs of commerce.

In the business sector, the economics of slavery followed the same patterns as in the educational field, in that expensive training and the lack of a market may have acted in combination as a strong disincentive to the development of free labor. But even more important was another combination: the lack of direct agency in Roman law along with the total control possible over slaves and dependants.[134] Moreover, having stable, long-term employees in positions where local knowledge of circumstance mattered was an important advantage. These forces also acted to create complex modes of domination, in which violence and incentives were both instrumental. The

---

[131] Gr. Nyss. Usur. 200 (Gebhardt: 200): ἂν δὲ καὶ ναυτικὸν ᾖ τὸ δάνεισμα, τοῖς αἰγιαλοῖς προσκάθηται, τὰς κινήσεις μεριμνᾷ τῶν ἀνέμων, συνεχῶς διερωτᾷ τοὺς καταίροντας, μή που ναυάγιον ἠκούσθη, μή που πλέοντες ἐκινδύνευσαν. Late Roman horoscopes reflect precisely such worries: see McCormick forthcoming.

[132] cf. Andreau 1999, 23.

[133] Aug. Psalm. 136.3 (CC 40: 20–22): *Navigare et negotiari magnum est; scire multas provincias, lucra undique capere, non esse obnoxium in civitate alicui potenti, semper peregrinari, et diversitate negotiorum et nationum animum pascere, et augmentis lucrorum divitem remeare.*

[134] Aubert 1994, 44; Kirschenbaum 1987.

Table 3.2 *The organization of business in the late empire*

Professional	Patrimonial
Merchants	Primary oversight (*procuratores, oikonomoi, phrontistes*)
Ship-captains	Agency (*actores, institores, epitropoi, pistikoi*)
Bankers	Management (*praepositi, vilici, oikonomoi, epitropoi*)
	Accounting (*dispensatores, tamiai*)
	Secretarial (*tabellarii, notarii*)
	Entrepreneurship (via *peculium*)

prominence of freedmen in business roles points to the use of manumission as a reward for trusted and proven slaves.[135]

Table 3.2 illustrates these two styles of commercial involvement and helps us to envision the role of slaves and freedmen in various capacities.

The professionals of late Roman business, *negotiatores* and *emporoi*, kept slaves in their employ. The greater merchants owned slaves in abundance.[136] A "wealthy Christ-loving merchant of Alexandria" sent goods to a monk via his slaves.[137] Even more modest traders, like the dealers in flax mentioned in Coptic sources, were assumed to have slaves who facilitated their operations.[138] Documentary evidence, thin though it is, concurs: a papyrus of AD 402 shows a ship-captain ordering a supply of wine through his slaves.[139] The evidence is richer in the east, but certainly western traders owned slaves, too. Ambrose offers the telling fact that even slave-traders had slaves.[140] The use of slaves as sailors and stevedores may be attested visually on shipping mosaics.[141] Merchants in the east continued to use slaves into the sixth century. Roman traders working the Red Sea routes took slaves with them.[142] A "man of business" sent his slave from Seleucia to Constantinople.[143] A merchant in the luxury trade of gems and pearls would board his ship with his slaves.[144] Slaves were used as permanent employees in a sector that entailed considerable travel and risk.

---

[135] Already Jones 1956, 186. Scheidel 2008; Temin 2004. See chapter 5 on slave management.
[136] Pall. H. Laus. 14 (Butler vol. 2: 37). Jones 1964, 870.
[137] Hist. mon. in Aeg. 14.20 (Festugière: 108): ἄνδρα τινὰ ἔμπορον Ἀλεξανδρέα εὐλαβῆ καὶ φιλόχριστον.
[138] *Four Martyrdoms from the Pierpont Morgan Coptic Codices* (Reymond and Barns) 52Rii and 54Vii.
[139] P. Haun. 68 (AD 402).   [140] Ambr. Psal. 43.42 (CSEL 64: 292).
[141] See the mosaic in McCormick 2001, 85, perhaps slaves.
[142] Procop. Bell. 1.20.4 (Haury and Wirth vol. 4: 107–8).
[143] Ioh. Mosch. Prat. 79 (PG 87.3: 2936): Ἦν τις ἀνὴρ πραγματευτής.
[144] Ioh. Mosch. Prat. 203 (PG 87.3: 3093).

The significance of slave labor was greater, and more visible, in the patrimonial style of business activity in the late empire.[145] As in the high empire, there were cultural and even legal barriers to aristocratic involvement in trade, leaving much of the commercial sector in the hands of professionals.[146] But the management of a great patrimony and the marketing of its products were inherently large business operations.[147] Illustrious and Elite households, comprising the top 1–1.5 percent of the population, controlled perhaps a fifth of the empire's annual income and an even larger share of its wealth.[148] Simply administering property on this scale was an extraordinary project that has left its traces throughout the late antique record. Moreover, the use of agents, clients, and financial intermediaries allowed elites to invest in commerce with varying degrees of risk and involvement. From the merchants "who belong to the powerful," mentioned in a law of AD 364, to the more indirect and shadowy "patrons" of the slave-dealers mentioned by Augustine, late Roman elites were implicated in commerce.[149] Slaves were instrumental, in both the direct administration of elite property and in the more indirect forms of elite involvement in trade.

It is notoriously difficult to assign precise, stable roles to the titles used to describe slave agents and managers in the Roman empire. The Romans had a bewildering array of words for their skilled slaves with different connotations in the legal and social spheres. It does not simplify matters that the Greek and Latin terms fail to overlap neatly.[150] Just as importantly, the degree of specialization within the slave staff varied between the more modest curial household and the grand senatorial *domus*. The head slave of a small curial household might be agent, accountant, manager, courier, and entrepreneur all in one, whereas a whole army of specialized slaves could fulfill these roles in larger houses. The sheer volume and variety of administrative work is reflected in the elaborate hierarchies which helped to manage the largest properties. John Chrysostom, preaching about slavery, compared the large house to a city because of the layers of management, "the rulers over the rulers."[151] Basil included among the slave staff of the rich man "innumerable slaves," from the "overseers and dispensers" down

---

[145] Andreau 1999, 64.   [146] CJ 4.63.3 (AD 409) and CJ 12.57.12 (AD 436). Jones 1964, 871.
[147] Vera 1983. D'Arms 1981, for the earlier period.   [148] See chapter 1.
[149] CT 13.1.5 (AD 364). On Aug. Ep. 10*, see chapter 2.
[150] Carlsen 2002 and Aubert 1994, 32–3, 142. Hier. Ep. 121.6 (CSEL 56: 22), says that an *oikonomos* is a *vilicus + dispensator*. Ausonius, p. 123, for the range of *epitropos*. For a Greek managerial staff in the third-century papyri, see Rathbone 1991, 58–87.
[151] Ioh. Chrys. In. Ephes. 22.2 (PG 62: 158): ἄρχοντες ἐπὶ ἄρχουσιν.

to the farmers and craftsmen.[152] Augustine knew that in a rich household
there were "many grades" within the hierarchy of slaves, and Libanius, too,
spoke of the numerous gradations within the household staff.[153]

It is possible to identify a variety of overlapping roles and to place them
in a rough hierarchy. At the top of the managerial pyramid sat the master's
primary overseer and agent, his procurator. Procurators were a prominent
element in late Roman society, and they wielded considerable authority. In
408, governors were reminded not to allow the "procurators of the powerful
to do anything illegal or illicit."[154] They figure in dozens of surviving fourth-
century laws, controlling property, instituting agents, and standing in for
their masters in litigation.[155] In the high empire, procurators were often
freeborn or freedmen, but in late antiquity there is considerable evidence
that procurators were freedmen or still slaves.[156] The highest-ranking slave
in Augustine's chain of command was the procurator.[157] Only trusted,
experienced slaves could be given control of "the keys, the property, the
household substance."[158] As high-status slaves, they were an easy target for
insinuations of hidden sexual misconduct between elite women and their
"primped procurators."[159] Symmachus instructed a provincial governor to
hunt down some runaway slaves and return them to his procurator.[160] In
Africa, procurators were the living presence of the distant senatorial class.[161]
The bishop of Hippo received his first reliable information about the sack
of Rome from a senator's procurator.[162]

Beneath the highest level of management, wealthy households required
an array of lesser agents to control their property, market their products,
and execute other commercial or financial acts. Business agents, *actores*,
epitropoi, *pragmateutai*, and *pistikoi*, are common in the fourth-century
sources.[163] *Actores*, like *procuratores*, were high-status slaves, in that they

---

[152] Bas. Hom. Div. 2.2 (Courtonne: 46–7): οἰκετῶν ἀριθμὸς ἄπειρος... ἐπίτροποι, ταμίαι.

[153] Aug. Psalm. 103.4.10 (CC 40: 1530): *quam multi sunt gradus.* Lib. Or. 25.57 (Foerster vol. 2: 564).

[154] CT 1.16.14 (AD 408): *ne quid potentium procuratores perperam inliciteque committant.*

[155] CT 2.12.1 (AD 363); CT 2.12.3 (AD 383); Dig. 14.3.5.18.

[156] CT 2.32.1 (AD 422); CT 4.12.5 (AD 362); CT 9.45.3 (AD 398); CT 9.29.2 (AD 391). Aug. Serm.
40.7 (PL 38: 246); Caes. Arel. Serm. 7.3 (CC 103: 39). For the earlier period, see Aubert 1994,
107–9, 143.

[157] Aug. Psalm. 103.4.10 (CC 40: 1530).

[158] Bars. Resp. 60 (SC 426: 296): τὰ κλεῖθρα καὶ τὰ ὑπάρχοντα αὐτοῦ καὶ τὴν οἰκετείαν. *Fides*:
Salv. Gub. 3.2 (MGH AA 1: 25). Gr. Nyss. Eun. 8.47 (Jaeger: 256).

[159] Hier. Iov. 1.47 (PL 23: 277): *procurator calamistratus.* Hier. Ep. 54.13 (CSEL 54: 479) and 79.9
(CSEL 55: 97).

[160] Symm. Ep. 9.140 (MGH AA 6.1: 273).

[161] Aug. Psalm. 131.6 (CC 40: 1914).   [162] Aug. Ep. 99.1 (CSEL 34.2: 533).

[163] Despite the damage to the first five books of the *Theodosian Code*, where the relevant laws would
have been gathered.

controlled property and other slaves.[164] An important constitution in the
Theodosian Code assumes that an *actor* was the sort of slave whom a free
woman might marry in a non-legal union; Augustine knew of free men who
sold themselves into slavery to become *actores*.[165] In one case Symmachus
asked a governor for help because "the *actores* who are entrusted with
the distant property of abstentees live as though free from the laws since,
situated afar, they feel no terror of their masters. Thus it is necessary for
judicial action to make them pay up for what is owed in rents." Symmachus
needed the governor to help his agent "extract what is owed from obligated
slaves."[166]

Actores could work in agriculture or other types of enterprise. Often these
were not separate ventures, for *actores* were involved in collecting rents,
selling the produce, and controlling the finances of an estate. The *actor*
had control over local accounts.[167] Late Roman laws assumed that senators
who lived in the capital collected income from faraway *actores*.[168] Their
activities gave them considerable economic opportunity. An inscription of
371 from Ephesus shows that the *actores rei privatae* in the province of Asia
were collecting rents from imperial estates; they were rendering 9,000 *solidi*
annually to the fisc, but an audit revealed that, with heavy exactions and
savvy marketing, they were actually making closer to 12,000 *solidi* a year.[169]
It is significant that, into the fourth century, *actores* are highly visible in
the epigraphic record, a sign of their ability to accumulate some financial
resources of their own.[170]

Because the roles of management and agency were inherently complex
and diverse, the Latin *actor* is particularly difficult to map onto the Greek
terminology. *Epitropos*, *pragmateutes*, and *pistikos* could all be equivalents
of *actor*.[171] *Epitropos* was the most important and common of these terms,
and it implied management of property and other slaves.[172] In a papyrus
of AD 338, we meet an *epitropos* overseeing the central management staff of
a large estate; he had several employees on his staff, helping him oversee

[164] CT 7.18.2 (AD 379). Ambrosiast. Comm. in Gal. 4.2 (CSEL 81.2: 42).
[165] CT 4.12.5 (AD 362). Aug. Ep. 24*.2 (CSEL 88: 127). Lepelley 1983.
[166] Symm. Ep. 9.6 (MGH AA 6.1: 236): *actores absentium, quibus res longinqua committitur, tamquam
soluti legibus vivunt, quoniam procul positis nullus dominorum terror incurrit. opus est igitur iudiciali
vigore, ut locationibus adscripta persolvant. . . debita ab obnoxiis servis eruenda.*
[167] CT 2.32.1 (AD 422); CT 11.15.1 (AD 361).   [168] CT 6.2.16 (AD 395).
[169] Chastagnol 1986.   [170] See Aubert 1994, 186, n. 242; Gsell 1932.
[171] A tax declaration in fourth-century Magnesia was made on behalf of the owner, Quadratus, by his
agent, Syneros, probably a slave: Kern, I.Magnesia, no. 122, line 14a, and Thonemann 2007, 473.
His title is abbreviated *prag*, which the editors understand as *pragmatikos*, but it could equally be
pragmateutès. cf. IGLS 1908 (Syria, AD 344).
[172] Ps.-Mac. Serm. 47.1.7 (Berthold vol. 2: 89).

the accounts, control the flow of goods (over a dozen types of foodstuffs) between the farms and the central unit, and communicate with the lower-level managers in the fields.[173] Sometimes, too, *epitropoi* were in the main household. Basil, urging Christians to be lenient towards their slaves on the Sabbath, advised them to give relief to the *epitropoi* responsible for their household income.[174] The *oikonomos* was a closely related figure. His job could certainly include agricultural management. Asterius imagined an *oikonomos* retiring, handing over keys, giving up control of the vines, gardens, and houses.[175]

Farm management will be discussed in chapter 4, but it is important to recognize that the role of *actores* and *epitropoi* ranged into direct oversight of agricultural labor. *Vilicus* remained the basic term for bailiff, farm manager. A master would ask his *vilicus* how the harvest looked.[176] The *vilicus* strove to produce a *fructum copiosum*.[177] There was a subtle difference in connotation between *actor* and *vilicus*: *actores* were closely involved in the financial management of estates, *vilici* in agricultural cultivation. An *actor*, moreover, might have financial responsibility over a number of estates, whereas a *vilicus* was responsible for an individual farm.[178] But these distinctions could be fluid, and from Columella to Ambrose the *actor* and *vilicus* could be mentioned in the same breath.[179] Ambrose claimed that "sometimes a *vilicus* or *actor agri* proves efficient, and he is brought into the urban staff."[180] *Vilici* were found with *coloni*, and *actores* were found whipping slaves.[181] There was probably a whole universe of lower-level overseers who are hard to detect in our souces – for instance, the slaves called "head farmers" in a fourth-century papyrus or the custodians overseeing the workers on the villa of Palladius.[182] The hazy boundaries between these managerial categories, and the discordant semantic ranges of the Greek and Latin terminology, are reflected in an artful letter of Ausonius, whose pretentious *vilicus* preferred to be called *epitropos*.[183]

Slaves also served as managers within the household staff. The operation of the household itself often demanded the ability to manage human

[173] P. Lips. 97 (AD 338): see chapter 4.   [174] Bas. Jej. 1.7 (PG 31: 176).
[175] Ast. Am. 2.9 (Datema: 22). Also in Philogel. 47 (Thierfelder: 46); Geopon. 2.44 (Beckh: 79) translates *vilicus* as *oikonomos* or *epitropos*.
[176] P. Nol. Ep. 39.3 (CSEL 29: 336).   [177] Petr. Chrys. Serm. 158 (CC 24B: 98).
[178] Aubert 1994, 192.   [179] Aubert 1994, 129–30, 190–1; Corbier 1981, 437.
[180] Ambr. Abr. 1.3.13 (CSEL 32.1: 511): *vilicus nonnumquam utilis est vel actor agri: confertur urbano.*
[181] Symm. Ep. 6.81 (MGH AA 6.1: 176); Salv. Gub. 4.3 (MGH AA 1: 38). The *actor* of Sidonius Apollinaris, Ep. 5.20 (MGH AA 8: 92–3), was mentioned along with the agricultural products of an estate.
[182] P. Lips. 97 (AD 337): 8.23 and 14.27. Pall. Op. ag. 2.10.4 (Martin: 62).
[183] Auson. Ep. 20 (Green: 219–22). See Aubert 1994, 141–3.

resources. "If someone is in charge of a house with a few slaves, he will deal with countless outbursts and worries."[184] Masters turned to slaves for help in managing the household.[185] "The administration of a house is like controlling a ship. When the master has the helm of the house, he is, like the captain, in charge of all. The one in charge, entrusted with the care of the rest of the slaves, is like the first mate and tells the master what is best. The other slaves, resembling sailors, each have their own concern and do what they are ordered."[186] The slave manager's work consisted of apportioning the food and sleep of the slaves, dividing their labor, watching their behavior, doling out reward and punishment.[187] The occupation of the slave manager could itself be a reward, a position of authority given to trusted slaves. The master "makes the good slave a friend and decorates him and puts him in charge of the *domus* and the *familia* and all the master's affairs."[188] Thus, the role became an incentive for a slave to climb within the household organization – a circumscribed form of mobility.[189] Often this role as domestic manager required the co-operation of the mistress. She found herself worrying about money, slaves, overseers, cooks, and seamstresses.[190] The manager could be her partner, subordinate, or substitute; Jerome thought it tasteful if a widow appointed a manager and stayed out of the way.[191]

Slave agents were used in a more restricted sense, too, charged to execute specific acts.[192] Libanius mentioned slaves of an Antiochene councilor sailing to an *emporium* in Sinope, via Constantinople, and in the same letter he empowered them to sell a property on his own behalf, too.[193] In another letter Libanius dispatched a group of his slaves to Cilicia to buy wood.[194] An Egyptian decurion, who seems to have been involved in the slave trade, used

---

[184] Ioh. Chrys. Stag. 3.4 (PG 47: 477–8): Εἰ γὰρ οἰκετῶν τις ὀλίγων ἐν οἰκίᾳ προεστὼς, καὶ παροξυσμῶν καὶ λύπης μυρίας ἔχει προφάσεις.

[185] Amm. 14.6.17 (Seyfarth vol. 1: 15). Dionisotti 1982, 17, 98. *Silentiarii*: Salv. Gub. 4.3 (MGH AA 1: 38).

[186] Thdt. Provid. 7.676C (PG 83: 676): Καὶ μὴν οἰκία καὶ ναῦς κατὰ τὴν οἰκονομίαν λίαν ἀλλήλαις ἐοίκασιν. Ὁ μὲν γὰρ δεσπότης, καθάπερ τις κυβερνήτης, τῶν τῆς οἰκίας οἰάκων ἐπειλημμένος, τοῖς πᾶσιν ἐφέστηκεν. ὁ δὲ τῶν οἰκετῶν πρωτεύων, ὁ τῶν ἄλλων ἁπάντων τὴν κηδεμονίαν πεπιστευμένος, τὸν πρωρέα μιμούμενος, διδάσκει τὸν δεσπότην ἃ νομίζει συμφέρειν. Τῶν δὲ ἄλλων οἰκετῶν, οἱ μὲν ναύταις παραπλησίως, μερικὰς ἐγκεχειρισμένοι φροντίδας, τὰ κελευόμενα πράττουσιν.

[187] Bars. Resp. 60 (SC 426: 296).

[188] Lact. Ir. 5.12 (SC 289: 108): *bonum adloquitur amice et ornat et domui ac familiae suisque rebus omnibus praeficit.*

[189] Aug. Psalm. 103.4.10 (CC 40: 1530).

[190] Ioh. Chrys. Virg. 73.1 (SC 125: 350).   [191] Hier. Ep. 79.8 (CSEL 55: 97).

[192] CJ 4.25.5 (AD 294) and CJ 4.25.6 (AD 294). Aubert 1994, 4, *passim*.

[193] Lib. Ep. 177 (Foerster vol. 10: 165).   [194] Lib. Ep. 568 (Foerster vol. 10: 535).

one of his slaves as his business agent, carrying out financial transactions that included slave sales.[195] The archive of Theophanes, reflecting his voyage from Hermopolis to Antioch, reveals that he had around three trusted slaves with him, who are glimpsed carrying out business both frivolous and weighty.[196] It is remarkable that this type of activity is visible at all in the fourth-century sources, for our knowledge of the slave *institor* comes first and foremost from the classical legal evidence.[197] The relevant sections of the *Theodosian Code* have been especially poorly transmitted, but it is at least worth noting that the codification of Justinian, not to mention other post-classical handbooks of Roman law, took care to include the Roman law of indirect agency.[198]

Slaves were employed in financial roles, as accountants and dispensers. Just as they contributed to the efficient use of human and agricultural resources, they were used to manage financial resources. In larger households *dispensatores* and *tamiai* filled specialized roles, whereas their tasks were probably integrated with those of management and agency in smaller households.[199] It was assumed that slaves would physically handle the money.[200] Slaves knew where masters kept the cash hidden.[201] A particularly paranoid and greedy man would not trust his money to a slave or to a banker.[202] Masters also might expect their slaves to keep track of household finances, the amount of reserves and outgoing expenditures. "As soon as we rise from bed, before we go to the forum . . . we call in the slave and ask for an account of expenses."[203] In an early fifth-century comedy written in Gaul, a master is portrayed as exceptionally overbearing and miserly for keeping track of all the expenses "in his own hand."[204]

Slaves served the late Roman household as secretaries and couriers, too. Perhaps these roles were effectively lower-level positions where slaves were

---

[195] P. Lips. 4 + P. Lips. 5 = M. Chr. 171 + P. Strasb. VI 594 (AD 293). Straus 2004, 330. See chapter 2.

[196] Matthews 2006, 95–6.

[197] Aubert 1994, 16, notes that the literary sources for *institores* treat them as traders or hucksters rather than agents. Among the only non-legal sources to suggest that *institores* were (slave) agents: *Chronographus anni CCCLIV* (MGH AA 9: 43); Claud. In Eutr. 1.192 (Hall: 150).

[198] Aubert 1994, 6, 52–3. PS 2.6–9; Inst. 4.7.

[199] For *tamiai*, Bas. Hom. Div. 2.2 (Courtonne: 46–7). For *dispensatores*, Aug. Util. cred. 1.24 (CSEL 25.1: 30).

[200] Ioh. Chrys. Laz. 2.5 (PG 48: 988); Ioh. Chrys. In 1 Tim. 16.2 (PG 62: 590); Ioh. Chrys. In. Rom. 21.3 (PG 60: 606); Aug. Serm. 345.3 (PLS 2: 204).

[201] Sometimes it was hidden so the slaves *wouldn't* know where it was: Aug. Serm. 38.8 (CC 41: 483).

[202] Gr. Nyss. Usur. 205 (Gebhardt: 205).

[203] Ioh. Chrys. Non ad grat. conc. 4 (PG 50: 660): Εὐθέως ἀναστάντες ἀπὸ τῆς κλίνης, πρὶν εἰς ἀγορὰν ἐμβαλεῖν . . . τὸν οἰκέτην καλέσαντες ἀπαιτοῦμεν λόγον τῶν δαπανηθέντων.

[204] Quer. (Randstrand: 39): *propria . . . manu*; chapter 6.

prepared for jobs of greater responsibility. Their importance is especially notable in the epistolary corpus of Symmachus, one of our best sources for the operations of a senatorial patrimony.[205] An army of low-ranking functionaries, like couriers (*tabellarii*), were instrumental in connecting Symmachus to his properties, and it is just possible to detect this giant class of senatorial emissaries in late antiquity, running their circuits to the provinces and back to the center, conveying information.[206] Above the lowest class of messengers, a group of secretaries (*notarii*) were prominent in the house of Symmachus. A Castor was active in Campania; Euscius seems to have shuttled back and forth from Sicily. This class of mid-level servile agents made possible the logistics of running a small empire in landed wealth.[207]

An underappreciated way in which slaves aided the household was in their role as letter-carriers. Epistolary contact was the lifeblood of political, cultural, and economic relations. The surviving portions of some letter collections – the thousands of letters of Libanius, hundreds for Symmachus and Augustine – point to the extraordinary integration of communication in the late Roman empire. Travel was no easy matter in the ancient world, even in a highly connected realm like the late Roman empire. There was no postal service for private citizens, so masters often delegated the work of correspondence to their slaves.[208] It is perhaps remarkable that masters could reliably depend on their slaves to travel hundreds of miles and then return home. This is proof of the psychological dimension of control, but also of the effective net for discovering runaways. "I think I have found your boy called Germanus who slipped away three years ago . . . "[209] Interestingly, the letter collections preserve a surprising amount of chatter about the anger and frustration over the imperfect services of slave couriers – like the slave messenger who told Libanius he would be

---

[205] Vera 1986b.

[206] Symm. Ep. 1.11 (MGH AA 6.1: 8); Symm. Ep. 1.13 (MGH AA 6.1: 9); Symm. Ep. 1.16 (MGH AA 6.1: 11); Symm. Ep. 1.57 (MGH AA 6.1: 27); Symm. Ep. 1.87 (MGH AA 6.1: 36); Symm. Ep. 2.48 (MGH AA 6.1: 57); Symm. Ep. 2.54 (MGH AA 6.1: 59); Symm. Ep. 3.4 (MGH AA 6.1: 71); Symm. Ep. 3.28 (MGH AA 6.1: 79); Symm. Ep. 3.30 (MGH AA 6.1: 80); Symm. Ep. 4.20 (MGH AA 6.1: 105); Symm. Ep. 4.28 (MGH AA 6.1: 107); Symm. Ep. 5.33 (MGH AA 6.1: 132); Symm. Ep. 5.61 (MGH AA 6.1: 141); Symm. Ep. 5.88 (MGH AA 6.1: 150); Symm. Ep. 7.16 (MGH AA 6.1: 181); Symm. Ep. 8.32 (MGH AA 6.1: 225); Caes. Arel. Serm. 7.3 (CC 103: 39).

[207] Castor: Symm. Ep. 6.9 (MGH AA 6.1: 155); Symm. Ep. 6.18 (MGH AA 6.1: 158). Euscius: Symm. Ep. 6.33 (MGH AA 6.1: 162); Symm. Ep. 8.68 (MGH AA 6.1: 233); Symm. Ep. 9.4–5 (MGH AA 6.1: 236). Vera 1986b, 256–7.

[208] Letourneur 2002, 132–3.

[209] Ennod. Ep. 3.19 (CSEL 6: 86): *fugacem puerum vestrum Germanum vocabulo, qui ante triennium lapsus est, me suspicor invenisse.*

unable deliver a return letter since he planned to vacation in Antioch for a while![210]

Finally, slaves were an essential part of the business world as semi-independent entrepreneurs.[211] Not only were slaves in the direct employ of patrimonial operations, they could be allotted a *peculium*, an account under their control and the master's ownership that allowed substantial opportunity for entrepreneurial activity.[212] John Chrysostom could re-work a Biblical parable into a scene drawn from everyday life at Antioch: imagine "your slave owed you one hundred gold coins, and someone owed him a little silver . . . "[213] These slaves had money, and they were (at the master's discretion) held to account for their earnings and expenses.[214] "Many slaves even have slaves" of their own; in a sermon delivered in North Africa, Augustine claimed that it "frequently happens that slaves have slaves in the *peculium*."[215] The use of the *peculium* allowed masters to participate in ventures while limiting their risk and intensifying the incentives to the slave.[216] The relevant titles of the *Theodosian Code* are poorly preserved, but an important constitution of AD 422 shows that the laws of agency and *peculium* were in use: a master was liable for acts he empowered agents to perform, and a slave could use his *peculium* as surety, but otherwise the master was insulated from liability.[217] The institution of the *peculium* also allowed masters to act as silent partners in unsavory forms of commerce, such as the slave trade, tavern-keeping, and prostitution. For reasons which are easy to understand, it is a challenge to see the direct links between the seedy side of the late ancient city and the illustrious patrimonies whose

---

[210] Lib. Ep. 650 (Foerster vol. 10: 593–4). Other troubles with slave couriers: Lib. Ep. 138 (Foerster vol. 10: 136–7); Lib. Ep. 624 (Foerster vol. 10: 574); Lib. Ep. 661 (Foerster vol. 10: 602); Bas. Ep. 58.1 (Courtonne: 145); Symm. Ep. 5.33 (MGH AA 6.1: 132); Symm. Ep. 6.8 (MGH AA 6.1: 155) particularly angry; Symm. Ep. 6.78 (MGH AA 6.1: 175); P. Nol. Ep. 5.21–2 (CSEL 29: 39). Syn. Ep. 106 (Garzya: 191).

[211] Juglar 1894, 30–40.

[212] Andreau 1999, 67; Aubert 1994, 65–70. Ast. Am. 2.6 (Datema: 20); Aug. Ord. 2.2.6 (CC 29: 109–10); Aug. Psalm. 49.17 (CC 38: 589). CJ 4.26.7 (AD 293).

[213] Ioh. Chrys. Ad pop. Ant. 20.6 (PG 49: 206): Εἴ τις οἰκέτης σὸς ὤφειλέ σοι χρυσίνους ἑκατόν, εἶτα ἐκείνῳ ἕτερός τις ὤφειλε ἀργύρια ὀλίγα . . . There are similarities to Mt 18:21–35, but the king has become a private individual in Chrysostom's audience, and the talents of silver have become gold coins!

[214] Ioh. Chrys. Dec. mill. tal. 4 (PG 51: 22); Ioh. Chrys. Hom. in Genes. 38.4 (PG 53: 355).

[215] Ioh. Chrys. In Mt. 59.4 (PG 58: 571): πολλοὶ γὰρ καὶ οἰκέται δούλους ἔχουσιν. Aug. Serm. 21.5 (Dolbeau: 275): *plerumque evenit ut servi peculiosi habeant servos.*

[216] Ioh. Chrys. Virg. 28.1 (SC 125: 184); Them. Or. 21.246d (Downey and Schenkl vol. 2: 22); Salv. Eccl. 3.7 (MGH AA 1: 148).

[217] CT 2.31.1 and 2.32.1 (AD 422). cf. CJ 4.26.10 (AD 294); CJ 4.26.12 (AD 294).

capital surely multiplied in bars and backalleys.[218] The *peculium*, as before, was the invisible pipeline between *honestas* and *lucra sordida*.

TEXTILE PRODUCTION AND SLAVE LABOR

The manufacture of textiles consumes a giant portion of human energy in a pre-modern society.[219] Textile production constituted, after food production, the most important sector of the late Roman economy. A history of ancient slavery must recognize the structural role of textile production in the slave system, and yet this represents a distinct challenge. The economics of the Roman textile industry have not been particularly well served by modern historians; there is not a single attempt to measure the overall dimensions of time and resources spent in the production of cloth in the Roman empire. Moreover, histories of slavery have almost systematically ignored textiles. Not only have the physical remains of the industry decomposed, economic historians have started with the assumption that labor is masculine and agricultural, thereby obscuring the significance of textile production, dominated as it was by women.[220] The problem runs even deeper when we consider the relation between textile production and the fate of late Roman slavery, since debates over continuity and transition have been framed entirely in terms of the countryside and measured solely by the criterion of farm labor. The interrelationship between textile production and slave labor must not only be emphasized, it must find a place in the way we evaluate the survival and transformation of the slave system in the late Roman empire.

From the simple tunics of the slave class to the silk garments of the aristocracy, the 50 million inhabitants of the late antique empire created an enormous, complex market for textiles. And although many peasants produced for their own needs, the textile sector was a *market* in the late empire. Eleven of the thirty-two sections in the Price Edict of Diocletian pertained to textiles, and the Edict offers an exceptionally fascinating glimpse of the sheer variety and steep hierarchy of the Roman vestimentary catalogue.[221] There are other signs of the industry's scale and complexity. A tantalizing papyrus from second- or third-century Oxyrhynchus suggests cloth exports of a volume that would not compare poorly with late medieval figures.[222]

[218] Purcell 1999 is evocative, esp. 154.
[219] Roth 2007, 53–118; Wild 2003, 2002, 1999, 1994, and 1970; Drinkwater 2001; Vicari 2001; Jongman 2000a; Wipszycka 1965; Calderini 1946.
[220] Above all Roth 2007.   [221] Horden and Purcell 2000, 352–63.   [222] Van Minnen 1986.

Textiles belonged among the bulk commodities which circulated in the late Roman empire; the market served the needs of much more than the aristocracy. We see the urban poor buying rather than making their own garments.[223] In the early fifth century, when an ascetic at Rome wished to wear humble attire, he bought an *Antiochene* cloak that had presumably traversed the Mediterranean.[224] The industrial fulleries which survive from the Roman period are striking archaeological evidence for the textile industry; they suggest organization and capital investment, and yet fulling has been estimated to contribute only 1 percent to the production cost of a finished textile.[225] Even as consistent a minimalist as Jones had to admit that the Roman textile trade was impressive.[226]

The bulk market was dominated by two textiles: linens and woollens. In both cases slave labor was a particularly suitable fit within the textile production process, which in the Roman empire was characterized by extremely limited levels of technology and low productivity.[227] We can identify four essential stages of the textile production process. The raw fibres had to be prepared, then spun into thread, which was woven into cloth which, in many cases, was finished by fulling, tailoring, or dyeing.[228] The first phase, the preparation of raw fibres, was essentially agricultural and took place on rural estates. It was the most capital-intensive phase, and most of the cost of finished textiles probably derived from the raw materials.[229] Because linens were made from flax, woollens from the fleece of sheep, the production of raw materials competed with other agricultural priorities. In some cases, not only the production of wool and flax, but the entire manufacturing process, including spinning, weaving, and fulling, was carried out on estates. What interests us now are the middle two phases, spinning and weaving, which could take place either in town or country (table 3.3).[230]

Spinning and weaving are separate stages, with distinct attributes. Spinning, the production of yarn, was routine, unskilled labor. Requiring only a spindle, distaff, and whorl, spinning entailed little capital expense beyond the raw material, but it was exceedingly laborious. It has been estimated that spinning occupied five – or, more realistically – ten times the amount

---

[223] Jones 1964, 848.   [224] Ger. Vit. Mel. 8 (Gorce: 142).
[225] Wilson 2004a, 2003 and 2001b, for an excellent micro-study of Timgad, emphasizing prosperity in the second–fourth centuries. For the estimated cost, Jongman 2000a, 191.
[226] Jones 1964, 848, and 1960.   [227] Wild 2002, 27; Horden and Purcell 2000, 360.
[228] Though wool might be dyed in the fleece. In general, see Wild 1970, 31–8. Vicari 2001, 1–8.
[229] Jongman 2000a. Roth 2007 may underestimate the costs of the raw materials.
[230] Compare the useful chart of Wild 1999, 30 and the discussion of Frayn 1984, 142–61.

Table 3.3 *The textile production process*

Preparation of fibers	→ Spinning	→ Weaving	→ Finishing
Rural	Household, workshop, or estate	Household, workshop, or estate	Urban
Ungendered	Feminine	Masculine or feminine	Masculine
Agricultural	Unspecialized	Allows specialization	Industrialized
High-capital	Low-capital	Medium-capital	High-capital

of labor as weaving: a tunic that took ten hours to weave required yarn that took 100 hours to spin.[231] Spinning represented a "bottleneck" in ancient textile production and might be distributed wherever there was surplus labor.[232] Spinning has also tended to be invisible in the historiography. Weaving was more complex. The Price Edict gives the maximum wages for various levels of weaving. Weaving required modest capital investment, in the form of a loom, and more importantly weaving could be of varying qualities, some of which required training. Thus we find apprenticeship contracts for weavers in the papyri, and weaving frequently appears as a specialized occupation in the legal and literary sources.[233]

In the ancient world, spinning and weaving were intrinsically suited for domestic labor. Hence, textile production was the quintessentially feminine labor.[234] The virtuous *lanifica* was a cultural stereotype firmly rooted in reality, its enduring resonance a testimony to the millennial absorption of women's work in the production of cloth.[235] Spinning was an exclusively female role, although males – and male slaves – could be employed as weavers.[236] It is important to understand why the production process itself made textile labor suited not only for the domestic sphere but also highly adaptive to the use of slave labor within the household. Labor-intensive, with low levels of technology and capital investment, there were few if any returns to scale in spinning and weaving.[237] Spinning particularly

---

[231] Roth 2007, 59; Wild 2002, 8; Carr 1999, 165.   [232] Wild 2003, 108–9, 2002, 29.
[233] Calderini 1946, 20.   [234] Lovén 1998a.   [235] Wild 1999, 33. Scheidel 1995, 205.
[236] P. Oxy 51.3617 (3C). P. Lips. 97 (AD 338). Claud. In. Eutr. 2 lines 380–5 (Hall: 181). Dig. 33.9.3.6; Dig. 7.8.12.6; Dig. 24.1.31.1; Dig. 33.7.16.2. Amm. 14.6.17 (Seyfarth vol. 1: 15): slave weavers, sex unclear. Roth 2007, 21: "weaving can be a male profession, spinning never is." Lovén 1998b, 75.
[237] Jongman 2000a, 193. The largest textile producer, the state, ran giant textile factories, yet also seems at times to have allotted production quotas to individual workers: Jones 1964, 836–7 and Soz. H. E. 5.15.7 (GCS 50: 214). Many, though not all, of the state's textile workers were slaves. See CT 10.20.2 (AD 357); CT 10.20.5 (AD 371); CT 10.20.7 (AD 372); CT 10.20.9 (AD 380); and especially CT 10.20.10 (AD 379) with Vicari 2001, 17; Sirks 1994.

was unskilled and required great amounts of time, but it did "not demand exclusive concentration" and was "typically carried out in conjunction with other low-intensity occupations."[238] Textile work was the sort of effort-intensive labor that was possible to extract through coercion; the necessary supervision was in the household, in the form of the mistress, whose labor cost little in the way of opportunities lost.[239] There was hardly room for slaves to shirk and nothing especially valuable for them to destroy. The requirements of textile production and the mechanics of slave exploitation went hand in hand.

The use of slave labor in textile production is attested in various kinds of households, but it was simply presumed that women, particularly slave-women, were constantly at work spinning and weaving. Textile production was embedded in all manner of households, great and humble. The smallest village households were involved in textile work.[240] The sixty-one sheep and forty goats in the household of Taësis and Kyrillous would have provided wool as a secondary product, some 50 to 100 pounds of fleece annually.[241] The textile work of slaves could also reward special training: in a papyrus of around 300, a woman from the village of Kellis apprenticed a slave "to learn the art of weaving."[242] In a "small household" of early fourth-century Hermopolis, an inheritance included four slaves, one of whom was a weaver.[243] At the very pinnacles of the social hierarchy, textile work was simply presumptive as well. The daughter of a Roman senator, Symmachus, sent her father a home-made garment for his birthday. In his return note, he thanked her and praised her for being a *matrona lanifica*, the ideal of womanhood: "You eschew those who sweep off to the lakes, and whether you are seated or walking around, you judge it the only delight of your sex to be amongst the wool and thread of the slave-girls."[244] The daughter of a Roman magnate oversaw the production of yarn and fabric in her household.

We should imagine that the use of female slave labor in textile work was pervasive among Agricultural, Bourgeois, Elite, and Illustrious house-holds alike. John Chrysostom imagined textile work as part of the normal

---

[238] Roth 2007, 106–7.
[239] The standard economic analyses of labor supervision neglect female work such as textile production: Scheidel 2008 (who, to be fair, has separately written a most lucid analysis of female labor in antiquity: Scheidel 1995–6a); Temin 2004; Fenoaltea 1984; Findlay 1975.
[240] Bagnall 1996, 34.   [241] For goat hair at Karanis, Batcheller 2001, 38–47.
[242] P. Kellis 19a: πρὸς μάθησιν τῆς γερδιακῆς τέχνης. cf. P. Kellis 71 (mid-fourth century). Forbes 1955, 330.
[243] Bagnall 1993, 229. P. Lips. 26 (fourth century).
[244] Symm. Ep. 6.67 (MGH AA 6.1: 172): *renuntias stagna verrentibus et residens aut obambulans inter pensa et foragines puellarum has solas arbitraris sexus tui esse delicias.*

"good order" in an Antiochene household. "In an *oikos* you may see many examples of good order. The mistress of the household sits in her chair with all propriety, and the slave-girls weave silently."[245] In this sermon there is no sense that Chrysostom was talking about particularly wealthy households. It was part of the everyday panorama in the towns where he preached: he spoke of women "often" swearing their slave-girls could not go to sleep without finishing their daily quota of work.[246] The papyri which show slaves performing textile work also seem to originate from rather ordinary households, such as those modest slave-owning families so prominent in the census records. Certainly Chrysostom did at times address wealthier households. In one treatise he described a girl's father who departed on a business trip, leaving his daughter at home in charge of a whole troop of newly bought slave-girls, putting them in rhythm with the wool-working.[247] The noisy murmurs of the "throngs of weavers" resounded throughout the wealthy Roman household.[248]

Textile work was organized differently in Bourgeois and Elite households. Jerome wrote a letter to Demetrias, a woman of the highest wealth and rank. He counseled her to guard her virginity and suggested constant labor as a means of occupying herself. "Keep wool always in your hands."[249] She could participate in the actual production process: "draw down the threads of the warp with your thumb . . . " Or, she could supervise: "examine what has been woven, correct errors that have been made, manage what is to be produced. If you will stay busy with such a variety of tasks, the day will never be too long."[250] Jerome presumed that the daughter of a Roman aristocrat could find the textile work of the household an absorbing diversion. The methods of weaving he described entailed not only the production of common woolen fabrics, but also a method of spinning "used widely for fine muslin in the East."[251] He expected that Demetrias' family would reward her financially for her work and that she could then spend this money on poor relief. All of this implies a rather large, organized, and commercially oriented enterprise.

---

[245] Ioh. Chrys. In 1 Cor. 36.5 (PG 61: 313): Ἐν οἰκίᾳ μὲν γὰρ πολλὴν καὶ εὐταξίαν ἴδοι τις ἄν. καὶ γὰρ ἡ κυρία τῆς οἰκίας ἐπὶ τοῦ θρόνου κάθηται μετὰ εὐσχημοσύνης ἁπάσης, καὶ αἱ θεραπαινίδες μετὰ τῆς ἡσυχίας ὑφαίνουσι.

[246] Ioh. Chrys. Ad pop. Ant. 14.1 (PG 49: 145).   [247] Ioh. Chrys. Subintr. 9.27 (Dumortier: 76–7).

[248] Hier. Helv. 20 (PL 23: 204): *textricum turba commurmurat.*

[249] Hier. Ep. 130.15 (CSEL 56: 195): *habeto lanam semper in manibus.*

[250] Hier. Ep. 130.15 (CSEL 56: 195): *vel staminis pollice fila deducito . . . quae texta sunt, perspice; quae errata, reprehende; quae facienda, constitue. si tantis operum varietatibus fueris occupata, numquam tibi dies longi erunt.*

[251] Wild 1970, 37.

In a context far removed from the elite corridors of Jerome's world, an anonymous North African preacher also drew on the relationship between Christian womanhood and the job of weaving. This African preacher, whose Latin lacked the grace but not the fire of Jerome's, thundered against drunkenness at martyrs' festivals. The wild atmosphere of these Christian celebrations turned women into lushes and threatened to throw the household into disarray. "The whole *domus* resounds with the clamors of the undisciplined *familia*. The weaving is neglected, abandoned, or done with utter carelessness... The mistress no longer sets up the looms for the purpose of weaving garments for chastity, the need for which she has long since dismissed from the household through drunkenness. The looms which she has withdrawn from the leisured slave-girls are given over to weaving – spider webs!"[252]

Despite the common moral agenda of Jerome and the anonymous preacher, there was a subtle difference in their respective economies of female modesty. Demetrias was encouraged to become an accessory to an established weaving installation in her household (one that was manufacturing woolen garments and fine fabrics). Her role was supplemental, a way to divert her and preserve her virginity. The mistress of the North African *domus* – a married woman – was the lynchpin of a small labor system. Without her supervision of the *familia*, the organization fell apart and the household became unproductive. These contrasts imply the broad range of ways that slaves might be integrated into productive processes in the ancient household among Bourgeois and Elite families. It is also notable that in late antiquity the cultural ideal of the *matrona lanifica*, the chaste wool-working woman in the tradition of Penelope and Lucretia, was so dominantly associated not just with spinning and weaving, but with *managing* the slaves who actually did the spinning and weaving.

Economic goals differed in smaller and larger households. Smaller slave-owning households may have directly consumed what they produced, so that the value was earned through making instead of buying finished products on the market. Textile work allowed slave-owners to recoup the costs of slaves.[253] Even without adequate data we can imagine, in rough outline, how this was possible.[254] A plain mass-produced tunic cost something like

---

[252] Ps.-Aug. Sobr. (PL 40: 1110): *indisciplinataeque familiae clamoribus domus omnis perstrepit. Lanificii vero aut negligens, aut nulla, aut abominabilis efficitur cura... Non tuendae castitatis causa telas ad texendum erigit, quae usum telae olim de domo per ebrietatem amisit: et telas quas ancillis otiantibus subtraxit, texendas araneis dedit* (African, fourth century).

[253] E.g. P. Brem. 63 (second century), for an earlier example. cf. Dig. 7.8.12.6.

[254] I offer these figures only as defensible guesses, at each stage probably underestimating profits.

1 *solidus* and required up to 100–150 hours of spinning and weaving to
make; labor costs are hard to calculate; a low but realistic estimate might
be one-third of the finished price.[255] If a slave-girl was worked five hours
a day in spinning and weaving for 300 days a year (higher and lower
amounts are conceivable), she did something like 1.5–3 *solidi* worth of textile work per year. Female slaves cost something like 5–15 *solidi* in the late
empire, so it would not have been unreasonable for a family – who may
have wanted a slave-girl to provide honor, comfort, and sexual availability
among other goods – to have expected to be able to make part or more of
her cost back.[256] With industry and frugality, higher profits were achiev-
able. Jerome knew of a monk who "out of thriftiness rather than greed left
behind on his death 100 *solidi* which he had made from weaving linen."[257]
If we imagine that slave-girls, like monks, lived on an exiguous diet, we
can see the opportunities the market provided to capitalize on a lifetime of
rote labor.[258]

Textile production in larger households, by contrast, was clearly organized for profit. Basil of Caesarea accused the late Roman aristocracy of
being avaricious, turning wheat, wine, *and wool* into gold.[259] Asterius of
Amasea characterized the rich man as one with "a multitude of slaves
weaving and houses full of clothes."[260] These households owned specialized textile workers: when Ammianus described the parade of slaves which
accompanied an elite Roman through the streets, specialized weavers were
a distinct category.[261] Textile production, both because of the rural context
of its basic materials and its multi-phase production process, defies any neat
categorization as agriculture or manufacture, rural or urban production. In
large, commercially oriented enterprises, rural and urban production could

[255] Time: Roth 2007, 81–2. Wild 2002, 31, reports some incredibly high figures. Carr 1999, 164–5.
Labor costs: Jongman 2000a, 191, shows that raw materials could be many times as expensive as
the cost of weaving, although at the lower end of quality their costs converged. He omits the cost
of spinning. cf. Wild 1994, 30–1 (who accounts for spinning and weaving and puts labor costs at
well over half the total, but omits finishing, transport, and marketing expenses). Final cost: Jones
1964, 850. A study of the basic cost structure of Roman textile production is a *desideratum*.
[256] Harper 2010, on prices.
[257] Hier. Ep. 22.54 (CSEL 54: 195): *parcior magis quam avarior... centum solidos, quos lina texendo
quaesierat, moriens dereliquit.*
[258] The archive of Theophanes (P.Ryl. 627 recto, col. viii) includes numerous textile implements for
the production of fine garments. Matthews 2006, 43–5, discusses the possible meanings of the
fragment, concluding that it is unconnected with Theophanes' journey. If the inventory does
describe his travel pack, however, it surely reflects the expectations that the slaves would spend any
free time weaving.
[259] Bas. Dest. horr. 5 (Courtonne: 25–6).
[260] Ast. Am. 3.13 (Datema: 36): καὶ ὁ πολλοὺς ἔχων δούλους ὑφάντας καὶ οἰκίας γεμούσας
ἐσθῆτος... cf. Dig. 33.7.16.2; Dig. 33.9.3.6; Dig. 33.7.12.6; Dig. 50.16.203.
[261] Amm. 14.6.17 (Seyfarth vol. 1: 15). cf. Dig. 32.61; Dig. 30.36.

have been integrated. In other words, land-owners could have produced their own raw materials in the countryside and concentrated the later phases of production, such as spinning and weaving, in their urban houses. As Jongman has persuasively argued, the production of raw materials competes with cereals and other foodstuffs for land. Hence the economics of location were a major factor in the organization of the textile industry. Regions like Pontus and Cappadocia, where Basil and Asterius describe commercial wool production, to say nothing of Gaul or Britain, were capable of devoting land to sheep-rearing. The fleece could be spun and woven on site, exported as raw material to be sold in urban markets, or finished in the land-owner's household and sold as finished cloth.

Textiles remain the most underestimated and understudied product of the Roman economy. Goods which never enter the market and thereby fail to be assigned exchange values are often ignored in conceptions of economic production; women's labor, and women's products like textiles, are prime examples.[262] But in the Roman case, where a vast and complex market developed for every phase of textile production – fibers, yarn, cloth, clothing – the neglect of the industry is even harder to explain. In a field where archaeology has done so much to invigorate discussion, perhaps the decomposition of wooden spindles and looms, the perishability of tunics and cloaks, is ultimately the culprit which has allowed textile work to escape the attention it deserves. But a history of slavery, especially one proposing that some two and a half million women found themselves enslaved in the late Roman empire, must account for the time and effort spent spinning and weaving as structural features of the slave system. Here was one of the major flows of capital that allowed middling households, rich households, and commercially oriented estates alike to use slave labor. The implements of the industry may be lost forever, like the "songs of the weaving women" that lilted through the streets of a late ancient city, but it is the historian's task to sense the vanished artifact and to hear the "rhythms" of those whose labor was taken in the endless cycles of the spindle and loom.[263]

AGRICULTURAL LABOR AND SMALL SLAVE-OWNING HOUSEHOLDS

In late Roman Egypt, a holy man went to a village and encountered its headman, who, without much prodding, described his record of achievement.

[262] Waring 1988.
[263] Hier. Vigil. 6 (PL 23: 345): *mulierum textrinas cantato.* cf. Ioh. Chrys. Subintr. 9.27 (Dumortier: 76–7).

The villager had been married faithfully for thirty years. He had three sons. He was hospitable to guests and generous to the poor. As a judge he had not shown favoritism even towards his children; the fruits of another's labor had never come into his house; he had tried to make peace whenever possible; he never took the finest fields for himself; his herds never grazed on the lands of others; no one could accuse his slaves of wrongdoing.[264] The good behavior of his slaves was included in this rather ordinary catalogue of virtues by an upright villager of the late Roman empire. Other papyri witness the violence and crime which masters might practice through their surrogates, so this was a real enough merit among a list of virtues aimed to minimize the inevitable tensions of living in a close-knit farming community.[265] But how extensive was slavery in this niche of Roman society?

That is a question the sources will never answer. Even the modestly comfortable dwellers of the countryside lie beyond the reach of the literary and legal sources. The discussion of small-scale slave-holding in the Roman countryside, moreover, is not an especially well-developed corner of the historiography. The classical Athenian household has garnered far more attention. Over the last several decades a debate has unraveled over the extent of slavery in ordinary peasant households in classical Athens. The evidence is impressionistic, of course, and ultimately the case turns on the level of stratification in the countryside and the time commitments of a democratic citizenry. A plausible argument can be made that widespread slave-ownership penetrated the stratum of wealthy peasants but not anywhere near the median Athenian household.[266]

Here we are trying to identify and to understand the economic behavior of slave-owning Agricultural households in the late Roman empire. In contrast to Bourgeois households, the primary substance of the family was absorbed in farming; in contrast to estates, discussed in chapter 4, the free family itself constituted one of the primary sources of labor on the farm. We are not, it should be emphasized, speaking of ordinary peasant households. Agricultural slave-owners constituted a class of rich peasants or leading villagers; to an Elite Roman, the rustic slave-owner would have cut a rather humble figure, but to his neighbors in the village, he was, like our Egyptian head-man, a powerful entity – a source of help in times of need, a mediator in seasons of conflict, and always a potential source of danger or violence.

---

[264] Hist. Mon. in Aeg. 14.13–14 (Festugière: 106).
[265] P. Kellis 23 (AD 353). Bagnall 1993, 236–7. See also CT 9.10.4 (AD 390).
[266] Foxhall 2007, 74–5; Cartledge 2001 and 1985; Gallant 1991, 30–3; Jameson 1977, for higher estimates; Wood 1983, for lower.

How would we even begin to gauge the extent of these households? The census records of Egypt indicate that, in the villages, 12 percent of households included slaves, who made up almost 9 percent of the rural population.[267] No census papyri survive from the fourth century, but at least impressionistically there is no decline of slavery. There is suggestive evidence. A law of AD 368 issued to the Prefect of Illyricum warned the agents of the governor not to harass ordinary citizens, including the "*rustici.*" For instance, the government agents were not to take "the slave or perhaps the ox" of a rustic for their own use.[268] Other laws protected the tax exemption of veterans settled as farmers; they were alloted something like 20 *iugera* – a healthy family plot but by no means an elite property – and it was assumed they might own slaves.[269] In the late empire it was assumed that an indebted tenant might even own slaves.[270] In the end there is no decisive evidence, and it is perhaps more important to recognize that the patterns of stratification in rural society made slave-ownership plausible. Documentary evidence suggests the existence of an upper tier of peasant families.[271] The "peasant" households which are discovered by rural survey are probably the remains of well-to-do families who could purchase durable materials.[272] Even the well-preserved villages of the Levant, which point to a broad base of peasant prosperity, regularly show signs of limited stratification at the top of the village.[273] The peasant in the Roman empire had as much opportunity to buy and sell, and to build wealth, as the Athenian householder.

The reasons behind the use of slave labor in the Agricultural household were complex, but we could identify the interplay of three factors: the multi-phase nature of agricultural production, the advantages of permanent, closely monitored labor versus the transaction costs of hiring labor, and the imbalances of the family life cycle which created gaps between family labor and family property. Like textiles, agricultural products are the result of a multi-phase process, in which different stages may be adaptable to different forms of labor. Plowing, sowing, and harvesting must be complemented by threshing, winnowing, and grinding. Harvesting and grinding deserve particular attention, because they required such different inputs in terms of labor: harvest work was intensive and highly time-specific, whereas grinding was not. Slaves were useful in harvest work precisely because the risks and transaction costs of finding seasonal labor were so high for a family. On the

[267] See chapter 1.   [268] CT 11.11.1 (AD 368): *servum eius vel forsitan bovem.*
[269] CT 7.20.8 (AD 364). Gallant 1991, 84–6 and Garnsey 1998b, 98–9, for subsistence farm sizes.
[270] CJ 8.14.5 (AD 294) and CT 2.30.1 (AD 315).   [271] See esp. Bagnall 1992, 133–4.
[272] cf. Rathbone 2008, for the earlier period.   [273] Hirschfeld 1997.

other hand, work like milling was structurally akin to textile labor in that
it was distributable and likewise found its way into the women's quarters.

An agricultural economy on the Roman scale required an extraordinary
amount of labor in food processing. Mills powered by animal energy were
common. Romans had also learned to harness the potential of water power
in the service of food production, especially by the late empire.[274] Palladius
recommended building a watermill to save the energy of human *or* animal
labor, and clearly variety of technology was normal.[275] Milling was a task
that could be hired out to specialized firms, even in village societies; on the
other hand, a household or an estate might process its food internally.[276]
The stock of equipment on the village farm of Taësis and Kyrillous, for
instance, included a grinding mill, and it is easy to imagine their slaves
being assigned to the task of grinding.[277]

Milling is the sort of work that makes any effort to distinguish between
productive, male labor and non-productive, female labor futile.[278] Late
antique authors associated milling with women and particularly with slave-
women, an association that was both proverbial and based in reality. Libanius could imagine that women and slave-women could not leave the mill
to participate in communal festivals.[279] Basil of Caesarea casually spoke of
a slave-girl working in the mill.[280] A third-century document recorded the
joint sale of a female slave, a mill, and all the instruments pertaining to the
mill.[281] In the sixth century, Cosmas Indicopleustes interpreted the passage
in the *Gospel of Matthew* that speaks of "two in the mill" by glossing, "and
when he says two slaves in the mill . . ."[282] The scripture says nothing of
slaves.

Work in the mill could be considered punishment, even for slaves. A
male slave might be relegated to the mill for not working hard or for
being suspected of theft.[283] The mill was listed alongside the fetter and
lash as a corrective instrument.[284] Procopius of Gaza claimed it was *the*
punishment for slave-women.[285] The distribution of labor was used as a
disciplinary mechanism. Augustine sheds further light on what made the
mill an especially degrading punishment. In North Africa, when rebellious

[274] Wilson 2002, 10–12. For the eastern empire, Wilson 2001a.
[275] Pall. Op. ag. 1.41 (Martin: 52).   [276] Bagnall 1996, 42.
[277] Indeed, household grinding mills were discovered during excavations at Karanis. A photograph of
  one *in situ* is available online at www.umich.edu/~kelseydb/Exhibits/Food/text/farm.html#grain.
[278] For an earlier period, Amouretti 1986, 213.   [279] Lib. Or. 53.19 (Foerster vol. 4: 64–5).
[280] Bas. Ep. 204.4 (Courtonne: 176).   [281] CPR 6.73 (AD 222–235).
[282] Cosm. Ind. Top. 5.241 (SC 141: 351–3): εἶτα καὶ τοὺς ἐν τῷ μύλῳ τοὺς δούλους λέγει . . .
[283] Lib. Or. 25.13 (Foerster vol. 2: 543); Lib. Decl. 1.147 (Foerster vol. 5: 98–9); Lib. Decl. 33.33 (Foerster
  vol. 7: 98); Aug. Spir. et litt. 33.58 (CSEL 60: 217); Bas. Hom. Mart. Iulit. 6 (PG 31: 252).
[284] Gr. Nyss. Bapt. Diff. (PG 46: 428).   [285] Procop. G. Is. (PG 87.2: 2444).

slaves declared themselves free and ripped their ownership documents, they then strapped their former masters to the mill and made them turn it "like the most contemptible animals, by the lash."[286] Is the significance of this act of revolt that masters had penalized slaves not merely by making them grind grain, but by fastening them into machines turned by animal labor and forcing them to push the wheel?

The schedule of agricultural labor could make the micro-economics of slavery particularly attractive. If one property of milling is that it was not especially time-sensitive, the busy harvest season creates a bottleneck: a family could only cultivate as much land as it was able to harvest. It has been plausibly argued that the smaller the household, the more likely that women were conscripted to "masculine" labor in the fields.[287] Household slaves who could be deployed to the fields would also, very neatly, expand the agricultural prowess of a family. Significantly, we hear that female slaves might also be deployed in masculine labor as necessary, and historically, the ability of slave status to override the constraints of gendered labor has been one of its most significant sources of efficiency.[288]

The use of slaves was compatible with the focus of households on safety over profit. Slaves ensured the availability of extra hands for the harvest. This not only saved the family from having to hire labor, but also of avoiding the transaction costs of looking for labor and the risks of not finding it. A worried letter from fourth-century Egypt illustrates the dangers of relying on free-market wage labor during harvest. The writer – perhaps a farm manager – fretted to the owner that workers had not shown up in the fields as expected. " . . . [with] Didymus to hire other slaves to work. He said to me that you do not have money. And if you want I will go there to hire workers, and I will work with them and clear the field. Write me back, but see that you do not neglect to respond to me about this. For you know, *it is the time*."[289] Interestingly, the letter informs us that slave-owners who did not urgently need their slaves' labor might capitalize on their slaves by

---

[286] Aug. Ep. 185.15 (CSEL 57: 14): *tamquam iumenta contemptibilia verbere.*

[287] Scheidel 1995–6a, 202–17.

[288] Stob. Anth. 4.28.21 (Hense and Wachsmuth vol. 5: 699): quoting Hierocles (second century). Pall. H. Laus. 23.5 (Butler vol. 2: 76). In the New World, Wright 2006, 111; Toman 2005.

[289] P. Lips. 111 (fourth century). The text is damaged but this is the sense of the passage: Διδύμῳ ὅτι δούλους μισθώ[ση/ἄλλους, ἵνα ἐ[ρ]γάσωσιν. εἶπέν μοι ὅτι ἀργύρια οὐκ ἔχε[ις,]/καὶ εἰ θέλεις με ἀπελθεῖν ἐκεῖ καὶ μισθῶσαι ἐργατας,/καὶ σὺν αὐτοῖς ἐργάσομαι καὶ καθαρίσομεν τὸ γεώργι[ο]ν./Ἀντίγραφόν μοι, ἀλλ' ὅρα μὴ ἀμελήσῃς ἀντιγραψαι μοι/περὶ τούτου. Οἶδας γάρ, ὅτι καιρός ἐστιν. It might make more sense if Didymus did not have the money (ὅτι ἀργύρια οὐκ ἔχει) rather than the landowner (ἔχεις), but either of these reconstructions is conceivable. Wilcken and Mitteis (M. Chr.) suggests an alternate reading, δὸς τοὺς μισθοὺς ἄλλους for δούλους μισθώ[ση ἄλλους but the latter is more sensible. The latter is also accepted by Das Papyrus-Projekt Halle-Jena-Leipzig.

renting them out to land-owners during the harvest season. Slave-renting may have been common.[290]

The essence of the Agricultural family is that it is a unit of both property and labor. Ultimately, sons and slaves were, as labor inputs, interchangeable. John Moschus repeated a vignette of rural life in late antique Palestine which illustrates this dynamic. There was a populous village. The people of the village kept large herds. "Every day at dawn they would gather at the gate of the village, and each would send off his own beasts with either his son or his slave. And the young ones would take the animals and some food and go out for the day until sunset, then return with the herds."[291] In this village animal husbandry was a supplementary pursuit, handed off to slaves and sons, but it could certainly have played a significant role in the household economy. In Agricultural households, slaves were flexible labor substitutes for the family.

An important structural limitation on the family as an economic unit is that it offers an inelastic supply of labor. If the family's proprietary resources exceeded its disposable labor, it would have been unable to exploit its property fully. The biological and proprietary rhythms of the family were often not in sync, and it is important to appreciate the constant dynamism of family formation and re-formation in a high-fertility, high-mortality society.[292] In the Roman empire, the slave trade was entwined with these perpetual demographic cycles, allowing the free family to respond as it experienced the unpredictable carousel of mortality. When the free element of the family was insufficient to meet the labor requirements of the family's property, slaves were one solution. "Those who are masters in this world obtain various services from their slaves. They send some slaves into the fields, to work the land and to protect the patrimony. They place other slaves, or the children of the slaves, if they are seen to be suitable and attractive, in the service of their households."[293] This is a revealing passage: slaves were used for *various* services, in order to *protect* the patrimony. It

---

[290] Salv. Gub. 6.18 (MGH AA 1: 83–4).

[291] Ioh. Mosch. Prat. 8* (Nissen: 361): καθ' ἑκάστην ἡμέραν ἕωθεν συνήθροιζον τὰ κτήνη πρὸς τὴν πύλην τῆς κώμης, καὶ ἕκαστος ἀπέστελλεν μετὰ τῶν ἰδίων ἀλόγων ὁ μὲν τὸν υἱόν, ὁ δὲ τὸν παῖδα αὐτοῦ. καὶ παραλαβόντες τὰ κτήνη οἱ παῖδες καὶ τὸν ἐπισιτισμὸν ἑαυτῶν ἐπορεύοντο καὶ διετέλουν ἐν τῷ ἀγρῷ ἕως ὀψίας, δύνοντος δὲ τοῦ ἡλίου συνεκόμιζον αὐτά. cf. Laes 2008, 247.

[292] Horden and Purcell 2000, 264; Gallant 1991, 60–112.

[293] Ps.-Ath. Vit. Syncl. 77 lines 760–4 (Abelarga: 242): οἱ κατὰ τὸν κόσμον δεσπόται διαφόρους οἰκετῶν ὑπηρεσίας κέκτηνται, καὶ τοὺς μὲν ἐν τοῖς χωρίοις ἐκπέμπουσι πρὸς τὸ τὰς γαίας ἐργάζεσθαι καὶ τὴν τοῦ γένους διαδοχὴν φυλάττειν, τοὺς δὲ ἐξ αὐτῶν γεννωμένους, ἐὰν ἐπιεικεῖς καὶ περικαλλεῖς θεάσωνται, ἐν τοῖς οἰκείοις οἴκοις μεθιστῶσι πρὸς τὴν ἑαυτῶν ὑπηρεσίαν.

unveils the form and function of household economic behavior. Slaves were a key ingredient in patrimonial strategy, the small-scale striving to keep the family's property profitable and to expand its ability to exploit land.

The potential energy of slaves, in textiles, milling, or as hired-out laborers, was highly fluid and helped to spread labor and diversify household output. This is why so many slaves are found in para-agricultural activities like fertilizing. Augustine and Asterius of Amasea both regarded fertilizing as "servile."[294] It might be an unattractive job, but fertilizing was the sort of activity a household could delegate to its slaves and thereby improve the fertility of land around the house. Slave labor was eminently flexible, and preaching on a scriptural parable (Luke 17:7–8) in which a slave is forced to work excessively, Peter Chrysologus could say, "How familiar! How this hits home! How relevant to everyday life, how common this teaching is! . . . for a slave, after waking before dawn, after a whole day of various and heavy labors, after a fearful and anxious inspection, in addition prepares his master's dinner . . ."[295]

By freeing the master's time, the slave's contribution to the economy was not always a net gain. There was a revealing joke in late antiquity that poked fun at a braggart. One day the man encountered his slave in the public square and asked, pompously, "How are my sheep doing?" The slave answered with too much information: "They're both fine. One is standing up, the other one is sleeping."[296] Behind the humor there is a certain truth. Some slaves, even slaves working in the field, must not have added to total agricultural production so much as enabled their masters to be the sort of busybody imagined in the joke. In a household, the slave's labor was not valued just in terms of bushels produced, but also by how much the master valued participating in public affairs, or simply loitering amidst the bustle of an ancient city. But we should not lose sight of that quiet majority of families in which labor was an all-consuming imperative. Theodoret observed that "many masters work no less than their slaves."[297] These working families, intent on maintaining their narrow supremacy over their fellow rustics, were a vital part of the slave system.

---

[294] Aug. Psalm. 80.10 (CC 39: 1125); Ast. Am. 3.13 (Datema: 36).

[295] Petr. Chrys. Serm. 161.3 (CC 24B: 996): *quam familiaris, quam vernacula, quam de cottidiano usu veniens, quam communis est ista doctrina! . . . Servus namque post vigilias antelucanas, post totius diei varios et duros labores, post trepidantes et anxios concursus, et parat domino suo cenam.* cf. Ambr. Luc. 8.31 (CC 14: 309).

[296] Philogel. 108 (Thierfelder: 68): Τί ποιοῦσι τὰ πρόβατα; ὁ δὲ εἶπε. Τὸ μὲν καθεύδει, τὸ δὲ ἵσταται. cf. Philogel. 47 (Thierfelder: 46).

[297] Thdt. Provid. 7.681A (PG 83: 681): πολλοὶ τῶν δεσποτῶν οὐκ ἔλαττον πονοῦσι τῶν οἰκετῶν.

CONCLUSION: SLAVERY, HOUSEHOLDS, AND
THE ROMAN ECONOMY

Labor is not an abstract sum of work performed in an economy. Its form
and function are inextricable from the way that a society is organized, and
in particular the way that a society organizes the only material imperative
which is as important as subsistence: reproduction. The family was the basic
unit of reproduction in ancient society, and equally the basic unit of labor
and property-ownership. Slavery was deeply embedded in the construction
of families and households. Indeed, there was a profound, psychological
recognition of this fact among the Romans, whose very conception of the
"family" did not center on the affective nuclear unit, but on a constellation
of relationships – biological, proprietary, residential – in which slavery was
truly a constant element.[298]

The attention that this model gives to the household as a unit redresses
the broad neglect of female slave labor.[299] There were millions of female
slaves in late Roman society. By focusing on the exchange of goods as a way
to measure the productive output of a society, the domestic and reproductive work of the household is excluded from the entire game of valuation.
The role of the household in enabling "productive" work is impossible
to measure relative to exchange value; the actual, social value of goods
like biological maintenance, child-rearing, food preparation, and so on,
remains unmeasured. The contribution of female slaves in food preparation, domestic upkeep, nursing, milling, and textile work was significant.
In particular, it requires no elaborate justification to say that the work of
female slaves in the textile industry was productive, by any definition of
the term. Textiles were the second most important sector of the economy.
The 50 million inhabitants of the late Roman empire required immense
quantities of textile labor, and household slavery was deeply implicated in
the economy of textile production.

The family is the most permanent, and among the most variable, of all
human institutions. Household slavery has been a persistent phenomenon
across Mediterranean history. But the patterns of production and consumption which prevailed in late antiquity were not the state of nature in
the Mediterranean. The late antique family was an extraordinary organism
because the Roman economy created an extraordinary environment. The
economy conditioned the way that reproduction, property, and labor were
interrelated. Under the empire, households had the capital to consume

---

[298] Harper forthcoming a; Shaw 1987a.   [299] Saller 2003, 185–6.

slaves on a scale that has no parallel in pre-modern Mediterranean history. Likewise, household slavery was integrated into small-scale systems of production, in particular textile work and family farming, which show how the primary unit of social life in the Roman world was shaped by the enormous power of the slave trade.

CHAPTER 4

Agricultural slavery: exchange, institutions, estates

THE PROBLEM OF ROMAN AGRICULTURAL SLAVERY

In a sermon on the *Gospel of Matthew*, John Chrysostom asked his audience to imagine a man who wished to become wealthy. The path to riches lay in farming the land and plying the sea. The priest simply assumed that lucrative, commercial agriculture entailed "buying fields and slaves."[1] In another sermon, Chrysostom thundered against the greed of his flock, whose members were endlessly scheming "how to buy land, how to buy slaves, and how to make money."[2] These sermons are part of a broad body of evidence that testifies to the importance of agricultural slavery in the late empire. Chrysostom's contemporaries, too, frequently noticed the prevalence of slavery in agricultural production. The imperial constitutions preserved in the *Theodosian Code* repeatedly confirm the existence of rural slaves, not only in theoretical terms, but in actual land transactions. The papyri of fourth-century Egypt document the presence of slaves on rural estates. The inscriptions of late antiquity provide incomparable testimony for large, slave-based properties, not least in the form of the remarkable stones uncovered on Thera. The evidence for agricultural slavery in the fourth century is abundant and credible – arguably as rich as for any period of classical antiquity.

Where do the slaves of Chrysostom's sermons, then, the rural slaves of the laws, papyri, and inscriptions, fit into our understanding of the late empire? Is there a narrative which explains their existence in structural terms, and not as an anachronistic holdover from an earlier epoch of slavery, or a phenomenon marginal to the main currents of the late Roman economy?[3] The history of agricultural slavery in the late republic and high

---

[1] Ioh. Chrys. In Mt. 24.11 (PG 57: 319): καὶ ἀγροὺς ὠνεῖσθαι καὶ ἀνδράποδα...

[2] Ioh. Chrys. In act. Apost. 32.2 (PG 60: 237): ὅπως μὲν ἀγρὸν ὠνησώμεθα, καὶ ὅπως ἀνδράποδα, καὶ ὅπως πλείω τὴν οὐσίαν ποιήσωμεν...

[3] Jones 1964, 794: "a survival from earlier times." Wickham 2005a, 262: "the basic economic shift from the slave to the feudal mode had already taken place well before 400." cf. Giardina 2007; Vera 1995.

empire conjures images of chained captives, condemned to a life sentence of hard labor on Italian villas. This was the age of the great slave revolts, the period spanned by Cato, Varro, and Columella. The story of agriculture in the middle ages, by contrast, evokes images of a countryside populated with serfs, an underclass of dependent peasants, legally free but bound to the land and weighed down with obligations to their lords. Stated in these terms, it is obvious why late antiquity has made an appealing backdrop for the transition from one period to the other. Late Roman labor relations have been a sort of missing link, an intermediary phase of evolution between two other, fully developed species of rural exploitation.[4]

This chapter aims to describe and explain the incidence of estate-based agricultural slavery in the long fourth century. Most historians who have spent time with the sources of the late empire have concluded that the evidence for slavery is compelling, so, although much of the testimony is gathered below, the emphasis has not been placed on simply cataloguing the evidence.[5] There is, remarkably enough, significant new evidence for late Roman slavery, and some of the old evidence, hiding in plain sight, has been too little noticed, but ultimately we will never have the data to judge precisely how much slave labor was used in the Roman countryside. Rather, what is most urgently needed is an attempt to explain the dynamics of slave labor in the late Roman economy. The greatest opportunities lie in the possibility of improving the framework within which we analyze the long-term dynamics of slavery in the Roman economy. In particular the debates over late Roman slavery have been hampered by the lingering influence, often implicit, of nineteenth-century models originating with Marx and Weber. Replacing the paradigm of the "transition narrative," which situates late Roman slavery on a continuum between ancient slavery and medieval serfdom, is imperative. This chapter proceeds by trying to uproot some of the misconceptions embedded in the transition narrative before offering an alternative model and then exploring the evidence.

FROM SLAVERY TO SERFDOM? PROBLEMS WITH THE TRANSITION MODEL OF LABOR

In his monumental history of the early medieval economy, Wickham observed that, despite its flaws, the story of a transition "from slavery

---

[4] Shaw 1998, 32.
[5] Vera 2007, 491, and 1986a, 407; Wickham 2005a, 262; Giliberti 1999, 52; MacMullen 1987, 377; Whittaker 1987.

to serfdom" remains an underlying metanarrative of late Roman social history.[6] The transition model, in fact, has proven irresistible, or at least irrepressible.[7] For Marxists, the inherent antagonisms of slave labor led to its transformation into medieval feudalism; in the Weberian tradition, the political capitalism of which slavery was a decisive part carried from its beginnings an expiry date: when conquest ended, the supply diminished, slave families were encouraged, and slaves became like serfs. These two traditions, in various permutations, have dominated the discussion of late Roman slavery for more than a century. They both operate on the premise that the labor system itself was evolving, progressively and uniformly, from one type of exploitation to another. Because the evolutionary paradigm has been so influential for so long, it may be useful to identify some of the specific habits of thought which it has nurtured. These assumptions account for the persistence of the transition paradigm even in the face of ambiguous or countervailing evidence. We can recognize four premises embedded in the narrative logic of transition "from" one labor system "to" another:[8]

(1) The idea of a transition from slavery to serfdom tends to assume that the scale of exploitation was static; the mechanics of oppression changed, not the quantity. This pattern of transformation obscures what was one of the most dynamic variables in the creation of the slave system: demand for estate-based labor. As we will see, it was the collapse of demand for commodities and therefore for controllable labor that was the driver of change after the fall of the Roman empire. By the late sixth century, there was simply less demand for estate labor. Wickham suggests that we should see the early medieval countryside in terms of a "peasant mode of production" where there was little extraction of surplus.[9] His framework greatly improves on narratives which claim that Roman slavery persisted deep into the early middle ages or which see medieval serfdom as a direct continuation or outgrowth of late Roman structures of power.[10] As the archaeology of trade and settlement shows, there was an important interlude of several centuries between phases of economic intensification. Literary evidence can be beguiling, but the hard evidence of stones and sherds challenges any narrative that posits a constant level of production or exploitation.

[6] Wickham 2005a, 259.
[7] Giliberti 1999, 8 (critically), on the "indubbia eleganza" of the scheme. De Martino 1993b, 789.
[8] Harper forthcoming c.   [9] Wickham 2005a, 261, 539; Henning 2008.
[10] For continuity, Hammer 2002; Grieser 1997; Pelteret 1995; Bonnassie 1991; in a qualified sense Banaji 2009.

(2) The paradigm of transition implies a uniform logic of exploitation in a given period or place. This habit of thought has been prominent among Marxists attempting to classify historical phases according to a mode of production. Often, this categorization is softened with the word "dominant."[11] This qualifier tries to close the gap between evidence for diversity and a view of society that ties the base to the superstructure. The dominant mode of production, if not quantitatively preponderant, determines the social structure. This style of thought is not confined to the Marxist tradition. It is often present in attempts to define "the" nature of Roman estate management: did tenancy prevail or direct management, were land-owners risk averse or profit-maximizing?[12] The evidence shows that Roman agriculture was inherently diverse, so that tenancy, slavery, wage labor, and peasants coexisted in the same countryside in response to the complex economies of agricultural production.[13] The tendency to think that a single logic of economic organization existed in a given space at a particular moment is exacerbated by the paucity of evidence. Often the discussion will congeal around a single striking testimony – Cato, Columella, Settefinestre – as though it were representative of an entire landscape or epoch. The challenge is to reconstruct a dynamic countryside where land-owners made an array of choices about production in response to the complex forces of supply and demand, risk and profit. Diversity was structural, not transitional.

(3) As a corollary of the tendency to describe pre-industrial agriculture in terms of a uniform logic, the transition model implies a single direction of change over time. Some accounts of the late Roman economy, even while recognizing that outcomes in the labor market were diverse, look for the combination of factors working in the same direction that led to the demise of ancient slavery. The desire to transcend monocausal explanation is laudable, but there is no guarantee that the relevant causal parameters were moving in the same direction. Not only was the labor system inherently diverse, it changed in fits, starts, and reversals. There is no reason to imagine that "decline" was a long, linear process. The amount of slave labor might rise and fall and rise again in response to local conditions, and one could even argue that slavery in the long fourth century might be considered an "epicycle" of Roman slavery.

[11] Vera 2007, 490. Or even a "dominant exception": Wickham 1984, 188. Carandini 1988, 318; Vera 1998, 308.
[12] See the judicious remarks of Carrié 2005, 298.
[13] Rightly, Hickey 2007; Banaji 2001, 200–2; Garnsey 1999b, 108.

The end of Roman slavery was not a foregone conclusion even as late as AD 400. We need a holistic model that can consider the range of forces acting simultaneously to promote and hinder the incidence of rural slavery.

(4) The transition paradigm, and here the legacy of the nineteenth century is most apparent, can lead to a search for intermediate stages of evolution, the "missing links" of labor history, in Shaw's apt phrase.[14] The late Roman slave system is supposed to differ from the early, authentic form of ancient slavery in such a way that made it closer to medieval serfdom. The existence of slave families is thought to characterize a new economy of servile labor in which slaves were allotted parcels of land and allowed to control their own productive units; in short they became "like *coloni*" and were assimilated with tenants to form a single class of dependent serfs.[15] This narrative has more to do with pre-fabricated models than the ancient evidence. It presupposes a form of all-male plantation slavery in the early period that is largely mythical. It refuses to admit, despite all the comparative evidence, that family life and slave labor are compatible. Most problematically, it has no basis in the fourth-century evidence, where "*servi quasi coloni*" are virtually unattested.[16] Sources which are ambiguous about the organization of labor, like Symmachus, the *Life of Melania the Younger*, and Palladius, have been read through a strong prism to make them evidence for the absence of plantation labor, and the model asks us to ignore too much evidence, both archaeological and literary, for elite control over the productive process in the late Roman countryside.[17] The labor system of the long fourth century was not in the throes of becoming the early medieval labor system.

Marx and Weber have cast a long shadow over the history of late Roman slavery. It is no slight against their contribution to say that the time has come to discard the seductive idea of a transition from Ancient Slavery to Medieval Feudalism. Having identified some of the lingering patterns of thought embedded in the narrative pattern of transition, let us now try to construct a new model of late Roman slavery.

---

[14] Shaw 1998, 32.

[15] Giardina 2007, 753: "'equalization.'" Whittaker and Grabar 1999, 698: "partial assimilation." Vera 1998, 320; Koptev 1995, 129; De Martino 1988b, 75: "assimilazione." Alföldy 1986, 203: "levelling." Wiedemann 1981, 40; Brockmeyer 1979, 50, 55, 225; Jones 1964, 795.

[16] Whittaker and Garnsey 1998, 295, "surprisingly little explicit mention." A textual search of the *Theodosian Code* reveals no occurences. cf. De Martino 1988b; Duncan-Jones, 1986, 297; Veyne 1981. Giliberti 1981, on the legal evidence of the earlier period.

[17] Banaji 2009, 68, notes the peculiar reading of the late Roman sources.

Table 4.1 *Finley's model of ancient slavery*

Privatization of property
Production and exchange of commodities
Unavailability of alternative labor source

EXCHANGE, INSTITUTIONS, ESTATES: THE LONG-TERM DYNAMICS OF SLAVE LABOR

It is important to ask not only why slavery declined, but more generally what forces promoted the use of slave labor. In his sweeping analysis of ancient slave systems, Finley offered a valuable model that sought to explain why large-scale rural slavery emerged in the classical world. He emphasized three factors (table 4.1).[18]

Finley's model, expressed most clearly in chapter 2 of his *Ancient Slavery and Modern Ideology*, was written against simplistic versions of the conquest thesis. His model, in other words, was articulated at a specific historiographical moment, and it presupposes an adequate supply of slaves. Finley was trying to illuminate the role of demand in the creation of the slave system. Demand for slaves required not only private ownership of property and the circulation of commodities – the products of slave labor – but the "unavailability" of an alternative source. Finley ascribed this unavailability to the dynamics of status. The abolition of debt bondage in late archaic Greece and republican Rome constrained the ability of landowners to exploit citizens, driving a wedge between freedom and slavery, free labor and slave labor. Stated differently, the institutional conditions of the Roman labor system re-directed demand away from free citizens and towards enslaved outsiders. This argument amounts to a critique of the Nieboer hypothesis in which a high land/labor ratio is the prime mover of slavery. In antiquity, the shortage of labor was not an effect of geographic expansion; it was politically created. Finley's model represented a breakthrough by posing the question of slavery's long-term development in dynamic terms, considering supply, demand, and institutions as parts of a single model.

In a more recent contribution, Scheidel has offered a characteristically illuminating model that modifies and extends Finley's insights.[19] His version identifies two decisive parameters and then considers their underlying dynamics (table 4.2).

---

[18] Finley 1998 (orig. 1980), 135–60. See Shaw 1998, 26–7.   [19] Scheidel 2008.

Table 4.2 *Scheidel's model of ancient slavery*

Demand for goods and services High real wages among free laborers	→ **SHORTAGE OF LABOR**
Accumulation of capital Physical access to enslavable persons	→ **ACCESS TO SLAVES**

The model is elegantly simple and analytically powerful. It is organized around the fundamentals of supply and demand. One of its prime
virtues is that it can explain the incidence of slavery under highly different
conditions. Scheidel argues that slave labor emerged in classical Athens
because it was cheap while wages were high and that similar conditions
perhaps existed in the late Roman republic. In the empire, by contrast,
slaves were dear but their labor was profitable, so that slavery persisted in
a high-equilibrium state. Indeed his model is a corrective against one of
the most persistent illusions about slave labor: that slaves are necessarily
cheap labor.[20] What matters is the ability to employ slave labor at a profit –
the marginal value of labor against the costs of a slave, which are often
high.[21]

The emphasis on supply is necessary and even obvious; no critique of the
conquest thesis should deny that the supply side was always an economic
constraint, as important as the demand side. But the dynamics of demand
are, analytically, more interesting and more challenging. Scheidel's model
begins by proposing that slave labor and free labor are in more or less direct
competition.[22] Land-owners used slave labor not just because free labor
was institutionally unavailable, as per Finley, but because it was expensive.
It was expensive because it was in short supply. It was in short supply due
to high levels of political/military commitment among the free population
or because of low population levels. This model explains why slave labor is
so prominent in late republican Italy (with its military mobilization) and
so exiguous in Roman Egypt (with its dense population).

Scheidel's model adds an important variable complicating the proposition that free and slave labor were in perfect competition in some sectors
of agriculture. He adopts Hanes' arguments about the role of transaction
costs in the employment of slave labor.[23] The risk of being unable to find
labor at sensitive times in the agricultural cycle, the time and effort spent

[20] cf. Wright 2006, 71. [21] cf. Morris 2002, 39, for Greece. [22] cf. Harper 2010.
[23] Wright 2006, 117–19; Hanes 1996.

contracting labor, and the turnover costs of re-training workers were all salient considerations. Slave labor was effectively an involuntary lifetime contract. Transaction costs, then, should be accounted for along with the raw market price of wage labor. Transaction costs amplified the effects of the demographic context, for "thick" labor markets like those in Egypt not only drove down wages, they reduced the risks and costs of the open labor market for land-owners. This model also explains why slave labor was adaptive to certain types of Mediterranean agriculture, such as grape and olive cultivation, that required both effort and care in the nature of the labor performed.[24] It thus represents an important advance in the application of institutional economics to ancient slavery by taking seriously the nature of the work regime and the type of labor employed.

Scheidel's account offers the most persuasive model we now have of ancient slavery, and it can be extended. In the model, demand for slaves is construed as a shortage of labor – "labour relative to exploitable resources."[25] But the components of demand were more complex, and there was no stable quantity at which labor was needed. Rather, demand for labor, especially controllable labor, fluctuated; this is especially important in late antiquity, when the fall of the empire prompted a dramatic reduction in the extent of commodity production. Moreover, the model is right to emphasize both demography and institutions, but there could be more emphasis on the latter. Long-term wage labor, for instance, is attested in the unusually "thick" labor markets of Egypt, but it is surprisingly hard to find in the west, particularly if we believe in massive population growth that should have encouraged the use of desperate free laborers.[26] Below we will attempt to extend the argument about transaction costs and insist even more strongly on the institutional dynamics of labor.

As Finley, Scheidel, and others have recognized, the persistence of slave labor presents something of a puzzle. If the demand for labor was one way or another politically created, then why did slave labor so long outlast the unique conditions of late republican Italy? After all, Columella is the most sophisticated advocate of slave labor among the agronomists, to say nothing of the abundant evidence for slave labor in the fourth century.[27] Finley allowed that rural slavery remained vigorous into the late empire. So does Scheidel, although with a rather tepid endorsement of the case for continuity ("may be largely illusionary") and with the suggestion that a

---

[24] Scheidel 2008, rightly critical of Fenoaltea 1984. On incentives, see chapter 5.
[25] Scheidel 2008, 116.
[26] Wickham 2005a, 276; Morley 1996, 127. Though cf. Dumont 1999.   [27] Roth 2007, 12.

Table 4.3 *Institutional model of Roman slavery*

Natural reproduction Internal enslavement Importation across frontiers	→ **SLAVE SUPPLY**
Demand for agricultural commodities Cost of free labor	→ **DEMAND FOR SLAVE LABOR**
Roman law of status, contract, and tenancy	→ **LEGAL MATRIX OF LABOR MARKET**
Estate management in intensive Mediterranean polyculture	→ **INSTITUTIONAL DYNAMICS OF LABOR**

"bloated system" may have survived into the high empire because of path dependence and the desire for domination itself.[28] But perhaps there is an explanation which does not have to dismiss the evidence as an illusion, nor to assume that late Roman slavery was based on an irrational lust for power as such.

In this new model, supply and demand remain fundamental, but legal institutions and the dynamics of estate management play a complementary role. Demand for slave labor, moreover, can be seen as a function not only of politically created shortages of free labor but also of demand for commodities. This model emphasizes the core determinants of supply and demand while preserving the insight of Finley that legal status mattered and the argument of Scheidel that slave labor had specific properties making it valuable in Mediterranean agriculture (table 4.3).

The incidence of slavery in the late empire should be considered in light of these four determinants: supply, demand, formal institutions, and the dynamics of estate management.

Chapter 2 has already made the case that the slave supply in late antiquity was stable and robust. Long-term changes in the slave system are probably not to be sought in the slave supply.[29] The demand for slave labor, on the other hand, was an especially important variable. Demand for rural labor on elite-owned estates was a function of demand for agricultural commodities. In Atlantic slave systems, the association between slavery and the production of cash crops is obvious.[30] In the case of Rome, slavery was

---

[28] Scheidel 2008, 126.
[29] Scheidel 2005a, 79: "arguments about supply have no place in discussions of the imperial slave system prior to the fifth century A.D."
[30] Fogel 1989. Wright 2006, 29, on the variety of crops.

closely associated with the production of staples for the market, especially wine, the first of the truly mass-market cash crops in human history.[31] It is not a flattering comment on humanity that the most intense forms of economic exploitation have been fed by consumer demand for psychotropic products. Urbanism and wine consumption expanded dramatically under Roman rule, and the late Roman empire remained home to a world-wide wine emporium notable for its volume and diversity.[32] Nor can we neglect the mass markets in olive oil, textiles, and even industrial goods whose production we find in the fourth-century countryside. Roman slavery is historically exceptional for being among the few pre-modern slave systems with strong links to exchange-oriented agricultural production. The great urban centers of the late empire, and the hundreds of substantial if second-tier cities, provided real, stable market demand for foodstuffs. The fourth century was, as its more outspoken spiritual advisers regularly noted, a world where control over land and labor could be turned into profit.[33]

If historians of the late republic and early empire are able to take for granted high, sustained levels of production beyond subsistence, the student of late antiquity will be more prepared to recognize long-term secular change in the overall output of the Mediterranean economy, with a massive decline in production and commodity exchange from the fifth century in the west and somewhat later in the east. Demand for labor is the primordial variable in the slave system and, at least over the long fourth century, demand remained strong. Demand for labor, though, did not automatically translate into demand for slave labor. Thus it is necessary to consider how land-owners chose what type of labor to employ. Cost was one consideration, but not the only one. Their decisions were constrained by the institutional environment created by Roman law and then shaped by the dynamics of estate management. In other words, Roman law and Mediterranean agriculture mediated between the raw demand for labor and the choice to use slave labor.

Roman law was an important influence in shaping the labor market of the fourth century – but not necessarily in the ways which are often supposed. The historiography has focused almost exclusively on the rise of the colonate. In the late empire the Roman government tried to levy a head tax (*capitatio*) on the rural population. The colonate is the name for the resulting fiscal system in which rural laborers (*coloni*) were tied

[31] In general Tchernia 1986.
[32] Morley 2007a; Tchernia 1986; Purcell 1985. Jongman 1988, 132–3, lower consumption estimates. Late antique wine: Pieri 2005; Kingsley 2002, 60.
[33] E.g. Ioh. Chrys. In act. Apost. 32.2 (PG 60: 237); Bas. Dest. horr. 5 (Courtonne: 25–6).

to their *origo*, their place of tax registration, in order to discharge their fiscal obligations.[34] Eventually, workers with no land of their own could be registered on the property of their land-owner, thereby limiting their mobility and possibly intensifying their dependence. Ominous language – rhetorical but disconcerting – spoke of *coloni* as "slaves of the land."[35] There is no need here for yet another extended discussion of the late Roman colonate, an institution which has received more than its share of attention, often at the expense of understanding how slave labor worked in the rural economy of the late empire.[36] Suffice it to say that Carrié's initial critique forever undermined the idea that the colonate was a "replacement" of the slave system or that it created an intermediate serf-like status between slavery and freedom. And because the enactments pertaining to *coloni* were truly fiscal in motivation, they are at best a highly distorted mirror of rural relations.

The real question is whether the fiscal rules of the late Roman state distorted the dynamics of the labor market.[37] Did the colonate, in other words, alter the way that landlords contracted tenant labor or modify the sort of control which landlords could obtain over free, tied workers – in a way that altered the value and competitiveness of slave labor? The immobility of rural laborers could have benefited land-owners, but only a few laws concerned the personal status of *coloni* relative to their land-owners. These laws gave land-owners the power of distraint over the property of the *colonus*, even as they afforded legal remedies against the abuse of the landlord's power.[38] More importantly, not all *coloni* were tenants, and as a fiscal category the label *coloni* indicates nothing about the organization of labor.[39] Many *coloni*, especially in the west, were tenants, who already lived in long-term customary relationships with their landlords. The colonate may have had little material effect on social relations or land-use strategies in this sector, particularly so long as the imperial government legislated against raising rents and provided remedy against abuse. On the other hand, if the colonate made it possible for land-owners to exert greater influence over the labor of permanent, estate-based workers, then it may have distorted the market for the sort of controllable labor offered by slavery. This, it

---

[34] Grey 2007a.

[35] CJ 11.52.1 (AD 393). Grey 2007a, on the use of slavery as an imperfect template for the obligations of *coloni*.

[36] Sirks 2008; Grey 2007a; Scheidel 2000; Lo Cascio 1997; Carrié 1983 and 1982; Eibach 1980.

[37] Esp. Kehoe 2007. Many elements of the colonate (mobility restriction, fiscal patronage) were long-standing. See Sel. Pap. 2.215 (AD 215) for the former, Rathbone 1991 for the latter.

[38] CJ 11.50.2 (AD 396).

[39] Sarris 2006, 128–9; Banaji 2001, 209–11. CJ 11.48.19 (Anastasius) is a crucial text.

seems, is what progressively occurred, from the fifth century, in the Roman east.

Only recently has it been appreciated that the colonate had fundamentally different effects in the east and the west.[40] In the east, in the fifth and sixth centuries, the fiscal rules of the colonate were enacted in the context of a strong state, a vibrant rural economy, and a labor market with a long tradition of year-round wage labor. In the west, the colonate developed in the context of a weakening state, a rural economy that was becoming ever more primitive, and a labor market without a tradition of wage labor. Hence, in the west, the constrictions on movement may have had only limited effects and mainly in the arena of long-term, low-risk, extensive land-use based on rent collection. In the east, the fiscal rules restricting the mobility of workers took effect in an economy where estate labor was in high demand, and where the pre-existence of free estate workers meant that the new institutional conditions may have created a viable and rather direct alternative to slave labor: *coloni adscripticii*, low-status free workers tied to estates. *Adscripticii* become detectable in the papyri of the fifth century and prominent in the documents of the sixth century.[41] By the time of the Justinianic codification, there was a coherent account of the legal position of the *adscripticius*.[42] There remained differences between *adscripticii* and slaves. But the crux of the matter is that in the east, the rules of the colonate may have distorted the labor market precisely at the point where demand for controllable labor made slavery so valuable to estate managers.

In comparative terms, the manipulation of landlessness and debt by land-owners are common means of acquiring and controlling agricultural labor.[43] In the absence of third-party governance, asymmetries of social power tend to override contractual norms between landlord and tenant. The Roman period, up to and including the fourth century, was exceptional as a phase of pre-modern history with a strong state, a sophisticated legal framework, and an active judicial apparatus.[44] It was not only the politicized peasantry of republican Italy which enjoyed protection from naked social coercion. Far from shamelessly augmenting the power of land-owners, the fourth-century government was earnestly concerned with limiting the forms of coercion in the countryside.[45] This claim stands in

---

[40] Sarris 2006; Banaji 2001 and 1997.   [41] Fikhman 2006, 190–250; Eibach 1980, 132–93.

[42] See Grey 2007a, for the fourth and fifth centuries, Sirks 2008 for the Justinianic period. De Martino 1993b, 798.

[43] Bush 1996; Banaji 1977.   [44] In general, Honoré 2004 and 1998; Harries 1999. See part III.

[45] E.g. CT 2.30.1 (AD 315); CJ 11.50.2.4 (AD 396); CT 1.29.5 (AD 370). Kehoe 2007, 19–20; Frakes 2001. Private land-owners also had to compete with the appealing and fair terms offered by the state as land-owner. Kehoe 2007, 77–8.

almost diametric opposition to the once pervasive assumption that the late empire was a period when an oppressive Roman state increasingly sanctioned or ignored forms of private coercion.[46] To understand the difference between the late Roman and early medieval countryside, it is imperative to weigh in the balance the entire institutional momentum of Roman law rather than a selection of laws pertaining to the fiscal status of rural laborers. On the whole, the Roman state limited the exercise of raw power in private relationships, and the transition to the medieval period should be described as a phase during which public institutions themselves decreased in relevance.[47] There was no serfdom in the Roman empire, and landowners looking to find labor could not take it by brute force from free workers.

Roman law thus created an environment in which land-owners could choose from three categories of labor: slavery, tenancy, and wage labor.[48] To a certain extent these types of labor were interchangeable, and therefore direct cost was a major influence on a land-owner's decisions. Wages, rents, and the price of slaves were interdependent.[49] But the specific properties of slavery, tenancy, and wage labor meant that they were imperfect substitutes. They differed in ways that were significant in the context of Mediterranean estate management. Slavery brought to the owner a set of property rights over a human being.[50] Tenancy encompassed a variety of relationships.[51] The nature of the contract and the form of the rent payment were essential variables within the practice of land leasing, but whether we imagine sharecropping, short-term leases, or long-term relationships, tenancy implies

[46] Still held by Finley 1998 (orig. 1980), 209–11.   [47] Whittaker 1987.

[48] It may be objected that this is too simplistic, and I would admit these are ideal types which help us observe and analyze the dynamics of labor competition. The scheme is vulnerable to claims that Roman rural relationships were socially embedded (Andreau and Maucourant 1999; Garnsey and Woolf 1989; the contributions in Garnsey 1988a). I would make several mitigating points. (1) We know of *no* dependant-run estates in the west, whereas slavery is assumed to be the means of running a large intensive farm. (2) The fourth-century countryside was highly Romanized, and with all of the evidence I find it hard to believe that archaic social forms persisted beneath our field of vision. (3) If you were a poor, desperate worker who wanted to become a permanent employee in the Roman empire, you *sold yourself into slavery* – it was the dominant institutional form of complete dependence. (4) See chapter 10, on enslavement, for the Roman state's efforts to regulate long-term labor rentals. (5) Roman land-owners may have been able to exploit their tenants, as is often emphasized, but were they able to build estates around such forms of abuse? (6) There was always diversity, but the fact that we hear so much about slave-based estates, so little about vague forms of social dependence being harnessed into estate labor, leads us to conclude that slavery was more important in the economics of estate management. None of this is to deny that many landlord–tenant relationships did entail various forms of social dependence.

[49] Lo Cascio 2009, 61.   [50] Wright 2006; Barzel 1997.

[51] Rowlandson 1999; Foxhall 1990. Tenancy was a form of *management* in the first place, and secondarily a form of labor. Tenants might use slaves on estates they rented: CJ 8.14.5 (AD 294); CT 2.30.1 (AD 315).

Table 4.4 *Labor and land-use decisions*

Decision 1: Control production or devolve?
   Devolve → Tenancy
   Control → Decision 2

Decision 2: Hire labor or buy laborers?
   Wages + Transaction costs > Cost of slaves → Buy slaves
   Wages + Transaction costs < Cost of slaves → Hire laborers

If Wages + Transaction costs AND Cost of slaves are both higher than rewards for   Control → Tenancy

lower levels of oversight.[52] Finally, in parts of the empire, land-owners were able to hire workers for pay. This form of labor is most apparent in Egypt, where the density of the population made wage labor possible. Seasonal harvest labor was common around the Mediterranean, but it is not clear that year-round wage labor was an option beyond Egypt and parts of the Near East.[53] This is a crucial fact, for (year-round) wage labor, where it is reliably and permanently available, shares certain properties with slavery. Long-term wage labor was adaptive to forms of estate management that entailed direct control over the productive process. Tenancy, by contrast, was a low-intensity, low-risk style of labor that reduced oversight by devolving management of the productive process to the laborer.

A land-owner in the Roman empire was thus faced with a hierarchy of interrelated decisions about land-use and labor. The competition between slavery and tenancy was based not only the cost of labor, but also on the desired level of control over the productive process. The competition between wage labor and slavery presupposes a desire to control the productive process, and in this case direct costs plus transaction costs constituted the basic grounds of competition (table 4.4).

This model has several advantages. It is built around the core determinants of supply and demand, but it recognizes the role of legal institutions and estate management. The cost of labor was a major consideration, but so too was the relation between the type of labor demanded and the specific properties of slavery, wage labor, and tenancy. This model, moreover, explains why various styles of land-use are evident within the same landscapes in the Roman world. Precisely because such a variety of forces were

---

[52] Kehoe 2007, the best account. Capogrossi Colognesi 1986; De Neeve 1984a.
[53] Wickham 2005a, 276. Scheidel 1994c, 153–233. cf. Dumont 1999. Garnsey 1999b, 102.

at play, outcomes in the labor market were complex; far from being dominated by a single mode of production, Roman countrysides were dynamic
and diverse places. Slavery, wage labor, and tenancy coexisted, at times even
on the same estate.[54] A land-owner might wish to diversify his portfolio,
using part of his land in a higher-intensity mode that entailed control over
labor while leasing other parts to reduce risk.[55] Even if Roman land-owners
did not develop a fully-fledged manorial system, divided between domanial
and dependent land, they did practice mixed forms of management that
were structurally analogous to the underlying principles of the bisectorial
estate.[56]

In this model slavery is predicted when direct control over production
is rewarding but wage labor is too expensive or too thin to form a pool
of dependable permanent labor. It is significant that large-scale estates run
by hired laborers are virtually unknown in the western provinces, where
rural settlement was dispersed, while intensively managed estates operated
with hired labor are in evidence just where we would predict: in Egypt.
From the third century onward, Egyptian elites began to construct large,
directly managed estates producing cash crops for the market.[57] The most
well-known property is of course the Appianus estate analyzed in detail
by Rathbone.[58] Here was a large estate, much of which was under direct
management. The estate's production strategies were organized around a
combination of rigorous cost controls and carefully calibrated responses to
market demand for wine. The estate's labor force was composed of short-
term (but not seasonal) hired laborers and long-term laborers known as
oiketai, some of whom may even have been slaves.[59] The densely settled Nile
corridor created thick labor markets where wage labor was affordable and
reliably available. In other parts of the empire where there were the same
incentives to control cash-crop production but wage labor was expensive
or unreliable, slavery might well have emerged.

Commercialized agriculture encourages elites to exert control over production, to invest in the countryside, and to intensify forms of land-use.
Wickham has used the systematic relationship between commercialization
and intensification (and the gradual decline of both) as one of the central framing devices for the transition from late Roman to early medieval
society.[60] Lucrative payoffs were to be found in direct management. But

[54] CT 9.42.7 (AD 369), a census formula. See pp. 165 and 174 for examples. "Mixed" estates in the
earlier period: Corbier 1981, 431. cf. Stone 2005, 12, on late medieval agriculture.
[55] Bagnall 2005, 198.   [56] Wickham 2005a, 273, offers judicious thoughts; Sarris 2004.
[57] Banaji 2001.   [58] Rathbone 1991.
[59] See p. 171 and appendix 1, but cf. Rathbone 1991, 106–16.   [60] Wickham 2005a, 265.

to appreciate why control over labor was rewarding, we must consider the specific processes entailed in intensive Mediterranean polyculture: the production of wheat, wine, oil, textiles, meat, and fruit products to be sold in urban markets.[61]

The first class of reasons could be called *technical efficiencies.* It is unclear whether, in certain types of tasks, managers can extract more efficient labor through "pain incentives." Low-skill effort-intensive labor, like mining or digging, may be more suited by its very nature to exploitative modes of labor.[62] While plowing, trenching, and other intrinsic requirements of Roman agriculture were low-skill and effort-intensive, Roman farming has never seemed to fit within a model where the technical efficiency of pain incentives was utterly decisive. Perhaps, though, other forms of technical efficiency did represent a salient factor in the economies of labor: specialization and returns to scale. If, for instance, specialized workers such as vintners could be profitably employed on farms exceeding the normal size of tenant plots, then there were advantages to organizing production in larger units. Indeed, there is considerable evidence for specialized workers on Roman estates, suggesting that one reward for control rather than devolution was the opportunity to utilize the particular skills of specialized laborers on larger farms. Slaves in specialized or managerial roles were not marginal to the labor force; these sorts of jobs were, in fact, utterly instrumental for intensive, market-oriented land-use.[63]

A second class of reasons why land-owners might benefit from control over production is even more important. These are institutional efficiencies – reasons why property rights in labor were remunerative.[64] In the Mediterranean context, three are particularly notable. The first is the relation between directly managed production and capital investment.[65] Output in intensive Mediterranean polyculture was particularly sensitive to levels of capital investment, namely pressing installations, tools, and livestock.[66] Expensive outlays for productive installations, iron tools, and animals (for draught, manure, and secondary products) were highly rewarding, yet they were difficult to combine with devolved management. Tenancy inherently discouraged capital investment, partly because tenants had little reason to invest in long-term improvements and because the principal cash

[61] cf. Morley 1996, 108–42, for intensification in Rome's hinterland.
[62] Temin 2004; Fenoaltea 1984. Scheidel 2008 and Wright 2006 are rightly critical of Fenoaltea's more sweeping claims.
[63] cf. the United States: Fogel and Engerman 1974, 40: "over 25 percent of males were managers, professionals, craftsmen, and semi-skilled workers."
[64] Wright 2006.   [65] Rathbone 2005, 264–8.   [66] For machines, Wilson 2002.

crops of the Roman empire, grapes and olives, take so long to mature.[67] Roman land-owners tried to create institutional solutions to this impasse.[68] This is hardly a sign that slavery was unviable – rather it is a sign that capital investment paid off and that land-owners had every reason to find ways to realize the potential returns from capital investments. There is always more than one way to skin a cat; the frictions between capital investment and tenancy were real but not insuperable.

A second institutional efficiency inherent in the control of labor was represented by the ability of the land-owner to mobilize labor at will. The estate operated as a firm, distributing labor by command rather than contract. It has often been emphasized that slave labor, as a form of fixed capital, may have been inefficient given the strong seasonality of Mediterranean agriculture.[69] Certainly even slave-based estates could maximize profits by hiring extra harvest labor.[70] At the same time, however, the ability to dispatch managers, shepherds, specialized workers such as craftsmen, even perhaps the *familiae urbanae*, represented a form of insurance against the risks of not being able to find labor at time-sensitive junctures in the production process.[71] More importantly, the land-owner's control over labor, especially over slave labor, could override gender norms which kept free women indoors.[72] The ability to exploit female labor maximally, often in the form of textile production, represented an advantage of slave labor.[73] In the US South, the exploitation of slave-women represented one of the principal comparative advantages of slave labor.[74] In the Roman world, with strongly gendered cultural conventions of labor and exceedingly low levels of textile technology that allowed cloth production to be organized on estates, the deployment of female slave labor was a prime element in the economy of slavery. Certainly the slave-based estate on Thera employed large numbers of female slaves.[75]

Finally, control over labor is efficient because it permits the land-owner to make decisions about allocation. The goals of a large, directly managed farm will differ from a tenant plot or a peasant farmstead. The estate can shoulder more risk than tenants or peasants, whose strategies will be organized around "safety first" rather than profit.[76] Of course, risk reduction was always a strategy of Mediterranean land-owners, and the role of "plantations," specialized in a single crop, has been exaggerated; the fourth-century estates we shall examine are exclusively polycultural.

[67] Kehoe 2007, 96. cf. Walsh 1985, for a modern comparison.   [68] Kehoe 2007, 56–62.
[69] On seasonality, Erdkamp 1999.   [70] Rathbone 1983.   [71] See pp. 172–3.
[72] Scheidel 1995–6.   [73] Roth 2007.   [74] Wright 2006, 106–11; Toman 2005.
[75] Harper 2008.   [76] Gallant 1991, 7.

Table 4.5 *Styles of land-use in the Roman empire*

Land-use	Intensive	Extensive
Labor	Controlled (Wage or slave)	Devolved (Tenancy)
Scale	Factory units	Family units
Capital investment	Higher (Installations, tools, animals)	Lower
Strategy	Profit	Safety
Product	Polyculture with cash-crop emphasis	Polyculture with cereal emphasis

The production strategies of the large and small land-owner may have differed only in degree, but this could make a significant difference in terms of profitability. Control over production, moreover, allowed the estate manager to respond year-by-year to market conditions. Larger land-owners, too, could store their product, not just as insurance against bad harvests, but in order to sell at opportune moments of scarcity and high prices – practices well attested in the late empire.[77]

This discussion is not meant to suggest that slavery was the only way of controlling labor or profiting from agriculture.[78] Rather, the goal is to recognize specifically what was entailed in intensive Mediterranean poly-culture and to see why control over labor was related to the processes of intensification. The deployment of labor was implicated in a series of decisions about land-use, capital investment, the organization of work, and crop allocations. Slavery, which by its nature allowed control over the laborer, had affinities with choices that entailed more intensive forms of agriculture. We could imagine intensive and extensive modes of land-use as two ends of a spectrum, with most land-owners falling somewhere between the two extremes (table 4.5).

This model is meant to describe the dynamics of a complex labor system, accounting for the primordial influence of supply and demand as they were refracted through the contexts of Roman law and Mediterranean estate management. It explains why slavery, tenancy, and wage labor are imperfect substitutes and posits two axes of competition beyond direct costs: transaction costs and estate management. The model allows demand for labor to derive from demand for commodities, rather than limiting its underlying causes to politically or demographically created conditions of

[77] McCormick forthcoming; Erdkamp 2002.
[78] Banaji 1992, is particularly lucid and has influenced the presentation here.

scarcity. The model predicts that slave labor would have been viable in the late empire where market conditions rewarded control over production and where wage labor was expensive or labor markets were thin. The test of the model is whether it can explain the patterns of slave employment attested in the late empire. It will be an advance if we can explain slavery as an integral part of the agrarian economy without having to dispose of the evidence by assuming that slave labor was anachronistic or marginal, the result of path dependence or a lust for domination.

SLAVE LABOR AND AGRICULTURAL ESTATES IN THE EASTERN MEDITERRANEAN

The eastern Mediterranean prospered in late antiquity.[79] The long fourth century was an expansionary phase of this cycle. How was labor, then, and specifically slave labor, implicated in this trajectory of growth? Slavery has played little role in the modern conceptualization of the eastern Mediterranean economy.[80] In a sense, this provides an opportunity to build from scratch a model of slave labor in the east. Even historians who have admitted that the evidence for late Roman slavery is abundant have allotted no constructive place for slave labor in the east, so that if we can demonstrate its significance there, we are well on our way to demanding a re-evaluation of how slavery fit into the productive systems of the later Roman empire. Moreover, the eastern context provides a laboratory for studying the effects of economic forces on the slave system, for surely no one would argue that the use of slaves in the eastern Mediterranean was driven by conquest or the mass military mobilization of the peasantry. Most importantly, the east offers documentary evidence. The most reliable quantitative evidence for slavery comes from the documents of the east.

In several ways the east was structurally different from the west. The settlement landscape in the east was everywhere dominated by villages, whereas the western countryside was characterized by a dispersed settlement pattern organized around a hierarchy of isolated habitations ranging from palatial villas to peasant farmsteads.[81] This division had profound

---

[79] The literature is cited in the Introduction.

[80] We should note that the so-called Great Estates of Egypt are documented from the late fifth century (Hickey 2007; Sarris 2006; Gascou 1985; Hardy 1931). For third-century Egypt, see Rathbone 1991. For fourth-century properties, Banaji 2001 and Bagnall 1993. The profile of estate ownership and land-use which emerges below suggests that fourth-century properties were closer to the third-century estates than the later ones, although diversity was always the norm.

[81] Wickham 2005a, 442; Chavarría and Lewit 2004, 16–17; Francovich and Hodges 2003, 32–6; Hirschfeld 1997.

repercussions for patterns of land tenure, estate management, and labor markets. Throughout the fourth century, western elites far outclassed their eastern peers in terms of wealth.[82] Of course, even the western senate hardly succeeded in carving up the entire countryside among a few great land-owners. But in the east we are presented with an ancient curial aristocracy, resident in the towns, with landed wealth that was considerable if modest by western standards. In the east we meet Elite land-owners but few Illustrious households. Many of these belonged to the revamped imperial service aristocracy; in the fourth century, the imperial state deliberately increased the senatorial order from around 600 to several thousand members, drawing on the provincial upper classes of the east.[83] This new service aristocracy was paid in gold which could then be re-invested in landed wealth.[84] These interlinking patterns of imperial service, capital investment, and commercial agriculture created men like Heliodorus, the man who started as a *garum* merchant, became a lawyer, and invested his wealth in slaves and land. After serving the emperor, he was rewarded with land and slaves in Greece and Macedonia.[85] His case demonstrates that slavery was integrated into the characteristic circuits of capital, land, and labor in the fourth century.

Documentary evidence confirms that Heliodorus was no aberration and that slavery was an integral component of agricultural production in the fourth-century east. Some of the best evidence for the deployment of rural labor in the Roman empire is preserved in a series of late antique census records.[86] Fragments of these census records, inscribed on stone, are fortuitously preserved from eleven cities, all in the Aegean islands or along the western coast of Asia Minor. They date to the fourth century, perhaps to the early 370s. They are a unique cache of evidence which offers an invaluable opportunity to test our model of agricultural slavery. The census records are an objective, random sample of data collected by the state as part of a fiscal assessment; this sort of documentary evidence is exceedingly rare outside Egypt. The inscriptions allow us to reconstruct, tentatively, the aggregate structures of land tenure and agricultural labor in an eastern countryside. These inscriptions are perhaps the only documents from antiquity that provide some quantitative data with which we can estimate the extent of slave labor in a given rural sector. Here, for once, we are not interpreting the mute data of archaeological survey, we are not

---

[82] Wickham 2005a, 162–3; Hendy 1985, 202–3; Jones 1964, 554–5.   [83] See chapter 1.
[84] Banaji 2001.
[85] Lib. Or. 62.46–8 (Foerster vol. 4: 370): quoted in chapter 1. PLRE 1: Heliodorus 3, 411.
[86] The following draws on Harper 2008.

vulnerable to the rhetorical exuberance or subjective slant of a witness, we are not forced to read normative texts as social description. We have a set of documents which reflect the status of laborers in a real ancient landscape.

Having emphasized the value of these documents, we should also recognize their limits. The inscriptions are fragmentary, and they require careful reconstruction. They are not standardized in their format or units of measure. On some of the stones, the physical totals of registered property have already been converted into fiscal units – *iuga* of land and *capita* of workers – according to a schedule which is unknown and debated.[87] In all cases, the tax liabilities are assigned to individual land-owners. The inscriptions measured the property of town dwellers, whose landed wealth was scattered across villages inside the territory of each city. The most complete register, from Magnesia on the Meander, suggests that urban residents owned on the order of 30 percent of the taxable land in the territory, a ratio which is consistent with parallel data from Egypt. The surviving fragments of the Magnesia register represent no more than about 8 percent of the original document; still, at least sixty-five different land-owners are attested in this sample, ranging from senators to very small-scale owners.[88] Five senators and six town councilors are present in the sample, evidence for the growth of the senate in the east. The largest properties at Magnesia, Thera, and Lesbos surpass 1,000 *iugera*; large estates were thus present, but this is hardly a landscape of *latifundia*. Invariably the properties are cobbled together from small plots, often spread across numerous villages; concentrated wealth was not contiguous wealth.

The documents attest the amount of registered labor – the capitation taxes for which the land-owner was responsible. A law of 371 stated that if a *colonus* owned any land of his own, he was to be inscribed on the census under his own property.[89] If, however, a *colonus* held no land, he was registered on the estate where he worked, and the land-owner was responsible for the capitation taxes. Thus, the extent of free, contract tenancy is almost invisible in the inscriptions. But not entirely invisible. The Magnesia inscription, because it records the tax liabilities owed by a large number of proprietors, gives some evidence for the patterns of registering laborers. Nearly all of the registered *capita* were associated with large properties, properties held by owners of high status, or owners from other cities

---

[87] On the *iugum*, see Harper 2008; Duncan-Jones 1990. Thonemann 2007 makes the best case for a large *iugum*.

[88] I.Magnesia no. 122, with new readings of Thonemann 2007.   [89] CT 11.1.14 (AD 371).

(and thus presumably wealthy land-owners). The numerous petty properties, mostly in the range of 10–20 *iugera*, had almost no *capita* associated
with them. This pattern would imply that registered labor was associated
with larger properties, even as smaller urban proprietors continued to lease
their land to villagers and peasants. Egypt provides parallel evidence which
confirms the continued importance of small-scale renting.[90]

The census inscriptions divide registered laborers into two categories:
slaves and *paroikoi*. It is likely that *paroikoi* were a mix of both tenants
(without land of their own) and estate employees. Unfortunately, none of
the inscriptions preserves a clear ratio of slave to free workers, and the well-
known estimates extrapolated by Jones are based on a faulty methodology.[91]
But it is possible to extract meaningful quantitative impressions about the
deployment of labor at Tralles, Thera, and Lesbos. Each sample testifies, unequivocally, to the significance of agricultural slavery, and in each
case we glimpse the outlines of different land-use and estate management
strategies.

The sample from Tralles is the smallest and also the most problematic.[92]
Jones argued that the apparent ratio of slaves to *paroikoi* was 1:5, so that
slaves were around 17 percent of the labor force. The numbers seem compromised by the inclusion of animals, and it is not clear that the category
of plain *capita* was necessarily composed of free *paroikoi*.[93] Some of these
may have been slaves, so that the number of slaves should probably be
seen as a minimum. The schedule used to convert individual humans into
capita is also somewhat uncertain, although somewhere between 1–2 persons per *caput* seems most likely.[94] The stone records the tax liability of
four different owners – three decurions and one priest (table 4.6).[95]

The glimpses of the countryside at Tralles reveal several distinct scales
and types of land-use. The large farm owned by the decurion Tatianus
was equipped with workers who were likely free, but he employed on the
order of eight to sixteen slaves, perhaps a permanent, core workforce that
included managers or technicians. Fulvius, the priest, held a small farm
which was worked by a few apparently free laborers, without employing
slaves. Kritias had two to four slaves to complement a larger staff of free
workers. Latron had four to eight slaves but no free workers. Latron's

[90] Bagnall 1997a, 1996, 119–21. cf. Rowlandson 1999 and 1996; Kehoe 1992, for the earlier period.
[91] Jones 1953. For criticisms, see Thonemann 2007 and Harper 2008.
[92] IGSK 36.1, no. 205; superior edition now available in Thonemann 2007.
[93] Jones 1953; Thonemann 2007, 458.
[94] CT 13.11.2 (AD 386) with CT 7.6.3 (AD 377). Jones 1953, 50.
[95] The figures presented from Tralles are converted using the small *iugum* and operate with the
simplifying assumption that all taxable land was arable.

Table 4.6 *Land and labor at Tralles*

	Slaves	*Paroikoi*	Land
Fulvius	0	4 to 8 workers	39 *iugera*
Tatianus	8 to 16 slaves	56 to 112 workers	616 *iugera*
Kritias	2 to 4 slaves	9 to 18 workers	251 *iugera*
Latron	4 to 8 slaves	0 workers	205 *iugera*

Table 4.7 *Land and labor on Lesbos*

Lesbos	Arable	Vine	Olive (no. trees)	No. plots	Labor
XII.2.76	1,514	109	5,511	16	22 slaves
XII.2.77	267	20	1,281	18	
XII.2.78	52	15	248	5	21 slaves
XII.2.79	594	19	2,000	5	

slaves would not have been sufficient to work a property of 205 *iugera*, and it seems possible that these slaves may have functioned as managers or overseers. Among this random slice of land-owners, slaves were a minority input in the labor force, but one which was instrumental in controlling production – the creation of a large curial estate, in the case of Tatianus, and the management of free workers, in the case of Latron.

The inscriptions from Lesbos and Thera are more informative. The surviving fragments record a total of roughly eight properties from the two islands. All of these estates would rank as medium-to-large-scale curial properties, and there are also hints of senatorial land-ownership. The stones are fragmentary, and it is difficult to reconstruct with certainty the total liability for any individual. From Lesbos, four stones survive.[96] We do not know who owned this land, nor the relationship between the individual stones. On the assumption that each stone represented a separate owner, there is information about four different properties (table 4.7).

Two stones (76 and 78) conserve information about the labor force. No. 76 records a large property with land scattered in sixteen villages. Labor was registered in only one location.[97] That plot was sizeable: ninety-one *iugera* of arable land, twenty *iugera* of vineyard, 352 olive trees, land

---

[96] IG XII.2 nos. 76–9.   [97] IG XII.2, no. 76, c–d.

for pasture, twenty oxen, fifty sheep, and twenty-two slaves. The estate is a prime example of intensive Mediterranean polyculture, with an emphasis on olives, and we can easily envision the diversity of its products. In the other villages listed on this stone, the owner had no tax liabilities for laborers, slave or free. It is likely that some of his land was worked by the slaves, some let out to tenants responsible for their own personal taxes, or some worked by laborers recorded on the lost part of the stone. This inscription also registered a handful of shepherds – at least some of them slaves, such as the one with the name Philodespotos.[98] No. 78 recorded a property with land in five villages. In one village, the owner was liable for taxes on twenty-one slaves.[99] Yet this particular farm included only five *iugera* of arable land, some vines, and 132 olive trees. This small plot may have done little more than house the slaves.

The manning ratios established by Duncan-Jones can give us a rough guide of how much labor would be needed for the amounts of registered land in the inscription.[100] On property no. 76 the twenty-two slaves of this land-owner may have been able to handle, roughly, a quarter to a third of the necessary work on the visible arable land. When the calculations are repeated for no. 78, it appears that the twenty-one slaves on this property provided too much labor for the holdings which are visible. Most likely the owner held other farms which were lost in the damage to the stone, and it is even possible that the same owner held all the farms on both stones. Yet in this small but random sample, we can see that slave labor was integral rather than marginal to the exploitation of elite-owned land on Lesbos.

The inscriptions from Thera offer the most stunning information about the use of slave labor in the eastern Mediterranean.[101] Like the inscriptions from Lesbos, these are fragmentary (table 4.8).

Although it is impossible to say what percentage of the total labor force on Thera was servile, the new inscription is, by any reckoning, remarkable. The attestation of over 152 slaves belonging to a single owner ranks as the most concrete, credible evidence for large-scale rural slavery in the entire Roman empire. This is the sort of property that led John Chrysostom to deplore the wealth of the eastern aristocracy, whose members he accused of owning "a thousand slaves, or two thousand."[102] Sometimes dismissed as outlandish rhetoric, the preacher's complaint looks ever more realistic

---

[98] Philodespotos implies slave status: Bagnall 1996, 126. cf. Solin 1996, 418–19. For slave shepherds see pp. 185–7.

[99] IG XII.2, no. 78, c.   [100] Duncan-Jones 1974, 327.

[101] Kiourtzian no. 142 a–g; Geroussi-Bendermacher 2005.

[102] Ioh. Chrys. In Mt. 63.4 (PG 58: 608): ἀνδραπόδων χιλίων, ἢ δὶς τοσούτων. See chapter 1.

Table 4.8 *Land and labor on Thera*

Thera	Land	Free	Slave
142a	504 *iugera* arable 79 *iugera* vine 554 olive trees	3	2
142b	614 *iugera* arable 162 *iugera* vine 1,420 olive trees	?	?
142c	528 *iugera* arable 120 *iugera* vine 586 olive trees	?	?
142d	?	18	?
New	?	?	152+

in light of the inscription from Thera, particularly if this property was just one of many held by the individual land-owner.

Wine production was an emphasis on Thera. The land, with its rich volcanic soil, was allotted between arable, vine, and olives at a ratio of 80, 17, and 3 percent, respectively. The inscriptions of Thera and Lesbos reveal agricultural specialization on the islands, but only within strict limits. On Lesbos, olive production was a greater priority, with the land allotted at 88, 6, and 6 percent among the three crops.[103] Estate-based animal husbandry was also an important complement to the cultivation of crops. These are some of the most objective data on land allocation from the entire Roman period, and they provide us valuable confirmation that specialization in crops such as grapes and olives occurred along the margins of a landscape dominated by grain cultivation. Even in the United States, large plantations enjoyed a productivity advantage because they could allocate marginally greater resources to cash-crop production, while subsistence agriculture frequently remained a priority.[104] In the ancient Mediterranean, it should be no surprise that agricultural specialization, even on large estates, was limited by the weight of arable farming.[105] But wine and olive oil were both specialized products of the Aegean, exported in bulk to Constantinople and beyond.[106]

---

[103] Assuming olive trees at 50 trees per *iugerum*: Thonemann 2007.   [104] Wright 2006 and 1978.
[105] Jongman 1988, on the predominance of arable farming, in Campania in the early empire. Morley 1996, 102. For the compatibility of wheat cultivation and slave labor, Scheidel 1994b; Spurr 1986.
[106] Reynolds 2005; Kingsley 2002; Karagiorgou 2001.

Slaves appear prominently in all three inscriptions which preserve information on the status of the laborers, and it is worth noting that there are also
hints of slaves from the other sites documented by the census inscriptions,
at Chios and Magnesia.[107] These small indications from Chios and Magnesia give additional reason to believe that land-owners at Tralles, Lesbos,
and Thera were not exceptional. These census inscriptions demonstrate the
intrinsic diversity of slave labor. No typical estate or single logic emerges
from the stones; slaves were owned in groups of 2, 4, 8, 16, 21, 22, and 152.
And the documents testify to the coexistence of slaves, tenants, and estate
workers within the same complex productive system.

The slaves were centrally managed rather than installed on separate plots
like tenants. The laborers appear to have been concentrated on individual centers, not dispersed across the land, a pattern which suggests that
habitation, and presumably work, was organized from above. The age structure of the slave population on Thera suggests the manumission of adult
males – this would lead us to believe that manumission was an incentive
used to motivate slaves and to create internal hierarchies on the estate.[108]
The cultivation and processing of care-intensive crops like grapes and
olives is certainly consistent with the presence of highly trained and trusted
slaves. The papyri offer corroborating evidence for the direct management
of agricultural labor on large farms of the fourth-century east.[109] So do
Greek manuals of estate management, like the *Geoponica*.[110] There we find
detailed accounts of worker oversight, such as the suggestion that workers
should be organized to balance the cost of supervision against the risk of
shirking: "If there are many workers, they should not all work together,
for they will be content to slacken off their efforts. But do not put them
in twos or threes, for this requires too many overseers . . . It is best, then, if
the workers are numerous, to deploy them in work gangs of ten, or if they
are few, in groups of five or six."[111] This is hardly the discourse of a society
based on a *rentier* elite.[112]

The census inscriptions are random, quantitative, officially measured,
and ideologically neutral. Thus, they constitute some of the best evidence

---

[107] Thonemann 2007, 474, also notes that the enormous capitation taxes due at places called "Barbaria"
and "Barbariane" may well reflect slave-ownership.
[108] Harper 2008.   [109] See pp. 172–5 for the papyri.
[110] Teall 1971, noting that agricultural literature began circulating more intensely in the fourth century.
[111] Geopon. 2.45.3-4 (Beckh: 80-1): Ἐὰν δὲ πολλοὶ ὦσιν ἐργάται, οὐ δεῖ πάντας ὁμοῦ ἐργάζεσθαι,
εὐκόλως γὰρ ῥαδιουργήσουσιν. οὔτε πάλιν ἀνὰ δύο ἢ τρεῖς, πολλῶν γὰρ δεήσονται
τῶν ἐπιστατούντων . . . κάλλιστον μὲν οὖν, ἐὰν πολλοὶ ὦσιν, εἰς δεκάδας τάσσειν τοὺς
ἐργαζομένους· ἐὰν δὲ ὀλίγοι, εἰς ἑξάδας, καὶ οὐ πεντάδας.
[112] Teall 1971, esp. 7 and n. 9, for further indications.

for rural labor to have survived from the fourth century, if not all of antiquity. This prompts two questions: how well do they fit within our institutional model of agricultural slavery, and how representative are they?

The productive system reflected in the census inscriptions is one in which the slave supply and the demand for labor created the basic conditions for slavery to flourish. Here on islands and coasts were communities with strong links to seaborne exchange networks. The price of slaves was apparently not prohibitive. The demand for slaves was a function of demand for commodities. The census inscriptions bring to life a landscape directly in the path of the powerful tow of urban demand emanating from the markets of fourth-century Constantinople. The islands, with their proximity to trading routes and easy access to waterborne transport, were an ideal location for market-oriented production. Moreover, slavery was apparently competitive with wage labor; perhaps the islands created "thin" labor markets that made it risky to rely on contract labor. But Lesbos is hardly a small or isolated island, and the use of slaves at inland Tralles suggests that the use of slavery was not purely an effect of the island ecology.[113] The census inscriptions document a landscape where various forms of tenancy were important, for small-scale urban land-owners and larger properties alike. The countryside was a patchwork with interlaced zones of intensively and extensively exploited land. Slavery was instrumental in the intensively managed estates in these regions.

How representative are the census inscriptions? The stones come from a region with strong market demand, good access to seaborne and riverborne trading networks, and an expansionary economy. Yet there is nothing which makes this region entirely exceptional. If there were documentary evidence from other parts of the eastern provinces near the coasts, close to markets, or connected to trading routes, we might expect the same mix of slavery and intensive estate management. Rural surveys have not been carried out at Lesbos, Tralles, or Thera, but archaeological research throughout the late antique east has consistently revealed a landscape of village-based estate centers and even isolated farmsteads. Certainly villages dominate the settlement landscape of the east, but large isolated farms do appear, especially near urban areas, market centers, and transport routes.[114] Well-explored areas like the coast of Palestine, the immediate hinterland of

---

[113] On Mediterranean islands, Horden and Purcell 2000, 224–30, 390.

[114] Sarris 2006; Chavarría and Lewit 2004, 19; Vanhaverbeke and Waelkens 2003, 246; Kingsley 2002, 63; Hirschfeld 1997; Mee and Forbes 1997, 88; Fejfer and Mathiesen 1992; Rossiter 1989 for literary evidence; Dar 1986, 23–5; Frost 1977.

Antioch, or the valleys of Lycia and Pisidia offer good examples.[115] Palestine, Syria, Asia Minor, and Greece have all yielded extensive evidence for the presence of expensive industrial-scale productive installations in villages, especially grape and olive presses.[116] A great wave of capital investment is evident throughout the eastern Mediterranean of late antiquity. Such investments are a signature of commercialization and intensification – not direct evidence for slavery, but a plausible context for the types of land-use with which slave labor had such affinities.

No one has allowed slavery much significance in the eastern provinces, so the census inscriptions at a minimum insist that slave labor needs to be reconsidered as a possible element in the productive system of the east. The only other source of documentary evidence is Egypt and, surprisingly, there was some use of slave labor in agriculture there too. In early imperial Egypt, land leasing seems to have predominated, and the evidence for agricultural slavery is generally recognized to be marginal.[117] With the rise of larger and more exchange-oriented estates in the third century, however, the picture becomes more complex.[118] The best-attested Egyptian estate of this period is the property of Appianus, known through the thousands of documents of a mid-level manager of the estate's land.[119] The property is of particular importance because no other ancient estate allows such insights into the daily operations, the multitude of decisions about production, storage, sale, personnel, and the accounting systems of antiquity as the Appianus estate. This estate of the mid-third century was a tightly managed machine, broken down into smaller units, organized principally around the production of wine for sale on the market.[120]

If the fourth-century evidence is never quite so rich, the extant papyri do provide unambiguous evidence for slave labor on a variety of properties in the late Roman period. A papyrus of 268, from a family with connections to the Alexandrian aristocracy, shows a property of over 1,000 arouras and around 22 slaves.[121] Nor was it only the highest stratum of the Alexandrian elite which owned slaves. In the will of a land-owner from the late third century, a master left his manager a gift of land, while requiring him to

---

[115] Casana 2004; Kingsley 2002, 65–7; Safrai 1994.
[116] For productive investments, see Morrison and Sodini 2002, 178–9; Gibson, Kingsley, and Clark 1999; Dar 1986, 152; Mayerson 1985. For slaves, Safrai 1994, 334–5.
[117] For leasing, Rowlandson 1996; Kehoe 1992. Bieżuńska-Małowist 1974–7, vol. 2, 83, agricultural slavery marginal.
[118] Banaji 2001.   [119] Rathbone 1991.
[120] Rathbone 1991, 88–147. On the status of the *oiketai*, see appendix 1.
[121] P. Flor. 1.50 (268). Banaji 2001, 110–11; Kehoe 1997, 130–1.

"stay in the service" of his sons, implying that he was a freedman.[122] He left his wife at least seven slaves, two of them freed on condition of *paramonê*. In 289, an Oxyrhynchite man objected to his appointment for office by pleading "poverty." His property included, at the least, a holding of 60 arouras, a building, slaves, calves, and a horse, all within one village.[123] He would seem to be an urban land-holder who had slaves stationed in a village to work his property.

The documents of estate management, which are relatively exiguous for the fourth century, confirm the presence of slaves, even in a small sample. From the village of Karanis, a local manager sent an agitated letter to the urban land-owner. The letter informed the owner that his slaves were misbehaving, "especially Eutyches," who refused to hand over the agricultural produce destined for the master and who insulted the manager.[124] He would not perform the work commanded of him, "which you will see for yourself when you come for an inspection."[125] This papyrus thus offers a glimpse of an urban land-holder who used slaves in exploiting his village property, which he occasionally visited in person for oversight. In a letter dated to 307, one Plutarch wrote to Philantinoos, who was the manager of an estate's holdings in a village outside Oxyrhynchus.[126] He ordered Philantinoos to "give my slaves eight artabas of wheat for their rations, calculated by the measure of a tenth of Apion, and eight only."[127] Plutarch was either the owner or the central manager of the estate. The letter dates to March, and it seems likely that he dispatched "his" slaves out to the village in advance of the harvest, with orders on the rations they should receive from the local manager.

One of the best documents of estate management from the fourth century is a fragmentary account book from Hermonthis, a town along the banks of the Nile in Upper Egypt.[128] The papyrus is the expense register of an estate manager for the first four months of the year 338. It tracks the flow of wheat and other foodstuffs among various installations which were centrally managed.[129] The estate was centered at Hermonthis; its

---

[122] P. Oxy. 2474 (third century, possibly late). Kehoe 1997, 131–2.

[123] P. Hamb. 268 (AD 289). cf. PSI 10.1102 (late third century, Oxyrhynchus?); P. Rain. Cent. 85 (AD 364–6).

[124] SB 11130 (Karanis, third/fourth century): Μάλιστα δὲ ὁ Εὐτυχῆς...

[125] SB 11130: ἃ καὶ ἐλθόντος σου ἐπόψῃ καὶ μαρτυρηθήσεταί σοι.

[126] P. Harr 2.233 (Oxyrhynchus, AD 307).

[127] P. Harr 2.233: δὸς εἰς διατροφὰς τοῖς πεδίοις μου μέτρῳ Ἀπίωνος δεκάτου πυροῦ ἀρτάβας ὀκτώ, γ(ίνονται) (ἀρτάβαι) η μ(όναι).

[128] See Bagnall 1996, 126–7.

[129] P. Lips. 97 (subsequent references are to the column and line number).

land was spread across at least thirteen plots in three different villages.[130] This is one of the rare opportunities to see inside a working, large-scale agricultural organization in the fourth century. The operation of the estate was overseen by a considerable managerial staff.[131] In the month of Mecheir, five names were listed as "from the command of Leontius," presumably the managerial staff.[132] Two of these were slaves. One, named Philokurios, was also paid during an irregular disbursement (during an off-month in the cycle), suggesting that he ranked higher than the mass of workers. As the harvest arrived, he was out with the other slaves, dispatched to work in the fields. This movement of personnel between the central unit and the field implies a certain amount of fluidity in the labor force, responsive to seasonal pressures. The estate also demonstrates the informal hierarchies which extended down into the fields, since it mentions two "lead farmers" who were paid rations in the account.[133]

The Hermonthis estate was a highly structured and centrally managed organism of some scale and complexity, centered around the production of wheat and the rearing of livestock.[134] Our knowledge of labor on the Hermonthis estate comes from the management staff's record of the rations dispersed to the workers. The account recorded the amount of wheat spent as a bimonthly ration for individual laborers, listed by name.[135] The laborers were organized in functional groups (table 4.9).

The labor force was nearly identical in both disbursement lists.[136] The main exception was the addition to the workforce of fourteen gardeners and eleven shepherds. This swelled the number of employees by nearly 20 percent, which might be expected at the onset of harvest. This could reflect nothing more than a convention of payment in this account, but more likely it demonstrates the mobilization of all available hands for the harvest time.

The status of the laborers is the most tantalizing question of the account. The document was an internal account, not an official public record, and it was written in its own terms. It was organized principally by function, not status, with the exception of a group of *paidaria*, who were certainly

---

[130] 4.2–17.   [131] 1.2.   [132] 3.6: τῶν μὲν ἐκ κελεύσεως Λεοντίου.

[133] 8.23 and 14.27: Ἀρχιγεώργοι.

[134] Bagnall 1996, 126, suggests the wheat outlays reflect ca. 2,000 arouras of land under cultivation.

[135] The document covers four months but only records individual wheat allotments for Mecheir and Pharmuthi.

[136] Only the categories of slave (fifteen), donkey rearer (two), and head farmer (two) were precisely consistent in number (though a slave named Horios has disappeared from the second list, and Philokurios joined it).

Table 4.9 The employees of the Hermonthis estate

Mecheir		Pharmuthi	
Function	No.	Function	No.
Cowhand (βουκόλος)	6	Cowhand	6
Asst. cowhand (ὑποβουκόλος)	3	Asst. cowhand	1
Wagoner (ἀμαξηλάτης)	10	Wagoner	7
Laborer (ἐργάτης)	12	Laborer	20
Irrigation machinist (ὀργανίτης)[1]	22	Irrigation machinist	21
Helper (βοηθός)	5	Helper	4
Donkey rearer (ὀνοτρόφος)	2	Donkey rearer	2
Head farmer (ἀρχιγεώργος)	2	Head farmer	2
Slave (παιδαρίον)	15	Slave	15
Trainee (ὑπουργός)[2]	2	Trainee	1
Camel driver (καμηλάτης)	3	Gardener (κηπουρος)	14
		Shepherd (ποίμην)	11
Total	**82**	**Total**	**104**

[1] Bagnall 1996, 126.
[2] For "ὑπουργος" as "trainee," cf. Geopon. 2.2 (Beckh: 34).

slaves.[137] This group accounted for roughly 20 percent of the workforce in Mecheir, closer to 15 percent in Pharmuthi. Other slaves were mentioned incidentally throughout the account – a weaver, a "trainee," and a group of slaves traveling on business down the river to Lykopolis. None of these other slaves were on the regular cycle of food rations that went out to the workers in the villages, so the total number of slaves on this estate

[137] Rathbone 2005, 263; Sarris 2004, 287; Bagnall 1996, 126; Bieżuńska-Małowist, 1974–7, vol. 2, 80–1. cf. SPP 20.106 and P. Haun. 3.68. In P. Oxy. 58.3960, *paidaria* were listed in explicit contrast to the "free" workers. PSI 8.953, of the sixth century, refers to the "παιδάρια Γοθθικά" of an estate. In legal transactions like sales, slaves are uniformly called *douloi* or *andrapoda*, whereas in this internal document they are simply "boys." Straus 1988, 849–50 is too careful to say that *paidarion* is, as a reflection of status, ambiguous. The word can mean "slave" or "young boy." It does not, however, mean anything else, and if a *paidarion* is unambiguously from context not a "boy," then he is a slave (Bieżuńska-Małowist, 1974–7, vol. 2, 11). The term was frequently used at Leukopetra, regardless of age (by contrast, *paidion* was used for young slaves): Petsas *et al.* 2000, 42. For literary examples, Gr. Nyss. Apoll. 208 (Müller vol. 3.1: 208), where *doulos*, *oiketês*, and *paidarion* are used in succession to vary the diction. Pall. H. Laus. 46 (Butler vol. 2: 135), where a free woman disguises herself as a slave (*paidarion*) to serve monks; the governor did not recognize that she was "free" (*eleuthera*). The *paidaria* in the papyri should not be "boys" on several accounts. First, one *paidarion*, Didymus, is called the elder, which at least suggests he is not a child. Secondly, Philokurios was paid on the management staff and then amongst the *paidaria*. Third, in this and other papyri, taxes are paid on the *paidaria*, whereas boys were not taxed until the age of fourteen in Egypt. Against my argument, in the Cairo Genizah, "boy" could have the sense of "worker": Goitein 1967–93, vol. 1, 131. But half a millennium is plenty of time for semantic evolution.

would be higher if the central office in town were included. The only woman listed in the entire account was a slave, Thaësis, on the managerial staff.[138] It seems improbable that Thaësis was the lone female slave on an estate of some hundred workers, and even the single attested specialized weaver implies a significant amount of spinning somewhere in the overall productive operation.[139] Whether women were few, only assigned to the central staff, or paid through male associates, they are practically invisible in the document.

The use of the term *paidarion* for slave, in a document where the workers were organized primarily by function, probably implies that the slaves were unspecialized laborers.[140] It is unclear whether all of the other employees, all of the shepherds, for example, were free. Their status was not specified in the document, and because they were categorized by function, it cannot be ruled out that some of them were specialized slaves. Among the specialized laborers, half were listed with a patronymic and half without.[141] That cannot stand as proof that they were slaves, but the inconsistency does throw their status into doubt.[142] Certainly, however, the Hermonthis document stands as proof that slave labor could account for one-sixth to one-fifth of an estate's workforce in an area of the empire where agricultural slavery has been considered a marginal phenomenon. The Hermonthis account provides glimpses into a large, centrally managed estate of the fourth century, devoted to raising livestock and cultivating grains. It demonstrates the possibility of a mixed labor force, in which an estate's demands elicited a strategic deployment that included both slaves and hired workers.

The evidence to hand for slaves in fourth-century Egypt is insistent.[143] There is no doubt that land leasing and wage labor were prominent, but the papyri would argue that slave labor had also gained a meaningful role in the operation of large estates in fourth-century Egypt. This is perhaps surprising, and it merits some attempt at explanation. From the third century onward, large, centrally managed estates, producing for the market,

---

[138] 3.6.   [139] cf. Roth 2007, 59.

[140] Bagnall 1996, 127. cf. Dumont 1999, for the agronomist's use of functional rather than status terms.

[141] None of the *paidaria* have patronymics with the possible exception of Ὡρίως Ἡμιστίου, 9.6, but there was another *paidarion* with the same name, so it may have been used to differentiate. cf. Matthews 2006, 95.

[142] When a worker was listed without a patronymic in Mecheir, he was listed without one in Pharmouthi.

[143] A receipt for clothing allocations to slaves from 355 or later included the names of thirty-eight slaves. SPP 20.106. See Bagnall 1996, 126, n. 78. A few of the slaves in this document had specialized functions, including three cooks, one weaver, and a carpenter. No job title was specified for the rest of the slaves, who were presumably unspecialized laborers. Other late Roman documents: BGU 1.34 = P. Charite 36 (322); P. Duk. Inv. 553 v (after 252).

are visible in Egypt. Tenancy remained, of course, the predominant form of land-use among elites. But with the new style of intensive commercialized agriculture came demand for controllable labor. With its high population density, Egypt nurtured the sort of thick labor markets that were largely capable of fulfilling demand for estate labor, but to judge by the documents of the fourth century, there was still room for the exploitation of slaves.

The literary sources of the east are impressionistic, but they do corroborate the evidence of the inscriptions and papyri. They suggest that slavery played an important role across the eastern core – into the Greek heartland, around Constantinople, along coastal Asia Minor, and in the hinterlands of other urban centers. The literary sources add specific cases of slave-owners. The example of Heliodorus, the merchant-turned-imperial servant, suggests that slave labor was used in the Greek heartland. The example of an imperial *agens in rebus* Aristophanes, a native of Corinth, provides further evidence. "Because of his great and lengthy absences, his orchards were laid to waste and his land deprived of cultivation. Some of his slaves have escaped, others learned to be lazy."[144] These estates included both arboriculture and arable cultivation, worked by slaves under the direct control of estate managers; when the oversight was removed, the slaves either fled or became unproductive. Basil of Caesarea knew a greedy official who had amassed "an abundance of land, farms and estates, herds, and slaves."[145] The laws add more cases.[146] On their own, these examples could never be decisive, but they show us that the patterns evident in the census inscriptions have left a trail in the literary and legal sources of the period.

The specific slave-owners can be paralleled by the generic testimony about private wealth. Basil of Caesarea and John Chrysostom are two of the most important contemporary social critics. We have already seen several examples in which Chrysostom assumed that market-oriented agriculture was synonymous with the acquisition of land and slaves.[147] Basil of Caesarea too described, critically, the slave-based wealth of the local aristocracy. In a series of sermons, Basil described the "rich man" who earned his fortune

[144] Lib. Or. 14.45 (Foerster vol. 2: 103): ἔπειθ᾽ οὗτος μακραῖς καὶ χρονίοις ἀπουσίαις, δι᾽ ἃς δένδρα τε ἐκκέκοπται καὶ γῆ γεωργίας ἐστέρηται, τῶν δὲ ἀνδραπόδων τὰ μὲν ἀπέδρα, τὰ δὲ ἀργεῖν ἔμαθε...
[145] Bas. Hom. Mart. Iulit. 1 (PG 31: col 237): γῆς τε πλῆθος... καὶ ἀγροὺς καὶ κώμας, καὶ βοσκήματα καὶ οἰκέτας.
[146] E.g. CT 12.1.96 (AD 383); CJ 11.63.3 (AD 383); CT 12.3.1 (AD 386).
[147] Ioh. Chrys. In Mt. 24.11 (PG 57: 319); Ioh. Chrys. In act. Apost. 32.2 (PG 60: 237).

through selling agricultural commodities like wheat, wine, and wool.[148] We should notice the absence of olives – it is too cold in Cappadocia to grow them – as a trace of realism in this portrait of commercial wealth. Basil considered textile production a major source of profit, as did Asterius. We sense behind these claims a style of agriculture distinct from the coastal wine and olive factories of the census inscriptions. The operations that Basil and Asterius described perhaps entailed animal husbandry on a large scale. They are plausibly describing the stock ranches which produced wool to be finished either on the estate or shipped in raw form to urban markets.

In another sermon we glimpse the productive base of the commercially savvy aristocrat whose wealth Basil criticized. "The rest of his slaves are innumerable and add up to extravagance. Overseers, dispensers, farmers, those skilled in every craft, both those who are necessary and those found for sumptuous pleasures..."[149] In Basil's mind, there were slaves who were necessary (productive) and unnecessary (pleasurable). Basil took special offense at the ranks of non-productive slaves in the service of the wealthy land-owner. More significantly, he assumed that slave labor was the foundation of the rich man's wealth. It is noteworthy that Basil was conscious of the organization of the slaves. He claimed that the owner would have slaves as managers, as financial agents, as trained technical workers, and as ordinary farmers. Of special interest are the slaves "trained in every craft," presumably such para-agricultural workers like blacksmiths, carpenters, textile workers, or industrial craftsmen.[150]

Certainly the sermons of Basil or Chrysostom were high on emotional content; they were not disinterested social reportage.[151] Basil's "rich man" was unremittingly greedy and violent. "Everywhere the eye [of the rich man] looks, it witnesses the image of his evil: here are the tears of the orphan, there is the misery of the widow, beyond, the poor who are battered by you and the slaves whom you have torn to shreds."[152] But these sermons cannot be dismissed as pure exaggerations. Both bishops assumed that slave labor

---

[148] Bas. Dest. horr. 5 (Courtonne: 25–6). See Rousseau 1994, 137–8.

[149] Bas. Hom. Div. 2.2 (Courtonne: 46–7): Τῶν ἄλλων οἰκετῶν ἀριθμὸς ἄπειρος πρὸς πᾶσαν αὐτοῖς πολυτέλειαν ἐξαρκῶν. ἐπίτροποι, ταμίαι, γεωργοί, παντοδαπῆς ἔμπειροι τέχνης, τῆς τε ἀναγκαίας καὶ τῆς πρὸς ἀπόλαυσιν καὶ τρυφὴν εὑρημένης... cf. Bas. Attend. 5 (Rudberg: 31).

[150] See pp. 189 and 194–5, on Melania the Younger and Palladius, for comparisons. cf. also CT. 9.42.7 (AD 369).

[151] The essays in Holman 2008 and Holman 2001.

[152] Bas. Hom. Div. 2.6 (Courtonne: 61): Ὅπου γὰρ ἂν περιαγάγῃς τὸν ὀφθαλμόν, ἐναργεῖς ὄψει τῶν κακῶν τὰς εἰκόνας. ἔνθεν τοῦ ὀρφανοῦ τὰ δάκρυα, ἐκεῖθεν τῆς χήρας τὸν στεναγμόν, ἑτέρωθεν τοὺς κατακονδυλισθέντας ὑπό σου πένητας. τοὺς οἰκέτας, οὓς κατέξαινες.

was at least partly responsible for the wealth of the aristocracy. They both gestured towards the complex managerial structures connecting the owner to the exploitation of his land, the diversity of the slave labor force, and the essential violence of the master's control. Undoubtedly, the extraction of rent from tenant farmers was an important means of exploiting the land, also described in the speeches of Libanius, Basil, and Chrysostom.[153] But the significant role of slave labor in these same documents has not found a place in the historiography of slavery. The literary sources confirm the conclusion drawn from the documentary evidence, that slave labor was vital in the control of agrarian production in the eastern core in the fourth century.

The history of rural labor in the late Roman east has been so focused on the rise of the colonate that an antithetical development has gone almost without comment: by all appearances, agricultural slavery reached its high tide in the eastern core during the fourth century. The traditional narratives, organized around the transition from ancient to feudal labor, have no way to account for rural slavery in the fourth-century east. Instead of military conquest (and by inference cheap *supply*), or a general scarcity of labor driven by military conscription, what must have driven the growth of slavery in this region was strong demand for farm labor among proprietors who were looking to exploit their landed wealth and who found slavery a suitable way of doing so. As the geographic co-ordinates of production and wealth changed in late antiquity, slavery remained integral to the ability of the Roman aristocracy to capitalize on its control over agricultural resources.

Nothing in this account would lead us to believe that slavery was dominant, numerically, in any corridor of the eastern Mediterranean. It was important, particularly in the parts of the countryside that were most integrated in commercial networks. We would predict that slave labor was most intensively used in the areas of the countryside most under the influence of market demand – the hinterland of the great cities, the regions lying near transport routes.[154] Slavery does not appear prominent in wide stretches of the east, in particular the inland villages of Syria and Palestine, a pattern which is probably not an accident of the surviving evidence. Even if we are ill-informed by documentary and literary evidence for the structures of wine and oil production in the interior Levant, this is one region of the

---

[153] Tenancy, Vera 1986a, esp. 378; MacMullen 1987, 364.
[154] Vanhaverbeke and Waelkens 2003, 251–60. Generally, see Fellmeth 2002; Morley 1996; De Neeve 1984b. Wilson 2004b, 573, archaeological, for the earlier period.

empire where it has been theorized that peasants were able to plug into market-oriented production with notable success while excluding larger land-owners.[155]

Although beyond the scope of this book, it is worth noting that agricultural slavery does not seem to have endured through the sixth century. There is some indication of slave labor on the great estates of Byzantine Egypt, although it is difficult to know how important these slaves were.[156] The *Novels* of Justinian show some attention to agricultural slavery.[157] It would be surprising if there were no slaves in this period, but it is increasingly hard to find rural slave labor in the subsequent periods of the late antique east.[158] How could we explain this pattern? In the east, slavery was forced to compete against the wage labor of a perennially "landless peasantry."[159] Continued population growth could have exacerbated the pressures on the peasantry and provided a safe reservoir of available labor.[160] More significantly, the colonate in the east played directly into the hands of estate-owners. In the east *coloni* were explicitly considered estate workers rather than tenants.[161] Rural workers bound to an estate suffered from an increasingly articulated set of restrictions from the mid-fifth century.[162] Strikingly, they begin to appear in the papyri at this same moment.[163] At the same time, the great estates of Egypt grew exponentially in comparison with their third- and fourth-century predecessors, as a new provincial aristocracy took hold.[164] Finally, it is worth noting that late antique prosperity was most stable in precisely the regions where agricultural slavery made no appreciable inroads, such as the high limestone villages of Syria. The eastward drift of slavery was stalled at the gates of the village culture in the Levant.

SLAVERY IN THE FOURTH-CENTURY WEST

If the history of agricultural slavery in the late Roman east has suffered from relative neglect, the battle lines in the debate over slavery in the west are all too clear. The transition narrative of Roman slavery describes the labor

---

[155] Wickham 2005a, 448. [156] Esp. Sarris 2006. [157] Rotman 2000, 503.
[158] Lenski 2010, "but five instances of agricultural slaves for the four centuries of Middle Byzantine history."
[159] Banaji 2009, 60. [160] Morrison and Sodini 2002, 172–6, for high population density.
[161] CJ 11.48.19 (Anastasius). [162] Eibach 1980, 132–93, esp. 151.
[163] Fikhman 2006, 190–250.
[164] Banaji 2001, 134–70, describes the "new aristocracy," esp. 136. Though see Hickey 2007, 297, for sensible cautions both about the size of the fifth- and sixth-century properties and possibly also the significance of *adscripticii*.

system of late antiquity as one in which slaves remained in large numbers but were now exploited "like tenants" on giant *latifundia*.[165] The concession that slaves were numerous in the late empire is an important one, for it shifts the discussion away from the question of whether or not there were slaves and towards the question of how they were used. The following pages will try to demonstrate that there is no compelling reason to believe in a wholesale transition from plantation slavery to servile tenancies in the fourth century. The idea that a radically transformative mode of plantation slavery was ever dominant does not rest on solid evidence.[166] It is all the more troublesome, then, that the theory of servile tenancy relies on a *lack* of evidence for plantation slavery rather than clear, positive attestation of tenant-slaves.

The effort to cast late antique slaves as tenants is focused on the aggregation of giant properties.[167] Giant properties are supposed to entail reduced supervision: Columella sensibly claimed that distant, arable-focused farms were better suited for free workers than slaves.[168] Thus, as the scale of private estates grew over the imperial period, slavery supposedly made less economic sense. Yet even the largest properties may have retained intensively managed sectors within a diverse overall portfolio that included geographically dispersed arable properties.[169] More importantly, we should not concentrate on the largest senatorial land-owners to the exclusion of lesser senatorial and municipal land-owners who were also a vital force in the rural economy. Nor should we overestimate the concentration of property; in fact the concentration of wealth in the late Roman west is one of those points of consensus that forms around little evidence and less critical analysis. The theory that wealth was increasingly concentrated rests on the most egregiously selective impressionism. The wealthiest stratum of the western senate owned properties of stunning proportions in the late empire, as they had before. But we still need to examine the countryside in aggregate. It is the overall tenurial structure of the countryside that matters, not just the most visible elements at the very top of the senatorial pyramid.[170]

The evidence in the west is even more inadequate than in the east. We have virtually no documentary sources, nor do we have the benefit of

---

[165] Giardina 2007, 1997b, and 1986; Vera 2007 and 1998. *Contra*, Samson 1989; Whittaker 1987.

[166] Roth 2007, 2005b, and 2005a; Scheidel 2005a, 1999, and 1997; Jongman 2003 and 1988; Rathbone 1983 and 1981. *Contra*, Carandini 1989b.

[167] Giardina 2007, 752; Carandini 1988, 32; Alföldy 1986, 187; Shtaerman 1964. Critically, Lewit 1991, 35; Bowman 1985; Percival 1976, 119; Jones 1953, 244. cf. Hickey 2008, 98, on Egypt.

[168] Colum. De re rust. 1.7.6–7 (Lundström: 38). cf. Whittaker and Garnsey 1998, 285, 291.

[169] Finley 1998 (orig. 1980), 201.   [170] Wickham 2005b, 353.

an agricultural writer from the fourth century. The investigation necessarily rests on literary evidence and archaeology. The literary evidence is
suggestive but inadequate; the archaeological evidence is fundamental, but
it is notoriously impossible to read settlements and ceramics as evidence for
structures of ownership or labor. For that very reason, the interpretation
of archaeology threatens to be shaped by prior convictions, a Rorschach
test. In fact, the dominance of the transition narrative, and specifically the
colonate, has encouraged a constricted reading of the material evidence.
The late Roman settlement pattern in the west was dominated by dispersed settlements – isolated farmsteads, rustic estate centers, and palatial
villas.[171] Yet this inherent diversity is often reduced to a few ideal types, so
that Settefinestre stands as the archaeological proof that plantation slavery
once dominated the countryside while a site like the villa at Piazza Armerina reveals the accumulation of larger proprietary units by the senatorial aristocracy and a style of extensive land-use based on the collection of
rents.[172]

This archaeological narrative offers a veneer of hard evidence to the
transition model, and it is especially seductive in light of the inherently
limited range of sources in our possession. Indeed, some villas do display
monumental characteristics without a clear relationship to production,
and tenancy was quantitatively the predominant form of labor. And yet we
might approach this account with two sets of questions. First, were slaves
used in the western provinces, such as Gaul, Britain, Spain, and Africa,
and in particular on Elite estates? In part the way we read the villa as the
trace of an economic system will shape our answer to this question. Our
model of intensive Mediterranean polyculture brings to the archaeological
evidence a more flexible paradigm for interpreting the relationship between
the material evidence and the structures of labor. Secondly, if we are not
looking for a transition from plantation management to rent collection,
what do the sources reveal about the use of slave labor on Illustrious
properties, concentrated mostly in Italy, Sicily, and Africa? The evidence
indicates that there was an important element of direct control over the
productive process, even on senatorial land. The one source that describes
a senatorial property of this period, the *Life of Melania the Younger*, points
towards direct control. This chapter proceeds first by surveying the evidence
for Elite estates and then by investigating Illustrious land-use in the triangle
of Italy, Sicily, and Africa.

---

[171] Brogiolo 2005, 7; Christie 2004, 11; Scott 2004; Sfameni 2004.
[172] Vera 1995 with the memorable slogan: dalla *villa perfecta* alla villa di Palladio.

SLAVES AND THE LAND IN THE WESTERN PROVINCES

We start with the literary evidence. The profits of western Elites were made, in part, on the backs of tenants.[173] Authors like Ambrose and Augustine furnish a vivid catalogue of abuses against tenants. Tenants were, undeniably, crucial to the deployment of labor by late Roman land-owners.[174] But the long-standing dominance of the colonate as a historiographical paradigm can pull the eye towards the interaction between landlords and tenants in the surviving literary evidence, away from the obvious admixture of slave labor in agricultural production in late antiquity. If most of the plentiful references to slavery in the works of late Roman authors like Augustine or Ambrose, Salvian or Caesarius, are not specific about the tasks performed by slaves, on occasion these texts are explicit about the function of slavery, and the casual assumption of an agricultural role for slavery is unmistakable.

Caesarius thought of vine-work as a type of labor performed by slaves.[175] Salvian assumed that masters called their slaves "to plow or to hoe, to break the land or prepare it for the vine" – effort-intensive labor suitable to coercive slave-driving.[176] Ennodius laughed at the drunken poetry he wrote as he watched his slaves stamp grapes to make his wine.[177] In a world in which the mundane realities of productive labor were filtered out of most cultural expression, these are precious glimpses of rustic life and the use of slaves in the cycle of agricultural labor. Notably, each of these passages strongly implies direct management, not land leasing. The association of slavery and viticulture in these passages also reflects the affinity between slavery and higher-risk, higher-investment forms of land allocation.[178] Specialized slave *vinitores* can be found deep into the post-Roman period.[179]

The paucity of documentary evidence is a major obstacle to understanding the diversity and dynamism of the countryside. Perhaps the only

---

[173] As before: Finley 1998 (orig. 1980), 211; Kehoe 1997 and 1992; De Neeve 1984a.

[174] Vera 1986a, 378, 401–2; Cracco Ruggini 1961.   [175] Caes. Arel. Serm. 1.8 (CC 103: 6).

[176] Salv. Gub. 7.2 (MGH AA 1: 85): *ad aratra aut ad ligones... ad scindendas terras... ad vineas pastinandas.*

[177] Ennod. Carm. 1.9, 2.67 (CSEL 6: 538 and 578); Ennod. Ep. 7.20 (CSEL 6: 188); cf. Ennod. Ep. 1.6 (CSEL 6: 16); Ep. 3.1 (CSEL 6: 71); Ep. 3.16 (CSEL 6: 84); Ep. 3.19 (CSEL 6: 86); Ep. 6.10 (CSEL 6: 155); Ep. 8.15 (CSEL 6: 210).

[178] Whatever the status of the workers (possibly slaves) depicted in the Severan-era "Labours of the Fields" mosaics from Cherchel, they depict close supervision in vine-work. Dunbabin 1978, plate XL, no. 102, lower left panel; Ferdi 2005, no. 94, 114–17.

[179] Wickham 2005a, 284–7.

sustained means of access to a western municipal aristocracy in late antiquity lies in the corpus of Augustine's writing. We can investigate his surviving sermons for what they have to say about rural slavery, appreciating that they are our only large body of contemporary evidence for a crucial element of late Roman society.[180] Slaves were an integral part of life in Hippo. The barbarian tribes of the semi-desert were an exotic notion to his coastal audience, but one thickened into reality by the example of slaves "before our own eyes every day."[181] A slave was something over which heirs might spar, something "everyday."[182] The slaves of Augustine's listeners were expected to labor in the vineyards of the master or, as punishment, were assigned to millwork.[183] Augustine also described the social uprisings triggered in the name of Donatism, which included not just migratory free laborers and tenants, but also agricultural slaves. Nor were these simply the slaves of absentee senatorial land-owners: "What master was not forced to live in fear of his slave, if the slave fled to the patronage of the Donatists? . . . "[184]

The sermons of Augustine defined the social and economic horizons of the Elite strata. It was a fundamentally acquisitive class, striving to acquire money, land, herds, and slaves. Slaves were, along with fields and herds, inevitably part of the portfolio of wealth that could be imagined by Augustine's listeners.[185] Happiness was measured in vines and cattle, an obedient wife, reverent children, fearful slaves.[186] The countryside around Hippo was divided amongst these land-holding classes. "Sometimes we are traversing a road, and we see a beautiful or prosperous *fundus*, and we say, 'Whose is that?' We say, 'it's his.' We say, 'what a blessed man.' How empty our speech! 'Blessed is the one who owns that *domus*. Blessed is the one who owns that *fundus*. Blessed is the one who owns those cattle. Blessed is the one who owns that slave. Blessed is the one whose *familia*

---

[180] Garnsey 1998a and 1996, 206–19; Klein 1988; Corcoran 1985; Giordiano 1980; Mary 1954.
[181] Aug. Ep. 199.12 (CSEL 57: 284): *cotidie . . . in promptu.* Aug. Psalm. 148.10 (CC 40: 2173).
[182] Aug. Civ. 11.16 (CC 48: 336); Aug. Serm. Dom. 1.19.59 (CC 35: 69–70); Aug. Util. iei. 13 (CC 46: 241). Everyday: Aug. Serm. resp. Psal. 4 (Dolbeau 28: 292); Aug. Ep. 199.12 (CSEL 57: 284); Aug. Psalm. 124.7 (CC 40: 1840–1).
[183] Aug. Spir. et litt. 33.58 (CSEL 60: 217).
[184] Aug. Ep. 185.15 (CSEL 57: 14): *quis non dominus servum suum timere compulsus est, si ad illorum patrocinium confugisset?* Aug. Ep. 108.18 (CSEL 34.2: 632). cf. CT 16.5.52 (AD 412) and possibly CT 7.19.1.3 (AD 399).
[185] Aug. Conf. 1.19.30 (CC 27: 16–17); Aug. Tract. Io. 8.4 (CC 36: 84); Aug. Ep. Io. (PL 25: 2003); Aug. Serm. 21.9 (CC 41: 285); Aug. Serm. 113.6 (PL 38: 651); Aug. Psalm. 48.2.7 (CC 38: 570); Aug. Psalm. 64.8 (CC 39: 830).
[186] Aug. Psalm. 136.5 (CC 40: 1966–7). See chapter 8.

that is.'"[187] It was not an imaginary scenario. Augustine spoke of a specific man who owned a *fundus* called Zubedi in the nearby district of Fussala. When his animals and slaves were possessed with evil spirits, it took an exorcism from a priest at Hippo to cast them out.[188]

If Augustine wanted his audience to envision a "great house" – though still one where the master was present – he conjured its intricate hierarchy of slaves:

The great house has a master and it has slaves, and the house keeps nearby it the slaves in the higher offices, in charge of clothing, the treasury, and the store rooms of the great property. It also has slaves in lowly services, subject to the power of the others, all the way down to cleaning the sewers. There are so many grades from the height of the procurator down to such extremely low forms of work. But if the great procurator should offend someone, it will be the punishment of the master to make him a doorkeeper in some far-off spot.[189]

This description is interesting not just for its awareness of a complex managerial hierarchy, but also for its intimation of careful spatial surveillance: certain slaves were near the house, some were distant. The estate covered enough space that slaves were posted in faraway spots and made to monitor the coming and going of the workers. Augustine imagined that the higher-ranked slaves were nearer the estate center, but he nevertheless implies a degree of control over the lower, more distant slaves.

Augustine's sermons are invaluable because they constitute the most important dossier of evidence for life in an ordinary western city of the late empire. They form a desperately needed if imperfect control on the lack of documentary data in the west and the overrepresentation of the senatorial class. The evidence of Augustine can remind us that the findings of archaeology do not have to be twisted into a scheme which posits fundamental shifts in the organization of production between the high and late empire. The curial class, in all its diversity, was a crucial force in controlling production, and it managed a subject labor force that

---

[187] Aug. Serm. 113.6 (PL 38: 651): *aliquando transimus viam, et videmus amoenissimos et uberes fundos, et dicimus: cuius est ille fundus? asseritur illius: et nos dicimus, beatus homo: vanitatem loquimur. beatus cuius est illa domus, beatus cuius est ille fundus, beatus cuius est illud pecus, beatus cuius est ille servus, beatus cuius est illa familia.*
[188] Aug. Civ. 22.8 (CC 48: 820).
[189] Aug. Psalm. 103.4.10 (CC 40: 1530): *domus ista magna habet dominum, habet servos, et in ipsis servis habet circa se proximos sibi in apparatibus melioribus vestium, thesaurorum, horreorum, magnarum possessionum; habet etiam servos in infimis ministeriis, ita subditis sibi potestatibus, ut quosdam habeat et ad mundandas cloacas; a summis procuratoribus usque ad extrema ista et infima ministeria quam multi sunt gradus. si ergo aliquis magnus procurator offendat, et poena domini sui, verbi gratia, fiat ostiarius in aliquo loco extremo.*

included both tenants and slaves. The story of Roman slavery is incomplete without accounting for the ordinary rich man, with his cattle, vines, and slaves, on the horizons of a late Roman town like Hippo. The imperial constitutions of the fourth century add highly credible evidence to the testimony of Augustine.[190]

Augustine's sermons also point us to a specific role of slave labor in the western countryside: the use of slaves as herders. Rearing animals was one of the most important slave occupations, from the age of the great revolts (instigated and organized by slave shepherds) to the fall of the Roman empire (when once again roving bands of transhumant shepherds threatened the security of Italy).[191] The search for ancient "modes of production" has directed attention towards crops rather than livestock, but animals were an integral part of Mediterranean farming, and indeed the very conception of wealth in late antiquity entailed owning land, herds, and slaves.[192] We should be attuned to hear this deep connection between wealth and the ownership of animals. Moreover, the persistent association between "herds and slaves," four-footed and man-footed creatures, is equally telling of a systematic affinity between livestock, slavery, and the accumulation of wealth in late antiquity.

We can distinguish two types (not stark alternatives) of livestock cultivation in Roman farming: estate-centered and transhumant.[193] In the first case, animals were integrated within a form of intensive Mediterranean estate management. In a series of articles, Kron has demonstrated that the Romans already practiced a form of convertible husbandry in which, rather than biennial fallow, arable land was turned over to pasture for several years to regenerate its soil nutrients.[194] In this process animals are essential, and they provide valuable draught power and secondary products besides. This style of land-use, in which agriculture and animal husbandry are fundamentally complementary, was capital-intensive. In the second case, the rearing of livestock is a primary and independent aim, and pasture must be sought away from the estate in seasonal transhumance. This form of husbandry required space and was often located in secondary regions where there was land to roam.

We have already seen several examples of integrated estate-centered animal husbandry, including the estates on Lesbos and at Hermonthis. Traces

[190] CT 10.1.2 (AD 357); CT 10.8.4 (AD 353); CT 7.19.1.3 (AD 399) probably Africa.
[191] Russi 1986.   [192] See p. 200. In general, Gabba 1988. Greece: Hodkinson 1988, 65.
[193] The essays in Whittaker 1988; esp. Garnsey 1988c, 201; Frayn 1984, 45–6.
[194] Kron 2005 and 2000.

of "estate-centered agro-pastoralism," consistent with seasonal transhumance or farm-based pasturage, are found archaeologically in late antiquity from North Africa to Palestine.[195] Estate-based livestock was a source and a sign of wealth, as the mosaic evidence for flocks on African *villae* attests.[196] Clearly not all slaves in animal rearing were herders roaming the distant hills: a Vandal in the fifth century made one of his slaves a cowherd "not far from Carthage, where he would be seen by everyone."[197] That manuring was a characteristically servile task is another sign of the integration of slavery, agriculture, and husbandry on the estate.[198]

At the same time, slavery was also adaptive to the practice of transhumant shepherding in late antiquity. Chapter 3 has cited passages from Basil and Asterius, in Cappadocia and Pontus, which made reference to the giant herds and weaving installations that were the center of great wealth. The emperor Julian knew a rich man with vast flocks of sheep, cattle, goats, and horses, tended by "both slave and free hired shepherds."[199] Augustine repeatedly mentioned slaves, presumably with some degree of mobility, using the master's brand even as they stole his sheep.[200] He also imagined good shepherds – simply presumed to be slaves – who tried to keep their master's flock intact.[201] Transhumance and textile production flourished in late antique Italy, and several laws in the *Theodosian Code* point to the close connection between pastoralism and brigandage in southern Italy.[202]

The economic advantages of animal husbandry are apparent. Meat, leather, and wool were valuable; manure contributed to intensive farming; female slave labor could be integrated with textile production. The use of slaves in estate-centered animal husbandry allowed close supervision of the workers, but the suitability of slave labor in more distant, transhumant styles of animal rearing is less obvious. Reduced supervision gave slaves the opportunity to steal or to flee, as the writings of Augustine illustrate. Certainly shepherding could be performed by slave or free workers, as the passage of Julian attests. Perhaps it was difficult to contract or to find enough free laborers for this sort of work, but the association between herds

---

[195] Mattingly and Hitchner 1995, 195; Hitchner 1994, 38. In the east, see Dar 1986, 203.

[196] E.g. from Tabarca, Sarnowski 1978, fig. 5, early fifth century; from the villa of Dar Buc Amméra, Aurigemma 1926, 88, fig. 54. Gsell 1932, 406.

[197] Vict. Vit. Hist. Pers. 1.44 (CSEL 7: 11): *haut procul Carthagine, ubi ab omnibus videretur*.

[198] On manuring, Kron 2005, 293.

[199] Iul. Imp. Or. 7.22 (Rochefort: 75), speaking of Constantine: ποιμένες δοῦλοί τε καὶ ἐλεύθεροι μισθωτοί.

[200] Aug. Ep. 105.1 (CSEL 34.2: 595–6); Aug. Cresc. 1.30.35 (CSEL 52.2: 355).

[201] Aug. Ep. 185.23 (CSEL 57: 22).

[202] See Volpe 1996, 285, textile industry in southern Italy; Vera 2002; Russi 1986.

and slaves is too tight and too enduring to believe that slave labor was not somehow intrinsically adaptive to animal husbandry, even when pasturage was distant.[203] Positive incentives surely complemented the use of pain incentives in his corner of the slave system to make slavery an effective form of labor.[204] The *peculium* might be used not only as incentive but also as security.[205] Certainly late ancient land-owners were aware of the dynamic relationship between risk, incentives, and profit:

> If a master were to commit his sheep into the care of his slave, without doubt he would consider whether the *peculium* of that slave was worth the value of his sheep. And he would reckon, "If the slave loses them, if the slave wastes them, if the slave consumes the sheep, he should have enough to return the value." The master would entrust his sheep therefore to a slave with sufficient means . . . [206]

If once upon a time Odysseus could bask in the pure loyalty of his herder, the late Roman master took out insurance! But from one end of antiquity to the other, slaves and animals were interdependent variables in the equation of wealth.

The literary evidence gathered so far suggests the use of slave labor by Elite land-holders in late antique Africa, northern Italy, and southern Gaul – socially and geographically outside the heartland of Illustrious property.[207] This has been an attempt to counterbalance the near-exclusive focus on the very largest senatorial properties, which have been the prime movers in the interdependent narratives of latifundism and the colonate. It is significant that, wherever there is documentary evidence, land-holding patterns appear highly stratified but hardly concentrated in a few hands. Settlement archaeology, moreover, has demonstrated the continuing vitality of mid-sized estate centers in the late empire, the sort of properties that could be plausibly associated with Elite land-owners.[208] At the same time, surveys and excavations have uncovered evidence for monumental villas in the fourth and fifth centuries that surely belonged to Illustrious households, the old senatorial class, the wealthiest 500 or so families of the empire. Indeed, while their extraordinary wealth is not to be the only focus of discussion, it is also not to be neglected.

---

[203] Hodkinson 1988, 55, for Greek slaves.
[204] Carlsen 1991, on the *magister pecoris* and the frequency of family life.
[205] CJ 4.26.10 (AD 294).
[206] Aug. Serm. 296.4 (Morin: 403): *si dominus homo servo suo commendaret oves suas, procul dubio cogitaret utrumnam peculium servi illius idoneum esset pretio ovium suarum, et diceret: si perdiderit, si dissipaverit, si consumpserit, habet unde reddat. commendaret ergo idoneo servo oves suas.*
[207] Also CT 10.12.1–2 (AD 368); CJ 11.53.2–3 (AD 371); CT 10.8.1 (AD 313), Italy.
[208] Brogiolo and Chavarría Arnau 2005; Lewit 2004.

There is still work to be done on the scale and organization of western properties in the late empire, but the richest senatorial families may have owned land on the order of tens of thousands of *iugera*, implying thousands or even tens of thousands of laborers.[209] Symmachus owned three suburban *villae* and no less than twelve *villae* in central Italy, plus land in southern Italy, Sicily, and Mauretania; Melania and Pinian owned estates in eight provinces.[210] Western senators were the only proprietors with truly multi-regional reach, but even their lands were concentrated in the triangle of Italy, Sicily, and North Africa. In aggregate, the senatorial order would have dominated, though not exclusively controlled, agricultural production in the western heartland.

Property ownership of this magnitude is often claimed to have under-mined the viability and profitability of slavery, as units of ownership became too large to manage closely. There is a kernel of truth here, since tenancy, reduced supervision costs, and arable cultivation were compatible. But as a framing narrative of fourth-century labor, this story has more to do with Marxist orthodoxy than the evidence of the period. As Finley long ago noted, what is relevant is the unit of exploitation, not ownership.[211] It is eminently plausible that wealthy senators collected rents from distant estates but maintained pockets of intensely managed land near markets or on their more valuable land. There is a clear logic of supervision and com-mercialization behind the prominence of "our slaves in the suburbs."[212] In short, with enormous properties that mimicked the dynamics of the rural economy as a whole, Illustrious households held diversified portfo-lios, mixing their products and their exposure to risk, combining slavery and tenancy without necessarily turning their slaves into tenants.

There are some important indications of managerial hierarchies, intensely managed units of property, and the use of slave labor on Illustri-ous land in the late empire. Chapter 3 has already explored the household of the senator Symmachus, which furnishes insights into the ways that a far-flung portfilio was managed.[213] The patrimony of Symmachus was a conglomerate agricultural firm run out of his household. Procurators, sec-retaries, and couriers connected the central staff to the local agents. On the ground *actores* and *vilici* oversaw the management of estates, the collection of rents, and the process of cultivation. Yet it would not have been pos-sible to control wealth on the senatorial scale without the visible hand of

---

[209] See p. 167.   [210] Seeck, MGH AA 6.1: xlv–xlvi.   [211] Finley 1998 (orig. 1980), 201.
[212] For Melania, see p. 192. On suburbs generally, Morley 1996, 83–107; Purcell 1995.
[213] Vera 1986b is fundamental.

imperial government. When Symmachus had to collect from a defaulting tenant "who with all of his *familia* has been bound to my house for a long time," he promptly wrote to the governor: "Your intervention can and must fill in for my presence."[214] On another occasion, Symmachus also asked a governor to recover fugitive slaves.[215] These letters are a reminder that the giant absentee wealth of the senatorial class was a collective feat of government enforcement and private management.[216]

Unfortunately the evidence for farm management in the fourth-century west is thin, for the simple reason that no contemporary agricultural writer has survived. The *Opus agriculturae* of Palladius belongs to the mid- or late fifth century, severely limiting its value as evidence for the style of land management in the fourth century.[217] Moreover, Palladius offers only a minimalist account of labor. The sheer diversity of opinion about his tract is a warning that we risk reading our own narratives of Roman agriculture into a pliable text.[218] With that caveat, the widespread notion that Palladius was running an estate where rent collection took precedence over direct management is difficult to maintain. The only time he mentioned tenants was in a passage that specifically advised an estate-owner *not* to lease out land to neighboring land-holders or tenants.[219] He advised the presence of the master on the estate, if possible, and the continual presence of a procurator, if not.[220] The entire cycle of work – plowing, sowing, harvesting, trimming, pressing, fertilizing – was organized centrally and supervised directly by the master's agents in the field.[221] He advised the owner to keep his own iron-workers, carpenters, jar- and cask-makers, on the estate, "lest the regular labor of rustics turns to the city for lack of these things."[222] The whole estate of Palladius was geared to intensify production through direct control.

---

[214] Symm. Ep. 9.11 (MGH AA 6.1: 238): *vicem praesentiae meae et possit et debeat tuus interventus inplere... dudum domui nostrae cum familia sua dicit obnoxium.* cf. Symm. Ep. 9.6 (MGH AA 6.1: 236).

[215] Symm. Ep. 9.140 (MGH AA 6.1: 273).

[216] E.g. CJ 11.48.12 (AD 396) and CJ 6.1.1–8 (from Diocletian to Theodosius).

[217] Martin 2003, VII–XX.

[218] For slaves, see Banaji 2009, 68; Grey 2007b; Rosafio 1994; MacMullen 1987, 375; Kuziščin 1979, 240–1. *Contra*, Wickham 2005a, 269; Vera 1999; Giardina 1986; Frézouls 1980; Shtaerman and Trofimova 1975, 336.

[219] Pall. Op. ag. 1.6.6 (Martin: 9).

[220] Pall. Op. ag. 1.6.1 (Martin: 7); Pall. Op. ag. 1.36.1 (Martin: 45).

[221] Rosafio 1994, 154. Pall. Op. ag. 2.10.4 (Rodgers: 62); Pall. Op. ag. 2.3.2 (Rodgers: 58). cf. Colum. 2.4.3 (Lundström: 61–2).

[222] Pall. Op. ag. 1.6.2 (Martin: 8): *ne a labore sollemni rusticos causa desiderandae urbis avertat.* MacMullen thought that the use of "*rustici*" was itself probative evidence of the servile status of these field laborers. The passage of Varro, 1.16.4, uses the phrase, *ne de fundo familia ab opere discedat.* Geopon. 2.49.2 (Beckh: 85) speaks of keeping the "γεωργοί" on the fields. The description certainly entails central management, possibly slave labor.

In the most explicit reference to slavery in his manual, Palladius advised his readers, "Do not appoint the head of the farm from among the beloved slaves, since trusting in previous affection, he will think he is unpunishable for his present faults."[223] At the very least, this passage implies that the estate of Palladius had farm managers who were slaves. But there is no way to know if such slaves were appointed to managerial positions from the urban staff or if they had risen through the ranks of the farm slaves. It is safest to read the manual of Palladius on its own terms, recognizing that his primary objective was to describe an efficient use of time, not of land or labor. The bulk of the manual is organized by the calendar, as the author describes the work suitable for each month of the year. This was Palladius' "idée de génie."[224] The concern with time is entirely compatible with sophisticated management of a tightly controlled labor force. If a land-owner owns agricultural labor in the form of slaves – a sort of fixed capital – he will be eager to distribute labor over the calendar in an efficient manner.[225] Palladius also considered the labor inputs of women and children: "there is not a woman who does not know how to raise chickens."[226]

Ultimately, it is wisest to remain something of an agnostic about the significance of Palladius for the status of labor in the western countryside. The archaeology of the fifth century would suggest that Palladius was writing as elite investment in agriculture and control of the productive process was breaking down, and his account could just as easily be seen as a reaction against this trend as an expression of it. The real significance of Palladius is that he reveals the whole spectrum of decisions about land allocation, labor management, intensification, storage, construction, and industrial production which faced a Roman land-owner. Even if Palladius was not running a plantation *à la* Columella, he clearly advocated control over the productive process on his estates. The villa of Palladius cannot be seen as the terminal point of a long movement away from the slave mode of production.

If Palladius is reticent about the status of labor, the literary evidence for Illustrious property in the fourth century offers ample evidence for the use of both slave labor and tenancy. Symmachus, for instance, certainly

---

[223] Pall. Op. ag. 1.6.18 (Martin: 13): *agri praesulem non ex dilectis tenere servulis ponas, quia fiducia praeteriti amoris ad inpunitatem culpae praesentis expectat*. Martin 2003, 112.

[224] Martin edn. of 2003, XXVI.   [225] Anderson and Gallman 1977. cf. Roth 2007, 16.

[226] Pall. Op. ag. 1.27.1 (Martin: 26): *Gallinas educare nulla mulier nescit*. 8.7.1 and 11.14.16 (Rodgers: 174–5 and 211): boys. This is not an argument against the presence of slaves (Vera 1999, 288), unless one believes the masculine army-barracks version of slavery. cf. Laes 2008, 247, for child slaves in the Julius mosaic. Campbell, Miers, and Miller 2006, comparatively, child slaves usually start by tending barn animals such as chickens or pigs.

employed tenants, for he is found collecting their rents, forgiving arrears, and lamenting their poverty.[227] But the presence of rural slaves haunts his letters, too, and not only on his own estates, but also those of his senatorial colleagues. In two separate cases which Symmachus judged during his tenure as urban prefect, inheritance disputes over senatorial estates involved the possession of rural slaves.[228] Another senator, Celsinus Titianus, must have also had slaves on his land, since Symmachus had to write him a letter of complaint when the workers "by a servile daring," had stolen a field.[229] These are impressionistic clues, but the larger significance of slave labor can be inferred from the senator's horror at the idea of conscripting slaves into the imperial army after the revolt of Gildo.[230] Both the proposal itself, and the frustration on the part of land-owners, suggest that slaves existed in some number.

There is evidence beyond Symmachus that slave labor was important on senatorial land in the late Roman west. The author of the *Augustan History*, writing in the late fourth century, assumed that an imperial pretender of the late third century, from northern Italy, could mobilize 2,000 of his own slaves, or that another emperor could try to replenish the wine industry of Etruria by "settling captive slaves there, planting the hills with vines, and producing wine through this project in such a manner that the fisc would receive none of the revenues, but everything would be given to the benefit of the Roman people."[231] Rutilius Namatianus claimed that his relative put down an insurrection with undertones of servile resistance in northern Gaul.[232] In 416–17, two Spanish brothers conscripted an army composed of "slaves and peasants" to repel the usurper Constantine.[233] Paulinus of Pella and the Gallic Chronicle reported social unrest involving slaves in fifth-century Gaul.[234] None of the sources are as specific or as credible as we would like, and they are too diffuse to be of much value, but they do reveal a contemporary belief that slaves occupied the countryside in masses.

---

[227] Vera 1986b, 258–9.
[228] Symm. Rel. 28.3 (MGH AA 6.1: 302–3); Symm. Rel. 48 (MGH AA 6.1: 316).
[229] Symm. Ep. 1.74 (MGH AA 6.1: 32): *servili ausu.*
[230] Symm. Ep. 6.64 (MGH AA 6.1: 171), although Symmachus does not specify how the slaves at issue were employed (*movent in usum militarem petita servitia*), the context suggests large numbers of able-bodied male slaves. See also chapter 6.
[231] SHA, Quadr. Tyr. 12.1–2 (Hohl vol. 2: 230); SHA, Div. Aur. 48.2 (Hohl vol. 2: 184–5): *illic familias captivas constituere, vitibus montes conserere atque ex eo opere vinum dare, ut nihil redituum fiscus acciperet, sed totum p. R. concederet.*
[232] Rutil. De red. lines 215–16 (Doblhofer: 104). Though see Minor 2000; Sánchez León 1996; Drinkwater 1989.
[233] Zos. 6.4.3 (Paschoud vol. 3.2: 8): πλῆθος οἰκετῶν καὶ γεωργῶν.
[234] Chron. Gall., a. 435 (MGH AA 9: 660). P. Pell. Euch. lines 329–42 (SC 209: 80). See chapter 6.

The only source which does provide real insight into an Illustrious property of the fourth century is the *Life of Melania*, written around 454 by a priest close to Melania in her later years.[235] Finley opened his chapter on late Roman slavery with this text because, if it is credible, it forces us to admit that slavery remained a vital institution.[236] The *Life* is a biography of a pious senatorial woman. At thirteen years of age, Melania was forced into marriage to ensure the biological succession of her family. By 405 Melania and her husband Pinian had lost two children, and her father passed away that year. The pair took a vow of abstinence. They spent the next two years with Paulinus at Nola, during which time Pinian would have turned twenty-five, at last old enough to assert full ownership over his patrimony.[237] Their plan to liquidate one of the largest properties in the empire met fierce resistance from the family of Pinian, whose brother Severus fomented resistance from the slaves. The slaves in the suburbs of Rome demanded that if they had to be sold, they wanted to be sold to Severus.[238] An independent report also contains oblique confirmation of this event, claiming that many of Melania's slaves were "unwilling" to be *freed* and demanded to pass into the ownership of Severus.[239] Both the motive and the means of using slave agitation in this sort of patrimonial jostling are plausible. Symmachus, as prefect of the city, had heard a case in which slaves had been provoked to cause trouble for inheritors.[240]

Melania and Pinian were shaken to see their slaves in rebellion, even – or especially – under the guidance of their relative. She reasoned to her husband, "If the slaves who are in the suburbs and under the power of our presence have dared to contradict us, what are the slaves in the other provinces, Spain, Italy, Apulia, Campania, Sicily, Africa, Numidia, Britain, and others farther still, likely to do?"[241] Slavery hardly seems confined to a small classical heartland. Melania and Pinian went to the imperial government, through the mediation of Serena, wife of Stilicho and cousin of the emperor Honorius. She heard their story and convinced Honorius

---

[235] In general, Clark 1984. For economic history, De Martino 1993b, 808–11; Giardina 1988.
[236] Finley 1998 (orig. 1980), 191; De Martino 1993b; MacMullen 1987, 374; Blazquez 1978, broadly accepting the *Life*'s reliability.
[237] Clark 1984, 100–1; Allard 1907.   [238] Geron. Vit. Mel. 10 (Gorce: 145–6).
[239] Pall. H. Laus. 61 (Butler: 156). Hardly a referendum on the "benevolence" of the Valerian clan, *contra* Barone Adesi 1990, 740; Gorce 1962, 145.
[240] Symm. Rel. 48 (MGH AA 6.1: 316).
[241] Geron. Vit. Mel. (lat.) 10.5 (Laurence: 172): *si hii qui in suburbano sunt constituti servi et sub praesentiae nostrae potestate aguntur haec nobis ausi sunt contradicere, quid facturi sunt illi qui in diversis aguntur provinciis, id est in Spaniis, Italia, Apulia, Campania, Sicilia, et Africa vel Numidia seu Britannia, aut procul in reliquis regionibus?*

to take their side. He gave orders that their properties were to be sold by imperial officials. It was a victory, but perhaps not the unqualified victory that the *Life* presents. Their property would be sold, by imperial agents and on the government's terms.[242]

While it is unclear whether Melania and Pinian originally intended to free or to sell their slaves, they were obviously slave-owners on a massive scale. Three different witnesses confirm the story. In the earliest testimony, Paulinus of Nola claimed that Pinian freed slaves (and debtors) all over the world.[243] The *Lausiac History* of Palladius, written around 420, is a second witness to the manumissions. Palladius is an informed but partial source who had actually stayed with Melania on her estates in 405. In his words, "She freed eight thousand of her slaves who were willing, for the rest were not willing but preferred to be the slaves of her brother. She let him have them all at three *solidi*."[244] There is some discrepancy between this report, that the slaves were to be manumitted, and the *Life*, in which they were to be sold.[245] It is clear though that in the end many slaves were sold to Severus, while many others were freed. The non-ascetic branch of the Valerian family managed to keep at least some of the patrimony together.[246] Palladius reckoned that Melania and Pinian were still able to manumit 8,000 slaves. The author of the *Life of Melania* claimed, "I would like to say how many thousands of slaves they gave freedom, if I could ascertain a number. So, lest I give a number too high or too low, and bring vainglory into this work (and besides, the number is known to God and to them), I pass on to something else."[247] The circumspection of this passage is notable. Relative to other religious biographies, the *Life of Melania the Younger* was a sober account, and its author did not balk at putting the total number of freed slaves in the thousands.[248]

The *Life* indicates that the properties of Melania and Pinian were spread across no fewer than eight provinces, yielding them an annual income of 120,000 *solidi*.[249] If we imagine that 80 percent of the income was earned

[242] Geron. Vit. Mel. 12 (Gorce: 153).   [243] P. Nol. Carm. 21 lines 255 ff. (CSEL 30: 166).

[244] Pall. H. Laus. 61 (Butler: 156): Ἠλευθέρωσε δὲ τὰ βουληθέντα ἀνδράποδα ὀκτακισχίλια, τὰ λοιπὰ γὰρ οὐκ ἐβουλήθησαν ἀλλ᾽ ᾑρήσαντο δουλεῦσαι τῷ ἀδελφῷ αὐτῆς. ᾧ παρεχώρησε πάντας ἀπὸ τριῶν νομισμάτων λαβεῖν.

[245] Giardina 1988, 136–8.

[246] The decree of Honorius may have been something of a compromise, since 3 *solidi* was a favorable sum: Jones 1964, 852. Harper 2010.

[247] Geron. Vit. Mel. (lat.) 34.5 (Laurence: 216): *vellem dicere quanta milia servorum libertati donaverunt, si numerum cognoscere potuissem; unde, ne plus aut minus pronuntians, vanam gloriam superducam (Deo et ipsis notum est), ad aliud transeam.*

[248] On the religious polemics of the *Life*, Clark 1984, 141–52.   [249] Hendy 1985, 202.

through farming, this income implies on the order of 55,000 *iuga* of land under their ownership.[250] That figure is something like the territory of several cities, and it would have required on the order of 25,000–50,000 laborers.[251] This is perhaps just possible among the very highest level of Roman land-owners. Certainly, the *Life* portrays two large rural estates of Melania in convincing detail. One was located on the coast of Sicily or Campania.[252] The devil tempted Melania with thoughts of "the precious statues or the various decorations, the many incomes or the immense register of people on the place. For this estate (*possessio*) had sixty *villae* around it, each with forty agricultural slaves."[253] The estate is described in the voice of Melania, as she may have remembered it years later in the presence of Gerontius. The seaside palace was surrounded by sixty *villae*, each with forty slaves, for a total of 2,400 slaves. The *Life* does not say how the slaves were managed, beyond the fact that they were organized into smaller production units. Perhaps the satellites were specialized or interdependent, and the breakdown into smaller groups may imply direct management. There is nothing in the text which indicates that these slaves were simply rent-paying tenants.[254] If management were entirely devolved, then why would the production be organized into units of forty laborers, rather than individual families? And why such regularity if these were not organized agricultural factories?

The *Life* described a second rural property far from the elegant seaside estate. When Melania made a sojourn to North Africa, she endowed the local church in Thagaste with "an estate that brought in an enormous income. The estate was bigger than the city itself, with a bath, many artisans working in gold, silver, and bronze, and two bishops, one of our

---

[250] Urban property investments of the Roman elite were considerable (Garnsey 1998b, 63–76), as were other financial, mercantile, and manufacturing interests. This land figure comes from assuming a rate of return equal to the roughly contemporary imperial estates in Asia (Chastagnol 1986).

[251] On manning ratios, see Spurr 1986, 133–46; Duncan-Jones 1974, 327.

[252] Marzano 2007, 47–81, on the *villa maritima* as an economic enterprise.

[253] Geron. Vit. Mel. (lat.) 18.3–4 (Laurence: 188–90): *pretiosa marmora et ornatos diversos vel multos reditus et censum eius immane. Habebat enim ipsa possessio sexaginta villas circa se habentes quadragintenos servos agricultores.* This last fact is unfortunately preserved only in the Latin version of the text. The better manuscript tradition (*CDE*) reports that each *villa* had 40 (*quadragintenos*) slaves, while an inferior version (*F*) has 400 slaves per *villa* (*quadringentenos*). The editor, Laurence, defers to the inferior tradition, since 24,000 slaves would be an "immense census" – 2,400 is immense enough! *Contra* MacMullen 1987, 374, the sentence should imply that each villa had 40 slaves, not that the *possessio* had 400 or 40 slaves in total. Whittaker and Garnsey 1998, 295, only consider the inferior reading (400 slaves) and consequently believe this was probably the total number of slaves rather that the number per unit. De Martino 1993b, 808, perceptively noted and favored this variant before the new critical edition.

[254] De Martino 1993b, 809. *Contra*, Vera 1986a, 407, 417.

faith and a heretic."[255] The status of the artisans on Melania's estate is not specified, although some of them certainly could have been slaves.[256] Strikingly, Gerontius admits to the presence of a Donatist bishop on the property. Not only is this another small sign of the author's honesty, it shows that on this center of agricultural and industrial production, peaceful management overrode orthodox piety.

The purpose of the *Life* was to describe the extraordinary piety of this late Roman matron. There is no need to be so credulous as to think every detail or figure is accurate. Even if she owned 8,000 slaves, it would not account for all the labor she needed to provide a 120,000 *solidi* income. But the *Life* is the only document of the fourth or early fifth centuries which describes the status of labor at the base of senatorial wealth. It is a story that is verified in many of its particulars, told by an author who is circumspect with numbers and honest even when inconvenient. Its orders of magnitude are plausible for the western Illustrious class, to which Melania and her family clearly belonged. The claim which most interests us, the claim of mass-scale slave-ownership, is confirmed by two other witnesses. The rural properties which are described add background to the sensational quantity of slaves. If Melania had lived in the last century BC, would not the story of her property be taken more or less at face value? This was not some great hoax. The *Life* is credible testimony that the wealth of a late Roman senator was unthinkable without *servi agricultores*.

The frustrating absence of documentary evidence and the primacy of literary evidence in the west makes it impossible to draw firm conclusions about the extent of rural slavery. This is one reason why archaeology, which can provide random and systematic data, seems to hold such hope for the interpretation of the limited literary evidence. If a type of settlement structure can be associated with social and economic patterns attested in the literature, then the extent of the latter could be judged by the spread of the former. But this has not proven possible, for archaeological finds typically do not allow conclusions about the structure of ownership or production. Even the interpretation of Settefinestre, one of the most remarkable excavations of a Roman site, remains controversial.[257] The economic interpretation of villas in the provinces and in the late empire

---

[255] Geron. Vit. Mel. (lat.) 21.4 (Laurence: 194): *possessionem multum praestantem reditum. Quae possessio maior erat etiam civitatis ipsius, habens balneum, artifices multos (aurifices, argentarios, et aerarios), et duos episcopos, unum nostrae fidei et alium haereticorum.* cf. CT 16.52 (AD 412).

[256] Bas. Hom. Div. 2.2 (Courtonne: 46–7); CT 9.42.7 (AD 369). cf. Palladius, p. 189.

[257] *Journal of Roman Archaeology* 2008 shows that it remains a lively issue. Within a few pages, Fentress 2008 vigorously defends the Carandini model, while Wilson 2008 offers an amusing anecdote about some of the identification methods at the excavation. Marzano 2007.

yields even more ambiguous results. Some have proposed that the on-site habitation of dependent workforces reflects the continuity of plantation slavery.[258] New excavations at the *Villa Magna* in Italy have uncovered what the archaeologists are cautiously but convincingly calling the "slave barracks," which certainly housed large numbers of laborers grouped into families in a single complex.[259] Yet others have resolutely argued that the monumental villas represent rent-collection centers for giant, tenant-run properties.[260] These are not mutually exclusive. We need to be able to imagine the data of rural survey in terms of a society as dynamic and complex as that reflected in the census inscriptions.[261]

More survey and excavation are unlikely to resolve this impasse, so long as the questions asked of the archaeological data are posed in unrealistically stark terms. The identification of the "slave mode of production" with plantation agriculture is deeply flawed. It is no surprise that the all-male, army-barracks model of plantation slavery is hard to find in the material evidence.[262] Villas, in all their variety, should be viewed as nodes of investment that reflect commercialization, intensification, and control over production. Threshing floors, presses, grain driers, storage facilities, craft workshops, textile implements, livestock pens, and residential quarters for dependants are signals which cannot be translated directly into conclusions about the form of labor, but they do reflect elite involvement in the productive process of the sort that made control over labor valuable.[263] These traces of investment are common on most mid-sized-to-large late Roman estates. At the same time, the absence of productive installations on some monumental sites should not be taken to reflect *rentier* land-owners rather than direct management. Monumental villas could have been related to productive *villae rusticae* in precisely the way reflected in the hierarchical integration of Melania's seaside palace and its slave-run satellites.

There is one type of material remain which can be read as straightforward evidence for the use of slave labor. A recent study by Henning contributes a chilling new proxy for physical coercion. It comes, moreover, from beyond the traditional heartland of central Italy. In the first systematic study of

---

[258] Esp. Samson 1989. Thompson 2003, 105, Spanish villas; Whittaker and Garnsey 1998, 296 (Sicily), 307 (Spain).

[259] Fentress, Goodson, and Maiuro 2009.   [260] Vera 2007, 496–7.

[261] cf. Brogiolo and Chavarría Arnau 2005, 34–9. Morley 1996, 99–100, on the earlier period.

[262] The stunning excavation of Settefinestre has probably discouraged the search for and identification of servile quarters near other villas in unattached huts, barns, and cottages: Webster 2008 and 2005, and Marzano 2007, esp. 131. Thompson 2003, 103–30.

[263] Chavarría Arnau 2004, 69; Scott 2004, 54; Van Ossel and Ouzoulias 2000, 155–6; Van Ossel 1992, 154–5.

iron finds on the villas of Gaul, he found a remarkable number of human shackles from third- and fourth-century villas.[264] The contexts of the finds, on rural estates, suggest that these are the relics of slave-based farming rather than simply the slave trade. Chains were, undoubtedly, a prominent tool of slave-ownership, and their preservation on northern villa sites must rank among the most important evidence for brute physical coercion in the rural sector of the northwestern Roman empire.[265]

What the archaeological data can most reliably provide is evidence for the long-term rhythms of intensification and abatement in the Roman economy. The archaeological record has demonstrated the vitality of villas in the western countryside of the fourth and early fifth centuries.[266] Yet there are good reasons to locate a decisive point of change in the middle of the fifth century. Wickham's *Framing the Early Middle Ages* describes a long process of involution that began in the fifth century, marked by the recession of market demand and by reduced levels of elite control over the countryside.[267] The pace of the change differed regionally, but the overall trajectory seems certain. Virtually no new aristocratic residences are detectible in the countryside of the fifth, sixth, and seventh centuries.[268] This is a solid and stunning fact: thousands of new villas have been found from the fourth century, only a handful from the next few hundred years. Villas continued to be occupied, in many cases.[269] Certainly new buildings continued to be built in wood.[270] The landscape was not abandoned. It was poorer, and less integrated into the circulation of goods, capital, and investment.[271] Coins, abundantly attested in fourth-century layers, vanish from the villas.[272] High-quality pottery becomes increasingly hard to find. "It seems clear that the Roman villa-estate, closely tied to a commercial market exchange, was no longer the basis of Roman exploitation."[273]

---

[264] Henning 2008; Thompson 2003, 217–44, and 1993, 149.

[265] Use of shackles to discipline slaves: Lact. Inst. 5.18 (CSEL 19.1: 461); Amm. 28.1.55 (Seyfarth vol. 2: 71); Ioh. Chrys. Ad pop. Ant. 9.3 (PG 49: 108); Ioh. Chrys. Lib. Repud. 2.1 (PG 51: 218); Ioh. Chrys. Virg. 41.2 (SC 125: 236–8); Ambr. Tob. 8.31 (CSEL 32.2: 535); Ambr. Psal. 118.3.6 (CSEL 62: 43); Lib. Or. 45.5 (Foerster vol. 3: 361); Lib. Or. 51.6 (Foerster vol. 4: 9); Lib. Decl. 1.41 (Foerster vol. 5: 36); Cyr. Jo. 4.387A (Pusey: 568); Bas. Hom. Mart. Iulit. 6 (PG 31: 252); Aug. Serm. 161.9 (PL 38: 883).

[266] Chavarría and Lewit 2004; Lewit 1991. Lewit 2004, VI–VII. Spain, Chavarría Arnau 2007. In Britain, Dark 2004. In northern Gaul, decline was far less abrupt than once believed: Lenz 2001; Van Ossel 1992. Southern Gaul: Balmelle 2001.

[267] Wickham 2005a, 265.

[268] Brogiolo and Chavarría Arnau 2005, 49–68; Chavarría and Lewit 2004, 26–7.

[269] Chavarría and Lewit 2004, 31; Ripoll and Arce 2000.

[270] Van Ossel and Ouzoulias 2000, 146.

[271] Brogiolo 2005, 9; Balmelle 2001, 115–17; Van Ossel 1997, 102; Dark 1996, 18–19.

[272] Christie 2004, 7.   [273] Lewit 2004, x.

This trajectory towards lower levels of investment and market-oriented production had tremendous effects on the slave system. Roman slavery was situated in the sectors of the economy most influenced by elite land-ownership and market-oriented production, and these were the sectors of the post-Roman countryside most devastated by the fall of Rome. What we witness in the fifth-century west is an "equilibrium flip," a shift away from a system where demand for commodities in urban markets created rewards that encouraged land-owners to take the risks of direct control over production. By the sixth century, the villa network was moribund, and villages became increasingly dominant nodes in the settlement system. If demography and institutional change explain the recession of slave labor in the east, it is the overall decline of commercialization that was the motive force of change in the west.

We see the aggregate effects of this flip spread out over several centuries in the countryside of the west. The flip was a change of direction, not a sudden and total collapse. It should be no surprise to find exceptions, to find slaves even in the sixth or seventh centuries. They are there. Papal letters demonstrate as much, as does the famous will of Remigius.[274] These texts, though, must be read within the framework of the archaeology.[275] The material evidence shows that intensely managed estates were marginal in the countryside of the sixth and seventh centuries. Even if there are apparent continuities in the textual evidence, archaeology insists that there was no transition from slavery to serfdom in the early medieval centuries. It is worth noting too that the bulk of the evidence for continuity in the immediate post-Roman period rests on the barbarian law codes, texts which are normative, Romanizing, and by no means limpid commentaries on the state of the countryside. There lies a deep caesura in the history of rural society in the post-Roman era, and when the impresarios of the Carolingian estate re-started the process of intensification, they did so in a fundamentally new economic and institutional context.[276]

CONCLUSIONS: RE-FRAMING THE END OF ROMAN SLAVERY

The central claim of this chapter is simple: there is abundant evidence for agricultural slavery in the fourth century which must be explained in economic terms. It would be hyper-skeptical to dismiss this much evidence as an illusion, and it is dangerous to dismiss fourth-century slavery

---

[274] See Banaji 2009, 69. Visigothic Spain, see Corcoran 2003.   [275] Francovich 2005, 349.
[276] See the Conclusion for further thoughts on the post-Roman west.

as somehow inexplicable in a truly economic analysis. The interpretation offered here parts from the Marxist tradition in several ways. It forgoes the usual narrative tropes of transition or crisis. It does not predict an inevitable dissolution of the slave system. It does not equate the slave mode of production with the all-male plantation and instead tries to understand the role of slavery within the logic of intensive Mediterranean estate management. In short, the toolbox used in this chapter is equipped with the terms of supply and demand, institutions and estate management, rather than modes of production, surplus extraction, contradiction, and crisis.

At the same time, this chapter differs from recent analyses of Roman slavery in the late republic and early empire. These, I would submit, reflect the lingering influence of the conquest thesis. We sense a form of the "Goldilocks principle" at work. Roman slavery emerged under a narrow set of conditions that were *just* right: the massive influx of capital to Italy, the commitments of the free citizenry, cheap slaves, and open markets for wine. These conditions were aligned ever so briefly, making the decline of slavery inevitable. But this explanatory matrix has trouble processing the evident vitality of slavery into the high empire, to say nothing of the fourth century. The account offered in this chapter tries to correct the model by allowing slavery a more constructive role in the production of commodities on Mediterranean estates. Here we part ways with Finley and his heirs who privilege the "negative" condition, the absence of alternatives to slave labor. The technical and institutional efficiencies of slave labor made it more stable than it often appears in recent literature. Slave labor was valuable and effective; it had its own momentum.

This chapter has repeatedly made one rhetorical argument in favor of its model: the geographic distribution of slave labor. The Greek census inscriptions alone would seem to undercut any interpretation which privileges political over economic explanation, conquest over capital. The slave labor which appears in the Aegean and Asia Minor, Egypt and North Africa, can be explained within a model that is organized around supply and demand, formal institutions and estate management. The Roman Mediterranean could be considered much like late medieval Europe, a place where the sweeping force of commercialization and the swings of demographic change had complex and varied effects based on institutions, location, and local factor endowments. But in the Roman context, there was no serfdom, and a strong state constricted the ability of land-owners to extract labor from peasants. In the Roman world, commercialization, intensification, and slavery were connected by a deep and sinister logic that made control over human chattel the road to riches. In the fourth

century, the rich man was not a feudal lord or a *rentier*. He was a man
of commerce and estate management. In the fourth century, the rich man
was a slave-owner.[277]

---

[277] Iul. Imp. Or. 7.22 (Rochefort vol. 2.1: 75); Ioh. Chrys. Thdr. 1.18.17 (SC 117: 192); Ioh. Chrys.
Oppug. 3.16 (PG 47: 377); Ioh. Chrys. In Mt. 24.11 (PG 57: 319); Ioh. Chrys. In Mt. 32.4 (PG
57: 375); Ioh. Chrys. In Mt. 59.4 (PG 57: 608); Them. Or. 33.365a (Downey and Schenkel: 207);
Sedul. Op. 1.26 (CSEL 10: 190); Ps.-Ath. Virg. 91 (CSCO 593: 34); Lib. Ep. 385.2 (Foerster vol. 10:
375); Lib. Or. 7.9 (Foerster vol. 1: 375); Lib. Or. 8.1 (Foerster vol. 10: 385); Lib. Or. 50.20 (Foerster
vol. 3: 480); Lib. Or. 51.6 (Foerster vol. 4: 9); Lib. Or. 62.46–7 (Foerster vol. 4: 370); Bas. Attend.
5 (Rudberg: 31); Bas. Hom. Mart. Iulit. 1 (PG 31: 238); Aug. Conf. 1.19.30 (CC 27: 16–17); Aug.
Tract. Io. 8.4 (CC 36: 84); Aug. Ep. Io. 3.11 (PL 25: 2003); Aug. Psal. 48.2.7 (CC 38: 570); Aug. Psal.
55.19 (CC 39: 691); Aug. Psal. 64.8 (CC 39: 830); Aug. Util. iei. 13 (CC 46: 241); Aug. Serm. 21.9
(CC 41: 285); Aug. Serm. 113.6 (PL 38: 651).

PART II

The making of honorable society

Introduction

IN SEARCH OF MASTERS AND SLAVES

The people of fourth-century Antioch were famously devoted to their theater.[1] Built under the patronage of Julius Caesar, the theater of Antioch stood, there in the sloping foothills of Mount Silpius, as a monument of the city's deep Roman past.[2] But it was not, in the late empire, a fossilized remain from an extinct culture. The theater was a vital institution, and the mainstream of theatrical culture in late antiquity was the comic mime.[3] Mime was a form of dramatic comedy played by unmasked actors.[4] Travesties of myth, lampoons of public figures, and ethnic mockery were common themes of this inherently irreverent genre. But the natural subject of the mime was the portrayal of everyday, domestic life. One description called mime "an imitation of life, encompassing the permissible and the shameful."[5] Peopled with a familiar array of stock characters, the mime act was a medium where the dramatic possibilities of the faithless wife, the clever slave, the harsh father, the fool, the parasite, and the miser were reconfigured in endless permutations. Masters and slaves were foremost among the stock characters of the genre.[6] The basic symbols and character types of late Roman mime were enmeshed in the webs of significance produced by a violent and rigidly hierarchical social order. The mime – part slapstick, part sitcom, part minstrel show – was an organic cultural expression of a slave society.

---

[1] Soler 2004; Leyerle 2001, 15. Iul. Imp. Mis. 8 (Lacombrade: 163).
[2] Ioh. Mal. 9.5 (Thurn: 163). Downey 1961, 155–6, posits a major renovation sponsored by Caesar.
[3] Classical genres were still performed, too, Webb 2008, 26; Leyerle 2001, 20–1; Jones 1993; Roueché 1993, 25.
[4] Webb 2008, 95–115; Malineau 2005; Wiemken 1972.
[5] Diom. Ars Gr. 491 (Keil: 491): μῖμός ἐστιν μίμησις βίου τά τε συγκεχωρημένα καὶ ἀσυγχώρητα περιέχων.
[6] E.g. Choric. Or. 32.110 (Foerster and Richtsteig: 369).

The mime act generated its comic energy through the presentation of characters drawn from real life and stylized by a literary heritage.[7] A character was prefigured by an ensemble of inherent qualities and relations to other characters that could be manipulated on stage. Very often, this comic manipulation was produced by an excess of violence and obscenity, verbal play and mock stupidity. Comedy is one of the most inscrutable realms of any culture, but even the most sensitive review will struggle to find the humor in some of the extant fragments of ancient mime. The fragments of mime that survive are, by any standard, violent and lewd. The late antique stage was filled with sex-crazed wives, pathologically abusive masters, and slaves whose bodies could sponge any amount of physical torment. One source referred to the "peals of slapping" that reverberated from the theater; visual representations show masters beating their slaves as though this were more or less the basic image of the mime act.[8] In one story a lascivious mistress found that her slave would not gratify her sexual wishes; he became the object of her sadistic obsession – his teeth were smashed in, he was separated from the slave-girl he loved, and eventually his throat was slit.[9] We can easily enough diagram the inversion of social protocols in this story: cuckoldry was the paradigmatic example of subversion enacted in ancient mime, and adultery with a slave was the ultimate transgression of the Roman social order.[10] It is much more challenging, at this remove, to understand why it was so funny. The laughter is truly alien.[11]

There are two reasons for evoking the lost world of the late Roman theater. The first is that mastery and slavery were distinctly prominent roles among the *dramatis personae* of late antique society. These roles, of course, played out differently within individual stories, according to the circumstances of the narrative and individual improvisation. But the inherent structural features of the character determined the individual's range of motion and defined the meaning of the individual's action. Secondly, the world of mime needs to be evoked precisely because it is so obscure to us. Mime was *the* popular cultural medium in the late empire; its performers were the great celebrities of the late ancient world. And yet, these comic stories of late antique masters and slaves have been lost; there is no late antique Menander or Plautus. This has more to do with the transmission of

---

[7] Webb 2008, 104: "culturally sanctioned images of human types..."
[8] Arnob. Adv. Nat. 7.33 (CSEL 4: 267): *salapittarum sonitu*. cf. Choric. Or. 32.147–54 (Foerster and Richsteig: 378–9). Webb 2008, plate 8. Welborn 2005, 70; Rouéché 2002, fig. 47, 267.
[9] P. Oxy. 3.413. Andreassi 1999; Wiemken 1972, 81–109.
[10] Webb 2008, 103, 109–11; Malineau 2005, 154–5. cf. Philogel. 251 (Thierfelder: 122).
[11] Webb 2008, 116–38. For Plautine comedy, McCarthy 2000.

cultural artifacts than the underlying realities of art or society. The textual corpus as it survives is not representative, and the challenge only deepens as we turn towards the texts that we do have.

A spectator sitting in the theater of late antique Antioch looked down, towards the city.[12] If the theater-goer gazed past the long, marble colonnade that ran along Antioch's main street, towards the island in the Orontes which housed the imperial palace and hippodrome, his eyes would have met the gleaming, gilded dome of the city's Great Church.[13] The church was founded by Constantine as a monument to his new faith. Theater and church stood as antipodes of a cultural contrast in the late Roman city. Priests railed against attendance at the theater, while mime troupes blasphemed the mysteries of Christianity.[14] Our sources are one-sided, but we gather the feeling that, despite strong imperial patronage and enthusiastic episcopal activism, the church had a less organic relationship with the city than did the theater. Nestled in the heart of the imperial quarter, emitting unmissable signals of imperial favor, the church remained the newcomer, if not the outsider, in the fourth-century city.

At a distance of over a millennium and a half, it is not immediately obvious that the church struggled to be heard amidst the bustle of the late Roman town. Whereas the words spoken on stage in the late empire can only be re-assembled from the most insufficient fragments, the words which echoed through the air of the Great Church survive in superabundance. John Chrysostom alone has left behind nearly 1,000 sermons.[15] Ironically, this inveterate enemy of the theater is our primary informant for the stage.[16] And his homiletic corpus leaves us in no doubt that mastery and slavery were as prominent in the mind of an aggressive preacher as they were in the mime act. His sermons form one of the great sources for the historian of everyday life in antiquity, and they have often been mined for their extraordinary detail. Yet we must be cautious. A preacher like John Chrysostom was a performer no less than the actors of the theater – in his case, a highly trained and marvelously talented one.[17]

His genuine rhetorical talent, his uncompromising attitude, and his sense of everyday life make John Chrysostom an unparalleled source for the realities of Roman slavery. Most of his sermons are exegetical, taking

[12] Amm. 23.5.3 (Seyfarth vol. 1: 302), with Downey 1961, 443–4. Generally, Uggeri 1998.
[13] For the colonnade (sponsored by Augustus) see Downey 1961, 16–17, 173 and for the church, 342–5.
[14] Webb 2008, 99–100. Banned by Justinian: Nov. 123.44 (AD 546).
[15] Mayer 2005.   [16] Leyerle 2001, 42–74.
[17] On homiletics in general, see Harper forthcoming d; Mayer 2008; the essays in Cunningham and Allen 1998; Sachot 1994; Olivar 1991; Bernardi 1968. On their use for social history, Maxwell 2006; Allen and Mayer 1993; MacMullen 1989. On the rhetorical aspects, Kinzig 1997.

their cue from a passage of scripture, but there was always for John a direct, contemporary application. This was how the priest, for example, following the words of Paul, found himself preaching for calmness in the household, against "clamor." For Chrysostom, the abuse of slaves was the primary example of how a household would lose its aura of repose:[18]

My teaching about clamor especially applies to the tribe of women. Women, whenever they become enraged at their slave-girls, fill the whole house with their raucousness. Often, if the house is built along some narrow way, all those nearby will hear her shouting and the wailing of the slave-girl. What could ever be more shameful than to hear this shrieking? For right away they all stick their heads in and ask, "What is going on there?" "So-and-so," someone replies, "is beating her own slave."[19]

Here is an extraordinarily vivid scene, drawn from the life of late Roman Antioch, where domestic walls were porous shields of privacy and the noises of the household drifted through the public air. This simple scene, sketched with the mastery of an accomplished stylist, conjured the basic dilemmas inherent in a slave society. In his better moments, John Chrysostom confronted those realities with a humane sensibility.[20] His more radical tendencies, however, were continually blunted by the pragmatic requirements of reforming a lukewarm congregation: "So what then, there is no need to beat slaves? That's not what I'm saying. For it is necessary, but do not do it constantly, nor without measure, nor for one's own faults, as I am always saying, nor for some little flaw in her service, but only if she is injuring her own soul."[21] The techniques of Greek rhetoric were second nature to Chrysostom, and we can watch him put himself in the persona of the ordinary Antiochene, only to glide effortlessly back into his own voice and his exhortation against excessive violence.[22]

The vividness of Chrysostom's preaching makes it evident that just behind the rhetorical façade lay the problems of social life in a late Roman city. The problem of female violence against slaves was all too real.[23] John

---

[18] The sermon that follows was a riff on Eph. 4:31.

[19] Ioh. Chrys. In Eph. 15.3 ff. (PG 62: 109–10): καὶ μάλιστα ἐντεῦθεν ταχέως ἁλίσκεται τὸ τῶν γυναικῶν γένος, αἵ, ὅταν ὀργίζωνται ταῖς θεραπαινίσι, τὴν οἰκίαν ἅπασαν τῆς κραυγῆς πληροῦσι τῆς ἑαυτῶν. πολλάκις δὲ καὶ εἰ παρὰ στενωπὸν τυγχάνοι ᾠκοδομημένη ἡ οἰκία, καὶ οἱ παριόντες ἅπαντες ἀκούουσιν αὐτῆς βοώσης, καὶ τῆς θεραπαινίδος ὀλολυζούσης. Τί τούτου γένοιτ᾽ ἂν ἀσχημονέστερόν ποτε τοῦ κωκυτοὺς ἀκούειν; Πᾶσαι γὰρ εὐθέως διακύψασαι, Τί δὴ γέγονεν, ἐρωτῶσιν, ἐκεῖ; Ἡ δεῖνα, φησί, τὴν δούλην τύπτει τὴν αὑτῆς.

[20] Beautifully evoked, with particular reference to the problem of poverty, by Brown 1988, 305–22.

[21] Ioh. Chrys. In Eph. 15.3 (PG 62: 109): Τί οὖν, οὐ χρὴ τύπτειν; Οὐ τοῦτο λέγω. δεῖ μὲν γὰρ, ἀλλὰ μήτε συνεχῶς, μήτε ἀμέτρως, μήτε ὑπὲρ τῶν οἰκείων ἀδικημάτων, ὅπερ ἀεί φημι, μήτε τῆς ὑπηρεσίας ἄν τι ἐλλείπῃ, ἀλλ᾽ εἰ τὴν ἑαυτῆς βλάπτει ψυχήν.

[22] See Uthemann 1998, for the rhetorical strategy.   [23] See chapters 7 and 8.

Chrysostom's sermon accepted that the physical coercion of slaves was an inevitable part of life, but he insisted that it was a practice in need of refinement:

> What is most disgraceful of all, some mistresses are so ruthless and harsh that when they lash their slaves, the stripes don't dissipate within the day. They take off the girl's clothes, call their husband in for it, and tie them to the couch ... You expose your naked slave-girl to your husband? And don't think it shameful? Then you further stimulate him and threaten shackles, first insulting the pitiable and suffering girl with innumerable slurs, calling her a witch, a runaway, a whore ... Should this happen in Christian houses? "But slaves are an evil tribe," you say, "and reckless and shameless and incorrigible." Yes, I know this. But there are other ways to maintain order – fear, threats, words – which are more effective and rescue you from shame ... What if she should happen to go to the bath, and there are stripes on her naked back, and she carries around the marks of cruelty? "But the tribe of slaves is unbearable if they get reprieve." Yes, I know this ... Some women are so out of line they uncover the slave-girls' heads and drag them by the hair. *Why are you all blushing?* This sermon isn't aimed at all of you, but towards those who are drawn into savagery ... If she appeared to you with her head uncovered, you would call it an offense, but when you strip her, it is not? ... I am saying this to you now not for their sake, but for you the free, so that you do nothing indecent or shameful, so that the free women do nothing to harm themselves ... [24]

The homily on clamorous mistresses became a dialogue between Chrysostom and the conventional wisdom of his age. He couched his appeal as a call for tranquil household management, a sort of rule that would reflect the master's honor and sense of easy command. Even if his approach was camouflaged in conservative language, it outed the more visceral, hidden presumptions of the master class towards its slave population: uninhibited

[24] Ioh. Chrys. In Eph. 15.3–4 (PG 62: 109–10): Καὶ τὸ δὴ πάντων αἰσχρότερον, εἰσὶν οὕτως ἄγριαι καὶ ἀπηνεῖς, ὡς ἐπὶ τοσοῦτον μαστίζειν, ὡς μηδὲ αὐθημερὸν τοὺς μώλωπας σβέννυσθαι. Γυμνώσασαι γὰρ τὰς κόρας, καὶ τὸν ἄνδρα ἐπὶ τοῦτο καλέσασαι, δεσμοῦσι πολλάκις πρὸς τοῖς σκίμποσιν ... ἀλλὰ γυμνοῖς τὴν παιδίσκην, καὶ δεικνύεις τῷ ἀνδρί; καὶ οὐκ αἰσχύνῃ μή σου καταγνῷ; καὶ ἐπιπλέον αὐτὸν παροξύνεις, καὶ ἀπειλεῖς δῆσειν, μυρία πρότερον λοιδορησαμένη τῇ ἀθλίᾳ καὶ ταλαιπώρῳ, Θεσσαλίδα, δραπέτριαν, προεστῶσαν καλοῦσα ... Ταῦτα ἐν Χριστιανῶν οἰκίαις γίνεσθαι ἔδει; Ἀλλὰ πονηρὸν τὸ γένος, φησὶ, καὶ ἰταμὸν καὶ ἀναίσχυντον καὶ ἀδιόρθωτον. Οἶδα κἀγώ. ἀλλ᾽ ἔστιν ἑτέρως ῥυθμίσαι, φόβοις, ἀπειλαῖς, ῥήμασι, κἀκείνην μειζόνως δυναμένοις δάκνειν, καὶ σὲ τῆς αἰσχύνης ἀπαλλάξαι ... Εἶτα ἐν βαλανείῳ ἐὰν δέῃ προελθεῖν, μώλωπες κατὰ τῶν νώτων γυμνουμένης αὐτῆς, καὶ τεκμήρια περιφέρει τῆς ὠμότητος. Ἀλλ᾽ ἀφόρητον, φησὶν, ἀνέσεως τυχὸν τὸ δουλικὸν γένος. Οἶδα κἀγώ ... Νυνὶ δὲ εἰς τοσοῦτό τινες ἀτοπίας ἥκουσιν, ὡς ἀποκαλύπτειν τὴν κεφαλὴν, καὶ ἀπὸ τριχῶν σύρειν τὰς θεραπαινίδας. Τί ἠρυθριάσατε πᾶσαι; Οὐ πρὸς πάσας ἡμῖν ὁ λόγος. ἀλλὰ πρὸς τὰς εἰς τὴν θηριωδίαν ἐξελκομένας ταύτην ...Ἂν μὲν οὖν γυμνῇ φανῇ σοι τῇ κεφαλῇ ἐκείνῃ, ὕβριν τὸ πρᾶγμα λέγεις. σὺ δὲ αὐτὴν γυμνοῦσα, οὐδὲν δεινὸν εἶναι φής; ... Ταῦτα ἡμῖν νῦν οὐχ ὑπὲρ ἐκείνων εἴρηται, ἀλλ᾽ ὑπὲρ ὑμῶν τῶν ἐλευθέρων, ὥστε μηδὲν ἄσεμνον, μηδὲν αἰσχρὸν ποιεῖν, ὥστε μὴ βλάπτειν ἑαυτάς.

by the normal rules of honor and shame, slaves were unbearable if not disciplined by continuous and brutal violence. Chrysostom was testing the limits of his audience. Men and women were physically separated in the nave, and we might imagine the preacher drawing his eyes slowly across the women's gallery as he unleashed his harshest words.[25] Having made them "all" blush, he retreated to the safer ground of improving upon the honor of free women and in doing so invoked an ancient discourse on the appropriate application of violence.[26]

This sermon, even as it sets out to amend the experience of the master–slave relationship, makes revealing assumptions about the nature of the relationship. It was a relationship of domination. Whether it was rhetorical posture or his own conviction, the preacher had to accept that slaves were literally "without shame." Slaves were consequently disciplined by violence, though Chrysostom would have preferred an arsenal of substitutes – fear, threats, words. Slavery activated the entire network of power in the household – the authority of the mistress, for instance, might rely upon the physical force of her husband. Above all, the sermon exposed how incurable the basic framework of master–slave relations remained in late antiquity. A truly passionate reformer like Chrysostom, whose suggestions were, in the end, relatively mild, was dancing along the edge of what his audience would bear to hear. His effort to mitigate the wild violence of household relationships was laced with caveats and equivocations (and a misogyny that was surely strategic). His solution was not to attack the root problem, domination itself, the *dominium* of one human over another. Chrysostom focused his energies on the excess violence of the relationship.

Chrysostom's sermons provide us unparalleled access to the ancient world. Here is the opportunity to step into a church sixteen hundred years in the past and listen to a popular preacher at an instant of momentous Christianization. Violence against slaves was something he was "always" preaching about. But, to be sure, this speech was not an unmediated reflection of social life. It was produced by a master of Greek rhetoric; it was prompted by reflection on a textual canon; it was shaped by an ancient discourse of polite mastery; it was stylized by the cultural personae of the master, the mistress, and the slave. But it would be unduly skeptical to deny the extraordinary value of this document. The palpable tension between preacher and audience, the dialectic between scriptural norm and everyday practice, is precisely what gives this sermon such authenticity. The homily on clamorous mistresses provides, in fact, an all too rare glimpse of the

---

[25] Mayer 1997, for the "dynamics of liturgical space."   [26] For which see McKeown 2007, 45.

collision between Christian norms and the inertia of social reality. More often we will have to make critical judgments without the benefit of a speaker who is so engaged and an audience who is so near.

In searching for the master–slave relationship, we must be conscious of what has been lost, even as we are critical of what has survived. It is no simple task to reconstruct the experience of mastery and slavery in the late empire. But by situating the preacher and the mime in the same cityscape, we begin to imagine a world that was still classical and becoming Christian. Most denizens of the late empire approached this dualism with a mind for accommodation.[27] In fact, what most bothered Chrysostom was his inability to keep his flock out of the theater. In both theater and church the inhabitant of a late Roman town encountered representations of mastery and slavery. If the ecclesiastical representation of slavery was solemn, while the theatrical version was farcical, both representations have something to tell us about a world where the basic social roles were shaped by the practices of domination. The rest of this Introduction will explore how we might begin to recover the realities of that world, first by looking at some old, problematic approaches before offering a new framework for assessing the lived experience of masters and slaves in the late empire.

"AMELIORATION" AND CHRISTIANIZATION

Most investigations into the experience of late Roman slavery have started in the church. This point of departure is understandable, since the patristic record is so dominant. More problematically, though, the relationship between Christianity and slavery was long studied in terms of "amelioration," the thesis that master–slave relations improved over time.[28] The idea of amelioration was so entrenched for so long that the debate was not *whether* amelioration happened, but whether Stoicism, Christianity, or economic change was to be credited.[29] Although it received brief if withering criticism from Finley, the amelioration thesis is one of those themes

---

[27] See, e.g., Salzman 2002.
[28] Allard 1876; Wallon, 1847, and Biot 1840 were foundational (Harrill 1995, 80–1, notes that Allard's book went through six editions). Material causes: Ciccotti 1899, 271–81; Pólay 1969. For concise statements of the amelioration thesis, see Gaudemet 1958, 564–7; Westermann 1955, 114–17. Significant efforts to assess the impact of late antique Christianity on slavery include Nathan 2000, 169–84; Klein 1999; Garnsey 1998a and 1996; Frend 1993; Waldstein 1990; MacMullen 1986a; Maraval 1970. For approaches to individual Christian authors, see Serfass 2006; Klein 2001, 2000 and 1988; Kontoulis 1993; Corcoran 1985; Giordiano 1980; Jaeger 1974; Mary 1954. The question of Christian influence on Roman slave law is independently vast: see part III.
[29] Wallon 1847, vol. 2, 1–46.

in the study of ancient slavery that has quietly faded from respectability. No one ever explained what evidence would justify the belief in a change of habits, nor by what mechanisms new cultural values could fundamentally transform the institution of slavery. It lacked basic plausibility, and probably few believe it any more.[30] Yet we must reckon with the lingering distortions introduced by a paradigm that managed to hold the field, after all, for at least a century.

The amelioration thesis quietly influenced which evidence was put into discussion. In a debate about *why* slavery was ameliorated, prescriptive evidence was more important than descriptive evidence. The abundant documentation about the realities of slavery, particularly in late antiquity, was marginalized during the nineteenth and early twentieth centuries, the great period of positivist research. Literary evidence that did not enter modern discourse in the age of Daremberg-Saglio and Pauly-Wissowa has tended never to enter circulation, relegating to oblivion a mass of important source material. Hence, the remarkable homily of John Chrysostom on clamorous mistresses has almost never received comment or notice.

The amelioration thesis, moreover, has promoted a profoundly impoverished analysis of Christianization. The amelioration thesis sets up a static model of the relationship between Christianity and slavery. In this account the Christian idea of slavery is located, optimistically, in the claim that there is neither Jew nor Greek, male nor female, slave nor free in the promise of salvation. This statement was the basis for a long-lived if superficial optimism about slavery in the Christian era, among ancient Christians and modern historians alike.[31] But the Christian reaction to slavery was neither simple nor stable. The conversion of society to the new religion was still underway in our period, an age of tremendous ideological upheaval. It is imperative to recognize that Christianization was a dynamic, ongoing, and largely unfinished process in our period.[32] Our sources must be seen within that process, not as expressions of a timeless Christian attitude towards slavery.

The fourth century was bookended by two monumental acts of Christianization – the legitimation of the new religion under Constantine and its final ascendance as the official public religion under Theodosius. In late antiquity pagan temples were closed, the old rites were outlawed, the church was given civil authority, and the new religion came to control

---

[30] Although, see Whittaker and Grabar 1999, 699; Cantarella 1996, 129; Kontoulis 1993, 338.

[31] Ancient optimism: e.g., Ioh. Chrys. In 1 Cor. 19.4–5 (PG 61: 155–7). Modern: Wallon 1847, vol. 3, 296–443. Wallon's book carried the vulgate of Gal. 3:28 as an epigraph.

[32] Maxwell 2006; the essays in Harris 2005; Markus 1990; MacMullen 1984.

the calendar of sacred festivity. The generation of Christian leadership on either side of 400, whence comes most of our evidence, was forced to think through the social implications of Christian doctrine in the wake of the church's successful *coup d'état*. The scriptural core of Christianity provided no articulate program of social reform and little impetus to change on the question of slavery. The command that slaves should "obey" their masters in the flesh, "with fear and trembling," allowed Christianity to absorb the slave system with a minimum of inconvenience.[33] But as waves of new Christians entered the folds of the church, bishops had to consider with a new urgency the relationship between scripture and society, to conceptualize what a Christian society might look like. For the church, our period was the age of thinking through.

In this age of thinking through, the optimistic slogans of earlier generations were gradually replaced by a view of slavery more familiar with the mundane realities of social life. John Chrysostom, for example, preached on the verse from *Titus* which commanded Christian slaves to obey their masters, in order to "adorn" the faith.[34] Chrysostom could admit that:

Among the unbelievers and indeed everywhere this fact is acknowledged, that the tribe of slaves is somehow unrestrained, dull, intractable, and has little potential to learn virtue. This is not because of nature, not at all, but because of poor nurturing and the neglect of their masters. Those who rule them are concerned with nothing at all except their services, and if they do somehow take any regard for the slaves, it is in the interest of their own convenience, so as not to be bothered by whoring, stealing, or drinking.[35]

Chrysostom took it for granted that slaves were troublesome, but he wanted to blame nurture, not nature. This was a remarkable observation on slavery, displaying a sort of sociological reasoning almost completely absent from ancient thought.[36] He went on to say that if Christianity could make slaves docile through fear of hell and judgment, it would be an *extraordinary* demonstration of Christianity's power. Chrysostom hoped to Christianize slavery by instilling obedience through fear of damnation. This sermon is an example of how the late Roman church staked out a position that

---

[33] For slavery in the early church, see Glancy 2002; Harrill 1995; Martin 1990.   [34] Titus 2:9–10.

[35] Ioh. Chrys. In Tit. 4.3 (PG 62: 685): Καὶ γὰρ καὶ παρ' αὐτοῖς, καὶ πανταχοῦ τοῦτο διωμολόγη-ται, ὅτι τὸ τῶν δούλων γένος ἰταμόν πώς ἐστι, δυσδιατύπωτον, δυστράπελον, οὐ σφόδρα ἐπιτήδειον πρὸς τὴν τῆς ἀρετῆς διδασκαλίαν, οὐ διὰ τὴν φύσιν, μὴ γένοιτο, ἀλλὰ διὰ τὴν ἀνα-τροφὴν καὶ τὴν ἀμέλειαν τὴν παρὰ τῶν δεσποτῶν. Ἐπειδὴ γὰρ πανταχοῦ οὐδενὸς ἑτέρου, ἀλλὰ τῆς αὐτῶν διακονίας οἱ κρατοῦντες αὐτῶν φροντίζουσιν. εἰ δέ που καὶ τῶν τρόπων ἐπιμεληθεῖεν, καὶ τοῦτο πάλιν διὰ τὴν αὐτῶν ἀνάπαυσιν πράττουσιν, ὥστε μὴ πράγματα αὐτοῖς παρέχειν ἢ πορνεύοντας, ἢ κλέπτοντας, ἢ μεθύοντας.

[36] cf. Salv. Gub. 4.3 (MGH AA 1: 38).

was closer to accommodation than abolition, even as it grappled with the spiritual implications of social arrangements.

In those generations of creative social discourse, new patterns of Christian thought would appear. The depth of Christian reflection on slavery was moving rapidly beyond the bare scriptural norms of the New Testament. At this fledgling stage, bishops were forced to recognize that the presence of this institution had unforeseen consequences for their spiritual program. By 400, there was simply less room for naiveté about the nature of slavery than during any previous stage of church history. This recognition helps us to take a proper measure of the interaction between slavery and Christianity in the late Roman empire. Even along the fringe of radical, thoughtful, and well-intentioned Christian leadership, there was an apprehension that slavery was beyond repair. Gregory of Nazianzus expressed the sentiment precisely. "To be a master over slaves is a fatal net! Harsh masters always become hateful, but slaves will trample a pious master without shame, the bad slaves can not be made mild, the good ones can not be made docile. They breathe sharp bile against both types of master beyond all reasoning."[37] It is this sort of candor that makes the late Roman sources so valuable.[38]

This deepening encounter between Christian leadership and ancient society gives us perspective on the tempo and trajectory of historical change. By underestimating the dynamism of Christianization, the amelioration thesis has obscured the process through which Christian and Roman ideologies became mutually enmeshed. It was precisely in the pivotal generations of the Theodosian dynasty that a Christian ideology of slavery began to solidify. It emerged in the context of a triumphant church that was progressively less able to offer itself as an alternative to life in the world. It emerged as Christian leaders like Augustine and Chrysostom found themselves pestered by the members of their congregation to explain, to justify, the institution of slavery.[39] It emerged as bishops assumed civil authority and were increasingly confronted with the sordid realities of the slave system.[40] The Christian ideology of slavery which emerged in the late fourth century represented neither a critique of, nor a challenge to, the Roman ideology of slavery, but rather a baptized version of it.

---

[37] Gr. Naz. Carm. 2.1.1 line 140f. (PG 37: 980–1): Πρῶτον μὲν δμώεσσιν ἀνασσέμεν, οἷον ὀλέθρου δίκτυον! οἳ πικροὺς μὲν ἀεὶ στυγέουσιν ἄνακτας, τοὺς δ᾽ ἱεροὺς πατέουσιν ἀναιδέες, οὔτε κακοῖσιν ἤπιοι, οὔτ᾽ ἀγαθοῖς εὐπειθέες. ἀμφοτέροις δὲ κέντρα χόλου πνείοντες ὑπὲρ νόον.

[38] *Contra* De Ste. Croix 1981, 425, that ancient Christians never recognized the effects of slavery upon the master, because of the "irresistible force of the class struggle."

[39] See the sermon cited at the beginning of chapter 1.

[40] Aug. Ep. 24*.1 (CSEL 88: 126). Lepelley 1983. On the *audientia episcopalis*, Rapp 2005, 242–52; Lenski 2001; Harries 1999, 191–211; Lamoreaux 1995, 143–67; Cimma 1989.

The Roman ideology of slavery was rooted in a civic status system.[41] To the extent that it was necessary to justify the existence of slavery, the ideology of conquest explained why slaves were slaves.[42] Slavery belonged to the *ius gentium*, the universal rules of the endless conflict inherent in the human condition.[43] War did the mental work of justifying slavery, but what is most striking is how little mental work was required.[44] The Roman ideology of slavery was inchoate, half-formed, precisely because it faced so little opposition. Late Roman Christianity absorbed this ideology but situated the inherent chaos and conflict of the human condition within a more encompassing theodicy. Slavery entered the world because of mankind's sin.[45] Some Christians would focus on the Fall in the Garden of Eden as the moment when sin, war, and eventually slavery entered the world; others noted that slavery did not appear in the Bible until Noah cursed the sons of Ham (an ominous linkage with a long future).[46] The church accepted the Roman civil ideology of slavery, but it was able to carry that ideology one step backwards towards an ultimate justification for the violence and apparent senselessness of the human condition in this *saeculum*.

The ancient church never questioned the essential justice of slavery. This should be no surprise; slavery was accepted in Old and New Testaments alike. At the same time, the church did encourage its followers to live with a set of values and aims detached from this world. In Augustine's characteristically clear formulation, Christians were to live for the city of God, even while in this transitory city of man. Chapter 8 will explore the considerable space this opened up for contests over the nature of authority and honor in late antiquity.[47] But during the life of this *saeculum*, the church was abundantly reconciled to the traditional structures of power. This accommodation had begun already in the earliest generations of Christianity, as is so evident from the *Haustafeln* that enjoin conscientious fulfillment of traditional social roles. The church accepted the harsh realities of this world, and with them the extraction of labor from slaves and the use of physical discipline to obtain it.

In one regard, the ancient church did stake out a position that was vehemently opposed to the accepted practices of the world it inherited: sexuality. This departure from pattern is so important that it throws into

---

[41] Above all Garnsey 1996.   [42] See the Introduction to part III.   [43] Dig. 1.5.4.

[44] Garnsey 2000, 407: "no Roman counterpart to Aristotle arose . . . Romans saw slavery as a structural feature of their society, an economic and political necessity, and that was that."

[45] See esp. Aug. Civ. 19.15 (CC 48: 682–3).

[46] Garnsey 1996, esp. 213–19. Ioh. Chrys. Serm. in Genes. 4.112–16 (SC 433: 228–32). Goldenberg 2003, for Ham's curse.

[47] See, e.g., Elm 1996.

even greater relief the church's general acceptance of most aspects of the slave system. The Christian leadership expended an uncanny portion of its energy in the reform of sexual morals. The most visible manifestation of this new sexual culture was the complete renunciation of sexual activity. The rise of Christian asceticism has garnered a great deal of historical attention, but chapter 7 will argue that the Christianization of sexuality cannot be seen as the triumph of a new attitude towards the body, or not only that. The Christian model of human sexuality came into direct conflict with the social configuration of ancient sexual norms. Christianity brought not just new sanctions for sexual behavior and new anxieties about the body, it brought new rules that contradicted the established sexual order of the Roman world, a sexual order that was inseparable from the slave system.

   We will trace this battle between Christian reformers and secular habits in detail. There is a stunning amount of evidence, and the pastoral efforts of the late Roman church offer a rare opportunity to see how pervasive the sexual exploitation of dishonored women truly was in the Roman empire. The same documents also reveal that the church, even in this area of praxis where it put such concentrated energy, was in an unwinnable battle. Its teachings ran against the overwhelming momentum of social structure. The rules which made some bodies visible and vulnerable were embedded deep in the nexus of honor and social reproduction. John Chrysostom could implore his flock to think of sex with slaves as a moral wrong, he could implore them to respect the bodies of honorable and shameful women alike, but in doing so he was casting stones against a sturdy edifice of ancient custom, founded in the very bedrock of the ancient city.[48] On questions of sexual conduct, Chrysostom could look across Antioch to the theater and sense his own isolation. The city surrounding him was a place where sexual behavior was channeled by social status.

A SOCIAL HISTORY OF SLAVERY: FRAMING THE QUESTIONS

Part II will explore the human relationships implicated in Roman slavery. In this pursuit it is especially important to ask the right questions. The agenda is not organized around an attempt to measure how "good" or "bad" ancient slavery was, much less to identify the moments of humanity which peek through the darkness of an abusive system. Finley and Bradley demonstrated the insuperable problems of evidence and method in such

---

[48] See chapter 7.

research.[49] All the evidence is from the slave-owner's point of view, and uncritical attention to legal or moral norms is no substitute for social history. We cannot be umpires, keeping score with examples of humanity and cruelty.[50] The core of Finley's intervention was the claim that slavery was a particular type of power relationship, systematically dehumanizing, based on violence.[51] This intervention had its place, but a more foundational approach to the problem is needed. These chapters try to extend and formalize Finley's insight that slavery was a particular type of relationship; they do so by programmatically exploring the interrelationship between structure and experience in the Roman slave system.

Structure and experience are the organizing concepts behind these chapters. By "structure" we mean the recurring patterns in the lives of masters and slaves that were immanent in systems of production and reproduction. The lives of masters and slaves were structured by what Giddens has called "rules and resources."[52] Slavery was the relationship of domination that emerged from the fact that one human owned another. The bond between master and slave was not a singular, super-historical entity. It was a repeating form of human interaction, a recurring cycle which, over and over again, began in a marketplace and ended with sale, death, manumission, or escape. This relationship had ends, and the actors in the relationship had means of achieving those ends. For masters, the purpose of the relationship was principally the extraction of labor, with intermediate ends such as obedience and submission. Masters were endowed, by the formal and informal rules of society, with the powers to pursue those ends. Slaves, who likely viewed the relationship as illegitimate and as a situation to be manipulated, sought physical security and private happiness. They were endowed with far less power to pursue their goals, but their agency was not negligible.

One aim of the chapters in part II is to demonstrate that the type of labor sought from the slave was of fundamental, structural importance.[53] Employment in the production of wheat, wine, oil, livestock, and textiles, in financial management, business agency, personal service, and so on, required different modes of management, different techniques of domination, with systematic effects for the master–slave relationship. Thus,

---

[49] Finley 1998 (orig. 1980), 161–90; Bradley 1994, 7, and 1987b, 18–20; see also Garrido-Hory 1981b.

[50] E.g. Klein 1999; Kudlien 1991. Hopkins 1993, 8–10, criticizing the "anecdotal" method; Scheidel 1993, too. McKeown 2007 reconstructs the polemical war between scholars who emphasize or de-emphasize the positive aspects of slavery.

[51] Patterson 1982 drew on Finley's insights and has in turn been influential in ancient history.

[52] Giddens 1984.   [53] Fenoaltea 1984. See Scheidel 2008 and Temin 2004.

the social history offered in part II is a direct extension of the economic history offered in part I. Labor, space, and gender were essential variables in the patterns of the master–slave relationship. In fact, it is impossible to speak of *the* master–slave relationship as a single type of relationship, in the sense which the amelioration thesis tended to encourage. The concept of experience forces us to appreciate the inherent dynamism and unpredictability of the relationship. The master–slave relationship was variable, but by identifying the most important factors behind the variation, we can hope to arrive at a more profound understanding of the forces at play in the late Roman slave system.

This approach has clear methodological advantages over past attempts to search for amelioration or humanity in the ancient slave system. We cannot hope that enough positivist research will truly reveal to us how good or bad Roman slavery really was – and that is not the point. This allows us to sidestep some of the pitfalls of the evidence. We do not have to trust every claim about the quality of master–slave relations, especially in rhetorical or normative texts. Even in the American slave system, where the evidence is so rich that scholars can debate the quantitative incidence of floggings, the important question is less how often slaves were whipped, than what whipping says about the nature of the relationship and the environment of fear that defined it.[54] The ancient sources do not give us the option of trying to reconstruct the relationship in hard, quantitative, or physical terms, but the goal can still be to trace the structure of the relationship.

A social history of slavery must also be situated within the social history of the Roman empire more generally. The last generation has witnessed tremendous advances in Roman social history. What kind of society inhabited the Roman Mediterranean? It was a society organized to offset high mortality through high fertility, especially in the form of marriage.[55] The Roman family was an essentially patriarchal institution, based on agnatic kinship structures, partible inheritance, and strong private property rights.[56] Marriage was a strictly monogamous relationship between a man and a free, honorable woman capable of producing an heir.[57] Economic production was principally agricultural, although historically exceptional rates of urbanism exerted a profound effect on all of Roman society.[58]

[54] Gutman 1975, 14–41.
[55] Scheidel 2001a and 2001b; Frier 2000; Bagnall and Frier 1994. See Harper forthcoming a; Beaucamp 1990–2, for basic continuities into late antiquity.
[56] Saller 2007a and 1994; Saller and Shaw 1984. Rawson and Weaver 1997; Dixon 1992; Rawson 1991 and 1986.
[57] Treggiari 1991. Scheidel 2009a, on monogamy.   [58] Erdkamp 2001; Bowman 2000; Parkins 1997.

Roman society was highly stratified, and its hierarchies were both formal and informal.[59] Roman society and its status system were profoundly shaped by Roman law. The law formally regulated rank and status, while the pursuit of wealth and honor provided the grounds of competition for status. Within these interlaced and dynamic structures, masters and slaves lived out their existence.

Chapters 5–8 unfold in a logical sequence that tries to capture the richness of the patterns underlying the master–slave relationship. Chapter 5 is focused on the master's effort to extract labor from the slave. Adopting an "incentive model," it tries to demonstrate the close relationship between the aims and techniques of domination. Chapter 6 explores these dynamics from the slave's perspective. Slaves could shirk, steal, retaliate, or flee; more profoundly, they could form families and resist collectively. Chapters 7 and 8 zoom out and view the place of the master–slave relationship in the broader structure of society. Chapter 7 considers the role of sexual exploitation in the Roman slave system. Slaves, deprived of sexual honor, were systemically exploited, and yet this remains one of the most neglected aspects of Roman slavery. Chapter 8 analyzes the concept of mastery and the importance of slave-ownership in generating honor for the master. In the ancient world, where the atomized individual was not the basic particle of social structure, one's place among others was determinative. The ultimate claim of these chapters is that slavery was elemental in the making of honorable society.

Roman society was a unique historical conjuncture, determined by systems of production and reproduction in which the use of slaves was instrumental. In the late empire it was still a classical society, with all that name implies about civic identity and formal hierarchy and sexual frankness, even as it was slowly becoming a Christian society. But just as the beguiling narrative of transition from Antiquity to Feudalism must be set aside to understand the material structure of late Roman slavery, so any evolutionary trajectory from Classical to Christian must be discarded to understand the volatile synthesis of the late imperial world. This society had no scripted destiny and was certainly not the germ of the medieval future. It was made up of the sum of human relationships, as men and women fought for survival, sought to fulfill their desires, strove for honor, and struggled to make sense of the experience.

The Christian critics of this society will be our principal guides. The best of them felt, with a profound dissatisfaction, the fury of the competition

[59] Formal hierarchies: Garnsey 1970. Economic hierarchies: Scheidel and Friesen 2009; Friesen 2004.

for honor which surrounded them. They felt it so keenly because they tried to teach the souls under their care *not* to take honor and meaning from their social roles. So it is telling that a preacher like John Chrysostom found in the theater a symbolic focus for his spiritual dissatisfaction. Life, he said, was like a stage:

When the dusk gathers and the play is finished, and everyone leaves, the masks come off... When the masks are gone, the illusion is over, and the truth is revealed. The one who played a free man on stage is a slave in the world outside... So it is in life and death. This world is the theater, our affairs here are but a role. Wealth and poverty, power and subjection, all such things... When this theater is closed, when these masks come off, each will be judged by his works rather than his wealth, his power, his honor, his office...[60]

Chrysostom knew that the theater was an organic expression of the society in which he lived and preached. It was a representation of a world where the roles of master and slave scripted the experience and the meanings which were possible for its actors.

[60] Ioh. Chrys. Laz. 6.5 (PG 48: 1034–5): ἐπειδὰν δὲ ἑσπέρα καταλάβῃ, καὶ λυθῇ τὸ θέατρον, καὶ πάντες ἀναχωρήσωσι, ῥίπτονται τὰ προσωπεῖα... Ἀπερρίφη τὰ προσωπεῖα, ἀπῆλθεν ἡ ἀπάτη, ἐδείχθη ἡ ἀλήθεια. καὶ εὑρίσκεται ὁ ἔνδον ἐλεύθερος, ἔξω δοῦλος... οὕτω καὶ ἐν τῷ βίῳ καὶ ἐν τῷ τέλει. τὰ παρόντα θέατρον, τὰ πράγματα ὑπόκρισις, πλοῦτος καὶ πενία, καὶ ἄρχων καὶ ἀρχόμενος, καὶ ὅσα τοιαῦτα... ὅταν λυθῇ τὸ θέατρον, ὅταν ῥιφῇ τὰ προσωπεῖα, ὅταν δοκιμάζηται ἕκαστος καὶ τὰ ἔργα αὐτοῦ, οὐχ ἕκαστος καὶ ὁ πλοῦτος αὐτοῦ, οὐχ ἕκαστος καὶ ἡ ἀρχὴ αὐτοῦ, οὐχ ἕκαστος καὶ ἡ τιμὴ αὐτοῦ, οὐχ ἕκαστος καὶ ἡ δυναστεία αὐτοῦ, ἀλλ' ἕκαστος καὶ τὰ ἔργα αὐτοῦ.

CHAPTER 5

Semper timere: *the aims and techniques of domination*

THE MASTER–SLAVE RELATIONSHIP

Seeking a metaphor to describe the mysterious compound of love and wrath which God was capable of showing towards mankind, Lactantius found in the figure of the slave-owner an evocative parallel. "The master calls the good slave a friend and decorates him and puts him in charge of the *domus* and the *familia* and all the master's affairs, but the bad slave he punishes with cursing, lashes, nudity, hunger, thirst, chains. The one is an example to the others not to sin, and the other is an example to good behavior, so that some are coerced by fear, others driven by honor."[1] The use of the most horrifying terrors and the promise of such conspicuous rewards belonged on the same spectrum. The spectrum described by Lactantius was not merely conjured to serve his rhetorical purpose, for as we will see the Roman master was vested with an exceptionally broad range of powers to reward and to punish. This chapter is an exploration of that spectrum. It is an attempt to understand the techniques of domination in Roman society and to uncover the systemic forces promoting the use of particular techniques. We cannot accept, with Lactantius, that some slaves were simply "good," others "bad." Instead we want to discover the choices made by masters and slaves as they tried to maneuver towards their desired ends.

Domination was the essential structure of the master–slave relationship, but history amply attests the wide variety of outcomes possible within this basic structure.[2] Although slavery is a cross-cultural category, a persistent type of human relationship, slavery was nevertheless experienced differently

---

[1] Lact. Ir. 5.12 (SC 289: 108): *bonum adloquitur amice et ornat et domui ac familiae suisque rebus omnibus praeficit, malum vero maledictis verberibus nuditate fame siti conpedibus punit, ut et hic exemplo ceteris sit ad non peccandum et ille ad promerendum, ut alios metus coerceat, alios honor provocet.*

[2] Patterson 1982 remains fundamental.

across time and space. The challenge is to understand both the hard structural features of the master–slave relationship and the patterns of variation.
This is possible, because the diversity of experience within slavery was not
random; outcomes were shaped by identifiable and repetitive conditions.
One of the most successful attempts to explain the manifest patterns of
diversity in slavery is the influential model of the economist Fenoaltea.[3]
Fenoaltea starts from the premise that the end of the master–slave relationship is the production of a good and then explains why the production of
different goods will encourage the use of different incentives by the master.
This "incentive model" is illuminating. This chapter will adopt the central insights of the model while adapting some of its more vulnerable and
empirically unsound applications. But as we approach the lived realities
of a slave system as massive and internally diverse as the Roman one, the
model is a useful way to organize the analysis.

The key insight of the incentive model is that the exploitation of slaves,
whether through pain or reward, required resources, and thus the management of slaves was subject to economies of scarcity. Various modes of
supervision and motivation were differentially effective according to the
type of work sought from the slave. The model describes the types of work
along a spectrum from effort-intensive to care-intensive. Effort-intensive
work required routine physical drudgery; care-intensive work required trust
and adaptibility, and it entailed the use of capital. The model describes the
incentives used to motivate slaves along a spectrum from pain to positive
rewards. Effort-intensive labor – mining, digging, plowing – can be efficiently extracted through the use of pain incentives, while care-intensive
activities – skilled crafts, financial administration – are more suitable for
positive incentives. Fenoaltea marshals a range of examples, but the demonstration is largely intuitive. Effort is compatible with anxiety and can be
performed by gangs supervised by drivers. Care is incompatible with physical anxiety; proximity to valuable capital makes sabotage risky; it is hard to
monitor slaves in roles that require dynamic response or technical skill. Few
slaves in mining were rewarded with manumission, while we do not see
slave-drivers following around procurators, pushing them to work. Masters
adjusted the ratio of pain and positive incentives to maximize output and
minimize cost.

The model has the great advantage of explaining why the occupational
structure and incentive structure of a slave system are dynamically interlinked. At the same time, the model is considerably more robust at the

---

[3] Fenoaltea 1984; Findlay 1975.

ends of the spectra it describes than anywhere in between. When either the effort/pain or care/reward pair is utterly dominant, the model holds up well, but life for most masters and slaves was lived between the extremes, so this is not an inconsiderable flaw. Indeed a number of empirical counter-examples to Fenoaltea's model have been adduced, and some glaring inconsistencies in his argument have been noted.[4] We might add that he neglects gender (his slave is implicitly male) and fails to account sufficiently for the dynamics of space – where and in what types of groups slaves lived. Moreover, because the internal logic of the model is intuitive, it becomes vulnerable when muddled by reality. What if care-intensive work did not place the slave in close proximity to valuable capital, or what if the arrangements of the domestic sphere meant that supervision costs were artificially low? Though Fenoaltea adumbrates the notion that masters used a "mix" of incentives, the imagery of a spectrum may imply that the master–slave relationship would reach a stable equilibrium at some specific balance. This does little justice to the real experience of slavery. The array of options available to the master was part of the terrifying uncertainty of the slave's experience. It is precisely the volatile compound of violence and reward that has made slavery a peculiar institution throughout its history.

The incentive model is the tool of an economist, and it can be enriched by infusing into it some of the insights produced by historians working on modern slavery. The last forty years have seen an ongoing debate over whether modern slavery should be seen as an essentially capitalist phenomenon or rather as a paternalist institution.[5] Both of these paradigms assume that the master's power was finite.[6] Historians have fleshed out the clinical terms of the incentive model to show that something more was at stake than a zero-sum adjustment between the *master's goals* and the *master's means* of achieving them. Slaves were active players, whose goals were more complex than avoidance of pain and pursuit of reward, and whose means were equally variable.[7] The contest, moreover, was temporal and cumulative – burdened by past structure and experience. And the contest was waged above the level of the individual. Fenoaltea's model subtly assumes an individual master and an individual slave as atomized participants in a struggle over motivation. The master–slave dynamic was mediated by the interrelationships between slaves and other slaves, and between masters and other masters.

---

[4] Scheidel 2008, esp. 107–11; Wright 2006.
[5] Johnson 1999; Oakes 1990; Fogel 1989; Fogel and Engerman 1974. For paternalism, Genovese 1974.
[6] Morris 1998 is an especially valuable overview.   [7] Morris 1998, 985.

The importance of family life among slaves immediately highlights the need to extend the incentive model. The model sets up financial reward and manumission as the standard positive incentives. These rewards describe the aims of some slaves – in particular, isolated male slaves practicing an independent craft who were incapable of being monitored. But something is missing. The evidence suggests that, at least in some slave systems, the space to pursue private relationships, especially family life, was a primary form of positive incentive. Crucially, master and slave viewed the allowance of privacy in incommensurable terms; what for the master was a *means* was for the slave an *end*. The interests of masters and slaves could overlap, even in relatively stable patterns. But it is imperative to recognize the slave's labor as something more than potential energy in need of motivation, because it was labor that belonged to a living, breathing, desiring, knowing agent. Slaves viewed "incentives" not just as motivation with a cost to the master, but as the opportunity to pursue their own private goals under adverse conditions.

The patterns evident in modern slavery help us identify the terms in which the dynamics of power played out, especially when the perpetually recurring contest between masters and slaves was situated between the extremes of pure slave-driving and pure reward, when the objects at stake were more complex than carrots and sticks. The historical record reminds us that the model must reckon with real historical actors who were only partially aware of their situation and who did not describe their condition in terms of differential efficiencies or maximizing outputs. Although sometimes slaves were told that they would receive incentive x for the performance of task y, or punishment a for the failure to perform task b, more often the tension between motivation and labor was experienced as a bundle of moralized expectations. The master made claims to *authority*, to the rightful possession and exercise of power; this authority demanded *submission*, the recognition of the master's claim to the slave's obedience and labor. The terms of negotiation between masters and slaves were thus hypostasized into these normative claims; in the words of Lactantius, the "good" or "faithful" slave was submissive and received rewards, while the "bad" slave was recalcitrant and earned punishments.

This chapter attempts to recover the structural patterns in the master–slave relationship in the late Roman empire. Labor, space, and gender are taken as fundamental ingredients in the experience of slavery. The incentive model should be used as a tool to illuminate the evidence which we have and to make us aware of the evidence which we may be missing. But the model should not be allowed to overwrite the ancient words which survive and which provide irreplaceable testimony from those who tried to exercise their tremendous but always finite power over the humans they owned.

THE AIMS OF DOMINATION

The expropriation of labor was the *telos*, the form-giving purpose of the master–slave relationship. "If you had a slave, who never stole or offended or contradicted you, who was always sober and such, but sat around in laziness and not fulfilling the service a slave owes the master, would you not lash and torture him?"[8] Fenoaltea's model distinguishes between care-intensive and effort-intensive labor, but how well do these categories fit the Roman slave system? Many Roman slaves, particularly in Illustrious and Elite households, were employed in finance, commerce, or business. Slaves were agents and managers, roles that required skill and trust. Libanius, for instance, dispatched slave agents to another city on business; this implies faith in the slaves to obey at a distance, where the master could not directly monitor the slave's actions. The trust was clearly fragile – Libanius sent a letter to a friend in the city asking him to keep an eye on the slaves.[9] Chapter 3 argued that the stupendous scale of the non-agricultural economy, in combination with primitive concepts of legal agency, made slavery instrumental in the commercial sector. Such slaves, with opportunities to acquire property and hope for manumission, were also among the most visible elements of the entire system. Yet the occupational structure reminds us that they were exceptional, and it would be a mistake to make conclusions about the experience of Roman slavery based solely on their experience.[10]

A larger number of Roman slaves were occupied in domestic roles. In large households, the domestic slaves were at the bottom of the pyramid; their supervision might be carried out by other slaves, and their intimacy with the master and mistress might be rather limited. In smaller households, by contrast, slaves were directly supervised by the master and especially the mistress. We should not fail to recognize that "control of the slaves" was a standard part of the Roman woman's responsibilities.[11] The

---

[8] Ioh. Chrys. In Ephes. 16.1 (PG 62: 112): εἴ τινα οἰκέτην ἔχοις, μήτε κλέπτοντα, μήτε ὑβρίζοντα, μήτε ἀντιλέγοντα, ἀλλὰ καὶ μέθης κρατοῦντα καὶ τῶν ἄλλων ἁπάντων, καθήμενον δὲ διαπαντὸς ἀργὸν, καὶ οὐδὲν τῶν ὀφειλόντων παρὰ οἰκέτου δεσπότῃ πληροῦσθαι ποιοῦντα, οὐ μαστιγώσεις, οὐ στρεβλώσεις αὐτόν;

[9] Lib. Ep. 177–8 (Foerster vol. 10: 165). cf. Lib. Ep. 568 (Foerster vol. 10: 535).

[10] Temin 2004, emphasizes this part of the slave system.   [11] See chapter 8.

domestic sphere, particularly in Bourgeois and Agricultural households, provided a venue for close supervision.[12] This fact is underemphasized in the traditional incentive model. The patterns of domestic labor do not easily fit along the spectrum of effort- and care-intensive labor. The ability to monitor slaves in close proximity created opportunity for intense exploitation. Textile work, in particular, was suited to domestic labor – routine, low-capital, easily measured and monitored.[13] The low levels of technology in spinning and weaving meant that there were no advantages to organizing production on a large scale. The Roman household was a small-scale sweatshop.

The same patterns of close supervision underlie the realities of slavery in Agricultural households. The incentive model, as Fenoaltea presented it, manifestly fails to explain why slavery was able to thrive in some types of agricultural production that were care-intensive.[14] At least part of the answer lies in the prevalence of the family farm. In Roman society as in the US South, modest farmers played a vital role in the slave system alongside more conspicuous plantation-owners. The small scale of organization made close monitoring more feasible. Masters who worked alongside their slaves could watch, measure, and motivate their slaves personally rather than through managerial intermediaries. In such contexts, too, the slave's private life and personal contacts were more likely to be co-ordinated around the free family. Slaves might always have solidarities with slaves in other households, and slaves found or created ways to maintain those solidarities through clandestine contact, but slaves in smaller households were inevitably more likely to be integrated into the free family.[15]

Slaves working on estates experienced a different set of constraints and opportunities. Estates opened the possibility for family and community bonds, while market-oriented farming was a double-edged sword that might make masters especially eager for co-operation, even as the labor of slaves was subjected to tighter discipline. The experience of slavery on estates was influenced by several interrelated factors: the organization of the work process, crop selection, and the dynamics of gender. Were slaves worked in gangs or allotted individual tasks?[16] How did the repertoire of Mediterranean crops affect the patterns of production and thus the rhythm of slave life?[17] To what extent were slave-women used in the fields?[18] Chapter 4 has proposed that estate-based slavery in the Roman empire was

---

[12] E.g. Ioh. Chrys. In 1 Cor. 36.5 (PG 61: 313).   [13] Roth 2007, 53–87. See chapter 3.
[14] Scheidel 2008, 108–9.   [15] See chapter 6.   [16] See esp. Morgan 1988.
[17] cf. Roth 2007, 95–6.   [18] Scheidel 1995–6a.

not organized around monocultural plantations worked by gangs. Nor were slaves used as tenants, allowed to control production on their own. Instead slaves were instrumental in the organization of estates practicing intensive Mediterranean polyculture. This has important implications. First, many agricultural slaves were managers and skilled craftsmen; some had positions of responsibility, others had specialized roles that required specialized skill or knowledge. This should not be surprising; even in the US South as many as 25 percent of adult male slaves were in skilled or supervisory roles.[19] Managerial roles were themselves an incentive, a form of promotion that encouraged effective labor. Moreover, the slave manager was a layer of insulation between the master and the slaves in the fields – with intrinsically complex effects. Finally, there are empirical and logical grounds to believe that rural slaves, particularly in management or crafts, had some prospect of manumission.[20]

Rural slave labor was clearly compatible with a variety of crops and work regimes in the Roman empire. The crops produced on slave-based estates included cereals, grapes, and olives, in addition to livestock and secondary products. There is no doubting that wine, oil, and textiles were the really lucrative commodities. Fenoaltea argued that slave labor was incompatible with care-intensive Mediterranean products like grapes and olives, and he even speculated that this incompatibility made Roman slavery unstable, bound for extinction.[21] This is a wildly incredible claim that does nothing so much as demonstrate the vulnerable basis of his arguments. Nevertheless, it is important to recognize that growing grapes is not like growing sugar cane, and olives are not like cotton. Fenoaltea's model overemphasizes the danger to valuable capital implements, and he too narrowly associates violence with gang-labor. By ignoring the role of the family as an instrument of domination, moreover, he relies on a reductive spectrum of carrots and sticks. The sheer longevity of the Roman slave system shows that slave labor, managed through careful dispensations of pain and reward, was compatible with intensive Mediterranean polyculture.

THE TECHNIQUES OF DOMINATION

Masters sought labor from their slaves, but they sought to extract it in the first place by securing the slave's submission. In other words, struggles over motivation were often conducted in the mystified language of authority and submission. Submission meant that the slave recognized the master's power

---

[19] Fogel and Engerman 1974, 40.   [20] Harper 2008.   [21] Fenoaltea 1984, 687.

as legitimate and internalized that recognition. Ideally, slaves accepted their condition without complaint. "The *maximum* vice of slaves is to contradict their masters and murmur amongst themselves when they are ordered to do something."[22] Contumacy was intolerable. It was "so arrogant" to ask the master why an order was given.[23] The manners and words of slaves were watched for signs of disrespect.[24] A slave lived in sharp fear of offending his master, "lest he order him to be whipped, to be put in shackles, to be imprisoned, to be wasted away in grinding grain . . . but when he feels the eyes of his master are absent," the slave behaved as he wished.[25] This claim hints at the awareness among masters that their slaves, in fact, might obey but not submit – the eternal anxiety of all relationships of domination. John Chrysostom struck precisely on this chord of anxiety when he promised masters that his religion could make slaves internally docile through fear of hell.[26]

The master's pursuit of the slave's submission began in the marketplace, preceding even legal ownership. Slaves were interrogated by future masters before they were bought. In a revealing passage, John Chrysostom explained that slaves were asked to consent to their sale.[27] Ambrose spoke of slaves choosing their masters.[28] The *Life of Aesop* played on the slave's ability to outwit the master while still in the slave market.[29] On the purchase block, the master tried to commute the abundance of his potential power into pre-approved consent, surrender; the slave manipulated the unfavorable condition to leverage his limited capacity to resist. This double movement – power trying to become authority, powerlessness grasping to negotiate – prefigured the basic dynamics of the master–slave relationship.

The first act of ownership was to change the name of the slave. This act of existential domination was the "symbol of mastery."[30] The imposition of a new name was a raw assertion of power; it preceded the possibility of trust or softer forms of control. It is significant that the act was by its nature *demonstrative*: "It is like someone buying a slave, how he often changes the slave's name and appearance and does everything

---

[22] Hier. Tit. 2 (PL 26: 585): *maximum servorum vitium est, dominis contradicere, et cum aliquid iusserint, secum mussitare.*
[23] Aug. Serm. 296.7 (Morin: 406): *tam superbus . . .*   [24] Ps.-Ath. Qu. Ant. 78 (PG 28: 645).
[25] Aug. Serm. 161.9 (PL 38: 883): *ne iubeat eum verberari, iubeat in compedes mitti, iubeat carcere includi, iubeat eum pistrino conteri . . . sed quando senserit absentes oculos domini sui . . .*
[26] Ioh. Chrys. In Tit. 4.3 (PG 62: 685).   [27] Ioh. Chrys. Catech. 2.5 (PG 49: 239).
[28] Ambr. Virg. 1.9.56 (Gori: 154–5).   [29] Vit. Aesop. 26 (Perry vol. 1: 43–4). Hopkins 1993.
[30] Ioh. Chrys. Hom. in Genes. 14.5 (PG 53: 116): σύμβολον δεσποτείας. Ioh. Chrys. Mut. Nom. 3.3 (PG 51: 137). cf. Turley 2000, 29; Patterson 1982, 54–5.

to make it completely obvious that the slave is his, in order to proclaim his mastery."[31] New slaves were then subjected to a trial period. The first days brought special scrutiny and tight surveillance. Trust was earned only through a long display of obedience.[32] This early period might be especially violent. A master would beat a slave just to "announce his enslavement."[33] Violence was used to imprint the ground rules of the master–slave relationship. Precisely because the exertion of violence required the expenditure of finite resources, it was best if it was done conspicuously and early, so that the slave recognized the inherent realities of his or her condition.

If domination was decorated with the language of authority and submission, legitimacy and obedience, in substance the practice of domination was determined by the realities of the master's power. The bedrock of this power was violence. It will take no long proof to claim that Roman society was unusually violent.[34] In a militaristic and patriarchal society with a taste for spectacular pain, the use of violence was hardly confined to slavery. Temin, in his discussion of Roman slavery, has argued that Roman society, like many pre-modern societies, was by our standards violent, and that therefore we should not overemphasize the role of violence in a slave system in which he claims "positive incentives were more important than negative incentives."[35] The Romans, to be sure, had a high quotient of tolerance for physical pain; but the very fact that they so often insisted on the association between slavery and horrific violence suggests that slavery had an integral part in the use of pain in their society. Roman society was so violent, in part, because it was a slave society, and the private habits of physical discipline familiarized and desensitized the Romans to the experience of violence.

The sources of the late empire provide extraordinary testimony to the use of violence as a mechanism of domination, and they allow us to explore the modes, strategies, and limits of violence in the slave system. Late antique society was suffused with an aura of mundane physical violence. The sources insist that violence was the normal mode of

---

[31] Ioh. Chrys. Hom. in Genes. 40.1 (PG 53: 568): Καὶ καθάπερ τις οἰκέτην κτησάμενος, πολλάκις καὶ τὸ ὄνομα αὐτοῦ μετατίθησι καὶ τὸ σχῆμα, καὶ πάντα ποιεῖ ὥστε κατάδηλον αὐτὸν ποιῆσαι, ἵνα διὰ πάντων κηρύττῃ τὴν δεσποτείαν. Slave sales often included the slave's name and the addendum "by whatever name he/she is called."

[32] Ioh. Chrys. In 1 Tim. 11.1 (PG 62: 553).

[33] Bas. Anc. Virg. 11 (PG 30: 689): δουλαγωγίας . . . ἐπαγγειλάμενος.

[34] The essays in Drake 2006; MacMullen 1986b. For public violence in the early empire, Coleman 1990. Dossey 2008 on domestic violence. cf. De Bruyn 1999, esp. 281–4.

[35] Temin 2004, 524–9.

master–slave relations, and given all that masters hoped to achieve from
domination it is perhaps not surprising that masters felt themselves
inevitably "compelled" to violence, as though the gravitational mechanics of the relationship demanded it. Harsh rule was normative, exercised by
thoughtful masters for the good of the *domus*.[36] It was the fault of the slave
that a master was cruel, so men and women of late antiquity thought.[37] If
words failed, the master was "forced to bring upon the slave fear and blows
and chains and such."[38] Violence was reckoned the fault of the slave and a
burden upon the slave-owner.

The instruction of slaves was reflexively considered in physical terms.[39]
The forms of physical violence over slaves in late antiquity were varied and
brutal, but there is no doubt that whipping was absolutely the fundamental
method of control.[40] In early sixth-century Gaza, the orator Choricius used
a public oration as an opportunity to retell a story recorded by Herodotus.
The Scythians were at war with their rebellious slaves; so long as they
fought the slaves with weapons, the uprising lingered, but as soon as the
masters took up their whips, the slaves remembered their servitude and
submitted.[41] Far from scholastic showboating, it was the sort of myth that
resonated with the master class across ten centuries of antiquity. Flogging
was a physical and psychological punishment; the whip was the icon of
mastery.[42]

To understand the practice of whipping, we must remember that men
and women in antiquity were much closer to the mundane physical coercion of animals. The lash was the instrument used to tame and to dominate
beasts of burden. It was a household device in an agricultural society. From
the experience of dominating their livestock, men won a brutish knowledge
of violent coercion, of how to break the will of another organism through
the use of pain.[43] Men of late antiquity looked at the act of disciplining
their slaves as not altogether different from controlling their animals. Slaves
were subhuman, "man-footed beings," *alogos*, deprived of the sense to rule
themselves.[44] The scourge gave masters the exhilaration of control. Critics

[36] Aug. Serm. D5.12 (Dolbeau: 82).   [37] Thdt. Prov. 7 (PG 83: 684D-685A).
[38] Marc. Diac. Vit. Porph. 73 (Grégoire and Kugener: 58): κατὰ ἀνάγκην τούτῳ ἐπάγει τὸν φόβον καὶ πληγὰς καὶ δεσμὰ καὶ ἄλλα τοιαῦτα.
[39] Gr. Nyss. Castig. 313 (PG 46: 313).
[40] See Saller 1994, 133–53. cf. Dal Lago and Katsari 2008, for the earlier period and comparatively.
[41] Choric. Or. 3.14 (Foerster and Richtsteig: 52).   [42] cf. Patterson 1982, 3.
[43] Aug. Psalm. 31(2).23 (CC 38: 241). cf. Apul. Met. 7.16–8 (Helm vol. 1: 166–8).
[44] *alogos*: Didym. In ep. cath. 27 (Zoepfl: 27). *Andrapoda* (man-footed beings) habitually mentioned with the *tetrapoda* (four-footed beasts), e.g. Gr. Naz. Or. 16.19 (PG 35: 961). Not fit to rule themselves, Thdt. Provid. 7.676B (PG 83: 676). See Hezser 2005, 56–7.

of astrology used this feeling of power over the future to ask – if the stars determine the course of events, why do masters spend such energy lashing their slaves?[45]

Lashing caused excruciating physical pain. The lacerations were visible for days, as slaves bore the "marks of cruelty" on their bodies.[46] Chrysostom warned masters they should not tear through the tunic when they beat their slaves, and he chided masters whose cruelty was evident on the slave's body when the slave was at the public bath.[47] Jerome called it an "everyday custom" for a slave to use the time between blows to ask for death as a reprieve.[48] Basil of Caesarea, criticizing the rich, said they could see their wicked deeds all around them, including the "slaves whom you have ripped to shreds."[49] The violence of lashing could of course be chaotic and disorderly. The incentive model should not lead us to forget that the actors involved were human beings, with all that implies about fallibility and passion and unpredictability, in which one party possessed extreme power over another. Iamblichus said that philosophers never lashed their slaves while they were still in a state of anger – implying that the average man did.[50] Masters might chase their slaves around the house punishing them.[51] Ammianus reported that a slave who was slow to serve received 300 lashes.[52] The context is clearly one of exaggeration, but the point to notice is that the blows were *numbered*. Chrysostom spoke of thirty or fifty lashes as a high number.[53] A really bad whipping was one in which the blows were "countless."[54] The violence imposed on slaves was applied in a calculated manner. If the pain became truly unbearable, the master might forgive "the rest of the blows" – but again, the quantification of pain is the striking fact.[55]

Pain was quantified because the art of mastery was based on a well-understood economy of violence. A master knew not to lash his slave "every day," but to endure through several days and then whip him on the back and "take his soul."[56] There could be a certain choreography to the

---

45 Eusebius, P.E. 6.6.17 (SC 266: 134); Ioh. Chrys. Hom. Goth. 8.6 (PG 63: 509).
46 Ioh. Chrys. In Ephes. 15.3 (PG 62: 109): τεκμήρια τῆς ὠμότητος.
47 Ioh. Chrys. In act. Apost. 15.4 (PG 60: 126).
48 Hier. Ep. 36.3 (CSEL 54: 271): cotidianae consuetudinis.
49 Bas. Hom. Div. 2.6 (Courtonne: 71): τοὺς οἰκέτας, οὓς κατέξαινες.
50 Iambl. Vit. Pyth. 31.197 (Klein: 141–2). An old trope: see Fitzgerald 2000, 35–6.
51 Ioh. Chrys. Hom. in Genes. 17.2 (PG 53: 136).
52 Amm. 28.4.16 (Seyfarth vol. 2: 80).   53 Ioh. Chrys. Adv. Iud. 8.6 (PG 48: 936–7).
54 Ioh. Chrys. Ad pop. Ant. 20.6 (PG 49: 206); Ioh. Chrys. In Mt. 38.5 (PG 57: 425).
55 Ioh. Chrys. Stelech. 2.4 (PG 47: 417): λοιπὸν τῶν πληγῶν.
56 Bars. Resp. 93 (SC 427: 394): καθ᾽ ἡμέραν . . . λαμβάνεις τὴν ψυχὴν αὐτοῦ.

practice of flogging. An angry master would not look at the slave.[57] The
master would recite the cause of offense.[58] The master would announce the
punishment not by speaking directly to the slaves, but by talking to another
person.[59] The denial of recognition to the slave added to the degradation of
corporal punishment. The punished body was expected to remain silent.[60]
The other slaves were expected to take the lesson to heart and quietly
observe; if a slave snickered at his colleague under the lash, the master's
anger might be transferred to him.[61] The effect of corporal punishment
was amplified by carefully selected, ostentatious examples. Violence against
slaves could be performed to maximize its visibility and thus its impact.
A slave might be locked up for the sake of teaching the other slaves.[62]
Conspicuous violence was a standard part of domination: "lashing one
slave often, he makes the rest more controlled through fear."[63] "Often,
when one of the slaves has been treated abusively, the whole rank of them
becomes terrified . . . "[64]

Whipping was used to maintain an environment charged with potential
violence.[65] A master watched the suffering slave and might consider mercy,
but by keeping the offense steadily in mind, he could finish the beating.[66]
Mercy might be perceived as weakness. Some masters had their friends
administer the lashing in order to avoid diminishing the climate of fear by
clemency.[67] Augustine preached mercy, but worried that someone would
ask, "'Shall discipline sleep?'" The bishop was quick to answer, "That's
not what I'm saying . . . and if you see your slave living badly, what other
punishment will you curb him with, if not the lash? Use it: do. God allows
it. In fact he is angered if you don't. But do it in a loving rather than
vindictive spirit."[68] Whether masters were really so reluctant, and whether
the pastoral efforts of an Augustine could really modulate the emotional
basis of lashing, slave-ownership and the scourge were, by any reckoning,
inseparable.

---

[57] Diod. Psalm. 12.2 (CCSG 6: 71); Ambr. Apol. Dav. 1.14.67 (SC 239: 168).
[58] Aen. Dial. 17 line 6 (Colonna: 17). The context refers to the punishment of sons or slaves.
[59] Ioh. Chrys. In 1 Cor. 14.1 (PG 61: 115).   [60] Ioh. Chrys. Serm. in Genes. 2.88–91 (SC 433: 188).
[61] Ioh. Chrys. In Mt. 80.4 (PG 58: 722).   [62] Ioh. Chrys. Oppug. 3.3 (PG 47: 352).
[63] Ioh. Chrys. Laz. 3.8 (PG 48: 1003): ἕνα πολλάκις μαστιγώσαντες οἰκέτην, τοὺς λοιποὺς σωφρον-
εστέρους ἐποίησαν τῷ φόβῳ.
[64] Ps.-Caes. Resp. 146 (Riedinger: 131): καὶ ἑνὸς πολλάκις οἰκέτου αἰκιζομένου πᾶσα τῶν οἰκετῶν ἡ
φάλαγξ πτήσσουσα . . .
[65] cf. Gutman 1975, 14–41.   [66] Ioh. Chrys. Psalm. 117.3 (PG 55: 330).
[67] Ioh. Chrys. Non ad grat. conc. 5 (PG 50: 661).
[68] Aug. Psalm. 102.14 (CC 40: 1464–5): *dormiet disciplina? . . . servumque ipsum tuum, si male viventem
videris, non poena aliqua, non verberibus refrenabis? fiat hoc, fiat: admittit deus, immo reprehendit, si
non fiat; sed animo dilectionis fac, non animo ultionis.*

Since private force was not constrained by due process, violence could be knowingly carried out against innocents. A little flogging might restore order after the day-to-day disruptions of the *pax domestica*.[69] Hurt feelings could easily be avenged on the bodies of slaves. Augustine theoretically had qualms about the beating of innocent slaves to spare the free, though in actual cases he was not slow to have slaves punished.[70] Slaves made easy scapegoats. It is notable that the physical coercion of slaves is described as simply routine, duteous, or perfunctory. If a slave had learned to steal, the master beat him whether it would change him or not, so that the master himself was absolved of any blame for negligence.[71] "The master has the power to use the mill, chains, whips, tattooing, torture, and so on, but if the slave is wicked, it cannot change him."[72] Violence against slaves was socially expected. It was so reflexive that it was exerted even where it was known to be futile.

The whip was only the most common mechanism of corporal punishment. Physical confinement was often mentioned, varying from public incarceration, private restrictions on movement, to, of course, shackles.[73] The use of manacles was the natural response if a slave was thought prone to flight. A slave might be identified by the black marks on his ankles.[74] Slaves of the same master might be chained together, to embarrass them and simultaneously hinder their mobility.[75] Chains were considered an essential instrument of slave-ownership, the very emblem of punishment.[76] Other forms of violence – beating, torture, distension, broken limbs – were used by masters.[77] A master could hand the slave over to a public official, the *carnifex*, for torture.[78] Nudity and other means of humiliation were inflicted on slaves – a most degrading reminder that the slave's body was not legally his own.[79] Slaves were placed on display in wooden stocks.[80] Slaves could be punished with reassignment, to the fields, for instance, or to sewage work.[81] It is impossible to say how often these methods were

[69] Aug. Conf. 9.9.20 (CC 27: 145–6).
[70] Aug. C. mendac. 9.22 (CSEL 41: 497). For an actual case, Aug. Ep. 8.2* (CSEL 88: 41–2).
[71] Lib. Or. 49.24 (Foerster vol. 3: 463).
[72] Lib. Decl. 1.147 (Foerster vol. 5: 98–9): ἐξουσία τοῖς δεσπόταις μύλωνος, πεδῶν, μαστίγων, στίξαι, στρεβλῶσαι, τούτους μέν, ἂν ὦσι πονηροί, οὐκ ἂν μεταβάλοιμεν . . .
[73] See chapter 4.   [74] Claud. In Eutr. 2 lines 342–5 (Hall: 179).
[75] Ioh. Chrys. Virgin. 41.2 (SC 125: 236–8).   [76] Cyr. Jo. 4.387A (Pusey: 568).
[77] Hist. Apoll. Reg. Tyr. 39 (Kortekaas: 366–8), fictional. Ioh. Chrys. In Ephes. 16.1 (PG 62: 112); Ioh. Chrys. Non iter. conj. lines 271–9 (SC 138: 184); Mir. Menas 2 (Detorakēs: 167–8).
[78] Zeno Tractatus 1.35.8 (CC 22: 90–1).
[79] Lact. Ir. 5.12 (SC 289: 108); Lib. Or. 25.13 (Foerster vol. 2: 543).
[80] Bas. Hom. Mart. Iulit. 6 (PG 31: 252): ἐν ξύλῳ.
[81] To fields: Ambr. Apol. Dav. 1.14.67 (SC 239: 168). To sewage: Aug. Lib. 3.9.27 (CC 29: 291).

employed; we have a qualitative, but not quantitative, insight. Many, creative, calculated, and depraved were the mechanisms of pain used to extract
labor from recalcitrant bodies.

Violence against slaves was loosely limited by social constraint and by
public law. In his sermon on *Ephesians*, John Chrysostom staked his argument against excessive violence on the moral foundation of preserving the
master's honor, invoking a long tradition which debated the limits of polite
violence.[82] Chrysostom latched onto the use of violence against slave-
women. Cultural protocols towards the use of violence against women can
have repercussions for the use of violence within slavery. In the modern
world, for instance, abolitionists clung to the emotive power of violence
against slave-women as a rhetorical strategy.[83] In an insightful study, Dossey
has shown that attitudes towards violence against women differed significantly in Latin and Greek cultures, with eastern societies more hesitant
to condone excessive physical force against women's bodies.[84] Chrysostom
was tapping into this reserve of cultural inhibition, even though violence
against slave-women was far more acceptable than violence against free
women. In the west domestic abuse found greater acceptance, and no
one seems to have blinked in the face of violence against female slaves.

There were few public limits on violence, and such as existed were
vague, impractical, and largely irrelevant. The Roman state, rather than
specific statutory limits, preferred to give governors jurisdiction over the
maintenance of public order. A law of Antoninus Pius, for example, forbade
individual masters from "atrocious savagery." The explicit purpose was to
avoid inciting trouble among slaves as a class.[85] Such laws are not rare
historically, even in the harshest slave societies.[86] The laws of Constantine
are an interesting case study in the Roman state's desire to maintain order
and decency without practically undermining the master's power. In 319,
Constantine decreed that if a master beat or confined his slave, and the
slave died, the master was free of guilt, regardless of how soon thereafter
the slave died.[87] But:

Lest the master use his right immoderately, he shall be charged with homicide
if he intentionally kills the slave with the blow of a stick or stone, or definitely
[i.e. regardless of "intention"] if the master inflicts a lethal wound with a spear,
or orders him hanged by a noose, or by a monstrous order commands him to be
thrown to his death, or fills him with a mortal poison, or has his body torn apart

---

[82] McKeown 2007, 45, 91; Hopkins 1993, 10.   [83] Paton 1996.   [84] Dossey 2008.
[85] Coll. 3.3.5–6: *atrociore saevitia*. cf. Dig. 1.6.2. Bradley 1987b, 126–9.
[86] Morris 1996, 162–82. Karasch 1987, 116–17, where law and practice are juxtaposed.
[87] Thus probably prompted by Jewish or Christian norms: see Stuiber 1978, 68. cf. Exodus 21.20–1
and Conc. Eliberritanum, canon 5 (Mansi vol. 2: 6).

by public punishments, ripping his sides with the claws of beasts or scorching his body by the application of fire, or if, with the savagery of the wild barbarians, in the midst of tortures, as their bodies go white, and black blood mixed with gore flows out, the master makes him die.[88]

The law is morbid and voyeuristic. It combined the love of high-flown rhetoric in Constantine's legislation with the presentation of imperial benevolence.[89] Constantine tried to create a distinction between death in the course of normal master–slave violence, which was perfectly acceptable, and deliberate death sentences or especially spectacular forms of death. Sadistic punishments were, notably, reserved for the state. In a law ten years later, Constantine reiterated the master's immunity from guilt if the slave died while being punished, this time without so much detail.[90] Constantine's legislation marks a regression from the standards of the high empire.[91] It was the last time on record that a Roman emperor meddled with the works of private discipline.

The incentive model of the master–slave relationship leads us to believe that violence was not exerted uniformly on all slaves. Unfortunately the evidence does not allow us to test this proposition in much detail. Surely most of the evidence, with its implicit focus on the master, belongs to a discourse which centers around the master's presence. In these sources we are typically near the slave-owner, which inevitably means we know more about slaves close to the person of the master. At the same time, the ubiquity of violence is remarkable, and few slaves were immune from its influence. Procurators can be found fleeing into a church for asylum.[92] Slaves were punished for being slow or lackadaisical in their service at table.[93] Cooks might be whipped for culinary mistakes.[94] Slaves who dropped a girl from her carriage were "ground into dust."[95] Failing to wake up the master at

---

[88] CT 9.12.1 (AD 319) though the date is uncertain because Constantine was not in Rome, where the subscription places him: *nec vero inmoderate suo iure utatur, sed tunc reus homicidii sit, si voluntate eum vel ictu fustis aut lapidis occiderit vel certe telo usus letale vulnus inflixerit aut suspendi laqueo praeceperit vel iussione taetra praecipitandum esse mandaverit aut veneni virus infuderit vel dilaniaverit poenis publicis corpus, ferarum vestigiis latera persecando vel exurendo admotis ignibus membra aut tabescentes artus atro sanguine permixta sanie defluentes prope in ipsis adegerit cruciatibus vitam linquere saevitia immanium barbarorum.* In this law, the drafter distinguished between (1) legitimate punishment with blows, sticks, stones, etc., which might accidentally kill the slave and was not illegal, (2) intentional (*voluntate*) killing of the slave by these means which was illegal, and (3) punishment of the slave by any of the means listed in this gruesome catalogue, in which case intent was irrelevant and the master was definitely (*certe*) liable. The text was included in nearly identical form in the CJ as 9.14.1.

[89] Stuiber 1978, 66; Sargenti 1938, 50–4.   [90] CT 9.12.2 (AD 329). Seeck 1919, 179.

[91] Waldstein 1990, 142.   [92] CT 9.45.3 (AD 398).

[93] Thdt. H. rel. 21.33 (SC 234: 120); Ioh. Chrys. In Mt. 36.5 (PG 57: 411).

[94] Ioh. Chrys. Virgin. 69.1 (SC 125: 342).   [95] Lib. Ep. 615 (Foerster vol. 10: 566–7): συντριβῆναι.

the right hour brought on a beating.[96] Servile estate managers who failed
to follow orders were severely corrected.[97]

Physical proximity might affect *who* administered violence, not *whether*
it was administered. A considerable proportion of slaves lived in close quarters with their masters. In small households with three or four slaves – who
slept on the master's floor, in a separate quarter of the house, or in the mule's
stall – masters might rule their slaves face-to-face.[98] But many "households"
were larger, more complex, and even in urban settings mastery was often
mediated through managerial personnel. It was said that masters *ordered*
their slaves to be beaten, insinuating that the actual deed was delegated.[99]
Managers – themselves slaves – were often in charge of the labor, rest, and
nutrition of the other slaves.[100] Some households were so large that slaves
might mutter about the master never hearing their complaints.[101]

Many masters were physically distant from their subordinates. The
wealthy held their property in scattered estates. Melania the Younger and
Pinian were said to own thousands of slaves, spread across properties in over
half-a-dozen modern Mediterranean countries. This did nothing to dim
the personal feelings of mastery. With the true sensibility of a grand Roman
matron, Melania was piqued when slaves on her estates "dared to contradict" her.[102] The domination of absentee land-owners was felt through
their intermediaries.[103] Fear was maintained – through agents, through the
government, through regular inspections.[104] John Chrysostom imagined
the rich household as a long chain of authority, with farms and overseers,
and rulers over the rulers, and the master at the top.[105] The master's power
was often refracted and relayed through several layers before it was felt by
the slave.

The practical effects of this power, as it flowed down the ladder of
domination through agents and managers, is largely beyond our ken. In
the American South, it has been appreciated how white slave overseers could

---

[96] Lib. Ep. 1446 (Foerster vol. 11: 483–4).   [97] Caes. Arel. Serm. 7.3 (CC 103: 39).

[98] Separate quarters: Aug. Locut. Hept. 116 (CC 33: 392). Mule's stall: Ioh. Chrys. In act Apost. 45.4
(PG 60: 319). Straw floor: Ioh. Chrys. Virgin. 70.2 (SC 125: 346). Master's floor: Gr. Naz. Or. 18.32
(PG 35: 1028).

[99] CT 9.12.1 (AD 319). Aug. Serm. 161.9 (PL 38: 883).

[100] Bars. Resp. 60 (SC 426: 296); Lib. Or. 25.57 (Foerster vol. 2: 564); Gr. Nyss. Eun. 8.47 (Jaeger:
256); Mart. Paes. Thecl. 52Rii (Reymond and Barns: 153).

[101] Aug. Psalm. 33.2.20 (CSEL 93.1A: 295).

[102] Vit. Mel. (lat.) 10.5 (Laurence: 172): *nobis ausi sunt contradicere.*

[103] Lib. Ep. 319 (Foerster vol. 10: 298–9); Lib. Or. 14.45 (Foerster vol. 2: 103); Ambrosiast. Comm.
Coloss. 2.17 (CSEL 81: 188).

[104] Government: Symm. Ep. 9.6 (MGH AA 6.1: 236). Agents: Salv. Gub. 4.3 (MGH AA 1: 38).
Inspections: SB 11130 (Karanis, third/fourth century).

[105] Ioh. Chrys. In Ephes. 22.2 (PG 62: 157).

act as a terrible proxy for the master's presence, intensifying the violence of the relationship while insulating the master's *politesse*.[106] On the other hand, most plantations used slave foremen, workers of the same status and race as the other slaves. These foremen were of necessity Janus-faced, responsible to the master yet often sensitive leaders capable of understanding their subordinates and cushioning the brutality of the system.[107] We can only wonder how the lack of a racial identity affected the solidarity of the ancient slave population. In antiquity, slave-drivers were usually slaves.[108] Certainly ancient slave management could be a terror for slaves: it was said that slaves might seem to belong to the master's agents, his *actores*. Slaves might flee for fear of the lash in the hands of these managers.[109] In the *Life of Aesop*, the slave manager who oversaw work in the fields was represented as capricious and sadistic, and only the clever Aesop was able to get past him to show the master how cruel his agent truly was.[110]

Fenoaltea's model perhaps understates the effectiveness of violence because it fails to grapple, fundamentally, with the nature of violence; the model assumes that violence is used in slave-driving, where pain is immediate and physical anxiety constant. This may describe some extreme forms of slavery, in mining or perhaps the sugar plantation. But it only poorly comprehends the more reserved and calculated use of violence in the Roman slave system. One sign of this carefully maintained threat of violence is the emphasis which Roman observers placed on the use of fear. Psychological violence was more effective than physical violence.[111] Masters recognized that it was much more efficient to turn the capacity for violence into the fear of violence. The slave "feared the master's shadow every day" – and a shadow could be everywhere at once.[112] The most wicked slaves could be made to fear brute physical pain.[113] Fear made slaves diligent in their labor; it motivated their actions.[114] "For to be a slave is in essence to fear, and to be the master's entirely, and to keep the master always in mind."[115] The use of fear is different from the use of immediate physical anxiety, and fear allowed the manipulation of slaves in a broader variety of tasks and supervisory arrangements.

---

[106] cf. Genovese 1974, 10–25.   [107] Paquette 2000.

[108] On the earlier period, Carlsen 1995. cf. Dal Lago and Katsari 2008, 210.

[109] Salv. Gub. 4.3 (MGH AA 1: 38). cf. Hopkins 1993, 16.

[110] Vit. Aesop 9 (Perry: 38). Hopkins 1993.   [111] Iul. Imp. Or. 9.15 (Rochefort: 163–4).

[112] Ioh. Chrys. Hom. in Genes. 50.2 (PG 53: 450): καθ' ἑκάστην ἡμέραν τὰς σκιὰς αὐτὰς δεδοικότες.

[113] Aug. Tract. Io. 43.7 (CC 36: 375).

[114] Hilar. Pict. Psalm. 2.45 (CSEL 22: 72); Dor. Doct. 14.157 (SC 92: 440).

[115] Olymp. In Plat. Alc. 160 (Westerink: 102): ὁ γὰρ δοῦλος ᾗ δοῦλος δέδιεν καὶ ὅλος ἐστὶ τοῦ δεσπότου, ἀεὶ ἐν νῷ αὐτὸν ἔχων.

Fear was perhaps the primary strategy of mastery in the Roman slave system. In the corpus of late antique writings, no attribute was more often associated with slavery than fear. It was the most keenly *felt* element of the relationship. "To fear is the symbol of slavery."[116] "Who does not know that the one who is a slave by nature and employed in a master's power cannot be without the emotion of fear? For fear is in a sense yoked to the very nature of slavery."[117] To fear was in the nature of slaves.[118] "Nothing is more particular to slavery than the eternal fear."[119] *Semper timere.* We hear so much of this emotion because it was precisely what masters sought from their slaves. "If a slave is under fear and the lash, and immediately trembles when anything is said to him by the master, lest he hear he is to be beaten, certainly the master rejoices in this situation."[120] Fear was a means of maintaining the constant labor and subjective annihilation demanded of slaves. Violence commuted into its potential, spread out into all corners of the relationship, tinged all interaction between masters and their human property.

Physical punishment was not the only means of corporal control over slaves, and psychological manipulation was not limited to the threat of violence. Perhaps nothing breaks down the strict dichotomy between pain and positive incentives like the use of food as a tool of domination in the Roman slave system. With a few important exceptions, the use of hunger and the promise of dietary satisfaction have been terribly neglected by ancient historians.[121] The use of food is less spectacular than the incidence of violence, but it gave masters considerable leverage to extract the submission and labor demanded of slaves. The use of hunger was a potentially dehumanizing method of control. Physical dependency was cultivated. "Slaves wait at the hands of their masters when they want to be nourished, so that they avoid a complete want of necessities . . . "[122] Masters considered

---

[116] Diod. Rom. 8.15 (Staab: 92): φοβεῖσθαι δουλείας σημεῖόν ἐστιν; Sever. Gab. Rom. 8.15 (Staab: 220): ὅπερ δουλείας ἐστὶ σημεῖον.

[117] Gr. Nyss. Eunom. 8.53 (Jaeger: 258): τίς γὰρ οὐκ οἶδεν ὅτι ὁ δοῦλος τῇ φύσει καὶ πρὸς δεσποτικὴν ἀνάγκην ἠσχολημένος οὐδὲ τοῦ κατὰ τὸν φόβον πάθους ἐκτὸς ἄν εἴη; συνέζευκται γάρ πως τῇ φύσει τῆς δουλείας ὁ φόβος.

[118] Symm. Ep. 9.53 (MGH AA 6.1: 251); Aug. Psalm. 18(2).10 (CC 38: 110); Aug. Psalm. 63.2 (CC 39: 809); Aug. Psalm. 77.12 (CC 39: 1077); Aug. Psalm. 118.17.1 (CC 40: 1719); Ioh. Chrys. Non iter. conj. lines 271–9 (SC 138: 184); Ambr. Psal. 118 5.46 (CSEL 62: 108).

[119] Ambr. Ios. 4.20 (CSEL 32.2: 87): *nihil enim tam speciale servitutis est quam semper timere.*

[120] Ps.-Mac. Serm. 47.1.7 (Berthold vol. 2: 89): ὁ δ' ἄλλος ὑπὸ φόβον ἐστὶ καὶ πληγάς, καὶ εἴ τι αὐτῷ λέγεται ὑπὸ τοῦ δεσπότου, τρέμων ταχέως ὑπακούει, μήπως ἐὰν παρακούσῃ τυπτηθῇ. ὁ γοῦν δεσπότης ἐπὶ τῷ τοιούτῳ χαίρει.

[121] Roth 2007, 38, and 2002, 209; De Martino 1993a.

[122] Cass. Psalm. 122.2 (CC 98: 1156): *Attendunt servi ad manus dominorum suorum, sive quando per eos desiderant enutriri, ut totius indigentiae necessitates evadant . . .* cf. Faust 1982, 103.

themselves gracious for feeding their slaves, and the physical layout of the
act – slaves waiting at the hands of the master – might be used to reinforce
the power structure behind the relationship.

Slaves received their food in rations. They were given their "measure
according to need, the daily ration allotted with economy" – enough to
keep them physically fit for labor.[123] In a comic setting, slaves were given
leftovers, but it was deducted from their allowance.[124] Some were fed on a
daily ration, which might have allowed the most minute physical control.[125]
Rural slaves might receive a monthly or bi-monthly ration, which could
have made the use of food a less fine-tuned means of control. Perhaps it
just raised the stakes.[126] A trustworthy slave, appointed as *oikonomos*, was
put in charge of the sleep and food allotments of the slaves.[127] It is most
revealing, and discomforting, that a well-fed slave was instantly suspected
of being a sexual favorite.[128] Hunger and starvation were important tools of
control. Lactantius listed hunger and thirst among the punishments meted
out to bad slaves.[129] Food was used to discipline the slaves to intensive
labor: a mistress swore to her slave-girl that unless she completed her quota
of work she would go to sleep without food.[130] Ammianus reported seeing
the emaciated bodies of slaves, worn out by squalor.[131] In lean years, slaves
were the first to go hungry.[132] Caesarius begged his Christians not to use
starvation against their slaves.[133]

Slaves, of course, ate separately from their masters.[134] The slave diet was
monotonous and unappealing. Theodoret said that slaves "eat bran bread,
and never enjoy even a little delicacy."[135] "The good *oikonomos* grinds the
grain and that which is better and cleaner he makes into bread for the
masters and the free ones, that which is worse he gives to the slaves, and
that which is still worse, from the husks, he gives to the pigs and the
cocks."[136] A medical text called the consumption of horse or donkey meat

---

[123] Thdt. Provid. 7.680A (PG 83: 680): ὁ δὲ τῇ χρείᾳ μετρῶν τὴν μετάληψιν, καὶ τὸν χοίνικα τὸν
διδόμενον οἰκονομικῶς διαιρῶν.

[124] Lib. Decl. 32.24 (Foerster vol. 7: 55).   [125] Ioh. Chrys. In Rom. 14.2 (PG 60: 526).

[126] P. Harr. 2.233 (AD 307). cf. P. Lips. 97 (AD 338); SPP 20.106 (AD 355–6); P. Haun. 3.68 (AD 402);
BGU 1.34 = P. Charite 36 (AD 322); P. Duk. Inv. 553 v (after 252); P. Bad. 4.95.

[127] Bars. Resp. 60 (SC 426: 296).   [128] Hier. Ep. 79.8 (CSEL 55: 97). See chapter 8.

[129] Lact. Ir. 5.12 (SC 289: 108).   [130] Ioh. Chrys. Ad pop. Ant. 14.1 (PG 49: 145).

[131] Amm. 28.1.55 (Foerster vol. 2: 71).   [132] Lib. Or. 16.21 (Foerster vol. 2: 169).

[133] Caes. Arel. Serm. 34.2 (CC 103: 148).   [134] Thdt. Int. Heb. 2.10 (PG 82: 694).

[135] Thdt. Provid. 7.680A (PG 83: 680): Ἄρτον ἐσθίει πιτυρίαν, οὐδὲ μικροῦ προσοψήματος ἀπο-
λαύων.

[136] Ioh. Philop. Gen. Anim. 114 (CAG 14.3: 114): ὁ ἀγαθὸς οἰκονόμος τοῦ ἀληλεσμένου σίτου τὸ
μὲν καθαρώτερον καὶ βέλτιον, οἷον τὸ σταῖς, ἀπεργάζεται ἄρτον τοῖς ἐλευθέροις καὶ τοῖς
δεσπόταις, τὸ δὲ χεῖρον τοῖς δούλοις, τὸ δ' ἔτι χεῖρον, οἷον τὰ πίτυρα, χοίροις καὶ ἀλεκτρυόσι.
cf. Aristotle, Gener. Anim. 744b.

"servile."[137] Another assumed that slaves were in poor health, "due to constant exposure and the bad humors of the slave diet."[138] In the archive of Theophanes, we can follow in unexpected detail the diet of a traveling party composed of a mixed group of free and slave members. Two levels of bread, fine and common, were regularly purchased, the former for the free members of the party, the latter for the slaves; occasionally the slaves were bought olives or real wine, and in one instance the "entire party of slaves was invited, as it were, to High Table to enjoy the same fare as their master."[139] Ultimately, though, as unappealing and conditional as the slave's diet was, at least it was relatively guaranteed. Paradoxically, the slave's body was a valuable possession, so the nutrition necessary for bare survival was probably more guaranteed to the slave than to the free poor, not a fact to be taken for granted in the ancient world.[140]

If masters thought themselves gracious for feeding their slaves, the practice of rationing food made them look upon their slaves as gluttons. It is a real measure of the chasm between masters and slaves that they could think of their dependants as "a band of complainers" – their allotment was "always insufficient for them."[141] A slave would say anything for his stomach.[142] Only Salvian of Marseilles admitted the obvious: slaves were accused of gluttony, precisely because "he has a greater desire for satiety who has often endured hunger."[143] Again, it is impossible to measure the extent of deliberately inflicted malnutrition. What our authors meant by the claim that masters "often" used hunger against their slaves is unknowable, but the certain fact is that hunger was potentially a blunt, bloodless weapon in the hands of the master.

DOMINATION THROUGH POSITIVE INCENTIVES

The master's power was not merely coercive. The master was also able to hold out the hope of various rewards to his slaves. The use of rewards intensified the effect of pain incentives, since the slave was presented with such a stark contrast between physical torment and material reward. Honor

---

[137] Orib. Coll. Med. 2.68 (CMG 6.1.1: 63).
[138] Pall. Med. In Hipp. sex. (Dietz vol. 2: 185): διὰ τὸ συνεχῶς τῷ ἀέρι προσομιλεῖν, καὶ διὰ τὸ κακόχυμον τῆς δουλικῆς διαίτης.
[139] Matthews 2006, 166.   [140] Chapters 2 and 10, for self-sale.
[141] Hier. Ep. 117.8 (CSEL 55: 431): *querulum servulorum genus est et, quantumcumque dederis, semper eis minus est.* Hier. Ep. 54.5 (CSEL 54: 470).
[142] Gr. Naz. Or. 21.16 (SC 270: 142).
[143] Salv. Gub. 4.3 (MGH AA 1: 38): *magis desiderat saturitatem qui famem saepe tolerarit.*

the good, whip the bad.[144] Slaves were treated with a combination of carrot and stick – a slave on the master's bad side might improve and earn higher trust than before.[145] It is precisely the mix which makes slavery such a peculiar relationship, which nurtured the belief in the slave's dependency and which gave the master's will such potency. In the Roman slave system, moreover, the master enjoyed an exceptionally deep reserve of positive incentives. Slaves could be rewarded with the master's esteem, promotion within the family, power over other slaves, nicer clothing, a little property.[146] Such petty emoluments were the wages of obedience, expropriated labor, and submission.

Other positive incentives were anything but petty. The four most important positive incentives in Roman slavery were promotion, *peculium*, family life, and manumission. The occupational structure outlined in chapters 3 and 4 demonstrates the significant space for internal hierarchies to develop within slavery. Slaves were prominent as managers, both within the domestic staff and in the fields. Ambrose claimed that promotion was based on performance.[147] The possibility of upward mobility acted as a powerful incentive to slaves to meet their master's expectations. Secondly, slaves could be rewarded with property of their own. Slaves of course could not legally own property, but the law allowed slaves to have a *peculium*, an account in their possession but which ultimately belonged to the master. This device allowed slaves to accumulate their own goods and to reap some of the fruits of their labor.[148] The *peculium* could also deepen the slave's dependence on the master, since it might act as a form of collateral for the slave's good behavior: the master giveth, the master taketh away.[149]

The *peculium* could be used as a formal or informal mechanism.[150] In some instances, the *peculium* was a carefully managed account. Particularly if a slave was a business agent or manager, the *peculium* was a devolution of responsibility that gave the slave a stake in the success of an enterprise. On the other hand, the *peculium* might encompass the more informal goods acquired by the slave. Historians have come to recognize what a

---

[144] Cyr. H. Catech. 18.4 (Reischl and Rupp vol. 2: 302).
[145] Ioh. Chrys. Thdr. 1.16.59 (SC 117: 180).
[146] Clothing: Aug. Lib. 3.11.34 (CC 29: 295). *Peculium*: Aug. Serm. 296.4 (Morin: 403). Positions of trust: Aug. Conf. 9.8.17 (CC 27: 143); Ambr. Abr. 1.3.13 (CSEL 32.1: 511); Aug. Psalm. 103.4.10 (CC 40: 1530).
[147] Ambr. Abr. 1.3.13 (CSEL 32.1: 511).   [148] Roth 2005a.
[149] E.g. Aug. Serm. 296.4 (Morin: 403). See chapter 4.
[150] Andreau 1999, 67; Aubert 1994, 65–70; Buckland 1908, 187–233.

significant role the "informal economy" played in modern slave systems.[151] Slaves used extra time or extra space – marginal lands, forests, gardens – to accumulate private goods. Masters could see the potential benefits of the informal economy. Slaves would supplement their own nutrition, and the industrious use of spare time was unobjectionable. Unfortunately we lack the evidence which would document the informal slave economy in the Roman world, but it was perhaps significant. Roth has argued that the nutrition outlays of the agricultural writers assume some additional input.[152] Probably rural slaves had more space and opportunity; Libanius claimed that, even in hard times, the slave always found a little something from the earth.[153] Palladius considered raising small animals like chickens an instrinsic activity of the female workers on an estate, and poultry is precisely the sort of good susceptible to informal ownership.[154] Late Roman authors assumed that the slave had some private goods, and we must imagine the invisible circuits of informal property that gave the slave a stake in his own labor, some material reward for carving out private space and time through obedience.

Chapter 6 explores in more detail the dynamics of the slave family, but we should discuss here the basic features of the Roman system which made the family such an important spur to motivation. The Roman slave system endured over an exceptionally long period of time, and chapter 2 has argued that the key to this longevity was natural reproduction. Few large-scale slave systems have been centered on agriculture; the cultivation of standard Mediterranean crops gave life a relatively normal rhythm for slaves – it sustained mortality rates and sex ratios which were not fundamental blocks to reproduction. Reproductive success is a sign that slaves enjoy some privacy and family opportunity.[155] Slaves in the countryside, owned in larger groups, probably enjoyed much more freedom to pursue family life, and the inscription from Thera encourages us to believe that the slaves on this estate enjoyed some success in creating spheres of privacy.

What is important to recognize in the context of this chapter is that family life had repercussions for the practice of domination. The strange tincture of the US slave system was largely due to the fact that the master–slave relationship was so colored by the prominence of slave families.[156] The slave family was at one and the same time an economic benefit to the master, for whom it represented reproduction and a means of discipline,

---

[151] Morris 1998, 994–1002; Berlin and Morgan 1993 and 1991.
[152] Roth 2007, 25–52, 2005a, and 2002. cf. Rathbone 1991, 111–12.
[153] Lib. Or. 25.67 (Foerster vol. 1: 570).   [154] Pall. Op. ag. 1.27.1 (Martin: 26).
[155] See chapter 2.   [156] See Morris 1998, 987; Gutman 1976.

and a subjective goal for the slave, for whom it represented a counter-weight to the dehumanization and degradation of enslavement. We have no slave diaries, no Works Progress Administration (WPA) interviews to tell us what family life meant to ancient slaves, but it takes no extraordinary feat of empathy to appreciate the significance of the slave family. The sources do, just occasionally, show that masters recognized the disciplinary potential of family life, as a way of literally domesticating their slaves and containing sexual energy. But because the slave family is so central to the slave's assertion of agency, further discussion is deferred to chapter 6, where we will explore this double character of the slave family as both an especially strong means of discipline and a highly charged arena of potential conflict.

The ultimate, shimmering reward for the slave was the promise of freedom.[157] In the study of incentives, manumission has typically enjoyed pride of place as the principal reward offered by the master in return for the slave's obedience. While it is fundamentally true that manumission was deeply implicated in the control of slaves, such a categorical statement is partly misleading. Clearly, not all manumissions came about as a reward for effective service. In the late empire, for instance, manumission might be prompted by Christian asceticism, as part of the liquidation of an earthly property.[158] Much more importantly, manumission might be prompted because of emotional or biological bonds between master and slave. The manumission of favorites, such as sexual partners or the master's illegitimate offspring, was a structurally important component of the Roman slave system.[159] As is only to be expected in a system as massive and interally complex as Roman slavery, causes were complex and to some extent unpredictable.

If manumission was not exclusively a tool of social control, it typically was. As Hopkins, Bradley, and others have demonstrated in the Roman case, manumission was a powerful incentive to extract the slave's co-operation.[160] Fenoaltea's model demonstrates why. Slaves employed in care-intensive labor were difficult to monitor, and it was counter-productive to foster intense malice when retaliation was costly. So the slave's motivation had to include the promise of positive rewards. Chief among these

---

[157] A list of essential studies would include López Barja de Quiroga 2007; Zelnick-Abramovitz 2005; Harrill 1995; Los 1995; Bradley 1987b, 81–112; Waldstein 1986; Fabre 1981; Garnsey 1981; Treggiari 1969a and 1969b; Veyne 1961; Duff 1928. For the legal form and effects of manumission, with relevant bibliography, see chapter 9 and especially chapter 12.

[158] See chapter 12.

[159] López Barja de Quiroga 2007, esp. 45–67; Weiler 2001; Smadja 1999, 366. Gaius, Inst. 1.18–19, on the exceptions to the *lex Aelia Sentia.* cf. Cole Libby and Paiva 2000, for Brazilian parallels.

[160] Bradley 1987b, 81–112; Hopkins 1978, 133–71.

was manumission. The incentive model shows why certain types of freedmen appear so prominently in Roman society. At the extreme, of course,
lies the wealthy freedman of imperial literature, but even more substantial
are the tens of thousands of freedmen who could afford to commemorate themselves in sepulchral inscriptions. Slaves who during their term of
enslavement had the most opportunity to acquire skills and capital were
those most likely to enjoy independence and success after their manumission, and it is these slaves whom we meet at the table of Trimalchio and in
the epigraphic record of Rome.[161]

Manumission was an important incentive, but like the spectrum of punishments and rewards, its use as a motivational technique was camouflaged
in ambiguous and moralized terms. Manumission *could* be held out as a
direct recompense for particular tasks: do this, become free.[162] More commonly, however, manumission was dangled as the reward for a long period
of obedient service. The faithful slave, who proved that he possessed *fides*,
was led to hope for freedom.[163] Some manumission rituals announced and
preached the value of *fides* – a virtue that combined the expectations of
labor, loyalty, and submission.[164] Manumission, of course, was at the master's discretion. It was given by the "grace or goodwill" of the master.[165]
This absolute control reinforced the master's power, and it influenced his
self-perception. A late antique joke told of the master who was aboard a
ship with his slaves when a storm arose. His slaves wept for their lives, but
he told them not to fear, since they had been freed in his will. The joke was
supposed to poke fun at the solipsism of the master, but it was a poignant
comment on the circularity of living in servitude as the price of freedom.[166]
Slaves were often freed by testament, a final act of conspicuous goodwill.[167]
Despite the fact that virtually every ancient slave's voice has been lost to
history, there are hints of betrayals and broken promises.[168] Many slaves,
moreover, were manumitted in their old age, after decades of expropriated
labor had left them tired, spent, or frail.[169]

Roman manumission was an incentive that the master could fine-tune
to his own advantage. Manumission took different forms and had different
effects in Roman law. At one extreme, Roman law permitted atypically

---

[161] Andreau 1993; Garnsey 1981; Veyne 1961.
[162] Hist. Apoll. Reg. Tyr. 31 (Kortekaas: 344); Herm. Past. 55.2 (SC 53: 228).
[163] Aug. Serm. 159.5 (PL 38: 870).
[164] Aug. Serm. 21.5–6 (CC 41: 281). cf. Bradley 1987b, 33–9; Wiedemann 1985, 164.
[165] Gr. Nyss. Tunc et ipse 6 (Downing: 6): δι' εὐνοίας ἢ χάριτος.
[166] Philogel. 25 (Thierfelder: 38).   [167] Ioh. Chrys. In Mt. 13.4 (PG 57: 215). Garnsey 1981, 31.
[168] Tac. Ann. 14.42–5 (Heubner: 332–4). cf. CJ 7.16.36 (AD 294).
[169] Ioh. Chrys. In 1 Tim. 16.2 (PG 62: 589).

generous terms of manumission that entailed citizenship and relative independence for the slave.[170] Particularly if a slave purchased his way out of
manumission, he might find himself in a position of considerable legal security and social independence.[171] This was not, apparently, altogether rare:
"for a slave can often get complete freedom, if he can ever gather money
to pay his value to the master."[172] Such arrangements, as Hopkins long ago
argued, promoted efficient labor and allowed the master to re-capitalize
in slaves.[173] Roman masters could also free their slaves on a variety of less
advantageous terms, and as patrons they could retain claims to respect
(*obsequium*) and more importantly labor (*operae*).[174] Manumitters could
also retain some claims, such as inheritance rights, to the property of freed
slaves, especially if the slave was freed informally.[175] In the east slaves were
often freed on the condition of continued service, either for a set term or
the life of the master; in the west testamentary manumission allowed the
master to set conditions on the slave's eventual liberation.[176] Chapter 12
will explore the changing institutional context of manumission in the late
empire, in which masters enjoyed even greater powers over their freedmen.
The noteworthy aspect of Roman manumission, from the vantage point
of discipline, is that the master could finely modulate the terms of reward
offered to the slave.

It is an enduring and ultimately unanswerable question how frequent
manumission was in Roman society.[177] The incentive model, because it
explains some of the underlying causes of manumission, at least prepares
us to expect a great diversity of outcomes within the system. There is
simply no decisive evidence at our disposal. Impressionistic evidence cuts
both ways. On the one hand, John Chrysostom claimed that even the
cruelest of men would not fail to honor a worthy slave by leaving freedom
and even a legacy to the slave in his will, but how many slaves were worthy
by this standard?[178] On the other hand, Theodoret claimed offhandedly
that most slaves would not become free.[179] The discussion for the earlier

---

[170] Garnsey 1981, 32–42.
[171] Buckland 1908, 636–46. See López Barja de Quiroga 2007, 90, on the different modalities of
manumission by purchase. Dig. 40.1.4. CJ 7.16.8 (AD 286) for a late Roman case.
[172] Ioh. Chrys. Virgin. 28.1 (SC 125: 184): Τούτῳ μὲν γὰρ ἔξεστι πολλάκις καὶ παντελοῦς ἐλευθερίας
τυχεῖν, εἰ δυνηθείη ποτὲ εὐπορήσας ἀργυρίου καταθεῖναι τὴν τιμὴν τῷ δεσπότῃ.
[173] Hopkins 1978, 133–71.   [174] See chapter 12.
[175] See esp. Sirks 1983 and 1981 on informal manumission.   [176] See chapter 9.
[177] Scheidel 1997, 160; Bradley 1994, 154–65 and 1987b, 81–112; Wiedemann 1985; Hopkins 1978, 115–
32. For a high estimate of manumission, Alföldy 1972. The case for high levels of manumission
has been renewed by Temin 2004, who makes an analytical but not empirical case for frequent
manumission. Also Lo Cascio 2002.
[178] Ioh. Chrys. In Mt. 13.4 (PG 57: 215).   [179] Thdt. Provid. 9.720 (PG 83: 720).

period has revolved around the *Digest* and the epigraphic material (which shows incontrovertibly that slaves were freed in massive numbers) along with a handful of literary sources to add color. The trouble lies in finding a random sample of data that would allow us to measure the frequency, and not just the volume, of manumission. The only potentially compelling data which have been adduced come from the census papyri of imperial Egypt. These reveal very few adult male slaves, and very few female slaves over the age of fifty.[180] This has been taken to imply that manumission was very extensive, but there are grounds for skepticism.[181]

First, the slave population of early imperial Egypt was not representative of the slave population as a whole. There is virtually no evidence for agricultural slavery in this period. In the early empire, Egypt exhibited slave-holding patterns dominated by Bourgeois and Agricultural households, with virtually no estate-based slavery. This was so because (1) in the early empire elite control of land in Egypt was relatively limited, (2) dense populations created thick labor markets for tenants and wage workers, and (3) commodity production was centered in the west, particularly in Italy. Roughly two-thirds of the slaves in the census papyri were females. Male slaves were probably pulled towards western markets, where their labor was most valuable; this same pattern is exhibited in the Delphic manumission inscriptions.[182] The male slaves in Egypt would have been employed in the most valuable roles, occupations involving skill and trust – the very roles most likely to entail manumission. The census papyri of the early empire, therefore, are probably not a representative sample.[183]

One imperfect but intriguing *comparandum* is the census inscription from Thera. This fourth-century tax register provides our only serious evidence for the demographic structure of a rural slave population in antiquity, and the contrasts with the Egyptian data are telling (figure 5.1).

The demographic structure of this population appears relatively "normal."[184] Tax evasion may lead to an understatement of adolescents and young adults, especially males; age rounding may artificially distort the age brackets towards the older cohorts. But the inscription suggests two relevant facts about manumission. First, the sheer number of older slaves demonstrates that manumission was not automatic. The rural data of Thera

---

[180] Bagnall and Frier 1994, 156–9.
[181] Used to suggest high levels of manumission in Scheidel 2005b, 4.   [182] See Hopkins 1978, 161–3.
[183] Another (admittedly imperfect) index lies in slave prices. If manumission was somewhat common from the age of thirty onward, we would expect the price of a slave in his twenties to decline, but such a pattern is not evident. Harper 2010. cf. Scheidel 2005b, 3.
[184] Harper 2008.

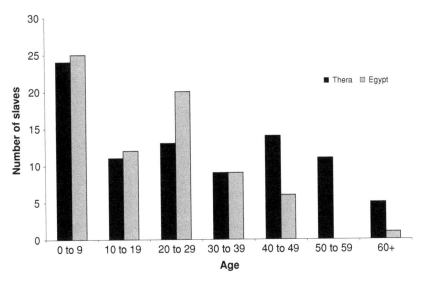

Figure 5.1 The age structure of two slave populations

are thus an important correction, or rather complement, to the predominantly Bourgeois data from Egypt. Secondly, the data hint that there was some male manumission. The imbalance of the population towards females in the adult population becomes more lopsided in the higher age cohorts, suggesting that some males and few females were freed. The assumption has been that rural slaves were rarely manumitted.[185] The Thera inscription shows that they had some hope. The data are very thin, but they are at least intuitively consistent with a model of estate-based agriculture in which managers, craftsmen, and skilled workers were important. Finally, we cannot resist calling attention to two slaves on another property, sixty and forty years old, named Lucky and Longtimer. Were they so named from birth – or renamed in a mocking spirit?[186]

Manumission was not an equal opportunity incentive. It was most common among slaves in positions of responsibility and skill, and these positions in turn were concentrated around the commercial interests of the Illustrious and Elite and to a lesser extent on their rural estates. Fenoaltea's model also helps us to understand how the extent of manumission could have changed over time. If a slave system is in an expansionary phase and slaves are in such abundant supply that they are cheap relative to free

[185] Bradley 1994, 163; Wiedemann 1985, 162–3; Duncan-Jones 1974, 25.
[186] Eutyche and Polychronios: IG 12.3.343 = Kiourtzian, 142a.

labor, slaves will begin to enter sectors of the economy where they act as substitutes for free labor.[187] For instance it may become cheaper to hire slave labor than to pay wages in industrial work. In such environments positive incentives are typically required, manumission chief among them. This pattern is unstable in the long term. Particularly if the slave supply is constricted, or if the free population grows (sending down wages), or if slaves are pulled into more valuable roles, the influx of slaves into occupations easily filled by free workers may be temporary. This pattern may partly characterize some elements of the slave system in classical Athens and late republican Rome. The Augustan manumission restrictions may have been enacted in response to such an environment. Chapters 3 and 4 have emphasized that the late empire was characterized by a mature slave system in a high-equilibrium state; in late antiquity slaves were deployed in roles where free labor was an imperfect substitute and where slavery was – for technical or institutional reasons – a highly competitive alternative. The incidence of manumission could ebb and flow in cycles, as changes in supply and demand shifted the occupational structure of the slave system.

CONCLUSIONS: DISCIPLINE, COMMODITIES, MARKETS

Earlier generations of Roman historians looked to measure the brutality of Roman slavery and to assess whether the quality of the master–slave relationship changed over time. Finley, Hopkins, and Bradley, among others, offered a withering critique of this agenda and presented a more realistic view of ancient slavery. The current challenge is to seek a holistic, structural account of the relations between masters and slaves. The goal is not to say *how bad* Roman slavery was, but rather to reconstruct the underlying forces shaping the slave's existence, to search for the specific texture of the slave's life. The basic contours of the slave's existence were determined by the nature of the labor which he or she was asked to perform. One distinctive aspect of the Roman slave system is the sheer diversity of roles occupied by slaves – from positions of extraordinary trust to positions of extreme drudgery and extreme exploitation. The techniques of domination were as varied as the aims of domination in Roman society. Roman law and Roman culture provided the array of tools necessary to allow the finely tuned manipulation required by such an internally segmented slave system.

For historians of modern slavery, the central problem in the reconstruction of the slave's experience has been to identify the precise mixture of

---

[187] Harper 2010; Scheidel 2008 and 2005b.

capitalism and paternalism in the master–slave relationship. The regimentation of time and work that defined the slave's existence was determined by the need for labor, but the human actors involved were mutually bound by the complex, reciprocal relations in which one side had most but not all of the power. The most ardent follower of Rostovtzeff would be wary of describing Roman slavery as part of a capitalist system, if "capitalism" is equated with its modern guise, in which the market permeates social relations and utterly dominates the labor system. But if ancient "capitalism" is taken in a more restricted sense, in which commercial forces begin to regiment time, to discipline the body and its labor, we can admit that there was a real relationship between the precocious development of market institutions in the Roman empire and the transmutation of human bodies into private property. Slavery went hand in hand with the proto-modernity of the Roman empire, with the irruption of commercial forces into the rhythms of social life. The greatest concentration of power, of violence, and of discipline in Roman society was slavery.

The defining trait of slavery lies in the extreme commodification of time and labor, in the commodification of the slave's whole existence. To reckon completely with the master–slave relationship, we should always remember that the interval of ownership was only part of the experience of slavery. The power of the master to trade his property was an ever-present reality.[188] The humiliation, the uncertainty, the severing of human ties – the sale of slaves exposed the deep structure of domination. It was the *right* of the master to move or sell slaves as he wished.[189] Although the velocity of circulation may have been slower in the ancient market than in the modern world, even in the US South it was the *potential* of re-sale, along with the reality, which made the chattel principle a terrifying existential problem for slaves.[190] It is impossible to say how often slaves were sold and re-sold in antiquity. It was considered a disgrace for a slave to have multiple masters.[191] An "un-useful" slave would have many masters.[192] There are several examples of bad, uncontrollable, or misbehaving slaves being re-sold.[193] Libanius said that a master would "hesitate to sell a good slave," but, after all, "hesitation" is not exactly profound reluctance.[194] All our sources blame the sale on the slave, never on the master, never on his

---

[188] Ioh. Chrys. Virgin. 57.2 (SC 125: 308).   [189] Ambr. Exc. 2.16 (CSEL 78: 259).
[190] cf. Johnson 1999.   [191] Claud. In Eutr. 1 lines 29–34 (Hall: 144).
[192] Ambr. Psal. 43.42 (CSEL 64: 292): *inhabilem*. Evagr. H.E. 3.1 (Bidez and Parmentier: 99).
[193] Ioh. Chrys. In 1 Thess. 11.3 (PG 62: 464); Syn. Ep. 45 (Garzya: 84–5). cf. Soz. H. E. 6.29.15 (GCS 50: 281).
[194] Lib. Decl. 18.9 (Foerster vol. 6: 248): εὔνους οἰκέτας ὀκνοῦμεν . . . ἀποδίδοσθαι.

desire for labor, his speculation in slaves, his wish to be rid of an unwanted servant.

There was a joke in late antiquity about a half-wit who walked to market to sell a jar. The handle (the word is the same as the word for "ear") had been broken off, and when someone asked him why he was selling a jar without a handle, he replied that he broke it off so the jar wouldn't hear it was being sold and run away.[195] The joke is the single ancient reference to the delicate process of re-selling a slave, to the machinations of a slave-owner who had determined to put his slave on the market. In the case of the American South, perhaps no process has so clearly demonstrated the contradiction and pain of the slave economy, and the means by which the market constantly betrayed the efforts of men and women to live with a bad system. It is a chastening reminder that we can only say so much about the human experience of ancient slavery.

[195] Philogel. 122 (Thierfelder: 72).

CHAPTER 6

Self, family, and community
among slaves

FROM THE SLAVE'S PERSPECTIVE

The only extant comedy from late antiquity is a Latin play composed in early fifth-century Gaul. Called the *Querolus* ("The Grumpy Old Man"), the work is a creative pastiche of traditional comic elements.[1] In the play we find the figure of the clever slave duly resurrected. In an atmosphere heavy with literary allusion, we are presented a litany of stereotypes about miserly masters and wily slaves. The slave – named Pantomalus, Every-evil – does not play a primary role in the plot, but he does deliver a lengthy monologue, on the vice of masters and the cunning intelligence of slaves. The speech is in the spirit of Plautus and, as a statement of the clever slave, lives up to its heritage. Although much neglected, this speech belongs to the handful of literary creations that reflect, through the dark and distorted prism of humor, the anxieties of those who sought to dominate slaves.[2]

"That all masters are wicked is a true and undeniably obvious fact. Yet I know – and all too well – that my master is the very worst. Oh, he isn't such a dangerous fellow, but he sure is a nasty ingrate."[3] So Pantomalus launches into his part. His monologue oscillates between ranting against masters and praising the cleverness of slaves. Pantomalus describes all the usual points of conflict between master and slave. Disputes over time and labor, food and drink, smoldered in every corner of the relationship, waiting to flare into open discord. "If there is a theft committed in the house, he curses as though it were a crime."[4] "If the wine has been adulterated or diluted

---

[1] Querol. (Ranstrand). Küppers 1989 for the literary texture of the work, and 1979, for the date around AD 415.

[2] But see Nathan 2000, 177. In general, Bradley 2000a; Fitzgerald 2000; McCarthy 2000; and Hopkins 1993.

[3] Querol. (Ranstrand: 38): *omnes quidem dominos malos esse constat et manifestissimum est. Verum satis sum expertus nihil esse deterius meo. Non quidem periculosus ille est homo, verum ingratus nimium et rancidus.*

[4] Querol. (Ranstrand: 38): *furtum si admissum domi fuerit, execratur tamquam aliquod scelus.*

with water, he knows right away."[5] One master would "give his slaves less food and more labor than was just."[6] This sense of a normative level of work and reward, which slaves grudgingly accepted, points to the uneasy accommodation between masters and slaves. Masters were supposed to know that their power rested on naked force, not legitimate authority, and that slaves accepted it conditionally. The master of Pantomalus had the rude habit of noticing too easily when his slaves were drunk, "seeing at one glance the amount and quality of wine in the face and on the lips of the slave, for he just won't be outmaneuvered or tricked in the way masters usually are."[7] In other words, an implicit truce, tolerating a zone of petty disobedience where master and slave tested each other's limits, was the normal mode of master–slave relations.

Pantomalus spoke in the double-entendre which was the stock-in-trade of the clever slave. This verbal dexterity symbolized the slave's understanding of both surface and depth in human relationships as in much else. Pantomalus described the way that men scrutinized gold coins – "and what could be more solid than the *solidus*?" This was more than a cheap pun. Pantomalus knew that with gold, as with slaves, looks could be deceiving. "Looks, age, color, nobility, letters, homeland, and weight, down to the smallest fraction, are questioned – in gold even more than in men."[8] The allusion to the slave being examined as a commodity on the auction block was unmistakable. No matter how carefully inspected, the slave always remained an unknown quantity because the master could never see that which was immaterial and inscrutable, the slave's interior self.

Pantomalus had a sort of indiscreet pride, for once he had broached the subject of the slave's true nature, he was unable to resist openly vaunting the hidden joys of the slave life. "We slaves are neither as sad nor as stupid as some think. Some say we're lazy because we nod off during the day."[9] The truth, though, was that the slave who rests in the daytime:

... is awake in the night. I think that mother nature has done nothing greater for mankind than to make the night. That is our day, that is when we do everything. Even if we are tempted to go by day, it is at night that we go to the baths. We

---

[5] Querol. (Ranstrand: 40): *vinum autem corruptum tenuatumque lymphis continuo intellegit.* cf. Philogel. 254 (Thierfelder: 122).

[6] Querol. (Ranstrand: 40): *servis alimenta minuit, opus autem plus iusto imperat.*

[7] Querol. (Ranstrand: 39–40): *modum qualitatemque vini in vultu et labiis primo conspectu videt [falli se prorsus non volt neque circumveniri ut solent].*

[8] Querol. (Ranstrand: 40): *quid tam simile quam solidus solido est? ... voltus, aetas et color, nobilitas, litteratura, patria, gravitas usque ad scriptulos quaeritur in auro plus quam in homine.*

[9] Querol. (Ranstrand: 41): *non sumus tamen tam miseri atque tam stulti quam quidam putant. Aliqui somnulentos nos esse credunt, quoniam somniculamur de die.*

bathe with the slave-girls and boys – ain't that the life of the free? Not everything is visible in the glowing light – but enough is. I hold a slave-girl in the flesh whom the master barely gets to see with her clothes on. I explore her front and back, I handle her flowing hair, I embrace her by my side, and we caress one another. What master is allowed to do that? The crown of our happiness is this: that amongst slaves there is no jealousy. We all steal and no one turns traitor, for we are all in it together. We watch out for the master and divert him, for slaves and slave-girls are in alliance... We have daily weddings, births, games, orgies, and holidays of the slave-girls – with all this, who wants to be manumitted![10]

In this extraordinary passage, Pantomalus describes the night as the counter-world of slaves, where they enjoyed the basic pleasures of life free from social and material constraint. The stupidity and laziness of the slave by day was a mask, worn to conceal the secret self that came to life in the master's absence. None of this, of course, is to be mistaken for a close description of reality. It is a textured literary production that has to be understood first in terms of its place in the play itself, where it serves to reinforce the contrast between appearance and reality, surface and depth, as well as to enrich the characterization of the greedy protagonist. Then, of course, the playwright was working within a long tradition of clever slaves and duped masters. But it must be admitted that the *Querolus* is not a stale or scholastic production. It refers to contemporary events, and its dialogue possesses an organic vitality. The speech of Pantomalus draws on the comic tradition, but the panegyric on the night was without precedent.[11] Pantomalus was, strictly speaking, extraneous to the plot, but his brief cameo showed him to be every bit the worthy successor of Pseudolus.

With a figure such as Pantomalus, the object of mimesis is not the actual character, but the charged tension between masters and slaves, the distance between authority and power, and the gulf between surface and truth, that indirectly reflect the realities of the master–slave relationship. The

[10] Querol. (Ranstrand: 41–2): *famulus qui diurnis quiescit horis, somni vigilat tempore. Nihil umquam melius in rebus humanis fecisse naturam quam noctem puto. Illa est dies nostra, tunc aguntur omnia. Nocte balneas adimus, quamvis sollicitet dies. Lavamus autem cum pedisequis et puellis: nonne haec est vita libera. Luminis autem vel splendoris illud subornatur, quod sufficiat, non quod publicet. Ego nudam teneo quam domino vestitam vix videre licet. Ego latera lustro, ego effusa capillorum metior volumina, adsideo amplector foveo foveor. Cuinam dominorum hoc licet? Illud autem nostrae felicitatis caput, quod inter nos zelotypi non sumus. Furta omnes facimus, fraudem tamen nemo patitur, quoniam totum hoc mutuum est. Dominos autem observamus atque excludimus, nam inter servos et ancillas una coniugatio est... nobis autem cotidie nuptiae, natales, ioca, debacchationes, ancillarum feriae. Propter hoc quidam nec manumitti volunt.* The final line, in one manuscript, reads: *propter hoc non omnes fugere servi, propter hoc quidam nec manumitti volunt.* See Reeve 1976, 22.
[11] The closest parallel is Phaed. Fab. 3.7 (Mueller: 23).

"night" is a symbol in the *Querolus* for those corners of the slave's existence which the master either could not, would not, or did not need to patrol. The play prompts us to look for the real sanctuaries of private existence that slaves were able to carve out for themselves. Chapter 5 explored the master's power and its ultimate finitude; this chapter explores the range of motion which was left to the slave. Following the speech of Pantomalus, the chapter will proceed by considering the slave's response in terms of self, family, and community. In other words, what could a slave do in response to his or her condition, and how was this response conditioned by relations with other slaves? No chapter in the book is more beset by empirical shortcomings, but it would be inexcusable not to gather what we do have and to imagine, in as orderly a fashion as we can, what we have lost. Even if we cannot observe it directly, the will of the slave is like the dark matter in the relation of domination – imperceptible in itself, all-important in its effects.

INDIVIDUAL REACTIONS

The master's domination of the slave was ends-oriented, and his power was finite. Both of these facts left the slave room to maneuver in pursuing his or her own private ends. The slave's options were limited and inherently unstable, and they were governed by the same conditions that influenced the master's techniques of domination. In other words, the slave's opportunities were shaped by the specific properties of the work demanded, the gender of the slave, and the physical organization of the workforce. And once again we must imagine great internal variety within the slave system, so that not all slaves had the same prospects for resistance, privacy, and community. This chapter, like chapter 5, is organized taxonomically, so that we can at least take inventory of the slave's options. The discussion begins with the isolated choices of the slave in response to his or her immediate condition, and then considers the role of family and community as responses to enslavement.

The first and simplest choice available to the slave was to shirk, to work as little as possible. Shirking always entailed a game of perception, for slaves had every reason to conceal their lack of effort as well as they could. The agronomist Palladius displayed a keen awareness of the problem. "I know not if it is this way with all masters, but to me it seems hard to find any middle way in the nature of slaves. So that if their nature will often undermine that which is profitable, it also mixes things to be hoped for with their opposites. Alacrity is a path to crime, while sloth appears as innocence, and as far as a slave is from efficiency, so far is he from perfidy."[12] In other words, a conspicuously motivated slave was cause for suspicion: his effort may have concealed even greater or more dangerous deceptions. Lack of motivation, by contrast, was normal, and a sign that a slave was not hiding more insidious forms of deviance or resistance. This dictum of Palladius betrays an intimate familiarity with the challenge of dominating slaves.

On the one hand, it was not impossible for slaves to take personal pride in their labor – the subjective value of work well done, regardless of who claimed the exchange value of the product.[13] But the ubiquitous stereotype of the slave as lazy is a sure sign that shirking was common. Laziness was the characteristic "vice of slaves, for whom the greatest of holidays is to lie down and move only a little or not at all."[14] In the eyes of the master, fear of violence was the only solution to the inherent laziness of slaves.[15] Correcting the laziness of slaves was a daily burden on the master.[16] In the *Querolus*, Pantomalus humorously explained that slaves were "lazy" because they stayed awake all night in revelry.[17] This is implausible as reality, but funny as a twist on the obvious ideological message of the stereotype. The joke was on the master who worried that his slave's laziness was due to mere lack of motivation: such a master was laughably clueless to the real nightmare going on right behind his back.

Not all slaves had equal opportunity to shirk. Slaves in close proximity to their masters, for instance, might be easier to supervise. Textile work may have lent itself to close surveillance and easy monitoring.[18] Work quotas were imposed.[19] Slaves working outside the house, in skilled roles or crafts, might be held accountable along the lines of a task system; a slave who was capable of earning 10 drachmae a day who only earned 5 was whipped or reassigned to degrading labor.[20] Palladius assumed that slaves working in agriculture had to be closely monitored to be kept from shirking: an overseer had to check the plough marks constantly to make sure the slaves were actually breaking ground and not simply scattering the top soil.[21]

---

[12] Pall. Insit. 2 (Rodgers: 293): *nescio utrum commune sit dominis: mihi difficile contigit in servilibus ingeniis invenire temperiem. Ita saepissime natura haec vitiat commodum, si quod est, et miscet optanda contrariis. Velocitas procurrit in facinus. Segnities figuram benignitatis imitatur et tantum recedit ab agilitate quantum recessit a scelere.*
[13] Above all Joshel 1992.
[14] Lib. Or. 3.4 (Foerster vol. 1: 269): ἀνδραπόδου νόσημα τοῦτο ἡγούμενος, ᾧ τὸ κεῖσθαι καὶ ἢ μηδὲν ἢ μικρὰ κινεῖσθαι ἑορτῶν ἡ μεγίστη.
[15] Lib. Or. 25.37 (Foerster vol. 2: 554).   [16] Ioh. Chrys. Virgin. 67 (SC 125: 336–8).
[17] Querol. (Randstrand: 41).   [18] Hier. Ep. 130.15 (CSEL 56: 195). See chapter 3.
[19] Ioh. Chrys. Ad pop. Ant. 14.1 (PG 49: 145).   [20] Lib. Decl 33.33 (Foerster vol. 7: 98).
[21] Pall. Op. ag. 2.10.4 and 2.3.2 (Martin: 62 and 58).

Libanius reported that the slaves of a man from Corinth learned to be lazy as soon as oversight was removed.[22]

If shirking was the primordial response of the slave, close behind was the choice to "steal." Of course the appropriation of the master's property was only "stealing" insofar as the master's claim to the property was legitimate; slaves might have reasonably objected to this claim, and in a practical sense they clearly did.[23] The threat of theft hung over the master–slave relationship, creating a haze of mistrust: "we hate our slaves" because they steal.[24] Theft was "daily."[25] Physical punishment was thought the only antidote to theft.[26] One of the principal advantages of asceticism, so claimed Chrysostom, was the peace of mind that came with not having to worry whether the slaves were stealing.[27] Just as slaves were reckoned "lazy" for trying to assert control of their time, slaves were considered prone to theft for trying to assert control over the fruits of their labor. Across antiquity, a trinity of negative stereotypes attached to slaves: they were lazy, gluttonous thieves.[28] From Aristophanes to the *Querolus*, the irresponsible, hungry, and pilfering slave was the object of public humor. These traits were an ideological interpretation of the fact that slaves, denied legal rights to their labor, opportunistically claimed time, food, and property where they could find it.[29]

Shirking and stealing were relatively low-risk forms of opportunism in which slaves could regularly indulge. Slaves had access to more desperate measures such as fight or flight. The use of physical violence against the master was a gamble with mortal consequences. Violence was always a potential outcome in a relationship fraught with distrust and ill-will. In the courtroom, for example, it was frankly confessed that "it is normal and universal and undeniable and altogether understood to say that a slave is the enemy of his masters."[30] Masters spoke of the unchanging hatred of slaves, the unalterable hostility.[31] The enemy within the household, the

---

[22] Lib. Or. 14.45 (Foerster vol. 1: 103).

[23] Ioh. Chrys. In 1 Cor. 35.6 (PG 61: 304); Ioh. Chrys. In Tit. 3.4 (PG 62: 685); Philogel. 254 (Thierfelder: 122); Claud. In Eutrop. 1 lines 193–5 (Hall: 150–1); Choric. Or. 23.5 (Foerster and Richtsteig: 254); Ambr. Off. 3.3.22 (CC 15: 161); Aug. Serm. nov. 4 (= 299A) (Dolbeau: 413); Caes. Arel. Serm. 15.2 (CC 103: 73).

[24] Bas. (dub.) Is. 1.50 (PG 30: 211): . . . τοὺς μὲν οἰκέτας μισοῦμεν.

[25] Ps.-Aug. Sobr. (PL 40: 1110).

[26] Ambr. Fug. 3.15 (CSEL 32.2: 175); Aug. Ep. 246.3 (CSEL 57: 584).

[27] Ioh. Chrys. Serm. in Gen. 1.276–82 (SC 433: 172).

[28] The stereotypes of course are not unique to Roman slavery: Turley 2000, 114–15.

[29] Joshel and Murnaghan 1998, 15.

[30] Sop. Ermog. tech. (RG 5: 42): ἃ ἐστι πρὸς ἀπόδειξιν γνωμικὰ καὶ καθολικὰ καὶ ἀναντίρρητα καὶ πᾶσι δοκοῦντα λέγειν, ὅτι τὸ δοῦλον δεσπόταις πολέμιον.

[31] Firm. Ep. 36 (SC 350: 154); Them. Or. 21.249C (Downey and Schenkl: 26).

hostis domesticus, was a menacing presence.[32] Violence against the master signaled that the terms of negotiation in the relationship had broken down. A slave might kill his master because "he feared excruciating torment."[33] Masters, too, might sense the gathering desperation of a slave and act with anticipatory violence: "you fear your slave will kill you, so you kill him."[34] A harsh master might not only turn his slaves into runaways; he might plant within them an irresistible urge to seek revenge: "for some it is enough to leave their evils behind, but others decide to take revenge too, and waiting for night they take vengeance with a sword for the blows and floggings they suffered."[35]

The potential escalation of violence was built into the relationship, but the use of violence by slaves was a sort of lurid danger that abided in the realm of dark fantasy. Horoscopes warned against stellar aspects foreboding servile violence.[36] Rhetorical exercises included sensational tales of sex-crazed mistresses suborning the slaves to kill their master; another story told of a general whose barbarian slaves ambushed him on a hunting expedition and killed him.[37] Murderous slaves were a type of bogeyman.[38] But they posed a real enough threat. Symmachus petitioned on behalf of a client to request governmental assistance in apprehending a fugitive, "lest an innocent house live any longer in fear of the deadly devices of a cheap slave."[39] An Alexandrian merchant left his wife and daughter at home with a slave, who plotted to attack them with a knife; they were miraculously saved when the slave was struck blind and turned the knife on himself.[40] A master's murder in Theoderic's Italy was punished by a thunderous royal decree: "you should use the torture of the law to punish the slaves who have slaughtered their master in a damnable crime . . . so that insofar as any slaves should be inspired by this worst example, they will be restrained by the spectacle of punishment."[41] For masters, the threat of reprisal from slaves was an unconscionable betrayal of the master–slave relationship and

---

[32] Ambrosiast. Comm. Rom. 8.2 (CSEL 81.1: 251).

[33] Aug. Lib. 1.4.9 (CC 29: 216): *sibi metuebat cruciatus graves*. cf. Eugip. Vit. Severin. 8 (SC 374: 202).

[34] Aug. Serm. 297.8 (PL 38: 1363): *times enim ne te occidat servus, et tu occidis servum.*

[35] Lib. Prog. 9.7.8–11 (Foerster vol. 8: 317–18): τοῖς μὲν γὰρ ἤρκεσεν ἀπελθοῦσιν ἀπηλλάχθαι κακῶν, τοῖς δ' ἔδοξε καὶ δίκην λαβεῖν. καὶ νύκτας ἀναμείναντες τῶν πληγῶν καὶ τῶν μαστίγων ξίφεσι τὴν δίκην ἔλαβον.

[36] Heph. Apot. 2.33 (Pingree: 215).   [37] Sopat. Diar. 314 (RG 8: 67) and Ermog. tech. (RG 5: 136).

[38] Aug. Serm. 113.4 (PL 38: 650).

[39] Symm. Ep. 4.48 (MGH AA 6.1: 114): *ne ulterius innocens domus commentis feralibus vilis mancipii terreatur.*

[40] Ioh. Mosch. Prat. 75 (PG 87.3: 2928).

[41] Cass. Var. 2.19 (CC 96: 70): *dominum suum plectibili scelere trucidantes . . . legum districtione resecetis, quatinus qui exemplis provocantur pessimis, poenis arceantur aspectis.*

a violation of its natural order. But however desperate and remote, it was a subtle, unspeakable check on unrestrained abuse against slaves, lest they make that ultimate choice.

One of the most enduring responses to enslavement was flight.[42] Flight was a common strategy of slaves. A law of AD 365 considered slave flight a matter to be handled by lower magistrates.[43] A law of 392 noted that vagrant slaves were a major nuisance to land-owners.[44] A law of AD 395 claimed that suits over fugitive slaves were an ordinary, even trifling affair.[45] None of these laws hint at any underlying crisis; flight was an inherent part of the slave-holding order, to be combated with vigor but not alarm. This was a society that was familiar with the risks and punishments of flight. Preachers and orators could draw on the mental repertoire of this society to evoke images of runaways dragged off in chains, of slaves soaking their chains in the river before fleeing, of masters hunting the countryside at night on slave-catching expeditions.[46] This was a society where newcomers were eyed carefully, under the default suspicion that an unfamiliar and able-bodied stranger might well be an escaped slave.[47] The most detailed horoscopes in late antique astrological manuals concerned fugitive slaves.[48] Flight was a permanent risk to the slave-owner, and the whole balance of power between masters and slaves was influenced by the hopes of flight and the odds of detection.

Flight took different forms and was spurred by different motives. It might be a response to the condition of enslavement as such.[49] But it was more often assumed that flight was prompted when the violence and abuse of the master became unbearable. Salvian pointed out that slaves chose to flee because they feared their impending punishment.[50] A slave would flee a harsh master and live in mortal fear of being caught.[51] It was something any master knew: "the slave flees the flogging master."[52] As we will see, flight was a severe risk to the slave, so it might require imminent and excruciating danger to shift the calculus in favor of flight. In other slave systems, flight was far more often practiced by men than women, and there is no reason

---

[42] Bellen 1971 remains fundamental but unconvincing that flight became more common in the fourth century (124). See Garnsey 1972, 207. On the legal sources, see Klingenberg 2005. Weiler 2003, 167–71.

[43] CT 1.29.2. Klingenberg 2005, 159–60. On the *defensor*, Frakes 2001.   [44] CT 10.10.20.

[45] CT 2.1.8. Klingenberg 2005, 160–1.

[46] Ioh. Chrys. Lib. Repud. 2.1 (PG 51: 218); Ioh. Chrys. Ad pop. Ant. 9.3 (PG 49: 108); Lib. Prog. 7.1.8 (Foerster vol. 8: 162).

[47] Ioh. Chrys. In Mt. 35.3 (PG 57: 409).   [48] Heph. Apot. 3.47 (Pingree: 317).

[49] Aug. Psalm. 148.10 (CC 40: 2173). See chapter 2.   [50] Salv. Gub. 4.3 (MGH AA 1: 38).

[51] Ioh. Chrys. Stag. 3.1 (PG 47: 476).

[52] Bas. Jej. 1.10 (PG 31: 184): Οἰκέτης δραπετεύει δεσπότην τύπτοντα.

to doubt the same held in Roman society.[53] But it was not impossible for females to flee: Theodoret told a harrowing story about a girl who fled her master rather than submit to his sexual demands.[54]

The master had at his disposal both private and public means to prevent and recover fugitive slaves. There was a deep mental association, surely derived from actual experience, between fugitive slaves and chains. Chains could be used as a preventive or punitive tool. Some slaves lugged their chains with them as they fled.[55] Synesius pithily imagined the consequences of being caught: "we flee, we are caught, we are punished, we are bound, we are sold."[56] A master would "first chain his fugitive slaves, then chain them together" to impair their mobility.[57] Flight, moreover, entailed the risk of painful vengeance if the slave was caught. The fugitive could expect to be "thrashed with the whip."[58] The fugitive slave deserved "lashes and chains and imprisonment and crucifixion and every type of punishment."[59] Fleeing was a high-stakes gamble.

The master could also use tattooing as a weapon to prevent or to punish flight.[60] To be tattooed on the forehead was a typical penalty for the fugitive.[61] Corporal marking was not rare. "Slaves are inscribed with the mark of their master."[62] Bellen argued that the passage implies a brand on the hand, but it is just as likely that it means a tattoo.[63] The Romans believed that the tendency to run away could be an innate characteristic of some slaves, who needed to be tattooed to prevent future episodes of flight.[64] "Retain me lest I flee," was the basic inscription.[65] Libanius imagined that a fugitive who returned to the master's good graces might someday be allowed to let his hair grow down over his forehead, covering the tattoo.[66] But the runaway went to his grave with the permanent marks of his vice.[67]

Constantine ended the practice of tattooing criminals on "the face, which is formed in the likeness of heavenly beauty," ordering instead

[53] Naragon 1994.   [54] Thdt. H. rel. 9.12 (SC 234: 426–8).
[55] Ioh. Chrys. Lib. Repud. 2.1 (PG 51: 218).
[56] Syn. Catast. 2.5 (Terzaghi: 292): φεύγομεν, ἁλισκόμεθα, τιτρωσκόμεθα, δεδέμεθα, πιπρασκόμεθα.
[57] Ioh. Chrys. Virgin. 41.2 (SC 125: 236–8): φυγάδες οἰκέται καθ᾽ ἑαυτοὺς δεδεμένοι καὶ πάλιν ἀλλήλοις συνδεδεμένοι.
[58] Aug. Ep. 185.21 (CSEL 57: 20): *flagellorum verbere*.
[59] Lact. Inst. 5.18 (CSEL 19.1: 460): *verberibus et vinculis et ergastulo et cruce et omni malo dignissimus iudicatur.*
[60] Gustafson 1997; Jones 1987.   [61] Lib. Decl. 1.147 (Foerster vol. 5: 98–9).
[62] Ambr. Valent. 58 (CSEL 73: 357): *charactere domini inscribuntur et servuli*.
[63] Bellen 1971, 26.   [64] Dig. 21.1.1. Buckland 1908, 267–8.
[65] E.g. CIL 15.7173: . . . *tene me ne fugia*. See the collection in Thurmond 1994.
[66] Lib. Or. 25.21 (Foerster vol. 2: 546–7).   [67] Agath. Hist. 5.4 (Keydell: 169).

that hands or calves be used for the same purpose.[68] Christianity may have created some uneasiness towards the use of penal tattoos. It has been argued that Christian attitudes towards tattooing encouraged the use of collars, clasped around neck of the slaves and carrying an identifying inscription, in place of tattooing.[69] Although the use of collars long pre-dates the triumph of Christianity, nearly forty collars and pendants survive from antiquity, and they are virtually all from the fourth century. "Retain me and return me to Apronianus Palatinus at the *mappa aurea* on the Aventine because I have fled": this inscribed collar was found around the neck of the slave's skeleton.[70] Many of the collars include Christian symbols such as crosses or the chi-rho. One even reads "I am the slave of Felix the archdeacon. Retain me lest I flee."[71] If these collars are to be explained by a Christian queasiness towards the use of facial tattoos, they are powerful testaments to the enduring risks of flight and the strict preventive measures against it.

The survival of so many artifacts of slavery from the fourth century is astonishing, and it has been noted that the vast majority of the collars appear to have come from Rome and its environs, from Christian slave-owners, and from imperial officials or bureaucrats.[72] The concentration of slave collars in these milieu may reflect a vogue among the imperial elite, but this will not explain the survival of slave collars from Africa or Sardinia.[73] We know, moreover, of one high imperial official, a Christian, who still used tattoos against his runaway slave in the fourth century: Ausonius. His scribe, Pergamus, tried to flee. But, Ausonius taunted, he ran as slowly as he wrote. Ausonius tattooed his forehead and wrote two epigrams about it, the second of which shows that the master either relented or had remorse – the slave's face, he said, bore the punishment for the crime committed by his legs.[74] In the early sixth century, Anastasius banned tattooing altogether. At that time tattooing was still closely associated with slavery, for his law stated "we are pleased to free slaves from the yoke of slavery; how is it then that we can deem those who are in freedom to bear the fate of a slave?"[75] Little else is heard of this law, and perhaps it was ultimately ineffective.[76] But

---

[68] CT 9.40.2 (AD 315): *facies, quae ad similitudinem pulchritudinis caelestis est figurata.*
[69] Thurmond 1994; Bellen 1971, 27–31.
[70] CIL 15.7182: *tene me et reboca me aproniano palatino ad mappa aurea in abentino quia fugi.*
[71] s [] *felicis arc diac tene me ne fugiam.* Thurmond 1994, 471; Sotgiu 1973–4.
[72] Esp. Thurmond 1994.   [73] E.g. ILS 9455 (Bulla Regia: see chapter 7). Sotgiu 1973–4 (Sardinia).
[74] Auson. Epig. 16–17 (Green: 70). See Fitzgerald 2000, 17.
[75] Ioh. Mal. 16.14 (Thurn: 328): . . . ὅτι ἡμῖν ἐστιν εὐχὴ τοὺς ἐν ζυγῷ δουλείας ἐλευθεροῦν. πῶς οὖν ἀνεξόμεθα τοὺς ἐν ἐλευθερίᾳ ὄντας ἄγεσθαι εἰς δουλικὴν τύχην.
[76] Agathias (see p. 257) still refers to tattooed runaways.

throughout our period, masters used physical markers – whether written on the brow or welded around the neck – to counteract the risk of flight.

Roman slave-owners had a powerful ally in the effort to reduce the risk of flight: the state. The state's apparatus for preventing, detecting, and punishing fugitives and those who would abet them was an indispensable prop of the slave system. The state came to the aid of slave-owners in several ways. First, under the rules of the Aedilician Edict, the state required vendors to declare slaves with a history of running away, and it enforced contractual warranties against flight.[77] Second, the state could punish runaway slaves. Constantine, or possibly Licinius, issued a law that any slave caught fleeing into barbarian territory was to be sent to the mines or to have his foot amputated.[78] Third, the state actively aided masters in the detection and recovery of runaway slaves. This is evident from the legal material, but also in surviving private letters where masters ask for or expect imperial assistance.[79] Perhaps most importantly, though, the state severely punished those who would assist fugitives. "No one leaves their master behind without knowing that there is a place they can hide themselves."[80] It was assumed that fugitive slaves usually sought out a new master rather than freedom, and the state provided fierce penalties for harboring fugitive slaves.[81]

The powerful man had better odds of mobilizing the system in his favor than the ordinary slave-owner; Augustine claimed that "the men who catch fugitives ask them from whom they have fled. And whenever they find a slave who has fled from some master of little power, they simply take him without fear, saying to themselves, 'this slave does not have the sort of master who could see that this will be investigated.'"[82] Moreover, private networks provided masters protection against the flight of their slaves. Acting on a tip, Libanius wrote a letter on behalf of a friend from Crete requesting help in the recovery of his fugitives.[83] Symmachus wrote a letter requesting help in a distant province.[84] Jerome saw the fugitive slave of a friend in Antioch; he was too busy to apprehend the runaway himself, but he passed along the notice of the slave's whereabouts.[85] Synesius notified friends in

---

[77] Buckland 1908, 52–68. CT 2.1.8 (AD 395) and CT 3.4.1 (AD 386).

[78] CJ 6.1.3 (AD 317–23). See Corcoran 1993.   [79] CJ 6.1.2 (AD 294). cf. Bellen 1971, 15.

[80] CJ 11.48.12 (AD 396): *nemo enim dominum suum deserit sciens nusquam sibi latendi locum esse derelictum.* Procop. Bell. 7.16.19 (Haury and Wirth: 366).

[81] CT 4.8.5 (AD 322); CJ 6.1.4 (AD 317); CJ 6.1.6 (AD 332); CJ 11.53.1 (AD 371). Bellen 1971, 58–63.

[82] Aug. Psalm. 138.10 (CC 40: 1997): *homines qui suscipiunt fugitivos, quaerunt ab eis, a quo fugerint; et quem servum invenerint alicuius domini minus potentis, tamquam sine ullo timore suscipiunt, dicentes in corde suo: non habet iste talem dominum a quo possit investigari.*

[83] Lib. Ep. 306 (Foerster vol. 10: 285–6).   [84] Symm. Ep. 9.140 (MGH AA 6.1: 273).

[85] Hier. Ep. 5.3 (CSEL 54: 23); cf. Ennod. Ep. 3.19 (CSEL 6: 86).

Alexandria to be on the lookout for his runaway slave.[86] The amount of
noise about runaway slaves in the late Roman literature is striking, but the
public and private mechanisms available to the master help us understand
why observers believed the average runaway faced poor odds. "His relief
lasted only a short spell, like a runaway slave who has fled his master."[87]

Flight came in different styles, along a full spectrum from true escape
to temporary asylum. Sometimes slaves carefully plotted the moment of
their getaway.[88] They could wait until the light of full moon allowed a
nocturnal escape.[89] They might travel afar, boarding a ship and changing
their identity.[90] But perhaps more often slaves used flight to avoid imminent abuse. Slaves could try to lower the stakes of running away by fleeing
to a friend of the master, seeking intercession.[91] In the late empire, slaves
could also flee to a Christian church.[92] Canon law commanded bishops
and priests to return the slave to the master, but only after trying to talk
down the master's anger.[93] The imperial state endorsed and reinforced the
church's role as a place of temporary asylum.[94] By the late fourth century,
the church was fully enmeshed in the hard realities of the master–slave relationship. Ecclesiastical networks were useful in the detection and recovery
of fugitives.[95] One saint's shrine even specialized in the production of
talismans that were thought to help in the discovery of runaway slaves![96]

The possibility of flight was one of the slave's primordial options, and
across the history of slavery it has been an important determinant in
the texture of master–slave relations. Although we cannot measure the
prospects of flight for a slave in the Roman empire, it does appear, in
the abundant, impressionistic evidence, that state and society threw up
a formidable net for the detection and return of fugitives. This net is a
mostly invisible skein, cast around the slave system and providing it with
essential form and coherence. In the later fifth and sixth centuries the
net came unraveled, and this invisible fact should not be underestimated.
The fragmentation of the imperial state was a silent but real shift in the

[86] Syn. Ep. 145 (Garzya: 255–6).
[87] Pall. H. Laus. 35 (Butler: 103): καὶ βραχεῖαν ἀναπνεύσας ὥραν, ὡς δραπετεύσας οἰκέτης δεσπότην.
[88] Procop. Bell. 7.16.19 (Haury and Wirth: 366).   [89] Ps.-Caes. Resp. 111 (Riedinger: 90).
[90] Lib. Ep. 306 (Foerster vol. 10: 285–6): runaways had fled from Crete to Antioch with a merchant. Ioh. Chrys. Mut. Nom. 3.3 (PG 51: 137).
[91] Ioh. Chrys. Adv. Iud. 8.6 (PG 48: 936–7).
[92] Ducloux 1994; Barone Adesi 1990; Langenfeld 1977, 107–209; Bellen 1971, 74–6.
[93] Nathan 2000, 173–5. Bas. Reg. fus. tract. 11 (PG 31: 948); Aug. Tract. Io. 41.4 (CC 36: 359); Socr. H.E. 7.33 (PG 67: 812–13).
[94] CT 9.45.3 (AD 398); CT 9.45.5 (AD 432).   [95] Firm. Ep. 36 (SC 350: 154).
[96] Chrysip. Enc. Theod. 73 (Sigalas: 73). cf. Bellen 1971, 9.

balance of forces in the slave system over the late fifth and sixth centuries, particularly in the west.[97]

THE SLAVE FAMILY

"This, no guardian nor any man of good will would do, not even those who gain possession of persons in the course of war: even they sell them as far as possible as a family. Further, those slave-merchants and traders who do anything shameless for profit, when they sell children who are siblings or a mother with children, even these, you well know, take a loss and sell them for less, this being the right thing to do." "It is necessary that the division of the properties be effected in a way that relationships among slaves are preserved intact among each owner. For who could bear that husbands be separated from wives, brothers from sisters, or parents from children?" "That an equal division of slaves, in number or value, is not always possible, and sometimes improper, when it cannot be exactly done without separating infant children from their mothers, which humanity forbids, and will not be countenanced in a Court of Equity: so, that a compensation for excess must, in such cases, be made and received in money . . ."[98]

These three strikingly similar sentiments come from places far removed in time and space: classical Athens, Constantine's Roman empire, and early nineteenth-century Virginia, respectively. Of the three, Constantine's has received the best press by far.[99] His law has often been interpreted as a sign of deeper change, as a surface reflection of a major underlying shift in attitude bringing respect for slaves as human beings. But, in Constantine's empire as in Athens and the United States, the slave remained chattel, and his or her private relations were entirely subject to the master's power, even if masters had reason to advertise their benevolence and goodwill towards their slaves. Juxtaposing these three statements should not only caution us away from giving Constantine too much credit; it should lead us to ask why the matter of slave families could evince such thick, emotional language of respect, even as the rules of the slave system were unyieldingly in favor of the master's power to override the slave's choices.

[97] cf. Bellen 1971, 43–4, post-Roman law codes.
[98] The first quote is a newly discovered fragment of Hyperides, *Against Timandros*: Jones 2008 (whose translation, based on a corrected text, I give); Handley, Austin, and Horváth 2007. The second is a law of Constantine, CT 2.25.1 of AD 325, in full below. The last is a court decision, *Fitzhugh* v. *Foote*, 7 Va. (3 Call) 13 (1801), cited in Higginbotham and Kopytoff 1989, 514–15.
[99] See p. 272.

Table 6.1 *Obstacles to family life*

Property formation	Chief obstacle
Illustrious/Elite urban	Sex imbalance
Illustrious/Elite rural	Work regime
Bourgeois or Agricultural	Lack of opportunity and inconvenience to free family

The study of the Roman slave family faces insurmountable obstacles.[100] The documents that survive were written by slave-owners, and nowhere was the conspiracy of silence towards the mundane injuries of the system so tightly in effect. Thus, an investigation of the Roman slave family must have limited aims. One feasible goal is to correct the view that a growing benevolence characterized the relations between masters and slaves in late antiquity in a way that promoted the development of stable family life among slaves. Secondly, we should at least gather the evidence for the slave family which does survive, woefully incomplete though it is. Most importantly, we should identify the dynamic structural factors which contributed to the makeup and breakdown of the slave family and its constituent parts. The attitude of the master was hardly the only or even the most important factor. We should look to the rules which framed the master's power over the slave family, the demographic and disciplinary forces at play, as well as the paternalist expectations which congealed around the tensions between economic interest and the subjective will of the slaves.

The demographic and occupational structure of the slave population proposed in part I is of primary importance for this investigation, for the slave's living and working conditions were the most powerful influence on his or her prospects for family life. The slave faced a number of different obstacles, but we could use our model of the slave population to identify the most important challenges to family formation. Schematically, we should imagine three principal types of situation faced by slaves, each with its own attendant challenges (table 6.1).

In larger urban households, greater specialization meant greater demand for male labor, so that some male slaves may have been unable to find female partners within the household.[101] Slaves in small households, while more often female than male, may have been discouraged from relationships or

---

[100] Martin 2003; Bradley 1987b, 47–80; Flory 1978; Bieżuńska-Małowist 1978.
[101] See chapter 1.

reproduction because of the inconvenience to the free family or the lack of opportunity to forge private bonds.[102] Slaves on rural estates had the greatest opportunity for family life; in part I we argued that the fertility of the rural slave population was not undermined by imbalanced sex ratios, devastating mortality patterns, or exceptional forms of agricultural labor.

The Thera inscription evokes like no other source the opportunities for family life enjoyed by slaves on rural estates. The demographic structure of the population suggests high levels of reproduction, which is in turn a sign of familial opportunity. Moreover, the ordering of the slaves' names on the stone implies that the slaves were organized, at least loosely, into family units.[103] The mother–child bond emerges most clearly from the inscription. A deficit of obvious "fathers" on the stone might be attributed to patterns of male manumission, so that, perhaps, some of the fathers had been freed at the time of the inscription. Whether slave alliances revolved around the mother–child bond, or whether the nuclear unit is obscured by the conventions of recording – and these interpretations are not entirely mutually exclusive – the stone from Thera does reveal significant space for forging private bonds. At the same time, the engraver of the stone, presumably an imperial functionary, was punctilious in *not* recognizing the relations among slaves. Whereas the other census inscriptions from Thera specify the relations between free individuals – father, wife, son, daughter – the list of slaves does not. Even in this accounting context, slave families were not recognized.

In urban habitats it is even harder to know how common slave families were. From a body of second- and third-century mortuary inscriptions, Martin has demonstrated the complexity of family life among slaves in Asia Minor.[104] Of course, a common factor was likely to select for slaves who enjoyed familial bonds and slaves able to inscribe funerary epitaphs: these are relatively well-off, perhaps managerial slaves.[105] In other words, it is hard to find a representative sample that would allow us to infer the *frequency* of family formation. Nevertheless what remains is intriguing. Families are well attested, marriages and parenthood are amply documented, and even a few extended families are indicated on the stones. In some cases, what appear to be nuclear families list the children as "of the mother" – a most interesting construction that may reflect the relative strength of the mother–child bond among slaves, a tendency which is corroborated

[102] cf. Gould 1997, for modern parallels.   [103] See Harper 2008.
[104] Martin 2003, 207–30.   [105] Martin 2003, 213.

below.[106] What emerges from these inscriptions, in short, is a half-seen world of immense complexity.

The papyri, too, offer fragmentary evidence for the existence of family life among urban slaves, even in small households. The picture is not always rosy. Many sales involved "homeborn" slaves.[107] In fact, homeborn slaves are strongly represented in the deeds of sale, which would seem to confirm the significance of natural reproduction in the maintenance of the slave population.[108] Moreover, the slave sales of Roman Egypt almost exclusively preserve transactions between individual owners.[109] This is a reminder that the slave trade was an ever-present reality, and it shows that slave sales would have been dictated by the revolving needs of the free family as it coursed through the life cycle.

The literary sources provide impressionistic evidence for the slave family. In the remarkable sermon of John Chrysostom which is quoted at the beginning of chapter 1, the preacher casually claimed that even slaves in "poor" households had wives and children.[110] Chrysostom's passage simply assumes that family relationships were normal even within these smaller households. In Chrysostom's image, the slave family recapitulated the dynamics of the free family: nuclear structure, male authority, control over the offspring. But this picture is static, and whether the free family and the slave family were truly made of similar stuff – and by similar processes – is another question.

There were three discrete links in the nuclear triangle: father–child, mother–child, husband–wife. Among slaves, these links were not equally strong. The slave father's position was tenuous at best.[111] It is remarkable that there is so little information, from any period of antiquity, about slave fathers. Augustine, preaching to a rowdy congregation at Carthage, tried to make an analogy from everyday life about a slave father and his son. If the slave son obeyed his biological father rather than the master, Augustine claimed, the son would be a perverter of order.[112] The Talmud stated in positive form the fundamental, guiding principle of family life among slaves: a slave had no legal relation to his or her father.[113]

---

[106] TAM 2.1032.
[107] Bradley 1987a and 1987b, 47–80. The sale of homeborn slaves remain prominent in the late papyri: P. Abinn. 64 (337–50). P. Oxy. 55.3784 (227 or 281, more likely the latter), a twelve-year-old slave girl was separated from her living mother. P. Oxy. 9.1209 (252–3). P. Ryl. 4.709 (early fourth century). P. Köln 5.232 (337–50).
[108] Bieżuńska-Małowist 1974–7, vol. 2, 113–14.
[109] On the vigor of the private slave trade, Straus 2004, 301–13.
[110] Ioh. Chrys. In Ephes. 22.2 (PG 62: 158).   [111] Joshel and Murnaghan 1998, 10.
[112] Aug. Serm. nov. D2.13 (Dolbeau: 338).   [113] Talmud Bavli, *Kiddushin*, 69a.

The devaluation of slave fatherhood was overdetermined. It allowed status to pass through the mother; questions of paternity were immaterial in disputes over status. It allowed free men sexual access to slave-women without losing proprietary control over their offspring. The legal separation of slaves from their fathers instantly deprived them of the main bonds of social intercourse. Slaves had only one name, a personal name without a patronymic or family nomenclature: it reinforced the isolation from their ancestry.[114] In court hearings that were a standard procedure in slave sales, the slave was interrogated about his past – his origin, his trader, his mother, his siblings.[115] Questions about his paternity were omitted. The slave sale lays bare the structure of the relationship between slave fathers and their children. It was a discretionary relationship that could be dissolved without consent and even imagined away in the market of human bodies. Young slaves were not infrequently sold with their mothers, yet there is not a single known case of a slave sold with a father. Slaves were forcibly deracinated, starting with the fiction that they had no relation to their fathers.

Relations between slave-women and their children were more substantive. Since a slave's status derived from the mother, this attachment confirmed the slavery of the child. It was often a recognized bond.[116] In manumissions and inheritance documents, children were sometimes freed or inherited with their mothers.[117] The developmental advantages to newborn slaves gave the master an obvious practical interest in affirming a slave's maternity, especially during the earliest years. Even so, this was a relation contingent upon the will of the master.[118]

Relations between slave husbands and wives are a murkier subject still. Surely, slave marriages could be affirming or affectionate, a way to repudiate the dehumanizing force of slavery. If society refused to recognize the legitimacy of slave marriages, slaves did not internalize this refusal. Slaves had their own world of meaning and selfhood which has been lost to us. We see the most important elements of that world only in occasional and inadvertent glimpses. Jerome, for instance, warned Christian women against being present at the wild revelry of "slave weddings."[119] In the *Querolus*, the night was described as the domain of independent slave culture, the scene for "weddings, births, games, bacchanals, and slave-girl festivals."[120]

---

[114] Ioh. Chrys. Mut. Nom. 3.3 (PG 51: 115).   [115] Straus 2004, 62–71. P. Herm. Rees 18 (AD 323).

[116] Straus 2004, 271.

[117] ISMDA no. 92. CPJ 3.473 (AD 291) = P. Oxy. 9.1205. Inheritance: Bradley 1987b, 67. P. Flor. 1.50 (AD 268). Zelnick-Abramovitz 2005, 163.

[118] Bagnall 1997b, 135: wet-nurses raising slave infants. Caes. Arel. Serm. 44.2 (CC 103: 196).

[119] Hier. Ep. 107.11 (CSEL 55: 302): *nuptiis servulorum.*

[120] Querol. (Randstrand: 74): *nuptiae, natales, ioca, debacchationes, ancillarum feriae.*

These rare hints of slave life point to the existence of a communal culture among slaves giving meaning to the life-course, a culture about which the sources are virtually silent.

Marriages between slaves were potentially subjected to the humiliation and powerlessness which characterized the slave system in general. The master might still use the slave's wife sexually.[121] Roman law held that "slaves can not make a legal accusation of adultery on account of a violated *contubernium*."[122] The *Historia Augusta* represents Aurelian acting as a private despot over his slaves, putting to death a slave-woman who committed "adultery" on her fellow slave-husband.[123] One slave, Sapaudulus, turned against his master after watching his wife being flogged.[124] Slave marriages existed at the pleasure, and often the compulsion, of the master. The Talmud was quite explicit that masters were in control of slave marriages.[125] "Many masters forced slaves" into marriage "against their will."[126] Libanius said that the slave was free of any worry about marriage, since it was entirely under the control of the master.[127] Even slaves who wanted to remain virgins were commanded to be given in marriage.[128] It is important to remember that where slave marriages did exist, we cannot assume that they were self-selected.

The nuclear triangle of the slave family was more fragile than Chrysostom's metaphor might have suggested. The axis of husband–wife relations was purely under the master's control. The line between fathers and children was the weakest link, offering little of value to the master and completely unrecognized in law. The connection between mothers and children was the most prominent of the three. It not only confirmed the status of the children, it also maximized the reproductive success of the slave family. But this, of course, was no guarantee against sale or separation. The only certainty about the slave family is that every angle was entirely at the discretion of the master. It is striking how rarely masters bothered to protest that they respected the slave family as an entity with intrinsic value. In the American South, where a thick paternalist discourse of slavery evolved, masters frequently claimed to respect and nurture the private bonds forged

---

[121] Talmud Bavli, *Sanhedrin*, 58b. The rabbis disapproved, but could only call it "theft" rather than "adultery."

[122] CJ 9.9.23 (AD 290): *servi ob violatum contubernium adulterii accusare non possunt.*

[123] SHA. Aurel. 49.3–5 (Hohl vol. 2: 185).   [124] Amm. 28.1.49 (Seyfarth vol. 2: 69).

[125] Talmud Bavli, *Kiddushin*, 15a.

[126] Ioh. Chrys. In Philem. 1.2 (PG 62: 706): Πολλοὶ πολλοὺς οἰκέτας ἠνάγκασαν... μὴ βουλομένους.

[127] Lib. Or. 25.66–7 (Foerster vol. 2: 569–70).   [128] Thdr. Mops. In Cor. 7.37 (Staab: 183).

among slaves, even if ample research gives the lie to their rhetoric.[129] From a comparative perspective, the Roman slave family developed relatively little independent value in the ideology of ancient slavery.

It is not as though the opportunity to express paternalistic sentiments was lacking. For instance, a letter of Libanius shows him, as a slave-owner, defending a union between his female slave and the male slave of another owner. Libanius wrote to an acquaintance, Melinianus, who had recently received his inheritance but relocated from Antioch to Cilicia. "You have a multitude of slaves, and among them there are many who take heart that under the circumstances you might want to see your friends (*tous philous*)."[130] Libanius took this as a chance to express a grievance about a slave marriage:

But, I think, you have been saying that you know about affection (*philein*), but in fact you do not really understand it. At the time when you were present here you did not take away the man, who is your slave, married to my slave-woman. But when he came to you, you kept him. More precisely, if it is against his will that you keep him, you are doing wrong. But also, if he is willingly staying there and you do not drive him back, you are still doing wrong. Don't let this become an unpleasant beginning between us.[131]

Libanius staked his argument on the grounds of *philia*, affection or friendship, the common idiom of late ancient epistolography. Libanius indicted Melinianus for doing an injustice to *philia*, deploying a resonant word that implied both a failure of friendship between the masters and a failure to protect their dependants.[132] Libanius expected Melinianus to force his slave back to his wife in Antioch, whether the slave liked it or not. It is impossible to say whether Libanius was interceding for his slave-woman, for himself, or both. Conceivably, he was offended by a man whose actions undercut his gentility as a slave-owner. Certainly, Libanius assumed that the master had complete control over his slaves and their relationships with other slaves. Most importantly, even as he acts as an advocate on behalf of his slave-woman (and let us not understate the decency of his actions) Libanius makes no appeal to the inherent value of the slaves' relations; his

---

[129] Morris 1996, 99–101.
[130] Lib. Ep. 567 (Foerster vol. 10: 534): καίτοι σοι καὶ πλῆθος οἰκετῶν κἂν τοῖς πολλοῖς εἰσί τινες, οἷς καὶ βουλομένῳ τοὺς φίλους ἰδεῖν ἦν περὶ τῶν ὄντων θαρρεῖν.
[131] Lib. Ep. 567 (Foerster vol. 10: 534): ἀλλ᾽, οἶμαι, τοῦ φιλεῖν μὲν εἶναι ἐπιστήμων ἔλεγες, ἦσθα δὲ οὐ πάνυ, ὃς καὶ τὸν ἄνθρωπον, ὃς ὑμέτερος ὢν ἡμετέρᾳ συνῴκησε δούλῃ, παρὼν μὲν οὐκ ἀπέσπασας, ἐλθόντα δὲ κατέχεις, μᾶλλον δέ, εἴτ᾽ ἄκοντα κατέχεις, ἀδικεῖς, εἴθ᾽ ἑκόντα καθήμενον οὐκ ἐξελαύνεις, ἀδικεῖς. ἀλλ᾽ ἐκεῖνος ἡμῖν μὴ γένοιτο δυσχεροῦς τινος ἀρχή.
[132] On *philia*, Cribiore 2007, 42. On *philia* as a word implying the reciprocal obligations of master and slave, see Zelnick-Abramovitz 2005, 39–60.

slave-woman's wishes could only be articulated as an extension of Libanius' self.

In one sermon, John Chrysostom narrated to his audience a remarkable story he had recently heard about an unfortunate slave-woman. The story highlights some of the emotional and material complexity of a slave marriage:

A certain slave-girl was yoked together with an evil man, a wicked and runaway slave, and she suffered much wrong from the man. She was about to be sold by her mistress, for the sins of her husband were too much, and the owner was a widow. On account of the diminution of her house, she could not punish him and had to sell him. But the widow thought it was unholy to separate man and woman, and, even though the girl was useful, decided to sell the two together rather than part them.[133]

The widow, unable to control her slave, had to sell him. But she thought it "unholy" to separate man and woman – although the slave-woman wanted to be separated. Chrysostom had little to say about the woman's "holiness," noteworthy in its own right, and he had not a negative word to say when, in the end, the slave-woman secured the separation she had sought. Most interesting is the way he claimed that the widow was selling the girl, *even though she was useful*. It was abnormal that the woman's feelings of holiness overrode her practical interest in the slave, not to mention the girl's own wishes to be free of her husband.

Probably the gravest threat to the stability of the slave family was not the heartlessness of a greedy master; rather, it was the intrinsic vulnerability of the slave's status as property when the master died or fell into debt.[134] Slaves were completely exposed to the vagaries of the proprietary pressures faced by free families.[135] As human property, the master's emotions, intentions, or beliefs might be secondary to the material imperatives which affected his actions. The rescripts of the late third century show us that slaves were often used as collateral on debt, a fate which left them dangerously exposed to the master's fortunes rather than his feelings.[136] A desperate letter of the

---

[133] Ioh. Chrys. In 1 Thess. 11.3 (PG 62: 464): Παιδίσκη τις ἀνδρὶ πονηρῷ συνεζευγμένη, μιαρῷ, δραπέτῃ, αὕτη, πολλὰ τοῦ ἀνδρὸς ἡμαρτηκότος, καὶ μέλλοντος ἀπεμπολεῖσθαι παρὰ τῆς δεσποίνης. καὶ γὰρ μείζονα συγγνώμης ἦν τὰ ἁμαρτήματα, καὶ χήρα ἦν ἡ γυνή, καὶ κολάζειν αὐτὸν λυμαινόμενον αὐτῆς τὴν οἰκίαν οὐκ ἴσχυεν, ἀλλ' ἔγνω ἀποδόσθαι. εἶτα ἀνόσιον εἶναι νομίζουσα ἡ δέσποινα διασπάσαι τῆς γυναικὸς τὸν ἄνδρα, κατεδέξατο καὶ χρησίμην οὖσαν τὴν κόρην ὑπὲρ τῆς ἀπαλλαγῆς τῆς ἐκείνου συναπεμπολῆσαι καὶ τὴν γυναῖκα.
[134] For modern parallels, Morris 1996, 99. [135] Bieżuńska-Małowist 1974–7, vol. 2, 126.
[136] E.g. CJ 4.24.11 (AD 293); CJ 2.36.3 (AD 294); CJ 8.27.15 (AD 294); CJ 7.45.8 (AD 294); CJ 8.13.25 (AD 294); CJ 8.13.26 (AD 294). See chapter 9.

fifth century, a poignant artifact of domestic crisis, brings such a scenario to life:

From Timios to Sophia, greetings. When Plusius caught me in Alexandria he seized me, but I couldn't find anything to give him. So please hurry up and put our little slave Artemidoros under mortgage. God willing, if I find a boat I will come to you quickly. Don't fail to do this, for I am seriously worried and starting to be abused. I have faith that God himself will take thought of us. I sold the *gaunakion* for ten artabae of grain. Now don't forget . . . [137]

Human property made for a complex and often contradictory phenomenon. Masters might argue that hard times *forced* them to sell particularly favored slaves – a nurse or a slave who was raised with the master.[138] But this reconstruction of events only proves that the deeper form of the relationship – owner and property – could be at odds with the self-perception of the master.

Probably the greatest prop of the slave family was the master's disciplinary and economic interests in allowing family life. Private life was used as an incentive to elicit obedience and labor from slaves; masters viewed it as a low-cost or even profitable means of garnering co-operation. "The aspects of slavery that could be most liberating and self-affirming for the slaves – family, economy, community – could become structures that made slavery profitable and enduring for the masters. On a structural level, then, dominance and resistance could become reciprocal, both perpetuating the conditions necessary to sustain the system."[139] This strategic view of slave marriage, from the master's perspective, is difficult to follow in the sources, but there is one – oblique – testimony which may be relevant. Jerome's *Life of Malchus* is the tale of a Syrian peasant-turned-monk enslaved by Saracens; it is a romantic saint's life which claims to be, and possibly is, based on a first-person informant.[140] The *Life of Malchus* was a story of sexual renunciation, and its hero was a slave who overcame obstacles to his chastity. The threat to Malchus' chastity, however, came not from temptation, nor from the sexual desires of the master or mistress. The sexual purity of Malchus came into conflict, deliberately, with his master's

---

[137] P. Amh. 2.144: Σοφία Τίμιος χαίρειν. εὗρον με Πλούσειος ἐπεὶ τῆς Ἀλεξανδρίας κατέσχεν με καὶ οὐδὲν εὗρον δοῦναι αὐτῷ. Σπούδασον οὖν τὸ μικρὸν παιδίον ἡμῶν Ἀρτεμίδωρον [.] θεῖναι ἐν ὑποθήκῃ, καὶ γὰρ ἐγὼ θεοῦ βουλήσει ἐὰν εὕρω πλοῖον ἔλθω ἐν τάχι πρὸς ὑμᾶς. Μὴ οὖν ἀμελήσεις τοῦ τοῦτο ποιῆσαι, καὶ γὰρ ἐγὼ ἐν πολλῇ μερίμνῃ καὶ θλείψει ὑπάρχω. Ἐλπείδα δὲ ἔχομεν εἰς τὸν θεὸν ἵνα αὐτος πρόνοιαν ἡμῶν ποιήσει. Τὸ γαυνάκιον ἐπράθη δί ἐμοῦ σείτου ἀρταβῶν δέκα. Μὴ ἀμελήσεις. . . . Bagnall 1993, 227. cf. P. Duk.inv. 527 R (3C); ISMDA no. 12.
[138] Lib. Or. 47.8 (Foerster vol. 3: 408).   [139] Morris 1998, 987.
[140] Leclerc and Morales 2007, 41; Rebenich 2002, 85.

methods of slave management. Jerome's narrative depended on a coherent explanation of the master's motives and objectives as a slave-owner.

Whether or not the *real* master (a Saracen, in the story) of a *real* slave named Malchus lies behind the *Life*, Jerome's explanation of the master's behavior is the sort of *datum* likely imported to the story from the author's own social background. After his capture, Malchus was made a shepherd by his masters. They saw that he was honest and effective, so they rewarded him with a slave wife. He tried to refuse, since he knew the girl's legal husband was alive. The master would hear nothing of it, and, sword in hand, forced him to take the wife.[141] Behind the dramatic embellishment lies a plausible, mundane usage of the master's power amply reflected in Roman sources. Marriage was a reward for good behavior and effective service, but it was a reward that the slave might not be able to refuse. "The marriage made us more endearing to the masters. We were beyond suspicion of running away."[142] The marriage made Malchus more reliable. The masters presumed that it gave them leverage through his emotional attachment to his wife. The masters "loved" him more after he was married, because their affection for Malchus was proportionate to the depth of his subjection. In the *Life of Malchus*, the link between permitting a slave family and the strategy of mastery was perfectly clear: discipline.

Slave families existed on a large scale in late antiquity, but ultimately they existed *de facto*, not *de iure*. This was not a technicality. The legal rule governing slave families in antiquity was peremptory: "with slaves there is no legitimate marriage."[143] The law was not blind to the existence of relations among slaves. "We do not refrain from using these names, that is, of relationships, even with slaves. So we say parents and children and brothers of slaves. But servile relationships have no relevance at law."[144] This was not legal purism – a case where the lawyers demanded a hard logic that was out of step with social reality. The state acknowledged the slave-owner's absolute property interest over the slave. Rules do not necessarily reflect behavior, but they are meaningful as expressions of power and invaluable as sources independent from what any individual master might say.

Scattered throughout the vast corpus of classical Roman law, there are only a handful of citations which reveal an awareness that the separation

---

[141] Hier. Vit. Malch. 6.2 (SC 508: 196).
[142] Hier. Vit. Malch. 6.9 (SC 508: 200): *amabiliores nos dominis fecerant nuptiae. Nulla fugae suspicio.*
[143] Ulp. Reg. 5.5: *cum servis nullum est connubium.* On this post-classical text (certainly after AD 320), Mercogliano 1997.
[144] Dig. 38.10.10.5: *non parcimus his nominibus, id est cognatorum, etiam in servis: itaque parentes et filios fratresque etiam servorum dicimus: sed ad leges serviles cognationes non pertinent.*

of slave families was a hardship on the slaves. In the one instance, the law interpreted grey areas in testaments to give slave families the benefit of the doubt.[145] The right of the slave-owner to dispose of his property as he pleased was inviolate. In another instance, a slave-buyer's rights were protected in a way that allowed him, at his discretion, to keep slave families together.[146] These two classical rules were low-cost benevolence; what is significant is just how rarely the state was willing to make what was surely a relatively common social custom (maintaining slave families) into anything like a general rule. The classical law's résumé of humanitarianism is short.[147]

The question then becomes whether things improved over time. The late Roman record is hardly more impressive, with the single possible exception of a law of Constantine. In 325 Constantine issued an imperial letter to his estate manager in Sardinia ordering him not to separate slave families during a division of property:

With regard to the imperial or emphyteutic estates of Sardinia that have now been distributed to various owners, it is necessary that the division of the properties be effected in a way that relationships among slaves are preserved intact among each owner. For who could bear that husbands be separated from wives, brothers from sisters, or parents from children? Therefore those who have carried off slaves separated among different owners are to be compelled to bring them back together. And anyone whose slaves re-locate on account of these required restorations shall receive back substitute slaves from the one who took them. Be on the alert, lest afterwards any grievances remain over the emotional separations of slaves throughout the province.[148]

The law shows that the emperor could be sensitive to the familial affections of his slaves. It was common for land to come into and pass out of the emperor's ownership. In this case, Constantine's manager in Sardinia had divided laborers among private owners in a way that obviously stirred discontent among the slaves. Word reached the emperor, who intervened on behalf of the slaves.

---

[145] Dig. 33.7.12.7. Herrmann-Otto 1994, 262–3; Zoz de Biasio 1983 (overly optimistic); Solazzi 1972, 580; Mañaricua 1940, 96. cf. Dig. 33.7.12.33; Dig. 50.16.220.1; Dig. 32.1.41.5; Dig. 32.41.2.
[146] Dig. 21.1.35.   [147] Herrmann-Otto 1994, 263.
[148] CT 2.25.1 (AD 325): *In Sardinia fundis patrimonialibus vel enfyteuticariis per diversos nunc dominos distributis oportuit sic possessionum fieri divisiones, ut integra apud possessorem unumquemque servorum agnatio permaneret. Quis enim ferat liberos a parentibus, a fratribus sorores, a viris coniuges segregari? Igitur qui dissociata in ius diversum mancipia traxerunt, in unum redigere eadem cogantur: ac si cui propter redintegrationem necessitudinum servi cesserint, vicaria per eum qui eosdem susceperit mancipia reddantur et invigila, ne per provinciam aliqua posthac querella super divisis mancipiorum affectibus perseveret.*

This letter was a directive to an imperial agent, not a general law.[149] Constantine was acting as an estate manager, not as a legislator. As with so many of Constantine's laws, this one was dripping with rhetoric. In addition to his advertised benevolence, Constantine had reproductive and disciplinary motives for protecting slave families. Constantine ordered that "no grievances" be allowed to persist. Slaves had very little power, but they might be willing to risk the most violent forms of resistance in the name of their relationships, giving imperial estate managers an incentive to recognize the slave family informally.[150] Moreover, in the 320s, Constantine was acutely sensitive to the reproduction of labor on his imperial estates. A major law of 320 had removed the legal penalties for free women who married the emperor's slaves, particularly on his estates.[151] Constantine's provision for slaves on his properties in Sardinia may indicate that stable family life was conducive to reproduction. The law was part of that benevolence which it was incumbent upon Roman emperors to demonstrate at least sporadically. It is equally revealing that Constantine's manager, in a routine division of property, was perfectly ready to separate slave families in the first place. Benevolence was discretionary, and we simply lack the evidence to have anything like a balanced image of ancient reality. It is important not to make too much of Constantine's law.[152]

The law issued to an imperial manager in Sardinia was collected during the sweep for legislation made by the editors of the *Theodosian Code* in the 430s. The fifth-century editors were instructed to collect all "general laws," but the notion of a "general" law did not readily correspond with the materials which the editors found.[153] Nevertheless, what was published in the *Theodosian Code* became general by virtue of its inclusion. Constantine's instructions to his estate manager thus obtained greater legal stature in the middle of the fifth century.[154] Parts of the *Theodosian Code* were re-issued in the compendium, the *Breviarium*, published in 506 by the king of the Visigoths. Laws published in this edition were appended by *Interpretationes*, stating in plain language the legal effect of the law.[155] In the *Interpretatio*, the application of Constantine's rule was widened so that

---

[149] Harper forthcoming b on the challenges the Theodosian editors faced in interpreting esp. Constantine's laws.

[150] Harris 1999, 66, for parallels.   [151] CT 4.12.3 (AD 320).

[152] E.g. Whittaker and Grabar 1999, 699; Cantarella 1996, 129; Koptev 1995, 131; MacMullen 1986a, 342; Firpo 1991, 113; Boulvert and Morabito 1982, 161; Treggiari 1979a, 196; Pólay 1969, 86–8; Mañaricua 1940, 190; Bonfante 1925, vol. 1, 151; Buckland 1908, 76.

[153] On *generalitas*, see part III.

[154] Melluso 2000, 149; Solazzi 1972, 576–81. Though cf. Sirks 2007.   [155] Matthews 2001.

it covered not only the division of imperial properties, but also private estates.[156] Though we cannot know how well enforced this provision was, the custom of maintaining slave families amidst the division of estates may have become a formal norm in the mid- to late fifth century (the period when, we have argued, the system went into severe decline). Certainly the *Justinianic Code* took Constantine's law and affirmed its general applicability.[157]

Constantine's law is not a sign of change driven by Christianity. The ancient church, in all the voluminous material it has left behind, bequeathed to posterity not a single statement encouraging the protection of the slave family. The silence is extraordinary, for the church was certainly conscious of private relationships among slaves. In the *Apostolic Constitutions*, Christian masters were told to provide fornicating slaves with a mate.[158] This hardly reflects autonomy for the slaves or respect for their relations. John Chrysostom commanded his flock to do the same – use marriage as a solution to the misbehavior of slaves.[159] Marriage for the late ancient church, even the marriage of slaves, was more of a stop-gap measure against fornication than a sacrosanct end in itself.

The inertia of the late antique church is best demonstrated by the rule preserved in the canons of Basil of Caesarea. Basil declared that "a slave-woman who gives herself in marriage against the will of her master is guilty of fornication. But if he approves, it is a marriage. So the one is a sexual sin, the other a marriage. The contracts of those subject to another have no force."[160] The church recognized the supreme authority of the slave-owner and was unwilling to countenance any infringement upon his contractual, legal rights. The church did not even protest the fact that the slave system overrode the formation of marriages within the community of believers. The collusion of the ancient church with the power of the master, enshrined in the canon law of late antiquity, speaks louder than any other witness to the vulnerable position of the slave family.

THE ROMAN SLAVE COMMUNITY

The publication of Blassingame's *Slave Community* and Genovese's *Roll, Jordan, Roll* in the early 1970s fundamentally altered the landscape of slave

---

[156] CT 2.25.1 *Interpretatio.*   [157] CJ 3.38.11. Melluso 2000, 149; Solazzi 1972, 577.
[158] Const. Ap. 8.32 (SC 336: 234–8).   [159] Ioh. Chrys. In Ephes. 15.3 (PG 62: 110).
[160] Bas. Ep. 199.40 (Courtonne: 162): Ἡ παρὰ γνώμην τοῦ δεσπότου ἀνδρὶ ἑαυτὴν ἐκδιδοῦσα ἐπόρνευσεν, ἡ δὲ μετὰ ταῦτα πεπαρρησιασμένῳ γάμῳ χρησαμένη ἐγήματο. Ὥστε ἐκεῖνο μὲν πορνεία, τοῦτο δὲ γάμος. Αἱ γὰρ συνθῆκαι τῶν ὑπεξουσίων οὐδὲν ἔχουσι βέβαιον.

studies.[161] These books focused the historian's attention on the relationships slaves made among themselves. The slave community was the context for the slave's individual existence, and it complicated the master's search for discipline. The slave community, moreover, nurtured the survival of a slave culture through which slaves invested their lives with meaning. The nature of the slave community, of course, differed widely across time and space, depending on the work regime and crop selection, the balance of homeborn and imported slaves, the stability of slave families, etc. But fundamentally, the existence of slave communities added an extra dimension to the exercise of domination and the practice of resistance.

It is an open question to what extent we can speak of slave communities in the Roman empire. For too long the discussion focused on whether or not Roman slaves formed a class.[162] "Class" is a stronger concept than "community," since it implies that bonds arise out of common working conditions, producing a group consciousness which in turn underlies a particular type of historical agency.[163] Finley and others argued that the Roman slave population was too internally segmented to form a class; instead slavery was a status.[164] Put another way, the occupational structure of Roman slavery blunted the formation of strong horizontal bonds across the slave population. Even though all slaves were property, and legally regulated as such in Roman law, the actual material conditions of the urban slave and the rural slave, the business manager and the mine laborer, differed too greatly to allow them to constitute a class. The discussion of ancient slave communities has, by and large, trailed off at this point.[165]

We need a structural account of the features of the Roman slave system that promoted or discouraged the formation of solidarities. "Solidarity" is an appropriately flexible term. It does not imply that bonds among slaves arose solely out of their material conditions, nor does it imply the development of a group consciousness that aimed to undermine the dominant structures of the slave system. Solidarity among slaves could arise spontaneously from a human desire for companionship and community, not strictly from a revolutionary spirit. The Roman slave population was internally segmented, and one pattern which served to undermine the extent and strength of slave communities was the proportion of slaves owned in small groups. In other words, the formation of vertical solidarities between the free family and its slaves acted to undercut the growth of a slave community.

---

[161] Genovese 1974; Blassingame 1972.   [162] Shaw 1998, 15–17, for an incisive overview.
[163] De Ste. Croix 1981, 31–69.   [164] Finley 1999 (orig. 1985), 183–8.
[165] Though see Joshel 1992; Harris 1988.

In Bourgeois and Agricultural households, the majority of the slave's human interaction came with the free members of the household. This might have nurtured feelings of loyalty across status.[166] A master might particularly love a slave who was born into his household or adopted when young.[167] A teacher might weep if his young master died.[168] A slave-girl assigned to a young mistress might have a bond of deep loyalty and shared affection.[169] A man and his slave may have grown up with the same nurse.[170] There is of course no reason to deny the emotions of warmth or trust which are not infrequently expressed in the sources. "He can be a slave and a friend, who is a good slave."[171] But he was a slave first, and that remained the bedrock of the relationship.

At the same time, life in the small household could have been claustrophobic and emotionally impoverished for the slave. Slaves found furtive ways to maintain contact and relations across the domestic bounds. Chores that required movement beyond the domestic zone, such as trips to the water well, provided an opportunity for sociability. In eighteenth-century New York, slaves gathered in the pre-dawn mist to collect water, and the well became a place for gossiping, flirting, and socializing beyond the master's eye.[172] In the letters of Aristaenetus, the lover of a slave-girl must wait until she fetches water before they can enjoy a surreptitious moment together: "Yesterday in the alley I whistled to Doris our usual signal. She stuck her head out, ever so slightly, shimmering like a shooting star, and softly said, 'I have heard your call, sweet one, but I am at a loss how I can get out. My master is here . . . .' But she came out soon, on the convincing excuse of needing to fetch water, pitcher under her arm."[173] In the indescribable bliss of the rendezvous, time stopped: "'so long as we are together, let us not squander this power which fleeting time gives us,' she said . . . The instant of union is more delicious and more desired when delayed by some obstacle."[174] Cynics can quibble that this is mere fiction,

---

[166] E.g. Gr. Nyss. Vit. Macr. 8 (SC 178: 166).
[167] P. Nol. Carm. 20.1 (CSEL 30: 143); Eus. H.E. 11.1 (SC 55: 154).
[168] Lib. Or. 58.10 (Foerster vol. 4: 186).   [169] Thdt. Ep. 70 (SC 98: 155).
[170] Bas. Ep. 37 (Courtonne: 80).
[171] Aug. Tract. Io. 85.1 (CC 36: 539): *potest igitur esse servus et amicus, qui servus est bonus.*
[172] Lepore 2005, 149, is especially evocative.
[173] Aristaen. Ep. 2.4 (Mazal: 71): Χθὲς ἐν τῷ στενωπῷ τὸ σύνηθες ὑπεσύριττον τῇ Δωρίδι. ἡ δὲ ὑπερκύψασα μόλις, ὡς λαμπρὸν ἀνέτειλεν ἄστρον, καὶ ἠρέμα φθεγγομένη φησίν. "ᾐσθόμην τοῦ συνθήματος, ὦ φιλότης. ἀλλὰ πρὸς τὴν κάθοδον ἀμηχανῶ. οὑμὸς πάρεστι δεσπότης" . . . ὅμως ὑδροφορῆσαι πιθανῶς προφασισαμένη κατέβη ταχύ, ἐπὶ λαιοῦ τοῖν ὤμοιν κομίζουσα τὴν κάλπιν. Drago 2007, 451–8.
[174] Aristaen. Ep. 2.4 (Mazal: 71): ἕως ἀλλήλους ἔχομεν, μὴ παραναλώσωμεν ἣν δίδωσιν ἡμῖν ὁ καιρὸς ὀξύρροπον ἐξουσίαν . . . ἡδίων γὰρ καὶ σφόδρα ποθεινὸς μετὰ δή τινα συμβᾶσαν δυσκολίαν τοῖς ἐρῶσιν ὁ γάμος.

but undoubtedly slaves bent space and time as they could to create havens for existence on their own terms.[175]

Vertical and horizontal solidarities were not strictly incompatible. At the same time, the power dynamics in the household threatened to fray the bonds between slaves. Julian mentioned that slaves who "set themselves to share their master's friends, interests and passions are cherished more than their fellow slaves."[176] If a slave was ordered to monitor or carry out punishment on another slave, he could sympathize with him.[177] Slaves could be vicious towards each other if given the chance. Many slaves had slaves, which created complex layers of domination.[178] Sometimes a group of slaves feared the good ones in the bunch, who had the master's confidence.[179] Sometimes a group of slaves feared the bad ones, who risked piquing the master's anger and bringing it down on them all.[180] Slaves resented it if other slaves showed them up, and they seethed with jealousy if a slave who had been disobedient returned to the master's favor.[181]

We know virtually nothing about slave cultures in Roman antiquity. Common beliefs and mutual loyalty can underwrite collective action, and we see hints of co-ordinated response by slaves when dire circumstances threatened. Consider, for example, the measure of Constantine protecting slave families on imperial estates in Sardinia. What brought these unbearable separations to the emperor's attention? Perhaps someone intervened on the slaves' behalf, but it is not hard to imagine the slaves' own agitation behind the imperial response.[182] When Melania the Younger planned to sell her slaves as part of her conversion to the ascetic life, the slaves went into rebellion. The *Life* presents her brother-in-law as a villain who fomented the resistance for his own benefit. While this is possible, it is also possible that the slaves made a demonstration of their collective power at a tense moment in order to tip events in their favor.[183]

It is difficult to say how far slaves were involved in acts of organized violence or even collective resistance in the late Roman empire. Certainly notices of servile agitation are strewn across the late antique record. We can organize these episodes, typologically, into three different categories:

---

[175] cf. Lib. Or. 25.66–7 (Foerster vol. 2: 569–70); Ioh. Chrys. Quod reg. 10.67 (Dumortier: 130–2).

[176] Iul. Imp. Ep. 89 (Bidez: 156): οἱ τοῖς ἑαυτῶν δεσπόταις συνδιατιθέμενοι περί τε φιλίας καὶ σπουδὰς καὶ ἔρωτας ἀγαπῶνται πλέον τῶν ὁμοδούλων.

[177] Ioh. Chrys. Ascens. 4 (PG 50: 448).

[178] Ioh. Chrys. In Mt. 59.4 (PG 58: 571); Aug. Serm. 21.5 (Dolbeau: 275).

[179] Ioh. Chrys. Hom. in Genes. 9.4 (PG 53: 79).

[180] Ioh. Chrys. Virgin. 46.4 (SC 125: 260); Ioh. Chrys. Serm. in Genes. 3.112–19 (SC 433: 212).

[181] Ast. Soph. Psalm. 25.1 (Richard: 187); Ps.-Mac. Serm. 22.1.2 (Berthold vol. 1: 224–5).

[182] cf. Huchthausen 1974, for petitions, and chapter 9.   [183] Geron. Vit. Mel. 10 (Gorce: 145–6).

(1) opportunistic mass desertion, (2) political violence, and (3) social violence or rebellion. To be sure, these were overlapping categories, but it is helpful to identify the specific modalities of each type of collective act and to scrutinize the particular limitations of the extant sources in each case.[184]

That slaves in the late Roman empire engaged in opportunistic mass desertion is not to be doubted. Organized flight was a communal variant of the individual slave's ability to flee, and the political conditions of the late empire created opportunities for slaves to flee *en masse*. Two particularly important episodes are recorded, on the eve of Adrianople and in the midst of Alaric's occupation of Italy. Ammianus Marcellinus claimed that the "multitude" who had been sold into slavery took the opportunity to rejoin their kinsmen as Roman control of the Danubian frontier slipped away.[185] A generation later, history repeated itself. Alaric and his army surrounded Rome, trying to negotiate a compromise with Honorius and the senate. As the negotiations wore on, Alaric allowed a brief reprieve in the form of a three-day market. Goods could enter the city, but it also gave slaves the chance to desert. According to Zosimus, "nearly all" the slaves of the city fled.[186] A few years later, Jerome mentioned the dregs of fugitives and slaves who had joined the Goths, and he imagined the shudder of joy which would result if only they were struck down by a lightning bolt from heaven![187] Throughout late antiquity, political turmoil and mass flight would go hand in hand.[188]

Even more numerous are the indications that slaves were mobilized in various forms of political violence. Slaves were a combustible element whose potential violence could be detonated as a political weapon. Certainly, extreme caution is in order: to accuse a political enemy of using slaves was a way of delegitimizing his cause.[189] Enrolling slaves was what usurpers and tyrants did. Proculus, who tried to seize power in AD 280, was said to have enlisted 2,000 of his own slaves in the campaign.[190] In fact, in late antiquity, no self-respecting usurper would fail to use the potential energy of servile violence for his political ends.[191] What is more surprising, and a sure sign that the use of slaves was not simply a tendentious accusation, is that some figures with varying shades of legitimacy were said to have

---

[184] Lenski 2009 (on the use of slaves in private armies); Bellen 1971, 108–15; Thompson 1952.

[185] Amm. 31.6.5 (Seyfarth vol. 2: 175): *multitudo*. cf. Eun. Fr. 42 (Blockley 60).

[186] Zos. 5.42.3 (Paschoud vol. 3.1: 63–4): σχεδὸν ἅπαντες. Heather 2005, 224, suggests that many of these slaves may have been captives on the invasion of Radagaisus. Bellen 1971, 111.

[187] Hier. Ep. 130.6 (CSEL 56: 181).   [188] E.g. Gelas. Ep. 14.14 (Theil: 370). Bellen 1971, 113.

[189] Lenski 2009, 152.   [190] SHA, Quadr. Tyr. 12.2 (Hohl vol. 2: 230).

[191] Notably Procopius: see Zos. 4.5.5 (Paschoud vol. 2.2: 266). And Tribigild: see Zos. 5.13.4 (Paschoud vol. 3.1: 20).

mobilized slaves too.[192] Two Spanish senators raised an entire army from their slaves and tenants to defend the government of Honorius.[193] Imperial laws underscore the reality of the threat in late antiquity.[194]

The use of slaves in civil violence had a long past in Roman history, but, in a perceptive analysis, Lenski has noted some distinct late antique trends. First, the late Roman state gradually lost its claims to a monopoly of violence.[195] The use of private bodyguards, often composed at least partly of slaves, is a sign of this development. Secondly, the abhorrence for enlisting slaves in the state's army was progressively eroded. This taboo has nearly always existed in slave systems, and has nearly as often been violated when circumstances required, but in the late empire we glimpse a particularly desperate debate over the use of slaves in the army and the breakdown of a long-standing Roman prohibition on the recruitment of slaves.[196] Finally, in late antiquity we can observe the use of private military retainers in a way that suggests a wholly different cultural matrix, a specifically Germanic tradition of militarized dependence.[197]

Clearly slaves were used in political violence in late antiquity – and they may have had their own purposes for choosing to participate – but the most interesting question is whether there were genuine slave revolts. Slave revolts are exceedingly rare in history.[198] It requires just the right convergence of circumstances to trigger a revolt: the presence of large numbers of slaves at a certain density, enough internal coherence within the slave population, effective leadership, and a window of opportunity created by external conditions.[199] Some of these criteria were met at various points in late antiquity, but there is no unambiguous evidence for a slave rebellion as such. There is considerable evidence, however, that slaves participated in social violence, sometimes alongside other disaffected elements of the population. Slaves in North Africa joined Donatist rebels and tormented their former masters.[200] Later they used the Vandal invasion as a chance to inflict revenge.[201] Rutilius Namatianus hinted, in ambiguous language, of

---

[192] Nepotianus, a relative of Constantine, employed a band of gladiators at Rome. Aur. Vict. 42.6 (Dufrainge: 61–2); Eutrop. Brev. 10.11 (Dietsch: 75–6); Socr. H.E. 2.25 (PG 67: 264–5); Soz. H.E. 4.1.2 (GCS 50: 140); Oros. Hist. adv. pag. 7.29.11 (Arnaud-Lindet: 81). See Lenski 2009, 152.

[193] Zos. 6.4.3 (Paschoud vol. 3.2: 8); Oros. Hist. adv. pag. 7.40.6 (Arnaud-Lindet: 119).

[194] CJ 9.12.10 (AD 468); Nov. Theod. 15.2 (AD 444); CT 9.10.4 (AD 390).   [195] Lenski 2009, 171.

[196] Esp. Hunt 1999 and the papers in Brown and Morgan 2006. Lenski 2009, 152–3. Esp. CT 7.13.16 (AD 406).

[197] Lenski 2009, 165–71.   [198] Urbainczyk 2008; Shaw 2001a; Bradley 1989.

[199] Genovese 1979.

[200] Aug. Ep. 185.15 (CSEL 57: 14); Aug. Ep. 108.18 (CSEL 34.2: 632). cf. CT 16.5.52 (AD 412) and possibly CT 7.19.1.3 (AD 399).

[201] Aug. Serm. 345.3 (PLS 2: 204). For the date, see Hill 1995, 66–7.

a social uprising in Armorica.[202] Paulinus of Pella reported that slaves in Bazas, a town of southern Gaul, joined with a few freeborn leaders to rebel and seize their masters' property.[203] The *Gallic Chronicle* recorded that in AD 435, all the slaves of Gaul, *omnia servitia*, entered rebellion.[204] This notice is short and not perfectly lucid. Some have imagined a slave revolt, others a peasants' movement, but these are not mutually exclusive. It is perfectly conceivable that the oppressed poor and slaves joined in revolt, just as they did over five centuries before in the great Sicilian rebellions.

The late empire offers no incidents of collective action by slaves with the same dramatic interest as a Spartacus (who remained a figure of morbid intrigue in late antiquity). At least no such record has survived. But it is noteworthy that the collective dissatisfaction of slaves was like a great store of charged energy in late Roman society, occasionally mobilized, always felt.

CONCLUSIONS

In AD 393 a group of twenty-nine Saxon captives, held under guard in Rome, committed a grisly mass suicide, strangling each other in turn with their bare hands, thereby refusing to participate in the public spectacles to which they were condemned. Symmachus, responsible for offering the games, took the news with annoyance but equanimity. What else could be expected from a tribe of men worse than Spartacus? Like Socrates, Symmachus tried to reckon his loss as a gain: at least their suicide brought Symmachus' edition of the games back within the prescribed limits.[205] The callous reception of this news by a man of great culture and authority is undoubtedly jarring. The fact that fourth-century society retained a taste for this sort of blood sport is equally noteworthy, although within only a few years the ancient tradition of gladiatorial combat would come to a sudden and dramatic halt.[206]

The Saxon captives chose private over public death. They were confronted with a situation that few slaves ever encountered in such stark terms. The Saxons refused to become a spectacular effigy of social death. Yet their refusal to submit to ritual execution reminds us that the "social death" of slavery was imaginary. Slaves were not mute, passive units of labor living out a barren existence at the master's mercy. The greatest hope for

---

[202] Rutil. De red. lines 215–16 (Doblhofer: 104). Minor 2000; Sánchez León 1996; Drinkwater 1989.
[203] P. Pell. Euch. lines 329–42 (SC 209: 80).   [204] Chron. Gall. a. 435 (MGH AA 9: 660).
[205] Symm. Ep. 2.46 (MGH AA 6.1: 57).   [206] See Jones 1964, 705–6.

most slaves was that their masters needed not simply their death, but their labor. The need for their labor allowed slaves a limited capacity to seek the basic goods of this life – physical security, human companionship. Life for slaves was not the carefree parade of wine and love described by Pantoma-lus, but neither was it the march towards death portrayed in the games. We do not have the archives and memoirs which the modern historian can explore in search of the life of the slave. Even if we did, the goal would not be to pronounce how harsh or humane ancient slavery was; it would be, rather, to understand the texture of life for those who were expected to live without power, to work without complaint, to obey without question. The goal would be to empathize with those who were "neither as sad nor as stupid" as their owners thought.

CHAPTER 7

Sex, status, and social reproduction

SLAVERY AND SEXUAL EXPLOITATION

The rhetorical talent of John Chrysostom derived not least from his intuitive sense of where he stood *vis-à-vis* his audience, an awareness of the distance between his claims and prevailing opinion. It was a skill he needed as he led his congregation through the logic of Paul's teaching that marriage was acceptable "on account of fornications," since it was "better to marry than to burn."[1] Chrysostom started his discussion on perfectly traditional grounds. Marriage was instituted for two reasons: the procreation of children and sexual self-control.[2] For the Romans, marriage was defined by reproductive intent, and marriage contracts explicitly declared that a union was intended to create children. Chrysostom, though, quickly tried to undermine this primary purpose of marriage: the earth was full and in no need of additional bodies. Moreover, in the post-resurrection age, the promise of eternal life nullified the need to live through future generations. This left only one purpose for marriage. Paul was right: marriage was a bulwark against sexual sins. Switching subtly from the ancient code of "self-control" to the Christian vocabulary of sin, Chrysostom went completely beyond his audience's expectations.[3] It was wrong for a married man to have sex, even with prostitutes or slaves. "What I am saying is illogical – but it's true."[4]

We need to explore the "logic" which Chrysostom was defying. Chrysostom juxtaposed his interpretation of Christian sexual boundaries with the ordinary rules of conduct. "I am not unaware that most think it is adultery only to violate a married woman. But *I* say that it is wicked and licentious to have an affair even with a public whore, a slave-girl, or any

---

[1] Brown 1988, 308.   [2] Ioh. Chrys. Propt. forn. 1.3 (PG 51: 213).
[3] Kirchhoff 1994; and below, on *porneia*, "fornication."
[4] Ioh. Chrys. Propt. forn. 1.4 (PG 51: 213): Εἰ γὰρ καὶ παράδοξόν ἐστι τὸ εἰρημένον, ἀλλ' ἀληθές.

281

other woman without a husband."[5] The preacher recognized that society's standards, which accepted dalliances between married men and their slaves or prostitutes, found a powerful ally in Roman law. "Do not show me the laws of the outside world, which say a woman committing adultery is to be brought to a trial, but that men with wives who do it with slave-girls are not considered guilty."[6] And if appeal to God's law was not enough, Chrysostom invoked the hope of a peaceful domestic scene. "Your wife did not come to you, and leave behind her father and mother and her entire household in order to be humiliated, so that you could prefer a cheap slave-girl to her and create countless wars."[7] His point required repetition: "Even a man commits adultery, if he has a wife but fulfills his lascivious desires with a slave-girl or any public whore."[8] Marital fidelity was the Christian path. "A wife (*gune eleuthera*) offers at once pleasure and security and joy and honor and order and a clean conscience."[9]

For Chrysostom, this was a personal crusade, and he promised to be persistent, so that his flock would "keep his words zealously, in public and at home, day and night, at the table and in bed, everywhere . . ."[10] But it was more than one man's obsession. Chrysostom's sermon brings into the foreground one of the central aspects of Roman slavery: its intimate relationship to sexual exploitation. The Christian preacher found himself surrounded by a culture in which the sexual abuse of slaves was commonplace and perfectly acceptable. Chrysostom had to combat a formidable social and cultural system that allowed and effectively encouraged masters to exploit the sexual vulnerability of their dependants.

Sexual exploitation is a common aspect of slavery, practiced in virtually every known slave society. In the most familiar case, the US South, the extent of sexual abuse could hardly be overestimated.[11] In the Roman

---

[5] Ioh. Chrys. Propt. forn. 1.4 (PG 51: 213): Οὐκ ἀγνοοῦμεν γὰρ ὅτι πολλοὶ μοιχείαν νομίζουσιν, ὅταν τις ὕπανδρον φθείρῃ γυναῖκα μόνον. ἐγὼ δὲ κἂν δημοσίᾳ πόρνῃ, κἂν θεραπαινίδι, κἂν ἄλλῃ τινὶ γυναικὶ ἄνδρα οὐκ ἐχούσῃ πρόσχῃ κακῶς καὶ ἀκολάστως.

[6] Ioh. Chrys. Propt. forn. 1.4 (PG 51: 214): Μὴ γάρ μοι τοὺς ἔξωθεν νόμους εἴπῃς νῦν, οἳ τὰς μὲν γυναῖκας μοιχευομένας εἰς δικαστήριον ἕλκουσι καὶ εὐθύνας ἀπαιτοῦσιν, ἄνδρας καὶ γυναῖκας ἔχοντας καὶ θεραπαινίσι προφθειρομένους οὐκ ἀπαιτοῦσιν εὐθύνας.

[7] Ioh. Chrys. Propt. forn. 1.4 (PG 51: 214): Οὐ γὰρ διὰ τοῦτο ἦλθεν ἡ γυνὴ πρὸς σέ, καὶ πατέρα καὶ μητέρα ἐγκατέλιπε καὶ τὸν οἶκον ἅπαντα, ἵνα καθυβρίζηται, ἵνα θεραπαινίδιον εὐτελὲς ἐπεισάγῃς αὐτῇ, ἵνα μυρίους ποιῇς πολέμους.

[8] Ioh. Chrys. Propt. forn. 1.4 (PG 51: 215): οὕτω καὶ ἄνδρα μοιχεύειν ἂν εἴποιμεν, κἂν εἰς θεραπαινίδα, κἂν εἰς ἡντιναοῦν δημώδη γυναῖκα ἀσελγαίνῃ, γυναῖκα ἔχων αὐτός.

[9] Ioh. Chrys. Propt. forn. 1.5 (PG 51: 217): Ἐπὶ γὰρ τῆς ἐλευθέρας γυναικὸς ὁμοῦ καὶ ἡδονὴ καὶ ἀσφάλεια καὶ ἄνεσις καὶ τιμὴ καὶ κόσμος καὶ συνειδὸς ἀγαθόν.

[10] Ioh. Chrys. Propt. forn. 1.5 (PG 51: 218): Μετὰ ἀκριβείας ταῦτα φυλάξαντες τὰ ῥήματα, καὶ ἐν ἀγορᾷ, καὶ ἐν οἰκίᾳ, καὶ ἐν ἡμέρᾳ, καὶ ἐν ἑσπέρᾳ, καὶ ἐπὶ τῆς τραπέζης, καὶ ἐπὶ τῆς εὐνῆς, καὶ πανταχοῦ.

[11] Genovese 1974, 413–31. Genetic evidence: Parra *et al.* 2001.

instance, the role of sexual exploitation in the slave system has been increasingly recognized. Indeed, it has become effectively obligatory to make some reference to the complete sexual availability of slaves in Roman antiquity. But if Finley could remark a generation ago that the "fundamental research remains to be done," that is substantially true to this day.[12] The sexual dimension of ancient slavery is one of the least systematically explored topics in the modern historical literature, and in consequence the full structural features of the practice have not been delineated. This chapter zooms out from the analysis of domination and resistance which occupied chapters 5 and 6 in order to consider more fully how slaves, and their bodies, figured in the structures of social reproduction in the late empire.

The neglect of this topic requires some explanation. The study of ancient sexuality has grown out of the study of canonical texts.[13] Even as ancient sexuality has become a central topic of investigation, it has been framed as a cultural problem. Historians have been sensitive to the range of meanings which sex was capable of carrying for various actors, to the moral and aesthetic constructions of sex.[14] Studies of gender, which inevitably raise questions of power, often make reference to the unquestioned patriarchy of the ancient world, but the focus has been on the difference between the categories of male and female, without always appreciating the entire social world within which those relations took shape.[15] In late antiquity, this problem has been exacerbated by the focus on asceticism, which makes the sexual renunciation of a militant fringe the sign of Christianization.[16] There has been too little systematic discussion of the social forces which were at work in the history of sex.[17] For the historian of slavery this is a serious sort of neglect, since the sexual exploitation of slaves was built into the social mechanics of sexuality in the Roman empire.

A second, more subtle, explanation also accounts for the lack of attention to the role of slavery in Roman sexuality. There is a latent tendency, derived from older, moralizing traditions (and immanent already in the Christian

---

[12] Finley 1998 (orig. 1980), 163. Shaw 1998, 46–7, "much research remains to be done." Williams 2010, 15–40, is probably the best account; Andreau and Descat 2006, 174–5, one page in a book-long treatment; Hezser 2005, 179; DuBois 2003, 101–13; Nettis 2000; Rousselle 1989; Bradley 1987b, 116–18; Veyne 1987, 77; Morabito 1986; Garrido-Hory 1981a; Kolendo 1981.

[13] Selectively, Skinner 2005; Nussbaum and Sihvola 2002; Greene 1998; Hallett and Skinner 1997; Richlin 1992; Halperin 1990; Halperin, Winkler, and Zeitlin 1990; Winkler 1990; Brown 1988; Rousselle 1988; Foucault 1986.

[14] E.g. Hallett and Skinner 1997, 3; Halperin 1990; Winkler 1990.   [15] Noted by DuBois 2003, 82.

[16] Brown 1988, 429, "a small and vociferous minority." Jacobs and Krawiec 2003. On asceticism, Clark 1999; Elm 1994.

[17] Cohen 1991a, for classical Greece. Saller 2007a and 1994 for the Roman family. McGinn 2004 and 1998, has inspired many of the arguments made here and in chapter 11.

critique) to think of the sexual exploitation of slaves as a sort of subjective failure, the indiscretion of the master, the outcome of individual choice: in short, a sin. Even our language threatens to import assumptions, since words like "abuse" or "rape" might imply individual culpability; hence "exploitation," with its more systemic connotations, is the keyword of this chapter.[18] The power of the individual master over the slave was, of course, instrumental in the exercise of sexual domination. The use of slaves as sexual objects is one of the most persistent, cross-cultural features of slave systems.[19] But the simple equation of private power does not catch the full depth of the relationship between slavery and sex in the Roman world. As Chrysostom recognized, the exploitation of slaves was ingrained in the whole fabric of late antique sexuality.

To sense the importance of sexual exploitation in Roman society, we can immediately draw a contrast between the ancient and modern contexts. The sexual abuse of slaves was disturbingly frequent in a society like the US South, where racial and religious barriers acted to deter, however ineffectively, this exercise of power.[20] In antiquity, race was not a factor. Moreover, religious considerations were of limited significance, even in the fourth century. John Chrysostom was not the only Christian to feel that he was on the outside looking in; those of his contemporaries who were most in touch with reality echoed the same sentiment. Christianity made a difference, and it would be cynical to deny that the sermonizing of the church could influence sexual habits. But the extensive historiographical discussion over the transition to Christian sexuality, as a cultural phenomenon that re-ordered the way men and women discussed sex and thought of the relation between body and self, threatens to draw our eyes away from the tremendous social continuities which made the sexual exploitation of slaves a pervasive practice. Precisely because Chrysostom was such an ardent and earnest reformer, he perceived the totality of his predicament.

This chapter has three goals. The first is to demonstrate that the sexual use of slaves was *institutionalized* in Roman society. Sexual exploitation was determined by the configuration of marriage, honor, and law in Roman society. The second aim is to show that slaves, prostitutes, and concubines were exploited as part of the same sexual system. The association between slavery and prostitution in Chrysostom's sermon was no accident. In a society where the ideology of honor determined which bodies were sexually available, the boundaries between the slave, the prostitute, and the

[18] cf. Genovese 1974, 415 "plantation miscengenation occurred with single girls under circumstances that varied from seduction to rape and typically fell between the two."
[19] Patterson 1982, 260–1. [20] Scheidel 2009a.

concubine were indistinct. The ideological connection between slavery and prostitution was reinforced by the fact that many prostitutes were slaves. Finally, we should try to evaluate the influence and the limits of Christianization. One of the most significant legacies of late antique Christianity was its stubborn insistence on the ideal of sexually exclusive marriage, and the radicalism of that commitment cannot be measured without recognizing its roots in a society where slavery was deeply embedded in the sexual economy. Christianity spawned a reform movement with a critical stance which exposed, like never before, the unspoken forces shaping ancient sexual habits. We can benefit from the fact that observers of late antiquity focused with new intensity on the social matrix of desire.

MARRIAGE AND SOCIAL REPRODUCTION IN THE ROMAN EMPIRE

Sex is a socially structured act; the terms, conditions, and opportunities which determine its incidence are profoundly shaped by society. Prior to the demographic transition of the nineteenth century, especially, patterns of sexual conduct were shaped by implacable material demands. Roman society reproduced itself, normatively, through the institution of monogamous marriage.[21] Greco-Roman monogamy was a peculiar institution, the exception rather than the rule in historical terms.[22] Marriage was the only sanctioned means of creating legitimate heirs in Roman society, and marriage could only occur with a free and honorable woman.[23] Marriage was the basic structuring principle of sexual boundaries throughout the Roman empire because sexual actors and sexual encounters were defined and categorized by their relationship to marital sexuality.

Ancient marriage was structured by its reproductive purpose. Marriage contracts in antiquity explicitly advertised its function, *procreandorum liberorum causa*, because it distinguished marriage from all other human relations.[24] The intention to reproduce an heir was the decisive marker of a publicly recognized marriage, which was otherwise a legally formless transaction.[25] As a reproductive strategy, ancient marriage worked. One

---

[21] Arjava 1996, 3.
[22] Scheidel 2009a; Herlihy 1995; Betzig 1992a and 1992b; MacDonald 1990. cf. Aug. Bon. conjug. 7.7 (CSEL 1: 197). On polygamy in ancient Judaism, Williams 2005; Satlow 2001, 188–92; Ilan 1996, 85–8. CJ 1.9.7 (AD 393).
[23] Slaves could not legally marry: Ulp. Reg. 5.5; Dig. 38.10.10.5. Freeborn men were prohibited from marriage with a prostitute: chapter 11.
[24] Caes. Arel. Serm. 44.3 (CC 103: 196–7); Aug. Serm. 9.18 (CC 41: 143); Bas. Anc. Virg. 38 (PG 30: 745).
[25] Evans Grubbs 2007, 86–7; Toubert 1998, 518–19; Arjava 1996, 206; Beaucamp 1990–2, vol. 1, 262–4; Gaudemet 1980, 126, 155; Wolff 1950, 293. See Harper forthcoming a.

of the most important contributions of historical demography has been the demonstration that ancient marriages were, in fact, very fertile.[26] The average married woman would have borne six children just to replace the population.[27] If the focus on reproductive intent seems overly austere, it is refreshing to read in the normative literature that marriage was, ideally, the locus of great emotional satisfaction, nor were marriages barren of erotic potential.[28] Ancient men and women did not marry for love, but they hoped to find it once they were joined. The function of marriage structured the relationship, even if it did not determine its content or subjective meaning.

The reproductive function of marriage was encouraged by a natalist ideology, but the most keenly felt pressures to reproduce were private in nature.[29] When ascetic radicals tried to dissuade men and women from marriage, they had to challenge converts to ignore the proprietary and psychological impetus to procreate. An ascetic like Jerome argued against the self-evident reasons to marry and reproduce: to pass on the family name, to have security in old age, and to transmit the patrimony to the next generation.[30] The reflexive protest against the ascetic was to ask, "to whom will I pass on my fields and my houses, my slaves and my money?"[31] Marriage was nature's solution to death.[32] Property was deeply connected with the desire to transcend the limits of mortality. There was an obvious psychological force operating in the desire for an heir: a son was the "greatest and highest honor" a man could have, especially if he looked like the father. "You would rather be the begetter of one son than the master of ten thousand slaves."[33]

The age structure of ancient marriage, which can be recovered from hard data, reinforces the impression taken from literary sources, and when we consider the dynamics of sex within and outside of marriage, age patterns should be a central consideration. Women were married young – as young as twelve.[34] By the late teens or twenty, practically all women were married.[35] Virginity was demanded of brides. A woman's sexual purity at

---

[26] Scheidel 2001b, 34; Bagnall and Frier 1994, 135–51.   [27] Bagnall and Frier 1994, 139.

[28] Dixon 2003 and 1992, 28–9; Treggiari 1991, 205–61. For late antiquity, see Cooper 2007a.

[29] Brown 1988, 5–32, for the claims of civic duty on the body. Arjava 1996, 77–80, on the Augustan laws.

[30] Hier. Adv. Iov. 1.47 (PL 23: 290).

[31] Ioh. Chrys. Oppug. 3.16 (PG 47: 377): Καὶ τίνι, φησί, καταλείψομεν τοὺς ἀγροὺς καὶ τὰς οἰκίας καὶ τὰ ἀνδράποδα καὶ τὸ χρυσίον;

[32] Choric. Or. 6.1.7 (Foerster and Richtsteig: 89).

[33] Gr. Naz. Or. 23.7 (PG 35: 296): εἰς τιμὴν μέγα καὶ μέγιστον ὁ σὸς υἱός . . . οὐκ ἂν δέξαιο μυρίων ἀνδραπόδων εἶναι μᾶλλον δεσπότης, ἢ ἑνὸς γεννήτωρ παιδός.

[34] Cloke 1995, 47–56.   [35] Scheidel 2001a, 20; Bagnall and Frier 1994, 112–15; Shaw 1987b.

the time of her marriage was obvious public knowledge – it was advertised in the aspects of the ceremony that symbolized her purity, like white veils or long hair.[36] Men married later, in their late twenties.[37] The average age difference between husband and wife was over seven years.[38] The burden of reproduction was spread as widely as possible across the fertile female population, and this meant that women were conscripted to marriage at a very young age, while men spent the first decade of sexual maturity without a spouse.

As its close association with reproduction might already imply, the relation between marriage and sexual norms was fundamentally different for men and women. For women, sex was normatively confined to marriage – an expectation that men went to some trouble to enforce. Men tried to justify this limit on female sexuality by appealing to concerns about legitimate succession.[39] "Marriage was instituted for two reasons – testation and child-production – neither of which can be saved after adultery... If men consort with a whole crowd of women, they do no harm to their own hearth, but if women commit sexual sin, they introduce alien heirs into their house and their line."[40] The concern with legitimacy, promoting obsession with female virginity at marriage and fidelity within marriage, was hardly unique to the Romans.[41] But it was a ferociously active principle in the social order of the Roman empire. The integrity of the Roman family rested on the chastity of its women.

The limits on female sexuality had both private and public enforcement mechanisms. The control over female sexuality started at home. Ambrose expected a husband to keep a close watch on his wife's eyes.[42] Augustine knew that if a woman stared out the window too long, she risked physical abuse from her husband.[43] Women without men, such as widows, were perceived as liminal, vulnerable.[44] The men of a family were charged with the surveillance of their wives and daughters, often through the agency of the slaves. In such proximity, slaves might be the first to know if a girl lost her virginity.[45] A wife under suspicion would have to answer to the slaves just to enter or leave her own home.[46] If the slaves were judged to

---

[36] Talmud Bavli, *Bava Basra*, 92b.   [37] Bagnall and Frier 1994, 116–21; Saller 1987a.
[38] Shaw 2002; Bagnall and Frier 1994, 118–19.   [39] Arjava 1996, 204.
[40] Ast. Am. Serm. 5.11 (Datema: 52): Γάμος γὰρ τούτων χάριν τῶν δύο συνίσταται, διαθέσεως καὶ παιδοποιΐας, ὧν οὐδέτερον μετὰ μοιχείας σώζεται... Οἱ μὲν γὰρ ἄνδρες, φασί, κἂν πάνυ πολλαῖς γυναιξὶ πλησιάσωσιν, οὐδὲν τῇ ἑστίᾳ λυμαίνονται. αἱ δὲ γυναῖκες, ἐξ ὧν ἁμαρτάνουσι, κληρονόμους ἀλλοτρίους ταῖς οἰκίαις καὶ τοῖς γένεσιν ἐπεισάγουσιν.
[41] Delaney 1987, 40–3.   [42] Ambr. Ios. 5.22 (CSEL 32.2: 88).
[43] Aug. Ep. 246.3 (CSEL 57: 584).   [44] Ioh. Chrys. Vid. 2.79–85 (SC 138: 118–20).
[45] Hist. Apoll. Reg. Tyr. 2 (Kortekaas: 280); Aristaen. Ep. 6 (Mazal: 15–16).
[46] Ioh. Chrys. Virgin. 52 (SC 125: 294).

be conscious of an illicit affair, they could expect the most violent reprisal. The master would "drink their blood and devour their flesh."[47] The state actively reinforced men in the effort to protect their women.[48] Under torture (and, of course, torture of the slaves) women could be pressed to admit affairs, real or imaginary.[49]

The dual burdens of purity and fertility weighed heavily upon the woman's experience of ancient marriage. For men, however, sex was not even normatively confined to marriage. Marriage was a patrimonial alliance, a relation with the explicit purpose of creating an heir. A wife was the woman with whom a man tried to create heirs. But this did not monopolize his use of sex. Men were not expected to enter marriage as virgins. They married at an older age than females.[50] Men spent their unmarried youths, from puberty to late marriage, in a time of proverbial license.[51] The young man was frankly "freer to love, more vulnerable to error, more exposed to weakness, more resistant to correction."[52] The life-course of ancient men by itself suggests wide, open spaces for extramarital sex. Philo of Alexandria, writing in the first century, described with unusual precision the importance of the life-course in shaping Greco-Roman sexual norms: "it is permitted for young men after their fourteenth year to use without shame whores, brothel-girls, and other women who make a profit with their body."[53] And even during marriage or afterwards, if a man survived his wife, marriage was no hard limit on his sexual options. To say that the Romans had a sexual "double standard" for men and women is to put it lightly.[54] There was no hypocrisy, no winking, in the Roman version: there were, frankly, two separate standards of behavior.

These interlocking forces – marriage, inheritance, demography – defined the social mechanics of sexuality in the Roman world. It is worth stressing how persistent these forces have been in circum-Mediterranean societies. They define a very long phase in the history of sexuality. In fact, this configuration, the transmission of property to legitimate heirs, created in a union with an honorable woman whose sexual activity was confined

---

[47] Ioh. Chrys. Psalm. 49.8 (PG 55: 253): τὸ αἷμα αὐτῶν ἐκπίοιεν, καὶ τῶν σαρκῶν ἀπογεύσαιντο.
[48] See chapter 11. Aug. Serm. 9.4 (CC 41: 115). cf. Cohen 1991b.
[49] E.g. Hier. Ep. 1 (CSEL 54: 1–3); Sopat. Diar. 289 (RG 5: 8); CT 9.7.4 (AD 385).   [50] Saller 1987a.
[51] E.g. Lib. Or. 2.12 (Foerster vol. 1: 243); Ps.-Aug. Sobr. (PL 40: 1110); Caes. Arel. Serm. 32.4 (CC 103: 142); Aristaen. Ep. 2.13 (Mazal: 86–7).
[52] Ambr. Psalm. CXVIII 16.45 (CSEL 62: 376): *ad amorem liberior, ad lapsum incautior, ad infirmitatem fragilior, ad correctionem durior est.*
[53] Philo Jos. 43 (Cohn: 70): ἐφεῖται μετὰ τὴν τεσσαρεσκαιδεκά την ἡλικίαν πόρναις καὶ χαμαιτύ-παις καὶ ταῖς ὅσαι μισθαρνοῦσιν ἐπὶ τοῖς σώμασι μετὰ πολλῆς ἀδείας χρῆσθαι. The words are in the mouth of Joseph, but the contemporary significance is clear.
[54] Stumpp 1998, 252; Treggiari 1991, 299.

to marriage, is practically sufficient to explain the sexual dimension of the honor–shame syndrome that is exhibited in so many Mediterranean societies. The honor–shame syndrome, in which female chastity is the touchstone of family honor, has shaped sexual norms in the Mediterranean for an imponderable length of time.[55] But this does not mean that it was incapable of being adapted, of taking particular forms within individual societies and cultures. The imposition of Christianity and Islam created a whole new layer of wrinkles in the system. But prior to the middle ages, two hallmarks of Roman civilization gave the honor–shame dynamic a distinctively Roman form: law and slavery.[56] To understand the way that sex was socially structured in the Roman period, it is necessary to account for these two, fundamental features of Roman society.

The double standard of sexual behavior, the operations of honor and shame, transcended any expression in public law, but nowhere was the decisive influence of power in ancient sexuality more apparent than in Roman civil law.[57] The law of sex and marriage, in its classical Roman form, was the creation of Augustus. The legislative reforms of Augustus, built around the *lex Iulia de adulteriis coercendis* and the *lex Iulia et Papia*, were among the most enduring and consequential social programs of antiquity.[58] By promulgating statutory penalties for the violation of honorable women, the Roman state became the arbiter of female honor. The Augustan legislation was meant to replace private vengeance with public justice, and it succeeded.[59] It was the only period of Mediterranean history during which a strong, unified state demanded the prerogative to resolve private conflicts over sexual honor.[60]

The Augustan laws categorized illicit sex under two rubrics: *adulterium* and *stuprum*. In both cases, "liability under the law always depended . . . on the status of the female partner to the sexual act at issue."[61] Men committed adultery only if they had sex with a married woman. For a married woman, sex with anyone other than her husband was adultery. *Stuprum*, illicit sexual violation, was a highly indeterminate crime that covered the remaining unmarried *matres familias*, women who possessed social honor, mainly widows and virgins from decent families.[62] *Stuprum* was left basically

---

[55] Horden and Purcell 2000, 485–523, 637–41. As they note (at 639), a historical survey of honor in the Mediterranean is desperately needed. McGinn 1998, 10–14; Kaster 1997; Cantarella 1991; Cohen 1991b. Bradley 2000b and Treggiari 1991, 311–13 offer cautions. Kaster 2005; Barton 2001; Lendon 1997 all discuss honor, principally in its masculine–competitive dimensions. See chapter 8.

[56] For the law, McGinn 1998, 13–14.   [57] See chapter 11.

[58] McGinn 1998 and 1991; Astolfi 1970.   [59] Cohen 1991b.

[60] Arjava 1996, 100.   [61] McGinn 1991, 343.

[62] Dig. 48.2.3.3; Dig. 48.5.9(8).pr; Dig. 48.5.11(10).pr.; Dig. 50.16.101. See Rizzelli 1987 and chapter 10.

290 The making of honorable society

undefined in positive law.[63] It was sex with honorable women, though a woman's sexual availability measured her honor. The jurists of the imperial period debated who belonged to the class of women "*in quas stuprum non committitur*" – with whom there is no illicit violation.[64] The debate itself is the crucial datum: the determination of honor and dishonor was left to judges and lawyers, to the mores of the litigious classes. The Roman state took a responsive position that required application to its procedures for enforcement. The Romans had no police force to monitor, seek out, or hunt down those who committed *stuprum*. But we should not underestimate the force of public law in crystallizing even the most intimate of social norms in Roman society.

The laws of Augustus limited male sexuality only indirectly. Male sexuality was not confined to marriage, but it was dangerous because it could be destructive of female chastity. The predatory sexuality of young men, the "*neoi*" or "*iuvenes*," was a persistent threat to a family's strategies. Men charged with protecting their wives and daughters recognized in other males a threat to family honor and the workings of marriage. The Augustan program enacted fearsome legislation protecting honorable females by public statute, and by the late empire, adultery was punishable with death.[65] Late Roman law represents an intensification, not a reconfiguration, of the Roman system of sexual honor.[66] The law was oriented towards protecting marriage as a reproductive and proprietary strategy, not to mention curbing the violence which ensued from violations of female honor. But it must be emphasized that this was a conscious effort to craft policy which exposed dishonored females to the remainder of male desire.[67] Sexual crime, *stuprum*, against one's slaves or against prostitutes was impossible by definition.[68] The law was a major prop of systemic sexual exploitation, and it is unsurprising that a critic like Chrysostom found in Roman law a powerful source of rival sexual norms.

The role of slavery marks a second particularity of the honor–shame complex under the Roman empire. A woman's honor came not only from

---

[63] McGinn 1991, 342–3. CJ 9.9.24 (AD 291).

[64] Dig. 25.7.1.1. With McGinn 1991, 350.   [65] Arjava 1996, 195–9.

[66] The essential studies are Arjava 1996; Evans Grubbs 1995; Beaucamp 1990–2.

[67] Dig. 1.6.2 quotes a rescript of Antoninus Pius which allowed governors to intervene when slaves sought refuge, "*si dominus in servos saevierit vel ad impudicitiam turpemque violationem compellat.*" cf. Dig. 1.12.1.8. There are several interpretive problems with the rescript. *Impudicitiam turpemque violationem* (a hendiadys?) implies some form of sexual transgression but is far from limpid. There is super-abundant evidence that later jurists and social observers were completely unaware of any limit on the sexual use of slaves. Nettis 2000, overly optimistic.

[68] Though slaves were private property and third parties might be punished for violations. PS 1.13.6; Dig. 47.10.25; Dig. 48.5.6.pr. Agathias, in Anth. Gr. 5.302 (Beckby: 432); Aug. Serm. 349.4 (PL 38: 1531). Dalla 1987, 44–7; Buckland 1908, 76.

her reputation or her behavior, but also from her legal status. The honor of free women, including their sexual honor, was constructed in opposition to legally dishonored women – slaves and prostitutes.[69] So Chrysostom could urge the men in his audience to remain faithful to their wives – their *"free women"* – and to avoid sexual affairs with slaves and prostitutes. In a fifth-century text, a girl who flouted social conventions by breaking out of her house was accused, by her furious mother, of "spurning a marriage worthy of her patrimony and preferring the shameful life of a prostitute or slave-girl!"[70] The honorable girl was reserved for *patrimonial* marriage, while the *shameful* life belonged to slaves and prostitutes. The quintessentially dishonored women of Roman antiquity were slaves and prostitutes. In the Roman period, they loom large on the sexual landscape. Without protection from the state or the private bonds of family, they were exposed to a system in which status and sexual honor were inseparable.

State and society deliberately made the bodies of dishonored females the safe outlet of male sexuality. We should be wary, even, of such hydraulic metaphors, insofar as they imply that sexual exploitation was an unfortunate outcome for excess sexual desire. The sexual exploitation of slaves and prostitutes was, materially and ideologically, a central, constructive feature of the Roman sexual economy. The social mechanics of sexuality under the Roman empire represented a conjuncture of the most elemental forces of pre-modern social life with two particular accents of Roman civilization: law and slavery. The need to reproduce the family as a human and proprietary unit, the hoarding of female chastity for this purpose, and the permissive, non-moral attitude towards male sexuality were basically primordial. The Leviathan of the Roman state had a policy of protecting the chastity of honorable females while deliberately exposing dishonored females. The legal system fused with the expansive slave system to create a remarkably stable pattern of sexuality, in which sexual dishonor was exploited in the interest of protecting the sexual honor of free women. The rest of this chapter explores the dynamics of sexual dishonor, in the case of slaves, prostitutes, and then concubines.

THE EFFECTS OF DISHONOR: THE EXPLOITATION OF SLAVES

A letter of Synesius recounted a sea voyage along the coast from Egypt back to his native Cyrene.[71] The ship ran aground in a storm, and the traveling

---

[69] Joshel and Murnaghan 1998, 4.
[70] Ps.-Bas. Sel. Vit. Thecl. 1.12 (Dagron: 216): ἡ τὸν μὲν εὐκλεῆ καὶ πάτριον ἀρνησαμένη γάμον, ἑταίρας δὲ καὶ θεραπαινίδος αἰσχρᾶς προελομένη βίον. On the text, Johnson 2006.
[71] Syn. Ep. 5 (Garzya: 25).

party fell desperately low on provisions. They came to depend on the local inhabitants of an isolated shore. The native women, so Synesius reports, had enormous breasts. When the locals saw a foreign woman, they wanted to see her naked chest:

> There was a certain young slave-girl from Pontus among us. Art and nature have conspired to make the slave appear more angular than the ants. Because of this there was great enthusiasm, and the slave-girl went around to the women. For three days the well-off women among these rustics called upon her, one after another, and she was so bold she would strip off her clothes! There's the story for you: from a tragedy to a comedy... [72]

The letter was a virtuoso integration of different genres to recount events which really happened. Synesius built up a sense of disaster to let it dissipate in a perverted joke. The slave appeared belatedly to a reader who was not forewarned about the social status of the women on board. Synesius introduced her status immediately before discussing her body. The slave-girl was sufficiently marginal to allow her exposure to curiosity of the natives. In this inverted world, she herself was able to capitalize on her own dishonor. In Synesius' account, she was complicit, they were satisfied, he was bemused.

As the letter reminds us, the slave body in antiquity was an object, an object sexually available to its legal owner. [73] We need to show not only that this was true in late antiquity, but why it was true. There was a deep connection between the chattel principle which reduced the slave to a commodity, the subjection to the power of the *dominus* at the household level, and the workings of honor at the social level. The slave's lack of honor as a sexual object took its essential form in the marketplace. Though we lack any slave's account of what it was like to be on the trading block, masters were occasionally willing to admit that it was humiliating. [74] Slave bodies were scrutinized, and the menstruation of female slaves was investigated. [75] They were also subjected to physical inspections to determine if they were

[72] Syn. Ep. 5 (Garzya: 25): ἡμῖν δὲ ἦν τι καὶ τῶν ἐκ τοῦ Πόντου θεραπαινίδιον, ὃ συνελθοῦσαι τέχνη καὶ φύσις ὑπὲρ τοὺς μύρμηκας ἔντομον ἔδειξαν. ἀμφὶ τοῦτο ἦν ἅπασα σπουδή, καὶ τοῦτο παρὰ τῶν γυναικῶν ἐνεπορεύετο, καὶ μετεπέμποντο αὐτὸ πρότριτα ἄλλη παρ' ἄλλης γυναῖκες τῶν ἀγρογειτόνων εὐδαίμονες. τὸ δὲ οὕτω τι σφόδρα ἰταμὸν ἦν ὥστε καὶ ἀποδύσασθαι. τοῦτό σοι δρᾶμα ἐκ τραγικοῦ κωμικόν... Ants (insects) were cut, notched (Arist. Hist. Anim. 487a), implying that the girl is scrawny, angular. On the trade in slaves from the Black Sea, Braund and Tsetskhladze 1989; Finley 1962.
[73] Hezser 2005, 179; Finley 1998 (orig. 1980), 163; Veyne 1987, 77; Garrido-Hory 1981a; Kolendo 1981.
[74] Lib. Or. 25.71 (Foerster vol. 2: 571); Ambr. Ep. 7.17 (CSEL 82: 51); Claud. In Eutr. 1 lines 35–41 (Hall: 144).
[75] Dig. 21.1.15.

virgins.[76] Lacking all privacy, here the slave's body and its sexual history
were objectified in the purest way. In a striking metaphor, Asterius of
Amasea referred to the way that female slaves for sale remained utterly
quiet.[77] Passive, powerless, slaves on the block were reduced to a physical
commodity, exposing the deep structure of the master–slave relationship.

A buyer might ask for a "maiden."[78] Virginity brought a premium in
the marketplace. One fictional captor abused his female captive on the first
night and then "wrapped her in seven robes," trying to conceal the fact.[79]
The rich prided themselves on the physical attractiveness of their female
slaves.[80] Many sought out "girls of the most elegant beauty" in the market.[81]
To increase their value, slave merchants applied cosmetics to their wares.[82]
Virginity and beauty were attributes that could be commuted into capital
by the seller. They were products that could be bought by consumers. "Just
as when you buy slave-girls, you check if they have been violated or are
untouched."[83] The Talmud speaks of the financial value of a slave's virginity
as though it were a straightforward and publicly known quantity.[84] The
price curve for slaves shows that only in their early teens did the average
price of female slaves match the average price of male slaves.[85] While this
has, rightly, been seen as an indication of the reproductive value of nubile
females and the productive value of all female slaves, female slaves also
represented an important sexual commodity.[86] The sexual past and the
sexual potential of a slave-woman were part of the bundled product for
sale in the slave market.

The slave market rent the possibility of sexual honor from the female
slave by removing her from a family. As a means by which the slave
market acted to dishonor slaves, this could not be overstated. In many
cases the market moved men and women great distances. With supply lines
stretching deep into Mauretania and the Red Sea, northern Europe and the
Asian steppe, this removal was often a fact of purely physical dimensions.[87]

---

[76] Ioh. Chrys. Quod reg. 2.37 (Dumortier: 100). cf. Ambr. Ep. 56.6–7 (CSEL 82: 87).
[77] Ast. Am. Serm. 5.7 (Datema: 49).
[78] Talmud Bavli, *Ketubot*, 40a. BGU 3.913 (AD 206) a twenty-year-old girl was sold and called a κοράσιον. For κοράσιον as a virgin slave: Petsas *et al.* 2000, 42–3.
[79] Talmud Bavli, *Gittin*, 58a.   [80] Ioh. Chrys. Virgin. 67 (SC 125: 336–8).
[81] Ambr. Ep. 7.12 (CSEL 82: 48): *puellulas formae elegantioris.*
[82] Orib. Coll. Med. 14.48 (CMG 6.1.1: 221).
[83] Ioh. Chrys. Quod reg. 2.37 (Dumortier: 100): ὥστε διαγνῶναι καθάπερ ἐπὶ τῶν ὠνουμένων θεραπαινίδων, τίς μὲν ἡ διεφθαρμένη, τίς δὲ ἡ ἀνέπαφος.
[84] Talmud Bavli, *Kethub*, 40b.
[85] *Edictum de pretiis rerum venalium*, 29 (Giacchero: 208). See Harper 2010; Saller 2003, 202.
[86] Scheidel 1996b, 67–79.
[87] E.g. Amm. 20.6.7 (Seyfarth vol. 1: 196); Aug. Ep. 10* (CSEL 88: 46–51); Ioh. Chrys. Mut. Nom. 1.1 (PG 51: 115).

Even if the trip was shorter, the deracination of the slave was confirmed by the legal processes of the slave sale. Transcripts from Egyptian papyri show slaves being interrogated about their past, with a systematic silence about paternal descent.[88] Slaves were cut off from their male relatives.[89] Yet a woman's honor was guaranteed by her father or husband. Men were the "protectors" of female honor, and a woman without men was a "city without a wall," in Chrysostom's metaphor.[90] The state operated without a positive definition of sexual honor precisely because it was something protected by a family who could sue for its honor in court.

The slave market reduced the body to an object without privacy. It reduced virginity, which in a free woman was a mark of honor, into a commodity which could be bought and sold. It, as a matter of routine, separated slaves from the social bonds that provided protection and access to social honor. And yet we must qualify the claim that slaves had utterly no claim to social honor, for in fact slaves might enjoy, or suffer, a sort of conditional, reflective honor as members of the *familia*. As a representative of the family, he or she might be expected to behave in a way that acknowledged the master's complete control and reflected the master's reputation. The sexual behavior of female slaves was thought in particular to reflect the honorable comportment of the mistress. The household slaves who attended the mistress on public excursions were an extension of her self-presentation. "Mistresses too are judged by the habits of their slave-women."[91] The chastity of the female slaves in a household was an emanation of the great honor of the mistress. And since not a few slaves were the illegitimate children of the master, the idea of family honor had a basis in biological relationships.[92]

Roman law recognized that raping someone else's slave might represent not only an assault on his proprietary interests, but could even "upset the entire fortune of the household."[93] A law of AD 343 claimed that pagans were selling their Christian slaves into prostitution "as a sort of mockery."[94] Basil knew that "it is a great fault for even a slave-girl to fill the house with ruin by giving herself in secret marriage or to affront the owner wantonly through her debauched life."[95] Sexual dishonor among

---

[88] E.g. P. Herm. Rees 18 (323). Straus 2004, 62–71.   [89] Talmud Bavli, *Kiddushin*, 69a.
[90] Ioh. Chrys. Vid. 2.79–85 (SC 138: 118–20): πόλις ἀτείχιστος.
[91] Hier. Ep. 79.9 (CSEL 55: 97): *ex ancillarum quoque moribus dominae iudicantur.*
[92] cf. McGinn 1998, 288–319.   [93] Dig. 1.18.21: *ad totius domus eversionem.*
[94] CT 15.8.1 (AD 343): *ludibriis quibusdam.*
[95] Bas. Ep. 199.18 (Courtonne: 156): Μέγα μὲν ἁμάρτημα καὶ δούλην λαθραίοις γάμοις ἑαυτὴν ἐπιδιδοῦσαν φθορᾶς ἀναπλῆσαι τὸν οἶκον καὶ καθυβρίζειν διὰ τοῦ πονηροῦ βίου τὸν κεκτημένον.

the free women, he quickly added, was a much greater disgrace.[96] But in the narrow urban societies of the Mediterranean, a slave's licentiousness was felt as a stain on the free household.[97] An interesting sermon from Alexandria drew this distinction between the public and private sphere. At festivals and spectacles, the nude bodies of dishonored women were on display in frankly exhibitionist entertainments, but household slaves were part of the private sphere and no master "would tolerate a slave-woman to commit fornication."[98] If caught, she could expect the lash.[99]

Masters cared a great deal about the sexual behavior of their slave-women. Ambrose mentioned a recent case in which a slave-girl was inspected and convicted of wrongdoing. Her master wanted a second opinion, so he called in a "wealthy and most experienced midwife" to re-inspect her... and "even now her status as a virgin is unclear."[100] This slave-girl, who was repeatedly inspected to determine her sexual history, was mentioned as an offhand example. This sort of *realia* is normally filtered out of our sources, but the story simply assumes that a master would expect to know the sexual history of his slave-women. Between the lines of this story, we sense how the female slave's residual access to the family's honor was not exactly liberating.

To the extent that female slaves had access to family honor, that honor was conditional (it was at the master's discretion) and reflective (it was rooted in the family's honor, not the slave's). Once slaves had been purchased, they found themselves under the complete authority of their owner. The slave could not choose which orders to follow; otherwise it was "the most insolent offense."[101] Sex was simply a domestic service. Legally, the master had no inhibition to the sexual abuse of his slaves. Sexual access was part of his proprietary interest. In Artemidorus' interpretation, if a master dreamt he was having sex with his slaves, it was a good omen, since it indicated he was enjoying his property.[102]

The household and its property were the sexual domain of the *pater familias*. This was expressed in an architectural idiom that delineated the house as the sphere of his unlimited power. Lactantius might urge Christian men to restrict their sexual lives "not merely to the household walls, but

---

[96] Ioh. Chrys. Sac. 3.13 (SC 272: 210), an identical sentiment.
[97] cf. early-modern Venice: Romano 1996, 67.
[98] Ps.-Ath. Fall. Diab. 8 (Casey: 9): καὶ δούλην μὲν πορνεύουσαν οὐκ ἀνέχῃ.
[99] Ioh. Chrys. In Ephes. 15.3 (PG 62: 109–10).
[100] Ambr. Ep. 56.8 (CSEL 82: 88): *peritissima et locupleti femina huiusmodi artis . . . tamen adhuc manet quaestio.*
[101] Salv. Gub. 3.7 (MGH AA 1: 31): *insolentissima abusione.*
[102] Artem. 1.78 (Pack: 51–2). See Winkler 1990, 17–44.

to the marriage bed itself."[103] But as an interlocutor replied to Augustine: "Would you rather I sleep with someone else's wife? . . . can I not do what I want in my own house?"[104] That reply, with its infinite sense of patriarchal power behind the private walls, was simply a reflexive answer to the bishop's meddling. It also gives perfect expression to the ancient notion that male desire was a fixed quantity whose expenditure was inevitable – it was only a matter of whether it would be inflicted on honorable or dishonorable women.

The sources concentrate on the exploitation of female slaves, but we must remember that same-sex exploitation was not rare. In Roman conceptions of sexuality, indeed in many pre-Christian systems, the distinction between active and passive sexual roles was important, at times more decisive than the biological sex of the parties involved.[105] There is strong evidence for the idea that masculinity in sexual behavior was associated with being the penetrator, regardless of whether the penetrated person was a man, woman, or boy.[106] Public law prohibited the penetration of freeborn men, but sex with male slaves – so long as the master played the active role – seems to have been socially accepted and not uncommon.[107] There is evidence for the practice in late antiquity, including sex with the household eunuchs.[108]

The operations of a sexual affair were naturally considered an exercise of the master's power, and the slave's agency is hard to map.[109] Of course, some slaves were accused of using magic, and it is not impossible to imagine slaves benefiting within the household from an affair.[110] From Ambrose to Agathias, it was a trope that masters became enslaved by their beautiful slave-girls.[111] Chrysostom urged men against "becoming enslaved to three-obol slave-girls," spending the day near the wool and spindle, filling their souls with the "ways and voices" of women.[112] These warnings hardly reflect

---

[103] Lact. Inst. 6.23 (CSEL 19.1: 568): *non modo intra privatos parietes, sed etiam praescripto lectuli . . .*

[104] Aug. Serm. 224.3 (PL 38: 1095): *numquid ad uxorem alienam vado? . . . an non licet mihi facere in domo mea quae volo?* This line may not be authentically Augustinian, though it is no later than the fifth century: Lambot 1969. The arguments of Lambot are not convincing (the next line is *non licet, non licet, non licet* – the answer to the question). cf. Aug. Serm. 69.3 (PL 38: 441); Aug. Serm. 82.10–11 (PL 38: 511).

[105] Williams 2010; Parker 1997.   [106] Walters 1997.   [107] Williams 2010; Cervellera 1982.

[108] E.g. Cyr. *Sermon against the Eunuchs*, in Geor. Mon. Chron. (de Boor vol. 2: 651–2); Gr. Nyss. Benef. 105–6 (Hermes 105–6); Claud. In Eutrop. 1 lines 61–75, lines 341–5 (Hall: 145–6 and 156). Guyot 1980, 59.

[109] Nettis 2000 is unduly optimistic.

[110] Thdt. H. rel. 8.13 (SC 234: 400). Ioh. Chrys. In Ephes. 15.3 (PG 62: 109), "Thessalian." Possibly the subtext of Ps.-Bas. Sel. Vit. Thecl. 2.20 (Dagron: 344), as it was at 2.42 (Dagron: 400), an actress. A slave having an affair with the mistress would become puffed up: Hier. Ep. 79.8 (CSEL 55: 97).

[111] Ambr. Ep. 7.12 (CSEL 82: 48); Agath. in Anth. Gr. 5.302 (Beckh: 432).

[112] Ioh. Chrys. Subintr. 10.73 (Dumortier: 82): . . . κορῶν τριωβολιμαίων ἀναδεξώμεθα ὑπηρεσίαν . . . καὶ ἤθη καὶ ῥήματα γυναικεῖα.

a real, stable means for slaves to obtain informal status in a household. Rather, they were appeals for self-mastery in the lexicon of dominance and masculinity. The master's prerogative over sexual affairs was one-sided and arbitrary: he could "take whichever girl was first available to the raging fury of his lust."[113]

In the voluminous evidence for sexual relations between masters and slaves in the late empire, there is strikingly little indication of genuine, mutual affection, whatever that may mean under the circumstances of a vastly asymmetrical power relationship. Nothing is preserved in the voice of those who experienced the sexual powerlessness of slavery. In fiction women forced into prostitution showed some slight capacity to resist. These women coerced into sex, that is, women who were sentenced to prostitution, might use menstruation or sexual diseases – real or invented – as a means of avoidance or delay.[114] Often, the women in these narratives are miraculously rescued in the small space of time they have bought themselves; this is a fantastic projection against a grim reality. True stories of humiliation and resistance have been silenced. One insight into the emotional consequence of enslavement is what the Romans feared when they were captured. "If you were to ask what is the most lamentable thing about captivity, immediately, without even thinking about it, one answers the shameful violation of women."[115] The sad reflections on what would happen to "Roman women and children" captured by barbarians was informed by an awareness of what slaves in Roman society suffered.[116]

From the meager hints at our disposal, we could infer that slaves refused to internalize the meanings of honor and shame which prevailed amongst the free.[117] Perhaps the most authentic echo of a slave's voice is the saying preserved in Petronius' *Satyricon*, a fiction whose fierce satire gives it an invaluable realistic edge: "there's no shame in doing what the master orders."[118] Synesius called the slave-girl who stripped for the natives "bold," but her actions imply an entirely different valuation of bodily privacy, of honor and shame, than what was current in Synesius' own circles.[119] It is

---

[113] Salv. Gub. 7.4 (MGH AA 1: 87): *in quamcumque eos primum feminam ardens impudicitiae furor traxerat.* The lack of slave's agency may be behind the statement in Bas. Ep. 46.4 (Courtonne: 121).

[114] Pall. H. Laus. 65 (Butler vol. 2: 161–2).

[115] Lib. Or. 59.157–8 (Foerster vol. 4: 288): εἰ γάρ τις ἔροιτο ὁντινοῦν, τί μάλιστα βαρύτατον ἀνθρώποις τῶν εἰωθότων λυπεῖν ἐν αἰχμαλώτῳ τύχῃ, εὐθὺς ἂν οὐδὲν περισκεψάμενος εἴποι τὴν τῶν γυναικῶν αἰσχύνην.

[116] Amm. 31.8.7–8 (Seyfarth vol. 2: 177).   [117] Barton 2001, 11–12.

[118] Petron. Sat. 75.11 (Mueller: 74): *nec turpe est quod dominus iubet.* Andreau 1993, 176–8; Garnsey 1981; Veyne 1961.

[119] cf. Athen. Deip. 13.582d (Kaibel vol. 3: 283): τί δ᾽ αἰσχρόν, εἰ μὴ τοῖσι χρωμένοις δοκεῖ; On this especially witty remark (a line of Euripides placed on the lips of a courtesan, transmitted from Machon via Athenaeus), McClure 2003, 96–7.

those circles which have produced the surviving record. In Achilles Tatius'
novel, the heroine was kidnapped, enslaved, and subjected to a gruesome
scene of manipulation in which the master tried to make her acquiesce to
unwanted sex.[120] Facing imminent torture, she refused to submit, declaring
proudly that though she was a naked, helpless woman, her one weapon
was her "freedom," a most resonant word implying all at once her true
status, her sexual honor, and her final reserve of internal subjectivity.[121] It
is a powerful passage that, while fictitious, betrays an intimacy with this
scenario. But, ultimately, it is the story of an honorable woman mistaken
for a slave, and we simply lack insight into the ancient slave's experience of
sexuality.

If the slave possessed only minor capacities for resistance, the master's
power faced other limits. It is imperative to recognize the external web
of soft constraints on the master's power. Slave-owning was a domestic
enterprise, and the dynamics of power were refracted through all the human
relations of the household. It is hard to say just how much sexual access
sons were given to the slaves. Jerome, urging fellow Christians to join him
in asceticism, imagined that a young John the Baptist had chosen a life
of locusts and honey over the *domus* of his mother and father because
of the inevitable ruin of his chastity – by the slave-girls of the family.[122]
It is a revealing letter of a late antique ascetic, who saw the world as a
place of households filled with sexual temptations for young men. The
relationships between sons and slaves were played out against the more
primary loyalty between father and son. The declamatory exercises of
late antiquity drew their popularity from the depiction of realistic fields of
tension; like modern crime stories, they exaggerated real issues for dramatic
effect.[123] In declamation exercises, the son who fell in love with his father's
slave or concubine triggered an amusing and often lethal sequence of
events.[124] It is hard to see the truth behind this fictional curtain. At the least
it confirms that the interaction between sons and slaves was triangulated
by other members of the household, and this was not always a peaceable
process.

The most important complication in the slave-owner's sexual use of
slaves was the mistress of the household, the *mater familias*. The Roman
period was a time when the institution of marriage flourished.[125] Marriages

---

[120] Ach. Tat. 6.20.2 (Garnaud: 184).
[121] Ach. Tat. 6.22 (Garnaud: 185): τὴν ἐλευθερίαν. Morales 2004, 200–3; Shaw 1996.
[122] Hier. Ep. 125.7 (CSEL 56: 125); P. Pell. Euch. lines 159–75 (SC 209: 68–9).
[123] Russell 1983, 21–39.
[124] Sopat. Diar. 318 (RG 8: 78–9). Also other genres: Aristaen. Ep. 1.13 (Mazal: 31–4).
[125] See p. 286.

could be affectionate, erotic, or peaceful. But just beneath the calm surface there lies an inevitable and ongoing play of power within the household, not a sweeping revolution in human behavior. Chrysostom could shrewdly try to ward off sexual affairs by warning husbands of the "wars" which inevitably ensued, although he recognized this might be a feeble weapon in his arsenal of arguments for fidelity.[126] When Christian radicals would try to convince women to shun marriage, a principal argument was that marriage meant inevitable frustration over the sexual relations between a husband and the slaves.[127] The processes which governed the *formation* of marriages were not fundamentally rooted in the dynamics of love and attraction. The position of the wife was often assimilated to "a sort of slavery" in late antiquity, and wives were subordinate to their husbands in the conception and operation of a household.[128] The humiliating affairs of the husband with the slaves were part of the wife's enslavement.[129]

The status of the *mater familias* in a household was complex and variable. Even at a disadvantage, the wife was a free woman who could leverage informal sources of honor to claim a better position in the house.[130] She might depend on the respect for her father's family, her wealth, her physical attractiveness, or simply savvy marital diplomacy. But these could fail a woman because ultimately the equation of power was stacked against her. Chrysostom warned that many "beautiful" ladies would fail to capture the sexual attentions of their husbands, who would prefer much lower women.[131] And if she was rich, he warned, it meant an abundance of slaves, among whom there would inevitably be a pretty one. Even if all she caught was the master's attention, the mistress would become distressed.[132]

The delicate position of the *mater familias* gave the biblical story of Abraham a particularly strange resonance among the church fathers.[133] In late antiquity many Christian men, knowing their scripture, proffered the example of Abraham to meddling bishops, who were in turn very cautious with the story of a master who used his slave-woman.[134] Abraham was too comprehensible. But Sarah, to late antique men and women, was an uncanny and mysterious figure. "What woman ever did such a thing, and

[126] Ioh. Chrys. Propt. forn. 1.4 (PG 51: 214): πολέμους.
[127] Ioh. Chrys. Virgin. 40.1 and 67 (SC 125: 232 and 336–8).   [128] Clark 1998, 113.
[129] Ioh. Chrys. Propt. forn. 1.4 (PG 51: 214).   [130] Hier. Iov. 1.28 (PL 23: 261). Hezser 2005, 75.
[131] Ioh. Chrys. Virgin. 57.3 (SC 125: 310): σφόδρα κατὰ τὴν τοῦ σώματος ὥραν.
[132] Ioh. Chrys. Virgin. 67 (SC 125: 336–8).   [133] Ioh. Chrys. In Ephes. 20.6 (PG 62: 143–4).
[134] Ambr. Parad. 13.65 (CSEL 32.1: 324); Ambr. Abr. 1.4.23 (CSEL 32.1: 518); Aug. Faust. 22.25 (CSEL 25.1: 620).

advised her husband to do this, or made room in her marriage bed for the slave-woman?"[135] The ensuing discord between Sarah and Hagar was seized upon as a natural consequence of the affair. Gregory of Nyssa would say, conscientiously, "It is hard indeed for legitimate wives when a slave-woman is suspected of being involved with the master."[136]

The mistress was forced to monitor the female slaves to ward off affairs with her husband. She could ask him reproachfully, "What have you been talking about with the slave-girl?"[137] The control of the mistress over the slaves was violent, and it is easy to imagine the force of jealousy at work in her physical abuse of the slave-women. Chrysostom played on the vicious irony of the situation, asking why women beat their slaves so ferociously that the slaves' clothes came off and thus exposed naked flesh to the master.[138] One of the most sobering documents of the late empire is a fourth-century canon of the Christian church which stipulated what to do in the case where a woman, "aflame with the frenzy of jealousy," killed her slave-girl.[139]

The overriding impression of the sources is that within the great variety of outcomes for marriage, a common danger lurked in the very center of the institution. The household was the site of a complex power struggle that involved the sexual use of slaves. In the end a late antique woman had no choice but to bear with the situation, "for who ever heard of a man taken to court for being found with his slave-woman?"[140] Only in the middle of the fifth century would the Roman state admit that a woman had legitimate grounds for divorce if her husband fornicated with loose women "in contempt of his own house and wife, while she is looking on" – a weak limit indeed, but one that, merely by broaching the subject in public discourse, broke new legal ground.[141] The marital relation existed within a broader family network where surveillance and violence, patriarchal power and available bodies, were part of a game in which the rules were aligned against women.

---

[135] Ioh. Chrys. Hom. in Genes. 38.1 (PG 53: 351): Τίς γὰρ ἂν ἕλοιτο πώποτε γυνὴ τοῦτο ποιῆσαι, ἢ συμβουλεῦσαι τῷ ἀνδρὶ τοῦτο, ἢ τῇ παιδίσκῃ τῆς εὐνῆς παραχωρῆσαι;

[136] Gr. Nyss. In diem lum. 230 (Gebhardt 230): χαλεπὸν γὰρ ταῖς νομίμοις γυναιξὶν ὑποπτευομένη δούλη πρὸς τὸν δεσπότην.

[137] Hier. Iov. 1.47 (PL 23: 289): *quid cum ancillula loquebaris?*

[138] Ioh. Chrys. In Ephes. 15.3 (PG 62: 109–10).

[139] *Conc. Eliberritanum*, canon 5: *furore zeli accensa...* (Mansi vol. 2: 6). Stuiber 1978, 69–70. For a case in Brazil, Karasch 1987, 114.

[140] Aug. Serm. 9.4 (CC 41: 115): *adductum virum ad forum, quia inventus est cum ancilla sua, numquam audierunt...*

[141] CJ 5.17.8.2 (AD 449): *vel ad contemptum sui domi suae ipsa inspiciente.* Arjava 1996, 204.

These sorts of household contests were a reality across a wide stretch of the social scale. Among the rich, the sexual use of slaves was endemic. Salvian could ask, "in Aquitania, what rich and noble quarter of the city was not like a brothel? What rich or powerful man did not wallow in the mire of his lust? . . . many mistresses managed to keep their right of power, but failed to keep their right of marriage unpolluted."[142] The sexual use of slaves was also inseparable from a style of urban entertainment. Dinner parties remained an important aspect of civic sociability in late antiquity. Slaves were provided for the sexual enjoyment of the guests.[143] These parties of the rich excited the anger of Christian critics. Spokesmen of a new social consciousness, like Gregory of Nyssa, would point out that as people starved, the rich demanded oysters and shellfish, served on bejeweled tableware; the presence of household entertainers compounded the insult: "jesters and mimes and citharists and singers and delicate speakers and musicians and female musicians and dancing girls and every kind of licentiousness, boys with effeminate hair, shameless girls . . . "[144] The night-time air of the late antique city rang with the sounds of these affairs, with their raucous drinking and music, and, inevitably, the sexual use of slaves. We hear often of "flute girls," a sort of slave trained in musical arts and used in erotic contexts.[145] Augustine knew of one backsliding Christian, an eighty-four-year-old widower, who had lived in celibacy for twenty-five years before giving into temptation and buying a flute girl for his pleasure.[146]

Not only rich masters used slaves as their sexual objects. The sexual availability of slaves was a fact with reverberations far down the social scale.[147] The masters who freed their slaves in the village of Leukopetra, recorded in a series of third-century inscriptions, were certainly not Roman magnates. Yet they give cause for suspicion of sexual liaisons with their slaves: slave-women were often freed with their young children, and some of these children have the name of the master.[148] Augustine's most outspoken

---

[142] Salv. Gub. 7.3–4 (MGH AA 1: 86–7): *Apud Aquitanicas vero quae civitas in locupletissima ac nobilissima sui parte non quasi lupanar fuit? Quis potentum ac divitum non in luto libidinis vixit? . . . habuerunt quidem multae integrum ius dominii, sed nulla ferme impollutum ius matrimonii.*

[143] Eun. Vit. 10.5 (Giangrande: 73).

[144] Gr. Nyss. Benef. 105 (van Heck: 105): γελωτοποιούς, μίμους, κιθαριστάς, ᾠδούς, κομψολόγους, μουσικούς, μουσικάς, ὀρχηστρίδας, πάντα τῆς ἀσελγείας τὸν ὁρμαθόν, παῖδας θηλυνομένους ταῖς κόμαις, κόρας ἀναιδεῖς.

[145] Lib. Decl. 32.38 (Foerster vol. 7: 63–4); Bas. (dub.) Is. 5.158 (PG 30: 376–7); Procop. H. arc. 9.12 (Haury and Wirth vol. 3: 58); Aug. Serm. 153.6 (PL 38: 828); Ael. Ep. 19 (Leone: 21).

[146] Aug. Iul. 3.11.22 (PL 44: 713).

[147] E.g. Hier. Ep. 69.5 (CSEL 54: 688). For discussion, see chapter 11.

[148] ISMDA nos. 63, 128. See chapter 9.

denunciation of sex with slaves came not at Hippo or Carthage, but a place named "Chusa," which can no longer even be identified.[149] The sermon, preached in the name of correcting the *quotidiana peccata*, contained an extended diatribe against the sexual use of slaves. Augustine knew he was the outlier, even in what was presumably a rural society: "if he tumbles around with his slave-girls, he is loved, he is accepted with praise, and calamities are turned into jokes."[150]

"Tumble around:" the pejorative implication is that the master wasted his own time and wounded himself. There is disturbingly little notice of the intersubjective dynamics of the encounter. The psychological effects of institutionalized sexual abuse on the master are no less opaque to us than the effects on the slave. It is hard to characterize the emotional dimension of a practice that was such an important part of the total sexual landscape of late antiquity. The inconsequentiality of sex between masters and slaves and the mass availability of utterly powerless women was a fact of late antique life. A cynical maxim was that "the lower a girl, the easier to ruin."[151] Despite the recognition that sex with slaves was an achievement of no real distinction, young Christians would still boast of their "conquests" among the slave-girls. "He wallows in the filth of lust with many slave-girls, and not only is he not punished, but he is congratulated by his comrades. They take turns bragging, who had done it more, confessing with foolish, roaring laughter."[152]

The feelings of one master towards his slave, or freedwoman, were recorded in a poem that survives. Ausonius penned a few verses about his "little Suebian girl" Bissula and sent them to a friend.[153] The piece was a fawning hymn to his "young girl." Ausonius' appreciation was not subtle: "My precious, my charmer, my toy, my love, my lust! A barbarian, but even you, ingénue, trump the Latin dames! Bissula, a rough name for a soft girl, a little rude to those who don't know you, but delicious in your master's ears."[154] He was taken with the physical characteristics – "a face like lilies and roses" – that marked Bissula as a northern European. Ausonius had

[149] Aug. Serm. 9 (CC 41). The Augustinian sermon with the most MSS of all. The Lorsch MS identified its location, "*habitus Chusa*." Lambot, CC 41, 100–2.
[150] Aug. Serm. 9.12 (CC 41: 131): *si quis volutatus fuerit cum ancillis suis, amatur, blande accipitur, convertuntur vulnera in ioca.*
[151] Hier. Ep. 125.7 (CSEL 56: 125): *quantum vilior earum condicio tanto facilior ruina est.* Caes. Arel. Serm. 41.3 (CC 103: 182).
[152] Caes. Arel. Serm. 42.3 (CC 103: 187): *vir cum multis ancillis in libidinis cloaca volutetur, non solum non puniatur, verum etiam a suis similibus conlaudetur; et sibi invicem loquentes, quis hoc amplius fecerit, cum risu et cachinno stultissimo confitentur.*
[153] Auson. Biss. 2 (Green: 131).
[154] Auson. Biss. 5 (Green: 132): *Delicium, blanditiae, ludus, amor, voluptas/barbara, sed quae Latias vincis alumna pupas,/Bissula, nomen tenerae rusticulum puellae,/horridulum non solitis sed domino venustum.* The name Bissula may be obscene: Kurfess 1953, 263.

an exotic object that combined the ideology of victory over the barbarians, so central in Roman slavery, with the sexual fantasy of an aging courtier. The epigram seems to be an authentic transcript of verse composed for domestic performance. It casts a faint light on an obscure corner of late antique life, but one where the main lines of political ideology, cultural classicism, and social stratification merged.

Ausonius was a Christian and a married man. In late antiquity Christian bishops seized on the elements of Roman society that had for centuries valorized the marriage relationship as an essential part of the social edifice.[155] The church found society especially receptive in its desire to protect female chastity; if "shame" and "sin" belonged to different idioms of moral discourse, they could be reconciled in the greater project of protecting females.[156] Preaching pre-marital virginity and marital fidelity for women was the easy part. Male sexuality was more resistant to change. The grandson of Ausonius, Paulinus of Pella, could write a poem of thanksgiving to God in which he, at the age of eighty, looked back on his youthful failings with the slave-girls. Paulinus could take solace in the fact that he had avoided "willing offers from the freeborn and been content to use the attractions of slaves in my house. I preferred this peccadillo to criminal offense and feared lest my reputation be smirched."[157] Sex with slaves was inconsequential, a conscious alternative to illegal and problematic sex with free women. Paulinus added that he had never seen his illegitimate children, but the very act of calling attention to his offspring might be seen as a crack in the vaunted code of silence that operated in the Roman aristocracy. The laity could lack the sensitivity of their bishops towards sex that had long been permitted and even considered a morally sound alternative to violating free women.

Scholars working in the wake of Foucault have shown that pre-Christian sexuality was not an uninhibited garden waiting for Christian repression. Folklore and medical wisdom warned men against overexpenditure which might drain their vital spirit. Philosophy commanded them to master the desires seething within the physical body. The social etiquette of the upper classes taught men to approach sex, marital and otherwise, in an orderly fashion. These ideas about sexuality have been construed as an entire sexual culture, oriented towards care for the self, shaped by the self-presentation of the civic upper classes.[158] Yet all of these ideas were firmly rooted in a society

---

[155] Harper forthcoming a; Cooper 2007a.   [156] Clark 1991, 229–34.
[157] P. Pell. Euch. lines 165–72 (SC 209: 68–70): *et ingenuis oblatis sponte caverem, contentus domus inlecebris famulantibus uti, quippe reus culpae potius quam criminis esse/praeponens famaque timens incurrere damna . . .*
[158] Brown 1988, 5–32; Rousselle 1988; Foucault 1986.

where male sexuality was given free expression within socially approved channels. Self-"mastery" was the language of male restraint because it was ultimately the only limit imposed on men in such a society.

Status was the iron rule of ancient sexuality. Power, at the individual and social level, must be integral to the history of sex. For every bishop fulminating against fornication in late antiquity, or every poet celebrating erotic love, there were also ships criss-crossing the sea loaded with bodies for sale.[159] Those bodies belonged to humans removed from the basic structures of protection in an aggressive and cruel society. They were, in definition and fact, denied all access to social honor. The law ensured that those bodies were a designated repository for the dangers of male sexuality. Whatever new ideas came to surround the ethics of the sexual act, slavery was part of a simple formula. An exasperated bishop sensed that slavery was an invincible obstacle to sexual self-control, even in the heart of a believer. "Nothing is more lamentable or miserable than for objects of delight to be immediately at hand... The compulsion of lust travels in a moment."[160] But we must recognize that this image of sexual exploitation, as the subjective failure of the master's self-control, threatens to distract us from the carefully established role of this act in the social configuration of ancient sexuality.

FROM PRIVATE TO PUBLIC WOMEN: PROSTITUTION
IN LATE ANTIQUITY

A late antique novel told the story of Tarsia, a beautiful and noble girl who – as often happened to beautiful and noble girls in the novel – was kidnapped by pirates and sold into slavery. When a greedy pimp caught wind that this attractive young slave was for sale, he went to the auction. The prince of the city, however, also desired Tarsia. Soon, pimp and prince were waging a bidding war for the girl. As the price soared, the prince decided to let the pimp have her. "When he puts her in the brothel, I will go in first and snatch her *nodum virginitatis* at a low price, and it will be as if I had bought her."[161] The ancient novel was an imaginative genre, more romance than realism.[162] But the story of Tarsia lays bare the sinister material and mental

[159] Clem. Paed. 3.22.1 (SC 158: 52).
[160] Caes. Arel. Serm. 41.3 (CC 103: 183): *nimium plangenda et miseranda condicio est, ubi cito praeterit quod delectat... Sub momento enim libidinis impetus transit.*
[161] Hist. Apoll. Reg. Tyr. 33 (Kortekaas: 352): *cum ille eam in prostibulo posuerit, intrabo prior ad eam et eripiam nodum virginitatis eius vili pretio, et erit michi ac si eam emerim.*
[162] For the representation of sexuality in the novel, see esp. Cooper 1996; Goldhill 1995; Konstan 1994a. On the *Historia Apollonii*, see Kortekaas 2007; Konstan 1994b.

links that connected slavery and prostitution in the ancient Mediterranean. The brothel was, like the slave market, a place where the human body was for sale. Prostitutes, like slaves, were unprotected by the bonds of family or the laws of state that guarded free women. Prostitutes were legally and socially dishonored. But prostitution and slavery were not just similar. For many slaves, the brothel waited at the end of the trade.

The study of Roman prostitution in the last generation has emphasized that slavery was integral to the economy of prostitution.[163] Prostitutes were very often slave-women, purchased by pimps eager to profit off the highly remunerative business of venal sex. Prostitution recapitulated, in an especially violent form, the essential coercion of the slave system.[164] The fundamental discovery of the new research has been that ancient prostitution, far from something repressed or deviant, played a central, defining role in the construction of sexuality in the Roman period. As McGinn in particular has demonstrated, the prostitute was defined through a process of differentiation from respectable women. As the ideological reverse of the *mater familias*, the prostitute was the embodiment of sexual dishonor. This has an immediate consequence for the historian: virtually all the ancient sources about prostitution descend from a perspective that was complicit in this construction of the prostitute. Since it is impossible to gain access to real prostitutes through the extant sources, the historian is required instead to decode the complex symbolic representation of prostitution.[165]

The purpose of this section is to place late antique prostitution in the context of these insights.[166] Slaves remained crucial to the sex industry in late antiquity. Moreover, throughout the fourth century, prostitution continued to be a privileged symbolic field in which late antique men and women discussed the social dynamics of sexuality. But most profoundly, we need to explore the ways in which slavery and prostitution were ideologically *and* materially interconnected. It was not a figure of speech when Chrysostom claimed, over and over again, that it was wrong for a man to have sex "with a slave-girl or a public whore." Slaves and prostitutes occupied the same role in the social mechanics of Roman sexuality, as the approved outlet for male sexual energies.[167] Their inherent sexual dishonor made prostitutes and slaves the solution to the dangerous problem of inevitable male sexual desire.

---

[163] Hezser 2005, 179–86; McGinn 2004 and 1998; Flemming 1999; Stumpp 1998; Sicari 1991; Leontsini 1989; Hirter 1960.

[164] McGinn 2004, 74; Flemming 1999, 58.   [165] McGinn 1998, 9.

[166] Late antique prostitution: Neri 1998, 200–33; Leontsini 1989.

[167] For the antiquity of this connection, Citti 1997.

The Roman prostitute was effectively the opposite of the honorable woman, the *mater familias*, in the civil law.[168] In Roman society the role of the *mater familias* was also constructed in opposition to the slave. The slave was an equally important, and in many ways more immediate, ideological foil to the *mater familias*. The resolution of this duality is plain: the *mater familias* was a woman with honor, while the prostitute and the slave were quintessentially without honor. The system of female sexual honor worked along a single spectrum. The free, honorable, sexually modest woman was at one end, while at the other was the dishonored, unfree, and sexually available woman. These attributes were integrated so that the honorable woman was described as free, the dishonored woman as unfree and promiscuous. Chrysostom, for instance, regularly contrasted the bodies of prostitutes with the bodies of *free* women: they were conceptual opposites.[169] The polarity between the free woman and the prostitute shows that the construction of sexual honor conflated legal status and sexual modesty. Nothing brings this out more clearly than the usage of the word "free woman," *eleuthera*, as a standard equivalent for respectable woman or wife.[170]

Recognizing this ideological equation between slaves and prostitutes helps us catch the fine register of the late Roman sexual idiom. As we have seen, in the fifth-century *Life and Miracles of Thekla*, the heroine's mother criticizes Thekla for acting like a prostitute or slave-girl instead of preserving her honor for "a marriage worthy of her patrimony."[171] The phrase shows us the binarism between patrimonial marriage for free and honorable women, on the one hand, and sexual promiscuity for unfree and publicly available women, on the other. Libanius likewise equated freedom, marriage, and honor in opposition to prostitution.[172] Roman lawyers assumed that the sexual honor of a *mater familias* would be socially visible by the clothes she wore, in distinction to the slavish or whorish dress of dishonorable women.[173] Mediterranean society under Roman rule had

---

[168] See chapter 11.
[169] Ioh. Chrys. Quod reg. 7.62 (Dumortier: 120); Ioh. Chrys. In Mt. 6.8 (PG 57: 72); Ioh. Chrys. Non iter. conj. lines 96–9 (SC 138: 168).
[170] Call. Vit. Hyp. 18.3 (SC 177: 182); Ioh. Mosch. Prat. 188 (PG 87c: 3065); Iambl. Vit. Pyth. 31.187 (Klein: 137); Pall. H. Laus. 17.6–9 (Butler vol. 2: 44); cf. Vivian, *Four Desert Fathers*, 106, for a Coptic equivalent. The sense of *eleuthera* as "marriageable or respectable woman" goes back to classical Greece: recognized by Omitowoju 2002, 88, 101, 206–7.
[171] Ps.-Bas. Sel. 1.12 (Dagron 216): πάτριον ἀρνησαμένη γάμον.
[172] Lib. Decl. 25.14 (Foerster vol. 6: 476). Also in Hier. Zach. 2.8 (CC 76A: 807) *mancipium* and *scortum* are generically associated with sexual dishonor.
[173] Ulpian in Dig. 47.10.15.15, with McGinn 1998, 160.

Table 7.1 *The binary division of female sexuality*

Sexuality structured by marriage	Sexuality structured outside marriage
Able to beget heirs	Not able to beget legitimate offspring
Modest	Promiscuous
Free	Servile

internalized a binary ideology that conflated eligibility for marriage, sexual honor, and social status (table 7.1).

The ideological association between slavery and prostitution makes it difficult to say how many prostitutes were legally slaves. Prostitutes were dishonored, whatever their legal status. If a slave-woman or prostitute conceived a child, it was in either case "shameful to you, a crime against the child, illegitimate because of you and poorly born."[174] Even if the father left the child money, "it is dishonored in the house, dishonored in the city, dishonored in the courts, both the child of a prostitute and of a slave."[175] Moreover, prostitution in many societies involves a degree of coercion that blurs the line between the woman's agency in becoming a prostitute and outright enslavement by the pimp. It is thus that, linguistically, materially, and conceptually, freedom and honor were conflated, while at the other end slavery, dishonor, and sexual availability converged.

The ancient evidence, which descends unanimously from the honorable classes, has been scrubbed of the details of life that would give direct access to the practice of ancient prostitution. But there is enough credible evidence to recognize the material connection between slavery and prostitution. The integration of the slave trade and the sex trade in the Roman empire was not merely imagined somewhere in the blind contempt of the upper classes; it was disturbingly real. The fictional scene in the slave market of Mytilene was a glimpse of the pimp at work.[176] The pimp was imagined as an owner, the *vilicus* as the manager. Though the *History of Apollonius* was a novel, it is one of the few representations of a pimp to survive and cannot be dismissed out of hand. Augustine delivered a sermon in which he momentarily addressed his discourse to pimps, calling them men who

174 Ioh. Chrys. In Rom. 24.3 (PG 60: 626): σὲ ᾔσχυνε, καὶ αὐτὸ ἠδίκηται διὰ σὲ νόθον καὶ δυσγενὲς γενόμενον.
175 Ioh. Chrys. In Rom. 24.3 (PG 60: 626): ἄτιμος ἐν οἰκίᾳ, ἄτιμος ἐν πόλει, ἄτιμος ἐν δικαστηρίῳ, καὶ ὁ ἐκ πόρνης καὶ ὁ ἐκ δούλης.
176 IG 14.2000 for a merchant of beauty. Clem. Paed. 3.22.1 (SC 158: 52).

"buy girls to prostitute them."[177] The purchase of women was, in his mind, a paradigmatic action of the pimp. A fifth-century rhetor, Syrianus, was offended that pimps gave their prostitutes the names of the muses.[178] Naming slaves was a definitive expression of the master's power, and thus another small, casual clue that many prostitutes were slaves.[179]

The auction block was not the only place to acquire slaves. Child exposure and captivity were two important sources of enslavement, and both could lead directly to the brothel. Christian authors warned against the exposure of infants, pointing out that the brothel was a natural destination for exposed children.[180] They conjured awful scenes of unwitting incest.[181] Though lurid and dramatic, the warnings presume that pimps would harvest bodies in order to prostitute them. Epiphanius spoke of a woman who was a prostitute and a captive – which he used as synonyms.[182] Any time an encounter with a prostitute was described in detail, the pimp appeared as an intermediary. Some Arians in Antioch tried to frame a bishop with a prostitute, and when it became a public scandal, only the pimp could resolve who had actually ordered the prostitute's services.[183] In a late antique joke, a man who wanted to sleep with a black prostitute asked the pimp, "how much do you charge for the night [i.e. the black one]?"[184] The situation suggests the importation of slaves.[185]

The sale of children into prostitution by their parents was another way in which the freeborn poor could have entered prostitution.[186] In a fourth-century papyrus, a poor elderly woman sued an Alexandrian councilor who murdered her daughter. The woman, grievously poor, had given her daughter to a pimp in return for sustenance. The transmission of her daughter to the pimp was a type of black-market transaction that would render the girl's legal status hard to classify; in late antiquity, the state struggled, largely without success, to maintain workable public rules in this arena of tangled social conflict.[187] The prostituted Alexandrian girl was never said to be a slave, but she was dishonored, deprived of modesty, and offered to everyone, "like a corpse."[188] The life of shame, like the life of slavery, entailed social death.

---

[177] Aug. Psalm. 128.6 (CC 40: 1885): *emens puellas ad prostitutionem.*
[178] Syrian. Comm. Herm. 44 (Rabe vol. 2: 44).
[179] Ioh. Chrys. Mut. Nom. 3.3 (PG 51: 115).   [180] Lact. Inst. 6.20 (CSEL 19.1: 559).
[181] Boswell 1988, 157. Tert. Apol. 9.18 (CC 1: 105); Clem. Paed. 3.21.5 (SC 158: 50).
[182] Epiph. Haer. 2.4, 3.10 (GCS 37: 17, 20).   [183] Ath. H. Ar. 20 (Opitz: 193).
[184] Philogel. 151a (Thierfelder: 82): Πόσου τὴν νύκτα μισθοῖς;
[185] For black slaves in late antiquity, see chapter 2.   [186] Hirter 1960, 78–9.   [187] See chapter 10.
[188] BGU 4.1024: ὡς νεκρά. Whether these were true crime stories or legal records is unclear. Keenan 1989, 15–23, is skeptical, Bagnall 1996, 196–8, more confident. Vuolanto 2003, 177.

John Chrysostom imagined a similar case in which a girl was sold into prostitution by her parents. If a parent sold a daughter to a pimp in order to prostitute her, and someone (in Chrysostom's metaphor, Jesus) then came along and redeemed her from that "slavery," the parents could no longer keep her in the brothel: "you have given her away, once and for all, and you have sold her."[189] Certainly this was a metaphor freighted with spiritual meaning, but it is nevertheless revealing that selling a daughter into prostitution came to mind as the perfect example of a parent's complete cessation of control over the daughter. Even for a freeborn girl, the entrance to the brothel was a passage into slavery.

One striking confirmation of the deep relationship between the slave trade and the flesh trade is the sudden realization, by bishops of the late fourth century, that it was problematic to describe as a "sin" the actions of those who lacked free will.[190] Basil of Caesarea was the first to evince awareness of this problem. "For while the slave-woman who was sold to a pimp is in sin by necessity, she who happens to belong to a well-born mistress was raised with sexual modesty, and on this account the one is forgiven, the other condemned."[191] "Sexual violations which occur through necessity are to be without blame."[192] Remarkably, these sentiments would come to affect imperial law, and a series of measures beginning in AD 428 sought to eliminate *coerced* prostitution, specifically including the prostitution of slaves.[193] The campaign reached a pitch under Justinian, who even commissioned an investigation into the flesh industry and found that it was still deeply intertwined with the slave trade.[194]

Ancient prostitution has left behind scant documentary evidence, but an intriguing papyrus hints at the complexity of the business and the role of slaves as prostitutes. The document concerned two pimps who owed a debt at Arsinoe in 265. The text is too fragmentary to allow a precise reconstruction of what happened, but pimps had been hired to run a brothel. The pimps not only owed money, they had sold off

---

[189] Ioh. Chrys. In 1 Cor. 18.2 (PG 61: 147): ἅπαξ γὰρ ἔδωκας καὶ ἐπώλησας.

[190] Glancy 1998, on the failure of the early church to confront the problem directly; Laiou 1993, esp. for later periods (and noting Basil's importance).

[191] Bas. Psalm. 32.5 (PG 29: col. 336): ἡ μὲν γὰρ πορνοβοσκῷ πραθεῖσα πρὸς ἀνάγκην ἐστὶν ἐν τῇ ἁμαρτίᾳ. ἡ δὲ εὐθὺς ἀγαθῆς δεσποίνης ἐπιτυχοῦσα συνεξετράφη τῇ παρθενίᾳ, διὰ τί αὕτη μὲν εὐηργετήθη, ἐκείνη δὲ κατεδικάσθη.

[192] Bas. Ep. 199.49 (Courtonne: 164): Αἱ πρὸς ἀνάγκην γενόμεναι φθοραὶ ἀνεύθυνοι ἔστωσαν.

[193] CT 15.8.2 (AD 428); Nov. Theod. 18 (AD 439); CJ 11.41.7 + CJ 1.4.14 (AD 457–68).

[194] Esp. Nov. Just. 4 (AD 535). These laws, often mischaracterized as a campaign against prostitution *per se*, occurred after the time-frame of this book but will be the subject of a future study by the author.

"a slave-woman, Kanthara," against orders.[195] It is a documentary confirmation of what novels, sermons, and folklore said about the status of women in prostitution. Yet the most evocative piece of evidence about the status of prostitutes in late antiquity is an artifact of North Africa. An iron slave-collar from Bulla Regia survives with the inscription, "I am a slutty prostitute. Retain me if I flee."[196] This fourth-century relic is a chilling confirmation that the life of prostitution was enforced within the entire apparatus of the master's power which rested, ultimately, on brute physical coercion, sanctioned by the public legitimacy of the slave regime.

Because of the nature of our evidence and the legal grey areas involved, it is not possible to guess in any meaningful sense what proportion of prostitutes were slave or free. The bulk of the evidence points towards the use of slaves, but the evidence is not a straightforward representation of reality. Moreover, there was a trend, particularly by the sixth century, towards representing poor women as prostitutes.[197] This, too, was certainly driven by the Christian ideological attention towards the poor and the church's construction of prostitution in particular.[198] There is reason to be pessimistic about the possibility of describing the realities of ancient prostitution.

The integration of sexual honor and legal status meant that this construction of sexual honor could extend far down the social scale. Certainly the elite and middle strata of society looked with suspicion on the sexual honor of the poor.[199] Though the self-perception and self-construction of the poor is largely hidden from the historical record, there is every reason to believe that, as in other slave systems, the poor clung ferociously to their free status and the sexual honor that accompanied it. In a revealing passage, John Chrysostom imagined the bitter jealousy that would fester in the minds of the decent poor, looking at the profits made by prostitutes who were the children of cooks, leatherworkers, or slaves. The poor man would grumble to himself, "I am a free man and freeborn. I have chosen decent labor, but I couldn't dream of such luxury."[200]

The affinity between prostitution and slavery also animated the terminology of the "public" whore. The word "public" was frequently paired with

---

[195] PSI 9.1055: δούλην ὄνομα Κανθάραν.
[196] ILS 9455: *adultera meretrix. tene me quia fugivi de Bulla R(e)g(ia).* The combination *"adultera meretrix"* is difficult. A slave obviously could not commit legal adultery. Here it is most likely used as a denigrating sexual insult, which I have tried to render by translating it as "slutty."
[197] But cf. Stumpp 1998, 37–42; Hirter 1960, 78.
[198] Brown 2002 and chapter 1.   [199] McGinn 1998, 28.
[200] Ioh. Chrys. In Mt. 69.4 (PG 58: 645): ἐγὼ δὲ ἐλεύθερος καὶ ἐξ ἐλευθέρων, δικαίους πόνους αἱρούμενος, οὐδὲ ὄναρ ταῦτα φαντασθῆναι δύναμαι.

the word "prostitute," and it was not simply an insult. It was a linguistic recognition of the fact that public prostitutes were an alternative to private slaves. For example, when Augustine enumerated the desires of the worldly man, prostitution was high on the list. The man would want, along with victory for the Roman army and general prosperity, "public prostitutes for any who wish to use them, but especially those who cannot afford private ones."[201] For Salvian, the houses of the rich were *like* brothels, because of the way that men used their slaves.[202] The brothel, on the other hand, was dirty, better suited for a poor clientele who could not afford to buy sex in the form of slaves.[203] Prostitution was the poor man's piece of the slave system.[204] The brothel was even patronized by slave men.[205] The language of "public prostitute" reflected the functional equivalence of prostitution and slavery in the economy of sexual honor.

Because the prostitute embodied female sexual promiscuity, prostitution acquired a significant symbolic place in the discourse of sexuality. Insofar as antiquity developed an articulate social theory of sexuality, one of its central tenets was that prostitution was a necessity. Rather, male desire was a necessity – "the necessity" was a nickname for the penis – and the exploitation of dishonored women was the correlate of this inevitable sexual energy.[206] In a famous anecdote, Cato the Elder, model of Roman virtue, congratulated an acquaintance exiting the brothel for avoiding other men's wives.[207] Cato enunciated the twin principles which justified the role of prostitution in the economy of sexual desire: male desire was an inevitable, dangerous quantity that had to be spent, and dishonored women were the solution to this threat. Just as revealing, a scholiast could not resist making an addendum to the anecdote, "Later, when Cato saw the young man leaving from that brothel often, the story goes that he said, 'Young man, I praised you for coming here sometimes – not for living at the place!'"[208] The story is a paradigm for the interface between pre-Christian attitudes towards sex and the social background to those ideas: the culture

[201] Aug. Civ. 2.20 (CC 47: 52): *abundent publica scorta vel propter omnes, quibus frui placuerit, vel propter eos maxime, qui habere privata non possunt.*
[202] Salv. Gub. 7.3 (MGH AA 1: 87).
[203] Flemming 1999, 45. "Poor": Petr. Alex. Div. 58 (Pearson and Vivian: 120).
[204] Stumpp 1998, 26–7.
[205] Procop. H. arc. 9.10 (Haury and Wirth vol. 3: 57). Ioh. Chrys. In Hebr. 15.3 (PG 63: 121). Flemming 1999, 45; Stumpp 1998, 176–9.
[206] Artem. 1.45 (Pack: 51–2): ἀναγκαῖον καλεῖται.
[207] Hor. Sat. 1.2 (Keller and Holder vol. 2: 14–15).
[208] Ps.-Acro. 1.2 (Keller vol. 2: 20): *postea cum frequentius eum exeuntem de eodem lupanari vidisset, dixisse fertur, adulescens ego te laudavi, tamquam huc intervenires, non tamquam hic habitares.*

of moderation coexisted organically with the exploitation of dishonored women.

The idea that prostitution held together a delicate balance of dangerous forces found echoes in the folk legend of the prostitute Lais. This semi-mythical figure was the most famous prostitute of antiquity and still provoked considerable interest in the late empire.[209] She had, the story went, become so popular amongst the young men of Corinth that she was a drain on the economic resources of the city. She was banished, but the youth simply turned their predatory sexuality on the free women of the city; the domino effect of honor killings depopulated Corinth. The proposed legislation to reintroduce her provided ancient orators with rich imaginary material for thinking about the role of prostitution in the ancient city.[210] The entire premise of the legend was that prostitution, however infelicitous, was safer than the alternative, a world in which competitive male sexuality threatened to boil over into incurable social violence.

Christian reformers clearly recognized the traditional social role of prostitution. Ambrose was frustrated that men felt virtuous for sparing other men's wives, while using the brothel "like a law of nature."[211] Salvian, in four words, has left the pithiest description of Roman sexual policy: forbidding adulteries, building brothels.[212] The double standard of sexual behavior was built into a patriarchal society, but the importance of the civil law in shaping these norms was unmistakable. Salvian was far from the only bishop to feel challenged by the weight of Roman law. Augustine's parishioners justified their behavior by appealing to the law. His only retort was that they should obey the law of heaven, not the law of the forum.[213] Lactantius pleaded for the superiority of divine over Roman law.[214] Ordinary Christians defended themselves against the moralizing of their bishops by appealing to the law.[215] The legality of prostitution solidified the use of the brothel into a moral right.

There is no stronger indication of the power of this ideology than the reception it received among some Christian intellectuals. One of the

[209] Geyer 1924, cols. 513–16. Lib. Decl. 25 (Foerster vol. 6: 470 f.); Iul. Imp. Or. 7.20 (Rochefort: 72–3); Auson. Epig. 18 (Green: 71); Synes. Ep. 3 (Garzya: 7); Steph. Ethn. 285, 382, and 647 (Meineke: 285, 382, 647); Aristaen. Ep. 1.1 (Mazal: 1); Agath. Anth. Gr. 5.302 (Beckby: 432).
[210] Lib. Decl. 25 (Foerster vol. 6: 470).
[211] Ambr. Abr. 2.11.78 (CSEL 32.1: 631): *tamquam naturae legi.*
[212] Salv. Gub. 7.22 (MGH AA 1: 101–2): *adulteria vetantes, lupanaria aedificantes.*
[213] Aug. Serm. 153.6 (PL 38: 828); Caes. Arel. Serm. 43.4 (CC 103: 191–2).
[214] Lact. Inst. 6.23 (CSEL 19.1: 565).   [215] Ioh. Chrys. Propt. forn. 1.4 (PG 51: 213–14).

most lucid statements of the social role of prostitution was Augustine's explanation in the *De ordine*:

What could claim to be more filthy and more worthless, more full of shame and defilement, than prostitutes and pimps and other pests of this kind? But take whores out of human affairs, and you will overturn everything because of lusts. Put them in the place of matrons, and you will ruin honor with fallenness and disgrace. Thus, they represent the most impure part of mankind by their habits and the most vile condition in the laws of order. Are there not in the bodies of living things certain parts which, if you tried to consider only these, you couldn't stand it? Nevertheless, the order of nature did not wish for things that are necessary to be lacking, but neither did it allow them, as they are dishonorable, to be conspicuous. Still, these imperfections, by holding their place, concede the better part to their superiors.[216]

For Augustine, prostitution was necessitated by the social mechanics of desire. He was merely expressing a conservative view of prostitution, embedded in Roman law, traditional in ancient thought. Prostitution was necessary for a greater order to prevail. Matrons enjoyed their place in society because prostitutes deflected dangerous lusts away from honorable women.[217] The "laws of order" were the foundation of the system. Augustine, no stranger to the world of procured sex, had a robust appreciation for the violent forces that prostitution held in check. If prostitutes were to be removed from society, not just the honor of free women, *everything* would be thrown into confusion. Men in late antiquity felt that, between

---

[216] Aug. Ord. 2.4.12 (CC 29: 114): *quid sordidius, quid inanius, dedecoris et turpitudinis plenius meretricibus lenonibus ceterisque hoc genus pestibus dici potest? aufer meretrices de rebus humanis, turbaveris omnia libidinibus; constitue matronarum loco, labe ac dedecore dehonestaveris. sic igitur hoc genus hominum per suos mores impurissimum vita, per ordinis leges condicione vilissimum. nonne in corporibus animantium quaedam membra, si sola adtendas, non possis adtendere? tamen ea naturae ordo nec, quia necessaria sunt, deesse voluit nec, quia indecora, eminere permisit. quae tamen deformia suos locos tenendo meliorem locum concessere melioribus.*

[217] McGinn 2004, 99–105, has adduced this passage of Augustine as an example of Christian advocacy for zoning. But this is to read later history into the passage. Augustine, employing an old metaphor of the body, said that prostitution had its *locus*. There is nothing to suggest he means this in a spatial sense; it is apparent that he means it has its *locus* in the social order (specifically, if prostitutes were given *the place* of free women – clearly neither in a corporal nor an urban-planning sense). In the passage, the social order is considered vertically, and prostitutes have their place at the bottom. Prostitutes concede the "better place" to their superiors – honorable women, who "are eminent." This does not mean that prostitution should be limited to particular quarters, just that prostitution allows honorable women to keep their honor and remain atop society. The passage in Aug. Civ. 14.18 (CC 48: 41), only says that sex with prostitutes is hidden, in precisely the same way that married intercourse was hidden. Other evidence is late: the tenth-century Patr. Const. 2.65 (Preger: 185–7), credits Constantine with establishing a brothel in the Zeugma district and limiting prostitution to this quarter. McGinn 2004, 93, this "defies belief." Dagron 1984, 139: "folklore."

continence and chaos, the sexual exploitation of dishonored women offered the only pragmatic choice.

PACTS OF LUST: CONCUBINAGE IN LATE ANTIQUITY

Concubinage in the Roman period was a peculiar institution, and unfortunately the Romans have left no systematic discussion of its conventions.[218] Concubinage was a refinement within a system where social honor demarcated the boundary between reproductive and recreational sex. Still, concubinage could mean different things in the Roman world, largely because it was defined in distinction to marriage.[219] The label of "concubinage" encompassed various types of non-marital partnerships. In the early empire, the prohibition of marriage for soldiers and the widespread lack of citizenship amongst the provincial inhabitants of the empire threw up considerable obstacles to legitimate marriage, *conubium*, in the Mediterranean.[220] In the late empire, when soldiers could marry and citizenship was universal, concubinage became ever more narrowly associated with partnerships between free men and low-status women forged for sexual, rather than procreative, aims. This form of concubinage, which we are concerned with here, can only be understood within the economy of sexual honor.

The role of concubinage in Roman society can be teased out by comparison with other forms of sexual encounter, namely marriage, slavery, and prostitution. Marriage was aimed at procreation; concubinage was meant to avoid reproduction. Roman marriage, though, was legally formless, in that it required neither document nor ceremony. The relative status of the partners might be the signal distinction between marriage and concubinage. In practice, a concubine was distinguished from a wife by the *tabulae coniugales* and the *iura dotalia*.[221] The wording of marriage contracts officially included the language *procreandorum liberorum causa*, while concubines were expected not to bear children.[222] Concubinage was meant to avoid producing *heirs*. Ancient birth control was imperfect, and concubines might become pregnant. "Whatever children these concubines conceive are born not free, but as slaves. And even after they're freed, they are not allowed to accept the inheritance of the father by any right or ordinance. So see whether it can be without sin, that the offspring

---

[218] Friedl 1996; McGinn 1991; Treggiari 1981, 59–81; Rawson 1974 marked a new era in the study of concubinage; Meyer 1895. For late antiquity, see Arjava 1996, 205–17, and Shanzer 2002.

[219] Friedl 1996, 45.   [220] Friedl 1996 emphasizes the impediments to marriage in the high empire.

[221] Hier. Ep. 69.5 (CSEL 54: 688). cf. Goody 1990, 406, 418.

[222] Aug. Conf. 4.2 (CC 27: 41), discussed on p. 319.

of noble blood is dishonored, or that from the finest of men slaves are born."[223] The production of illegitimate children was the unintended side effect of concubinage, but by law it was not allowed to interfere with the inheritance.[224]

The line between concubinage and the sexual use of household slaves is harder to distinguish. When late antique men spoke, the two practices were often blurred.[225] The same arbitrary use of power was at work. For an extreme example, a concubine might be casually swapped around in the household. In one fictional vignette, a doctor examined a man's ill son only to find the true cause of his malady: a crush on his father's concubine. This good doctor managed to obtain the only cure. He convinced the father to give way to the boy with the concubine.[226] Concubines, as slaves, might also be traded around for sale on the market: the wife of the emperor Justin, Lupicina, was purportedly concubine to several men before rising to the level of empress.[227] This was invective, but what made it doubly vicious was the claim that she was forced to be the lover of several men prior to Justin. It is impossible to know the extent to which the upper-class bias against pre-owned women affected men of middling social rank.

What separated concubinage from the straightforward sexual access of a master to his slaves was that concubinage was an informal pact, a more enduring and even semi-public relationship between the two unequals. We catch something of this public aspect in a bishop's vitriol towards the institution: concubinage is worse than adultery because it was done "with an impudent face while the whole populace looks on."[228] In a world that carefully sequestered its women behind private walls, it is hard to understand exactly how a concubine, as opposed to a wife or a slave, was open to public knowledge, though it is not impossible to imagine they could act as escorts in public or during social outings. Sex with slaves was a private use of mere property, while having a concubine was an

---

[223] Caes. Arel. Serm. 42.5 (CC 103: 188): *ut quoscumque ipsae concubinae conceperint, non liberi, sed servi nascantur. Unde etiam post acceptam libertatem hereditatem patris nulla lege et nullo ordine accipere permittuntur. Et iam videte utrum sine peccato esse possit, ubi decus generosi sanguinis ita humiliatur, ut de hominibus nobilissimis servi nascantur.*

[224] After Constantine: see chapter 11.

[225] Hier. Iov. 1.44 (PL 23: 287); Hier. Ep. 69.5 (CSEL 54: 688); Gr. Nyss. In cant. 15.6.8 (Langerbeck: 462–5); Ast. Soph. Psalm. 11.9 (Richard: 80); Aug. Epist. 259.3 (CSEL 57: 612–13); Salv. Gub. 4.5 (MGH AA 1: 40).

[226] Aristaen. 1.13 (Mazal: 34), obviously fictional.

[227] Procop. H. arc. 6.17 (Haury and Wirth vol. 3: 41). Tendentious but revealing that she was called a δούλη τε καὶ βάρβαρος.

[228] Caes. Arel. Serm. 43.4 (CC 103: 191–2): *fronte inpudentissima . . . toto populo vidente.*

acknowledged relationship. It was even possible to seek public penalties against a concubine who was guilty of infidelity.[229]

Concubinage was analogous to prostitution, except that the concubine was privately held and unique to the master. "Someone will say, 'but she is not a prostitute, she is my concubine.' Do you have a wife, you who say this? 'I have.' So she is a prostitute. She is a prostitute whoever she is... *Non licet, non licet, non licet.* They are all going to hell."[230] Despite Augustine's vituperation, it was not uncommon to regard concubinage as a lesser evil than prostitution. In a world saturated with dishonored, available women, concubinage was regarded as a tidy, temperate alternative to prostitution.[231] Salvian of Marseilles would say, tongue in cheek, that "in comparison concubinage may seem a kind of chastity, since this means to be content with a few wives and to contain the bridles of lust in a set number of women."[232] But he was merely giving a hostile expression to what many men actually thought. For John Chrysostom, concubinage was an instance of mistaking vice and virtue.[233] Continence, of course, was not a uniquely Christian virtue. The rhetor Libanius would brag that as a youth he had avoided what was not easy to avoid, namely the sort of revelry that involved hired sex.[234] But it was known that he had a concubine. Sexual restraint is a relative concept, and it is one of the more subtle clues to the overwhelming availability of sex with dishonored women that concubinage was reckoned a form of moderation.

Concubinage was distinct from marriage by its function: it was a recreational rather than a reproductive partnership. It was distinct from prostitution and slavery by its form. This explains how a figure like Lais, that mythical icon of sensuality in antiquity, could be spoken of as a slave, a prostitute, and a concubine in one breath. Synesius claimed that the *cursus honorum* of Lais began with her origins as a slave from Sicily, continued with a term as concubine to a ship-captain and subsequently to an orator, then included a period as concubine to a fellow slave, until finally she plied her trade around town as a prostitute.[235] Slavery, concubinage, and prostitution were indistinct points on the continuum of sexual dishonor.

---

[229] Dig. 48.5.14.

[230] Aug. Serm. 224.3 (PL 38: 1095): *dicere habet nescio quis, "sed meretrix non est, concubina mea est." Habes uxorem, qui hoc dicis? "Habeo." Illa ergo velis nolis meretrix est... non licet, non licet, non licet. In gehennam eunt.* See p. 302, on the transmission of this sermon.

[231] Arjava 1996, 209.

[232] Salv. Gub. 4.5 (MGH AA 1: 40): *hoc in comparatione supradictorum flagitiorum quasi genus est castitatis uxoribus paucis esse contentum et intra certum coniugum numerum frenum libidinum continere.*

[233] Ioh. Chrys. In act. Apost. 48.3 (PG 60: 336).

[234] Lib. Or. 1.22 (Foerster vol. 1: 93); Lib. Or. 2.12 (Foerster vol. 1: 243).

[235] Synes. Ep. 3 (Garzya: 7).

The links between slavery and concubinage were not merely ideological. The sources of the late empire suggest that many if not most concubines were slaves or freedwomen. Concubinage was thus a direct continuation of the master's power. "My slave-woman is my concubine."[236] The relationship between a man and his concubine was an affair of asymmetrical power. Christian opponents of concubinage could latch on to well-worn arguments about the risks of falling in love with a social inferior. One author could warn that "a concubine is a household slave who enslaves the free man."[237] Often, the concubine was the freedwoman of her master.[238] Freeing the woman gave her an added element of respectability and further protected her from the advances of other men.[239] It was indecorous, however, for a man to take a freedwoman other than his own former slave as a concubine, since female slaves were presumed to have been violated by their masters.[240] Moreover – in the Roman instance and cross-culturally – it is a distinctive feature of concubinage that the woman, dishonored, is severed from the other ties of kinship which guarantee a woman's informal status *vis-à-vis* her husband. The concubine was on her own.[241]

If the bulk of the evidence implies that concubines were servile, reality was not cut-and-dry. In the fourth-century redaction of the *Apostolic Constitutions*, a Christian who had a concubine should "cease the relationship if she is a slave and marry someone legally, or if the woman is free, marry her according to law."[242] The crucial fact was that a woman taken as a concubine should not have social honor. In order for the man to avoid incurring the penalties for *stuprum*, the woman could not have a legally defensible claim to sexual respectability.[243] The policy of the Roman state was essentially reactive, responding to disputes over sexual honor that bubbled into conflict. Women without the protection of a family (the type of women who receive little authentic representation in the source material) would be prime candidates for concubinage. Moreover, actresses or prostitutes, members of legally dishonorable professions which exposed women to the public gaze, could legally be taken as concubines.[244]

---

[236] Aug. Serm. 224.3 (PL 38: 1095): *ancilla mea concubina mea est.*
[237] Ast. Soph. Psalm. 11.9 (Richard: 80): Παλλακὴ γάρ ἐστι κατοικίδιος δούλη, καταδουλοῦσα τὸν ἐλεύθερον.
[238] Arjava 1996, 207.   [239] Dig. 48.5.14.   [240] McGinn 1991, 353.   [241] Goody 1976, 46–7.
[242] Const. Ap. 8.32 (SC 336: 237): εἰ μὲν δούλην, παυσάσθω καὶ νόμῳ γαμείτω, εἰ δὲ ἐλευθέραν, ἐκγαμείτω αὐτὴν νόμῳ.
[243] Dig 25.7.1.1, with McGinn 1991, 350.
[244] E.g. Lib. Or. 14.60 (Foerster vol. 2: 108–9); Ps.-Bas. Sel. Vit. Thecl. 2.42 (Dagron: 400). On the status of actresses in late antiquity, see Webb 2002.

Concubinage was a "self-regulating" social practice with legal validity, recognized by the laws of Augustus.[245] Constantine decreed – in line with the best practice of the aristocracy – that a man could not have a wife and concubine simultaneously.[246] This theoretically made the informal, social limits on concubinage a matter of public enforcement, but there are examples of men keeping multiple, servile mistresses. Augustine would not offer condolences to a widower, since he had good report that "the number of your concubines grows daily."[247] Salvian could speak of men with "crowds of concubines."[248] Augustine urged members of his flock not to have a wife and concubine concurrently.[249] A fifth-century woman intervened with a holy man, not a civil agent, to counteract the concubine who had put a spell on her husband.[250]

The blurring of the lines between prostitutes, slaves, and concubines in ancient texts is revealing, for it shows that concubinage *per se* was not so important as the system of sexual honor in general. Concubinage was part of the broader sexual economy that only limited men's sexual activity to keep it from violating honorable women or interfering with proprietary strategies. Significantly, the two late antique men known to us most intimately from their personal letters and autobiographies – Augustine and Libanius – both had a concubine... and a son by the concubine. Their biographies illuminate the conventions, and contradictions, of concubinage. The case of Augustine presents us with a climber from the provincial aristocracy who delayed marriage in the interest of finding a suitable mate. Though we have only oblique clues to the nature of the relationship, Augustine kept a concubine for some fourteen years, a woman whose name we never know, the mother of his only son, Adeodatus.[251] "With her I learned by my own experience the difference between the sort of marital unions contracted for the sake of procreation and those pacts made for sexual love, in which children are born against our wishes, although once they are born they

---

[245] McGinn 1991, 336.   [246] CJ 5.26.1 (AD 326). See chapter II.
[247] Aug. Ep. 259.3 (CSEL 57: 612–13): *crescit in dies pellicum numerus...*
[248] Salv. Gub. 4.6 (MGH AA I: 41): *turbas concubinarum.*
[249] Aug. Serm. 392.2 (PG 39: 1710).   [250] Thdt. H. rel. 8.13 (SC 234: 400).
[251] Shanzer 2002, is illuminating but suggests more strongly than I would that the relationship was quasi-marital and that the woman was perhaps a social equal. The passages which insinuate marital substance are allusive at best while Augustine clearly distinguishes between marriage and sexual partnerships in his own context. He directly states that after dismissing his first concubine he "procured another one," which implies the high-status/low-status sexual dynamic. The passages which liken Augustine's relationship to marriage are late and self-serving. Augustine's claim that his concubinage was superior to mere fornication has good parallels in the passages on p. 316 which show that men thought of concubinage as a moderate form of non-marital sexuality. And as Libanius shows, men could be coy about the status of their partners.

compel our affection."[252] We could not expect a more lucid statement of the difference between marriage and concubinage.

Augustine's biography illustrates the essential contradictions of concubinage: concubines might get in the way, emotionally, of socially appropriate marriages, and though concubines were not supposed to produce heirs, lack of control over fertility made this goal unrealistic. Augustine dismissed his concubine after a fourteen-year relationship when he, at the age of thirty-one, was engaged to a ten-year-old girl of high social status. Since the legal age for marriage was twelve, Augustine "procured another" concubine, presumably without the same risk of emotional attachment, for the two years he had to wait.[253] These women provide a human context to his plea, "Give me chastity and continence, but not yet." Augustine's sin was not simple carousing. He procured his sex in the form of concubines, whom he could acquire and reject as circumstances demanded. It is perhaps with a note of personal remorse that he could advise the young men of his flock against concubinage, warning them that they would have to send away their partners when the time for marriage arrived.[254]

The patterns of ancient demography conspired with the system of sexual honor to give concubinage a structural role in society. As the case of Augustine illustrates, Roman men, particularly those who might entertain designs on a strategic marriage, married late. They plotted to earn money first and then later, when they had it, to marry a richer wife.[255] For the decade-plus between pubescence and marriage, concubinage was always an option. "You will say, I am a *iuvenis*, and I cannot conquer my lust or overcome my libido."[256] Concubinage was a holding pattern for the young in a society when full manhood – control over property, wife, and house – often began around the age of thirty. Not only did men marry later than women, they often survived their wives. Widowers were not uncommon in an age of primitive medical knowledge and hazardous pressures on the fertility of free women.[257] If a man already had an heir, concubinage offered a form of sexual companionship that would not interfere with his testamentary strategy. Roman emperors, for instance, took concubines in

---

[252] Aug. Conf. 4.2 (CC 27: 41): *in qua sane experirer exemplo meo quid distaret inter coniugalis placiti modum, quod foederatum esset generandi gratia, et pactum libidinosi amoris, ubi proles etiam contra votum nascitur, quamvis iam nata cogat se diligi.*

[253] Aug. Conf. 6.15 (CC 27: 90): *procuravi aliam.*   [254] Aug. Serm. 392.2 (PL 38: 1710).

[255] Caes. Arel. Serm. 43.4 (CC 103: 191–2); Aug. Bon. coniug. 5.5 (CSEL 41: 193–4). See chapter 11.

[256] Caes. Arel. Serm. 32.4 (CC 103: 142): *Sed dicit aliquis: iuvenis sum, et ideo voluptatem vincere et libidinem superare non possum.*

[257] Bagnall and Frier 1994, 123: if a man at twenty-five and a woman at fifteen married, there was a 25 percent chance that one or both would die within ten years.

their old age, since the existence of superfluous heirs might have such dire consequences.[258]

The church treated concubinage as a sin. Yet it is hard to discern any radical influence on the habits of concubinage. "Bad Christians" had concubines.[259] Caesarius of Arles demanded his congregation not have intercourse with concubines in the holy days leading up to the nativity cycle: hardly a sign of the church's ability to impose a revolution in behavior.[260] To its credit, the church was generally understanding in its attitude towards women forced into concubinage, though it insisted that they remain monogamous regardless of circumstances.[261] And the church could always enforce a stricter code within its own clergy.[262]

A preacher like Caesarius of Arles sensed that his stand against concubinage might imperil his missionary success: "I worry that some will get mad at me rather than themselves..."[263] His sermon, he said, was like a mirror held up to his audience so they could see their own faults, and he urged them not to be like a woman who breaks her mirror because of her own appearance. "Perhaps some who are not stained with this abuse will say, why not suspend the offenders from communion?... Well, if one or two or four or five dared perform such crimes... The good priests do what they can, they strive in perfect charity to preach and sigh heavily, and they pour out groans and roars. Since there is such an infinite multitude they cannot exert the severity of ecclesiastical discipline, but warning and praying for the sinners they might provoke them to repentance."[264] Here was an earnest and aggressive agent of the church's pastoral mission, struggling in vain against the tides of secular sexuality. In Arles, a vital outpost of urban life in the west, the realities of the Mediterranean slave trade meant that the church found itself contending against the sexual reverberations of a status system much older than the Christian faith.

CHRISTIANIZATION AND CHANGE

The Christianization of human sexuality is one of the signal transformations in the passage between imperial Rome and late antiquity. The triumph

---

[258] McGinn 1991, 337.   [259] Aug. Serm. 251.2 (PL 38: 1168): *malos christianos.*
[260] Caes. Arel. Serm. 188.3 (CC 103: 768).
[261] Const. Ap. 8.32 (SC 336: 237–8).   [262] Hier. Ep. 69.5 (CSEL 54: 688).
[263] Caes. Arel. Serm. 42.6 (CC 103: 189): *timeo ne sint aliqui, qui nobis potius quam sibi velint irasci...*
[264] Caes. Arel. Serm. 43.5 (CC 103: 192): *Sed forte illi, qui isto peccato non sunt maculati, dicunt: quare, qui hoc agunt, a communione non suspenduntur?... Si enim unus aut duo aut quattuor vel quinque mala ista facere praesumerent... Faciunt tamen boni sacerdotes quod possunt, et cum perfecta caritate contendunt orare et suspirare iugiter, et gemitus ac rugitus effundunt; ut in quibus propter infinitam multitudinem non possunt severitatem vel disciplinam ecclesiasticam exercere, monendo vel orando pro eis possint eos vel aliquando ad paenitentiam provocare.*

of the church in the fourth century mediated one of the most important ideological transformations in pre-modern history.[265] This revolution fostered changes in both attitudes and habits. The rise of Christian sexuality crystallized a new conception of the relationship between the body and the self. Sexual acts gained a new dimension of moral significance. These new cultural values effected a change in sexual behavior, however difficult to measure that may be.[266]

The findings of this chapter suggest that change must be measured not only by the shift towards new ideas of the body and new valuations of sexual behavior, but by the extent to which new values cut across the social moorings of ancient sexual norms. The centrality of slavery and prostitution, of honor and shame, in the Roman sexual system suggests that there is a deficiency in current discussion. This deficiency is a variation on the problematic way in which ancient sexuality has been studied. Ancient sexuality has been construed as a cultural phenomenon – a system in which sexual acts were imagined or assigned moral and aesthetic value. Yet this chapter has argued that sexuality, and the transition to a Christianized sexual culture, must be considered in social terms, too. The social aspects of Roman sexuality pose a problem for any narrative of radical change, precisely because the social parameters of sexuality, embedded in the imperatives of a high-mortality, high-fertility society, changed so little.

In late antiquity, Christian reformers vociferously opposed the habits of mainstream Roman sexuality. And they recognized that they were taking aim at a coherent socio-legal system. "The laws of Caesar are one thing, the laws of Christ another. Their Papinian commanded something quite different than our Paul. Among them, the bridles of sexual restraint are unloosed for men. They condemn only *stuprum* and *adulterium*, letting lust run wild through whorehouses and slave-girls – as though social status determined what was an offense, and not sexual desire."[267] With these words, Jerome offered the clearest assessment of the chasm separating Roman from Christian sexuality. Law and slavery gave Roman sexuality its particular shape. Roman sexual norms were immanent in a social system; the Christian construction of sexuality descended from an alien set of religious values.

Jerome set up an opposition between "us," Christians, and "them," Romans. It is noteworthy that this social observer of the late fourth

---

[265] Gaca 2003, on the differences between Christian sexuality and earlier modes of self-restraint.
[266] MacMullen 1986, is a notable attempt.
[267] Hier. Ep. 77.3 (CSEL 55: 39): *aliae sunt leges caesarum, aliae christi; aliud papinianus, aliud paulus noster praecipit. apud illos in viris pudicitiae frena laxantur et solo stupro atque adulterio condemnato passim per lupanaria et ancillulas libido permittitur, quasi culpam dignitas faciat, non voluptas.*

century continued to see Christian sexuality as the radical, separate, minority view in opposition to mainstream culture. Jerome may offer a skewed sensibility on proper sexual conduct, but his observation raises an important qualification to any narrative of Christianization. Even in the late fourth century, it is necessary to question the extent to which social habits had been Christianized. The long process of conversion must itself be part of the story.

Christian sexuality was rooted in Pauline scripture.[268] Paul simultaneously lauded celibacy while allowing marriage, "to avoid fornications."[269] The crucial passage of his *First Letter to the Corinthians* became the focal point of Christian reflection on human sexuality, and it was these very words which, three-and-a-half centuries later, prompted Chrysostom's diatribe against sex with prostitutes and slaves. For Paul, the sexual alternatives open to a man were celibacy, marriage, and *porneia*. That word, translated *fornicatio* in Latin and hence "fornication" in the English lexicon of Biblical language, can be misleading. It is a gloss that threatens to be meaningless, since the English word "fornication" is unused outside of religious contexts. It has been debated whether Paul meant "prostitution," a narrow reading of *porneia*, or all extra-marital sex.[270] But this is a false dichotomy. *Porneia* was a metonym for the casual sex permitted in Roman culture, drawing on the ideological association between prostitution and sexual dishonor. *Porneia* must be understood in terms of a system in which male sexuality was given free rein to exploit dishonored women: prostitutes, concubines, and slaves. Paul's use of *porneia* operated by reference to an entire culture of sexuality that permitted casual sex with dishonorable women.[271]

The Pauline doctrine of marriage laid the groundwork for the assimilation of the Christian religion within Mediterranean society. The startling silence of early Christian texts towards sex with slaves has been appropriately interpreted as an unwillingness to confront sexual abuse directly.[272] The church in its early stages was unable or unwilling to offer voluble opposition to the sexual exploitation of slaves. The legalization of Christianity in the fourth century marked a new departure. Christianity became the

---

[268] Deming 1995; Niederwimmer 1975.   [269] Fitzmyer 2008, 273–87.

[270] Osiek 2003; Gaca 2003; Glancy 1998; Kirchhoff 1994; Jensen 1978; Molina 1972.

[271] Greg. Nys. Ep. Can. ad Let. 3 (Mühlenberg: 5–6) provides an especially clear definition: *porneia*, in contrast to *moicheia*, was sex which did no harm to a third party (namely, a male with an interest in the sexual honor of the woman). *Pace* Gaca, who overemphasizes the fact that religious exogamy could be construed as *porneia*, Gregory's definition shows that the primary meaning of *porneia* was sex which ancient society accepted because the woman had no claim to honor but which Christianity treated as a sin. See now Harper forthcoming e.

[272] Osiek 2003; Glancy 1998; Brown 1988, 23 f.

state religion. Conformism became possible. Augustine knew that drunks, pimps, gamblers, and astrologers walked through his church; other bishops worried that men and women in their audience were there simply to flirt.[273] A distinction between the "good" and "bad" Christian emerged.[274] Complete silence on delicate social issues, like the master's sexual power over the slave, was increasingly impossible. This helps us to appreciate the position of Christian leadership in the fourth and fifth centuries. The earliest systematic critiques of the sexual exploitation of slaves occur in late antiquity, precisely when the church became a mass institution and was forced to consider the distance between society and its doctrines.

Perhaps the most meaningful distinction between Christian and Roman marriage was the emphasis that Christianity placed on sexual exclusivity.[275] It is too easy to take this stance for granted. Greco-Roman societies were monogamous, but the practices of slavery and prostitution permitted sexual polygyny.[276] Christianity adopted the form of monogamy and made it the exclusive venue of legitimate sexual activity. This was a radical turn. One surviving author of the Roman empire, Musonius Rufus, made an unambiguous case for sexually exclusive marriage.[277] But there is no comparison between the isolated and feeble injunctions of a philosopher, and the rise of a mass-scale religion claiming to determine the eternal fate of the soul. The norm of sexually exclusive marriage is one of the primary legacies of the late Roman church to future ages, and by recognizing the slave society in which this legacy first took shape, we can recognize how radical the idea truly was.

The bishops from the generation on either side of 400 represented a particular phase in the ongoing dialectic between Christian sexuality and secular society. This period saw the entrenchment of a regular clergy that set down duteously to the task of trying to Christianize society. These great pastoral generations produced men like Augustine, who worked assiduously to improve the manners of his flock, lecturing at length in his rural parishes on the immorality of taking liberties with slave-girls.[278] The documents of these generations on either side of 400 offer a privileged but particular window onto the transformation of ancient sexuality. As a dialogue between the bishops and their audience, they constitute a uniquely rich body of

---

[273] E.g. Aug. Serm. 127.1 (PL 38: 1875); Cyr. H. Procatech. 5 (Reischl and Rupp: 8).
[274] Aug. Serm. 251.2 (PL 38: 1168).
[275] Harper forthcoming a.   [276] Scheidel 2009a; Betzig 1992a and 1992b.
[277] See Treggiari 1991, 220–3; Lutz 1947. Pythagoreanism also seems to have taught sexually exclusive marriage along with more stringent forms of asceticism: Philostr. Vit. A. 1.13 (Jones vol. 1: 60).
[278] See p. 302: Aug. Serm. 9.12 (CC 41: 131).

evidence that allows a comparison between the prescriptive ideas of the church and the state of social habits. The verdict which emerges is that the basilica was surrounded by a culture of sexuality whose actual practices were much closer to Roman than Christian norms. This pastoral dialogue is shockingly vivid, and the accumulation of evidence militates against the skeptical conclusion that these bishops just had a dour view of the world.

This chapter has presented a synchronic account of how the sexual system of antiquity disposed of slaves, framed at a moment of intense conflict; that is all that the sources will allow. The social history of sexuality in the centuries after Christian triumph was a series of permutations between the habits of power and the constant sermonizing of the church. It is not possible to track the ongoing encounter, parish by parish, between Christian preaching and the customs of secular sexuality. The endurance of the latter should not be underestimated. Not until much deeper into late antiquity, or even the early middle ages, did marriage become fully "Christian" – in the sense that social legitimacy required it to be a sacrament performed by a priest at an altar, and it is only in the Germanic and middle Byzantine law codes that we are clearly across a divide, in a society where the dominant, public sexual culture was nominally Christian.[279] The first stirrings of these changes belong to our period, but the Mediterranean societies of the late empire were still, in their deep structure, ancient societies.

The sixth century has left behind one of the most pessimistic responses to the erotic universe that the collision between ancient and Christian sexuality had created:

Where is the way to Eros? In the streets, you will regret the greed for luxury of the obscene prostitute. If you seek it in the virgin's bed, you are forced into lawful wedlock or face the penalties for violating an honorable woman. Who could bear to rouse the joyless love of a legitimate wife! That is like being dragged to pay a debt. Adultery is the worst, though, so let it be gone from Eros, and put the perverse obsession for boys there with it . . . If you mix with your own slave-girl, you will suffer a reversal of fortune, and you yourself become the slave of your captive. But if you look outside your household, you are branded with shame by the law which hunts out the violation of other men's slaves. So it was that Diogenes fled all this, and, having no need of Lais, sang a marriage hymn to his hand![280]

---

[279] On marriage, Toubert 1998, 534–5; Reynolds 1994, 153; Duby 1978; Daudet 1941. On sexual laws, Cass. Var. 9.18 (CC 96: 368–9); Laiou 1993, 117–19. See chapter 11.

[280] Agath. in Anth. Gr. 5.302 (Beckby: 432): Ποίην τις πρὸς ἔρωτας ἴοι τρίβον; ἐν μὲν ἀγυιαῖς μαχλάδος οἰμώξεις χρυσομανῆ σπατάλην. εἰ δ᾽ἐπὶ παρθενικῆς πελάσοις λέχος, ἐς γάμον ἥξεις ἔννομον ἢ ποινὰς τὰς περὶ τῶν φθορέων. κουριδίαις δὲ γυναιξὶν ἀτερπέα κύπριν ἐγείρειν τίς κεν ὑποτλαίη, πρὸς χρέος ἑλκόμενος; μοίχια λέκτρα κάκιστα καὶ ἔκτοθέν εἰσιν ἐρώτων, ὧν μέτα παιδομανὴς κείσθω ἀλιτροσύνη . . . εἰ δὲ μιγῇς ἰδίῃ θεραπαινίδι, τλῆθι καὶ αὐτὸς δοῦλος

The lament of Agathias stands as the last statement of an ancient synthesis.[281] The poem reflects the endurance of old boundaries, which mapped the social landscape of eros deep into late antiquity. Significantly, Agathias placed the poem at the end of his collection of erotic epigrams.[282] The poem represented an artist's cynicism towards a world in which sex was venal, dangerous, duteous, illegal, sinful, or inextricably mixed with power. Quite purposefully, quite poignantly, he chose to end his collection of poetic fantasy with this tragi-comic note. Agathias was a student of law and poetry alike. He knew well enough there was no Lais who could redeem the world which the rules of status and sin had, in combination, wrought.

ἐναλλάγδην δμωΐδι γινόμενος. εἰ δὲ καὶ ὀθνείη, τότε σοι νόμος αἶσχος ἀνάψει, ὕβριν ἀνιχνεύων δώματος ἀλλοτρίου. πάντ᾽ ἄρα Διογένης ἔφυγεν τάδε, τὸν δ᾽ ὑμέναιον ἤειδεν παλάμη Λαΐδος οὐ χατέων.

[281] Cameron 1970, 29.
[282] Cameron 1970, 17. McCail 1971 on the significance of the epigram's placement.

CHAPTER 8

Mastery and the making of honor

THE *DOMUS FELIX* IN LATE ANTIQUITY

In the late 410s, Augustine preached a sermon on the 137th *Psalm* to his flock at Hippo. The *Psalm* was set in the Babylonian captivity and represented for Augustine a lyrical reflection on spiritual exile. The sermon was a conversation between the bishop and his regular crowd, but in the preacher's words we sense an Augustine preoccupied with writing his *City of God*. He urged his Christians to be strangers in this transitory world, not to be a "willow on the waters of Babylon," but rather to look towards the "everlasting Jerusalem." This pastoral Augustine was a man who had an unfailing sense of what it meant to cling to life in the world:

> When you are well and the things of this earth smile upon you, when nothing of yours dies, none of your vines is ruined, nor does hail fall upon them, nor do they become sterile, your casks turn not sour, nor do your cattle bear dead offspring, you hold every dignity the world has to offer, you have friends everywhere who live and keep your friendship, you lack not clients, your children revere you, your slaves quake utterly before you, and your wife is agreeable, then your house is called happy.[1]

Augustine knew what the Christian gospel asked his parishioners to leave behind. He was asking them to re-orient, fundamentally, their ingrained sense of desire and ambition. He knew the pulse of honor which quickened the blood in a world where the good life was measured in terms of vines and cattle, clients and friends, and an obedient family. And Augustine knew that the *domus felix*, in late antiquity, was inconceivable without its slaves, cowering in visible submission to their master.

---

[1] Aug. Psalm. 136.5 (CC 40: 1966–7): *cum autem bene est tibi, arrident omnia saecularia, nullus tuorum obiit, nihil in vinea tua forte vel aruit, vel grandinatum est, vel sterile apparuit, non acuit cupa tua, non abortum passum est pecus tuum, non exhonoratus es in aliqua dignitate secundum saeculum constitutus, undique amici tui et vivunt et servant tibi amicitiam, clientes non desunt, filii obsequuntur, servi contremiscunt, coniux concors, felix dicitur domus.*

Augustine was antiquity's most profound psychologist, and in his *City of God* he diagnosed mastery – with its need to feel the fear of the slaves – as a symptom of sin. The *libido dominandi*, the lust for domination, was the prime agent of secular history that impelled states towards war and a dangerous presence in the heart of every human.[2] Augustine's assessment is a significant comment on his surroundings in the fourth and fifth century. Outside of a slave-holding society, it is difficult to appreciate the felt force of this drive. In the late empire, mastery was an experience and an end in itself. It was a role with an established place in the public and private order of Roman society. Mastery was a realm of social practice with conventions and expectations that were inseparable from the circulation of honor and the pursuit of happiness in the late Roman empire. This chapter is an attempt to recover something of the experience of mastery which Augustine felt so keenly when he asked his Christians to live in spiritual exile from the world.

There was an expression in late antiquity, "where there is no slave, there is no master."[3] That expression represents the chief claim of this chapter, and it is revealing that the sentiment could appear with such clarity in a popular adage of the late empire. There was a fundamental difference between being free and being a slave-owner. Like slavery, slave-ownership was an existential proposition. To possess, to dominate a human being was a practice that had consequences for the master's perception and projection of himself. While the sources scarcely allow us to know what it was like to be a slave in late antiquity, the master class was more vocal about its own experiences, and it is therefore incumbent on the historian to reflect upon what it meant to be not just an owner of slaves, but a master of them.

HONOR AND STATUS IN THE LATE ROMAN WORLD

Honor is an elusive concept, easier to detect than define. It can seem to be present and tangible, and at the same time protean. An anthropologist working in the Mediterranean defined honor as the public recognition of the individual's socially-determined worth.[4] Honor has been defined by a historian of the US South as that cluster of ethical rules which binds individuals in a community together, regulating their behavior in both the private and public spheres.[5] Aristotle said that honor consists of the "signs

---

[2] Aug. Psalm. 1.1 (CSEL 93.1A: 67); Aug. Civ. 19.15 (CC 48: 682–3).
[3] Hilar. Pict. Trin. 11.13 (CC 62A: 542): *et secundum commune iudicium, ubi non est servus, neque dominus est.*
[4] Pitt-Rivers 1977, 1. [5] Wyatt-Brown 1986.

of recognition for worthy action."[6] Honor, we could say, is the public recognition of the individual's worth, achieved through right behavior. Expectations of right behavior were socially determined, since masters and slaves, men and women, matrons and prostitutes were held to different standards of comportment.

These brief definitions reveal why honor has been such a slippery term: both the expected behavior and the codes of recognition change from one society to another. Honor is not an eternal, unchanging substance.[7] Accordingly, the concept of honor is liable to conjure up wildly incommensurate images. What does a man of the late Roman empire have to do with a twentieth-century Greek shepherd, or a dueling southerner of the nineteenth century? We need to seek out the specific workings of honor in late Roman society.[8] We are justified in doing so because the inhabitants of the late Roman Mediterranean recognized the significance of honor and used the language of honor in their day-to-day discourse about social life.[9]

Mediterranean cultures have often associated honor, principally a male virtue, with shame, a concept inextricable from female sexual modesty.[10] Male honor had to be earned, female honor had to be protected. This pattern held in the late empire. Nevertheless, any attempt to import into the Roman past the categories of honor and shame, as formulated by anthropologists, must account for two fundamental features of Roman society: the state and the slave system. Mediterranean society under Roman rule existed within a *formal* hierarchy, in which the organization of social status was centrally regulated by a system of official rules and fine gradations. Late antique men and women were highly sensitive to the hierarchy of order enforced by the Roman state.[11] This formal, statist hierarchy not only regulated the narrow distinctions of aristocratic rank, it enforced the most fundamental of all status distinctions: the line between slavery and freedom.[12] To an extent rare in Mediterranean history, social status in the Roman period was formally organized by the central government.

The absence of slavery from the wider discussion of Mediterranean honor is surprising. The mechanics of social honor are expressed with unusual

---

[6] Arist. Rhet. 1.5.9: τιμὴ δ' ἐστὶν μὲν σημεῖον εὐεργετικῆς εὐδοξίας.

[7] Horden and Purcell 2000, 485–523; the essays in Gilmore 1987a. Peristiany 1966 was seminal.

[8] McGinn 1998, 12, has sensible remarks on the social differences between the complex urban societies of the Roman Mediterranean and the face-to-face villages infiltrated by modern anthropologists.

[9] The Latin lexicon of honor–shame revolved around *honestas, pudor,* and *infamia*; the Greek, τιμή, αἰδώς, and αἰσχύνη. A comprehensive social–linguistic survey (such as Kaster 1997 for *pudor*) is needed.

[10] Giovannini 1997, 61.   [11] Jones 1964, 523–62.   [12] See part III.

clarity in slave societies.[13] "The concern for honor appears to be most pronounced in those societies where the gulf separating the upper from the lower classes is widest. Because the inequitable distribution of power reached its extreme in slavery, the master's obsession with honor reached corresponding heights."[14] The sexual dimensions of honor, to which slaves were denied access, was vital in the demarcation of corporal boundaries. Chapter 7 has explored the constructive role of shame in patterns of social reproduction, and this chapter forms a complementary exploration of the role of slavery in the making of honor. Slave-owning, domination, was elemental in the creation of honor. The very act of denying honor to slaves, the violence and codes of behavior that it required, were instrumental in the circulation of honor.

We are searching, then, for the workings of honor in a society that was formally hierarchical and exceptionally stratified. In comparative terms, Roman society was one of the most complex pre-modern societies; there was a dizzying distance between the highest *vir illustris* and the lowest slave, and there were innumerable gradations in between. But slaves formed a solid and impassable foundation at the bottom of the social order, and the line between slavery and freedom was the clearest boundary of all.

"CLOSELY-WATCHED HOUSEHOLDS"

The household was the basic social unit of Roman society, and the Roman household has been evocatively described by Kate Cooper as a "closely-watched" institution.[15] Private behavior and public honor were closely linked. There survived into the late empire the permanent distinction between the things of the *agora*, which belonged to men, and things of the *oikia*, which pertained to women.[16] We err, though, if we read into this divide the modern dichotomy of state and society, or if we confuse the private sphere with privacy. One of the characteristic traits of the Roman household was that it was, in deliberately calculated ways, laid open to view. When the *dominus* was in control of his *domus*, its members were not hidden away and silent. "A defining characteristic of the successful *dominus* was his ability to elicit visibly willing recognition of his authority from subordinates within the household system."[17] The game of honor revolved around the observable enactment of social roles, and those roles derived from the individual's place in the household.

---

[13] Wyatt-Brown 1986; Patterson 1982, 10–12.   [14] Oakes 1990, 15.   [15] Cooper 2007b.
[16] Ioh. Chrys. Virgin. 73.1 (SC 125: 350); Ioh. Chrys. Ad pop. Ant. 14.1 (PG 49: 145).
[17] Cooper 2007b, 7.

The word *pater familias* nicely summarized the role of the free, honorable man as both master and father, *dominus et pater*. Lactantius found the metaphor capable of expressing deep and mysterious theological truths:

So he is to be called *pater*, because he bestows upon us so many and such great things, and he is to be *dominus*, because he has the ultimate power to chastise and to punish. Even the logic of the civil law demonstrates that the *pater* and the *dominus* are one and the same . . . It is obvious that the title of *pater* also encompasses the slaves, since it is followed by *familias*, while the word *familia* includes the children, since *pater* precedes it. Whence it is clear that he is both *pater* to the slaves and *dominus* to the children . . . On this account he is called the *pater familias*, since he is endowed with a sort of double power. He should be indulgent, because he is a *pater*, and he should maintain order, because he is a *dominus* . . . [18]

It would be hard to find a more culturally resonant statement of Roman paternalist attitudes.

Mastery was a normal part of becoming an adult. The role of master was often associated with marriage, because each was a passage into adulthood. The assumption of manhood meant taking control of a household, of a wife and slaves.[19] It belonged with marriage, taxes, educating children, and farming in the catalogue of worries that faced the average man.[20] The role of the *pater familias* made hard demands on adult men. It required a man to be generous but firm, gracious but violent, all at the same time. It shaped the master's self-perception. Without reference to the cumbersome logic of Aristotle's natural slave theory, men of late antiquity knew instinctively that masters and slaves were compounded differently. Slave-owners thought of themselves as naturally fit to rule: they knew how to steer the ship of self in a way that slaves never could.[21] This self-perception was potentially contradicted by the violent underpinnings of their authority: the very exercise of power threatened to expose the master as unstable, unfit, or poorly composed.[22] Masters were bothered by the excessive anger that inferiors could cause in their well-ordered souls. In the voice of a man about to speak in the forum, late antique men could detect an unusual,

[18] Lact. Inst. 4.3 (CSEL 19.1: 280–1): *pater ideo appellandus est, quia nobis multa et magna largitur, dominus ideo, quia castigandi ac puniendi habet maximam potestatem. dominum vero eundem esse qui sit pater etiam iuris civilis ratio demonstrat . . . videlicet nomen patris conplectitur etiam servos, quia 'familias' sequitur, et nomen familiae conplectitur etiam filios, quia 'pater' antecedit. unde apparet eundem ipsum et patrem esse servorum et dominum filiorum . . . quodsi propterea pater familias nominatur, ut appareat eum duplici potestate praeditum, quia et indulgere debet, quia pater est, et cohercere, quia dominus . . .*
[19] Hier. Ep. 14.3 (CSEL 54: 47–8); Gr. Nyss. Benef. 96–8 (van Heck: 96–8); Aug. Ep. 246.3 (CSEL 57: 584). In general Saller 1987b and 1984.
[20] Bas. Ep. 2.2 (Courtonne: 6), quoted in chapter 3.
[21] Them. Or. 26.321C (Downey and Schenkl: 135).   [22] Hopkins 1993, 10.

lingering furor towards his slaves.[23] It was best to bear light murmuring from the slaves or pretend not to hear it at all.[24] The good man was never bitter towards his slaves.[25] Masters were supposed to be a little indulgent, especially to their young slaves.[26] Rather than lose his temper, he might coolly ask the offending slave, "Perhaps I am your master?"[27]

This high sense of honor was made by violence. "To teach or chasten foolish slaves, it is a great honor, and not a simple praise, when one is able to expel wickedness using private violence against those who are the most evil."[28] Domestic order was not static; it was a dynamic tension, requiring the constant intervention of a violent authority figure, a master. Honor derived from the possession of complete control over one's domestic domain. Masters were measured by the firmness of their rule over the household. It was a consuming role. The mastery of slaves was the "first and everyday example of power."[29] Masters sat in daily judgment, punishing and pardoning their slaves.[30] The control of slaves brought into the house a power that was, frankly, a little like God's.[31] "Whatever a master does to his own slave, undeservedly or in anger, willfully or ignorantly, forgetfully or intentionally, knowingly or unknowingly, it is final, it is right, it is law."[32]

If masters were genteel, educated, and capable of rational conduct, slaves by contrast were unrestrained and irrational. They were literally "shameless." A slave was someone whom "shame" did not deter, only fear of harm.[33] Slaves had no respect for modesty or chastity, only a fear of punishment. Slaves feared being caught rather than the misdeed itself.[34] Consequently, slaves had to be disciplined with constant violence. As Chrysostom admitted in his sermon against clamorous mistresses, slaves were known to be "reckless and shameless and incorrigible" unless conditioned by the expectation of violence.[35] Constant fear was considered the only antidote to the internal shamelessness of slaves.

---

[23] Ambr. Sacram. 4.19 (CSEL 73: 80).
[24] Hier. Eccl. 7.23 (CC 72: 310); Gr. Naz. Carm. 2.1.19 line 2 (PG 37: 1271).
[25] Auson. Prof. 3 (Green: 44).   [26] Aug. Psalm. 134.12 (CC 40: 1946).
[27] Aug. Tract. Io. 37.3 (CC 36: 333): *forsitan dominus tuus sum.*
[28] Ioh. Chrys. Hab. eun. spir. 3.7 (PG 51: 287): οἰκέτας ἀγνώμονας παιδεύειν καὶ σωφρονίζειν, ἀλλὰ καὶ ἐγκώμιον μέγιστον, καὶ οὐχ ὁ τυχὼν ἔπαινος, ὅτι τοὺς πρὸς τοσαύτην κατενεχθέντας κακίαν ἠδυνήθη διὰ τῆς οἰκείας σφοδρότητος ἀπαλλάξαι τῆς πονηρίας.
[29] Aug. Psalm. 124.7 (CC 40: 1840–1): *prima et quotidiana potestas hominis in hominem domini est in servum.* Aug. Serm. D21.4 (Dolbeau: 273–4); Ioh. Chrys. Virgin. 67 (SC 125 (336–7).
[30] Ioh. Chrys. In 2 Tim. 3.3 (PG 62: 616).   [31] Salv. Gub. 4.2 (MGH AA 1: 37).
[32] Petr. Chrys. Serm. 161.3 (CC 24B: 996–7): *quicquid dominus indebite, iracunde, libens, nolens, oblitus, cogitans, sciens, nesciens circa servum fecerit, iudicium, iustitia, lex est.*
[33] Fitzgerald 2000, 41–2.
[34] Ambr. Ep. 56.14 (CSEL 82: 171); Gr. Nyss. Vit. Mos. 2.320 (SC 1²: 326).
[35] Ioh. Chrys. In Ephes. 15.3 (PG 62: 109).

Bathed in violence, the master's supremacy of honor was re-affirmed in the most ordinary codes of interaction. Slaves did not address the master by name.[36] Slaves could not speak to their masters in the way they were spoken to.[37] Masters could hiss, whistle, curse at the slaves.[38] The regular use of the title "boy," regardless of age, emphasized the diminutive scale of recognition offered to slaves.[39] In a masculine society, it was a devastating reminder that slaves were denied access to the normal stages of development and selfhood. Slaves did not look their masters in the eye.[40] Servile eyes were fixed on the floor.[41] If a slave did look into the master's eyes, it was a grievance on a par with contumacious speech or even running away.[42] The corporal taboo is a significant detail. The master–slave relationship was not simply a relationship of asymmetrical power with high odds of being abrasive; it was a peculiar type of relationship, circumscribed by codes of conduct. A relationship in which the parties do not have enough mutual respect to lock eyes is not fertile ground for genuine human affections.

The culture of honor produced elaborate and uncanny rules about zones of movement and modes of physical contact. Certain types of labor were branded as dishonorable, and these were characteristically delegated to slaves. So it was that John Chrysostom would allow Christian priests to own a few slaves, in order that they should not have to do any shameful labor themselves.[43] This consisted mainly in menial or degrading personal service. We should not forget that slaves served their masters in the bath, and the master's body was accessible to slaves precisely because the slave was beneath social dignity.[44] Wet-nursing could also be reckoned servile, and mothers who breast-fed their own children might be considered "shameful."[45] Sewage work was characteristically slave-like.[46]

---

[36] Ioh. Chrys. Ad pop. Ant. 8.5 (PG 49: 96). cf. Patterson 1982, 56.
[37] Aug. Psalm. 58.1.15 (CC 39: 741).
[38] Hissing: Heliod. Schol. in Dion. 3 (GG vol. 3: 310). Aug. Civ. 9.19 (CC 47: 267); Aug. Psalm. 73.16 (CC 39: 1015), pagans curse at their slaves by calling them "Satan."
[39] E.g. Bas. Ep. 333.1 (Courtonne: 201); Lib. Decl. 32.49 (Foerster vol. 7: 69). Finley 1998 (orig. 1980), 164. *Contra* Kudlien 1991, 39.
[40] Gr. Naz. Ep. 17 (Gallay vol. 1: 25).   [41] Gr. Naz. Carm. 2.1.1 line 401 (PG 37: 1000).
[42] Lib. Or. 5.12 (Foerster vol. 1: 308).
[43] Ioh. Chrys. In Philip. 9.4 (PG 62: 251). See chapter 3.
[44] Dionisotti 1982, sections 59–64, 116; Lib. Or. 25.28 (Foerster vol. 2: 550–1); Thdt. H. rel. 4.15 (SC 234: 235); Ps.-Bas. Sel. Vit. Thecl. 2.19 (Dagron: 342); Amm. 28.4.8–9 (Seyfarth vol. 2: 78); Ioh. Chrys. In 1 Cor. 40.5 (PG 61: 353–4); Ioh. Chrys. In Ephes. 22.2 (PG 62: 157); Talmud Bavli, *Kethub* 62a; Philogel. 23 (Thierfelder: 36); Lib. Decl. 26.19 (Foerster vol. 6: 523); Hier. Ep. 107.11 (CSEL 55: 302); Claud. In Eutr. 1 lines 105–9 (Hall: 147); Mirac. Steph. 2.7 (PL 41: 847); Fagan 1999, 29; Brown 1988, 315.
[45] See chapter 3, esp. Ps.-Chrys. In Psalm. 50 (PG 55: 572).
[46] Aug. Psalm. 103.4.10 (CC 40: 1530); Ast. Am. Serm. 3.13 (Datema: 36).

One of the principal elements of honor, across Mediterranean history, is wealth.[47] The Roman aristocracy was explicitly grounded on wealth. Wickham has reminded us of this rather astounding fact; medieval aristocracies were military or royal, not civilian, elites.[48] Wealth was the path to prominence, and slaves, like land, were central in the ideology of wealth. To be rich was to own "land and slaves."[49] Slaves were a primary article of conspicuous consumption. Slaves not only constituted and created honorable wealth, they were visible wealth. Slaves were part of the public presence of the master. Along the streets and colonnades of the late antique city, masters marched with their slaves following in train. Ammianus has vividly described the importance of slaves in the habits of Roman showmanship. So concerned was the master with appearances that not even the cook was left at home, and Ammianus was critical of those who dragged their slaves, dusty from kitchen work, through the streets.[50] According to Chrysostom, upper-class men paraded through the city with a herd of slaves and anything less was considered shameful.[51]

It would be a mistake to believe that slaves, because they were an article of conspicuous consumption, were mere props to the master's self-image. In the Roman slave system, any strict division between production and consumption becomes a false dichotomy. Slaves were not an ornamental accessory of wealth already achieved. Through the domination of slaves, and through the labor of the slave, honor was made. The slave system offered the chance for ascent to those with guts and drive. The slave market was a place of opportunity, a place where potential labor could be bought and transformed into wealth. The inscriptions of a Greek village record the fate of a man who borrowed money to buy slaves but found himself ultimately unable to repay his debts: he lost everything, including the slaves.[52] Others succeeded. Augustine knew a "poor man" at Hippo who started with nothing but by "his own labors" had bought several slaves.[53] A cleric who had been raised by St. Martin had nothing to his name, but eventually Martin learned that he had started raising horses and buying slaves – not only barbarian slaves, but also slave-girls who were not unattractive![54] The slave market was a place where a mere man could become a master.

---

[47] Gilmore 1987b, 6.   [48] Wickham 2005a, 153–258, esp. 158.   [49] See n. 277 in chapter 4.
[50] Amm. 14.6.16–17 (Seyfarth vol. 1: 15). cf. Amm. 28.4.8–9 (Seyfarth vol. 2: 78).
[51] Ioh. Chrys. In 1 Cor. 40.5 (PG 61: 353–4).
[52] ISMDA no. 12, with Petsas *et al.* 2000, 90. See chapter 9.
[53] Aug. Serm. 356.6 (Lambot vol. 1: 136): *homo pauper est . . . de laboribus suis . . . emerat aliquos servulos.*
[54] Sulp. Sev. Dial. 3.15 (CSEL 1: 213).

Clothing was used to advertise social status. Outward appearances made one's claim to social honor immediately visible.[55] The free man was honorable and could be spotted by his clothing and his attendants, while slaves were dishonored and equally marked by their poor or simple dress. If they switched clothing, it would be shameful.[56] In late Roman art, the slave's costume varied but the simple tunic was a clear advertisement of slave status.[57] This sort of marking allowed society to recognize and to enforce appropriate deference: if a crowd saw a man's slave abusing him publicly, they would rush to his aid.[58] These codes of appearance were ritually inverted once a year. Transgressive holidays, in which masters and slaves traded places for a day, continued long into late antiquity.[59] Slaves were allotted a moment of rest and reprieve, while the normal rules of interaction were temporarily suspended.[60] But only to an extent: Libanius said it was a time for jesting, but the slaves knew there were unspoken limits on what could actually be said and done.[61]

The circulation of honor depends upon the recognition of individual worth by society. But the honor derived from slaves could create delicate angles of recognition. Masters expected to be autocrats over their own private subjects, claiming a monopoly on their slaves' ability to express recognition of worth: masters took offense if their slaves praised other masters.[62] Likewise, it was dangerous to judge someone else's slaves.[63] It was shameful if someone said they honored you because of your slaves.[64] Paradoxically, it was thought that slaves imitated their masters.[65] Slaves were expected to be miniature selves of their owner, mimicking his or her manners, speech, and grace. Slaves existed socially only through the master.[66] They should praise no one except their master, and they had no access to recognition except from the master – like the moon, cold and gray, emitting no light but reflecting the master's luminous honor.

The proximity of slaves, and their integration in the master's private sphere, made their submission imperative. Their intimacy with the free members of the household was hazardous.[67] Slaves were a dangerous source

---

[55] Dig. 47.10.15.15.   [56] Sever. Gab. Genes. (PG 56: 519).
[57] See Dunbabin 2003a, for slaves in late Roman art. Schumacher 2001; Sittl 1890, 156–7.
[58] Dion. Ar. Ep. 8.3 (Heil and Ritter: 182–3).   [59] Auson. Ec. lib. 16 (Green: 102).
[60] Lib. Or. 9.11 (Foerster vol. 1: 395–6); Lib. Prog. 12.5.11 (Foerster vol. 8: 476).
[61] Lib. Or. 16.36 (Foerster vol. 2: 174).   [62] Ioh. Chrys. In Mt. 11.8 (PG 57: 201).
[63] Hier. Ep. 45.1 (CSEL 54: 324). cf. the actual case in Bas. Ep. 72 and 73 (Courtonne: 169–72).
[64] Ioh. Chrys. In Coloss. 7.3 (PG 62: 347).
[65] Lib. Ep. 1106.1 (Foerster vol. 11: 212); Hier. Ep. 79.9 (CSEL 55: 97). cf. Salv. Gub. 8.3 (MGH AA 1: 106). Wiedemann 1981, 61.
[66] Though slaves of course did not agree: Barton 2001, 11–12; Joshel 1992. See chapter 6.
[67] Barton 2001, 21.

of leaks. In a world where appearances of submission and order were all-important, rumor could be as damaging as reality. Decent society officially held that servile chatter was categorically unreliable, even as it fed insatiably on gossip emanating from the slave quarters: "slaves make amends for their grievances in the only way they can: accusations . . . and mankind is always ready to believe the worst, so the rumor that starts at home soon flies in public."[68] Roman laws show that emperors could not make up their minds whether slave informants should be brutally tortured or gloriously rewarded; they wanted it both ways, of course.[69]

Servile intimacy was always a double-edged sword. In Roman society, slaves "knew their master inside out. They knew him in all his vulnerability, with his trousers down – rather as a wife does, but without the tender feelings or the commitment of a lifetime."[70] Masters and mistresses might have sex in front of the slaves. So, in the Talmud, "It is written: Stay here by yourselves with the donkey, which can be interpreted to mean: Slaves constitute a people that are similar to a donkey in terms of their legal status. Because of this similarity, cohabitation in their presence is permitted . . . " Not everyone was eager to perform before the invisible crowd: "Rabbah bar Rav Huna, before engaging in intimacy with his wife, would jingle the bells of the canopy surrounding his bed," signaling the slaves to depart.[71]

It is worth pausing at some length over the contradictions of intimacy in the late Roman world. The centrality of female chastity in the construction of family honor and the physical proximity of slaves to the women of the household was a point of incandescent tension. Late antique society was gripped by fear of the sexual threat of slave men. This fear was the result of a patriarchal fixation, sharpened by Christianity, on female virtue, and late antique legislation only intensified the public's attention. Mistresses who used their slaves as sexual objects had long been the butt of comedy.[72] Men of earlier periods did not view sex between slaves and free women as a joke, but it is interesting that the classical law had made no provisions regarding sex between a mistress and her own slaves: the problem was truly relegated to the private sphere.[73] Constantine, however, issued strong legislation

---

[68] Hier. Ep. 117.8 (CSEL 55: 431): *doloremque suum solis, quod possunt, detractationibus consolantur . . . facilius mala credunt homines et, quodcumque domi fingitur, rumor in publico fit.*
[69] CT 9.5.1 (AD 320); CT 9.9.1 (AD 326); CT 9.24.1 (AD 326); CT 9.6.1–2 (AD 376).
[70] Hopkins 1993, 22.
[71] Talmud Bavli, *Niddah*, 17a. The translation is from the Schottenstein Edition. cf. also *Gittin*, 58a. Aug. Civ. 14.18 (CC 48: 41), slaves and others sent from the room on the wedding night.
[72] Fountoulakis 2007; Hopkins 1993, 17. P. Oxy. 3.413. Philogel. 251 (Thierfelder: 122).
[73] cf. Parker 2007.

penalizing affairs with slaves and encouraging anyone with knowledge to blow the whistle on such affairs.[74] He brought the problem more than ever under the public gaze.

In a society where slaves were always in the shadows, and in which the bodies of masters and slaves were dangerously close, this was a menacing shift. In vivid detail, John Chrysostom described the violent jealousy of the husband, who would imagine his wife having sex with the slaves out of paranoid delusion, and he cited it as a practical reason for a young woman to avoid marriage.[75] Jerome, the self-appointed czar of aristocratic female chastity, was constantly bothered by the problem:

A woman's reputation for sexual virtue is a fragile thing, like a precious flower that breaks in the soft breeze and is ruined by the light wind. It is especially vulnerable when she is of an age which allows her to fall into vice, but lacks the authority of a husband, whose shadow is the protection of a wife. What business does a widow have among a crowd of slaves? Among a herd of servants? . . . I know many women who keep their gates closed to the public, but have not avoided suspicions of disgrace with slaves. The slaves have become suspect by their fancy appearance or their noticeably well-fed bodies. . . [76]

Jerome's letter reveals the dangers of a private sphere that was *too* private, beyond the public gaze. He evoked the peering eyes of the city, which watched avidly for outward signs of what went on behind the veil of privacy. The public would scrutinize the dress and comportment of slaves for suspicious "tells" (it is not encouraging that a well-fed slave was a probable indication of intense favoritism). This was not just Jerome's lurid imagination. The danger of male slaves permeated late antique culture, religious and secular. No handbook of virginity was complete without severe warnings.[77] Jewish sources indicate that women could buy female, but not male, slaves.[78] Astrological handbooks gave star charts to predict if a woman would sleep with a slave.[79] A late antique jokebook took aim at a husband cuckolded by his own slave.[80] The "true crime" stories in the late

[74] CT 9.9.1 (AD 329). See chapter 11. [75] Ioh. Chrys. Virgin. 52 (SC 125: 88–96).
[76] Hier. Ep. 79.8 (CSEL 55: 97): *tenera res in feminis fama pudicitiae est et quasi flos pulcherrimus cito ad levem marcescit auram levique flatu corrumpitur, maxime ubi et aetas consentit ad vitium et maritalis deest auctoritas, cuius umbra tutamen uxoris est. quid facit vidua inter familiae multitudinem, inter ministrorum greges? . . . scio multas clausis ad publicum foribus non caruisse infamia servulorum, quos suspectos faciebat aut cultus inmodicus aut crassi corporis . . .*
[77] Bas. Anc. Virg. 61–2 (PG 30: 796–7); Hier. Ep. 22.12 (CSEL 54: 159); Ps.-Bas. Hom. Virg. 2.38 (Amand and Moons: 43); Gr. Naz. Or. 44.8 (PG 36: 616); Pall. H. Laus. 28 (Butler vol. 2: 83–4), probably a slave.
[78] Talmud Bavli, *Bava Metzia*, 71a. [79] E.g. Heph. Apot. 2.21 (Pingree 176–8).
[80] Philogel. 251 (Thierfelder: 122).

antique declamations took affairs between mistresses and slaves as a theme ripe for legal disputation.[81] Late antique society stood at alert, watching and worrying about the sexual risk posed by its unfree men.

The incubus of male slave sexuality cannot be separated from an important subplot in the history of late antique slavery: the castration of male slaves. Eunuchs had been a fixture of royal courts in the near east, and the late antique court bustled with eunuch functionaries. The eunuchs of the imperial court have been explained in terms of late antique political sociology.[82] Indeed, the study of eunuchs in the late Roman empire has been basically limited to considerations of the imperial court or questions of gender.[83] What has gone without sufficient attention is the fact that the Roman empire saw a distinct escalation of the practice of keeping eunuchs in the private domain, which would become characteristic of the Byzantine aristocracy.[84] The rise of eunuchs in the aristocratic households of the Roman empire stemmed from an effort to de-sexualize male slaves in the most fundamental way.

Eunuchs had been stripped of the *officium patris nomenque mariti*, which made them the perfect foil to the masculine, sexualized *pater familias*.[85] They were at a premium because of their debilitation. A eunuch's "sole virtue" was to protect the chastity of females in the house.[86] But their unrestricted intimacy with the woman's quarters was wrought with contradiction, and unkind stereotypes quickly accumulated around the figure of the eunuch. They were greedy beyond measure, a greed made insane by the fact that the eunuch had no offspring to succeed to his property.[87] One late antique medical text claims, nonchalantly, that "most of them are savage-minded, loathsome, malicious, so on and so forth."[88] While these caricatures have been noted and ascribed to political hostility towards the imperial eunuchs, they are slight compared to the frequency and intensity with which another charge was laid against eunuchs: sexual perversion.

[81] Sopat. Diar. 314 (RG 8: 67).   [82] Above all, Hopkins 1978, 172–96.

[83] Noted by Tougher 2002, 143, and 1997. Gender: Ringrose 2003; Kuefler 2001. Politics: Scholten 1995; Schlinkert 1994; Hopkins 1978, 172–96.

[84] Esp. Guyot 1980, 52–4; Stevenson 1995. For the Byzantine period, Ringrose 2003.

[85] Claud. In Eutr. 1 lines 47–50 (Hall: 145).

[86] Claud. In Eutr. 1 lines 98–100 (Hall: 147): *unica virtus . . .* cf. Hier. Ep. 22.16 (CSEL 54: 163–4); Hier. Ep. 54.13 (CSEL 54: 479); Hier. Ep. 66.13 (CSEL 54: 664); Hier. Ep. 107.11 (CSEL 55: 302). Gift for a woman: Aug. Serm. nov. D16.17 (Dolbeau: 337). Conspicuous consumption of eunuchs: Amm. 14.6.16 (Seyfarth vol. 1: 15); Ioh. Chrys. In Rom. 4.4 (PG 60: 421).

[87] Ps.-Bas. Sel. Vit. Thecl. 2.9 (Dagron: 304); Claud. In Eutr. 1 lines 222–5 (Hall: 152).

[88] Adamantius Iud. Phys. 2.3 (SPGL vol. 1: 351–2): ὡς τὸ πολὺ εἰσιν ὠμόφρονες, δολεροί, κακοῦργοι, ἕτεροι δὲ ἑτέρων μᾶλλον.

Nothing more luridly illustrates the obsessive fears of late ancient men than the growing urban legend of eunuch sexuality. Having resorted to castration to neutralize the sexual threat of male slaves, masters were gnawed by the doubt that the effort had failed.

We can track the spread of this fear in some detail.[89] The earliest extant Christian document to offer a systematic warning about eunuch sexuality, complete with case histories, was the treatise on virginity by the physician and bishop Basil of Ancyra:

On the other hand they say that those who are virile enough for reproductive intercourse, with only the testicles removed, rage even more keenly and uncontrollably for copulation, and not only rage for it, but as it seems to them to be without danger, they violate the women they take. For they say that being castrated, the passages which the semen uses to pass from the kidneys and loins up to the remnant of their manhood are closed... By wickedly making their castration a sort of bait, they seduce and more shamelessly have intercourse with women. A natural man... spends his seed and his lust is relaxed. The man who does not have the ability to empty that which stimulates him has hardly finished his work before his weariness is overcome and, they say, he is raging again...[90]

According to Basil eunuchs seduced women by offering a clinical explanation to reassure them that sex was undetectable. This obviously draws on an old form of misogyny – women were untrustworthy or weak and given the opportunity would cheat on their husbands. There is even a trace of insecurity in his argument that the castrated man might be *more* virile, in a sense, because unable to discharge his energy:

This is not just derived from the principles of nature, but experience in our lifetime has attested it to me. An old man, grey and venerable, told me of a woman who said to him that a eunuch trusted by her husband, the master, mixed sordidly with her like a man. And she said he was even more audacious in the deed because of the castration, emboldened by knowing he wouldn't procreate. And he was not the only one, but another man, a kindred spirit of mine who would not lie, said that a virgin who was a canon in the church lamented to him that a eunuch had come

---

[89] Guyot 1980, 65. But for early examples, Parker 2007, 290. Apul. Met. 8.25–7 (Helm: 197–8); Philostr. Vit. A. 1.37 (Jones vol. 1: 122).

[90] Bas. Anc. Virg. 61 (PG 30: 796): Τοὺς γὰρ μετὰ τὸ ἀνδρωθῆναι πρὸς συνουσίαν τὰ παιδογόνα μόρια μόνους τοὺς διδύμους ἀποτεμόντας φασὶ δριμύτερόν τε καὶ ἄσχετον πρὸς τὰς συνουσίας οἰστρεῖσθαι, καὶ οὐκ οἰστρεῖσθαι μόνον, ἀλλὰ καί, ὡς αὐτοῖς δοκεῖ, ἀκινδύνως φθείρειν τὰς προστυχούσας. Φασὶ γὰρ ὅτι, ἀποκοπέντων κάτωθεν τῶν διδύμων, οἵ τῆς γονῆς ἀπὸ ὀσφύος καὶ νεφρῶν ἐπὶ τὸ λοιπὸν μόριον διάκονοι γίνονται, μύουσι μὲν μετὰ τὴν τομὴν ἄνω οἱ πόροι... Δέλεαρ δὲ τὴν τῶν διδύμων εὐνουχίαν τῇ γυναικὶ εἰς ἀπάτην δεινῶς ποιησάμενος, ἀκολαστότερον μίγνυται. Ὁ μὲν γὰρ κατὰ φύσιν ἔχων ἀνήρ... ἐξῆς ἐκπεσόντος τοῦ σπόρου διαφορηθείς, τὴν ἐπιθυμίαν καταμαραίνεται. ὁ δὲ οὐκ ἔχων ὅθεν τὸ γαργαλίζον κενώσῃ, μόγις τοῦ πόνου ὑφίησιν, ἄχρις ἂν κάματος τοῦτον, φασί, λυσσῶντα ἐκλύσῃ.

to her bed and embraced her passionately and, though bodies united, he could not fulfill his lust. So, he used his teeth, his bites revealing his feral madness for copulation... Two witnesses are enough for proof, so let me not say more... For even if he is a eunuch, he is a man by nature.[91]

Basil, writing in the mid-fourth century, was careful to offer reliable case histories. The themes he broached – an audacious attitude towards sterile intercourse, creativity in the sexual act, indefatigability – would quickly became simple truisms. Claudian's invective against Eutropius deployed a series of double-entendres insinuating that Eutropius rose to power by offering manual, oral, and anal sex to the right people.[92] In the love letters of Aristaenetus, the efforts of a eunuch have become a byword for sexual futility.[93] Cyril of Alexandria gave a sensationalist sermon accusing eunuchs of using their "hands and fingers to violate pitiful women... Thus it is said rightly by the Wise man," – here is one of the great misuses of scripture (*Wisdom of Solomon* 3:14) in late antiquity – "'blessed is the eunuch, who with his hand hath wrought no iniquity.'"[94]

These documents reveal a streak of vicious and anxious humor aimed at a figure who was the opposite of the free, masculine *dominus*. The school exercises of Libanius preserve a short speech written in the voice of an "amorous eunuch." The speech was an exhibition in mockery.[95] Other orators would debate whether a eunuch could be accused of adultery – the sort of sophistic training that kept the attention of schoolboys.[96] The cruel mockery and paranoid fear of eunuch sexuality yielded some of the most explicit descriptions of carnal activity to survive from late antiquity. Eunuchs are relatively well documented in late antiquity because their

---

[91] Bas. Anc. 61–2 (PG 30: 796–7): Ταῦτα οὐχ ὁ τῆς φύσεως λόγος μόνον, ἀλλὰ καὶ ἡ πεῖρα δὲ πρὸς τὸν βίον ἡμῶν ἐμαρτύρατο, ὡς πρὸς ἐμέ τις τῶν αἰδεσίμων καὶ πολιᾷ καὶ βίῳ παλαιὸς ἀνὴρ, ἐξομολογησαμένης πρὸς αὐτὸν γυναικός, ἀπεφθέγξατο. Ἔφασκε γὰρ τὴν γυναῖκα πρὸς αὐτὸν εἰρηκέναι, ὅτι ὁ πεπιστευμένος αὐτὴν παρὰ τοῦ ἀνδρὸς εἴτε δεσπότου εὐνοῦχος ὡς ἀνὴρ αὐτῇ ἀκολάστως ἐμίγνυτο. Καὶ κατετόλμα, φησί, πλέον τῆς πράξεως, διὰ τὸ ἄγονον αὐτοῦ τῷ ἀτοκίῳ θαρρῶν. Οὐχ οὗτος δὲ μόνον, ἀλλὰ καὶ ἕτερός τις τῶν ὁμοψύχων ἡμῖν, οὐκ ἂν ταχέως ψευσάμενος, εἴρηκεν. ὅτι παρθένος τις τῆς Ἐκκλησίας κανονικὴ πρὸς αὐτὸν ἀπωδύρετο, ὅτι ἐπὶ τῆς κοίτης αὐτῆς γενόμενός τις εὐνοῦχος, περιεπτύσσετο μὲν αὐτὴν ἐμπαθῶς, καὶ ἐμφὺς ὅλος ὅλη, ἐπεὶ μὴ εἶχεν ὅπως τὰ τῆς ἐπιθυμίας ἐργάσηται, τοῖς ὀδοῦσιν ἐκέχρητο, ζέουσαν ἐν τῇ σαρκὶ τῆς μίξεως τὴν λύσσαν τοῖς δήγμασιν ἀγρίως ἐμφαίνων... Καὶ δύο δὲ ἀνθρώπων ἡ μαρτυρία ἀληθής ἐστιν, ἵνα μὴ καὶ ἑτέρους πλείονας καταλέγοντες... Κἂν εὐνοῦχος γὰρ ᾖ, ἀλλ' ἀνήρ ἐστι τὴν φύσιν.

[92] Claud. In Eutr. 1 lines 358–70 (Hall: 157). Long 1996, 121–34.   [93] Aristaen. Ep. 1.21 (Mazal: 51).

[94] Cyr. Sermon against the Eunuchs, preserved in Geor. Mon. Chron. (de Boor vol. 2: 651–2): διὰ χειρὸς καὶ δακτύλου φθείρειν τὰς ἀθλίας γυναῖκας... καὶ τοῦτο δηλῶν ὁ σοφὸς ἀριδήλως ἔφη. μακάριος εὐνοῦχος ὁ μὴ ἐργασάμενος ἐν χειρὶ ἀνόμημα.

[95] Lib. Prog. 11.26 (Foerster vol. 8: 434–5). Possibly descended from ridicule of the sophist Favorinus? See Gleason 1995, 132–8.

[96] Sopat. Ermog. Tech. 95 (RG 5: 95).

mutilation highlighted a problem of paramount importance in late antique sources. By no means were most male slaves castrated; eunuchs were highly expensive and probably limited to Illustrious and Elite households.[97] The lurid sexual threat of the eunuch is, rather, the revealing exception. The eunuch was the ultimate contradiction: an emasculated creature set up to defend the chastity of the house, and yet whose access threatened to undermine the sexual reputation upon which the house's honor was built.

In Augustine's description of the *domus felix*, the wife stood in a "harmonious" relationship to the *pater familias*. With the language of harmony, Augustine evoked a prominent theme in Roman marital ideology, the ideal of concord.[98] The Romans valorized marriage as an affective partnership. If the marriage relationship remained firmly rooted in patriarchal power structures, the husband–wife bond was nevertheless the central strand in the Roman family. Roman conceptions of the family, by the late empire, had long since focused on the married couple as the nucleus of a new family rather than as extensions of a greater agnatic lineage.[99] In late antiquity Roman law was increasingly forced to recognize the realities of conjugal property, even though these patterns cut across the strong agnatic tendencies of Roman rules of succession.[100] The figure of the wife, in Roman society, was a subordinate partner – but partnership rather than subordination was the historical aberration. This partnership extended to mastery of the slaves. The Roman wife, the Roman mother, was also a Roman mistress of slaves.

More than the *pater familias* might have cared to admit, the different strands of the *domus felix* – master–slave, husband–wife, father–children – were intertwined. The persona of the *mater familias* was indelibly shaped by the presence of slaves. The Roman wife was more than just a passive, subordinate, sexually chaste partner; she played a medial role in the family as a slave-owner. From the woman carried in her litter by the muscle of her slaves, to the more humble Bourgeois matron who was careful to be seen with her single slave-girl, status shaped the lives of women.[101] For the upper and middling strata of Roman society, in particular, the ownership of slaves became interleaved, in delicate and subtle ways, with the maintenance and projection of feminine respectability. Women owned

---

[97] See CJ 7.7.1 (AD 530), where eunuchs cost at least two-and-a-half times an ordinary slave.
[98] Treggiari 1991, 245–53.
[99] For the late empire, see Harper forthcoming a and Cooper 2007a. Earlier periods: Saller and Shaw 1984.
[100] Beaucamp 1989.
[101] For litter-bearers and attendants, see, e.g., Hier. Ep. 22.16 (CSEL 54: 163–4); Hier. Ep. 66.13 (CSEL 54: 664); Lib. Ep. 615 (Foerster vol. 10: 566–7).

their own slaves and often had a separate contingent of slaves in their service.[102] For girls, marriage was a passage into adulthood, a world of childbearing, childrearing, and management of the slaves.[103] The good wife was devoted to household order, and her characteristic pose was sitting at the loom, supervising the slave-women in their weaving.[104]

The sermon of John Chrysostom on clamorous mistresses, analyzed in the Introduction to part II, reveals more complex striations when seen in this light.[105] The sermon transports us to a late ancient world where the role of the mistress was defined by her control over the slaves, where the household was open to public view, and where violence always threatened to overflow its proper bounds. Chrysostom staked his argument on preserving the honor of free women, whose abuse of slaves threatened to become unseemly. The noises of domestic clamor drifted into the public air, and those in the street "peeped," "stuck their heads in," to see what was transpiring. The bishop, by describing in such uncomfortable detail the practices of the Antiochene household, was able to make "all" the women in his audience blush – the physical sign of shame.[106] Chrysostom evoked a nightmarish failure of the household to maintain its good, honorable order, and the mistress's inability to control the slaves was at the center of this failure. Chrysostom the preacher was able to hammer with pinpoint accuracy on this delicate nerve.

Late Roman mistresses partook of that inscrutable superiority which stuck to the master class. One ascetic woman who sold all her property and dressed like her slave-girls could still be "told apart by the way she walked more effortlessly."[107] Slaves were supposed to stand in awe of the mistress. There was no image of tranquility like "the din of licentious slave-girls that is utterly silenced at the appearance of a wise mistress."[108] It was an awe based on fear: "some slave-girl, who likes to laugh, puts on airs when the mistress isn't home, but she becomes silent when the mistress suddenly appears, made well-behaved by fear."[109] Feminine mastery was mediated

[102] Bas. Anc. Virg. 62 (PG 30: 797); Ioh. Chrys. Ad pop. Ant. 13.2 (PG 49: 138); Hier. Vit. Hil. 8.1 (Bastiansen: 88); Hier. Ep. 22.16 (CSEL 54: 163–4).
[103] Ioh. Chrys. Virgin. 75.3 (SC 125: 360); Ast. Am. 5.7 (Datema: 48).
[104] Ps.-Aug. Sobr. (PL 40: 1110), Africa, fourth century. cf. Ioh. Chrys. Subintr. 9.27 (Dumortier: 76–7).
[105] Ioh. Chrys. In Ephes. 15.31 f. (PG 62: 109–10).   [106] See Kaster 1997, 7–8.
[107] Hier. Ep. 39.1 (CSEL 54: 294): *dinoscebatur, quod neglectius incedebat.*
[108] Bas. Attend. 7 (Rudberg: 35): οἷον θεραπαινίδων ἀκολάστων θορύβου κατασιγασθέντος δεσποίνης τινὸς σώφρονος παρουσίᾳ.
[109] Choric. Or. 20.60 (Foerster and Richtsteig: 243): ὥσπερ γὰρ θεράπαινά τις φιλόγελως οὐ παρούσης μὲν οἴκοι τῆς κεκτημένης κομψεύεται, ἄφνω δὲ φανείσης αὐτῆς ἠρεμεῖ σωφρονοῦσα τῷ δέει.

through the husband. Ideally, the slaves obeyed her and feared the master.[110] Of course, we hear of cruel mistresses, their harshness in the absence of the master, and hard widows.[111] But slave-ownership was treacherous for widows. They might have to sell an abusive slave.[112] The belligerent behavior of slaves was advertised as one of the hardest aspects of widowhood.[113] Without the violent presence of a husband, the dynamics of household power were drastically altered.

The position of the mistress *vis-à-vis* the slaves was ambiguous. She was free, and thus had access to networks of honor and power through which she could control slaves. The potential violence of the husband, in particular, activated her power. Her mastery was most secure when it was augmented by the sure assent and physical control of a male relative. If a woman lost the favor of her husband, the dynamics of slavery could be made to turn against her. A mistress suspected of adultery was put under tight surveillance, and the slaves were given the authority to monitor her movements. It would be her turn to "fear and tremble."[114] In a papyrus of the fourth century, we can actually watch a young marriage fall apart, as the husband uses physical and verbal violence against his wife and the slaves, locking the slaves in the wine cellar for a week. Later, he gave all the keys to the slaves but hid them from his wife. She extracted a promise from him, in front of the bishop, to change his ways. He still vexed his wife about a slave-woman whom he suspected of stealing, and ultimately he threatened to take a public woman as a mistress in a month's time – in the words of the poor wife, "God knows these things are true."[115]

Women in the Roman empire were subjected to the code of enforced privacy which is a common characteristic in Mediterranean history.[116] But the rules of privacy were suspended for women who were attended by their male relatives, or their slaves. When John Chrysostom preached against the ostentatious display of slaves, he imagined a woman replying to him, "How is it not *shameful* for a decent woman (literally "a free woman," i.e. a "wife") to walk around with only one or two slaves?"[117] A woman at the baths *without* a slave, for instance, was a scandalous bit of gossip.[118] Indeed,

---

[110] Ioh. Chrys. Non iter. conj. lines 271–9 (SC 138: 184).
[111] Ioh. Chrys. Vid. 5.350–4 (SC 138: 144); Choric. Or. 26.50 (Foerster and Richtsteig: 298).
[112] Ioh. Chrys. In 1 Thess. 11.3 (PG 62: 464).
[113] Bas. Anc. Virg. 23 (PG 30: 717); Gr. Nyss. Virg. 3.8 (SC 119: 292); Hier. Ep. 54.6 (CSEL 54: 97).
[114] Ioh. Chrys. Virgin. 52 (SC 125: 288–96).
[115] P. Oxy. 6.903 (fourth century): ταῦτα δὲ οἶδεν ὁ θ(εός). See Clark 1998, 126.
[116] CT 2.12.21 (AD 315). See Arjava 1996, 243–54.
[117] Ioh. Chrys. In Hebr. 28.4 (PG 63: 197–8): Καὶ πῶς οὐκ αἰσχύνη, φησὶν, ἐστὶ τὸ μετὰ δύο οἰκετῶν τὴν ἐλευθέραν βαδίζειν;
[118] Lib. Decl. 26.19 (Foerster vol. 6: 523).

it was the ownership of slaves that allowed middle- and upper-class women to flout the conventions of privacy that kept ancient women cloistered. The importance of slavery in constructing spatial boundaries for women has received little mention by modern historians. Women could be seen in public, but never alone.[119]

The relations between children and slaves were also unpredictable, but in this case because the child was still in preparation for mastery. Certainly the interaction between the slaves and the children of the master might be warm. The slaves were present at the birth of the master's child and maybe even given their freedom on that day.[120] In a world that required its men to be stern, slaves might be more uninhibited around children than the father. It was slaves who "made scary or funny faces" at the children.[121] Many of the jobs given to slaves encouraged a sort of intimacy. Female slaves might nurse the free children; nurses could enjoy a sort of informal emotional bond with the children.[122] Children had slaves assigned to them as escorts and guardians.[123] Tutors might be especially fond of their young charges.[124] Young masters and mistresses could have a comrade in the household, a sort of friendship that could cut across the father's desire to control his children and his slaves both.[125] Of course, many of them may have been half-siblings to their slaves, whether the relation was acknowledged or not.

The relationship between free children and slaves could mimic the dialectics of master–slave relations in general, but the child's youth distorted the power dynamics. Older slaves might be able to out-maneuver their young masters. In the *Confessions*, Augustine recounted a story about his mother Monica as a young girl. The slave-woman who customarily accompanied her to the wine cellar accused her of being a lush, out of resentment.[126] The little mistress was so shaken (*percussa*) at the accusation from an inferior that it "saved" her from alcohol, and the breach of normal propriety made such an impression that she obviously repeated it to her son decades later.[127]

We should not underestimate the role of corporal punishment in the practices of childrearing in antiquity.[128] It was a hard world, accustomed to the exercise of brutal violence, and physical discipline was regularly enforced on the free children as well as the slaves. Yet ultimately the

---

[119] MacMullen 1990, 162–8, is the best treatment, recognizing that the difference in habits of public exposure were not driven by an east–west cultural divide, but by status differences.

[120] Birthday: Ioh. Chrys. Eleem. 3 (PG 51: 265). Present at birth: Aug. Serm. 61.9 (PL 38: 412).

[121] Ioh. Chrys. Adv. Iud. 1.3 (PG 48: 848): προσωπεῖα δεικνύντες φοβερὰ καὶ καταγέλαστα.

[122] Aug. Conf. 9.8.17 (CC 27: 143). On nursing, see chapter 3, and Joshel 1986.

[123] Ioh. Chrys. Ad pop. Ant. 16.4 (PG 49: 168); Choric. Or. 32.85 (Foerster and Richtsteig: 363).

[124] Lib. Or. 58.10 (Foerster vol. 4: 186). See chapter 3.   [125] E.g. Hier. Ep. 107.9 (CSEL 55: 300).

[126] Aug. Conf. 9.8.18 (CC 27: 144).   [127] Clark 1998.   [128] De Bruyn 1999.

punishment and even the nature of obedience expected of sons was distinct from that of slaves.[129] "Just as fear means something different in the case of the wife and the case of the slave, so there is a distinction in the obedience expected of sons and of slaves."[130] "Often the *pater familias* will order his son to be corrected by his most wicked slaves, while he prepares the inheritance for one, and the leg-irons for the other."[131] The inheritance provided the structural framework of the family. The marriage between husband and wife was supposed to create an heir. The children were raised with the purpose of passing on the patrimony. The father's power over his children was absolute and despotic; if it resembled his control over the slaves, the inheritance was the decisive difference.

A son was prepared for the inheritance by which he would succeed as master. Late antique children acquired knowledge of mastery from their elders. That rough education, the process by which children were groomed to be masters, was the sort of ineffable, generational instruction never recorded in writing.[132] But in one document that has survived the hazards of transmission, we can just hear a faint echo of how young men were instilled with the sense of honor that would make them into masters. Hiding deep in the *Corpus Glossariorum Latinorum* is a revealing school exercise, one used to teach Latin to young men. It is the familiar sort of "see Jane run" narrative, except that the quotidian scene of the late ancient world was an argument about status and power:[133]

Do you insult me, you wicked person? You will be crucified. You do evil and you do not know that it is bad for you. Why is that? Because I am a freeborn man, but you are a vile slave. Keep quiet. You want to learn something? I am not your equal. No, you liar? I want to learn if you are a slave or a freedman. I do not give you a reason. Why is that? Because you do not deserve one. Let us go to your master. Perhaps – for I am a freeborn man known to all and a *pater familias*. It is obvious from your face. Let us go.[134]

---

[129] The point is also made by Hezser 2005, 71–2.

[130] Hier. Ephes. 3.6 (PL 26: 576): *ut sicut inter servum et uxorem habet metus diversitatem: ita et inter filios et servos obedientia discreparet.*

[131] Aug. Psalm. 117.13 (CC 40: 1662): *saepe filios paterfamilias per nequissimos servos emendari iubet, cum illis hereditatem, illis compedes praeparet.* Ps.-Mac. Hom. spir. 13 (Dörries, Klostermann, and Krüger: 120).

[132] On the American South: Wyatt-Brown 1986, 80–1.

[133] Rochette 2008, 94; Ferri 2008, 120–1, for the date, early-to-mid-fourth century.

[134] Colloq. Harl. 18 (CGL 3: 642): *Maledicis me, malum caput? Crucifigaris. Male facis et nescis quod non expedit tibi. Qua re? Quoniam ego ingenuus homo sum, tu autem nequam servus. Silentium habe. Vis ergo discere. Non sum tibi par. Non, inpostor? Volo discere utrum servus esse aut libertus. Non do tibi rationem. Qua re? Quoniam non es dignus. Eamus ad dominum tuum. Fortasse. Ego enim ingenuus omnibus notus et pater familias. Apparet a facie tua. Eamus nos.*

The innocuous, schoolbook language stands in utter contrast to the gigantic arrogance of the passage. The exercise was meant to teach more than just reading.[135] In this public encounter, the young man – the *pater familias* – claimed to discern his opponent's status from his face, the cipher of a man's interior self. The sense of honor among masters was not inborn, as they may have wished to believe; it was deliberately cultivated from a tender age in the next generation. Mastery was achieved by nurture, rather than nature, but it ran deep in ancient society.[136]

CONCLUSION: MASTERY AND SPIRITUAL MISGIVINGS

The study of mastery is an essential component of a history of slavery, and it also yields privileged insights into the encounter between late Roman Christianity and slavery. Mastery was, to an extent not sufficiently recognized, the zone of conflict between the slave system and the triumphant religion. This is nowhere more evident than in the only extant critique of slavery to survive from antiquity. From all of antiquity, we know of only a handful of critics of slavery. The opponents of Aristotle held that slavery was unnatural (but not necessarily unjust); myths of a Golden Age imagined a time of peace and equality; Philo reported that the Essenes refused to own slaves because it was unjust.[137] By far the most remarkable and categorical statement of opposition to slavery survives in an exegetical sermon of Gregory of Nyssa.[138] The sermon centered on the verse of *Ecclesiastes* in which the author confessed that "I got me servants and maidens." The king's great wealth, including his slaves, inflated his pride. There was, Gregory claimed, an especially insidious connection between the ownership of slaves and the experience of pride.[139]

"If a man makes that which truly belongs to God into his own private property, by allotting himself sovereignty over his own race, and thinks himself the master of men and women, what could follow but an arrogance exceeding all nature from the one who sees himself as something other than the ones who are ruled?"[140] Gregory argued that slavery was based on an

---

[135] Bradley 1994, 26; Bloomer 1997, 73, on the colloquia as exercises in socialization.
[136] Gleason 1995, the classic account of masculinity as an achieved state in Roman culture.
[137] Arist. Pol. 1253b20–3 (see Cambiano 1987); Urbainczyk 2008, 75–81, on egalitarian myths; Philo, Prob. 79–80 (Cohn vol. 6: 15–16), with Garnsey 1996, 78–9.
[138] Garnsey 1996, 81–2.   [139] Gr. Nyss. Hom. in Eccl. 4.1 (SC 416: 224).
[140] Gr. Nyss. Hom. in Eccl. 4.1 (SC 416: 224): ὁ οὖν κτῆμα ἑαυτοῦ τὸ τοῦ θεοῦ κτῆμα ποιούμενος ἐπιμερίζων τε τῷ γένει τὴν δυναστείαν, ὡς ἀνδρῶν τε ἅμα καὶ γυναικῶν ἑαυτὸν κύριον οἴεσθαι, τί ἄλλο καὶ οὐχὶ διαβαίνει τῇ ὑπερηφανίᾳ τὴν φύσιν, ἄλλο τι ἑαυτὸν παρὰ τοὺς ἀρχομένους βλέπων;

unjustified division of nature into mastery and slavery. He attacked slavery by questioning, philosophically, the paradigmatic act of the slave system: the sale. With penetrating insight, he asked how the human being, the rational creation of God, could be given a "price." What, he asked, could have the same market value as human nature? "How much does rationality cost? How many obols for the image of God? How many staters did you get for selling the God-formed man?"[141]

Gregory's sermon was a remarkable document, in some ways anticipating the moral groundwork and poetry of the abolitionist movement by nearly a millennium-and-a-half. He would tell masters that they and their slaves shared the same origin, the same life, the same sufferings. Master and slave breathed the same air, saw the same sun, ate the same food, and their two bodies became one dust after death.[142] But even this lone radical statement of opposition to slavery was not an abolitionist tract. Gregory's opposition to slavery never congealed into a political argument.[143] It arose in the context of opposition to pride. His moral reasoning was aimed not to achieve social justice, but to offer refinement for philosophical Christians. His sermons on *Ecclesiastes* were not even popular preaching. He branded them as a sort of rarefied teaching suitable for those advanced in the wisdom of Christian mysteries.[144]

The sermon of Gregory is a complex document. It is a work of exegesis; it is a Neo-Platonic attack on natural slave theory, informed by Gregory's view that all men and women were created rational; it is a visceral objection to the contemporary practices of the slave trade.[145] But the sermon also demands to be read as an attack on pride. That was its beginning and end. Gregory was more concerned about *mastery*, in fact, than *slavery*. This truth in no way undermines the beauty or even significance of the text. Gregory's sermon is simply not an assertion of natural rights, in any modern sense, even if the underlying values he espoused were pregnant with such potential. Gregory's sermon, as it exists, stands as a call for spiritual regeneration through the disavowal of earthly wealth and honor. Slavery, or rather mastery, stood as a looming obstacle in the way of such change.

---

[141] Gr. Nyss. Hom. in Eccl. 4.1 (SC 416: 228): πόσου κέρματος ἐτιμήσω τὸν λόγον; πόσοις ὀβολοῖς τὴν εἰκόνα τοῦ θεοῦ ἀντεστάθμησας; πόσων στατήρων τὴν θεόπλαστον φύσιν ἀπενεπόλησας;

[142] Gr. Nyss. Hom. in Eccl. 4.1 (SC 416: 230–2).   [143] Kontoulis 1993, 232; Moriarty 1993, 65–6.

[144] Gr. Nyss. Hom. in Eccl. 1.1 (SC 416: 106).

[145] Dennis 1982, on the importance of man's rational nature at creation for Gregory's critique.

The Christian church fundamentally accepted the practice and ideology of slavery. The church could accept the existence of mastery and slavery as social roles, and it could even allow that they were just, but it insisted that there were values which transcended these roles, there was a scale of good and evil which did not take its measurements from the place of mastery and slavery in the world. This transvaluation of all values was what Nietzsche called, not imperceptively, a slave revolt in morals. But he saw it, through the lens of modern Europe, as a *révolution accompli*. In late antiquity this revolution was highly incomplete and its outcome entirely uncertain.

The fourth century was a particularly intense phase of accommodation and conflict between values old and new. The burgeoning ascetic wing of the church stood as a stark challenge to those who believed that life in the world could be reconciled with Christian salvation. The ascetic effort to live out the re-valuation of values even involved manipulating the store of symbols used to advertise honor and shame, mastery and slavery. The ascetic who renounced ordinary social life did more than abandon property ownership, he (or she) lived in a manner that inverted the normal signs of social valuation. Clothing, for instance, was a universal marker of status. Long before the monastic habit had become a standardized costume, the pioneering ascetics of the fourth century took off their honorable clothes to don the humble attire of the slave.[146] Some radicals went further still. A more drastic act of inversion entailed marking the body, with tattoos. Tattoos were a viscerally evocative sign of enslavement, even of a degraded form of subjection. For those who voluntarily tattooed themselves, marking the body was at once a sign of utter submission to God and a powerful inversion of symbolic hierarchies.[147]

The ascetic celebrities of late antiquity formed a spiritual *avant garde* who deliberately and conspicuously posed the conflict between secular and religious values in the starkest possible terms. In its pastoral guise, the church appears as an institution more committed to reconciling traditional social structure and new spiritual values. Bishops like Augustine preached the possibility of spiritual change within society, a mystical form of spiritual exile in the midst of the earthly city. Augustine insisted that abandoning the world was not the only path of Christian righteousness; otherwise, Paul was being deceptive when he "so diligently set houses in good order with clear doctrine, preaching and teaching what wives owed their husbands,

---

[146] E.g. Ioh. Chrys. Oppug. 2.2 (PG 47: 333); Hier. Ep. 77.2 (CSEL 55: 38).
[147] See Elm 2004 and 1996.

husbands their wives, children their parents, parents their children, slaves their masters, masters their slaves – for how could these be done without a *domus*?"[148] This is the voice of a man in the trenches, disheartened by strategies of abandoning the world.

It was always Augustine who had the most vivid and sympathetic sense of the contradictions between Christianity and the emotional tendrils which connected men and women to life on earth. Augustine located the desire for mastery not quite within the realm of conscious choice, but deeper, in the psychic constitution of the fallen human self. The *libido dominandi* was an indistinct force, seething within the human soul, which could be blunted by sacramental grace but never cured in this life. It was inseparable from the welter of ambitions and physical desires which motivated human action. For Augustine, slavery was unnatural, in the sense that it was not located in man's essence; there were no natural slaves. For Augustine, slavery was inevitable, but it was a secondary consequence of mankind's sinful state. On the other hand, there was no one, in this lapsarian world, who was free from the lust of power, who did not crave recognition and human glory. For Augustine, slavery was secondary, conventional; mastery was natural.

---

[148] Aug. Ep. 157.30 (CSEL 44: 478): *domos tam diligenter doctrinae sanitate componit admonens et praecipiens, quales se praebere debeant uxores viris, viri uxoribus, filii parentibus, parentes filiis, servi dominis, domini servis; nam quo modo haec agi possunt sine domo . . .*

PART III

The imperial order

Introduction

AN ORDER IMPOSED

Late Roman statecraft was famously ceremonial.[1] In a far-flung empire, ruled by a bureaucratic monarchy, political ceremony became a vital interface between the state and its subjects. The movements of the emperor, the victories of the army, the cycles of the civic calendar were all celebrated with lavish spectacles. But military success and imperial itineration were unpredictable. Only the civic calendar provided the regular rhythms of celebration and display on which the late Roman state relied. In this cycle, no event was more significant than the annual installation of new consuls.[2] Late antique political ceremony has been well served in modern scholarship, and the ceremonies surrounding the annual installation of new consuls have been the object of detailed scrutiny. Nevertheless, an important part of the annual ceremony has been almost entirely neglected: the consular manumission of slaves. As part of their installation, the new consuls performed a public manumission, a ceremonial act freighted with ideological significance. The manumission of slaves by the Roman consuls on the first of the year symbolized, in especially compact form, the whole institutional order of the Roman state and its status system.

The consular installation was an imperial ritual synchronized with the natural cycles of Mediterranean festivity, coinciding with the wild atmosphere of the Kalends of January; the Kalends became a sort of universal holiday in late antiquity.[3] The manumission of slaves occurred on the first day of the New Year's games, on the Kalends itself, marking the consul's assumption of office. Ammianus' description of the manumission ceremony in

---

[1] McCormick 1987 and 1985; MacCormack 1981.
[2] Cameron 1976; Meslin 1970; Göll 1859, esp. 606–7.
[3] Meslin 1970. Lib. Or. 9.4–11 (Foerster vol. 1: 394–6); Lib. Or. 16.36 (Foerster vol. 2: 174); Lib. Prog. 12.5.11 (Foerster vol. 8: 476).

AD 362 makes this evident. On the "*day* of the Kalends of January," the new consul Mamertinus was presiding over the circus games while the slaves to be manumitted were led up to him "according to custom."[4] The emperor Julian was present and immediately declared them free. Ammianus was emphatic that this act occurred on the very day of installation: Julian, when reminded that the jurisdiction belonged to another *on that day*, immediately confessed that he was guilty of a mistake and fined himself ten pounds of gold. This story yields an unexpected insight, too: manumission was such a routine chore for the emperor that Julian absent-mindedly pronounced the slaves free, "as he was used to doing."[5]

The earliest references to the consular manumission come from the reign of Julian, although the ceremony probably originated earlier, perhaps in the reign of Constantine when the ordinary consulate began to re-claim the tremendous prestige it would enjoy throughout late antiquity.[6] The consul received a panegyric on assuming office; remarkably, no fewer than three of the extant panegyrics reach their climax with a call for the day's proceedings to continue in the form of manumitting slaves.[7] The passage of Ammianus confirms that the manumission ritual was part of the installation, held in conjunction with the games, races, and shows. The manumission seems to have taken place after the *processus consularis*, either before or near the beginning of the games. Ammianus implies that the manumission of AD 362 took place specifically in the circus, and indeed in Constantinople the *processus consularis* ended in the hippodrome.[8] In Rome it ended in the Atrium Libertatis of Trajan's Forum, where Sidonius describes the western consul manumitting slaves.[9]

Consular manumission condensed and advertised in a dramatic public ritual the array of political justifications that supported Roman statecraft. The consular manumission sat at the nexus of two of the most enduring themes in late Roman ideology: the rule of law and eternal victory. In the late empire, the office of the consul was practically a symbol; as the old magistracies of the republic withered into oblivion, the consulate remained the highest civilian honor.[10] The pageantry of the consulate celebrated an office and, by extension, a constitution that was imponderably ancient. The

---

[4] Amm. 22.7.1 (Seyfarth vol. 1: 258): *Calendarum Ianuariarum die . . . ex more.*
[5] Amm. 22.7.2 (Seyfarth vol. 1: 258): *ut solebat.*
[6] Amm. 22.7.2 (Seyfarth vol. 1: 258). Bagnall *et al.* 1987, 4 (arguing that Constantine "did no more than regularize an obvious tendency").
[7] Lib. Or. 12.101 (Foerster vol. 2: 44–5); Claud. De quart. cons. Hon. lines 612–15 (Hall: 83); Sid. Carm. 2.544–6 (Mohr: 255).
[8] Olovsdotter 2005, 180; Tondo 1967, 180–1. See also Heucke 1994, 77–80.
[9] Sid. Carm. 2.544–9 (Mohr: 255). Tondo 1967, 183.   [10] Bagnall *et al.* 1987, 1–6; Jones 1964, 532–4.

practical duties of the consul were limited to the provision of the games, but the manumission of slaves on the Kalends represented one legal act still performed by the magistrate. The manumission symbolized the legitimacy of the state and its laws. In the late empire, Roman emperors were careful to rule through the medium of public law. The story in Ammianus' history perfectly captures what was at stake in the consular manumission. Julian fined himself for failing to observe the façade of constitutional governance. Emperors "though not bound by the laws, live by the laws. They properly treat themselves as if bound by law."[11] Claudian's panegyric emphasized the importance of *Libertas* and *Lex* expressed by the consular manumission.[12] Both Malalas and Claudian derived the origins of consular manumission from the story of the first consul, Brutus, whose slave alerted him to the designs of the tyrant Tarquinius.[13] They could believe it was a tradition maintained across the centuries, connecting past and present through the continual re-enactment of political mythology.[14]

The ultimate sanction of the state's power, the source of its ideological legitimacy, was military victory.[15] The late Roman state was a triumphal monarchy. The imperial columns, coins, medallions, diptychs, and panegyrics of late antiquity constantly remind us that no element of Roman imperial ideology remained so powerful as the claim of eternal victory. The consular manumission ceremony was an expression of this ideology. In a formula of consular appointment, Cassiodorus claimed that the power of the consul, specifically the manumission of slaves, was justified by the eternal victory of the Roman state.[16] Libanius' speech of AD 363 conjured an image of Roman soldiers dining in Susa, served by enslaved Persians, just before concluding his speech with a call for the manumission.[17] In his panegyric for Anthemius, Sidonius finished his speech with a call for the consul to manumit the slaves, so that the armies could advance and capture new ones.[18] The spectacle of slaves hauled before the consul, whose office gave him the majestic right of making them Roman citizens, expressed the orderly control of the *oikoumenê* which the Roman government claimed to exert. The annual rite of consular manumission represented the continuous parade of military victories which justified the state's power.

---

[11] Honoré 2004, 131.   [12] Claud. De quart. cons. Hon. lines 612–15 (Hall: 83).
[13] Ioh. Mal. 7.9 (Thurn: 139–40). Tondo 1967, 182.
[14] Reflected too in the consul's costume: Olovdotter 2005, 71.   [15] Above all McCormick 1987.
[16] Cass. Var. 6.1 (CC 96: 224).   [17] Lib. Or. 12.100 (Foerster vol. 2: 44–5).
[18] Sid. Carm. 2.544–6 (Mohr: 255).

In late antiquity the ideology of victory was closely linked to the rule of Roman law.[19] Late antiquity was the age of Mediterranean-wide supremacy for Roman private law.[20] A fourth-century historian imagined that the ultimate goal of Roman victory was to bring Roman law to the entire world: "our laws and our judges will be everywhere."[21] That was a strikingly practical way to put it: judges were the institutional personnel who would carry the laws to the ends of the empire. If consuls were the symbolic embodiment of Roman institutions, judges were the living flesh of Roman law. Roman law was real because the state deployed an army of officials across the Mediterranean to enforce it.[22] Justice was the domain of the governor, the responsible judicial agent in each province. Significantly, provincial governors acted out a version of the consular manumission during the new year's celebration.[23] The manumission of slaves answered, like nothing else, the need to display victory over the barbarians and to express the legal order of Roman society. By ceremonially manumitting slaves on the Kalends of January, the Roman state chose to perform, in the electric public atmosphere of the New Year's games, its claim to regulate the social order.

The act of consular manumission in late antiquity acquired tremendous cultural cachet. The ritual of consular manumission came to provide a language for talking about political expectations. Claudian's invective against Eutropius could use the act of consular manumission as a symbol of everything wrong with the eastern consul of AD 399: on assuming the office, the former slave – who had never earned his freedom, according to Claudian – was about to pollute the sacred rites of manumission.[24] The slaves manumitted by the rebel Heraclian while he was consul had to be re-manumitted since "the rites of the consulate were polluted by his crime."[25] For Libanius, by contrast, Julian's tenure of the consulship in AD 363 fulfilled the ideals of a proper ruler. The slaves manumitted by Julian were the luckiest ever to be freed, since they were manumitted by a consul who ruled his own soul in freedom.[26]

We should not underestimate the force of the ideology expressed in the consular manumission ceremony. The Mediterranean world of late

---

[19] E.g. Amm. 14.6.5 (Seyfarth vol. 1: 12).   [20] Honoré 2004.
[21] SHA, Prob. 20.6 (Hohl vol. 2: 219): *ubique Romanae leges, ubique iudices nostri.*
[22] Slootjes 2006, 47–76; Jones 1964, 374, 386–7, overly negative.
[23] Ioh. Mal. 7.9 (Thurn: 140). cf. Auson. Grat. act. 7 (Green: 151), which implies a public aspect to the empire-wide celebration of the Kalends.
[24] Claud. In Eutr. 1 lines 309–11 (Hall: 155).
[25] CT 15.14.12 (AD 413): *scelere eius sollemnitatem consulatus esse pollutam.*
[26] Lib. Or. 12.101 (Foerster vol. 2: 44–5).

antiquity was one in which a strong imperial state furnished the rules that gave objective form and public legitimacy to the slave system. In a letter from early fifth-century Africa, we have heard the desperate voice of a bishop appeal to a distant emperor because slave-traders were abducting free Romans, not *"real slaves."*[27] In actuality, the slave trade carried an eclectic mix of barbarians and native Romans, homebred slaves, kidnapped children, imported strangers, and true captives.[28] But the Roman state made slavery a unitary and overriding legal category. The force of the conquest mentality, backed by the apparatus of the imperial administration, meant that even a shrewd visionary like Augustine could express, as an internalized habit of thought, a belief in the legitimacy of the status system. Slavery was a politically created reality, buried in the consciousness of late antique men and women, but the unity and objectivity of the slave system were not the state of nature in the Mediterranean. Slave status was part of the public order imposed by the Roman Leviathan.

STATUS AS AN INSTITUTIONAL PROBLEM

The object of these chapters is to scrutinize the institutional nuts-and-bolts of slave status in order to understand how the Roman state tried to make good on the symbolism of the manumission ceremony. The focus is on the institutional foundations of slave status from the late third century to the completion of the *Theodosian Code* in AD 438. This investigation is an integral component of a revisionist history of slavery. The law codes have been primary evidence in histories of slavery's decline.[29] In some accounts, the laws are supposed to reflect underlying social changes which corresponded with the decline of slavery – the law as a symptom or sign of slavery's decay. In others, the legal enactments are supposed to have catalyzed or contributed to the disintegration of the system – so that slavery was "Christianized" or undermined by a new regime of status. It is necessary to question these received views, but an equally important objective is to gain an understanding of the positive role of the Roman state in maintaining the status system. A slave system so massive and complex was inherently unstable, and it required constant, active regulation. The legal record reflects the constant institutional activity required to govern a slave society.

[27] Aug. Ep. 10*.2 (CSEL 88: 47): *veros...servos.*   [28] See chapter 2.
[29] Yuge 1982, 145: "die bedeutendsten Quellen für den Niedergang der antiken Sklaverei." Boulvert 1984; Härtel 1975, 240.

The choice of status as a focus of study is specific. There is little discussion of the colonate in these chapters, both because the legal framework of the colonate has been so extensively explored and because slave status in Roman law remained clearly distinct.[30] Moreover, there is in these pages little attention to the internal substance of slave status – to the specific disabilities or the limited protections afforded to slaves by the public authorities.[31] This is partly because the inner nature of slave status changed very little in the fourth and fifth centuries. On the other hand, the regulation of status itself, the edges of slave status, the passages between freedom and slavery – these occasioned constant activity, and they have left a highly visible trail in the legal record of the fourth century.

There were various forms of personal legal status in Roman law, depending on age, gender, relation to others, wealth, civic origins, etc.[32] But slavery was a distinct type of legal status, because it alone meant that the person was an object of ownership. The Roman law of slavery is an extension of the Roman law of property, and the idea of property is juristically the foundation of slave status.[33] All property is a public affair, because property requires a publicly mediated system of rules by which the community allots exclusive power over things, including the human being as an owned thing.[34] In late Roman society, the civil law was the primary means of mediating property ownership. It provided the rules and ultimately the coercive apparatus which made property rights functional and enforceable – in other words, legitimate.[35] The Roman laws regulating slave status were first and foremost an extension of the system by which some humans could be owned and traded as chattel.

Fourth-century men and women were perfectly aware of the role of the imperial state in maintaining the property system. "When we take wives, make a will, or are about to buy slaves, houses, fields, and such, we do it not according to private form, but as the imperial laws command."[36] The link between public law and the order of property was perceived as the *raison d'être* for the civil law. "God made the rich and the poor from

---

[30] On the colonate, see Sirks 2008; Grey 2007a; Scheidel 2000; Lo Cascio 1997; Marcone 1988; Carrié 1983 and 1982; Eibach 1980.
[31] Watson 1987; Boulvert and Morabito 1982; Robleda 1976; Buckland 1908, are the essential treatments.
[32] On the salience of citizenship in the late empire, Mathisen 2006.
[33] Compare Morris 1996, 42, for modern parallels.
[34] Barzel 1997, 3–4. cf. Patterson 1982, 30–1. For a property-based definition of slavery, see chapter 1.
[35] Meyer 2004.
[36] Ioh. Chrys. Ad pop. Ant. 16.2 (PG 49: 164): κἂν γυναῖκας ἀγώμεθα, κἂν διαθήκας ποιῶμεν, κἂν οἰκέτας ὠνεῖσθαι μέλλωμεν, κἂν οἰκίας, κἂν ἀγροὺς, κἂν ὁτιοῦν ἕτερον ποιεῖν, οὐκ οἰκείᾳ γνώμῃ ταῦτα πράττομεν, ἀλλ' ὅπως ἂν ἐκεῖνοι (sc. νόμοι βασιλικοί) διατάξωσι.

one clay, and one earth nurtures rich and poor alike. But by the law of man, one says, 'That is my villa, that is my house, that is my slave.' By the law of man, thus by the law of the emperors ... But what is the emperor to me, you ask? It is by his right that you possess land. Take away the laws of the emperors, and who would dare to say, 'This is my villa, this is my slave, this is my house?' Humans have accepted the laws of kings so that they can possess just such things."[37]

We can see the fundamental relationship between slave status and the property system at work in the administrative routines of the slave trade. To take one example, in December of 323, an Egyptian named Firmus brought his new slave before a panel of lower-level officials to certify the slave's status and complete the paperwork on his purchase of the slave.[38] The hearing was a routine part of commercial life in late antique Egypt: these proceedings appear in the mid-second century AD and are well attested throughout the third and fourth.[39] The officials asked Patricius, "Are you slave or free?" He replied: "slave." They asked who his owner was: "Firmus." They asked where he came from: "Rescupum."[40] They asked him who sold him: "Nicostratus." They asked if his mother was a slave: "Yes." Her name: "Hesychion." Siblings: "Yes, one, Eutychius." Is he a slave too: "Yes." The slave's laconic answers – whether these were the sullen replies of a slave on the block, anxious co-operation before a new master, or merely what the master found useful to record – guaranteed his status.[41] The questions put to him were an effort to draw an imaginary line back to an objective foundation for his status. The certification of his status underwrote the legitimacy of his sale.

The scene with Patricius is a paradigm for the law of status in antiquity. The state was the stabilizing force in the slave system, because it had the authority to provide publicly valid rules of status. In antiquity, the state was an absolute precondition for a slave system of any scale and

---

[37] Aug. Tract. Io. 6.25 (CC 36: 66): *pauperes et divites deus de uno limo fecit, et pauperes et divites una terra supportat. iure tamen humano dicit: haec villa mea est, haec domus mea, hic servus meus est. iure ergo humano, iure imperatorum ... sed quid mihi est imperator? secundum ius ipsius possides terram. aut tolle iura imperatorum, et quis audet dicere: mea est illa villa, aut meus est ille servus, aut domus haec mea est? ut teneantur ista ab hominibus, iura acceperunt regum.* cf. Wood 1988, 130–1.

[38] P. Herm. Rees 18. For the date, see Bagnall and Worp 1978, 108–9.   [39] Straus 2004, 62–71.

[40] The editors of the papyrus (accepted by Bieżuńska-Małowist, 1974–7, vol. 2, 37) suggest that this unknown place name (Ρεσκούπου) may be Resculum in Dacia, but the reading of the papyrus is secure, and it seems more likely that Rescupum is an unknown locale, beyond the southeastern zone of Roman power, where a vigorous slave trade is certainly attested in late antiquity (see chapter 2). Moreover, the littoral of the Arabian sea was covered with towns whose names begin with "Ras" – Arabic for "head," often with the connotation of "harbor."

[41] Straus 2004, 70.

complexity to emerge and survive. The state was instrumental in ancient slavery, perhaps even more so than in modern slave systems, for at least one obvious structural reason: ancient slavery was not race-based. The practice of "marking" status could not rely on the insidiously useful marker of skin color. "Only with difficulty can one distinguish a free man from a slave."[42] Marking status sometimes took a vestimentary or onomastic form in antiquity, but it remained, fundamentally, the role of the state to furnish the rules and enforcement mechanisms which classified some bodies as chattel.[43] In late antiquity, if the status or ownership of a slave was in doubt, it could be resolved in a courtroom.[44] Libanius had "often" heard court cases deciding the fate of a single slave in which both sides had brilliant, loquacious attorneys.[45] Census-takers noted whether an individual was free or slave; there was no in-between.[46] Disputed or ambiguous cases could be resolved according to a set of rules. Slave status was concrete and objective because it was backed by the majesty, machinery, and coercive power of the state. "The slave is a slave absolutely."[47]

The period covered by these chapters, the long fourth century, is in many ways a discrete phase in the history of Roman law.[48] For most of our period, the Roman empire remained a political unity, and down to the end of our period legal unity at least remained a realistic ambition. This was also an age of universal citizenship, at least for most free inhabitants of the empire.[49] Neither before nor since was Roman civil law applied on such a scale. This fact lies behind the production of the legal evidence which is at our disposal. Throughout these chapters, the nature of the source material will be a prominent concern. It is imperative not to mistake change in the nature of the sources for change in the nature of law or institutions.[50] From the classical period of Roman law, we possess far more juridical commentary than statutory law or administrative correspondence. This imparts some of the legal elegance associated with classical jurisprudence. The late Roman sources thrust us headfirst into the messy world of practice, of enforcement and administration, and in a context of universal citizenship. In the legal texts of the fourth and fifth century, the aura of immaculate

---

[42] Dig. 18.1.5: *difficile dinosci potest liber homo a servo.*
[43] For vestimentary codes, see chapter 8; for onomastic, see appendix 1.
[44] E.g. the titles CJ 7.16 and CT 4.8, *de liberali causa*, analyzed in chapter 9.
[45] Lib. Or. 45.18 (Foerster vol. 3: 367).
[46] E.g. Lact. Mort. 23.2 (Creed: 26). Eibach 1980 and Carrié 1982 on the absence of an intermediate status; Sirks 2008, for the formalization of the adscripticiate in the sixth century.
[47] Gr. Nyss. Eun. 8.44 (Jaeger: 255): ὁ δοῦλος δοῦλος πάντως ἐστίν.
[48] See esp. Honoré 2004; Harries 1999.   [49] See chapter 9.
[50] A point underscored by Liebs 2008b.

reasoning has vanished, supplanted by the coarse dialect of an imperial administration.

An institutional history by its very nature fixes our attention on the interface between legal rules and social practice. The legal sources of the long fourth century are many and diverse, but two sources in particular dominate our knowledge of this period: the Diocletianic rescripts preserved in the *Justinianic Code* and the imperial constitutions, from Constantine to Theodosius II, collected in the *Theodosian Code*. These, in turn, are very different witnesses to the legal regime of Roman slavery, each valuable in a distinct way. Rescripts are short statements of existing law issued by the emperor's chancery in response to a petition.[51] They re-iterate prevailing legal rules in the context of specific cases. A litigant in a private dispute could petition the emperor for a statement of the pertinent legal rule. In response, the petitioner would receive a legal opinion drafted by an imperial secretary and undersigned by the emperor. A rescript was a weighty opinion which the litigant could tender before a judge. The rescripts show us Roman law as it came into play in the ordinary disputes of some rather humble denizens of the empire; the codes show us the energy of the Diocletianic administration and its commitment to enforcing classical Roman law.

The documents of the *Theodosian Code* are altogether different. The *Theodosian Code* was commissioned in AD 429 and completed in AD 438 under the sponsorship of Theodosius II.[52] His code was a collection of laws from the time of Constantine up to his own day. It was the most ambitious effort at codification yet attempted, and although the commissioning acts survive, the precise nature and purpose of the *Theodosian Code* remain debated. Theodosius II called for the inclusion of all generally valid imperial laws.[53] This included imperial edicts and speeches to the senate, and more importantly letters issued by the emperor to imperial agents, especially praetorian prefects and governors.[54] The bulk of the *Theodosian Code* consists of letters from the emperor to his officials, typically written in the florid epistolary style of late Latin. The editors of the *Theodosian Code* were empowered to whittle the documents they found down to their legal core and to classify them under relevant titles of the code.[55] Every law as we now possess it is profoundly shaped by three phases of its

---

[51] Corcoran 2000, 42–73; Honoré 1994, 33–70; Turpin 1991; Coriat 1985; Williams 1980; Wilcken 1920. See chapter 9.

[52] Sirks 2007; Matthews 2000; Harries 1999; Honoré 1998; Harries and Wood 1993; Archi 1976.

[53] See Harper forthcoming b; Sirks 2007, 19–23, 70–2; Matthews 2000, 65–71; Harries 1999, 24–5; Honoré 1998, 128–9; van der Wal 1981; Bianchini 1979.

[54] Sirks 2007, 85–6.   [55] CT 1.1.6 (AD 435).

existence: its original enactment, its treatment by the editors, and a highly complex and incomplete transmission history.[56] The *Theodosian Code* is no straightforward guide to legal practice in the fourth century.

Constant awareness of the nature of the sources is one methodological premise of these chapters; another is careful construction of the questions we ask. The study of post-classical law has often been pursued as a study of change. The most influential narratives of late Roman slave law posit that social changes underlie post-classical developments. Indeed, three culprits have traditionally been assigned a role in the development of slave law in late antiquity: the rise of Christianity, the confusion or merger of the lower classes (including slaves and tenants), and the influence of provincial customs. A major contention of part III is that these narratives are an unsatisfactory way to *frame* the history of slave law in late antiquity.

The thesis of Christianization has been obvious and pervasive.[57] It bears a broader resemblance to the amelioration narrative of ancient slavery, in which the influence of Stoicism and then Christianity humanized master–slave relations and mitigated the horrors of slavery.[58] In many cases, influence is undeniable, but it is worth taking stock of the nature of "Christian" slave law, particularly as it existed in the fourth century. The enactments most clearly attributable to Christian influence almost exclusively concerned those areas where a new, public religion touched the practice of slavery in an institutional sense. So, for instance, Jewish and eventually pagan ownership of Christian slaves was circumscribed, manumission was brought from temples into the church, asylum was Christianized, and rules (generally restrictive) concerning the ordination of slaves developed.[59] The "Christian" enactments had more to do with legitimizing the new faith than with the changing substance of slavery. Christianity did little to affect the substance or modalities of slave status in Roman law, particularly before Justinian. A number of excellent studies over the last generation have reconsidered Christian influence and taken its proper measure.[60] Thus, throughout these chapters it will be unnecessary to belabor the point that Christian influence was limited and oblique.

In recent scholarship, the theory of Christianization has been on the wane, but a more resistant narrative trope has been the "merger" of the

---

[56] Harper forthcoming b.
[57] Firpo 1991; Carcaterra 1990; Waldstein 1990; Caron 1983; Langenfeld 1977; Fabbrini 1965; Biondi 1952–4; Imbert 1949; Dupont 1937; Jonkers 1933–4.
[58] Westermann 1955, 114–17.
[59] In general, Herrmann-Otto 2008; Langenfeld 1977. Asylum: Ducloux 1994; Barone Adesi 1990. Jewish owners: De Bonfils 1993. Manumission in the church: chapter 12.
[60] Arjava 1996; Evans Grubbs 1995; Beaucamp 1990–2; Sargenti 1986 and 1938, 7–25.

lower classes in late antiquity.[61] It has affinities with the narratives of the third-century crisis and the colonate, in which the condition of tenants and slaves was gradually assimilated.[62] It is thus related to evolutionary meta-narratives about the transition from slavery to serfdom.[63] More generally, it is insinuated that slave status was less meaningful in the late empire than in earlier periods.[64] Or, in related versions of the theory, the late Roman laws which enforced distinctions of status are read as *reactions against* an under-lying breakdown of the status system.[65] But under scrutiny, this narrative is highly misleading. It is worth pausing for a moment over the problems in this theory, which has been pervasive in accounts of the period.

First, the "merger" thesis misconstrues the nature of the sources. It has paid far too little attention to the evidentiary basis of the claim that slave status was progressively losing its clear definition. To compare the elegant juridical logic of the *Digest* with the late Roman constitutions is to compare apples and oranges.[66] Whenever there are documents of practice from the classical period, the image which emerges seems much closer to the tangled realities which we see in the late empire.[67] Ambiguous or disputed cases of status were a natural part of the system, prompted by a narrow range of concrete and recurring scenarios, typically involving illicit changes of status, manumission, or sexual relationships. Conflict and confusion around legal status had existed in the earlier period, so the goal of these chapters is to explain why these problems increasingly ended up in Roman courts and on the mind of Roman law-makers.[68] The state's response is a sign of slavery's vitality, not its decadence.

Second, the "merger" thesis misconstrues the nature of Roman society. The setting of late antique law was a sprawling, Mediterranean empire, "a militarily-created hegemony of immense land mass that harbored hun-dreds, if not thousands, of different societies."[69] The 50 million inhabitants of the late empire lived in a traditional society, rooted in agricultural pro-duction and shaped by the demands of a high-mortality, high-fertility demographic regime. But by pre-modern standards it was an exceptionally

---

[61] It is notable that the theories of "merger" and "status confusion" have not been defended in the form of a sustained, large-scale work, but they surface in most treatments of the period. Specific citations will be found throughout chapters 9–12. E.g. Vuolanto 2003, 191; McGinn 1997, 109; Arjava 1996, 207; Evans Grubbs 1995, 271, 277, and 1993, 140.

[62] Sargenti 1938, 1.   [63] Jones 1964, 795–6; Češka 1964, 113.   [64] Alföldy 1986, 191.

[65] E.g. Andreau and Descat 2006, 258–9; Evans Grubbs 1995, 277, and 1993, 140; Thébert 1993, 167–73. Garnsey 1996, 101. Garnsey 2004, 141, however, is critical of this view, and has influenced the argument made here.

[66] Evans Grubbs 2005, 126.   [67] E.g. Metzger 2000; Plin. Ep. 10.29–30 (Mynors: 305). Dig. 1.14.3.

[68] Grey forthcoming.   [69] Shaw 2000, 361.

complex and stratified society, with extensive urbanization, astounding divergences of wealth, and great regional diversity, organized under the umbrella of Roman administration. It should be radically unsurprising that fissures appear in the effort to order status centrally or that at different times the imperial administration tried to use different templates to classify the social hierarchy. The overemphasized distinction between *honestiores* and *humiliores*, or the well-known impediments which appear with respect to *coloni*, show us the central administration face-to-face with the kaleidoscopic social realities of a vast empire.[70] It is a testament to the success of the Roman state that we are surprised by logical blemishes in the order of status.

Third, the "merger" thesis misconstrues the nature of slave status. Slave status was unlike any other form of status, because it uniquely had as its consequence the effect of making the person an object of ownership. The essence of slave status lay not in the deprivations of power or privilege of the slave *vis-à-vis* the master. Slave status provided institutional validation that the slave was chattel. So, even if the lowest *coloni* of the late empire faced certain legal restrictions because of their fiscal condition (for instance the inability to bring certain charges against their landlords), these restricted rights amounted to something categorically different from slave status because a *colonus* could not be bought or sold.[71] Chapter 4 indeed has argued that, particularly in the fifth- and sixth-century east, the colonate deformed the market for estate labor. But slave status remained a distinct fate. Even the laws which rhetorically assimilate slaves and *coloni* are careful to maintain a legal division between the two, because the status of *servi* and *coloni* entailed different effects, even if both slaves and *coloni* represented a form of coercible labor.

If neither Christianization nor the breakdown of slave status can explain the development of post-classical slave law, a final alternative lies in the influence of provincial custom. Sometimes the "vulgar law" of the western empire is credited with a leading role in late Roman legislation, at other times change is ascribed to "orientalizing" tendencies.[72] This narrative risks being overstated, magnifying differences of legal idiom into radical substantive change.[73] There is an element of truth in this narrative, however, which makes it important to recognize that the adoption of alternative legal

---

[70] See Rilinger 1988; Garnsey 1970, 278–80; Cardascia 1950.   [71] Sirks 2008, on the disabilities.
[72] On "vulgar law," see esp. the critical overview of Liebs 2008b. Wieacker 1955; Levy 1951. Mitteis 1891, for eastern influences. See chapter 9, for further bibliography.
[73] See esp. Voss 1982.

customs was not based on an abstract preference for provincial norms, nor a breakdown of legal culture, but rather a pragmatic reshuffling of legal priorities. And certainly the provincialization of Roman law was ad hoc and should not be seen as an overarching trajectory of late Roman law.

In all of these evolutionary models of slave law, there is a latent assumption about the nature of classical Roman law. These models imply that the law of slavery in the classical period was pure slave law, the direct expression of a slave society, whereas late law was a corruption from the classical ideal. Yet the classical law was a bundle of compromises between conflicting goals, practical and symbolic. A major subtext of these chapters is that Roman civil law in its classical form was deficient. At crucial moments in the law of slavery, it rested upon open fictions, gentlemen's agreements, lax enforcement, and purposeful ambiguities that became increasingly difficult to manage in the late empire. In case after case, understanding these points of tension in the classical law is the key to decoding the significance of changes within the law. Late Roman legislation on slavery was driven not by external stimuli, but by a shifting balance between old, competing interests. This is not to claim that external influences had no role, for they surely did. But to take their true measure, it is first necessary to understand the intrinsic dynamics of slave status and the often imperfect means of regulating slave status in the classical law.

AN INSTITUTIONAL HISTORY OF SLAVE STATUS IN THE LATE EMPIRE

Chapters 9–12 explore the institutional foundations of slave status in the late empire. Chapter 9 stands apart from the other three and acts as a sort of prolegomenon. This organization is justified, in the first place, by the nature of the evidence. Chapter 9 is set earlier chronologically and focused on the rescripts which are preserved in the *Justinianic Code*, while chapters 10–12 cover the period known through the imperial constitutions of the *Theodosian Code*. This organization is also rooted in the shape of the argument. The rescripts bring to life the world of conflict behind the law of slavery; they allow us to see the points of tension that generated litigation. The rescripts analyzed in chapter 9 show that Diocletian adhered to classical standards of jurisprudence.[74] Constantine, by contrast, emerges as the focal point of chapters 10–12, since during his reign pragmatism

---

[74] Corcoran 2006.

began to intrude on the classical logic of slave status. The most significant reforms of Roman slave law were clustered in his reign. Legal enactments over the next century tended to be amendments to the Constantinian dispensation.

The roots of late antique legal institutions lay in the third century. The Antonine Constitution extended citizenship to all free inhabitants of the empire, thus altering the scope and jurisdiction of Roman private law.[75] Universal citizenship did not impose a change of habits among the new citizens, but it increased the odds that a dispute would end up in Roman jurisdiction. The flood of litigation coursing through the channels of Roman justice in the third century is perceptible. It is hard to follow the diffusion of Roman slave law in the dark decades of the mid-third century, but chapter 9 opens by making opportunistic use of a series of manumission inscriptions from an isolated Macedonian village. These inscriptions reflect the inherent tensions in slave status and bring to life the procedural interface between citizens and the law in the wake of the Antonine Constitution. Above all they evoke the physical challenge faced by the state in projecting its claim to regulate slave status across a Mediterranean empire. The chapter then moves to the imperial chancery of Diocletian to analyze how the same tensions were manifested in conflicts that reached the judicial center of the Roman world. This chapter argues that universal citizenship increased the points of contact between a Mediterranean slave system and Roman civil law. The rescripts are artifacts of this institutional transformation.

Chapter 10 analyzes the legal rules which handled the sale of children into slavery and the enslavement of exposed infants. Such "internal" Mediterranean sources had always been vital to the slave supply. This chapter demonstrates that universal citizenship intensified the contradiction between these sources of the slave trade and the ideal that the birth status of the Roman citizen was inviolable. Constantine tried to legislate a delicate compromise, but it appears from later evidence that the state struggled to find stable legal norms which reconciled these competing interests. These laws have almost always been read either as a sign of economic crisis or of Christianization. The theory of crisis is wholly unconvincing, while the influence of Christianity in these laws has often been overstated. In the legal dossier on the sale and exposure of children, we watch a rather earnest and ultimately unsuccessful attempt to create workable rules for this untidy realm of social practice.

---

[75] See chapter 9.

Chapter 11 is a complement to chapter 7's discussion on sexual honor in Roman society. Sex with slaves was an arena of dense, conflicting interests. The sexual exploitation of slaves was common in ancient society, but it created many human contradictions that became the object of public legislation. The state tried to maintain a community of honor, guarding the reputation of free women and excluding servile children from social dignity. On these matters, the late antique state was decidedly more interventionist than the high imperial government. Classical Roman law had depended heavily on the good behavior of the upper classes. It is possible that Christianity intensified the state's aggressive protection of female sexual honor, but there are no substantive differences between fourth-century sexual boundaries and earlier, socially determined sexual rules. The late Roman state's more aggressive stance towards the problem of illegitimate children, chapter 11 will argue, is explainable in terms of new patterns of elite formation. In maintaining a community of honor in late antiquity, the means employed by the state changed, but not the ends it sought.

Chapter 12 is an attempt to characterize the shifting institutional framework of manumission and patron–freedman relations. Until the fourth century, the state claimed to control the mechanisms of formal manumission and to oversee the relationship between former slaves and their patrons. But in the reign of Constantine, the church was granted the right to perform formal manumissions and to mediate patron–freedmen relations. The creation of Christian manumission was not part of an ideological revolution aimed at emancipation. As proof, we should consider the laws of Constantine which hardened the legal regime governing the patron–freedman relationship. These were a simplification which enshrined the already robust power of the patron in statute. Both reforms were essentially pragmatic. The state granted a major institutional prerogative to a non-state entity. In the end, the church consolidated its power to manumit slaves and continued to do so long after the Roman state had disappeared.

Slave status was an institutional problem of classifying bodies as human chattel. The widening jurisdiction of Roman private law in civil disputes exposed the inadequacies of the classical rules. Late Roman legislation had a different center of gravity; it often provided a simpler if more functional framework for defusing tensions. This pattern was the deep structure of change, visible in diverse points of law. If this conclusion in some sense prevents us from being able to translate late Roman legislation into neat models of underlying change or reality, it at least helps us understand the permanent frictions of ancient slavery and the truly unique, pan-Mediterranean scale of late Roman statecraft. The Roman state absorbed the duties of regulating slavery on an unprecedented scale, only to crumble, irreversibly in the west, more slowly in the east. By understanding the importance of the state in the slave system, we can begin to appreciate the invisible revolution in the history of slavery that was the dissolution of the Roman empire.

CHAPTER 9

Citizenship and civil conflict: slave status after the Antonine Constitution

ROMAN LAW BEYOND ROME

Late in the third century, the Greek rhetor Menander of Laodicea composed a handbook on oratory.[1] He advised the rhetor praising a city to laud all the traditional elements of civic vanity: architecture and athletic victories, festivals and favorite sons. The formula had centuries of Greek antiquity behind it, but in one respect times were changing. "In matters of state," he wrote, "one considers whether the city fastidiously observes the customs and affairs of law, such as inheritances and female succession to property. But this aspect of praise is now obsolete, since the laws of the Romans are used by all."[2] Though he did repeat the point, this was more than the wistfulness of a hidebound scholar. Menander was witness to the passing of an age. The third century saw the immemorial pluralism of the Mediterranean give way, in the field of law, to the universalizing impulses of the Roman state. Hundreds of cities, each with its own local traditions, lost their prerogative to regulate the inevitable dangers of social living in antiquity. Inheritance disputes, paternal power, forms of female tutorship, slave-holding – all came progressively under the compass of Roman civil law.

The roots of this transformation lay in AD 212, when the Roman emperor Caracalla felt moved to honor the gods by extending Roman citizenship to virtually all free inhabitants of the empire.[3] While the spread of Roman citizenship had been ongoing for centuries, universal citizenship was a watershed.[4] Nevertheless, the material effects of the Antonine Constitution

---

[1] The attribution may be false, Heath 2004, 127–31. More generally, Russell and Wilson 1981, XI–XXXIV.

[2] Men. Rhet. Epid. 1.364.10 (Russell and Wilson: 68): ἐν μὲν τοῖς κοινοῖς εἰ τὰ νόμιμα καὶ περὶ ὦν οἱ νόμοι τίθεται ἀκριβῶς ἡ πόλις, κλῆρον ἐπικλήρων, καὶ ὅσα ἄλλα μέρη νόμων. ἀλλὰ καὶ τοῦτο τὸ μέρος διὰ τὸ τοῖς κοινοῖς χρῆσθαι τῶν Ῥωμαίων νόμοις ἄχρηστον. Modrzejewski 1982, 347, for κλῆρον ἐπικλήρων. Garnsey 2004, 148–9; Lepelley 1996, 212–13.

[3] P. Giss. 40. Dig. 1.5.17. Bouraselis 1989, 189–98; Sherwin White 1973, 380–94; Sasse 1958.

[4] Garnsey 2004, 135. In general, Modrzejewski 1970.

were neither swift nor dramatic. The new citizens did not wake up one bright morning in 212 and begin to re-order their lives with the Praetor's Edict as their guide. The accommodation between social practice and Roman civil law was a long, complex, and uncertain process. Ludwig Mitteis, in a brilliant insight, recognized the conflicting systems of private law in the documents of the period and posited a grand conflict between Roman and provincial rules; other scholars have argued for varying degrees of formal tolerance by the Roman state; the truth lies somewhere in the middle.[5] The state's response across the third century was ad hoc. In some arenas of social practice, old customs proved sturdy; in others change was more rapid; in many respects Roman law and provincial custom were not radically dissimilar.[6] The general darkness of the mid-third century makes it exceedingly difficult to follow the relation between law, citizenship, and social practice in the decades between the Antonine Constitution and the age of Diocletian. This was a phase of legal twilight, as the local and the imperial mingled in a way that is only dimly perceptible.[7] Towards the end of the century, as Menander was writing, the pendulum swung decisively towards centralization and standardization.[8]

To trace the effects of the Antonine Constitution in a given area of social practice, such as slavery, it is necessary to understand the institutional tensions specific to that area of practice. This chapter argues that slavery is intrinsically wrought with conflict and that certain areas of structural tension regularly occasioned legal disputes. Manumission and the obligations of freedmen, mixed-status sexual partnerships, the transmission of status and illicit loss of status – these were perennial sources of conflict, in the early as in the late empire. Litigation arising from these aspects of slavery was the primary point of contact between Roman law and social practice. Of course, long before universal citizenship, non-Roman inhabitants of the empire had variously imitated Roman rules and appealed to Roman authorities for resolution of their quarrels.[9] But in the aftermath of the Antonine Constitution, and especially in the reign of Diocletian, Roman law increasingly shaped social practice as citizens adapted to a new

---

[5] See Garnsey 2004, 146–7 and Modrzejewski 1970, esp. 348–9, for summaries of the problem. Modrzejewski 1988, 1982, and 1974; Arangio-Ruiz 1974, esp. 294; Sherwin White 1973, 392; Schönbauer 1931; Taubenschlag 1930; Mitteis 1891.

[6] cf. Evans Grubbs 2005, 95, on family law.   [7] Watson 1974 and 1973.

[8] Garnsey 2004, 148; Lepelley 1996.

[9] Documentary discoveries are re-configuring what we know about the pace of Romanization. González 1986, esp. chapters 86 and 87. The Babatha archive: Cotton 1993. From a vast bibliography, see Peachin 2007, for a cautious recent exploration of informal adjudication by Roman military officials (esp. n. 66 on the difficulty of knowing *what kind* of law was applied in such instances).

regime of legitimacy in which disputes increasingly found their way into jurisdictions where Roman law was decisive.

This chapter begins by making opportunistic use of a series of recently published manumission inscriptions from a Greek village. The inscriptions offer a rare window onto the institutional history of the third century; they take us directly into a part of the empire impacted by the sudden spread of citizenship. The inscriptions evoke a slave society where conflict was constantly bubbling to the surface, and they reveal the local institutions through which these conflicts were resolved. The chapter then turns to the rescripts of Diocletian, which provide us a different vantage on the same patterns of conflict. The rescripts reflect the effort of Diocletian to adjudicate, in terms of Roman law, the endless stream of legal quarrels arising from slavery. The dense record of legal activity preserved in the *Hermogenian Code* takes us inside the judicial docket of the imperial chancery and provides an unparalleled glimpse of the sheer volume of litigation generated by the slave system. Nearly one out of every four cases which survive pertained to slavery. This snapshot provides an invaluable measure of the role of the state in maintaining the institutional foundations of slave status.

LEUKOPETRA: ROMAN LAW AND LOCAL CUSTOM

A collapsed temple covered with inscriptions was found by accident at the village of Leukopetra in the 1960s.[10] The inscriptions commemorate manumissions performed under the patronage of the "autochthonous mother of the gods," a local goddess whose priests and priestesses presided over the act. The freed slaves took the goddess as their protector and were expected to serve her temple on festival days.[11] The village of Leukopetra lay on the slopes of Mount Bermion above the river Haliacmon in southern Macedonia, to the southwest of Beroea. The region around Beroea flourished under the empire, and Leukopetra lay in the hinterland of this efflorescence.[12]

---

[10] Petsas *et al.* 2000.

[11] Sacral consecrations were true manumissions: Petsas *et al.* 2000, 32–5, summarizes the debate, with concluding arguments at 52. Zelnick-Abramovitz 2005, 86–99; Ricl 1995 and 1993; Cameron 1939b. The opposite view, Bömer 1960 and Latte 1920. Now Ricl 2001, esp. 132–5. Cameron 1939b reads like a point-by-point refutation, and the rationale of Petsas *et al.* 2000 (at p. 52) is convincing: the goddess received the services of the former slave on a few appointed festival days, the master frequently enjoyed the "continued service" (παραμονή) characteristically associated with Greek manumissions. Meyer 2002 is right to suggest that it was a structural difference between manumission at Leukopetra and manumission in Roman law which must have determined the events described below.

[12] Tataki 1988, esp. 456–96. Petsas *et al.* 2000, 23–8.

The milieu was bustling with country grandees, farmers, peasants, and debtors. For these men and women, their human merchandise could be the object of risky speculation: Flavius Eutrapelos borrowed 1,000 *denarii* to buy a slave named Felix but found himself unable to pay it back. He lost everything out of the deal.[13] These inscriptions reveal a world isolated, rural, and otherwise irretrievably lost: a little satellite of a slave-holding society, tucked into the mountainous folds of southern Macedonia.

The corpus provides roughly 120 inscriptions that bring to life the realities of slavery – and the inherent tensions of slave status – over the years AD 170–250. The physical geography is essential context, for it conjures both the awesome reach of Roman administration and the material difficulty of enforcing a complex law on a galaxy of local societies. Leukopetra can seem like an archaic holdover of millennial survivals, largely untouched by Roman time.[14] Yet equally remarkable is the extent to which the distant structures of empire slowly but inexorably shaped life in a remote village. The *pax Romana* brought security and prosperity, incubating little societies of petty aristocrats and middling elites. It was guarded by a professional army protecting faraway borders, though at Leukopetra we find a veteran manumitting his slaves – a little slave family.[15] The village was connected, in the first instance, to Beroea, a city of exuberant Romanization.[16] Beroea was the gateway to the wider world of law and markets, where a villager might go to find a governor making his circuit or a merchant peddling the wares of an empire. It was a full day's walk.[17]

The surest token of Romanization in the decades before the Antonine Constitution was the spread of citizenship among the wealthy or cultured classes.[18] The Ulpii, Aelii, and Aurelii of the east became ambassadors of Roman culture and law. The story of manumission at Leukopetra is inextricable from the biographies of such local elites who had won the Roman citizenship. The first known dedication at the shrine was made by a woman with the suggestive name Tiberia Claudia Procla.[19] Between 170 and 212, nearly 40 percent of the manumitters were Roman citizens. Some manumitters bore imperial *gentilicia*, others used the *tria nomina*.[20]

---

[13] ISMDA no. 12, with Petsas *et al.* 2000, 90.
[14] Hatzopoulos 2004, 45–53; Petsas *et al.* 2000, 41, "contexte juridique manifestement grec."
[15] ISMDA nos. 86, 95.   [16] Tataki 1988, 435–513.
[17] Epigraphy attests the names of 1,380 Beroeans, 430 Leukopetrans. Only two names appear in both places, suggesting interaction but certainly a divide between the city and country populations. Meyer 2002, 138; Petsas *et al.* 2000, 23.
[18] Sherwin White 1973, 251–87.   [19] ISMDA no. 2.
[20] E.g. ISMDA no. 12; ISMDA no. 29. Nine female manumitters cited the *ius trium liberorum*. Three of these were before 212.

The pattern is even more striking among the priests who presided over the manumissions: eighteen of the twenty priests and priestesses before 212 had Roman *gentilicia*.[21] The impresarios of sacral manumission in Leukopetra, at this temple of the "autochthonous" mother of the gods, were Roman citizens.[22]

Though Roman citizenship had made inroads into this society before 212, the impact of Caracalla's decree was strikingly immediate:

In the Augustan year 244, national year 360, in the shrine of the Autochthonous Mother before the goddess, by the command of the eminent governor Marcus Ulpius Tertullianus Aquila. I, Aurelius Posidonios, formerly son of Mestys, and also called Pantakianos, dedicate a slave-girl named Ammia and her children Posidonios and Nikon. I have deposited their pledges in the arms of the goddess.[23]

Inscribed in AD 212/13, Aurelius Posidonius not only bore the *gentilicium* given to new citizens, he still listed his former patronymic ("formerly son of Mestys"). Aurelius Posidonios has the honor of being the earliest attested beneficiary of universal citizenship.[24]

This inscription was the first of many that would mention the Roman governor, Marcus Ulpius Tertullianus Aquila. Tertullianus was already known from two inscriptions in southern Asia Minor. An inscription from Cremna in Pisidia marked it as his hometown.[25] An inscription from Balboura, undated, indicated that he held the office of *curator* at Attaleia.[26] He was governor in Macedonia in 213. The name Tertullianus was relatively uncommon, but three others are known: the African Christian, a legate of Moesia known from coins (241–4), and a late second-century jurist known from nine citations in the *Digest*.[27] It is tempting to suggest an identity between the governor of Macedonia and the jurist.[28] This identification would put Tertullianus squarely within an important pattern in the administration of the Severan empire: the promotion of legally educated easterners into positions of authority. Ulpian is an obvious example. An even better parallel is Licinius Rufinus, the jurist from Lydia.[29] Both

---

[21] Tataki 1988, 469–71; Sherwin White 1973, 263.   [22] Already Nörr 1969.

[23] ISMDA no. 63: Ἔτους ΔΜΣ τ[ο]ῦ κὲ <Γ>ΞΤ/σεβαστοῦ ἐν Αὐ[τ]όχθονι ἐπὶ/τῇ θεῷ κατὰ κ[έ]λευσιν τοῦ/κρατίστου ἡγ[εμό]νος Μ Ου Τερ-/τυλλιανοῦ Ἀκ[υλάο]υ Αὐρήλιος Πο-/σιδώνιος ὁ [πρὶν] Μέστυος ὁ κὲ/Πανтακιανὸς χαρίζομε πεδίσκην ὀνόματι Ἀμμίαν/κὲ τέκνα αὐτῆς Ποσιδώνι[ν]/κὲ Νείκωνα ὧν κὲ τὰς ἀσ-/φαλείας ἀπεθέμ[η]ν εἰς τὰς/ἀνκάλας τῆς θεοῦ. On the reading of "M Ου," see Ricl 2001, 151.

[24] cf. Gillam 1965, for other early examples.

[25] I. Pisidia, IGSK 57, no. 44. Horsley and Mitchell 2000, 55–8.

[26] IGRR 3.474, lines 27–9. Jones 1940, 136–8.   [27] PIR¹ III, "T" nos. 89, 306.

[28] Jones 2005. Also Sarikakis 1977, 106–7.   [29] Millar 1999.

Licinius' hometown of Thyatira and Tertullianus' native Cremna were mixed Greek and Roman societies and "could well have nurtured a Roman administrator and jurist."[30] Tertullianus may be another eastern lawyer in the government after the extension of universal citizenship.[31] These were the crack troops in the administration of a vast, multi-cultural empire, increasingly under the influence of Roman civil law.

Twenty surviving inscriptions at Leukopetra mentioned Tertullianus, nineteen with reference to his *apophasis*.[32] Commentators have been ambiguous or taken *apophasis* to mean "edict."[33] It makes intuitive sense that the Roman governor would have issued an edict outlining rules for manumission: in the wake of universal citizenship, the lawyer–governor issued a special edict explaining Roman rules of manumission. But *apophasis* does not mean edict. *Apophasis* is, unambiguously, a precise technical translation of the Latin word *sententia*: the judgment rendered in a civil trial.[34] Roman governors were judges. This is a fundamental point. The Antonine Constitution gave all inhabitants the opportunity, an "entry ticket," to apply to Roman jurisdiction.[35] This was a quiet revolution whose effects are hard to trace in a third century not famous for its abundant documentation. The *sententia* of Tertullianus was part of a reactive, judicial model of private law, and it was used by a new citizen immediately. The mechanism by which the law was applied is more than a procedural footnote. The machinery is the story.[36]

The *sententia* of the governor would have resolved the case at hand. At Leukopetra, though, the governor's decision was cited for decades at the shrine, as though it validated local procedure or provided guidelines pertinent to the practice of manumission. Judgments were cited by citizens as sources of legal authority.[37] As judge, Tertullianus had wide scope in

---

[30] Jones 2005, 269.   [31] cf. Philostrat. Vit. A. 5.36 (Jones vol. 2: 76–8).

[32] The first inscription refers to his "command" ("*keleusin*" – not a technical term) which disposed of the case at hand; subsequent inscriptions refer (presumably but not absolutely certainly to this same judgment) in technical language to an *apophasis*.

[33] E.g. Ricl 2001, 129; Sarikakis 1977, 106. cf. Jones 2005, 169. Meyer 2002, 139: "judgment or edict."

[34] Mason 1974, 25, 130. Bilingual IGRR 1.860. P. Tebt. 2.286. IG 2².1092 = SEG 12.95 records a decision of the prefect of Greece ca. 175 (line 32). Early third century: SEG 17.759 (line 11). An edict is almost always a *diatagma* (Mason 1974, 127). There is no basis for considering an *apophasis* an edict. Berger 1953, "*sententia*."

[35] Garnsey 2004, 147.   [36] Garnsey 2004, 149; Arangio-Ruiz 1974, 293.

[37] Dig. 1.3.38. cf. Dig. 36.1.67.2; Dig. 48.2.18. PS 5.5a.6; PS 5.12.6. CJ 7.45.2; CJ 7.45.4; CJ 7.64.1. A parallel is found at Eleusis. The prefect issued an *apophasis* defining any violation of the arrangement of the sanctuary's endowment as a public crime, *sacrilegium*. The *apophasis* was prominently displayed in an inscription and set a precedent that endured for decades. IG 2².1092 = SEG 12.95 = Oliver 1952.

issuing his verdict.[38] That single charged encounter at Leukopetra was the primary meeting point between manumission practices at the shrine and the Roman law of slavery. The details of the case and the content of the *apophasis* are unknown, but cautious speculation may narrow the possibilities. It is hardly surprising that a private suit involving manumission reached the governor. Manumissions could easily embroil the participants in conflict.[39] The manumission inscriptions at Leukopetra, even though they are celebratory artifacts, reflect the barely submerged fears about the volatile pressures of the slave system. Manumission, at its legal core, was the assurance that a slave could no longer be bought or sold. The judicious definition of Buckland is precise: manumission was "a release not merely from the owner's control, but from all possibility of being owned."[40] Manumission shuffled, but did not sever, the ties between the master and slave. The most plausible cause of a civil dispute over a manumission would concern the relationship between a patron and a freedman.[41]

This possibility is strengthened by the fact that there was a material difference in the way that eastern custom and Roman law handled the relationship between patrons and freedmen. The legal regime governing the status of freedmen in Roman civil law was complex.[42] The bond between patrons and their freedmen was grounded in terms of *obsequium* and *operae*.[43] Simply by virtue of the manumission, the freedman owed the patron a deep form of social respect, *obsequium*, that also, ominously, limited his legal capacity to act against the patron.[44] More variably, the freedmen often owed the patron labor – *operae*. In Roman law *operae* were quantities of labor set by the patron and the freedman.[45] They were created by an oath or a stipulation that, theoretically, had to occur after the manumission, because agreements with slaves were non-binding.[46] Because *operae* were created not by the act of manumission, but by an agreement between two free parties, disputes were adjudicated as breaches of obligation.[47]

In the east, where manumission was commonly performed in sacral contexts, patron–freedmen relationships were frequently governed by clauses that required the freedman to remain in the service of the patron for a

[38] Turpin 1999; Kaser 1996, 435–45.   [39] See pp. 385–6.
[40] Buckland 1908, 438. cf. Samuel 1965.   [41] cf. Zelnick-Abramovitz 2005, 273–306.
[42] Dig. 37.14. Quadrato 1996; Masi Doria 1993; Waldstein 1986; Sirks 1983, 1981; Treggiari 1969a; Kaser 1938.
[43] Boulvert and Morabito 1982, 122–3.   [44] Treggiari 1969a, 69–81; Duff 1928, 36–43.
[45] Waldstein 1986, 51–69, 209–99. Dig. 37.14.19.   [46] Waldstein 1986, 239–64.
[47] Waldstein 1986, 345–77.

specified term: *paramonê* obligations.[48] The structure of patron–freedmen relations is critical to the history of manumission, yet it is an unsolved mystery how Roman law would have regarded *paramonê* clauses.[49] *Paramonê* clauses are attested as early as the third century BC at Delphi, and they became increasingly prominent over the period 100 BC–AD 100.[50] *Paramonê* agreements were highly analogous to *operae* contracts. A. E. Samuel proved that *paramonê* clauses, like *operae* agreements, occurred, in a technical, legal sense, after the manumission.[51] But there were two potential differences between *operae* and *paramonê*: the nature of the labor owed and the methods of enforcement. Whereas *operae* were fixed, limited units of labor, *paramonê* were thoroughgoing service contracts, sometimes of unlimited duration. This distinction should not be overdrawn, since *paramonê* agreements were diverse and highly flexible.[52] And a good Roman example of something very like general service is preserved in the rubble at Herculaneum, where a mother and daughter, though freed, remained in the house of their former master.[53]

Probably the most significant difference between *operae* and *paramonê* lay in enforcement. Because *operae* were formally owed through a contractual stipulation, Roman patrons could seek legal redress against freedmen who did not fulfill their *operae*. Essentially, they could pursue a civil suit for failure to fulfill a legal obligation.[54] The institutional basis of *paramonê* agreements is a topic too little discussed.[55] A few articulate inscriptions imply that the penalty for a freedman who failed to fulfill a *paramonê* agreement was annulment of the manumission.[56] It was as if it never happened. How, exactly, this was accomplished is not something the sources willingly reveal. Among the manumission inscriptions at Delphi, a few specified the mode of enforcement.[57] *Paramonê* clauses could declare that in the event of a dispute over the fulfillment of services, the case was to be adjudicated by a panel of three men.[58] These typically involved the priests.[59] Similarly, in Jewish manumission inscriptions from the Bosporus, "the synagogue is bound to uphold the contract between owner and now freed slave."[60] The analogies are distant in time and space, but

[48] Zelnick-Abramovitz 2005, 222–48; Gibson 1999, 36–49; Nörr 1969; Calderini 1908.
[49] Such a study was called for by Nörr 1969, 636. Waldstein's juridical approach and chronological parameters have left the problem unsolved. In general, see Hopkins 1978, 133–78; Samuel 1965, 221–311; Westermann 1948. *Paramonê* customs survive into Islamic civilization: Crone 1987, esp. 69–73.
[50] Hopkins 1978, 133–78. [51] Samuel 1965, 274–5. [52] Zelnick-Abramovitz 2005, 225–7.
[53] Metzger 2000; Gardner 1986. [54] Waldstein 1986, 345–77.
[55] Zelnick-Abramovitz 2005, 273–306, on a much earlier period. [56] Samuel 1965, 275.
[57] Samuel 1965, 276–9; Sokolowski 1954. [58] Samuel 1965, 277.
[59] GDI 2049, 2072, 2073, 1971. cf. Zachos 2007, 118, for other examples. [60] Gibson 1999, 150.

nevertheless furnish an indication of something so obvious that it was probably assumed: slave-owners disposed of a large reserve of self-help, while temples provided the institutional grounding of *paramonê* obligations and a possible venue for mediating disputed cases.[61]

The general silence about a patron's means of enforcing service obligations may hint that, in reality, patrons in the eastern Mediterranean enjoyed wide, brutish power over their freedmen. There was an obvious danger in the possibility that the master or his heirs would abuse or re-enslave freedmen unfairly. Unambiguously, the gods became the protectors of the freedmen. At Leukopetra and elsewhere, the god or goddess was considered the slave's new "master."[62] The gods could issue terrible threats to those who would harm freedmen, including financial penalties.[63] Moreover, religious shrines acted as the archival repository for manumission documents. The inscriptions themselves were commemorative, not legal, documents, but temples would store ownership deeds and manumission papers. At Leukopetra the presiding priest was scrupulously mentioned in every manumission inscription. Whereas in Roman law the secular administration formed the institutional basis for relations between patrons and freedmen, in the east this role was often played by temples.[64] Even under the Roman empire, the limits of imperial power – materially and formally – left pockets like Leukopetra where local societies developed their own methods of mediating complex and tension-filled public enactments.

After the Antonine Constitution, the new citizens at Leukopetra, perhaps embroiled in a dispute about *paramonê* obligations, appealed to the governor's jurisdiction. There is a corroborating detail that this is precisely what was at stake in the civil case heard by Tertullianus. In the first inscription to mention the governor's decision, Posidonios manumitted three slaves. He added: *I have stowed their pledges in the arms of the goddess.*[65] The Greek *asphaleia* is equivalent to the Latin *cautio* and most commonly means, in Roman law, an express declaration of an obligation, a secondary guarantee that an obligation would be fulfilled.[66] It was a method of confirming obligations, making them actionable under Roman law.[67] In the first inscription to mention the governor, an obligation was assured in terms of Roman law and put in the hands of the priests.

---

[61] Zelnick-Abramovitz 2005, 233–4, 254–62.   [62] E.g. ISMDA no. 12.
[63] ISMDA no. 51, with Petsas *et al.* 2000, 119. ISMDA no. 71. In inscriptions at Edessa, the penalty for unlawfully seizing freedmen was a fine payable to the fisc. Cameron 1939b, 147.
[64] Patterson has noted that where the state was weak, sacral manumission was prominent: Patterson 1982, 238; Andreau 1993, 180.
[65] ISMDA no. 63.   [66] Berger 1953, 384; Leonhard 1899, cols. 1814–19.
[67] Arangio-Ruiz 1974, 287, notes that stipulation became a makeshift way of making private contracts in the provinces actionable under Roman law in the third century.

It is likely that the *sententia* of Tertullianus resolved a dispute over the obligations of freedmen, but we cannot reconstruct the substance of his verdict. Did the governor instruct the locals on the guidelines of Roman civil law? It certainly does not seem that his judgment altered the pre-existing framework of *paramonê* obligations. The inscriptions at the shrine evoked the same routines of manumission. In October of 239, for example, a citizen named Aurelia Asklepiodora manumitted a boy Herakleon, a ten-year-old homeborn slave.[68] Herakleon was bound to serve Aurelia for the remainder of her life. Perhaps Tertullianus' resolution was of a different nature. Roman governors, though they were judicially active, could appoint high-status substitutes as judges, particularly in petty cases.[69] This makes it conceivable that Tertullianus ruled on the case at hand and more generally confirmed the ability of the local priests to mediate disputes over patron–freedman relations at the temple. This reconstruction would explain the placement of guarantees in the arms of the goddess and the continuing reference to manumissions "according to the decision of the governor." This can only be a hypothesis, but if it is correct, Tertullianus effected an elegant reconciliation of Roman institutions and local custom, and one that seems tolerant of existing practices such as *paramonê*.[70]

Besides the visibility of the Roman governor, the only other change detectable in the inscriptions from Leukopetra is a new tendency to mention a slave's homeborn status. Before 212, there was not a single reference to the fact that a slave was born in the master's household. After universal citizenship, fully 20 percent of the inscriptions, sixteen in total, refer to the homeborn origins of a slave. This is surely not because birth to slave-mothers suddenly became more prominent in Macedonia after 212. The fact that masters increasingly declared the homeborn status of their slaves should be seen as an artifact of recording habits, not as a reflection of underlying change in the supply system of Roman slavery. Why, then, did masters in this remote Macedonian village feel the need to record the origins of their slaves in manumission inscriptions?

The inscriptions suggest that, by declaring the homeborn status of their slaves, masters were affirming their legal claim to the slave as property.[71] The assertion of homeborn status acted as an assertion of property rights. The mention of homeborn status fell in exactly the same place in the formula as the mention of purchase.[72] The claim of birth to a slave-mother,

---

[68] ISMDA no. 91.
[69] Turpin 1999, 523; González 1986, 147–243; Crook 1967a, 78; Steinwater 1916. Dig. 1.16.6.1.
[70] cf. Modrzejewski 1970, 353–4.   [71] cf. Herrmann-Otto 1994, 21–8.   [72] Petsas *et al.* 2000, 47.

for example, was emphasized in an inscription where a slave boy named Herakleon was manumitted: "it was born to me from my slave-woman."[73] This association between homeborn origins and proof of legal status was accented in another inscription. Olia Alexandra freed two slaves, Parhesia and Antigona, born to her by her slave Paramone:

AD 238/9

I, Olia Alexandra dedicated to the Autochthonous Mother of the Gods two slave-women named Parhesia and Antigona, who were sworn to the goddess from their very birth, who were born to me from my slave-woman Parmone, and whom I gave with my own hands, by a signed instrument which has been witnessed and given to Ioulianos Demetrios. No one shall be the master of these slaves except the goddess herself.[74]

The inscription drew a tight connection between the fact that the slaves were homeborn and given by the master's own hands (ταῖς ἰδίαις χιρσίν) and that this was written up in a subscribed legal instrument (διὰ χειρὸς) given to the priests certifying the act.[75] The analogy with the document of purchase is clear. The fact of the slaves' birth into Julia's household was transmuted into an assurance of ownership and handed to the priest in the same way that certificates of purchase were surrendered in other inscriptions.[76]

Knowledge about birth origins was essential in the event of a dispute over status or ownership.[77] What we are watching at Leukopetra is not a radical material transformation in the wake of universal citizenship, but a slow accommodation to the new, imperial-wide regime of legitimacy in the sphere of property rights.[78] The inscriptions from Leukopetra thus provide an invaluable perspective on the legal history of the third century. The effects of the Antonine Constitution were immediate but limited. Institutional change, not social change, is the substance of the story. The single most suggestive fact is that in the aftermath of universal citizenship, a

---

73 ISMDA no. 91: τὸ γενηθέν μοι ἐκ παιδίσκης μου.

74 ISMDA no. 90: Ὠλία Ἀλεξάνδρα/ἐχαριζάμην Μητρὶ/θεῶν Αὐτόχθονι παί-/δισκας δύο ὀνόμασιν/Παρησίαν καὶ Ἀντιγόναν ἃς καὶ ἀ-/πὸ βρεφῶν κατωνόμασα τῆ/θεῷ αἵτινές μοι ἐγεννήθ(η)σαν/ἐκ παιδίσκης μου Παρμόνις ἃ(ς)/<ἃς> παρέδωκα ταῖς ἰδίαις χιρσίν/ἃς καὶ διὰ χειρὸς μεμαρτυρωμέν(η)ς/ἥτις ἐδόθη Ἰουλιανῷ Δημητρί-/ῳ τῷ ἱερεῖ τούτων δὲ τῶν σω-/μάτων οὐδείς ἔστε κύριος ἢ μό-/νη ἡ θεός. cf. Ricl 2001, 152, for the correct reading of μεμαρτυρωμέν(η)ς.

75 LSJ, "χείρ," 6. cf. ISMDA no. 51. Ricl 2001, 149, 152. On the importance of written documents, Zelnick-Abramovitz 2005, 205.

76 Petsas *et al.* 2000, 151.

77 Marcus Aurelius required the registration of illegitimate free children in order to facilitate the resolution of status disputes. SHA, Marc. 9.7–9 (Hohl: 55) with Schulz 1942, 78–91.

78 cf. Meyer 2004, 206–15.

lawsuit from a new citizen in this remote place reached the Roman governor almost instantaneously. It is easy to imagine the proliferation of cases which could now have entered the court of a Roman governor. The new influx of civil-law disputes would have disproportionately represented places where citizenship was less advanced before 212: that is the east, the countryside, the middling classes. This extraordinary cache of documentary evidence provides social depth to the institutional dynamics of manumission in late antiquity. The inscriptions from Leukopetra also illuminate the complex background to the legal activity of Diocletian.

BACK TO THE CENTER: DIOCLETIAN'S RESCRIPTS

If the middle decades of the third century are lodged in relative obscurity, the late third century is far better documented. This record is due not least to the fact that the reformist emperor Diocletian brought a new vigor to the imperial government. His administration is responsible, directly or indirectly, for the survival of imperial rescripts in massive bulk. The two major collections of imperial rescripts, the *Codex Gregorianus* and the *Codex Hermogenianus*, were compiled during his reign, though it is unclear if these were private or officially sponsored compilations.[79] These codes were subsequently edited by Justinian and published in the *Justinianic Code*, whence they have descended to us. In all, over 2,500 imperial rescripts survive from the late second and third centuries. More importantly, over 850 rescripts are bunched within a two-year period following Diocletian's establishment of the tetrarchy, AD 293–4.[80] These rescripts provide unparalleled access to the legal docket of the imperial court, and they suggest how important slavery remained in Roman society during this period.

A rescript is an official imperial response to a citizen's petition.[81] Some details of the rescript process are obscure, but the outlines are clear.[82] Citizens involved in a dispute could bring their troubles in person to the imperial court hoping for a statement of law or even an imperial favor.[83] Petitions were handled by a court officer, the *a libellis* and later the *magister*

---

[79] On these two codes, see Corcoran 2000, 24–42; Honoré 1994, 48–9, 182–3 for imperial sponsorship. Corcoran 2004, 65, against official endorsement. Sirks 2007, 9–10, "the question of whether they were official remains open."

[80] Corcoran 2000, 26–8. On the structure of the *Codex Hermogenianus*, esp. Cenderelli 1965.

[81] On rescripts, Corcoran 2000, 42–73; Honoré 1994, 33–70; Coriat 1985; Wilcken 1920. Following common practice, we refer throughout to rescripts, while technically it would be more specific to speak of private rescripts or *subscriptiones*. *Rescripta* also included *epistulae* written for imperial officials.

[82] Honoré 1994, 43–8; Williams 1980.   [83] Honoré 1994, 37–8; Turpin 1991, 102.

libellorum, who was normally a trained legal authority.[84] Although the rescript carried the emperor's signature – and authority – the rescripts were drafted by the legal officer, and individual styles can be detected behind the composition of the rescripts.[85] A rescript was not a judicial ruling. It was not a finding of fact. Rescripts stated existing law, providing the parties of the dispute with the relevant rules governing the case.[86] At times the rescripts reflect the high-handed tone of jurists faced with provincials ignorant of Roman rules: "It is a most well-known tenet of the law that a child cannot be made a slave by an agreement with its mother."[87] Having received a statement of law, litigants then had to take their case before a competent judicial authority, typically a provincial governor, to obtain a ruling. The rescripts offer a glimpse of the routine application of Roman law in civil suits. The rescripts "show us a far more diverse range of men and women, both geographically and socially, than do the authors of classical literature and even the legal writers of the Digest."[88]

The compilations of the Diocletianic era mark a new turn in the history of Roman legal literature, away from the treatise format of the classical jurist, towards the systematization of imperial enactments characteristic of the late empire. The two tetrarchic compilations also differ from one another in important ways. The *Codex Gregorianus* gathered imperial rescripts from the age of Hadrian down to AD 291. The *Codex Hermogenianus*, by contrast, gathered imperial rescripts exclusively from the years 293 and 294 (although subsequent laws were added in later editions).[89] The Code was probably assembled by the same Hermogenianus who composed a handbook of Roman law and who seems to have served as Diocletian's *magister libellorum* in precisely these same years.[90] In other words, the *Codex Hermogenianus* is a collection of rescripts compiled by the imperial official responsible for their composition. The code may well have been planned even as Hermogenianus composed the rescripts. There is no reason to believe that every rescript from these years was included in his code. It has been estimated that four to five rescripts a day was normal, but higher or lower numbers are easily possible.[91] At the rate of just over one rescript per day, the code of Hermogenian may have included only a fraction of the

[84] Corcoran 2000, 45.   [85] Honoré 1994, 56–70.
[86] Corcoran 2000, 49; Honoré 1994, 33: "a free legal advice service." cf. Turpin 1991, 116, "a sort of high-pressure summons."
[87] CJ 2.4.26 (AD 294): *transactione matris filios eius non posse servos fieri notissimi iuris est.* Compare CJ 3.15.2 (AD 294); CJ 4.10.12 (AD 294); CJ 7.16.37 (AD 294).
[88] Evans Grubbs 2005, 125.   [89] Corcoran 2000, 35–7; Liebs 1987, 137–43; Cenderelli 1965.
[90] Honoré 1994, 163–81; Liebs 1987, 36–52.   [91] Honoré 1994, 45; Williams 1974.

business he handled as *magister libellorum* yet, in terms of volume, what remains is a truly remarkable mass of material.[92]

We possess documents from some 864 petitioners heard by the imperial court over a two-year period.[93] In these years Diocletian moved along the Danubian frontier. Diocletian opened the year 293 in Sirmium, and by April he was in Byzantium; over the summer he passed through Adrianople, Beroea, Serdica, and Viminacium before returning to winter at Sirmium. In 294 the emperor passed most of the year along the Danube before moving to Byzantium in November and eventually to Nicomedia for the rest of the year.[94] The 864 cases cover virtually the entire spectrum of Roman law – property, liability, procedure, etc.[95] Of these 864 cases, no fewer than 185 of them involved slavery.[96] This extraordinary frequency confirms, in an especially concrete way, the dictum of Finley that "there was no action or belief or institution in Graeco-Roman antiquity that was not one way or other affected by the possibility that someone involved *might be* a slave."[97] We do not know the selection principles of Hermogenianus, but certainly his *Codex* had a practical juridical purpose, not an antiquarian one; at the very least it shows us what a contemporary jurist thought was a sample of important case law.[98] These rescripts are doubly valuable because they are not theoretical documents; they are traces of actual cases which filtered their way to the central docket of the empire over a span of two years.[99]

In their original form, the rescripts may have included more details about the facts of the case, but as we have them they have been stripped of context to leave behind relatively bare statements of law. Sometimes the original details still peek through and evoke the veritable legal soap operas that prompted the litigation. In one instance, a slave was allowed to bring forward information pertinent to her master's death; in such grave circumstances slaves were allowed to interact with authorities.[100] In another example, a legal tutor had fallen in love with the slave-woman of his young charge; the tutor tried to make the slave-woman his heir, but the property simply passed to her owner, the boy.[101] More than one case involved a slave who had embezzled his own *peculium*, giving it to a third

[92] Corcoran 2000, 30.
[93] This number and the corresponding dates are based on the palingenesia of T. Honoré (online at iuscivile.com). cf. Corcoran 2000, 26–7; Honoré 1994, 163–81, 203–31.
[94] Barnes 1982, 53–5.   [95] Corcoran 2000, 111.   [96] See appendix 2 for a complete list.
[97] Finley 1998 (orig. 1980), 133.   [98] Cenderelli 1965, 112.
[99] Huchthausen 1974; Watson 1974, 1122.
[100] CJ 1.19.1 (AD 290); see too CJ 7.13.1. Evans Grubbs 2000.
[101] CJ 6.27.3 (17 December, 293). Henceforth, the rescripts from 293 and 294 are dated with a specific month and day, in order to evoke the constant flow of judicial business. See appendix 2.

party who then used it to buy the slave – the master was paid, unbeknownst to him, with his own money![102] One rescript reports a particularly piquant tale: a woman named Theodora claimed that her late mother's husband (her "step-father") was a slave.[103] Her mother and the slave had colluded to pretend he was freeborn and had even gone before a Roman judge to have him declared freeborn under the rules of *postliminium*. Whatever prompted Theodora to file suit – an inheritance seems likely – it is worth noting that her mother's fraud was perpetrated through the legal system. The mother, in fact, showed a keen awareness that she could not marry her own freedman and had to have him declared freeborn.[104] The daughter took the case to court, exposed her dead mother, and presumably won her battle.[105]

The advent of universal citizenship meant that the Roman state was burdened, on a new scale, with providing a forum and a set of rules for settling disputes arising from the slave system. The rescripts involving slavery are classified under dozens of different titles in the *Justinianic Code*, ranging from "On Testamentary Manumission" to "On Torture." Slavery produced a bewildering variety of court cases, but what is more striking is the fact that the vast majority of disputes revolved around only a handful of recurring scenarios. If we try to categorize the disputes, not in legal terms, but in social terms, the breakdown is revealing.

Table 9.1 represents the patterns of litigation arising from the slave system. These categories are not hard and fast, and more importantly they frequently overlap. Often, for example, a dispute over status arose because of mixed-status sex, or ownership was ambiguous because of a will, or heirs fought against a manumission. Appendix 2 lists the Hermogenian rescripts individually. The extensive overlap between these categories only underscores the point that the disputes arose from a relatively delimited range of problems.

The disputes over ownership generally turned on questions of proper claim to title over the slave. For example, if an owner sold or alienated a slave-woman who subsequently gave birth, he had no claim to own the children.[106] If a master's slave was stolen and then sold, the sale did not affect the original owner's *dominium*, and he did not have to pay to recover his property.[107] Most of the cases about slavery which we have classified

---

[102] CJ 4.49.7 (15 April, 293); CJ 4.36.1 (1 October, 293).
[103] CJ 7.20.1 (AD 290).   [104] See chapter 11.
[105] cf. Evans Grubbs 1995, 276–7, and 1993, who interprets the rescript as a sign of "status confusion."
[106] CJ 3.32.12 (8 April, 293).   [107] CJ 3.32.23 (16 November, 294).

Table 9.1 *Causes of disputes involving slaves*

Category	Number
Status	45
Ownership	28
Manumission	26
Crime	19
Inheritance	18
Postliminium	12
Sex	10
Agency	8
Wills	7
Fugitives	4
Peculium	4
Torture	4
Total	**185**

as "crime" involved, one way or another, the theft of slaves – slaves were a highly valuable and highly mobile form of property, worth the risks of stealing.[108] Sometimes the rescripts set out proper procedure for resolving cases of ownership: first determine possession, then *dominium*.[109] Slaves could be tortured to extract evidence in cases involving their ownership.[110] Many of the cases involved complicated transactions, often concerned with loans. The guardian of a minor had (illicitly) pledged a slave on a loan for himself.[111] Slaves working an estate that was pledged for a loan could not be claimed by the creditor.[112] A slave's labor could be contracted to a creditor in return for a loan, but after the labor was completed the creditor's claims expired.[113] In many instances we sense that one party's case was exceptionally weak: one debtor tried to claim that he no longer had to repay a loan because the slave pledged as collateral had died![114]

Disputes over status were a common type of litigation represented in the rescripts. Most of these rescripts survive in CJ 7.16, *De liberali causa*, one of the longest titles in the entire *Justinianic Code*.[115] *Causae liberales* were

[108] CJ 6.2.9 (7 February, 293); CJ 7.27.2 (9 April, 293); CJ 6.2.10 (13 April, 293); CJ 6.2.12 (15 October, 293); CJ 9.20.10 (5 November, 293); CJ 7.26.7 (8 February, 294); CJ 6.2.16 (1 August, 294); CJ 9.20.14 (4 December, 294).
[109] CJ 3.32.13 (13 April, 293).   [110] CJ 9.41.12 (13 May, 293).
[111] CJ 8.15.7 (27 December, 293).   [112] CJ 8.14.5 (21 January, 294).
[113] CJ 8.42.20 (28 October, 294).   [114] CJ 8.13.25 (26 December, 294).
[115] Notably, this title in the *Hermogenian Code* may have included even *more* rescripts, some of which Justinian's editors moved to other titles: Cenderelli 1965, 112, 169.

civil cases governed by specific procedures; the same procedures governed the case when a free man was charged with being a slave, and when a slave claimed to be a free man.[116] Because liberty was at stake, *causae liberales* could only be heard by high-ranking judges such as provincial governors.[117] The person whose status was in question was held to be free until the case was resolved, but he or she did have to find an agent to pursue the case, an *adsertor libertatis*.[118] The classical law seems to have barred torture in status cases, but by the time of Diocletian it was apparently allowed.[119] The burden of proof was always on the plaintiff, regardless of whether the case was *ex libertate in servitutem* or *ex servitute in libertatem*. But the alleged slave could only obtain the more advantageous position of defendant if he was in possession of liberty in good faith at the time of the charge; a fugitive, for instance, did not have the presumption of freedom, nor did physical detention automatically put the burden on the alleged slave.[120] In the event of an unbreakable tie, judges were to decide for freedom on the principle of *favor libertatis*.[121]

Roman civil procedure had no firm rules of evidence and relied heavily on oral testimony.[122] In status disputes, written documents had a strong effect but were not ultimately decisive.[123] Questions of status ultimately rested on the anxious words of human beings in close-knit groups hauled before a judge. "The absence of a certificate does not preclude proof of [free] birth, nor does a forgery take away from the truth. Since every proof put forth consistent with the law ought to be admitted for the discovery of the truth, the governor of the province who has admitted the case, with all the formalities completed, will see that the dispute over status is decided between you as the rule of law allows."[124] In another case, the refusal to produce documents of manumission was behind a dispute over status.[125] In

---

[116] Buckland 1908, 652, "essential to a comprehensive view of the topic of slavery." In general, Lenski forthcoming; Herrmann-Otto 1999; Huchthausen 1974; Franciosi 1961; Buckland 1908, 652–75. Dig. 40.12; PS 5.1.

[117] CJ 3.3.2 (AD 294); CJ 7.14.9 (7 March, 294); CJ 7.16.11 (14 April, 293); CJ 7.16.15 (10 May, 293); Dig. 4.8.32.7.

[118] Buckland 1908, 655–6. CJ 7.16.14 (28 April, 293); Dig. 40.12.24. CT 4.8.9 (AD 392) eliminated the need for an *adsertor* if a person who had been living *in libertate* for twenty years or had performed public offices was accused of being a slave. Justinian eliminated the need for an *adsertor* altogether: CJ 7.17.1 (AD 529).

[119] No torture: Dig. 48.18.10.6. Torture: CJ 9.41.9 (AD 290). Corcoran 2000, 109.

[120] CJ 4.19.15 (27 December, 293). Dig. 40.12.7.5; Dig. 40.12.10–2. Buckland 1908, 660–1.

[121] Dig. 40.1.24.pr. Huchthausen 1976.   [122] Dig. 22.3–5. CJ 4.19–21.   [123] Meyer 2004, 217.

[124] CJ 7.16.15 (10 May, 293): *nec omissa professio probationem generis excludit nec falsa simulata veritatem minuit. Cum itaque ad examinationem veri omnis iure prodita debeat admitti probatio, aditus praeses provinciae sollemnibus ordinatis, prout iuris ratio patitur, causam liberalem inter vos decidi providebit.*

[125] CJ 7.16.25 (9 February, 294).

other cases we even sense the bad faith behind the conflict. A patron could not rescind the manumission, and the judge could compel him to tender the manumission documents.[126] Heirs, as we will see below, frequently opposed manumissions performed by their parents.

The procedural aspects of a trial *de liberali causa* would be the subject of several major reforms under Constantine. The earliest of these dealt with the problem of children born to mothers whose status was in question while the case was pending: their birth did not extend or renew the time limits for the trial and their status followed their mother's.[127] In July of 322 Constantine issued a sweeping law overhauling the selection of *adsertores*.[128] If a person in possession of liberty was accused of being a slave, but could not find an *adsertor* to stand for his liberty, the alleged slave was led around the province wearing a sign indicating the need of a sponsor. Furthermore, if no sponsor was found and the person was enslaved, but the enslaved party subsequently found a sponsor and renewed the case, he or she started from the presumption of liberty – a significant advantage that placed the burden of proof on the putative *dominus*.[129] Constantine also raised the penalties exacted from those who claimed a free person was a slave and lost the case: one slave in retribution for each they had claimed.[130] In this and subsequent laws, Constantine presented himself as a champion of *libertas*.[131] He was manifestly more concerned about claims *ex libertate in servitutem* than those *ex servitute in libertatem*, but this does not alter the fact that he was an emperor earnestly concerned to protect the freedom of his citizens – so long as it was legitimate – under Roman law.

Of the thirty-two rescripts from AD 293–4 in the Justinianic title *De liberali causa*, ten derived from cases involving an illicit change of status.[132] The Roman state claimed the exclusive power to regulate status; legal status was objectively determinable by a system of rules that could not be overridden by private agreement. The passage to freedom had to be performed by an act of manumission, not simply intent: a man who bought his domestic partner from slavery, for instance, had to manumit

---

[126] CJ 7.16.26 (9 March, 294).   [127] CT 4.8.4 (AD 322).
[128] CT 4.8.5 (AD 322).   [129] See esp. Lenski forthcoming.
[130] Formerly, malicious accusations of slave status were *iniuria* (see CJ 7.16.31 of 294), but Constantine decided that a penalty was due from anyone who tried to claim a slave and lost. Lenski forthcoming argues, on the basis of CT 4.8.8, that the penalty was probably paid to the fisc. Previous penalties: PS 5.1.7. cf. CJ 7.16.31 (11 October, 294); Dig. 47.10.12; Dig. 40.12.39.1.
[131] Lenski forthcoming.
[132] CJ 7.16.10 (14 April, 293); CJ 7.16.11 (14 April, 293); CJ 7.16.16 (10 May, 293); CJ 7.16.21 (7 October, 293); CJ 7.16.22 (27 November, 293); CJ 7.16.29 (11 October, 294); CJ 7.16.34 (13 November, 294); CJ 7.16.36 (17 December, 294); CJ 7.16.37 (17 December, 294); CJ 7.16.39 (26 December, 294).

her for her to become free.[133] More problematic was the passage to slavery; it was never permissible through private act.[134] A free person could not be enslaved without their knowledge or will. One presumably poor woman had entered the service of a family who, after some time, included her in their daughter's dowry as though she were chattel. This of course did not render her a slave.[135] Even if the free man or woman consented, they could not alter their status.[136] Chapter 10 explores in more detail this murky area of Roman law. Constantine tried to create a new, pragmatic compromise between legal theory and social practice, and the prominence of these disputes in the rescripts helps us to envision the problems which lay behind his enactments.

Many of the status disputes in the rescripts can be traced back, ultimately, to the fact that mixed-status relationships were a prominent feature of Roman slavery. These encounters were of variable duration and intent, from simple rape to long-term partnerships. It was an iron rule of the *ius gentium* that legal status passed through the mother in the absence of legitimate marriage. The rescripts show that sex between free men and their servile women created a permanent tension between biological relationships and legal status. Diocletian consistently held that the father's status was irrelevant.[137] The complicated, multi-generational conflicts behind the rescripts are sometimes evident: one declared that only the mother's status – not the grandmother's – was relevant.[138] In another case, a child was born to a slave-mother. The owner, who was the child's master and father, sold the slave-child, who was unable to obtain freedom by reimbursing the new owner for his costs.[139] The sexual relationship itself might create ambiguity. The emperor ruled that a freeborn woman did not lose her status simply because she endured the sexual dishonor of being a concubine.[140] Sexual or biological links would have increased the chances that a slave might find someone willing to serve as an *adsertor* to defend his or her legal claims. Chapter 11 will explore in more detail the tensions between law and practice, but the rescripts immediately evoke the endless stream of conflict in a slave society where free and slave blood were perpetually mixed.

At least twelve of the rescripts in CJ 7.16 were related to manumission.[141] In all, a total of fifty-one rescripts, more than one out of four cases about

---

[133] CJ 7.16.29 (11 October, 294). [134] CJ 7.16.10 (14 April, 293).
[135] CJ 7.16.16 (10 May, 293). [136] CJ 7.16.39 (26 December, 294).
[137] CJ 7.16.11 (14 April, 293). [138] CJ 7.16.28 (10 April, 294).
[139] CJ 7.16.12 (14 April, 293). [140] CJ 7.16.34 (13 November, 294).
[141] CJ 7.16.12 (14 April, 293); CJ 7.16.19 (27 August, 293); CJ 7.16.20 (27 August, 293); CJ 7.16.22 (27 November, 293); CJ 7.16.23 (29 December, 293); CJ 7.16.25 (9 February, 294); CJ 7.16.26 (9 March, 294); CJ 7.16.29 (11 October, 294); CJ 7.16.30 (11 October, 294); CJ 7.16.32 (5 November, 294); CJ 7.16.33 (10 November, 294); CJ 7.16.36 (17 December, 294).

slavery from AD 293–4, related to manumission. Conflict was inherent in the practice of manumission. Manumission generated litigation because it reshuffled the obligations and duties which bound master and slave together.[142] Patrons and freedmen held different expectations about this new balance of power. Patrons demanded continuing respect and labor, and they often found that the new arrangement was not to their satisfaction. The chancery of Diocletian heard petition after petition from freedmen whose patrons tried to revoke the manumission. If a master paid back a freedman the ransom price he had given for his freedom, the manumission could not be annulled.[143] In line with the classical law, Diocletian ruled that lack of respect was insufficient grounds for revoking manumission.[144] The inscriptions of Leukopetra reflect precisely the tensions which are so visible in the rescripts of Diocletian, and they help us to envision the world of human conflict which smoldered just beneath the surface of the legal codes. The different customs prevailing in the east and west may be further responsible for the prominence of conflicts over manumission in the rescripts. Classical Roman law had "sought to strike a balance between conflicting interests," and it is precisely these legal balancing acts which were thrown out of equilibrium by the new institutional setting of late antique law.[145]

Manumission also generated conflict because it was a flashpoint of competing forces within the family. Manumission was an act of paternalistic grace and an essential means of controlling slaves.[146] The dream of freedom was elemental in the creation of incentives to good behavior.[147] At the same time, manumission relinquished a certain amount of control over the bodies and labor of integral units of the family. It diminished the patrimony. Manumission was a delicate act in the taut economy of household power, and heirs frequently asserted their own counter-claims against the arrangements worked out between their parents and the slaves. Asterius of Amasea described how a son might wish death upon his father and seethe with anger if he had to watch the father release a slave into freedom.[148] Conflicts over inheritance were an unrelenting source of litigation. It was no accident that Menander, reflecting on the ascendancy of Roman law, thought of inheritance disputes as the prime example of legal conflict. In a homily delivered around 411, Augustine evoked the episode from the *Gospel of Luke* in which a man interrupted Jesus to ask for mediation in

---

[142] See pp. 373–4 and chapter 12.   [143] CJ 7.16.33 (10 November, 294).
[144] CJ 7.16.30 (11 October, 294).   [145] Treggiari 1969a, 81.
[146] Bradley 1987b, 81–112; Hopkins 1978, 115–32.   [147] See chapter 5.
[148] Ast. Am. Serm. 3.11 (Datema: 34).

an inheritance dispute.[149] Augustine riffed on the story by imagining two brothers as they measured out gold, silver, slaves, cattle, and fields to divide their patrimony. The sons were so stingy that they could not wait for their father to die. "Each strives by lawsuits and quarrels to gain ownership of his own share, and the old man cries, 'What are you doing? I'm still alive. Just wait a little until I die, and then you can carve up my *domus*!'"[150]

Throughout the Diocletianic rescripts we see heirs fighting tooth and nail to undermine, prevent, or undo manumissions performed by their parents.[151] Heirs contested manumissions in every way conceivable, including fraud, forgery, and bad faith.[152] One heir tried to contend that without his signature, a testamentary manumission was invalid.[153] Another heir declined to follow his father's "recommendation" of freedom for a slave – the law was indeed on his side.[154] Heirs tried to demand labor services beyond those stipulated by the decedent.[155] Heirs fought amongst themselves over the services of freedmen.[156] Heirs tried to argue that the freedmen appointed as curators during their minority should remain in slavery.[157] Diocletian's rescripts suggest what an administrative burden it was to be responsible for mediating the tensions between inheritance and manumission.

There is nothing specifically late antique about these axes of conflict. The relation between free sons and slave sons, and the relation between slaves and heirs, were paradigmatic sites of discord. In the *Letter to the Galatians*, Paul gave a chilling interpretation of the story of Isaac and Ishmael. The scenario was re-worked for audiences that understood well what it meant.[158] In a second-century parable, a man rewarded an exceptionally obedient slave with freedom and property. The master decided, "'He has pleased me greatly. In exchange for the work he has done I want to make him a fellow heir with my son . . .' The master's son approved of the idea that the slave should become his fellow heir."[159] We are supposed to be struck by the

---

[149] Luke 12:13.
[150] Aug. Util. iei. 13 (CC 46: 241): *litibus et contentionibus studeant ad vindicandas sibi quisque partes suas, exclamat senex: "quid facitis? adhuc vivo. expectate paululum mortem meam, tunc secate domum meam."*
[151] Huchthausen 1974, 254–5.
[152] CJ 7.2.12 (1 December, 293); see Tellegen Couperus 1982. CJ 7.16.18 (15 July, 293); CJ 7.4.2 (AD 208–13). cf. CJ 7.2.6 (Gordian); CJ 7.4.1 (AD 197).
[153] CJ 7.16.32 (5 November, 294).   [154] CJ 7.4.12 (15 April, 294).
[155] CJ 6.3.5 (AD 212); CJ 6.3.10 (AD 225).   [156] CJ 7.16.23 (29 December, 293).
[157] CJ 7.16.35 (5 December, 294).   [158] Gal. 4:30. See chapter 11.
[159] Herm. Past. 55.7–9 (SC 53: 228): καὶ ἐμοὶ λίαν ἤρεσεν. ἀντὶ τούτου οὖν τοῦ ἔργου οὗ εἰργάσατο θέλω αὐτὸν συγκληρονόμον τῷ υἱῷ μου ποιῆσαι . . . ταύτῃ τῇ γνώμῃ ὁ υἱὸς τοῦ δεσπότου συνηυδόκησεν αὐτῷ, ἵνα συγκληρονόμος γένηται ὁ δοῦλος τῷ υἱῷ.

peaceful ending. Heirs were the real losers in manumission acts, and from one end of antiquity to the other, Greek inscriptions show the continuity of this problem.[160] In the late empire, Roman civil law stood eye to eye with these primordial frictions.

The rescripts of the late third century have sometimes been read as though they narrate the tabescence of the slave system: the reactionaries of the Roman state were engaged in a long, hopeless battle against the death of an old order.[161] But status disputes can be a sign of the vigor and complexity of the status system. The rescripts exhibit human beings waging fearsome legal battles over questions of status. A *causa liberalis* was a dispute, and it takes two to litigate. The emperor and his officials did not expend such energy to resolve empty scuffles. To interpret the rescripts as a sign of the slave system's breakdown is to assume that society itself was heading in a certain direction that progressively yielded more legal conflict. But we have no idea how much legal conflict was a "normal" part of the system, and it is only under these rare circumstances of codification that we can glimpse the amount of legal conflict which a Roman emperor encountered. Most importantly, the number of disputes in the late third century was not necessarily a function of total litigation, but of the total amount which ended up in Roman jurisdiction.[162] There was no abstract confusion about status, only a multitude of conflicts over power and property, increasingly adjudicated in a Roman court.

The rescripts echo the whirring gears of a legal machine bent on applying Roman private law in civil disputes throughout the empire; it is no stretch to see the Diocletianic rescripts as part of a programmatic effort to enforce Roman rules after decades of informal tolerance and simple inertia in the face of a dizzying array of local habits.[163] The compression of documents in the *Codex Hermogenianus* is a hint of the bustling energy of the new tetrarchy. Clearly Diocletian's reign marked an important phase in the history of Roman administration, but there were important precedents in the third century. The Severan period marked the beginning of a great shift from senatorial to equestrian officials.[164] Men like Tertullianus, equestrians with legal and practical experience, replaced the leisured classes in the activity of government. During the 230s and 240s, a coterie of men hardened by practical experience came into power, presaging the creation of a late antique bureaucracy.[165] The volume of legal business necessitated the creation of

---

[160] Hellenistic Butrint: Cabanes 1974. cf. too Schaps 1976, 63–4. Middle Byzantine: Rotman 2004, 176–81. See Zelnick-Abramovitz 2005, 139.
[161] Evans Grubbs 1995, 269, 271, 277; Huchthausen 1974.   [162] Corcoran 2006, 40.
[163] Evans Grubbs 2005, 95.   [164] Potter 2004, 76–82.   [165] Potter 2004, 229–32.

new posts. A new magistrate, the *praetor de liberalibus causis* at Rome, was first attested in the 210s.[166] This official had specific jurisdiction over status disputes. The Severan period was also "clearly the turning point" in the practice of appointing deputy emperors, *iudices vice Caesaris*.[167] This was directly correlated to the burden of legal business, and it made the civil law operational in the depths of crisis. The most "sweeping change" was the rise of deputy governors.[168] This office, typically held by equestrians with imperial experience, became common, and it was undoubtedly related to judicial activity.[169] Together, these reforms can be read as signs of institutional strain and adjustment, plausibly linked to the effects of the Antonine Constitution.

The long reign of Diocletian marked a particular moment in the spread of Roman private law.[170] "His aims were conservative and even reactionary, his methods radical."[171] His rescripts show a determined effort to fulfill the emperor's role as the bulwark of Roman law. Dividing provinces into smaller units and divesting governors of military responsibilities was a variation of the practice of appointing vice-governors and an effort to improve the system of justice. The compilation of rescripts, officially sponsored or not, was part of a movement to standardize legal business.[172] Diocletian was more emphatic about the enforcement of Roman rules than other third-century emperors.[173] In that sense, Diocletian's reign might be considered the apogee of legal classicism, but his reign also betrays the beginnings of a new age.[174] The elaborate rhetoric of Diocletianic laws became a fundamental aspect of all subsequent legal writing. The tendency to issue imperial edicts became ever more common, revealing an activist style of government.[175] Constantine would carry this style to new lengths.[176] Diocletian's reorganization of the *scrinia* was responsible, either immediately or shortly after his reign, for the effective subordination of the *magister libellorum*, as the imperial *quaestor* became the principal architect of legal policy.[177]

The nature of our sources distorts the picture: the rescripts of the third century reflect the enforcement of existing law in civil disputes, while the imperial constitutions of the fourth century were administrative acts or reforms of the law.[178] Still, the image of change from Diocletian to

---

[166] Franciosi 1961, 126–7.   [167] Peachin 1996.   [168] Peachin 1996, 154.
[169] Peachin 1996, 155.   [170] Garnsey 2004, 148; Honoré 1994, 135–8.
[171] Honoré 1994, 183.   [172] Corcoran 2000, 42; Turpin 1987.
[173] Garnsey 2004, 148; Lepelley 1996; Erim and Reynolds 1969.   [174] Corcoran 2006, esp. 49.
[175] Feissel 1995.   [176] Humfress 2006, 213, for Constantine as an innovator.
[177] Harries 1988.   [178] Corcoran 2000, 3.

Constantine is not a mirage. The classical law reached its high tide, but this was still an uncertain triumph. The rigorist classicism of Diocletian may have been a more compressed phenomenon than the sources make it appear. In the reign of Constantine, the state finally succumbed to a wave of practical legislation on precisely the delicate points of law which appear over and over in the rescripts: private changes of status, the contradictions between sex and status, and institutional control of manumission and patron–freedman relationships. As chapters 10–12 will demonstrate, the reign of Constantine marked a pragmatic turn in the regulation of a slave society.

CHAPTER 10

The enslavement of Mediterranean bodies: child exposure and child sale

STARS, STRANGERS, AND SLAVES

The Roman empire of the fourth century was home to a litigious society. A one-time lawyer in the age of Constantine, Firmicus Maternus, described the legal system, unflatteringly, as a world of greed, mischief, revenge, and graft.[1] So Firmicus retired from the legal profession to a more satisfying occupation: astrology. He authored "l'ouvrage d'astrologie le plus complet de ceux que nous a laissés l'Antiquité."[2] His work is a bewildering farrago, the product of ancient man's millennial intimacy with the sky.[3] Astrology in late antiquity was an exact science.[4] The disposition of the stars was imprinted on the soul of the infant at birth, and a professional like Firmicus could read destiny in a birthday.[5] Firmicus offered the horoscopes of emperors, slaves, and everything in between. The stars might decree that a slave would never be freed, or that a slave would be freed at a young age.[6] Slavery is omnipresent in the social–astronomical imagination of Firmicus, yet, nowhere is there to be found a barbarian slave hauled across some faraway border.[7] For Firmicus – writing in Sicily – if the stars had a malevolent aspect, anyone could become a slave.

It is noteworthy that the single most detailed chart in his work foretold the fate of exposed infants.[8] The unmistakable impression is that exposure awaited not a few of the human bodies who passed into the world. The exposed infant had, in reality, the most indeterminate future of all. Surely this lengthy horoscope whispers the collective despair of parents forced to

---

[1] Firm. Math. 4.pr.1 (Monat vol. 2: 125). Harries 1999, on Roman legal culture; Liebs 1987, 81–9, on Firmicus. cf. Lib. Or. 45.18 (Foerster vol. 3: 367); Ast. Am. 3.8 (Datema: 32); Aug. Util. iei. 13 (CC 46: 241). For a late medieval parallel, Smail 2003.

[2] Monat vol. 1: 8–10: born in Syracuse around 300, retired and began the *Mathesis* in 337.

[3] But not a mere pastiche: Harries 1999, 138–9; Grodzynski 1984, 397–403. cf. Boswell 1988, 80.

[4] Van der Meer 1978, 60–7.   [5] Firm. Math. 1.5.6 (Monat vol. 1: 66).

[6] Book 7 section 4 is entirely devoted to slaves.

[7] Though locals might be captured, e.g. Firm. Math. 4.10.4 (Monat vol. 2: 145).

[8] Firm. Math. 7.2.1–26 (Monat vol. 3: 151–60).

expose their children. Many exposed infants, it seems, met their end as easy prey for hungry animals.[9] Others were collected – some raised as sons, others as slaves.[10] The legal evidence of the late Roman empire will suggest that these horoscopes were not pure fancy or thoughtless convention; the state was forced to address, from a practical perspective, the indeterminate fate of the foundling. As both a lawyer and then an astrologer in the age of Constantine, Firmicus Maternus encountered infant exposure, an enduring Mediterranean practice. Both occupations would have given him cause to reflect on the nature of status, the indeterminacy of newborn life, and the unpredictable fate that awaited many a child in antiquity left to the whim of strangers.

THE JURIDICAL REGIME OF ENSLAVEMENT: BETWEEN LAW AND PRACTICE

This chapter explores changes of status in late Roman society.[11] In particular, it is focused on the separate but closely related practices – child exposure, child sale, and various forms of child "rental" – by which infants and children might pass from freedom into slavery. A long, complex, and significant series of legal enactments in late antiquity dealt with the problem of enslavement in its various guises. Traditionally, the legal enactments have been seen in one of two ways. On the one hand, the trail of legislation has been interpreted as a sign of economic crisis. In this narrative, imperial efforts to regulate enslavement were a symptom of growing social instability – to put it crudely, laws on enslavement reflect an increasing incidence of illicit enslavement.[12] Secondly, the laws on enslavement have been interpreted through the lens of Christianization. In this view, new approaches to enslavement pursued by the later emperors are related to Christian teachings on social questions – or, more broadly, to Christian ideology.[13] Both of these interpretations raise an important question of method: how can laws be used to understand social practice or social change?

This chapter tries to demonstrate that the effort to diagnose the laws on enslavement as a symptom of some external cause – be it social or

---

[9] Firm. Math. 7.2.9 (Monat vol. 3: 155). See Harris 1994.
[10] cf. Lact. Inst. 6.20.21–6 (CSEL 19.1: 559–60). cf. Taubenschlag 1944, 55.
[11] Evans Grubbs 2009b; Tate 2008a; Vuolanto 2003; Memmer 1991; Dalla 1988; Martini 1988; Gebbia 1987; Sargenti 1986 and 1938; Nardi 1984 and 1978; Fossati Vanzetti 1983; Humbert 1983; Kaser 1975, 132, 204–5; Mayer-Maly 1958; Dupont 1937, 26–8, 137–44; Volterra 1937; Mitteis 1891, 358–64.
[12] Vuolanto 2003, 191, is rightly critical that the evidence does not reflect the actual incidence of sale or exposure.
[13] Sargenti 1986, 19; Fossati Vanzetti 1983, 201; Dupont 1937, 27; Buckland 1908, 402.

ideological change – is misguided. Instead, the focus should be placed upon the institutional dimension of legal status in the Roman empire. There was, even under the late republic and early empire, a potentially massive contradiction between law and practice. The Roman slave system relied upon the enslavement of Mediterranean infants and children, but child exposure and child sale were not recognized modes of enslavement in classical law. Once that contradiction is placed at the center of the interpretation, then it becomes clear that the legal regime of enslavement was intrinsically problematic, and the late Roman laws can be read as part of an effort to address a structurally contradictory aspect of social life in the Roman empire. The contradictions between law and reality were in fact exacerbated in the late empire by the advent of universal citizenship, which re-configured the channels of access to Roman legal remedies. The law of enslavement in the late empire, far from a decline in the salience of status, reflects an ongoing search for a stable institutional framework for the slave system.

It is worth imagining the scale of these practices. Chapter 2 has already outlined the importance of internal enslavement in the Roman empire. The Roman slave trade had always relied heavily upon a Mediterranean supply of unfree bodies in order to maintain the slave population.[14] Enslavement, for demographic and economic reasons, was structurally embedded in Roman society. The exposure of infants was endemic in world of staggeringly high fertility and few safe methods of contraception or abortion. Parents exposed their offspring for a variety of reasons: poverty, patrimonial planning, illegitimacy.[15] In times of scarcity, cyclical and inevitable in the Mediterranean environment, the practice of child exposure was intensified. There were occasional criticisms of child exposure, but at least until the late empire, the practice was quietly accepted as a necessary part of life. It was perfectly legal. Greek and Roman observers universally assumed that child exposure was normal and extensive; comparative evidence suggests that a ghastly percentage of all newborns could be exposed in a pre-modern society. Most of these surely died, but many were adopted or harvested for slavery, even though these fates, as we will see, were not recognized in classical Roman law.

Child sale is an even murkier subject, primarily because it lies so far outside the blinkers of our upper-class sources. In the literary record, the sale of children is usually represented as a practice of "other" peoples who supposedly valued freedom less than the Greeks and the Romans; in

---

[14] Harris 1994; Ramin and Veyne 1981, 475.   [15] cf. chapter 2.

late antiquity, this ideological construction gives way to a new Christian concern for the poor, and we begin to see for the first time descriptions of parents forced by hardship to sell their children.[16] The sale of children was often assimilated, or disguised, as a rental of labor or an apprenticeship.[17] It was illegal to pledge children as security for a debt, since that exposed them too dangerously to claims of ownership, but it was legal to contract their labor.[18] The Roman empire always remained an agglomeration of underdeveloped societies, with high rates of mortality and astonishing levels of material stratification. The majority of the population, at all times, lived on the edge of subsistence.[19] Structural shocks – climatic, family mortality, etc. – always threatened to push parts of the population below subsistence and induce desperate gambits for survival. Child rental and child sale were built into these vicious material cycles.

Practice is one thing; law another.[20] Classical Roman law was guided by the principle that birth status was absolute, objective, and unalterable by private contract. "No price can be placed on a free man."[21] Slaves were imagined to be those captured in war or biologically descended – through their mother – from such captives.[22] There were a handful of other means of legitimate enslavement, such as penal servitude, but these were rare. The state's desire to control the line between freedom and slavery was directly required by the property system, and the Roman government was concerned to keep the line between slavery and freedom a *public* prerogative. "A private pact cannot make a man anyone's slave or freedman."[23] Slavery makes a human being into a piece of property; all property is by nature a public concern, since property is the inherently *exclusive* right to own, to use, and to transfer.[24] Papinian wrote that "by reason of the regular, daily traffic in slaves, it was in the public interest to adopt the rule which we have, for we frequently in ignorance buy free men."[25] The state guaranteed the legitimacy of the property system by enforcing clear, public rules of status.

Despite the abstract guarantees of inviolable status, classical Roman law handled the cases of enslaved adults, children, and exposed infants in

---

[16] Esp. Vuolanto 2003, 170 ff.   [17] Vuolanto 2003, 189–97.   [18] Dig. 20.3.5; PS 5.1.1.
[19] Scheidel and Friesen 2009.   [20] Ramin and Veyne 1981 remains the best treatment.
[21] PS 5.1.1: *homo enim liber nullo pretio aestimatur.*
[22] Dig. 1.5.4–5. cf. Ambrosiast. Comm. Coloss. 4.1–3 (CSEL 81: 202); Aug. Civ. 19.15 (CC 48: 682–3).
[23] Dig. 40.12.37: *conventio privata neque servum quemquam neque libertum alicuius facere potest.* Dig. 40.5.53.
[24] Barzel 1997.
[25] Dig. 41.3.44; adapted from Watson: *ibi propter adsiduam et cottidianam comparationem servorum ita constitui publice interfuit, nam frequenter ignorantia liberos emimus.* CJ 8.44.18 (AD 293); CJ 8.44.24 (AD 294); CJ 8.44.25 (AD 294). In general, Söllner 2000.

different ways. In the case of adults sold into slavery, Roman law harbored a number of exceptions that in effect permitted the passage from freedom to slavery. "Also, nothing at all prohibits free men who have allowed themselves to be sold or to be transferred into slavery for any reason, even if they are beyond twenty years old, from re-claiming freedom, unless perhaps they allowed themselves to be sold in order to share in the price. If anyone under twenty years of age allows himself to be sold to share in the price, this will not damage his claim after twenty years of age."[26] The law protected the slave-owner who bought, unknowingly, a free adult who had sold himself into slavery to share in the price.[27] If the free man knowingly connived at having himself sold as a slave to share in the profit then he was denied the ability to return to free status; he was barred from *vindicatio in libertatem*.[28] If the owner had known the man was free, he could not expect legal rights to his "property."[29] Likewise, if the man truly did not know he was free, and subsequently learned this, he could re-claim his freedom. Thus, only sale to defraud an unknowing buyer rendered the free man a slave. This seems to have been a deliberate loophole and one that might have encouraged the use of slave-dealers as middle-men to insulate the buyer from danger.[30] Ramin and Veyne have characterized this corner of Roman law as deliberately *trompeuse*.[31]

In the case of children, Roman law was adamant. "It is a manifest principle of law that children cannot be transferred into another's power by their parents by any title of sale or donation, any right of pledge, or any other means, not even under the pretext of ignorance of the one receiving them."[32] Free children were absolutely protected against being sold into slavery.[33] Regardless of their knowledge, regardless of the buyer's knowledge, a sale transacted before the free child was twenty years of age was absolutely null and void.[34] The state was serious about enforcing the prohibition on selling children into slavery, and parents might even find

---

[26] Dig. 40.12.7.pr-1: *Liberis etiam hominibus, maxime si maiores viginti annis venum se dari passi sunt vel in servitutem quaqua ratione deduci, nihil obest, quo minus possint in libertatem proclamare, nisi forte se venum dari passi sunt, ut participaverint pretium. 1. Si quis minor viginti annis ad partiendum pretium venum se dari passus est, nihil ei hoc post viginti annos nocebit.* See Söllner 2000, 86.

[27] Fossati Vanzetti 1983, 179; Buckland 1908, 427–36. Dig. 18.1.4–6; Dig. 40.12.7.2; Dig. 40.12.16.2.

[28] Ramin and Veyne 1981, 488–9. Dig. 1.5.5.1; Dig. 40.12.7; Dig. 40.12.14. Inst. 1.3.4. Hadrian sometimes allowed exceptions, if the slave paid back the purchase price: Dig. 40.14.2.

[29] Buckland 1908, 353. [30] Ramin and Veyne 1981, 475. [31] Ramin and Veyne 1981, 490.

[32] CJ 4.43.1 (AD 294): *Liberos a parentibus neque venditionis neque donationis titulo neque pignoris iure aut quolibet alio modo, nec sub praetextu ignorantiae accipientis in alium transferri posse manifesti iuris est.*

[33] Vuolanto 2003, 179; Buckland 1908, 427–36.

[34] Dig. 4.4.9.4 implies that some lenience might be allowed up to twenty-five.

themselves liable to punishment.[35] Kidnapping, likewise, was a violation of public law and obviously incurred the opposition of the state.[36] Parents could rent out the labor of their children, but such contracts had no bearing on the legal status of the child.

Exposure posed the most serious dilemmas for the government. Parents could legally expose their newborn infants, but this act could do no damage to the birth status of the child. The child not only remained free if born to a free woman, servile if born to a slave-woman, the father's claim of *patria potestas* was unbroken.[37] The most important evidence survives in the letters of Pliny to Trajan. During his tenure as governor of Bithynia, Pliny faced the predicament of exposed infants who had been enslaved but later re-claimed their freedom.[38] He wrote to Trajan for a legal ruling.[39] Two related issues were at stake: the "status and maintenance costs" of enslaved foundlings.[40] Pliny could find no general rule which applied to his province and referred to Trajan for guidance. Trajan responded, noting that he was unable to find a general rule. Trajan found archived letters of Domitian to two governors, but since these did not concern Bithynia, he ruled that free foundlings could recover their freedom through a civil suit *without* repaying the cost of their maintenance (*alimenta*).

Trajan held that freeborn status was inviolable, that the enslavement of freeborn infants, even exposed infants, had no validity in Roman law, and that no obstacles, such as repayment of maintenance costs, could impede the return to freedom.[41] It is interesting, historically, that no general rule had developed before the second century and equally striking that Roman governors were content to enforce local custom. But Trajan's advice seems to have become the standard approach for Roman governance, and in the eyes of the law, neither status nor *patria potestas* was affected by exposure.[42] The real issue before Pliny centered on the question of *alimenta*. The repayment of *alimenta* represented a mediated solution to the problem of enslaved foundlings. Trajan ruled that the principles of legal status supervened any need to compensate the *nutritor*, who invested time, money, and expectations in the foundling. Trajan's decision became the standard of Roman classical law, particularly in the *Digest*, where no trace of *alimenta*

---

[35] Melluso 2000, 33–4; Fossati Vanzetti 1983, 180–1, criminal. Vuolanto 2003, 181; Lambertini 1987, not. CJ 3.15.2 (AD 294). cf. Dig. 48.15.6.2.
[36] Dig. 1.18.13. cf. Dig. 48.15. CJ 9.20.   [37] Fossati Vanzetti 1983, 182–3. Dig. 22.6.1.2; Dig. 40.4.29.
[38] Harris 1994, 6; Cameron 1939a, 49–50; Mommsen 1905, 11–12; Mitteis 1891, 127–8.
[39] Plin. Ep. 10.65 (Mynors 323–4).
[40] Plin. Ep. 10.65 (Mynors 323–4): *de condicione et alimentis eorum.*   [41] Cameron 1939a, 49.
[42] Dig. 40.4.29; Dig. 22.6.1.2. Evans Grubbs 2009b, 120; Memmer 1991, 33–6; Taubenschlag 1944, 55. *Contra*, Vuolanto 2003, 181.

payments are found. But there are hints that, in reality, the practice of reimbursing *nutritores* endured.[43]

The enslavement of freeborn persons was invalid in Roman law yet structurally integral to the slave trade. A landmark article by Ramin and Veyne first traced this profound fissure between the law and practice.[44] They noted that bad faith and poor access to the legal system insulated the slave trade from the principles of law. Unless a slave – rather, an advocate for the slave – filed suit, the state would not intervene.[45] The consequences for harassment of the master, in a world where there were few limits on the corporal abuse against slaves, would surely have made legal action unattractive. Moreover, many children who had been exposed or sold as infants would be ignorant of their own origins.[46] Slave-traders also stood between "illegal" internal sources and slave-owners. Criminal charges might be hard to file against a slave-dealer.[47] The slave trade could move bodies great distances. Moreover, the civil law belonged to the Roman citizen, and only gradually did this privilege spread throughout the first two centuries of the empire. Economically backward areas, like the rural highlands of interior Asia Minor, were continual wells of the slave trade, yet they were among the least Romanized elements of the empire. This was hardly coincidental.

When a suit for freedom did reach a court, governors and emperors could be earnest judges – or at least later lawyers saw fit to codify the cases which made them look earnest.[48] The rescripts show that Diocletian was perfectly willing to rule in favor of freedom in cases of sale or exposure. In fact, if the classical rule was imperfectly enforced in the high empire, then Diocletian was perhaps more traditional than the tradition. His reign witnessed the firm and deliberate application of the classical principle. In cases of self-sale, the sale of children, and the exposure of free infants, Diocletian unequivocally ruled in favor of the inalienability of birth status. Not

---

[43] Lanfranchi 1938, 268–71. Ps.-Quint. Decl. 278 (Winterbottom: 86–8); Ps.-Quint. Decl. 278.pr. (Winterbottom: 86). Sen. Contr. 9.3.pr (Winterbottom vol. 2: 262); Quint. Inst. 7.1.14 and 9.2.89 (Winterbottom vol. 2: 369, 509). See the comments of Boswell 1988, 56. cf. also CJ 8.51.1 (AD 224) in which the reclamation of a slave who had been exposed without the master's knowledge or consent was allowed, so long as restitution for expenses incurred was paid. In CJ 5.4.16, Diocletian ruled in a complex case that the consent of a birth-father who had exposed a daughter was still necessary for her marriage, so strong was *patria potestas*. If he refused to consent to the marriage, however (and thus reasserted in a strong sense his *patria potestas* in a way damaging to the *nutritor*), he owed *alimenta* to the *nutritor* (Memmer 1991, 38).

[44] Ramin and Veyne 1981, 474.   [45] Ramin and Veyne 1981, 479.

[46] Dio. Or. 15.22–23 (Arnim: 232–41).

[47] CJ 8.44.18 (AD 293); CJ 8.44.24 (AD 294); CJ 8.44.25 (AD 294); CJ 3.15.2 (AD 294).

[48] cf. Cameron 1939a, 49.

coincidentally, the tetrarchy produced the first documentary evidence for the sale of children. The collision between the realities of enslavement and a stridently classicizing legal policy produced this evidence. The survival of case law from the late third-century rescripts is not a proxy measure of the material incidence of child sale. It always existed, and Diocletian's battle represented an exceptional campaign against it, rooted in his desire to adjudicate disputes according to Roman private law.[49]

Diocletian's rescripts sound a discernible note of impatience.[50] "It is a certain principle of law that free men can not change their condition and become slaves by any private pact or transaction of business."[51] "If you have sold your free son to your son-in-law, who being so closely related to you cannot plead ignorance, there is no right to charge one another with a crime."[52] "It is fitting that even free men who hold out that they are slaves cannot change their status."[53] The enforcement of public, inviolable liberty was a crucial theme in the Diocletianic program. Yet the inalienability of liberty could be a real nuisance to the slave-owner. The rescripts record not a few cases of owners who suddenly saw their property vanish. If a child was declared freeborn, he or she was not a piece of property. The Roman principle of inalienable birth status, when enforced, destabilized the property claims of *individual* slave-owners, while reinforcing the *social* legitimacy of the slave system.

High principles of freedom and a vigorous slave trade were a potent, if unstable, combination. The problem came to a head in the reign of Constantine. Several constitutions from his tenure – difficult and seemingly contradictory – show that this problem was of pressing relevance to the early fourth-century state. Constantine's laws were the fulcrum of late antique reform, for it was in his reign that the rigorist classicism of Diocletian's chancery finally gave way to a less purist approach. In the wake of Constantine's reforms, the state – and eventually the church – struggled to maintain stable rules for the problem of enslavement.

SALE AND EXPOSURE IN THE AGE OF CONSTANTINE

The evidence for the legal regime of enslavement in late antiquity is complicated. The basic facts are uncertain: the attribution of important laws, the

---

[49] Memmer 1991, 45.　　[50] CJ 2.4.26 (AD 294). Quoted in chapter 9. cf. CJ 4.10.12 (AD 294).

[51] CJ 7.16.10 (AD 293): *liberos privatis pactis vel actus quacumque administrati ratione non posse mutata condicione servos fieri certi iuris est.* Compare CJ 7.14.8 (AD 293); CJ 7.20.2 (AD 294).

[52] CJ 7.16.37 (AD 294): *Si filium tuum liberum genero vendidisti, qui tam proxima necessitudine coniunctus condicionis ignorantiam simulare non potest, utrisque sociis criminis accusator deest.*

[53] CJ 7.16.39 (AD 294): *Liberos velut servos profitentes statum eorum mutare non posse constat.*

precise meaning and effect of some enactments, and more profoundly the long-term sequence of reform. Best, then, to start with an unambiguous statement. A private rescript of Constantine, dated to 315 and issued in Rome, shows Constantine following Diocletian, enforcing the classical line on the sale of children:

It is not at all permissible for freeborn children to be reduced to slavery at a price and is not sanctioned by our untroubled age, nor should freeborn status be unjustly injured under the maintenance of the sale which was transacted. Therefore it is right to go to a judge with jurisdiction, who shall see to it that these things are accomplished in a hearing for freedom as they are supposed to be determined in these disputes and who will give a hearing to the parties according to the judicial discipline.[54]

In this legal opinion, Constantine held that the reduction of free children into slavery at a price was "not at all permissible." The party in question was instructed to seek out freedom through a status hearing before a Roman judge. Constantine, in 315, appeared absolutely in line with the classical dogma which had been the standard of Roman law since at least Trajan. Birth status was objective, inviolable, and not subject to private alteration.

Confusion arises immediately, however, because in the very same collection of rescripts, the next entry shows an emperor of 313 – two years *earlier* – taking what appears to be the opposite view:

Since you declare that you have bought a newborn slave at a certain price, which you say you have paid and secured with a written document, this principle has been ordered by us for some time now: that, if one should wish to recover his child, then give the master another slave in its place or the price at which its value is reckoned. Even now, if you bought it for a certain price from its parents, we hold that you possess the right of property. No one, however, except a relative, is permitted to make a claim on the child.[55]

This law, though it claims such a principle had long been ordered, is the first extant document of Roman law which admitted that the sale of a child

[54] FV 33 (AD 315): *Ingenuos progenitos servitutis adfligi dispendiis minime oportere etiam nostri temporis tranquillitate sancitur, nec sub obtentu initae venditionis inlicite decet ingenuitatem infringi. Quare iudicem competentem adire par est, qui in liberali causa ea faciet compleri, quae in huiuscemodi contentionibus ordinari consuerunt, secundum iudiciariam disciplinam partibus audientiam praebiturus.*

[55] FV 34 (AD 313): *Cum profitearis te certa quantitate mancipium ex sanguine comparasse, cuius pretium te exsolvisse dicis et instrumentis esse firmatum, hoc a nobis iam olim praescriptum est, quod, si voluerit liberum suum reciperare, tunc in eius locum mancipium domino dare aut pretium quo valuisset numeraret. Etiamnunc, si a suis parentibus certo pretio comparasti, ius dominii possidere te existimamus. Nullum autem ex gentilibus liberum adprobari licet.*

was legally valid.[56] The master had the right to hold the slave as property.[57] Notably, nothing about this law smacks of theoretical considerations: we are on the practical plane, a property dispute and a state trying to decide how to adjudicate it. If the parents or relatives wished to vindicate the child, they had to offer compensation to the slave-owner: another slave in its place or the cash value of the slave. Enormous conclusions have sometimes been drawn from this rescript, along the lines of the claim that "beginning in 313, Constantine legalized the selling of free children into slavery."[58]

The dissonance of the two rescripts is not a little indecorous, and Sargenti has offered a persuasive solution.[59] The law of 313, recognizing the sale of newborns, originated from the court of Licinius and reflected current practice in the eastern empire. Sargenti's hypothesis is strengthened by comparison with another law of Licinius which has survived. Issued 15 May, 314, the rescript declares that "it has been deemed best that in all matters justice and fairness are preferable to the reasoning of strict legal principle."[60] It was within the powers of the Roman emperor to respond to petitioners by granting them a favor or exception to the law, but this rescript certainly sounds more categorical. Licinius claimed to enforce a sense of justice and equity rather than strict legal principle.[61] It may signal a subtle criticism of the hyper-classical approach favored by Diocletian – whose rescripts use the idiom of *ratio iuris* more often than the language of justice or fairness.[62]

The decision announced in FV 34 would seem just and equitable, from a slave-owner's point of view, since he would be reimbursed for releasing the "slave" from his ownership. It might also seem reasonable from the point of view of the slave or the slave's intercessor, if it made a return to freedom more practicable. Certainly, this ruling did not represent the strict reasoning of classical law. FV 34 resembles the practice of re-claiming title or *potestas* over a foundling by the repayment of *alimenta*, but there is a discrepancy between *alimenta* payments and FV 34. FV 34 ordered that the slave-owner be paid, not *alimenta*, but a substitute slave or the cash value of the slave. The principle is similar but not identical. The language

---

[56] Some reconcile the two rescripts by hairsplitting the meaning of this constitution, arguing that it licensed something other than full ownership over the slave: e.g. Nardi 1984; Dupont 1937, 137–44. Sargenti 1986, 10, rightly characterizes such approaches as "veramente disperati."

[57] On *ius dominii*, Fossati Vanzetti 1983, 190.   [58] Harris 1994, 21.

[59] Sargenti 1986, 12–15. Seeck's re-datings do not work: Simon 1977, 37–8.

[60] CJ 3.1.8 (AD 314): *placuit in omnibus rebus praecipuam esse iustitiae aequitatisque quam stricti iuris rationem.*

[61] Corcoran 2000, 280, and 1993, for the Licinian provenance.

[62] E.g. CJ 3.32.24 (AD 294); CJ 4.14.6 (AD 293). On child sale, see CJ 2.4.26 (AD 294); CJ 4.43.1 (AD 294).

of a *iustum pretium* is found in several rescripts, and the idea is not alien to Roman law.[63] It made gains in the fourth century.[64] FV 34 did not copy the custom of *alimenta* payment. It adopted the underlying principle – financial restitution for the *nutritor* or slave-owner – but took a form of reimbursement in Roman law.

The primary objection to seeing FV 34 as an act of Licinius is that it survives in the *Fragmenta Vaticana*. The FV was a private collection of imperial constitutions compiled between 318 and 321.[65] It appears utterly dominated by western rescripts, partly because Licinius' name has been haphazardly erased throughout the collection.[66] Licinius' name survives in the *subscriptio* of at least five rescripts in the FV.[67] It seems originally to have been in the subscript in question, FV 34, too.[68] Even if the FV is a western compilation, it is not impossible that eastern rescripts have found their way into the collection. It is entirely possible that after the Battle of Cibalae some eastern public archives came into western possession.[69] Moreover, there was a "tetrarchic fervour for amassing rescripts," and particularly with private compilations such as the *Fragmenta Vaticana*, put together by interested legal scholars, interesting rescripts could have traveled across territories.[70] A third edition of the *Codex Hermogenianus*, published sometime before 324, included several laws of Licinius.[71] The inclusion of FV 34 in a largely western collection thus only suggests, but does not prove, that it was Constantinian.

---

[63] E.g. CJ 4.44.2 (AD 285); CJ 4.44.8 (AD 293); CJ 4.46.2 (Diocletian and Maximian); CJ 5.18.6 (AD 290 or 293).

[64] De Bonfils 1993, 57–87. *Competens* is common in Constantinian's laws (CT 4.12.1 of 314, CT 8.10.1 of 314, CT 5.10.1 of 329), maybe another slight piece of evidence against his authorship of FV 34.

[65] Mommsen, *Collectio librorum iuris anteiustiniani*, vol. 3, 11–13. De Filipi 1997, 16–24.

[66] Mommsen remarked that the name of Licinius in the FV was "obscurato magis quam sublato": *Collectio librorum iuris anteiustiniani*, vol. 3, 12. Simon 1977, 36–7, sees this as an insuperable objection to Sargenti's reconstruction.

[67] FV 32, 33, 273, 274, 287.

[68] FV 34 had an *inscriptio* with multiple emperors: *Augg. et caess. Flaviae Aprillae*. Yet the *subscriptio* read: *Subscr. XII kal. augg. Constantino aug. III conss*. Because of the nonsensical *augg* in the date Mommsen emended it to *aug*. Because Licinius is not named, he changed the plural *conss* to *cons*. But the change from *conss* to *cons* may be unnecessary. The *subscriptio* made no mention of Licinius, who became consul for the third time some time in 313 after defeating Maximinus in April. But the *inscriptio* indicated multiple emperors (*Augg. et Caess*), and the manuscript reading indicated multiple consuls. In other words, the *subscriptio*, very plausibly, originally said: *Subscr. XII kal. aug. Constantino et Licinio augg. III conss*. This reconstruction gives some explanation for the text as it stands. cf. Liebs 1987, 157, who sees the *inscriptio* as a reflection of the situation between 321 and 324.

[69] Licinius and the court fled his capital at Sirmium in "disturbed circumstances." Barnes 1981, 68. On the date, see chapter 12.

[70] Corcoran 2000, 37, and 2004, 57.   [71] Corcoran 2000, 36–7.

It must remain distinctly possible that FV 34 was Constantinian; emperors, after all, do not have to be consistent. But there are further grounds for believing that Constantine staunchly enforced the classical line on status throughout the first decades of his reign. No fewer than three subsequent laws exhibit Constantine's sincere and proactive efforts to protect the inviolability of birth status. Two laws, one issued to Italy and another to Africa, instructed imperial officials to advertise the availability of public support for parents pressed by poverty to give up their children by sale or exposure.[72] Constantine opened the public storehouses to needy parents, for "it is abhorrent to our values to permit anyone to be overwhelmed by hunger or to give in to such an undignified outrage."[73] These were acts of imperial welfare, imitating the *alimenta* schemes of Trajan, designed to prevent parents from taking desperate measures that endangered the freeborn status of their children.[74]

An even more revealing law of Constantine was issued in February of 323, during the emperor's stay at Thessalonica, on the eastern fringe of his territories, in an atmosphere of open hostility before the final and decisive military encounter with Licinius.[75] This lengthy law, CT 4.8.6, was emphatically devoted to classical principles and their enforcement. It opens with a remarkable flourish proclaiming the inviolability of birth status: "So devoted to liberty were our ancestors that fathers, who were allotted the power of life and death over their children, were not allowed to take away liberty."[76] This is perhaps the clearest statement of the tension between the expansive powers of the father and the inviolability of birth status. Even the fictitious power of life and death over the child did not extend to the right to change the status of the child. Status was determined by public rules, not private power.

CT 4.8.6 was a complex response to a complex problem: free persons who were sold into slavery as minors but committed acts after attaining majority which could be construed as consent to their condition. A passage in the *Digest* claimed that a minor sold into slavery who took part of the price after turning twenty could be denied a return to freedom.[77] Constantine's law qualified this rule in a way favorable to the person enslaved. The provisions of CT 4.8.6 are so specific that Lenski suggests the law "found its origins in

---

[72] CT 11.27.1 (AD 315, *contra* Seeck); CT 11.27.2 (AD 322).
[73] CT 11.27.2: *abhorret enim nostris moribus, ut quemquam fame confici vel ad indignum facinus prorumpere concedamus.*
[74] Corbier 2001, 65.   [75] Barnes 1981, 76–7.
[76] CT 4.8.6: *Libertati a maioribus tantum inpensum est, ut patribus, quibus ius vitae in liberos necisque potestas permissa est, eripere libertatem non liceret.* Shaw 2001b, 66–7.
[77] Dig. 40.12.7.

a particular incident," as indeed general enactments preserved in the CT often did.[78] Constantine ruled, first, that if a minor was sold into slavery and subsequently became a slave agent, *actor*, of his "master," his acts as an agent did not prejudice his rightful claim to freedom. Furthermore, even if he had transacted his own sale on behalf of his master, this act did not constitute the sort of knowledge or consent that would deny him the right to re-claim his freedom.[79]

CT 4.8.6 extended the protections for those who had a rightful claim to liberty originating in their minority. Constantine declared that if a slave was manumitted while a minor but subsequently undertook acts which might have damaged his claim to freedom, it did no damage to his status.[80] If manumission was forgotten or practically ignored because the freedman stayed in the service of the master, it did not change his status. This law was issued at Thessalonica, in the same region of the empire as the shrine at Leukopetra where many slaves were freed at a young age.[81] It is plausible that a child, manumitted in his or her youth, may have been unaware of his or her status, especially if the child continued serving under a *paramonê* agreement. CT 4.8.6 was the first evidence that the protection of minors applied to cases of "forgotten" manumission, but it was perfectly in line with classical reasoning. Constantine elaborated upon the original doctrine, perhaps in response to litigation engendered in this region by the practice of manumitting the young.[82] The constitution of 323 was loaded with the language of high principles; it was also a thoughtful piece of legislation with practical implications. CT 4.8.6 addressed a thorny issue in the classical law and ruled, as did many of Constantine's laws in the first two decades of his reign, on the side of freedom. The technicality of the measure shows that the law is truly a document in the administrative history of a litigious slave-holding society.

Constantine, while emperor of the west, remained actively committed to the classical rules on the inalienability of birth status. Particularly if FV 34, recognizing the sale of an infant, belonged to Licinius, a pattern emerges. Diocletian and then Constantine upheld the strict standards of Roman classical law. But this campaign of purist classicism may have been one strategy of governance among others. The survival of source material – the

[78] Lenski forthcoming.   [79] CT 4.8.6.1–2.   [80] CT 4.8.6.3.
[81] E.g. ISMDA no. 3 (5 years old), no. 20 (1 and 8 year olds), no. 25 (6 years old), etc.
[82] In the rest of this constitution, Constantine explained the rules that should govern the fate of property in the possession of the slave who successfully re-claimed his freedom. Because slave agents and managers were particularly likely to have a *peculium*, these provisions were a response to a serious concern. Property which originally belonged to the master was to be returned, while any property the "slave" had acquired through gift or testament he could keep as his own: CT 4.8.6.4–7.

dominance of the codes of Gregorianus and Hermogenianus, transmitted via Justinian – may well distort the image of Roman legal history over the late third and early fourth centuries. The government of the other tetrarchs is clouded by the subsequent success of these codes. The willingness to rule in favor of "justice and equity" rather than the "strict reasoning" of classical law adds important depth to the development of Constantine's legislative program after he became sole emperor.

NEW DIRECTIONS: CONSTANTINIAN CHANGE

Over his long reign, spanning more than three decades, Constantine's approach to law was not static.[83] Constantine always showed signs of a pragmatic, reformist bent. His recognition of *manumissio in ecclesia* as well as a major reform edict issued *Ad Populum* in 320 were significant measures.[84] After Constantine became the sole ruler of the empire, however, the pace of legal reform distinctly accelerated. Indeed, by 329, Constantine flip-flopped and recognized the legal validity of enslaving sold or exposed infants. A constitution given at Serdica and issued to Italy shows that after five years as sole emperor, Constantine departed from the classical principle which he had so loudly proclaimed in his law of AD 323:

According to the enactments of former emperors, if anyone shall purchase in legitimate fashion a newborn infant or arrange to nourish it, he shall hold the power of obtaining its service. So that, after some years if someone should sue for its freedom or assert property rights over it as a slave, he must hand over a substitute of the same kind or pay the price which it is worth. For whoever has paid an appropriate price and drawn up a title, has such certain rights of possession that he can freely pledge the slave in the payment of his debt. Any who try to contravene this law will be subject to penalties.[85]

The law is extraordinary in several regards, and it is by no means perfectly lucid. The law was the first known instance in Roman jurisprudence to treat the sale and exposure of infants jointly.[86] The law recognized the property rights of the slave-owner, albeit in language that is not without

---

[83] See also chapter 11.   [84] Evans Grubbs 1995, 103–39; Gaudemet 1992.

[85] CT 5.10.1 (AD 329): *Secundum statuta priorum principum si quis a sanguine infantem quoquo modo legitime conparaverit vel nutriendum putaverit, obtinendi eius servitii habeat potestatem: ita ut, si quis post seriem annorum ad libertatem eum repetat vel servum defendat, eiusdem modi alium praestet aut pretium, quod potest valere, exsolvat. Qui enim pretium conpetens instrumento confecto dederit, ita debet firmiter possidere, ut et distrahendi pro suo debito causam liberam habeat: poenae subiciendis his, qui contra hanc legem venire temptaverint.* CJ 4.43.2, altered by the Justinianic editors: Fossati Vanzetti 1983, 219.

[86] De Bonfils 1995, 516–19; Sargenti 1986, 16–17. *Contra*, Fossati Vanzetti 1983, 197.

difficulties. Constantine commanded that in order for the slave to be freed or re-claimed (in the case where a slave infant had been exposed), the current slave-owner had to be compensated the market value of the slave, either in the form of a substitute slave or the cash equivalent. The law represented the triumph of pragmatism over dogmatism on the question of enslavement.[87]

The legal status of the enslaved infants in CT 5.10.1 has been the subject of extensive discussion. Notably, the law refers to the slave-owner's *potestas obtinendi servitii* and confirms his capacity with the words *firmiter possidere*. Some have held that the phrase intends something other than slavery.[88] Others argue it is plainly a periphrasis for slavery.[89] In the late empire the semantic range of *possessio* was extended to the point where it could designate ownership.[90] Moreover, the Constantinian chancery was not rigorous in its use of legal terminology. The constitutions of Constantine, especially from late in his reign, were suffused with rhetoric.[91] Circumlocutions for legal terms were common, so it would be dangerous to read the phrase against its apparent sense. The slave was re-called *ad libertatem* – a clear indication that the law dealt with freedom and slavery. So complete were the buyer's rights that he could use the slave as a pledge on a debt – a scenario which would have exposed the slave to the ownership of the creditor in the event of default.[92] It is revealing that the language of *firma possessio* was otherwise exclusively used for real estate.[93] Rather than trying to parse the meaning of these terms in order to iron out the sharp changes in Constantine's policy over the years, we should recognize that the emperor adapted his stance and his legal drafters struggled to find the appropriate language for what was a delicate realm of regulation.

The opening phrase of CT 5.10.1 – "according to the enactments of former emperors" – poses another mystery.[94] Every emperor between Trajan and Diocletian, so far as we know, enforced the inalienability of liberty. But the attribution of FV 34 to Licinius helps to solve the mystery. FV 34 was a rescript, which merely shows how Licinius judged a particular case. It was not a general law. Whether Licinius himself or another emperor initially gave imperial sanction to the custom must remain unknown, but Constantine could invoke precedent as a guide for his reform. It is certainly

---

[87] Ramin and Veyne 1981 would call it "réalisme."
[88] Nardi 1978, 83–4; Cannata 1962, 80; Dupont 1937, 139–42, "n'est pas véritablement esclave."
[89] Sargenti 1986, 16; Fossati Vanzetti 1983, 191.   [90] Levy 1951, 21–31.
[91] Voss 1982. cf. CT 9.9.1, of 329.
[92] Hence parents could not use their children as pledges. Dig. 20.3.5; PS 5.1.1.
[93] Cannata 1962, 81.   [94] Sargenti 1938, 31–2.

plausible that it was the eastern tetrarchs who were permissive towards this custom. That Constantine's law was issued to the heartland of the western empire leaves no doubt he intended it as a general rule.

Constantine's legislation exhibited another affinity with FV 34. The constitution of 329 specified children who were bought *a sanguine*; the rescript of AD 313 concerned a child who had been purchased *sanguinolentus*. The idea is alien to classical Roman law: it occurs nowhere in the *Digest*. The vocabulary of "newly born" slaves, however, did appear frequently in late Greek manumission inscriptions.[95] Interestingly, the emperors were specific about the law's application to newborns.[96] This standard may have an ideological kinship with the folk belief that fathers had to recognize the legitimacy of a newborn child in a ritual act. CT 5.10.1 certainly signals a residual abhorrence towards the arbitrary passage between different statuses. The limitation to newborns circumscribed the period of uncertainty to a narrow window at the beginning of a child's life.[97] It was an effort to have it both ways: the practical custom which protected an important component of the Roman slave supply and a status regime in which the state prevented private changes of status.

It is imperative to recognize that CT 5.10.1 was not about the act of exposure or sale *per se*. The law was about conflicts over property and status which arose from the contradiction between an important input to the slave supply and the state's rules of status. Diocletian, and for a period Constantine, had tried to uproot the non-classical norms of the empire. But ultimately the classical law could not withstand the burden of its own triumph. As Roman citizenship spread around the empire, the state was confronted with the contradictions of status. Inside a courtroom, the inalienability of birth status could be an inconvenience to the individual slave-holder.[98] Constantine's reform underwrote an insurance policy on behalf of individual slave-owners.[99] He admitted into official practice a type of dispute resolution which was probably already practiced in wide stretches of the empire.

Constantine found that tinkering with the system was a delicate operation. The law of 329 had introduced a new linkage between sale and exposure into the public law of the empire. His initial legislation did

---

[95] Six times at Leukopetra: Petsas *et al.* 2000, 47. ISMDA nos. 39, 71, 86, 94, 103, 128.
[96] Vuolanto 2003, 182–3.
[97] Connected with the *dies lustricus*, the day of purification and naming, the eighth day for girls, the ninth for boys, which "marked the entry of the child into the family and society." Corbier 2001, 55.
[98] CJ 8.44.18 (AD 293); CJ 8.44.24 (AD 294); CJ 8.44.25 (AD 294). See also CJ 7.16.10 (AD 293); CJ 7.14.8 (AD 293); CJ 7.20.2 (AD 294).
[99] Not, per Memmer 1991, 55, that Diocletian's measures had increased the incidence of exposure.

not stop the legal harassment of slaveholders. A law of 331 was explicitly designed to do just that:

Whoever takes a male or female that has been cast out of a household with the knowledge and consent of the father or master, and raises it to strength with his own provisions, he shall hold it under that same status which he wished it to have when he collected it, that is whether he wishes it to be a child or a slave. Let all harassment by reclamation be absolutely done away with for those who will have lately expelled slave or free newborns from their household knowingly and by their own will.[100]

CT 5.9.1 dealt exclusively with exposed infants, and it superseded the provisions established just two years earlier in 329. It did not alter the rules for selling infants. Nor did it return to the classical rule on child exposure. The law marked a further advance for the rights of *nutritores*. Now their claim to the exposed infant was absolutely secure from disturbance, even should the birth parent offer reimbursement, so long as the child had been exposed with the knowledge and consent of the father or master. After protecting the slave-owner's right to claim compensation in 329, Constantine moved more radically in the same direction in 331, protecting the full rights over the foundling, regardless of its birth status. The *nutritor* acquired *patria potestas* (if he chose to take the infant as a *filius*) or *dominium* (if a *servus*). The ability to adopt through collection was a significant reform in its own right. Notably, the decision to adopt or enslave the foundling was to be made when the infant was collected – status was not a thing to be held in suspense.

There has been a broad consensus that the laws of 329 and 331 were the product of miserable economic times.[101] But the laws of Constantine are evidence that exposure was a *legal* problem in a new way, not that it was a *social* problem on a larger scale. Exposure was a primitive mechanism of family planning, which only links it in a very complicated fashion to the economy. It was hardly a practice or a problem unique to late antiquity.[102] The age of Constantine, moreover, should hardly be classified as miserable.

---

[100] CT 5.9.1 (AD 331): *Quicumque puerum vel puellam, proiectam de domo patris vel domini voluntate scientiaque, collegerit ac suis alimentis ad robur provexerit, eundem retineat sub eodem statu, quem apud se collectum voluerit agitare, hoc est sive filium sive servum eum esse maluerit: omni repetitionis inquietudine penitus submovenda eorum, qui servos aut liberos scientes propria voluntate domo recens natos abiecerint.*

[101] Firpo 1991, 115: "crisi." Memmer 1991, 66: "Hungersnöten." Boswell 1988, 72: "insecurity." Sargenti 1986, 19: "diffusa povertà." Fossati Vanzetti 1983, 187 and 199: "crisi demografica." Nardi 1978, 71: "in tempi di miseria e dura." Kaser 1975, 205; Cannata 1962, 79; Sargenti 1938, 39; Dupont 1937, 27; Mitteis 1891, 362.

[102] Bagnall 1997b; Harris 1994.

Running on decades of external military success, his reign was a period of broad economic resurgence.[103] No one has interpreted the high levels of child exposure witnessed in the earlier period as a sign of a deep economic depression. Putting Constantine's laws in the context of crisis and gloom deploys an outmoded stereotype of the late empire and associates that image of the late Roman economy, oddly, with his reign.

It has often been said that this law somehow represents Constantine's effort to save the lives of newborns by incentivizing the collection of infants.[104] Perhaps, but we must beware of special pleading for the Christian emperor. After all, Constantine's latter law did not reform a system in which slave-owners were at risk of suddenly losing their slaves. He reformed a system that had already been edging towards slave-owners' rights by guaranteeing them compensation.[105] Tellingly, Constantine neither criminalized nor discouraged exposure as such. The law concerned the status of collected infants. And, even if the law simultaneously protected the rights of adoptive parents to foundlings, the right to hold an exposed infant in slavery is a strange reward for benevolent child-collecting. The church opposed exposure and had compassion for the outcast, but nothing in the substance or language of the law corresponds very closely to ancient Christian thought.[106] The law was clear about its purpose: to eliminate "every harassment by lawsuits for freedom."[107] This is evidence for the problem as Constantine saw it: the legal insecurity arising from the inviolability of birth status. This enactment was a solid victory for the power of adoptive parents and slave-holders.

The classical law of the high empire was not the pure expression of a slave system. It contained within its intricate rules many dangerous negotiations, balanced between principle and practice. The rules of status sat uneasily with the realities of enslavement in the Roman Mediterranean, already in the early empire. Time gradually re-worked the balance. The boundaries of citizenship and the boundaries of imperial power were now coterminous; the state, with its dream of a universal law, was increasingly confronted with the intrinsic contradictions of the system; the diffusion of this law into environments with an ingrained mode of resolution destabilized the power of ownership. The custom of compensation offered a pragmatic alternative,

---

[103] See the Introduction.
[104] Sargenti 1986, 19; Fossati Vanzetti 1983, 201; Dupont 1937, 27; Buckland 1908, 402. The position is rightly ridiculed by Harris 1994, 21; Boswell 1988, 72. See Evans Grubbs 2009b, for a cautious attempt to find a middle ground.
[105] So too Tate 2008a, 131.   [106] Tate 2008a, esp. 131–2.
[107] *Repetere* is technical language: Berger 1953, 675.

but ultimately exposure was a source of the slave supply which had to be protected unconditionally. The Roman slave system was ferociously addicted to the internal consumption of slaves, and Constantine was one of the only emperors who tried to confront the tensions between the law of status and the practices of enslavement directly.

TEN THOUSAND TEARS: THE SALE OF CHILDREN AFTER CONSTANTINE

By the end of Constantine's reign, the enslavement of foundlings was permitted by the state, while the sale of infants was recognized but might be undone by compensation to the slave-owner. The laws recognized a difference between the sale of an *infant* and the sale of a *child*. In the *Codex Justinianus*, Constantine's measure allowing the sale of infants appeared after a rescript of Diocletian clearly forbidding all forms of selling, giving, or pledging children.[108] The two laws made up the entire title: the sale of children was void, the sale of newborns was valid. Constantine's law recognizing the sale of newborns was the last legal reference to the sale of infants. It appears that the sale of newborns into slavery remained licit throughout late antiquity, though the practice is ill-documented.[109] The sale of children, despite its prohibition, was an ongoing practice. If the laws of Constantine on sold or exposed infants had an influence in this realm, it was in recognizing that mediated settlement was more practical than strict principle. The *sale of children* in the centuries after Constantine should also be viewed as a realm of social practice where legal principles and economic reality posed a challenge for imperial administration.

The literary sources of the fourth century track a remarkable shift in perspective on the phenomenon of selling children into slavery. Classical authors, from Herodotus to Philostratus, regularly attributed the practice to other peoples. Late antique authors, conversely, represented the sale of children as a tragedy which afflicted individual victims among the decent poor of Roman society. This change in perspective did not follow a change in reality. It reflects, instead, the broader boundaries of Roman society in the late ancient Mediterranean and a virtual revolution in the ideology of wealth and poverty. The shift of emphasis to the poor in late antiquity – in some ways, it would be better to say the creation of the poor as a

---

[108] CJ 4.43.1–2.   [109] Vuolanto 2003, 185.

discrete social category – was driven by the leadership of the Christian church.[110]

The most extraordinary artifact of the church's concern for the sale of children is a sermon delivered by Basil of Caesarea. The speech is particularly interesting because it can be put in a specific context: a food shortage which visited Caesarea in 369 or 370.[111] At least three sermons survive from the spring and summer of 369, and they afford us our only opportunity to watch an ancient city, a provincial capital, brace itself against the unpredictability of the Mediterranean climate.[112] In the sermon which Basil gave early in the summer, as the population made steely calculations on its stores of food, Basil preached a sermon urging land-owners to open up their storehouses to the people of the city and not to wait until the depth of the famine.[113] To add *pathos*, Basil conjured a remarkable scene of the poor family suffering through the drought:

How can I put before your eyes the suffering of the poor? The poor man is looking about the house, sees no gold, and never will. He has some possessions and clothes of the type which the poor own, worth but a few obols. What to do then? He turns his eyes at last to his children, to take them to the market and find a way to put off death. Consider the battle between hunger and fatherly disposition... Imagine his deliberations. "Which will I sell first? Which will the grain merchant like best? The oldest? But I respect his age. The youngest? I pity his youth who doesn't yet understand misery. This one is the very picture of his parents, that one is rather clever. Damn this misery, what have I become?... How can I come to the table as though the money justified my deed?" But he goes, and with ten thousand tears, sells his most beloved son.[114]

Even as we recognize the artful rhetorical construction of the sermon, it would be overly critical to deny that this passage has a poignant streak

---

[110] Vuolanto 2003, 173. Brown 2002. *Contra*, e.g., Memmer 1991, 71.

[111] Garnsey 1988b, 22–3; Lenski 1996. On these sermons, esp. Holman 2001.

[112] Following Bernardi 1968, 60–4. cf. Rousseau 1994, 137.

[113] Rousseau 1994, 138. Bas. Dest. horr. 3 (Courtonne: 23).

[114] Bas. Dest. horr. 4 (Courtonne: 25–7): Πῶς σοι ὑπ' ὄψιν ἀγάγω τὰ πάθη τοῦ πένητος; Ἐκεῖνος, περισκεψάμενος τὰ ἔνδον, ὁρᾷ, ὅτι χρυσὸς μὲν αὐτῷ οὔτε ἐστὶν, οὔτε γενήσεται πώποτε. σκεύη δὲ καὶ ἐσθὴς, τοιαῦτα, οἷα ἂν γένηται πτωχῶν κτήματα, ὀλίγων τὰ πάντα ὀβολῶν ἄξια. Τί οὖν; Ἐπὶ τοὺς παῖδας λοιπὸν ἄγει τὸν ὀφθαλμόν, ὥστε, αὐτοὺς ἀγαγὼν εἰς τὸ πρατήριον, ἐντεῦθεν εὑράσθαι τοῦ θανάτου παραμυθίαν. Νόησον ἐνταῦθα μάχην ἀνάγκης λιμοῦ, καὶ διαθέσεως πατρικῆς... Καὶ οἷα βουλεύεται ὁ πατήρ; Τίνα πρῶτον τούτων ἀπεμπολήσω; Τίνα δὲ ἡδέως ὁ σιτοπώλης ὄψεται; Ἐπὶ τὸν πρεσβύτατον ἔλθω; Ἀλλὰ δυσωποῦμαι αὐτοῦ τὰ πρεσβεῖα. Ἀλλὰ τὸν νεώτατον; Ἀλλ' ἐλεῶ αὐτοῦ τὴν ἡλικίαν ἀναισθητοῦσαν τῶν συμφορῶν. Οὗτος ἐναργεῖς σώζει τῶν γονέων τοὺς χαρακτῆρας. ἐκεῖνος ἐπιτηδείως ἔχει πρὸς τὰ μαθήματα. Φεῦ τῆς ἀμηχανίας! Τίς γένωμαι;... Πῶς ἐπὶ τὴν τράπεζαν ἔλθω, ἐκ τοιαύτης προφάσεως τὴν εὐπορίαν ἔχουσαν; Καὶ ὁ μὲν μετὰ μυρίων δακρύων τὸν φίλτατον τῶν παίδων ἀπεμπολήσων ἔρχεται.

of social realism. The sermon helps us to understand the nature of child sale, which was prompted by quick, violent strokes of fortune that landed ancient families in these desperate situations. The sale of children in late antiquity was not a new phenomenon brought on by a long-term recession. Before Basil, we have no one to tell us how food crises afflicted the poor in places like Cappadocia. Basil's advocacy on behalf of the poor was part of a wider movement of Christianization, and his very words were adaptable to conditions in other parts of the empire.

Ambrose, in one of his most stirring works, borrowed the image of the poor father deliberating whether to sell his child.[115] It was not a case of simple plagiarism: Ambrose elaborated convincingly on the relationship between market manipulation of grain prices, the extreme wealth of the upper classes, and the desperate poverty of the free poor forced to sell their children into slavery. Ambrose was a former Roman governor, conscious of Roman law.[116] It is meaningful that he could talk in detail about the sale of children without any intimation of legal prohibitions against it. He even deployed legal jargon to describe the transaction of selling a child.[117] Ambrose claimed that "very many fathers sell their children by the authority of parenthood."[118] The sermons of Ambrose, in conjunction with other sources from the period, suggest that in the fourth century, the Roman state gave tacit sanction, perhaps even limited recognition, to the validity of selling children. Again, what we are witnessing is a subtle change in the relation between law and society. The rental of child labor is not attested in the classical law or imperial literature, even though it was clearly practiced. "The leasing out of children's labor did not interest the elite" – during the high empire.[119] The late Roman state, by contrast, began to recognize and regulate the rental of child labor.

No legal enactment marking this development of state policy has survived.[120] It is clear from the scraps of evidence which survive that the state remained hesitant and non-committal about its position on the temporary sale of children. A law of Theodosius, from 391, is a revealing index of the state's compromised position:

---

[115] Ambr. Nab. 5.19.25 (CSEL 32.2: 477–80). McGuire 1927, 4–6.
[116] E.g. Ambr. Abr. 1.3.19 (CSEL 32.1: 515): see chapter 11. Also Sargenti and Siola 1991. Ambr. Iac. 1.3.12 (CSEL 32.2: 12–13). See chapter 12.
[117] E.g. Ambr. Nab. 5.23 (CSEL 32.2: 479); Ambr. Nab. 5.25 (CSEL 32.2: 480). And especially Ambr. Tob. 8.29 (CSEL 32.2: 534). Zucker 1933, 19–21.
[118] Ambr. Tob. 8.29 (CSEL 32.2: 534): *vendit plerumque et pater liberos auctoritate generationis.*
[119] Vuolanto 2003, 196.
[120] See Vuolanto 2003, 189, but not convincing on its origins in CT 4.8.6 (for which see pp. 402–3).

All those who have been sold into slavery by the miserable fortune of their parents, while they were in need of subsistence, shall be returned to their native freeborn status. Nor indeed should anyone, whom a freeborn person has rendered service for a sufficient amount of time, insist on a reimbursement of the price.[121]

The law, as it exists, was a retroactive administrative measure undoing previous sales. It stated no general principle of law allowing or prohibiting the sale of children. The law of Theodosius included a vaguely worded clause which denied the slave-owner the capacity to demand compensation. This denial, however, was not categorical – the slave-owner was not reimbursed, so long as the child had "rendered service for reasonable amount of time."[122] Presumably, governors retained the judicial authority to settle the case-by-case implications of the open-ended phrase. Mediation, here, was more practical than abstract, categorical rules.

The chancery of Theodosius ruled that children sold under material necessity could re-claim their freedom. Beginning with Constantine, there was a new emphasis on the material circumstances which forced parents to sell their children.[123] A rule, which cannot be dated precisely, preserved in the *Sentences of Paul* echoed this distinction:[124]

Whoever, under threat of extreme necessity or for the sake of sustenance, sells their own children, shall not prejudice their freeborn status. For a free man has no price. Thus children cannot be given as pledge or insurance (and a conspiring creditor is banished on this account). Parents may nevertheless rent the labor of their children.[125]

Here a statement of the classical principle, that freedom could not be sold, was combined with a late antique compromise which allowed parents to rent the labor of their children without affecting their status.[126] The explicit power to "rent" out a child's labor is perhaps the earliest legal notice of what had long been actual practice.[127] The right to rent a child's labor was, it seems, subsequently accompanied by statutory restrictions which

---

[121] CT 3.3.1 (AD 391): *Omnes, quos parentum miseranda fortuna in servitium, dum victum requirit, addixit, ingenuitati pristinae reformentur. Nec sane remunerationem pretii debet exposcere, cui non minimi temporis spatio satisfecit ingenui.*

[122] *Contra* Vuolanto 2003, 185.   [123] CT 11.27.1–2.

[124] Fossati Vanzetti 1983, 208, would put PS 5.1.1 after 451. Given CT 3.3.1, the letters of Augustine, and Nov. Val. 33, a fifth-century date is plausible. On the PS, Liebs 2008a and 1993; Levy 1945. See also chapter 11.

[125] PS 5.1.1: *Qui contemplatione extremae necessitatis aut alimentorum gratia filios suos vendiderint, statui ingenuitatis eorum non praeiudicant: homo enim liber nullo pretio aestimatur. Idem nec pignori ab his aut fiduciae dari possunt: ex quo facto sciens creditor deportatur. Operae tamen eorum locari possunt.* Vuolanto 2003, 181.

[126] Memmer 1991, 72, assimilates CT 3.3.1 with a *locatio operarum*.   [127] See Vuolanto 2003.

are mentioned only in literary sources. In the 420s Augustine claimed that Roman law allowed parents to rent their children for twenty-five years.[128] Augustine had a good working knowledge of Roman law.[129] The bishop of Hippo even found himself adjudicating complicated disputes which involved the sale of children. One was so convoluted that he wrote to a lawyer for a professional opinion: "I am asking also whether free fathers can sell their children into *perpetual* slavery?"[130] To Augustine, the line between renting and selling children was all too thin.[131]

A law of Valentinian III, from 451, shows the late Roman state still trying to balance the interests of the freeborn child sold into slavery and the claims of those who paid for free children. The proximate cause of Valentinian's measure was a "most awful famine which ravaged all of Italy" (another reminder that child sale was endemic to the Mediterranean, but periodic).[132] Valentinian showed an awareness of the material causes underlying the problem: "men were forced to sell their children and relatives to obviate the peril of impending death."[133] "For there is nothing which desperation for his life will not make a man do. The man who is starving thinks of nothing as shameful or forbidden."[134]

Valentinian's policy shows how far pragmatism had invaded purist legal reasoning. "Therefore, I allow no prejudice to afflict free status, which the most wise founders of justice and law especially wished to be respected. Renewing the statutes of our ancestors, I declare any sale of freeborn persons provoked by the recent famine to be abolished."[135] Valentinian could pose as a defender of the classical standard – invoking the classical jurists and the inviolability of freeborn status. Of course, he added a condition which would have profoundly offended their logic of freedom: "this shall be done

---

[128] Aug. Ep. 24*.1 and 10*.2 (CSEL 88: 126 and 47). Humbert 1983, 189–203, though wrong about Constantine's law. cf. Memmer 1991, 83–4, for hints of similar limits in the *Sententiae Syriacae*. Willvonseder 1983 believes that the child's labor can only be rented up to the time when he/she would turn twenty-five years old. This is not a natural reading of Augustine's Latin, and the parallel evidence (*Lex Romana Curiensis* and the Interpretation to 4.8.6) is not probative, but the interpretation remains possible.

[129] Gebbia 1997, 216.

[130] Aug. Ep. 24*.1 (CSEL 88: 126–7): *quaero etiam utrum liberi patres possunt vendere filios in perpetuam servitutem?*

[131] Aug. Ep. 24*.1 (CSEL 88: 126).

[132] Nov. Val. 33 (AD 451): *obscoenissimam famem per totam italiam.*

[133] Nov. Val. 33: *coactosque homines filios et parentes vendere, ut discrimen instantis mortis effugerent.*

[134] Nov. Val. 33: *Nihil est enim, ad quod non desperatio salutis impellat: nil turpe, nil vetitum credit esuriens.*

[135] Nov. Val. 33: *Igitur libero statui, cui specialiter sapientissimi conditores iuris legesque voluerunt esse consultum, nullum praeiudicium patior irrogari; renovans statuta maiorum, venditionem censeo summoveri, quam praedicta fames de ingenuis fieri persuasit.*

in such a way, naturally, that the buyer receives compensation for the price plus one-fifth."[136] Yet it is important to admit that the classical law was not a temple of legal reasoning against which later law must be judged. By the middle of the fifth century, it was simply possible to reconcile in a lawyer's mind the permanence of freeborn status and the compensation paid to a buyer.

The *Novel* included a final disposition which reiterated a late legal standard whose original enactment has – again – been lost to us. "Of course, should anyone make a prohibited sale to the barbarians, or transfer a purchased freeborn person across the sea, let him know that he will render six ounces of gold to the accounts of the fisc."[137] This proviso, also mentioned by Augustine, is important, for it recognized a crucial limitation that kept the victim from becoming a chattel slave.[138] The need to legislate against re-selling the freeborn to barbarians or transporting them across the sea proves just how close the condition of the "rented" child was to chattel slavery. But it also shows that the Roman state was determined to limit the power over freeborn persons by keeping them out of the slave trade.

Valentinian's law was issued for Italy. It is hard to determine the legal status or prevalence of child sale in the east.[139] Presumably it went on much as before – in times of famine, debt, or hardship, in the shadowy zone between legal form and social oppression.[140] Within a sphere of legal activity such as the sale of children, we should not be surprised by a trail of inconsistent and patently ineffective legislation. The sale of children into slavery was a predominantly lower-class activity, one caused by immovable material and ecological causes, and one that sat at the intersection of conflicting interests – the principle of inalienable birth status and the realities of power. The fact that the late Roman state failed to establish clear or lasting norms is simply a reflection on the material limits of the state's power and its unwillingness to exert great energy in this arena of social activity. It is dangerous to assert that the "classical" and "post-classical" rules in any simple way reflect the different nature of classical and post-classical society.

The final word on the sale of children in Roman law belongs to Justinian, whose unique mixture of legal classicism and Christian influence

---

[136] Nov. Val. 33: *ita sane, ut emptor pretium sub quintae adiectione recipiat.*
[137] Nov. Val. 33: *Si quis sane barbaris venditionem prohibitam fecerit, vel emptum ingenuum ad transmarina transtulerit, sciat, se sex auri uncias fisci viribus illaturum.*
[138] Aug. Ep. 10*.2 and 10*.3 (CSEL 88: 46–8).
[139] For Basil and CT 3.3.1, see pp. 410–12. Lib. Or. 46.23 (Foerster vol. 3: 390).
[140] Fikhman 1995. cf. BGU 4.1024 (late fourth century), on which see chapter 7.

was enshrined in his codification. Under the title of his *Codex* regulating the sale of children, Justinian included the rescript of Diocletian stating that no child could be sold, pledged, or donated into slavery.[141] Justinian thus overturned any subsequent legislation recognizing the sale of children – which probably accounts for the poor state of our knowledge about the issue. Justinian's compilation also included an edited version of Constantine's law permitting the sale of newborns. "If anyone, due to extreme poverty or need, should sell a newborn son or daughter for the sake of subsistence, it is valid only in this instance, and the buyer has the capacity to obtain its service."[142] Justinian pasted onto the law about *newborns* the phraseology of "poverty and need" which had become common in late Roman laws about the sale of *children*. He made "extreme" material circumstance the only case in which the sale of newborns was valid. Justinian fought against the sale of children late into his reign, but it is uncertain how effective the law could have been against inveterate habits so determined by the convergence of social and environmental factors.[143]

In the west the sale of infants continued to be legal under the standard created by Constantine and enshrined in the *Theodosian Code*. The rental of child labor was allowed with fluctuating degrees of complicity from the state. The last word from the west goes to a letter preserved by Cassiodorus. Athalaric, king of Ostrogothic Italy under the regency of his mother, issued a command in 527 to his governor in Lucania to restore order in the region, which was the site of an important rural festival. The commodities of "diligent Campania, lush Bruttium, bounteous Calabria, hardy Apulia" were sold at the fair, which had been converted from a pagan celebration into a Christian feast.[144] Cassiodorus described the vista of the festival stretching over the valley:

You will see there the plains spread out, sparkling with beautiful market tents, and houses of the moment suddenly thrown up with lovely woven branches, and the people dashing about, laughing and singing. Although you won't spy there any urban buildings, you will see the ornaments of a renowned city. There are boys and girls, both sexes, at the prime age, whom captivity did not put under a price, but freedom. Their parents rightly sell them, since they profit from this very slavery.

---

[141] CJ 4.43.1.
[142] CJ 4.43.2: *Si quis propter nimiam paupertatem egestatemque victus causa filium filiamve sanguinolentos vendiderit, venditione in hoc tantummodo casu valente emptor obtinendi eius servitii habeat facultatem.* Surely the same as CT 5.10.1, but see Melluso 2000, 37–42 for the various possibilities.
[143] Nov. 134.7 (AD 556).
[144] Cass. Var. 8.33 (CC 96: 262): *industriosa mittit Campania aut opulenti Bruttii aut Calabri peculiosi aut Apuli idonei.*

For there can be no doubt that they are improved as slaves, who are transferred from agricultural labor to urban servitude.[145]

The slave market was the first feature of the country fair that made it resemble a city.[146] The transactions described by Cassiodorus certainly cannot be sales of infants, since the children were at a "prime age." The statutory law of the Ostrogothic kingdom had regurgitated the language of the *Sentences of Paul*: sales could not prejudice a freeborn child's status, though parents could rent their labor.[147] The emperor's legal spokesman, Cassiodorus, apologized for this slavery rather than articulating any qualms about its validity. In 527, the governor of the Ostrogothic state, a remnant of the Roman order, was concerned in the first place to establish security at the festival. He probably worried a good deal less about enforcing the finer, theoretical distinctions of the private law inherited from the Romans.[148]

EXPOSURE AND ENSLAVEMENT AFTER CONSTANTINE

As with the sale of children, imperial policy on the enslavement of foundlings fluctuated in the period after Constantine, though the right to enslave exposed infants remained a firm standard until Justinian's reign in the east, even longer in the west.[149] The most significant enactment was issued by Valentinian in 374:

Let everyone rear his own offspring. If, though, anyone considers that a child is to be exposed, he will be subject to the penalty which has been established. But we allow neither masters nor patrons the right to re-claim such infants, if a benevolent spirit of mercy should have collected those who were exposed to some form of death by these very same ones. For he cannot say something is his which he condemned to perish.[150]

---

[145] Cass. Var. 8.33 (CC 96: 262): *videas enim illic conlucere pulcherrimis stationibus latissimos campos et de amoenis frondibus intextas subito momentaneas domos, populorum cantantium laetantiumque discursum. Ubi licet non conspicias operam moenium, videas tamen opinatissimae civitatis ornatum. Praesto sunt pueri ac puellae diverso sexu atque aetate conspicui, quos non fecit captivitas esse sub pretio, sed libertas: hos merito parentes vendunt, quoniam de ipsa famulatione proficiunt. Dubium quippe non est servos posse meliorari, qui de labore agrorum ad urbana servitia transferuntur.*

[146] cf. Horden and Purcell 2000, 388.   [147] Ed. Theod. 94–5.

[148] A rural–urban cycle of enslavement endured throughout Mediterranean history. For a late medieval example, Stuard 1983.

[149] Boswell 1988, 71.

[150] CJ 8.51.2 (AD 374): *Unusquisque subolem suam nutriat. Quod si exponendam putaverit, animadversioni quae constituta est subiacebit. Sed nec dominis vel patronis repetendi aditum relinquimus, si ab ipsis expositos quodammodo ad mortem voluntas misericordiae amica collegerit: nec enim dicere suum poterit, quem pereuntem contempsit.*

The law is difficult for two reasons, textual and substantive. The law divides into two parts, one enjoining everyone to raise their children under threat of an unspecified penalty, the other asserting that masters and patrons had no right to re-claim exposed infants. The language of the latter part is identical to a law of Honorius from 412 preserved in the *Theodosian Code*.[151] The law of Valentinian survives only in the *Justinianic Code*. It is thus conceivable that the first part of the law was interpolated by the Justinianic editors, or that the second part was mistakenly included by the editors, or that both *Codes* are accurate, and the chancery of Honorius simply recycled the language of the Valentinian law.

The question of the law's textual integrity is of course inseparable from the question of the law's substance. It is normally assumed that the first part of the enactment is a sort of "criminal law" designed to punish parents who expose their children. The second part of the law has been read as handling a separate aspect of the problem of exposure, denying patrons and masters the capacity to re-claim the exposed children of their slaves and freedmen. But there is in fact an elegant way of resolving the apparent problems with the law, if we recognize that Valentinian's measure did not criminalize child exposure. It would be strange if such an important reform as the prohibition of child exposure was mentioned only vaguely in this single constitution – no other law from the late empire assumed that child exposure was illegal.[152] If, however, the "penalty" which had been established was nothing other than the loss of a parent's legal right to re-claim the exposed infant, the law begins to make coherent sense.

The first part of Valentinian's law warned *parents* that they – in the wake of Constantine's reform of 331 – had no right to assert the freedom of their exposed children. Such was the established penalty for child exposure. The second part of the law then modified Constantine's rule. Constantine's law had allowed the enslavement of foundlings who were exposed with the *knowledge and consent* of the *pater familias* or *dominus*. This could easily have created a legal grey area. If a man's slave or freedwoman exposed a newborn, his knowledge and consent might be much more ambiguous than if his own child were exposed. Valentinian eliminated this grey area by denying masters and patrons the ability to lodge such claims. So the two parts of his law represent a smooth progression of thought – it was already established that parents lost the rights to their children whom they exposed with knowledge and consent, likewise masters the children whom they exposed with their knowledge and consent. But whereas the

---

[151] CT 5.9.2. [152] On PS 2.24.10 see p. 418.

knowledge and consent of a parent, presumably close to the newborn
infant, was presumptive, the knowledge and consent of a master or patron
was too uncertain. Valentinian decreed that masters and patrons lost the
rights over exposed children, period. This resolution both explains the
law of Valentinian in its own terms and removes the odd notion that
Valentinian criminalized child exposure, which was clearly permitted by
the *Theodosian Code*.[153]

It is hard to believe that Valentinian penalized child exposure, or if he
did, that it was a general or lasting measure. One piece of evidence often
brought in support of this view is based on a patent misinterpretation.
A passage of the *Digest*, from the post-classical *Sentences of Paul*, might
seem to refer to exposure as a crime. "Not only one who suffocates a
newborn is considered to kill it, but also he who casts it out and denies
it nourishment and he who sets it out in public places for the sake of a
mercy which he himself does not have."[154] But this passage appears in a
title of the *Digest* concerned with the recognition of obligations between
parents and children, such as obligatory support for parents in their old
age. In other words, exposure is not equated to homicide as a crime –
only as an act which was sufficient to discontinue any residual obligations
from the child to his parents. It is the logical corollary of the principle
which was implicit in the laws of Constantine and Valentinian: the brief
window at the beginning of an infant's life was a period of uncertainty,
and just as the father or master might break *patria potestas* or *dominium* by
permitting the exposure, so the exposed child's duty to the parents was
broken by this metaphorical social death.[155]

Valentinian's supposed opposition to child exposure cannot be seen as
a sign of contemporary Christian sentiment. Christian authors had long
opposed child exposure, on the grounds of humanity towards the children,
but with an emphasis on the sexual causes and consequences of exposure.
Early Christian authors were obsessed with the possibility that an exposed
child would be enslaved in a brothel.[156] By the late fourth century, the
argument had shifted: Augustine urged married Christians to limit their
sexual activity to procreative sex. The exposure of unwanted children was,
for him, an open confession of excess marital congress.[157] Tate has argued

[153] Its absence from the *Theodosian Code* also militates against any connection to CT 9.14.1 (AD 374).
Rightly skeptical, Tate 2008a, 133. *Contra*, Fossati Vanzetti 1983, 213.
[154] Dig. 25.3.4: *Necare videtur non tantum is qui partum praefocat, sed et is qui abicit et qui alimonia
denegat et is qui publicis locis misericordiae causa exponit, quam ipse non habet.*
[155] cf. Corbier 2001, 59.
[156] Tert. Apol. 9.18 (CC 1: 105); Clem. Paed. 3.21.5 (SC 158: 50); Lact. Inst. 6.20.22 (CSEL 19.1: 559).
[157] Aug. Nupt. 1.15.17 (CSEL 42: 229–30).

that the positive language describing the *misericordia* of the collector reflects Christian rhetoric, and this much is likely; as he notes, the influence was more rhetorical than substantive.[158] The most developed Christian view in this period was offered by Basil of Caesarea. Basil distinguished between exposure prompted by poverty and exposure caused by a desire to conceal sexual sin.[159] The woman who exposed a child to hide sin was judged a murderer, but the woman who exposed because of necessity was pardoned. The preoccupation with sex in early Christian thought on child exposure is nowhere more apparent. Basil's letter is a good barometer of elite Christian opinion, and it is highly unlikely that Valentinian, not a particularly spiritual Christian, was ahead of the church on the question by issuing a blanket prohibition of child exposure.

The laws of the fifth century are in fact informative about the earliest phase of "Christianized" child exposure. Beginning in 412, the state directly implicated the church in the problems of child exposure. Honorius reaffirmed the absolute rights of the collector, on one condition: "if, that is, the notarized testimony of a bishop is obtained, which, in the interest of certainty, should happen entirely without delay."[160] Constantine had denied fathers, who *knowingly and willingly* exposed their infants, the right to re-claim them. But in subsequent decades, the ability of masters or patrons to re-claim an infant was a touchy legal issue, precisely because their knowledge and consent of the act might be ambiguous. Valentinian denied them outright the ability to sue, and under Honorius the state wished to consolidate the rule by using the church as a mechanism for certifying the collector's right to the exposed infant.[161] This measure built upon a pre-existing standard, by which the collector of the infant could have the child certified as a slave by public notaries: Honorius allowed the church to fulfill this civil role as well.[162]

The standard created by Honorius, permitting the church to certify the collection of exposed infants, remained the standard throughout the fifth century. This rule is clearly documented in a series of Gallic church councils, which explicitly ratified the role of the church in handling child exposure. The council held in 442 at Vaison declared, for instance, that exposed children were "now more exposed to the dogs than to compassion,

---

[158] Tate 2008a, 134.   [159] Bas. Ep. 217.52 (Courtonne vol. 2: 210).

[160] CT 5.9.2 (AD 412): *si modo testis episcopalis subscriptio fuerit subsecuta, de qua nulla penitus ad securitatem possit esse cunctatio.*

[161] Memmer 1991, 85–6.

[162] Memmer 1991, 92. Const. Sirm. 5 (AD 419), issued again after a famine, allowed masters to re-claim infants or dependants by repaying double the purchase price and expenses. This should be seen as a particular exception.

because fear of legal harassment has so turned humane intention away from the teachings of mercy."[163] Following imperial law, the church would certify the collector's claim to the child, and the priest was even to announce the act from the altar. The one who had exposed the child had a ten-day grace period, after which any claim was lost. "If anyone steps forward as an accuser or a re-claimer against a collector who has obeyed these provisions, he will be penalized as a homicide according to the discipline of the church."[164] This canon reflects the church's clear opposition to child exposure, although it is noteworthy that interference with the collector, rather than exposure *per se*, was the focus of ecclesiastical discipline. The private decision to expose was effectively beyond the reach of the church, but fights over status were within its competence, and it used this window of involvement to make its view known. The argument could be made that this was the same motivation behind Constantine's laws (protect the rights of the collector as a proxy battle against the effects of exposure), but Constantine, unlike the church, never penalized the child exposer who subsequently claimed back the child.

The fifth-century church furnished an institutional framework for the substantive standard which Constantine had created. Later councils affirmed that the church should act as the public notary certifying the collector's power over the infant.[165] Constantine's rule, that the collector had an impenetrable claim to the infant, remained the basic principle of law. Constantine's rule was also observed in the east into the late fifth century, as is clear from the interpretation provided in the *Syro-Roman Lawbook*. This collection of short, legal commentaries includes a section on the question of whether exposed infants could be enslaved: if anyone "collects a boy or girl, a child of adultery or poverty, whose parents do not recognize it, whether at a church or a bath, and nourishes and raises it with milk" they had the legal right to choose its status.[166] With no reference to the church's institutional involvement nor of any prohibition on exposure, the

---

[163] Conc. Vas. can. 9–10 (CC 148: 100–1): *non misericordiae iam sed canibus exponi . . . calumniatorum metu.* "Calumnia" means vexing with legal disputes, frivolous lawsuits. Berger 1953, 378. E.g. Gaius, *Institutiones*, 4.17.

[164] Conc. Vas. can. 9–10 (CC 148: 100–1): *si quis post hanc diligentissimam sanctionem expositorum hoc ordine collectorum repetitor vel calumniator extiterit, ut homicida ecclesiastica districtione feriatur.* This resulted in excommunication: Conc. Venet. (AD 461–91) canon 1 (CC 148: 151); Conc. Agath. (AD 506) canon 37 (CC 148: 208).

[165] Conc. Arel. II canon 52 (CC 148: 124); Conc. Agath. canon 24 (CC 148: 204).

[166] *Syro-Roman Lawbook*, 86. I am translating Selb's German translation of the Syriac: "Wenn ein Mann einen Jungen oder ein Mädchen, ein Kind des Ehebruchs oder ein Kind der Armut, dessen Eltern ihm nicht bekannt sind, (auf)nimmt, entweder aus einer Kirche oder aus einem Badehaus (βαλανεῖον) es mit Milch aufzieht und es (auch) nach der Milch ernährt."

Syro-Roman Lawbook gives the impression that exposure and enslavement carried on in the east with the full approval of the civil law.

Not until Justinian did the rules of exposure and enslavement change drastically, in the parts of the Mediterranean which remained under his power. Justinian's law on exposure was a radical departure, without any precedent in previous jurisprudence.[167] Justinian ruled, in emphatic terms, that the exposed infant was free, freeborn, and fully endowed with the rights which attended the free citizen.[168] Regardless of whether the exposed infant was male or female, the offspring of a free or servile woman, the newborn became free by virtue of its exposure. Justinian granted the person who collected the infant no capacity to hold it as a slave, a freedman, a client, a dependent tenant, or in any other condition which would at all impair its rights. He positively affirmed the rights of the infant to acquire and transmit property. Justinian's law takes the idea that collection was a deed of mercy "to its apparent logical conclusion: if the collection of an exposed infant is an act of piety, then it cannot lead to the enslavement of the child."[169] Justinian commanded all provincial governors, as well as all bishops, to obey his law.

Justinian instituted a truly revolutionary policy on child exposure.[170] It was not a return to the classical law – which held that status, based on the infant's birth-mother, was inviolable – for Justinian held that even exposed slaves became free. In other words, lest there be any risk that an exposed freeborn child was claimed as a slave, he pre-emptively ruled in favor of freedom without allowing the question of status to arise. Justinian's ideological predilection for freedom, *favor libertatis*, was a prominent theme in both his legislative agenda and his political propaganda.[171] Between Constantine and Justinian, considerations of pragmatism – reducing litigation, providing workable procedures for certifying rights over the exposed, compromising between principles of law and the slave trade – drove imperial policy. Under Justinian, policy was written in the clear logic of a reformist and ideological chancery. In this case, policy emanated from the center, rather than through a dialectical interaction between imperial center and social praxis.

Justinian's law, certainly, did not put an end to child exposure, nor even legal cases arising from the collection of foundlings. Decades later, in 556, a priest of the church in Thessalonica informed Justinian of legal disputes arising over the status of foundlings. Justinian replied with an

---

[167] Tate 2008a; Melluso 2000, 43–7.   [168] CJ 8.51.3 (AD 529).   [169] Tate 2008a, 138.
[170] Tate 2008a.   [171] Melluso 2000, 46–7.

indignant rescript, condemning anyone who would expose an infant and then re-claim it as a slave. The problem at Thessalonica was specifically the exposure of slave infants and their re-call by the original master.[172] Justinian ruled that anyone who re-claimed an infant into slavery was guilty of "many outrages": specifically, murder and legal harassment.[173] He decided they should be punished in the most harsh manner, "who by their shamelessness announced their own crimes."[174] The foundlings were declared free, even if the accuser could produce convincing evidence for the child's native slave status. The penalty for anyone who violated this law – or allowed it to be violated – was 5 pounds of gold. Justinian called child exposure murder, though it is noteworthy that he only redressed the problem insofar as it was connected with the *re-call* of the exposed infant into slavery – the double crime of exposure and reclamation. There was still no mention of the independent penalty for exposing an infant. The penalty was punitive (the equivalent of some eighteen prime-age slaves), but still not the regular punishment for homicide, normally a capital offense.[175]

It is most striking that even Justinian's radical and lengthy laws on exposure made no reference to state-imposed punishment for exposing infants. The best way to understand this conundrum is by adding nuance to our understanding of imperial "policy." Justinian opposed exposure and in particular the enslavement of foundlings. It is much more doubtful, however, that the imperial state waged an active campaign against this incurable habit, embedded in the demography of the ancient world. Instead, the determination of legal status was the state's angle of approach.[176] This was an area which it claimed a traditional prerogative to control; the state did not police the private decision of whether or not to raise an infant. Right through the end of Justinian's legislative career, the issue of legal status remained the primary contact between the Roman state and the practice of exposure. It is precisely these points of contact which must be identified and studied, if there is to be any hope of using the laws as social history.

CONCLUSION: ENSLAVEMENT AND THE STATE IN LATE ANTIQUITY

The late Roman law of exposure is comprehensible only if legal texts are read not as a mirror of social change, but as the product of a continuous effort to arbitrate the flashpoint where demographic cycles, the slave trade, and the state's claim to provide rules for status all collided. We begin

[172] Nov. 153 (AD 556).   [173] Nov. 153: πολλά... ἐγκλήματα.
[174] Nov. 153: ἐκ τῆς ἀναιδείας τῆς ἐναγωγῆς ἴδια ἐγκλήματα προσαγγείλαντας.
[175] Harper 2010, on slave prices. cf. Dig. 48.19, on punishments.   [176] cf. Vuolanto 2003, 204.

to sense certain long-term rhythms in the interaction between state and society. After a cycle of ad hoc accommodation, the reign of Diocletian and the early part Constantine's imperial tenure stand out as moments of rigorous classicism. But during Constantine's reign, a more pragmatic tone took hold, and forms of negotiated settlement ultimately prevailed over the abstract rules of status. The laws of the long fourth century cannot be ascribed to the breakdown of legal status nor, in any substantive way, to Christian ideology. These laws represent an entirely new phase in the relationship between Roman institutions and underlying social practices.

Constantine's reign emerges as the pivot of reform on the problem of enslavement. The laws of Constantine are illuminating precisely because they unveil the multitude of interests at work in the problem of enslavement. After the reign of Constantine, the Roman state struggled to find stable legal norms. The enslavement of exposed infants remained licit until the age of Justinian, and the empire even conscripted the Christian church into the business of certifying the collection of exposed infants. The sale of infants presumably remained valid, though it is the sort of practice which is woefully underrepresented in the sources. The sale of children is a legal phenomenon which is even more obscure in the historical record. The state afforded the practice limited recognition with certain ad hoc conditions, namely limits on the time of service and restrictions on re-selling the child. This hardly points to drastic social change; instead, we are watching the late Roman state undertake the challenge of earnest governance in the face of these inveterate habits.

The Mediterranean and its patchwork of peoples should always remain in the foreground. The fundamental change in late antiquity, which did not manifest itself instantaneously, was universal citizenship. The rules of status provided by the state grounded the public legitimacy of the slave system. But perspective is in order. The laws of the late Roman emperors applied on a scale without precedent. The late Roman laws on enslavement tell a story of how the Roman state tried, and often struggled, to create rules which could be enforced in an area of irremediable social conflict in a massive imperial slave society. Ultimately, the laws of late antiquity are more about change within the state than change within society.

CHAPTER II

The community of honor: the state and sexuality

"THE CHILD OF THE SLAVE-WOMAN": A BRIEF HISTORY

The patriarch Abraham had a son, Ishmael, by the slave-woman of his barren wife. When God made his wife fertile, the slave-woman and her son were unceremoniously "sent away." The Abraham scenario was paradigmatic in a way that transcended the millennia, across radically different epochs of history and radically different formations of state and society. The Abraham story, with its polarities between free wife and slave-woman, free son and slave son, inheritance and disinheritance, provided theologians and preachers with a stock of powerful metaphors that resonated in the experience of their audiences. But within the constant re-telling of the story, slight variations of detail charted underlying change in the way that this tale of slavery, sex, and inheritance was received by people of the book.

Around AD 54 the apostle Paul re-worked the story in his letter to the Galatians. Paul wrote in the idiom of customary practice in the eastern Mediterranean.[1] In his hands, the story of the nomadic patriarch was translated into the culture of the Greek city. Paul stressed the similarity of free and slave sons, especially before the free son's assumption of majority. Paul's solution to the inevitable discord between Isaac and Ishmael was drastic and simple: "Cast out the slave-woman and her son, for the child of the slave-woman shall not be heir with the son of the free woman."[2] Paul's allegory accessed a world of fluid custom, in which slave sons might

---

[1] Garnsey 1997, 106, suggests the influence of Roman law. Such influence is plausible, but the tutelage of minors was widely practiced in systems of law in the eastern Mediterranean: Taubenschlag 1944, 119–36. The decisive clue seems that the child assumes majority at the time appointed by the father. Roman guardianship ended at puberty, but persons *sui iuris* passed into the care of a *curator* until the age of twenty-five, a time set in statute: Jolowicz 1932, 251–2. Whereas peregrine fathers in Egypt often set the end of the guardianship, Roman papyri in Egypt do not: Taubenschlag 1944, 126.

[2] Gal. 4:30: Ἔκβαλε τὴν παιδίσκην καὶ τὸν υἱὸν αὐτῆς, οὐ γὰρ μὴ κληρονομήσει ὁ υἱὸς τῆς παιδίσκης μετὰ τοῦ υἱοῦ τῆς ἐλευθέρας. Glancy 2002, 34–8.

be made legitimate or, equally, cast away.[3] The raw power of the father to choose his son as an heir, or to throw out his servile offspring, was the decisive element. It is a candid glimpse of the universal patriarchy that was the basic cell of social life in the ancient Mediterranean.

Over three centuries later, around 387, the same story could be heard echoing throughout the basilica of a late antique city like Milan. But when Ambrose turned to the life of the patriarch for the moral instruction of his flock, there was a palpable anxiety in the air. Rarely has a sexual liaison with a slave received such elaborate rationalization: the story was meant to show that Abraham was "just a man, belonging to the tribe and the frailty of mankind."[4] It happened "before the law of Moses, before the gospel." Even more, it was excusable because "such was the rarity of the human species after the flood." And above all, Abraham had taken Hagar "not burned by some desire of raging lust," but, thankfully, "for the purposes of posterity and creating progeny."[5] His affair with Hagar was dutiful, perfunctory.

Ambrose was concerned that his Christians might find in the example of Abraham a justification for their sins.[6] "Therefore, let men learn not to spurn marriage nor to unite themselves with inferiors. Nor let them create children of such sort who cannot be heirs, so that thought for transmitting the patrimony will make them seek honorable marriage, even if no care for modesty will."[7] For Ambrose, a liaison with a slave was not only licentious, but it would fail to create a legitimate heir anyway. Having served as governor before becoming bishop, Ambrose spoke knowledgeably and precisely.

The exegesis of the Abraham story is a subtle reflection of historical change. Ambrose the Christian moralist focused unrelentingly on the sexual encounter between Abraham and Hagar itself. Ambrose the former governor used a language that was no longer the loose idiom of patriarchal power. He re-created the story using the lexicon of Roman law. The relation between Abraham and Hagar was, for him, a *contubernium*, an extra-legal

---

[3] For a parallel, Talmud Bavli, *Bava Basra* 127b (not approved by the rabbis). cf. Firm. Math. 7.6.9 (Monat vol. 3: 172).

[4] Ambr. Abr. 1.4.22 (CSEL 32.1: 517): *sed unus e numero et fragilitate universorum hominum.*

[5] Ambr. Abr. 1.4.24–5 (CSEL 32.1: 518–19): *ante legem Moysi et ante evangelium fuit . . . non ardore aliquo vagae successus libidinis . . . sed studio quaerendae posteritatis et propagandae subolis, adhuc post diluvium raritas erat generis humani.*

[6] cf. Ambr. Parad. 13.65 (CSEL 32.1: 324); Aug. Faust. 22.25 (CSEL 25.1: 620).

[7] Ambr. Abr. 1.3.19 (CSEL 32.1: 515): *Discant ergo homines coniugia non spernere, nec sibi sociare inpares; ne huiusmodi suscipiant liberos, quos heredes habere non possint; ut vel transfundendae hereditatis contemplatione, si nullo contuitu pudoris moventur, digno studeant matrimonio.*

union in the civil law. Moreover, the warning that servile offspring could
not inherit closely mirrored late antique legislation on sex, status, and
property. The distance between Paul and Ambrose should not be measured
in terms of social change, for the components of the story remained the
same – and all-too-comprehensible for the audiences of both writers. The
salient difference lay in the ambition of the late Roman state to control
status across the Mediterranean world.

THE COMMUNITY OF HONOR: QUID LICEAT, ET QUID HONESTUM SIT

This chapter forms a pendant to chapter 7, which explored the role of sexual exploitation in the Roman slave system. In this chapter, the abundant
legal material, interesting and revealing in its own right, is placed under
scrutiny. Chapter 7 argued that the sexual abuse of slaves was an integral
part of Roman social structure. The system of social honor simultaneously
protected respectable women, whose sexuality was conscripted to the reproduction of legitimate heirs, and exposed the bodies of dishonored women –
principally slaves, prostitutes, and concubines – to sexual exploitation. The
state was complicit in this scheme; the state's laws shaped and stabilized
social practice. This chapter uses the late antique legal record as a window
onto the role of the state in the sexual system of Mediterranean society in
the late empire.

   The late Roman laws on mixed-status sex have traditionally been interpreted in terms of Christian influence; over the last generation, however,
a sweeping revisionist view has prevailed. The work of Sargenti, Evans
Grubbs, Beaucamp, Arjava, McGinn, and others, has effected an extraordinary change of perspective, so that it will not even be necessary to belabor
the point that late Roman laws on mixed-status sex were not, principally, a
reflection of Christianization.[8] There are, of course, exceptions: the crack-
down on homosexuality, the restrictions on Jews and heretics, and the
prohibition of forcible prostitution were clearly influenced by Christianity,
but these are exceptions which only demonstrate the boundaries of Christian influence.[9] Justinian's reign, moreover, must be considered a distinct
break with the immediate past, for it was a period during which religious
motives occupied a larger place in statecraft.[10] But for our period, the

---

[8] McGinn 1999 and 1997; Arjava 1996; Evans Grubbs 1995; Beaucamp 1990–2; Sargenti 1986.
[9] Homosexuality, see CT 9.7.3 (AD 342), and Dalla 1987. Jews, e.g. CT 3.7.2 (AD 388). Forcible
   prostitution, esp. CT 15.8.2 (AD 428), Neri 1998, and Leontsini 1989.
[10] See Beaucamp 1990–2, vol. 1, e.g. 201.

long fourth century, Christian influence no longer represents a dominant interpretive paradigm.

Precisely because the idea of Christian influence for so long provided an easy explanation, the thorough debunking of the last generation has left a void. Into the breach have crept some doubtful alternatives. To cite only the most important accounts, Evans Grubbs has posited "widespread status confusion" behind the series of late antique enactments.[11] McGinn sees the laws as the effect of "the leveling of status distinctions among the lower orders from the third century on. One aspect of this was the decline of slavery; what is more, the social and legal distinctions between the slave and free poor were eroded."[12] With the disappearance of Christianity as a one-size-fits-all explanation, older stereotypes of the late empire are re-emerging.[13] There are two problems with this interpretation. First, the state was not *repressing* mixed-status sex. It was trying to manage the inherent tensions in a society which encouraged the sexual use of slaves but maintained a strict status system. Secondly, the late Roman state was not responding to a new problem. The problem of inter-status sex was nothing new. Inscriptions and papyri make it abundantly obvious that every permutation of mixed-status sex existed across antiquity.[14] The same is true of all slave systems.[15]

The claim that fourth-century laws were a reactionary response to under-lying status confusion is logically and empirically unsound, and it is a goal of this chapter to suggest better ways to explain the late antique legal evidence. In doing so, it is imperative to resist the temptation to overinterpret the evidence we have. As we examine the "changes" to the state's rules which are reflected in the *Theodosian Code*, we must always imagine the place of these changes in their entire institutional framework. Ultimately, what is notable about the late Roman legal dossier is just how little the rules governing marriage and sexuality changed.[16] The most vexing issues for late Roman emperors were questions such as whether or not illegitimate children could receive a small part of an inheritance, whether bar workers

---

[11] Evans Grubbs 1995, 271, 277, and 1993, 140. Arjava 1996, 207.   [12] McGinn 1997, 109.

[13] Andreau and Descat 2006, 258–9; De Martino 1988b, 79; Garnsey 1996, 101, but cf. Garnsey 2004, 141.

[14] Ptolemaic Egypt, free women and slave-men: Bieżuńska-Małowist 1974–7, vol. 1, 50, 109–10, 120. See P. Cair. Zen. 4.59620 and 59621. Free men and slave-women: P. Petrie 1.16. Roman Egypt: free women, slave men. Arsinoite census record: P. Brux. 19, lines 23–5. Taubenschlag 1944, 54–5. Bieżuńska-Małowist 1974–7, vol. 2, 132. Free men, slave-women: P. Lugd. Bat. 13.14, 35–40. Taubenschlag 1944, 83. Bieżuńska-Małowist 1974–7, vol. 2, 115. Herrmann-Otto 1994, 67 ff.; Gardner 1989, 236–57; Weaver 1986; Treggiari 1981, 68–9; Rawson 1974. Watson 1991, 132–9, on Dig. 16.3.27.

[15] Patterson 1982.   [16] Beaucamp 1990–2, vol. 1, 140.

were inside or outside the community of honor, or what procedures should govern the enslavement of free women cohabiting with slaves. These are historical problems that deserve close attention, so long as they are seen against the much larger backdrop of continuity. In historical perspective, the requirements for legitimate marriage and the public criminalization of *adulterium* were the truly foundational rules, and they changed little.

Roman regulation of sexuality was built upon the "two pillars of Augustan social legislation" – the *lex Iulia de adulteriis coercendis* and the *lex Iulia et Papia*.[17] The former established public penalties for certain sexual violations, the latter outlined the rules for legitimate marriage. With this pair of laws, the first emperor created a social order that was to prove remarkably stable. The *lex Iulia de adulteriis coercendis* established public penalties for two categories of sexual transgression, *adulterium* and *stuprum*.[18] The law used these two words rather indiscriminately, to the consternation of some jurists.[19] *Adulterium* was the violation of a married woman; *stuprum* was the violation of virgins or widows.[20] Sexual crime was determined by the status of the female partner.[21] The types of sexual contact criminalized by Augustus were, of course, socially illicit and had long been so. The Augustan reforms are best seen as the assumption on the part of the state to regulate a sphere of social life where private force had prevailed.[22] Indeed, the Augustan laws only partly arrogated this role, leaving some limited space for private violence. A father, for instance, could kill his daughter and an adulterer caught *in flagrante*.[23] A husband was denied this right, unless the adulterer was of dishonored status, a prostitute, or a slave.[24] Otherwise, public mechanisms of justice prevailed.

With the Augustan social legislation, the state became involved in the business of guarding sexual honor. This role required the state to define, however loosely, which women were eligible for protection, and here the state's reliance on underlying patterns of social honor are most in evidence. The Roman state provided public protection for the sexual honor of *matres familias*, yet it did not define *matres familias* in detail.[25] A *mater familias*

---

[17] McGinn 1997, 75. For the *lex Iulia et Papia*, a composite term, see McGinn 1998, 70–1. In general, Astolfi 1970.

[18] For possible further inclusions, see McGinn 1998, 140–1. Adultery was clearly the focus.

[19] Papinian in Dig. 48.5.6.1. Modestinus in Dig. 50.16.101.pr.

[20] Rizzelli 1987; Dig. 48.5.6.1. For women whose status or lack of sexual honor rendered them exempt, McGinn 1998, 194–202. *Stuprum* could be committed against free men or boys, but this was not regulated under the *lex Iulia*.

[21] McGinn 1991, 343; Beaucamp 1990–2, vol. I, 139.

[22] McGinn 1998, 141; Arjava 1996, 200; Cohen 1991b.

[23] Dig. 48.5.24(23). PS 2.26.1.   [24] Dig. 48.5.25(24). PS 2.26.4.   [25] McGinn 1998, 147–56.

was a woman with sexual honor: "we ought to accept as a *mater familias* she who has not lived dishonorably. For it is behavior that distinguishes and separates the *mater familias* from other women. So it matters not at all whether she is a married woman or a widow, a freeborn or freed woman, since neither marriages nor births make a *mater familias*, but good morals."[26] Despite the ostensible emphasis on behavior over status in this definition, the two were inseparably fused.[27] Clearly the woman's social status was of primary importance, for the boundaries of sexual honor emerge most clearly in the contrast between *matres familias* and women who were obviously outside the state's protection, particularly prostitutes and slaves.

The laws placed some women outside the bounds of public protection. Slaves were implicitly denied any access to public mechanisms of defense. "The *lex Iulia* pertains to *adulterium* and *stuprum* suffered among free persons only."[28] The slave-owner whose slave was violated by a third party could sue for injury to his property, but this was a matter of property law, not the *lex Iulia*. Equally importantly, the adultery statute excluded prostitutes from its provisions.[29] The *lex Iulia* exempted women who openly made a profit with their bodies from legal protection.[30] This statutory definition of the prostitute hovered, uncertainly, between promiscuity and venality.[31] One jurist noted that the criterion of "openness" would not exclude the prostitute whose business was furtive, while other jurists could contend that "openness" was the decisive element, so that even the woman who did not accept payment was a prostitute.[32] This ambivalence was not fatal because the law relied upon, and reinforced, an underlying social logic of sexual honor. The *mater familias* emerged as a foil to the prostitute: one the chaste woman bearing the burden of legitimate procreation, the other a promiscuous woman whose body could never be the vessel for honorable reproduction.[33]

---

[26] Dig. 50.16.46: *Matrem familias accipere debemus eam, quae non inhoneste vixit: matrem enim familias a ceteris feminis mores discernunt atque separant. Proinde nihil intererit, nupta sit an vidua, ingenua sit an libertina: nam neque nuptiae neque natales faciunt matrem familias, sed boni mores.*

[27] McGinn 1998, 9, 153, noting that the *lex Iulia* facilitated the semantic transition of *mater familias* from "wife" to "respectable woman." Beaucamp 1990–2, vol. 1, 202–3. cf. the discussion of *eleuthera* in chapter 7.

[28] Dig. 48.5.6: *Inter liberas tantum personas adulterium stuprumve passas lex Iulia locum habet.* cf. Dig. 48.5.35(34); CJ 9.9.23 (AD 290).

[29] Dig. 25.7.3; CJ 9.9.22 (AD 290). McGinn 1998, 197.

[30] McGinn 1998, 99–102: *qui quaeve palam corpore quaestum facit fecerit.*   [31] McGinn 1998, 123–39.

[32] Marcellus: Dig. 23.2.41.pr. Ulpian: Dig. 23.2.43.3, quoting Octavenus.

[33] See chapter 7, for late Roman sources on this ideological construction.

Ulpian's definition of the prostitute comes in a commentary on the marriage laws. The Augustan marriage laws were closely related – ideologically, practically, and historically – to the adultery law.[34] The Roman law of marriage left some women, such as prostitutes and, of course, slaves, ineligible for *iustum matrimonium* with any freeborn men.[35] More significantly, the highest order of Roman society, the senatorial order, was held to an even higher standard. A member of the order and his male descendants to the fourth generation were prohibited from marrying freedwomen or other categories of socially marginal women such as actresses.[36] The prohibitions which applied generally to the freeborn, namely the ban on marrying prostitutes, applied equally to the senatorial order.[37] With these rules, the highest echelon of Roman society was set apart, providing a particularly visible model of the interrelation between social status and private behavior. The considerable (if not exact) overlap with the adultery law was no accident. The same women who were denied access to the state's protection of female sexual honor were ineligible for legitimate marriage.

The state defined and thereby stabilized the community of honor. In doing so, it relied heavily and often tacitly on underlying patterns of social behavior. "Beyond the bedrock of legislative text and a thin strand of juristic commentary subsisted an ocean of prejudice."[38] Roman law provided a relatively minimalist template for regulating the habits of social reproduction. In its classical form, Roman law left many questions without detailed answers. What was the difference between a wife and a concubine?[39] Could a freeborn woman ever be a sexual partner without liability for *stuprum*?[40] The classical law provided only loose guidance on these questions, ultimately relying on judges to sort out what was legal, what was honorable.[41] The state's strategy, crafted by Augustus, worked: the Augustan regime endured across the centuries with minor variation and still provided the foundational rules of sex and marriage in the late empire. Late Roman laws, in fact, reflect *old* rather than *new* sexual values, including the belief that some women were beneath the state's protection. In the official words of Constantine, there were women whose "lowness of life" rendered their sexual honor "unworthy of notice by the public law."[42]

The late Roman state fundamentally accepted the social prejudices of the Augustan order, even if it was forced to sharpen the application of

[34] McGinn 1998, 207. Dig. 23.2.43.1.   [35] Dig. 23.2.43. Astolfi 1970, 31–8.
[36] Dig. 23.2.44.pr. Astolfi 1970, 16–38.   [37] Dig. 23.44.8.   [38] McGinn 1997, 111.
[39] See p. 451.   [40] McGinn 1991. Dig. 25.7.3.
[41] Dig. 23.2.42: *quid liceat considerandum est, sed et quid honestum sit.*
[42] CT 9.7.1 (AD 326): *quas vilitas vitae dignas legum observatione non credidit.*

some of the rules. In the late empire we witness a double movement. The first consistent trend is that the regulations protecting female honor were hardened: the penalties for violation were increased, the lines defining the circle of honor became clearer, the state played a larger role in protecting the sexual honor of decent women.[43] The patterns outlined in chapters 9 and 10 – the rise of universal citizenship and the inherent tensions within the praxis of slavery – often lie behind these developments, as necessary if not sufficient background to the reforms. What is distinct about late Roman law-making is the fact that "post-classical law comes to reflect prevailing social morality less ambiguously than in previous centuries."[44]

The second tendency in the late antique legislation is rather more complex. While men continued to exploit the bodies of dishonored women with the complicity of the state, emperors struggled to find an appropriate rule to govern the transmission of property to illegitimate children. This was not a new problem, but in late antiquity the code of silence which had prevailed among the early imperial elite broke down.[45] Behind this pattern, the reconstitution of the aristocracy looms large. It would be hard to overestimate, as a factor behind the laws regulating illegitimate children, the updraft of new men through the ranks of the imperial service into the higher orders of Roman society. The new elite was a decisive social dynamic of the fourth century. The expected good behavior of the aristocracy had always been instrumental to the state's minimalist regulation of sex and marriage. The new patterns of elite formation undermined the strategic economy of the state's rules.

A broader citizen base, a more aggressive state, a lower tolerance for ambiguity, a lack of confidence in the good behavior of the upper orders: these led the late Roman state to ratify in public law elements of practice that had been lightly handled in the classical period. The core principles of honor and shame, and their fusion with the dynamics of status, remained fundamentally the same in the late empire. The first Christian emperor, in particular, showed little creativity in the substance of his moral imagination. Free women were the bearers of sexual honor. Men were given immense sexual freedom within the established boundaries – so long as this sexual freedom did not result in heirs. In late antiquity, the values behind public law changed less than the mechanisms used by the state to enforce those values.

---

[43] Beaucamp 1990–2, a sharpening of traditional patriarchy. Evans Grubbs 1995, a reaction against status confusion. For Arjava 1996, a ratification of long-standing trends.
[44] McGinn 1999, 69.   [45] On the earlier aristocracy, see Syme 1960.

FREE WOMEN, UNFREE MEN, AND THE STATE

This chapter proceeds by examining the legal regulations bearing on mixed-status sex, first along the axis of free women and slave-men, then free men and slave-women. In Roman law, unions between free female citizens and slave-men were regulated under the provisions of the *senatus consultum Claudianum* (SCC). The SCC was enacted in AD 52.[46] Weaver noted that the SCC was not implemented on moral grounds (if so it was "singularly late and ill-conceived"), and Sirks has demonstrated that its primary purpose was to protect the master's authority over his slaves.[47] The SCC, in short, was not concerned with sexual contact *per se*. In its late classical form, the SCC allotted the owner of the slave two responses to the union. He could permit the union and claim the woman as his *liberta*, or he could, following a formal procedure, enslave the woman and claim her subsequent offspring as his slaves too.[48] The SCC was one of the few ways that free persons could lose their status in civil law, but the option to reduce the woman to slavery was purely at the discretion of the slave's master.

The SCC regulated unions between free women and slave-men throughout late antiquity, and the details of its application were modified in a series of laws preserved in the *Theodosian Code*. These laws, preserved in CT 4.12, were long interpreted as evidence for new, Christian attitudes towards sexuality or mixed-status unions.[49] The suggestion of Christian motivation is particularly unconvincing, and Evans Grubbs has thoroughly demolished the thesis of religious influence, arguing instead that the laws were a reactionary effort to enforce social boundaries in an age of status confusion.[50] But this solution is contestable, in the first instance because it makes the unjustified assumption that the laws are reactions *against* underlying change. Restatements and adjustments to the law were a "normal" part of governing: the SCC had been tweaked virtually every generation or so since its inception. Moreover, the *Theodosian Code* is a beguiling friend to the historian. The editorial process which brought together various laws under individual titles has influenced the way modern historians view the laws, a fact with important consequences for the interpretation of CT 4.12.[51]

---

[46] Tac. Ann. 12.53 (Heubner: 263); Gaius Inst. 1.84, 91, 160; PS 2.21ᵃ.1–18. Harper forthcoming b; Sirks 2005; Weaver 1986 and 1964; Voss 1985; Kaser 1975, 289; Crook 1967b; Hoetink 1959; Buckland 1908, 412–18.

[47] Sirks 2005, 148; Weaver 1972, 162–9.

[48] See esp. Weaver 1986, 167, n. 6, and Crook 1967b, 7–8, for the modification of Hadrian.

[49] Murga 1982; Murga Gener 1981; Andreotti 1965; Biondi 1952–4.

[50] Evans Grubbs 1995, 277; Arjava 1996, 221–3; Navarra 1990.   [51] Harper forthcoming b.

The first law in CT 4.12 was posted on 1 April, 314. There has been some doubt whether the law belongs to Constantine or Licinius, but the case for attributing it to Constantine is ultimately much stronger:[52]

If any free women, having suffered violence from slaves or anyone else, have been joined against their will to men of slave status, they must obtain restitution with the appropriate severity of the law. If, on the other hand, a woman should be forgetful of her social respectability, she must lose her freedom, and her children must be the slaves of the master whose slave she has joined in illegitimate union. This law should also be observed for the past.[53]

The law exhibits a perfectly conservative attitude. This law imagined two mutually exclusive scenarios. In the first case, the law ordered authorities to give legal restitution to women forced to join with slaves "against their will": they were allowed to return to freedom. The second part of the law was in balance with the first: it provided for women who voluntarily remained with their servile husbands. Women who stayed with their servile husbands were described as "forgetful of their social respectability" – the psychological counterweight of "against their will."[54] In other words, a woman whose union to a slave was not against her will had forgotten her social respectability and thus remained subject to the provisions of the SCC. She remained enslaved.

Other texts mention that the SCC could only be applied after a series of warnings, while CT 4.12.1 mentions none of these procedural requirements, so it has often been assumed that this law abrogated these procedures.[55] But this argument misunderstands the nature of the constitutions in the *Theodosian Code*, which often arise from particular circumstances. Occasionally, it is possible to reconstruct the original situation in which a constitution was issued. CT 4.12.1 shares both linguistic and substantive similarities with CT 5.8.1, a law posted just twelve days before CT 4.12.1.[56] CT 5.8.1 commanded that free people enslaved under the tyrant, Maxentius, be restored to their rightful status without waiting for the intervention of a court.[57] This provision is extraordinary, because it bypasses the whole apparatus of *causae liberales*. It would be absurd to read CT 5.8.1 as a procedural

[52] Evans Grubbs 1995, 264–5.
[53] CT 4.12.1: *Si quae mulieres liberae vel a servis vel a quolibet alio vim perpessae contra voluntatem suam servilis condicionis hominibus iunctae sint, competenti legum severitate vindictam consequantur. Si qua autem mulier suae sit immemor honestatis, libertatem amittat atque eius filii servi sint domini, cuius se contubernio coniunxit. Quam legem et de praeterito custodiri oportet.*
[54] *Immemor* means negligent of one's free status: CT 4.10.2 and CT 12.1.92.
[55] Arjava 1996, 222; Evans Grubbs 1995, 266; Beaucamp 1990–2, vol. 1, 186; Voss 1985, 138–9; Yuge 1982, 148; Andreotti 1965, 8; Buckland 1908, 413. Critically, Albanese 1991 (orig. 1951), 91–2.
[56] Seeck 1919, 162.　　[57] CT 5.8.1: *... natalibus suis restituere nec expectata iudicis interpellatione.*

reform of Roman law and not as a momentary suspension of procedure in a contingent situation. The same holds for CT 4.12.1. CT 4.12.1 may even have been a clarification of CT 5.8.1, directing officials how to act when a woman who had lost her status under Maxentius prefered to remain with a servile husband. As Lenski has noted, the *ex post facto* clause at the end of CT 4.12.1 is an indication that the law was "designed to rescind claims to freedom by *ingenuae* who had been enslaved under Maxentius legitimately but then took advantage of Constantine's blanket grant of *libertas* to escape their condition."[58]

The inclusion of this law in title CT 4.12 makes it appear to be a general reform of the SCC itself rather than a clarification of its application in the spring of 314. The problem is compounded when multiple laws are gathered in a title, so that later enactments appear as reactions to earlier measures. This illusion of development is precisely what has happened in the case of CT 4.12. CT 4.12.1 has always been seen as the beginning of a series of laws adjusting the procedures of the SCC, but in fact it was a discrete act of imperial administration in very particular conditions. The second law in the title, CT 4.12.2, looks entirely different once CT 4.12.1 has been properly placed in its context. Given in January of 317, the law is lost. Only the subscription and a post-codification commentary on the law survive:

> Interpretation. The third denunciation according to the *senatus consultum Claudianum* is to happen in the presence of seven witnesses who are Roman citizens.[59]

The purpose of CT 4.12.2 is not clear. In general our knowledge of the procedure involved in the SCC is poor. This is the first mention of the requirement of three warnings and of seven witnesses, but we do not know whether this law created the requirements. There is reason to believe that the triple denunciation was classical.[60] The specification of the formal requirements in the *Interpretatio* is a signal that the law mentioned the procedure but does not constitute proof that the law altered it. The interpretation, insofar as its language may reflect the constitution itself, implies that seven witnesses were required at the *third* denunciation.[61] Perhaps Constantine's innovation lies in the statutory requirement of seven witnesses. Constantine seems to have preferred witnesses and oaths to legal

---

[58] Lenski forthcoming.

[59] CT 4.12.2: *Interpretatio. Septem testibus civibus Romanis praesentibus tertio ex senatus consulto Claudiano denuntiandum.*

[60] Albanese 1991 (orig. 1951). Gaius, *Inst.* 1.91 and 1.160 mentions denunciation, but not a triple denunciation.

[61] Albanese 1991 (orig. 1951).

formalism.[62] Moreover, in the first decades of his rule, Constantine represented himself as the champion of *libertas*, so that stringent procedural requirements for enslavement would cohere with the thrust of his legislative program.[63] If we cannot say with certainty that CT 4.12.2 altered the application of the SCC, it is safe to conclude that CT 4.12.1 and CT 4.12.2 do not represent the beginning of a back-and-forth adjustment of the SCC. They are two separate acts which have been brought together by the fifth-century editors.

The idea of a back-and-forth struggle over the procedural requirements for the SCC has been a red herring, first leading historians to view it as a proxy battle over religious values, more recently as a sign of the state's uncertain reaction against the breakdown of legal status. These readings have obscured what was truly Constantine's first major reform of the SCC. CT 4.12.3 was part of a major edict of Constantine issued *Ad Populum* from Serdica in January of 320.[64] CT 4.12.3, reforming the SCC, is of a piece with the other laws in the edict:

Since the old law compels freeborn women joined in *contubernium* with fiscal slaves to a dissolution of their birth rights, without any lenience granted to ignorance or age, it is indeed proper that the chains of such unions be avoided. If, in fact, a free woman either unknowingly or even willingly shall join with a fiscal slave, she shall suffer no damage to her freeborn status. The offspring, too, who are born of a fiscal slave father and free mother, shall hold a middle destiny. As the children of slave men and the illegitimate children of free women, they shall be Latins, who, though absolved of the necessity of servitude, will nevertheless be held by the privilege of a patron. We wish this law to be observed both in the case of fiscal slaves and those adhering by origin to the patrimonial estates and to emphyteutic properties and those who belong to the staff of the *res privata*. For we take away nothing from the old law with regard to municipalities. Nor do we wish the slaves of any city to be joined in association with this law, so that the cities shall hold the full power of the old prohibition. If blind error, plain ignorance, or the slip of weak youthfulness throw a woman into these snares of *contubernium*, she shall be exempt from our sanctions.[65]

---

[62] E.g. CJ 1.13.1 (AD 316) with Soz. H.E. 1.9.6 (GCS 50: 21); CT 8.12.5 (AD 333); CJ 6.23.15 and CJ 6.37.21 (see p. 479).

[63] Esp. CT 4.8.5 (AD 322). Lenski forthcoming.

[64] Tate 2008c; Matthews 2000, 236–41; Evans Grubbs 1995, 119–20; Gaudemet 1992; Seeck 1919, 59–61; Mommsen, *Prolegomena*, vol. 1, ccxiv–ccxv.

[65] CT 4.12.3: *Cum ius vetus ingenuas fiscalium servorum contubernio coniunctas ad decoctionem natalium cogat nulla vel ignorantiae venia tributa vel aetati, placet coniunctionum quidem talium vincula vitari, sin vero mulier ingenua vel ignara vel etiam volens cum servo fiscali convenerit, nullum eam ingenui status damnum sustinere, subolem vero, quae patre servo fiscali, matre nascetur ingenua, mediam tenere fortunam, ut servorum liberi et liberarum spurii latini sint, qui, licet servitutis necessitate solvantur,*

This law eliminated the effects of the SCC for women married to fiscal slaves, while making their children freedmen. The first line declared that the "chains of such unions" were to be avoided. This sentence has been misconstrued. The *vincula talium coniunctionum* were to be avoided. *Vincula* here was an artful word, but it was synecdoche, not metaphor – not the "bonds of such unions."[66] CT 4.12.3 declared that the *chains* of such unions should be avoided, and it was meant very literally. The chains of slavery – caused by the application of the SCC – were to be avoided. The law explicitly declared that free women in relationships with fiscal slaves were no longer to be enslaved.

With this law, the emperor ceded his right as a slave-owner to enslave women who engaged in relationships with his slaves, but he retained certain claims against the offspring of such unions. The law decreed that children born from these mixed-status unions were to follow "a middle destiny." Specifically, the children were to become *Latini*, the equivalent of slaves who had been freed informally or without meeting the requirements for formal manumission outlined by Augustus.[67] The emperor retained a claim on the children as their patron. By this legal fiction, he would have enjoyed the power to claim labor and respect from the children.[68] Moreover, as *Latini*, the offspring would never be able to create a legally valid will, so that their property returned to their manumitter – in this case, the emperor, their fictive patron.[69] The law applied only to the emperor's slaves. It did not change the rules for private or municipal slaves.[70] Private and municipal slave-owners were still able to penalize free women who married their slaves.[71]

What motivated Constantine's law of 320? To answer this question, we must consider the original context of the SCC. The SCC was passed in AD 52. Weaver has shown that the problems of mixed-status marriage would have been especially obvious to the emperor, whose slave staff assumed an enormous role in domestic and administrative positions over the first

---

patroni tamen privilegio tenebuntur. quod ius et in fiscalibus servis et in patrimoniorum fundorum origini cohercentes et ad emphyteuticaria praedia et qui ad privatarum rerum nostrarum corpora pertinent servari volumus. nihil enim rebus publicis ex antiquo iure detrahimus nec ad consortium huius legis volumus urbium quarumcumque servitia copulari ut civitates integram teneant interdicti veteris potestatem. si vel error improvidus vel simplex ignorantia vel aetatis infirmae lapsus in has contubernii plagas depulerit, haec nostris sanctionibus sit excepta. For this reconstruction of the text, see Harper forthcoming b.
[66] Evans Grubbs 1995, 266; Pharr 1952, 93.
[67] Weaver 1997, 30–4; Sirks 1983 and 1981. See also Voss 1985, 136; Buckland 1908, 533–51. See chapter 12.
[68] Masi Doria 1993; Waldstein 1986.   [69] Salv. 3.7.31 (SC 176: 264), with discussion in chapter 12.
[70] On municipal slaves, see esp. Lenski 2006a; Weiß 2004.   [71] PS 2.21ª.14. See p. 438 on CT 4.12.4.

century.[72] The *familia Caesaris* was a social paradox; many of the emperor's male slaves were able to marry freeborn women. The SCC reinforced the emperor's power over his male slaves and at the same time gave him a claim on the offspring of his slaves' "wives."[73] Constantine, then, repealed the SCC for precisely those women who chose to enter unions with fiscal slaves. He thus withdrew the SCC from the service of one of its most important applications, but his measure made sense in terms of fourth-century conditions. Imperial slaves held a different role in late Roman society. By the third century, servile clerks employed by imperial administrators were gradually overtaken by the military *officia* with which they had long coexisted; then, under Diocletian, the civil and military functions of administration were formally separated.[74] The domestic side of the imperial slave family continued to exist, but on a more limited scale, and in positions around the court rather than in the civil service. The imperial court was increasingly staffed by eunuchs, who obviated the need to apply the SCC.[75]

When the emperor thought of imperial slaves in the fourth century, he imagined his workers on imperial estates.[76] Constantine removed the serious disincentive, slavery, that awaited any woman who wished to marry a servile worker on imperial land. We can imagine that this increased the likelihood of domestic stability and reproduction among his agricultural workforce. Constantine was more concerned with the reproduction of his rural labor force than with exoteric marriages at the clerical level of the *familia Caesaris*. Given the composition of the imperial slave family, Constantine's legislation of 320 was a pragmatic response to the contemporary situation. CT 4.12.3 made particular sense in light of fourth-century fiscal policy. Those who were liable for the capitation tax were assigned an *origo*, a place of fiscal registration, which they were not free to abandon.[77] A laborer might be registered to an imperial estate, so even though the emperor did not enslave the offspring of the mixed-status union, he could rest assured of receiving their continuing service. Like the original enactment of the SCC, its reform in 320 was driven by practical concerns related to the imperial treasury.

The SCC was rooted in concerns about power and property; it provided the slave-owner redress against the threat of losing control over his male

---

[72] Weaver 1972, 162–9.
[73] Sirks 2005, emphasizes the master's control as the motivation of the law.
[74] Demandt 1998, 212–23; Jones 1964, 42–62, and 1949, 38–55.   [75] See chapter 8.
[76] On imperial property Bransbourg 2008; Delmaire 1989; Chastagnol 1986; Jones 1964, 416; His 1896. For slave workers, see CT 11.9.1 (AD 323); CT 11.9.2 (AD 337); CT 10.8.4 (AD 346); CT 10.1.2 (AD 357).
[77] Grey 2007a.

slaves. It was not particularly concerned with moral questions arising from these unions, nor was it an act of social engineering aimed to prevent mixed-status relationships. Indeed, the master's right to determine the woman's fate marked the limited interventionism of the state in the realm of mixed-status unions. But a fourth law of Constantine, issued in 331, marked a new direction:[78]

Any woman who mixes herself in a non-legal union with a slave after this law, even if she has not been notified by the formal warnings as the ancient law held, loses her free status.[79]

A number of interpretive difficulties surround this constitution, in part because it is so fragmentarily preserved.[80] CT 4.12.4 dissolved the requirement of legal warning before a woman could be enslaved. We must ask, though, whether the purpose of CT 4.12.4 was to reform the procedure required to carry out the SCC or, more radically, to eliminate altogether the private slave-owner's discretion. Although the law is laconic, it is possible that it was not only the legal *process* that Constantine amended. Constantine's law mandated that any woman who mixed in *contubernium* with a slave automatically lost her status as a consequence. The dispositive verb was "she loses." On this interpretation, Constantine set up a public penalty for women who "mixed" – which was precisely his word – with slaves.[81] If so, a law that had originally been discretionary and intended to protect a master's power became, in 331, a law truly opposed to mixed-status unions as such.

The short notice of this change is disappointingly slight evidence for such a critical shift in the purpose of the law. But this interpretation is more convincing when set beside another near-contemporary law of Constantine on sex between women and slaves. The SCC regulated the problem of free women cohabiting with *servi alieni*: the slaves of other masters. In the classical law, there is scant mention of sex between mistresses and slaves. A husband could accuse his wife and a slave of adultery but, more ominously, the husband retained the private right to kill a servile adulterer.[82] The first statute in all of Roman law to address sexual liaisons as such between free women and their own slaves came from Constantine in 329:[83]

---

[78] Navarra 1990.
[79] CT 4.12.4: *Quaecumque mulierum post hanc legem servi contubernio se miscuerit, et non conventa per denuntiationes, sicut ius statuebat antiquum, statum libertatis amittat.*
[80] Harper forthcoming b.
[81] *Misceo* implies both intermarriage and the carnal union of two people. TLL vol. 8, cols. 1086–7.
[82] Dig. 1.12.1.5; Dig. 48.2.5. Gamauf 2007, 161; Parker 2007, 294–5; Arjava 1996, 194, 226.
[83] Barnes 1982, 78; Seeck 1919, 179.

If a woman is revealed to be having a hidden liaison with a slave, let her be sentenced to capital punishment, and the reprobate slave sent to the flames. And let everyone have the capacity to report this public crime, let it be a full duty to declare it, let even a slave have permission to make an accusation, which if it is true shall bring him freedom, though if it is false, a penalty waits . . . [84]

The law was a thundering attack on sex as such between women and slaves, but it was obscure at the critical moment. The highly literary, and not legal, language of the constitution has been perceptively noticed by Evans Grubbs.[85] The name given to the crime itself, *occulte rem habere*, could imply adultery, or an illicit *contubernium* or, if the ambiguity is intentional, both. This ambiguity becomes much more interesting when we recognize that CT 9.9.1 says nothing specific about a woman's "own" slaves. Only the fifth-century title specifies *servi proprii*.[86] Conceivably, the law intended for any woman detected having a covert relationship with a slave, *proprius* or *alienus*, to suffer the penalties outlined in CT 9.9.1.

One of the most striking elements of CT 9.9.1 was the large base of eligible informers.[87] Constantine passed adultery legislation in 326 that had strictly limited the public's right to denounce an adulteress: only the woman's family could denounce her.[88] CT 9.9.1 emphatically asserted the capacity of the public, the government, and even slaves to denounce a woman having an affair with a slave. CT 9.9.1 highlights the intensity of prejudice against these types of relations. For centuries Roman emperors and lawyers had left such matters to the private sphere.[89] To judge from the gaping silence, sex between free women and slaves was a matter about which lawyers did not speak.[90] CT 9.9.1 represented an assumption on the part of the state to protect female honor in situations where women were not privately protected by a father or husband. Constantine's reign betrays an unusual zeal on behalf of female honor – an issue on which the Christian church and traditional social prejudices were in agreement.[91] This interpretation of CT 4.12.4 and 9.9.1 accords well with the tenor of his later rule.[92]

---

[84] CT 9.9.1 (AD 329): *si qua cum servo occulte rem habere detegitur, capitali sententia subiugetur, tradendo ignibus verberone, sitque omnibus facultas crimen publicum arguendi, sit officio copia nuntiandi, sit etiam servo licentia deferendi, cui probato crimine libertas dabitur, cum falsae accusationi poena immineat . . .*

[85] Evans Grubbs 1995, 274. [86] Bassanelli Sommariva 2003, esp. 226–9.

[87] Evans Grubbs 1995, 275.

[88] CT 9.7.2 (AD 326). Evans Grubbs 1995, 208–9; Beaucamp 1990–2, vol. I, 146–7.

[89] Coll. 4.3.2–4; Coll. 4.12.3. Arjava 1996, 194; Beaucamp 1990–2, vol. I, 141–5; Shaw 1987a, 29.

[90] Though see Dig. 1.12.1.5; Dig. 48.2.5. Gamauf 2007, 161; Parker 2007, 294–5.

[91] Herrmann-Otto 2008, 364, CT 9.9.1: "hat nichts mit christlichen Moralvorstellungen zu tun." Similarly, Navarra 1990. cf. Waldstein 1990; Soraci 1983.

[92] See, e.g., CT 9.24.1 (AD 326).

CT 9.9.1 and CT 4.12.4 would represent, in tandem, a subtle yet pivotal change in the state's regulation of the intersection between legal status and sexuality. Constantine took a fateful step in 326, when he decided to regulate relations between free women and slaves with CT 9.9.1. Perhaps his penalties against women who committed the crime described by *occulte rem habere* prompted a question: what if the slave's master consented to the affair, as the SCC had long allowed? CT 4.12.4 then was passed to eliminate the master's discretion, creating a public penalty for women entering unions with slaves. CT 4.12.4 could even have been a clarification, rather than an independently motivated reform. This would have denatured the SCC, turning a law constructed to guarantee the master's power into a law about status and sex *per se*. Together, these laws show the assumption by the state of the power to decide the fate of women involved in unions with slaves. Traditional ideas of status and honor, the aggressive attitude of the state, and a zeal unleashed against the relationship itself – rather than just its potential to destabilize property – conspired to produce Constantine's legislative program.

Regardless of whether CT 4.12.4 amended the procedural requirements of the SCC or more broadly eliminated the private slave-owner's discretion, it was too radical to bear for Julian, who rescinded the law in 362.[93] He favored, instead, the old, moderate legal regime provided by the system of denunciations, which protected the power of private slave-owners but otherwise turned a blind eye to the partnerships of lower-class women. Julian's restoration of the SCC proved appealing to subsequent emperors. After Julian the rules and procedures pertaining to the SCC remained stable down to the time of Justinian. A handful of laws show the SCC in operation throughout late antiquity. The old social prejudices continued to prevail, as is particularly evident in a law of Valens from 366: "If lust is worth more than liberty to a lascivious woman, she has been made a slave not by war, not by purchase, but by marriage, so that her children shall lie under the yoke of slavery. For it is obvious that she wished to be a slave who regretted being a free woman."[94] The law conflated sexual and social transgression. If Christianization was behind this law, it was Christian influence of a form already outlined by Constantine, in which the religion

---

[93] CT 4.12.5 (AD 362).

[94] CT 4.12.6 (AD 366): *Si apud libidinosam mulierem plus valuit cupiditas quam libertas, ancilla facta est non bello, non praemio, sed conubio, ita ut eius filii iugo servitutis subiaceant. manifestum est enim ancillam esse voluisse eam, quam liberam esse paenituit.*

accepted and at times even hardened traditional social boundaries.[95] The substance of the rule remained unchanged.

The SCC was aimed primarily at lower-class women who would enter unequal marriages in the first place. The implicit abhorrence for unions between decent women and slaves is reflected in the classical rule against a free woman marrying her own *libertus*. Again, the standards of social honor were more important than positive law. Some free women were former slaves, and they might want to marry their *de facto* husbands: they could even buy their husbands for this purpose. The jurists were grudgingly tolerant of such lower-class activity. Ulpian wrote that if a woman was so ignoble as to find such a marriage honorable, a judge should not stop it.[96] Yet Septimius Severus punished a freedman who married into the family of his patroness. Septimius ordered the judge to render a verdict "fitting the manners of my reign, which finds such unions loathsome."[97] There was no stable, universal rule, and the civil law was purposefully vague. This ambiguity would eventually prove problematic. In 468 Anthemius issued a law in response to the case of a woman named Julia, who implored the emperor not to punish her for marrying a freedman of her household. She was worried because "a rule of the honorable Constantine does not permit, under the most strict severity, a *domina* to be inflamed by embraces with her slaves."[98] She argued that she should be immune since she was married to a freedman, not a slave. Anthemius ruled that her marriage – and any similar marriages – were valid if already contracted. In the future such marriages were disallowed, thus closing an ambiguity that had existed in Roman law since at least the age of the Severans.

The SCC was retired in AD 533 by Justinian, whose laws consistently defended the ideal of *libertas*; Justinian refused to allow this means of enslavement to continue.[99] The fortunes of the SCC in late antiquity reflect neither a proxy struggle over religious values, nor an institutional scramble to counteract a tide of mixed-status sex. Instead the history of the SCC reflects the ongoing effort to regulate the human complications of slavery in a vast Mediterranean empire. In the late empire, there were two major changes to the law. Constantine, in light of the altered composition

[95] cf. Petron. Sat. 126.5 (Mueller: 149). [96] Dig. 23.2.13. cf. Dig. 40.2.14.1.
[97] CJ 5.4.3 (AD 196): *moribus temporum meorum congruentem... huiusmodi coniunctiones odiosas.* cf. PS 2.19.9.
[98] Nov. Anthem. 1 (AD 468): *quod venerabilis sanctio Constantini dominam servorum suorum conplexibus inflammari districtissimo rigore non patitur.*
[99] On this complex reform, see Melluso 2000, 47–50; Beaucamp 1990–2, vol. 1, 191–5. Voss 1985 and Bianchini 1984, on the afterlife of rules on mixed-status reproduction.

of the imperial slave corps, changed the rules bearing on the emperor's slaves. Then, later in his reign, he took a much harder stance against sex between free women and slaves. The values were not new, nor were they particularly Christian, although the protection of female sexual honor was certainly compatible with Christianity. The aggressive posture of the state was new. The willingness to prohibit sex between women and their own slaves was an expansion of the state's role; the automatic enslavement of any woman cohabiting with a slave represented an unwillingness to leave her fate indeterminate. Constantine's successors did not sustain his zeal, and the rules would return to their classical form. But status and sexuality remained interlocking systems in late antiquity, in a society held together by the rules of the imperial state.

WELL-ORDERED EXPLOITATION: FREE MEN, SLAVE-WOMEN

The Roman slave system was a sex racket established by and for men of the higher classes. The power of free men over servile women was exerted in multifarious ways, from the use of brothels or transitory amours at the whim of the master to durable relations of companionship between partners of unequal status.[100] Nothing, perhaps, brings us so close to the manner in which the institutionalization of gross power differences brushed the routines of private life in the ancient world. The sexual exploitation of servile women was grounded in the law of marriage and adultery, by which the Roman state left dishonored women unprotected by public power. The state was more than complicit by silence, however, since these public rules actively structured the nature and direction of sexual exploitation.[101] Fear of the law was a check on sex with free, honorable women outside of marriage.[102] Augustine was right that the legal order deflected male lust away from decent women towards dishonored women.[103] While criminalizing the sexual violation of *matres familias*, Roman law allowed male sexuality untrammeled access to the bodies of prostitutes and slaves.[104]

Roman law enabled the sexual exploitation of dishonored women, but a tension lurked at the heart of the system. On the one hand, state and society encouraged the sexual exploitation of dishonored women, on a massive

---

[100] Chapter 7 has laid out the abundant evidence.
[101] Salv. Gub. 7.22 (MGH AA 1: 101–2): quoted in chapter 7.
[102] E.g. Agath. in Anth. Gr. 5.302 (Beckby: 432); P. Pell. Euch. lines 165–72 (SC 209: 68–70).
[103] Aug. Ord. 2.4.12 (CC 29: 114).   [104] Hier. Ep. 77.3 (CSEL 55: 39).

scale, in the name of protecting decent women. On the other hand, the state expected that, without strong public intervention, illegitimate children would not seep into the ranks of honest society. This was a dangerous assumption. The state expected men with legitimate children not to adopt servile offspring, although by the procedure of *adrogatio*, Roman law did allow men to adopt children, including natural sons who were freedmen, if there was good cause.[105] Adrogation, however, was an exceptional technique.[106] By the late empire, adrogation could only be effected by imperial rescript.[107] Yet it hardly needs saying that, across history, aristocracies and illegitimacy have gone hand in hand. Different societies have disposed of the "problem" of illegitimate children in different ways. The Romans, as Syme noted, were notable only for the extraordinary discretion they showed about their extra-marital offspring.[108] But in the late empire, the invisible illegitimates became increasingly visible. To understand the legal developments in the areas of marriage, concubinage, and illegitimate offspring, we will have to ask why the effects of mixed-status sex are more visible in late antiquity.

The most notable changes to the law of marriage and adultery, at least as they relate to the definition of the community of honor, congregate in the reign of Constantine. Constantine emerges as a sort of second Augustus, the creator of a new yet deeply conservative order founded on social and moral legislation.[109] Despite the manifest significance of Constantine's reforms, and the considerable attention they have received in modern scholarship, there remains extensive debate and even confusion over the precise nature and intent of his program.[110] The evidence for Constantine's reforms survives only in tatters. This poor state of affairs is explained in part by the highly imperfect transmission of the first five books of the *Theodosian Code*, but even more profoundly by the difficulties which the Theodosian editors themselves had in collecting the laws of the early fourth century. We should proceed, then, by cautiously considering in turn the chronology, substance, and purpose of the Constantinian dispensation.

Efforts to interpret Constantine's program usually begin with close readings of the individual constitutions, but it is worth zooming out and trying

---

[105] CT 2.19.1 (AD 319). Arjava 1996, 211.
[106] Dig. 1.7.46. Dig. 1.7 for *adrogatio*. Freedmen: Dig. 1.7.15.2–3; Dig. 1.5.27; Dig. 23.3.32. In general, see esp. Gardner 1989.
[107] CJ 8.47.6 (AD 293).   [108] Syme 1960.
[109] McGinn 1999, 69; Evans Grubbs 1995, 289; Lepelley 1986.
[110] McGinn 1999; Evans Grubbs 1995, 283–94; Astolfi 1993; Luchetti 1990, 15–16; Wieling 1990; Navarra 1988; Wolff 1945; Sargenti 1938, 132–6.

to establish the broader rhythm of reform. Already as emperor of the west, Constantine had revealed his reformist streak, but the pace of reform distinctly accelerated in the last decade of Constantine's reign, after he became the first sole ruler of the empire in over forty years. The laws relevant to the adultery exemptions and the marriage prohibitions cluster in the last ten years of his reign. A circumstantial case can be made for the year 326 as the moment of a single coherent reform act, reinvigorating the *lex Iulia de adulteriis coercendis* and the *lex Iulia et Papia.*[III]

The year 326 was a portentous moment. Having conquered the east, Constantine announced plans to found a new capital on the site of Byzantium in 324.[112] In 326 Constantine returned to Rome to celebrate his *vicennalia.*[113] A major re-ordering of the Roman aristocracy took place in Constantine's reign, and Chastagnol has argued for 326 as a crucial date, since after that year the equestrian order (with the exception of its highest tier, the *perfectissimi*) disappears, and the senatorial order began a massive expansion.[114] Constantine, like Augustus, simultaneously reformed the aristocracy and regulated private morals. There are traces of this reform package in the law codes: CT 9.7.1, which treats exemptions to the adultery statute, and more significantly, a small fragment of an *Ad Populum* edict preserved in the *Justinianic Code*, regulating the practice of concubinage.[115] Concubinage, as we will see, sits squarely at the intersection of aristocratic marriage prohibitions and adultery exemptions. If this reconstruction is correct, then in 326 Constantine implemented a sweeping reform, renewing the Augustan program for a specifically late antique social order.

That the principal enactments of a major reform have been lost to us is not in doubt. The crucial title, CT 4.6, is missing its first law in the manuscripts; later laws refer back to Constantinian measures which are not extant; fourth- and fifth-century observers assume legal rules whose creation is not attested in the legal codes.[116] From these scattered clues we can reconstruct, at least in outline, the substance of Constantine's reforms. The reform seems to have included four components (whether deriving ultimately from one original edict or developing piecemeal):

[III] Seeck 1919, 63, connects the laws on adultery and concubinage (CJ 5.26.1) and places them in 326; on pp. 447–9 I argue that the missing marriage reform (known through CT 4.6.3) and the amnesty for freeborn *concubinae* (known through CJ 5.27.5) also belong in this context.
[112] Lenski 2006c, 77–8.   [113] Barnes 1982, 76–7.
[114] Chastagnol 1988; Evans Grubbs 1995, 24. Lepelley 1986, stresses long-term processes over a single moment of reform.
[115] CJ 5.26.1 (AD 326).   [116] See p. 453.

(1) A reform of the adultery statute, including new rules on eligible accusers and a clearer definition of the women exempt from its application.

(2) An amnesty for men in a relationship with a *concubina ingenua*, providing the temporary opportunity to convert the union into a marriage.

(3) An expansion of the Augustan marriage restrictions.

(4) A prohibition on the transmission of property to illegitimate children.

(1) In 326 Constantine amended the *lex Iulia*. A law posted at Nicomedia on 25 April, for instance, restricted the public's right to accuse a married woman of adultery; only her husband and close kin could lay charges.[117] There was, in these very same months, discussion over which women were exempt from the adultery statute. The *lex Iulia* offered a minimalist definition of the community of honor. *Matres familias* were to be protected; the state would not punish sexual violations of women "who openly make or will have made a profit with their bodies." This definition prompted a long juristic debate, but the Roman state could operate with a minimalist statutory definition because the state's approach was responsive: it required application to the legal process, rather than state police surveillance, to activate the state's protection.

We could easily imagine that, given the reliance on underlying social prejudices, questions about the reach of the adultery exemptions arose in practice. In 326 the issue of definition surfaced in public discourse. Already Ulpian had made the observation that the brothel was not the only locus of prostitution. "We say that she has openly made a profit not only if she prostitutes herself in a brothel, but equally if she, as is common, fails to guard her modesty in a tavern or an inn or any other place."[118] The tavern was a notorious den of commercial sex.[119] In 326 Constantine created a "prostitute analogue" – another statutory exemption from the *lex Iulia*.[120] Constantine ruled that in adultery cases, it must be determined whether the woman was "the mistress or servant of the tavern."[121] If the woman owned the place of business, she was not excluded from protection by the state. If, however, the woman was a barmaid who served the "wines of intemperance" to the customers, then men who had sex with her were not liable under the *lex Iulia*.[122] Here we see the traditional prejudice against

---

[117] CT 9.7.2 (AD 326). Evans Grubbs 1995, 205–16.

[118] Dig. 23.2.43.pr: *Palam quaestum facere dicemus non tantum eam, quae in lupanario se prostituit, verum etiam si qua (ut adsolet) in taberna cauponia vel qua alia pudori suo non parcit.* cf. CJ 4.56.3 (AD 225).

[119] McGinn 2004, 16–22.　　[120] The label is from McGinn 1997.

[121] CT 9.7.1 (AD 326): *utrum domina cauponae an ministra fuerit.* Bassanelli Sommariva 1988. I would argue that Constantine's law was something more than a decision brought about by a specific case.

[122] CT 9.7.1 (AD 326): *intemperantiae vina.*

lower-class women exposed to public view. This reform was not a radical substantive change, but rather a slightly amended definition of the circle of women who were, like slaves and prostitutes, beyond public protection. Constantine cemented prejudice into law by considering any barmaid, *ipso facto*, a woman without sexual honor.

The amorphous body of post-classical law known as the *Sentences of Paul* (PS) preserves other signs of deliberation over the exemptions from the adultery law; the PS claims that the *lex Iulia* did not apply to women who "publicly oversee the sale of merchandise or the operation of a tavern."[123] This rule poses several problems. First, it is difficult to map the oversight of tavern operations onto Constantine's distinction between bar-owner and barmaid: are we to imagine "oversight" here to involve the sort of direct activity that rendered a woman's honor suspect?[124] Secondly, it is unclear if this rule belongs before or after Constantine's law.[125] If the passage pre-dates the law of 326, then CT 9.7.1 could be seen as a clarification allowing women who owned taverns to defend their honor publicly. If the passage post-dates 326, then Constantine may have changed his mind and opted not to extend protection to female tavern-owners. Constantine's reform of the Augustan marriage law forbade members of the upper classes from marrying, among others, tavern-owners and women who oversaw the sale of goods (see p. 449).[126] McGinn has argued that the rules hardened over Constantine's reign.[127] This reconstruction is possible, but if we locate Constantine's marriage reform in 326, then the likelier resolution is that Constantine distinguished bar-owners and barmaids for the purposes of the adultery law, while forbidding elite men to marry any woman associated with a tavern.[128]

PS 2.26.11 adds women who "publicly oversee the sale of merchandise" to the list of women outside the state's protection. This is "such an egregious piece of misogyny" that we must consider whether it is perhaps a "periphrasis for prostitute" or procuress.[129] Certainly, the inclusion of vendors among prostitutes could reflect extreme upper-class bias towards poor women exposed to public view. But the title on the *lex Iulia* in the *Theodosian Code* does not exempt these women from public protection, and

---

[123] PS 2.26.11: *publice mercibus vel tabernis exercendis procurant.* Bassanelli Sommariva 1988; Manfredini 1988; Rizzelli 1988.

[124] Manfredini 1988, 340–1; Rizzelli 1988, 740.

[125] On the date of the PS, see Liebs 2008a and 1993; Levy 1945. Liebs argues that most of it originates from around 300. Certain amendments were clearly made over the fourth and fifth centuries, but the interpretation of PS 2.26.11 offered here would allow the traditional date to stand.

[126] Beaucamp 1990–2, vol. I, 203–4.   [127] McGinn 1997, 94–7.

[128] Evans Grubbs 1995, 291.   [129] McGinn 1997, 96, concluding it is probably not.

neither did the corresponding titles in the *Justinianic Code* or the *Digest*. Probably, as before, social notions of honor continued to be the defining factor. In the late sixth century, a woman who owned a tavern was called an "honorable woman."[130] If Constantine intended a sweeping re-definition of sexual honor, to exclude all women who sold goods publicly, there is no sign he had any effect. The important and certain fact is that in 326 Constantine amended the statutory definition of women excluded from the adultery statute; he was trying to define the community of honor, in part by declaring who lay outside its privileged bounds.[131] There is nothing in Constantine's reform to indicate a significant departure from the older assumptions about social status and sexual honor. Constantine, ultimately, tinkered with public law in a way that sharpened traditional prejudices against poor, publicly visible women in unsavory employments or environs.

(2) Constantine also sought to define the community of honor, and to ensure its continuous reproduction, by enacting a series of laws about proper marriage partners. It is remarkable that Constantine's reforms have left such a mark in the sources, while the actual measures have been lost. The components of his reform can only be reconstructed from secondary enforcement laws, from later imperial constitutions, and from literary testimony. It is clear that, as part of his reforms, Constantine offered a temporary amnesty to any man currently living with a freeborn concubine, allowing them to marry and to consider the offspring born before or afterwards as fully legitimate.[132] This measure is only known obliquely through a law of 477 in which the emperor Zeno revived the amnesty.[133] If Zeno's use of legal history is to be trusted, Constantine issued a dispensation to those who were in a long-term relationship with a freeborn woman, allowing them to declare it a valid marriage.[134] The law was specific, though, that this dispensation only applied to men without a wife who were in relations with *freeborn* women. The law did not apply to slaves and freedwomen, normally the partner in concubinage.[135] Since Roman marriage was largely formless, and status was a decisive factor in distinguishing marriage from concubinage, this law was an effort to legitimize what were *de*

---

[130] Ioh. Mosch. Prat. 188 (PG 87.3: 3065).
[131] There are still other signs that the definition of women unworthy of the state's protection was an issue. A legal text, dating after AD 320, shows that freeborn men were prohibited from marrying slave-women manumitted by a pimp or procuress. Reg. Ulp. 13.2, with McGinn 1997, 87–9. Mercogliano 1997, on the text generally.
[132] Temporary: Evans Grubbs 1995, 298; Luchetti 1990, 179.   [133] CJ 5.27.5.
[134] Evans Grubbs 1995, 296–7; Luchetti 1990, 180–2; Navarra 1988, 461–3.
[135] Typically freedwomen: Arjava 1996, 207.

facto marriages into *de iure* marriages. The law "applied only to women who could (and probably should) have been living in *iustum matrimonium*, not *concubinitas*, in the first place."[136]

It is impossible to date a reform known only through a late fifth-century notice, but some investigators have connected the amnesty for freeborn concubines with another constitution, preserved in the *Justinianic Code*.[137] CJ 5.26.1 asserted that it was illegal to have a wife and a concubine simultaneously.[138] This was no substantive innovation, for concubinage was not supposed to be practiced simultaneously with marriage; Constantine was merely enforcing from the imperial center the best social practices of the aristocracy.[139] CJ 5.26.1 was part of an *Ad Populum* edict, and the copy preserved in the *Justinianic Code* was posted at Caesarea on 14 June of 326.[140] The date of CJ 5.26.1 is doubly significant, for it is also tempting to connect the amnesty law with Constantine's reform of the Augustan marriage prohibitions, as a measure that offered one chance to any man living in a relationship with a freeborn concubine to marry her. This chain of connections – one undated reform (extension of marriage prohibitions) tied to another undated reform (amnesty for freeborn concubines) associated with a dated law (CJ 5.26.1) – is tenuous, but it does possess a certain logical coherence suggesting a major reform in 326.

(3) Constantine revised and extended the Augustan marriage prohibitions. The social legislation of Augustus prohibited members of the senatorial order, and their descendants to four generations, from intermarriage with lower-class women. The prohibited category included freedwomen, actors, actresses, and their offspring. The same law forbade all *ingenui* from marriage with pimps, prostitutes, and adulteresses.[141] These laws were designed to mark off the upper classes and prevent mixing between the governing elite and servile or humble echelons of imperial society. The classical law thus came closest to "policing" honor, inheritance, and marriage practices in this uppermost tier of society. The symbolic value of monitoring the highly visible senatorial order must be considered an important part of the overall economy of the Augustan package. Constantine tried to re-calibrate the Augustan rules in the context of the fourth-century aristocracy, an aristocracy of his own making.

---

[136] Evans Grubbs 1995, 298.   [137] Esp. Navarra 1988, 461.
[138] CJ 5.26.1 (AD 326). Sargenti 1986, 37–8. cf. PS 2.20.1.
[139] Arjava 1996, 208. See Treggiari 1981, 77–8; Rawson 1974, 288.
[140] A *proposita* date signals that the law was originally recovered from somewhere other than the central archives: Matthews 2000, 61. cf. Sirks 2007, 140. CJ 5.26.1 was part of a larger edict: Evans Grubbs 1995, 298; Luchetti 1990, 185; Sargenti 1938, 133.
[141] See above. McGinn 1998, 93; Astolfi 1970, 31–2.

Constantine supplemented the Augustan restrictions by extending the class of prohibited women and by making the restrictions apply to a much broader swath of the aristocracy: in other words, his law expanded the size of the elite at the top and the untouchables at the bottom.[142] The enacting law is again lost, and its content can only be imperfectly reconstructed from complementary legislation. The primary evidence is CT 4.6.3, a constitution of 336. According to this law, the marriage restrictions applied not just to the senatorial order, but to "senators or *perfectissimi* or any who are honored with the duumvirate or the quinquennalitate of a city or the emblems of a *flamen* or priest of a province." If any man within these social categories tried to legitimize, "either by their own sentence or by the privilege of imperial rescript, any children born from a slave or a freedwoman or the daughter of a freedwoman, be they full citizens or Latins, or from an actress or the daughter of an actress, or a barkeeper or the daughter of a barkeeper, be they humble or absolutely base, or from the daughter of a pimp or a gladiator, or from a woman who sold goods to the public," the man was to lose his status and his citizenship.[143]

In CT 4.6.3 Constantine punished men of the higher orders who did any of three things: he punished men who considered the children of these mixed-status unions legitimate, who gave property to the children, or who gave property to the woman. The men were not allowed to reckon the children legitimate "by their own sentence or by the privilege of imperial rescript."[144] This clause prohibited adrogation, making it illegal for these men to seek the adoption of their illegitimate children.[145] Then the law prohibited in detail the transmission of property to the women or children.[146] Strictly speaking, this law punished members of the elite who tried to legitimize or to transfer property to their children from lowborn women. It is important to be specific: this law did not ban such

---

[142] McGinn 1999, 60; Sargenti 1986, 40–5.

[143] CT 4.6.3 (AD 336): *senatores seu perfectissimos, vel quos in civitatibus duumviralitas vel quinquennalitas vel flamonii vel sacerdotii provinciae ornamenta condecorant . . . si ex ancilla vel ancillae filia vel liberta vel libertae filia, sive romana facta seu latina, vel scaenica vel scaenicae filia, vel ex tabernaria vel ex tabernari filia vel humili vel abiecta vel lenonis vel harenarii filia vel quae mercimoniis publicis praefuit.* The final clause (omitted in CJ), about a certain son of Licinianus, has sometimes been interpreted as a reference to an unknown illegitimate son of Licinius. While possible, it has never added insight into the law, and it is unlikely anyway: McGinn 1999, 63.

[144] CT 4.6.3 (AD 336): *susceptos filios in numero legitimorum habere voluerint aut proprio iudicio aut nostri praerogativa rescripti.* Pharr 1952, 86, interprets *proprio iudicio* as "last will and testament," but the natural sense of *iudicium* without a modifier such as *supremum* is judgment. cf. Berger 1953, 520.

[145] Gardner 1989, 243, suggested that the original Augustan legislation prohibited senators from adopting their freed slaves.

[146] Concubines could, before Constantine, receive testamentary bequests. McGinn 1991, 346.

marriages, nor did it discourage concubinage.[147] It does imply that an earlier law, which is now lost, must have banned intermarriage between the men of the specified high ranks and these categories of women.[148] We do not know when this reform was passed, but there are grounds, as argued above, to suppose the year 326. CT 4.6.3 reflects these reforms and demonstrates the emperor's desire to prevent men from circumventing the law in practice.[149]

Constantine's marriage restrictions applied to a broad, specifically late Roman aristocracy. Constantine included not only senators but also *perfectissimi*, men holding high rank in the equestrian order.[150] This represents a delayed effect of Diocletian's re-organization of the empire and his preference for equestrian officers; the absence of equestrian grades other than *perfectissimi* in Constantine's law is notable and provides a *terminus post quem* of 326, when ranks such as *egregii* disappear from the historical record.[151] Constantine also included the top municipal magistrates, duumvirs, *quinquennales*, and flamens, who formed a "core elite within the decurionate."[152] Now, men of the senatorial and official aristocracy, including the highest civil and religious magistrates in each city, were set apart, on the emperor's command, in their family strategies.

Constantine's law was not railing against an imaginary problem. Third-century rescripts demonstrate the assumption of municipal office by slaves, especially slaves who were the natural children of fathers that held the same office. In one case, the status of an office-holder was questioned before a court, and Diocletian informed him that his father's civil honors were not evidence for the son's status.[153] Another slave had apparently attained the level of a *principalis* – the distinguished core of the civic council.[154] Such rescripts reveal the odd matrix of power in small societies. Many town councils must have been far removed from the illustrious prestige of the urban senates which dominate our imagination. The slaves of powerful families could have an informal social clout, especially those who shared in the bloodline of the curial class. While the performance of curial duties was an honor, it was also a burden, so it is no surprise to find civic councils conscripting the natural offspring of its members to duty. Amidst these complex, tugging forces, illegitimate sons might find themselves

---

[147] Astolfi 1993, who, however, sees an opposition to concubinage.
[148] Nov. Marc. 4 (AD 454) assumes as much.
[149] CT 4.6.3 (and the fragmentary 4.6.2) carry a *proposita* date from Carthage, implying recovery from the provincial rather than central archives.
[150] Jones 1964, 48–9, 526–7.   [151] Chastagnol 1988.   [152] McGinn 1999, 64.
[153] CJ 7.16.11 (AD 293). Also CJ 7.16.38 (AD 294); CJ 10.33.1 (Diocletian); CJ 10.33.2 (Diocletian).
[154] CJ 7.16.41 (Constantine).

holding office or dignity. The stringent rules that protected the purity of the senatorial aristocracy were extended by Constantine down to the level of local dignitaries.

Constantine's law also expanded the category of women who had been deemed impermissible marriage partners by Augustus. Augustus had placed actresses, their daughters, and freedwomen off limits for members of the senatorial order. Constantine included slaves, freedwomen, actresses and the daughters of all these, as well as tavern-keepers, the daughters of tavern-keepers, pimps, or gladiators, women who sold goods to the public, and women described as *humiles vel abiectae*. This list expands the ranks of women who could not marry into the highest tier of Roman society, but it does so in no particularly radical way.[155] It is important to note, as well, that this is not precisely a list of prohibited marriage partners – the mention of slave-women would be nonsensical. It is a list of women who may be sexual partners but whose children the man may not legitimize or leave property. The list thus realistically reflects the sort of freeborn women, without sexual honor, who may have become concubines.[156] The prohibition on marriage is implicit, but we do not have the list of forbidden partners as Constantine outlined it. The list presented here in 4.6.3 does forbid marriage to tavern-keepers (without distinguishing bar-owners from barmaids) and to women who sold goods to the public: the ruling elite could not intermarry with poor, publicly exposed women.

Constantine's list of unsuitable partners included women *humiles vel abiectae*. This category has been the object of considerable modern discussion, but it was confusing already in late antiquity, because the emperor Marcian had to issue a constitution in 454 to clarify the meaning of Constantine's terms.[157] Marcian ruled that Constantine had not intended to stigmatize poor, free women and that the phrase was a secondary description of the dishonored women specifically named within the law. It is not clear that this is truly what Constantine meant; it is not even clear whether the phrase refers to two types of women or represents a hendiadys describing one group.[158] The terms *humilis* and *abiecta* do not correspond to the category of *humiliores* in opposition to *honestiores*, a modern scholarly construction which has been vastly overused in the study of late Roman society.[159] Ultimately it is not possible to know exactly what Constantine

---

[155] McGinn 1999, 65, notes that the Constantinian reform is supplementary to the Augustan reform.
[156] Always a "delicate question" in Roman law, Arjava 1996, 207; McGinn 1991.
[157] Nov. Marc. 4 (AD 454). McGinn 1997, 78–86; Evans Grubbs 1995, 292–4; Beaucamp 1990–2, vol. I, 286–7.
[158] McGinn 1997, 82, for a survey of modern opinions.
[159] *Contra* Sargenti 1986, 41–2. In general, see Rilinger 1988; Garnsey 1970, 278–80; Cardascia 1950.

meant, but it is worth noting that late Roman laws, Constantine's in particular, were highly rhetorical, which often obscured precise constructions.[160] Moreover, CT 4.6.3 was an enforcement mechanism: the categories may have been clearer in the original enactment. CT 4.6.3 was meant to prohibit the legitimization of offspring from concubines. Though concubines were usually freedwomen, sometimes they were freeborn but socially marginal, and Constantine probably wanted to be inclusive.[161] Upper-class men could not legitimize or give property to their illegitimate children.

(4) CT 4.6.3 outlawed property transfers from men of the highest classes to illegitimate children born from various categories of prohibited women: "whatever the father will have given to such children, whether he will have called them *legitimi* or *naturales*, all of it having been taken back, it shall be returned to the legitimate offspring."[162] Subsequent constitutions preserved in the same title of the *Theodosian Code*, CT 4.6, along with a host of patristic sources, demonstrate that Constantine banned *all* men, not simply the upper-class men covered under his marriage law, from leaving testamentary bequests to illegitimate offspring.[163] In fact a Constantinian measure seems to have introduced a new terminology, distinguishing clearly between *filii legitimi* and *filii naturales*.[164] This measure is, yet again, missing from the surviving dossier of Constantine's laws. This raises a vexing problem, one that has never been satisfactorily resolved and is often simply glossed over.[165] Later emperors, starting with Valentinian, tried to temper Constantine's ban on leaving property to illegitimate children.[166] These laws specifically ascribe the original rule to Constantine, and they never mention any limitation to men of the upper classes.[167] In classical Roman law it was permitted for fathers to leave their illegitimate children legacies in a will, but from Constantine's reign this practice seems to have become illegal.[168]

Literary sources provide parallel testimony. Ambrose, as we saw at the beginning of this chapter, warned men not to create children with slaves

---

[160] Robinson 2000; Harries 1999, 42; Honoré 1998, 127; Voss 1982.

[161] McGinn 1997, 83, "inevitably and perhaps deliberately imprecise."

[162] CT 4.6.3 (AD 336): *(quidq)uid talibus liberis pater donaverit, sive illos legitimos (seu natur)ales dixerit, totum retractum legitimae subo(li redda)tur.*

[163] Wolff 1945, 38; Bonfante 1925, 318, for a general ban.   [164] Wolff 1945, 24.

[165] The best presentation of the problem is Wieling 1990, 460. Many treatments of the later laws in CT 4.6 never explain where the original prohibition on gifts to *naturales* originated. Tate 2008b, 2; Arjava 1996, 213–14; Evans Grubbs 1995, 300.

[166] CT 4.6.4 (AD 371): see p. 458.

[167] CT 4.6.4 and 4.6.5. Nov. 89 (AD 539) explicitly claims that the regulation of illegitimate children began with Constantine.

[168] Dig. 28.6.45; Dig. 34.9.16. Wieling 1990.

and concubines, because such children "could not be heirs."[169] Sometime between 385 and 410, Asterius of Antioch claimed that "the laws of the Romans do not permit a slave to receive the inheritance."[170] Caesarius of Arles claimed that servile children born of a concubine, even when freed, could "by no law and no order" receive the inheritance.[171] As Arjava has noted, these authors may mean simply that "bastards could not be made sole heirs," but Libanius and the laws in the *Theodosian Code* suggest that indeed a wholesale ban on donations and legacies was at issue.[172] Regardless, none of these authors give any indication that the rule only applied to men of the upper classes. The legal and literary evidence both suggest that there was a separate enactment, in the reign of Constantine, limiting and probably banning the transmission of property to illegitimate children, whether their father belonged to the aristocracy or not.

This reconstruction raises a question about CT 4.6.3. If an earlier measure of Constantine had already made it illegal to leave property to illegitimate children, then why was the law of 336 even necessary?[173] What did it do? This is a hard question, but it is often difficult to know the exact motivation or innovation of a given law in the *Theodosian Code*. Because we are manifestly missing the law by which Constantine expanded the Augustan inheritance restrictions, scholars – even when they explicitly recognize that CT 4.6.3 was not the original measure – are in the habit of treating it as the marriage reform.[174] But CT 4.6.3 created neither the new Constantinian marriage prohibitions nor the ban on gifts to illegitimate children. Its purpose must lie in some detail which is less obvious to us: perhaps it innovated in prohibiting gifts *inter vivos* from upper-class fathers to illegitimate children, perhaps its novelty lay in the ban on seeking an exception through imperial rescript, perhaps its penalties were harsher than those in the original law. Because CT 4.6.3 reflects other laws which have been lost, it is impossible to know with certainty how it differed from those laws.

---

[169] Ambr. Abr. 1.3.19 (CSEL 32.1: 515): *quos heredes habere non possint.*

[170] Ast. Soph. Psalm. 11.11 (Richard: 80): Δοῦλον οἱ νόμοι Ῥωμαίων κληρονόμον οὐ παραδέχονται. For the date, see Kinzig 1990, 227.

[171] Caes. Arel. Serm. 42.5 (CC 103: 188): *nulla lege et nullo ordine.* As with many sermons, this descends in the manuscript tradition of Augustine, too, Aug. Serm. 288.5 (PL 39: 2291).

[172] Arjava 1996, 215.

[173] Wolff 1945, 38, one of the few to deal with the problem, places a general ban after CT 4.6.3, in the small window of time before Constantine's death.

[174] The fact that this was not the law which banned the marriages explains why Constantine only names the men involved (*senatores*), not their descendants, the entire *ordo*, or female members of the aristocracy; it explains why there is no mention of unions prohibited to *ingenui*; it explains why a union (obviously non-marital) with a slave is put into consideration.

Constantine's reform package could be reconstructed as follows. In 326, as sole emperor, Constantine announced plans to establish a new capital and traveled from the east to Rome to celebrate the twentieth year of his power. He made major changes to the system of aristocratic rank and privilege, expanding the senate and narrowing the equestrian order. He issued a series of reforms – whether jointly or separately – re-invigorating the Augustan social program. He adjusted the law of adultery, restricting eligible informers and clarifying which women were beneath its protections. Constantine extended the Augustan marriage prohibitions, applying the rules to a broader elite and to a wider set of dishonored women. He allowed men a temporary opportunity to marry a freeborn concubine and to consider their children legitimate. Otherwise, illegitimate children could no longer receive legacies. Eventually, he ruled that members of the elite could not give property to their illegitimate offspring *inter vivos*; elite men were even prohibited from seeking an imperial rescript to legitimize their offspring.

What prompted Constantine's reforms? Christian opposition to concubinage was long suspected, but this is a highly unconvincing explanation.[175] A desire to combat eastern habits of concubinage has also been suggested, but on close inspection this theory does little to explain the timing, substance, or even the geographic scope of Constantine's reforms.[176] Recent interpreters have rightly stressed the social dimensions of Constantine's reforms: *sexual* regulation in the Roman empire was inseparable from *social* regulation. The rules on unequal unions and illegitimate children were concerned with the maintenance of social hierarchies rather than sexual behavior as such. But Constantine's reforms are not a signal that these hierarchies were unraveling in the late empire. Concubinage was one of those practices whose operations were only lightly regulated in the classical law; the early imperial state trusted the "self-regulating" good behavior of the upper classes.[177] In the late empire we see long-standing patterns of social behavior increasingly prescribed by law. The new style of statecraft is the decisive change.

The motives behind Constantine's reforms, or Augustus' for that matter, are complex. Both reforms occurred at a time of change and reconstitution for the governing classes. Still, this is context, not cause. The desire to legislate social boundaries takes us into the deeper psychological strata of an imperial regime and a slave-holding society. The charisma accrued by

[175] Van de Wiel 1978; Biondi 1952–4, vol. 3, 191; Dupont 1937, 126.
[176] Wolff 1945. See the criticisms of Tate 2008b, 7–8.   [177] McGinn 1991, 336.

one class through its separation, its elevation, can be imputed as a partial motive.[178] Constantine's broader application of marriage restrictions – not just to senators and *perfectissimi*, but to the local gentry – guaranteed that in every outpost of Roman civilization, a narrow class of men and women would be visibly demarcated, superior and liminal, in their ancestry and alliances. In an empire stretching thousands of miles, containing millions of inhabitants, it was a useful way to create countless little images of the ideal social order: a display and a reinforcement of the rigid stratification at the heart of Roman law and imperial society. Constantine's laws were no more a sign of crisis or the breakdown of the slave system than were those of Augustus – each emperor's reforms represented a monumental attempt to regulate the way in which the sexual dynamics of a massive and complex slave system interacted with the workings of property, status, and honor.

CONCUBINAGE AND ILLEGITIMACY AFTER CONSTANTINE

The fate of illegitimate children remained an intractable problem throughout late antiquity. *Aegrescit medendo*: Constantine's response aggravated the tension. It was a radical departure to punish men for transferring property to their servile offspring. Even later emperors found Constantine's rule unduly harsh. Constantine's reforms instigated a protracted effort to find the right balance among conflicting interests. Three subsequent phases are apparent.[179] The first lasted throughout the fourth and early fifth centuries and pitted the strict rules of Constantine against a slightly more lenient attitude. A second phase, in the mid-to-late fifth century, saw a new force intrude on the scene: the crisis of the curial councils and the willingness to conscript anyone with a claim to curial property. A final phase was marked by the reforms of Justinian, whose motives and methods were, as usual, *sui generis*.[180]

Why was the problem of illegitimacy so immovable in late antiquity? This development must be seen as the result of several convergent factors. First, concubinage. As chapter 7 has shown, sex with slaves not only took the form of sporadic abuse; men could enter long-term, publicly visible relationships with lower-class or servile women, expressly for the purpose of companionship rather than legitimate reproduction. Concubinage was interwoven in the demographic fabric of Roman society, for it was especially common in the years men passed between puberty and marriage, or

[178] McGinn 1997, 98; Evans Grubbs 1995, 289.
[179] Tate 2008b; Beaucamp 1990–2, vol. I, 197–201; Luchetti 1990, 26–33; Meyer 1895, 134–42.
[180] Melluso 2000, 152–71; Beaucamp 1990–2, vol. I, 201.

in the years after the death of a wife. Yet concubinage was legally formless. The state assumed that the line between marriage and concubinage would be understood in terms of legally informal categories.[181] Roman marriage itself required intent but not a ceremony or registration. The legal status of the partners might in fact be the criterion differentiating marriage from concubinage.[182] The clarity of the distinction between marriage and concubinage was inversely related to the social distance between the man and woman: amongst the highest echelons of society, it was obvious if a man's female partner was a proper aristocratic wife or a servile girl-friend. Amongst the middle or lower classes, these distinctions were less apparent.

The indistinct line between marriage and concubinage was thus especially vulnerable to manipulation, and this may have become an even more acute problem in late antiquity. The fourth century, in particular, was a period during which the Roman aristocracy was thoroughly restructured.[183] The process began with Diocletian but was taken in fundamentally new directions under Constantine. Constantine not only founded a new senate, he drastically increased the size of the senatorial order – which eventually grew from some 600 to 6,000 members.[184] This growth slowly phased out the equestrian order, and it drew heavily from the ranks of the town councils, a process which was audibly painful for the curial classes.[185] At the same time, the new aristocracy was built around imperial service; the "imperialization" of the Roman aristocracy created new avenues of ascent and new opportunities for men of humble origins to attain high status. There were, by the standards of the Julio-Claudian days, some shady characters walking through the corridors of power in the late Roman world.[186] They brought with them their private predilections and habits.

In the late Roman empire we witness a particularly sharp version of what has been called the "eternal tension between social mobility and social hierarchy."[187] The reconstitution of the aristocracy, and the new modes of social mobility, had a profound effect on marital strategy. Marriage was an important strategic ploy for the social riser; a union with a socially prestigious woman – or, often, girl – advertised social arrival and created politically useful alliances. Some of the most characteristic figures of late

---

[181] McGinn 1991, 336.
[182] Arjava 1996, 205; Evans Grubbs 1995, 294; Thomas 1984, 234; Rawson 1974, 287–90.
[183] Heather 1998 is the best general overview. Zuckerman 1998; Dagron 1974, 119–210; Chastagnol 1988 and 1976; Lepelley 1986; Jones 1964, 523–35. Banaji 2001, 101–70, for an economic profile.
[184] Heather 1998, 196–7.   [185] Laniado 2002, 7; Whittow 1990.
[186] Evans Grubbs 1995, 287. In general, MacMullen 1964; Hopkins 1961.   [187] McGinn 1997, 85.

antiquity – Augustine and Ausonius – are perfect examples of the strategic use of marriage.[188] Concubinage is to be seen in light of these broader social movements.[189] It was used strategically by men who delayed finding a wife until they could secure a more favorable marriage. In the hostile description of a Christian bishop, "they think to themselves that first they will acquire unjust wealth and filthy lucre through many connivances and thefts, and afterwards, perversely, they will take wives who are richer or more noble than they themselves are."[190] Concubinage was used as a holding pattern by upwardly mobile men. Augustine described the man who "attached himself to a woman for a time, and later, because of his offices or wealth, found another woman worthy to take as his equal: by this very spirit he is an adulterer!"[191] He should have known. Augustine was unusual only for his extraordinary success. "We see many who because of their poverty decline to undertake the burden of a wife and keep their slave-girls for wives and have children by them which they raise as their own. If perchance these men are enriched and earn for their women the right of the *stola* from the emperor, suddenly they are submitted to the apostle's yoke and forced to receive the women as wives. But if on account of their humble status they cannot petition for an imperial rescript, the laws of church and the laws of state will be at odds."[192]

The intrinsic dynamics of concubinage, along with the re-composition of the late Roman aristocracy, made the issue of illegitimate children acutely problematic in the fourth century. But what forced the issue to the surface was the attempt of Constantine to ban altogether the transmission of property to illegitimate children. This was an unprecedented measure, and under Valentinian, the rules of Constantine against such transmission were softened. He ruled that the laws of Constantine were to remain in effect, but that it was permitted to leave up to one-fourth of an inheritance to illegitimate children, in the absence of legitimate heirs. If legitimate heirs

---

[188] For Ausonius, Evans Grubbs 2009a, 202–6; Sivan 1993, 49–66; Hopkins 1961. For Augustine, Shanzer 2002 and Shaw 1987a.

[189] Harper forthcoming a; Evans Grubbs 1995, 295.

[190] Caes. Arel. Serm. 43.4 (CC 103: 191–2): *tractant enim apud se, ut prius de multis calumniis et rapinis iniustas divitias et iniqua lucra conquirant, et postea contra rationem plus nobiles quam ipsi sunt vel divitiores uxores accipiant.*

[191] Aug. Bon. conj. 5.5 (CSEL 41: 193–4): *aliquam sibi vir ad tempus adhibuerit, donec aliam dignam vel honoribus vel facultatibus suis inveniat, quam conparem ducat, ipso animo adulter est.*

[192] Hier. Ep. 69.5 (CSEL 54: 688): *multos videmus ob nimiam paupertatem uxorum sarcinam declinare et ancillulas suas habere pro uxoribus susceptosque ex his liberos colere ut proprios. si forte ditati ab imperatore stolas illis meruerint, confestim apostolo colla submittet et invitus inter uxores eas recipere cogetur; sin autem principale rescriptum eadem tenuitas inpetrare non quiverit, cum romanis legibus scita ecclesiae mutabuntur.*

existed, it was permitted to leave only one-twelfth of the estate to the illegitimate child.[193] It was still illegal for a representative of the upper classes to marry a socially dishonored woman, such as a slave, prostitute, or freedwoman, but if children were born from sexual relationships or concubinage, they were allowed to receive property in the will.

The effect of Valentinian's measure on the curial class can be followed in a surprisingly intimate way, for Libanius has described his feelings towards the law. Descended from a wealthy curial family, he was engaged to a cousin who died before their marriage. He remained unmarried and took a concubine. In a private letter, he wrote that his son, Cimon, was born from a concubine who was "a good mother, though not a free one."[194] Libanius raised Cimon as a legitimate son and provided him with a liberal education. Valentian's measure would have provided Libanius and his son some relief, and Libanius looked upon Valentinian's law as a stroke of good fortune, which freed him from "the immense distress that the same day would be the end of me and a day of impoverishment and extreme hardship for my son."[195]

The lenient measure of Valentinian was not to endure. Libanius claimed that his law was repealed by another which returned to the hard line of Constantine against illegitimate offspring.[196] In this environment, Libanius candidly admitted, he fully intended to funnel his estate through trusted friends who would take care of his son. This is precisely the sort of legal maneuvering which Constantine had foreseen, and Libanius knew that it was dangerous. Perhaps the return to the harsh standard mentioned by Libanius was only effected in the east, because in 397 the western emperor Honorius again returned to the harsh rule.[197] By this time none of it mattered for Libanius, whose son had preceded him in death in 391. At the close of the fourth century, Constantine's hard line prevailed across the empire. It was obviously difficult for the fourth-century state to find a suitable balance among these conflicting interests: the desire to cleanse the upper classes from illegitimate lines, the regularity of sexual partnerships between high-status men and servile women, and the affection which a father might have for his natural children.

Over the next generation, the rules would continue to waver, switching between harsh and lenient, before settling on the more lax principle that

---

[193] CT 4.6.4 (AD 371). Tate 2008b, suggests a link with CT 15.7.2 (AD 371).

[194] Lib. Ep. 1063.5 (Foerster vol. 11: 187): ἐκ μητρὸς ἀγαθῆς, εἰ καὶ μὴ ἐλευθέρας.

[195] Lib. Or. 1.145 (Foerster vol. 1: 153): ἥ με πολλῆς τε καὶ βαρείας ἠλευθέρωσεν ἀνίας, ὡς τῆς αὐτῆς ἡμέρας τελευτὴν μὲν ἐμοί, πτωχείαν δὲ ἐκείνῳ τὴν ἐσχάτην οἰσούσης.

[196] Lib. Or. 1.195 (Foerster vol. 1: 171).   [197] CT 4.6.5 (AD 397).

illegitimate children could inherit one-fourth of the estate in the absence of heirs, or one-twelfth if heirs existed.[198] Amidst this flip-flopping, there was no intimation that an illegitimate child, born of a servile concubine, could be made a legitimate heir. Then, in 442 a new concern intruded upon an already complex problem. Theodosius II ruled that in the absence of proper heirs, a councilor could not only bestow a portion of his estate on illegitimate children, he could bequeath the entire estate to the child so long as the new heir was assigned a place on the town council.[199] The plight of the councils, particularly by the fifth century, was an inexorable problem. It is not hard to understand how, by suspending the social prejudice against servile ancestry, all could benefit from the arrangement which Theodosius II allowed, in particular the council.[200] Of course, the suspension of social prejudice could be stomached only when no other heir was available and in response to one of the most chronic fiscal problems of the late empire.

In the sixth century, the state's position towards illegitimate children became increasingly liberalized. The emperor Anastasius authored a remarkable law in 517, granting the prerogative to anyone without legitimate children to make their illegitimate children into legal and proper heirs by marrying the concubine mother.[201] This law made permanent the temporary devices of Constantine and Zeno, and it did not require the mother to be an *ingenua*; the law evinces none of the usual prejudice against illegitimate children of low or servile mothers.[202] Any Abraham, without an Isaac, could have married Hagar and made Ishmael his heir. This law lasted on the books only two years, when Justin rescinded it, pardoning any who had already taken advantage of the dispensation but ruling that, in the future, "everyone should know that legitimate posterity is to be sought only in legitimate marriage, as though the aforementioned law had never been brought forth."[203]

Justinian would carry out a more circumscribed liberalization of Roman policy towards illegitimate children.[204] He issued an edict which made it easier to legitimize children born from a freedwoman or slave concubine.[205] In 528 Justinian increased the amount of an estate that could be left to

[198] See most recently Tate 2008b, 20–34. cf. Arjava 1998; Sargenti 1981.
[199] Nov. Theod. 22 (AD 442).   [200] Luchetti 1990, 65–172.
[201] CJ 5.27.6 (AD 517). Luchetti 1990, 202–16.
[202] See, for this interpretation, Navarra 1988, 465–8.
[203] CJ 5.27.7 (AD 519): *In posterum vero sciant omnes legitimis matrimoniis legitimam sibi posteritatem quaerendam, ac si praedicta constitutio lata non esset.*
[204] Arjava 1996, 216; Evans Grubbs 1995, 304.
[205] Nov. 18.11 (AD 536). Nov. 74 (AD 538). Still on the condition that no legitimate children existed. Nov. 78.3–4 (539). Melluso 2000, 158–62.

illegitimate children: one-half of the property, in the absence of legitimate heirs.[206] A series of rules made it progressively easier to legitimize offspring by enrolling them in a town council.[207] Justinian passed other measures which were favorable to servile women kept as concubines and the children born of these relationships. He ruled that if a slave-woman was kept as a concubine, a master was free to dispose of her as he wished during his lifetime or in his will. The slave-holder's rights were supreme. But, if his will made no disposition at all concerning the slave-woman kept as a concubine or her children, the legitimate heirs lost control over the woman and the children, who became free.[208] In another law, Justinian ruled that any testament in which the decedent explicitly declared a slave to be his illegitimate son was equivalent to an order to manumit the slave son.[209]

By 539 it was necessary to issue a lengthy law, preserved as *Novel* 89, giving systematic expression to Justinian's reforms. This *Novel* provides insight into the motivations – and limits – of Justinian's program. The emperor's favor towards illegitimate servile children was part of his broader ideological agenda of promoting *libertas*. *Novel* 89 expounded in a most systematic manner the state of the law on illegitimate children, even offering a guided tour through the history of Roman legislation on the question. Justinian's reform was interesting but not as radical as it may seem at first. It represented the triumph of his ideology of freedom over the social prejudices which existed against illegitimate and servile children – within limits. The social importance of Justinian's legislation should not be overemphasized. Only by enrollment in the council, marriage to a freed concubine, or imperial favor could legitimation be enacted; these were, to be sure, exceptional cases. Justinian explicitly attacked the measure of Anastasius which had permitted the father to legitimize his illegitimate children by his own decision. Justinian maintained a sharp distinction between marriage and concubinage, and he did nothing to discourage the sexual abuse of servile women. The sexual rights of slave-owners over their slave-women remained absolutely unfettered throughout late antiquity.

CONCLUSION: FROM ANTIQUITY TO THE MIDDLE AGES

The legislative record of late antiquity shows the rules being modified, and not the rules in their totality. Thus, an ongoing effort to tweak the rules in one tricky corner of the law can draw our eyes away from the center of

---

[206] CJ 5.27.8 (AD 528).   [207] Nov. 38.2 (AD 536); Nov. 89.2 (AD 539).
[208] CJ 7.15.3 (AD 531). cf. CJ 6.4.4.3.   [209] CJ 7.6.1.10 (AD 531).

the rules, the substance of the law as it related to society. This danger is particularly acute with the legislation on sex and status in late antiquity. We should never lose sight of the fact that the rules of *adulterium* and *stuprum* were the foundational law of the late Roman state and remained so through the reign of Justinian. These rules were part of a particular configuration between state and society that began, symbolically at least, with Augustus, and lasted throughout the entire late Roman period. The Roman law of sex was harmonized with a system of social reproduction in which property was passed to legitimate heirs created by legal, monogamous unions. As a consequence, ancient Mediterranean society placed great stress on the sexual honor of respectable women. Women married young, men married late. All of these factors created a sexual system in which dishonored women became the socially accepted outlet for surplus male sexuality. The sexual exploitation of slaves was institutionalized by society, and the Roman state colluded in this system. The state's aims were to establish rules for the transmission of property, to minimize social violence from conflicts over sexuality, to protect honorable women, to maintain the rules of status which legitimated the slave system, and to endorse a symbolic order of society, in which the ruling classes were purified of dishonored ancestry.

The core values of the Roman state changed remarkably little. The relation between sexual boundaries and social boundaries perdured, and the state remained a fundamental prop of the sexual system. The late Roman state was more aggressive, less subtle, in the construction and enforcement of its rules. This is partly, but not fully, an effect of the type of documents we possess – florid public pronouncements rather than juristic theory. But there is no doubt that the reign of Constantine, particularly the period of his sole rule, saw a distinct effort to harden the old rules and to enforce them more violently. Constantine's successors would not always continue his hard line. His stricter version of the SCC was not to last, while his rules against the transmission of property to illegitimate children were a matter of ongoing debate. Nevertheless, it is not until the sixth century that we sense deeper, more fundamental change: the abolition of the SCC after half a millennium, the liberalization of rules for legitimizing offspring. Even if the law in the age of Justinian does not present a radically different appearance, the structural integrity of the ancient system, beneath the surface, seems fragmented.

The fourth century was a late phase of a truly Roman configuration of state and society, in which the law shaped and stabilized social practice in a way that was truly in sync with the circuits of power in a patriarchal, slave-owning society. This configuration of state and society would be more fundamentally ruptured in the post-Roman period. By 533–4, one of the most powerful figures in the west, Athalaric, could promulgate a law against adultery – punishing *married men* for their "illicit lust." The law even disallowed sexual relationships between married men and their slaves.[210] The *Lex Visigothorum* instituted vicious penalties against prostitutes themselves.[211] These laws sit across a conceptual divide so enormous it is impossible to compare them with the public norms of the ancient world. In the east these laws came later, eventually protecting slaves from the sexual advances of the master.[212] Only such re-incarnations of the imperial state were willing to protect the sexual privacy of slaves against the master's power. This created a whole new configuration of state and society in the realm of sex, one without the organic coherence between patriarchy, property, and public law. The new configuration belongs to the medieval and modern worlds. Once the state intervenes even theoretically against the use of human chattel as private sexual objects, we have truly left behind the ancient world.

[210] Cass. Var. 9.18 (CC 96: 368–9).   [211] LV 3.4.17.   [212] Laiou 1993, 117–19.

CHAPTER 12

Rites of manumission, rights of the freed

THE LATE ANTIQUE EQUILIBRIUM: BETWEEN CHURCH AND STATE

On Easter day in 379, Gregory of Nyssa delivered a homily in which he described the atmosphere of joy and celebration which suffused the holiest day of the Christian calendar in late antiquity. The roads were empty, he declared, and the fields left without workers. All came to church in honor of the resurrected Christ. Indeed, in his native Cappadocia, it was unusual to see all of society's elements gathered together:[1]

The wife with the full complement of the household rejoices in celebration. The husband and the children and the slaves and all who share the hearth rejoice. Just like a swarm of bees that is newly born, away from the beehive for the first time in the air and the light, jointly clusters upon the branch of a tree, in the same way on this festival all the generations of the household run together to the hearth.[2]

The presence of the "full complement of the household," including the mistress and the slaves, made the communal gathering at Easter exceptional. The attendance of slaves was more than just decoration for the family on a public holiday, although it was that too.[3] The paschal season accrued a broad ritual importance in early Christianity, and in late antiquity the sacred liturgy absorbed a rite with tremendous secular importance, the manumission of slaves.[4]

The presence of slaves among the Easter crowd led Gregory to reflect on the nature of Christian manumission. Christians, he declared, freed their

---

[1] On the probable date (379) and location (Caesarea), Danielou 1955. Generally, see Spira and Klock 1981.
[2] Gr. Nyss. Pasch. 249 (Gebhardt: 249): ἡ ἔγγαμος ὅλῳ τῷ πληρώματι τῆς οἰκίας ἑορτάζουσα χαίρει. νῦν γὰρ αὐτῇ καὶ ὁ σύνοικος καὶ οἱ παῖδες καὶ οἱ οἰκέται καὶ πάντες ἐφέστιοι ἀγάλλονται. καὶ ὥσπερ τὸ σμῆνος τῶν μελισσῶν τὸ νέον καὶ ἀρτίτοκον πρῶτον τῆς καταδύσεως ἢ τῶν καλαθίσκων πρὸς τὸν ἀέρα καὶ τὸ φῶς ἐξιπτάμενον ἄθρουν ὁμοῦ καὶ συνημμένον ἑνὶ κλάδῳ δένδρου προσπλάσσεται, οὕτως ἐπὶ ταύτης τῆς ἑορτῆς ὁλόκληρα τὰ γένη πρὸς τὰς ἑστίας συντρέχει.
[3] On conspicuous consumption, see chapter 8.   [4] Rapp 2005, 240–1. CJ 3.12.7 (AD 392).

463

slaves "by the good and philanthropic proclamation of the church." This style of manumission he contrasted with secular forms of the manumission ceremony. Gregory claimed that Christian manumission was not accomplished "by a disgraceful slapping of the face, releasing slaves from blows with a blow." Christians did not perform the manumission of slaves in front of the populace "under the lofty tribunal, marking the beginning of liberty full of hubris and arrogance."[5] The secular manumission ceremony described by Gregory included the *alapa*, the ritual slap to the forehead, which marked the slave's passage into freedom. This slap was used in civil manumissions effected before a Roman magistrate, but Gregory's point of reference was perhaps more specific. Gregory was probably referring to the version of this ceremony carried out on the first of the year ("in pomp"), by the new consuls and by provincial governors, amidst wild celebration of the festivities which marked the annual installation of new officials. He contrasted this public ritual with the Christian rite, carried out according to Gregory with all the solemn dignity that the church could muster.

In Gregory's mind, the contrast between the rituals of church and the rituals of state was the surface reflection of a deeper rift between sacred and profane manumission. But Gregory is guilty of overstating the differences between ecclesiastical and civil manumission. It was under the direct authority of the imperial government that the Christian church was able to free slaves openly and legally. Gregory lived only a few generations after Constantine legitimized the practice of freeing slaves within the Catholic church, a significant grant of civil authority to a non-state entity. But Gregory also lived at a moment when both church and state were vital forces in Mediterranean society. It is significant that the consular manumission ceremony, the symbolic expression of the state's claim to regulate legal status was, for Gregory, the counterpoint of ecclesiastical manumission. This equilibrium is distinctly late Roman.

The church took the authority to manumit slaves from the empire. But ultimately, the institutions of the church would outlast the very state whence that authority originally flowed. The history of manumission in late antiquity is the story of this complex institutional transformation, in which the fourth-century church absorbed some civil functions of the state, in which church and state coexisted over a long cycle, but in which the state

---

[5] Gr. Nyss. Pasch. 250 (Gebhardt: 250): ὁ δοῦλος ἐλευθεροῦται τῷ ἀγαθῷ καὶ φιλανθρώπῳ τῆς ἐκκλησίας κηρύγματι οὐ ῥαπιζόμενος ἀσχημόνως κατὰ τῆς παρειᾶς καὶ πληγῇ τῆς πληγῆς ἀφιέμενος οὐδὲ ὥσπερ ἐν πομπῇ τῷ δήμῳ δεικνύμενος ἐφ᾽ ὑψηλῷ βήματι, ὕβριν δὲ ἔχων καὶ ἐρυθριασμὸν τὴν ἀρχὴν τῆς ἐλευθερίας.

eventually fragmented, leaving the church as the primary public institution in vast stretches of former imperial territory. Already a fifth-century juristic text could claim that there were three types of formal manumission – "by testament, in the church, or before the consul" – implying that ecclesiastical manumission had practically displaced manumission before a magistrate, with the single, majestic exception of the consular ceremony.[6] Even in the east, where a strong state survived, ecclesiastical manumission became the principal mode of freeing slaves by the sixth century.[7] Above all, this process must be described as an institutional, not an ideological, moral, or social revolution. Despite Gregory's optimism, the rise of Christianity did not revolutionize the ethical and emotional basis of manumission. Manumission, its causes and effects, never broke free from its secular moorings in late antiquity.

MANUMISSION IN THE ROMAN EMPIRE: FORMS AND EFFECTS

Chapter 5 has explored the complexity of manumission as a social institution somewhere between generosity and social control. This chapter explores manumission as a legal institution.[8] The late Roman Mediterranean was a world still profoundly shaped by the first emperor Augustus and his laws. Roman manumission in its classical form can be broadly categorized into two types, depending on the effect: manumission with Roman citizenship and manumission without full citizenship. To yield citizenship, the manumission had to be carried out by either of two methods, *vindicta* or *testamento*.[9] Manumission *vindicta* was accomplished by a master in his lifetime; it could be effected only by a Roman magistrate.[10] Manumission *testamento*, by contrast, did not require the intervention of a public magistrate. It is, plausibly, thought to have become the principal type of formal manumission in the empire, although the Augustan *lex Fufia Caninia* limited the proportion of slaves that a master could manumit in his will.[11] The method of manumission by testament carried the additional benefit to the

---

[6] Epit. Gai. 1.1: *testamento aut in ecclesia aut ante consulem.*   [7] Melluso 2000, 62.

[8] López Barja de Quiroga 2007; Watson 1987, 23–35; Buckland 1908, 437–597. Sirks 1983 and 1981 for informal manumission. Waldstein 1986; Treggiari 1969a, on freedmen. For manumission in late antiquity, see esp. Sargenti 1938, 59–70.

[9] Gaius, Inst. 1.17. Fr. Dos. 5. *Censu* was obsolete already in the imperial period: see Buckland 1908, 439–40.

[10] Dig. 40.2, with Wacke 1982, 127–34. cf. López Barja de Quiroga 2007, 16–34; Meylan 1953; and Lévy-Bruhl 1936 for different reconstructions. CJ 7.1.4 (AD 319) and PS 2.25.4, for the competent magistrates.

[11] Dig. 40.4, on testamentary manumission. Buckland 1908, 460. On the *lex Fufia Caninia*, Gardner 1991.

master that he could attach certain conditions, such as a specified term of service to his heirs, as a condition of the manumission.[12]

To grant citizenship, manumission not only had to be carried out in one of these two recognized forms by the Quiritary owner of the slave, the parties to the transaction had to meet certain requirements laid out by Augustus in the *lex Aelia Sentia*.[13] The manumittor had to be twenty years of age, the slave thirty.[14] The age of thirty was not a threshold that automatically or even normally brought freedom to the Roman slave, but it was the closest thing to a standard age of manumission which the Romans had. If the slave was under thirty, then upon manumission he or she became free but not a citizen.[15] There were certain situations in which the age requirements could be legally circumvented, and the law allowed full freedom with citizenship if the master secured formal approval.[16] A slave freed informally or without meeting the requirements of the *lex Aelia Sentia* could later be given full citizenship.[17]

A slave who was manumitted informally obtained freedom but not citizenship; likewise a manumission performed by an owner under twenty or on behalf of a slave under thirty.[18] Informal manumission cannot have been rare, particularly for masters who wished to free their slaves *inter vivos* but did not go before a magistrate. There were many informal rituals of manumission, which are somewhat obscured by the nature of the historical record; the umbrella term which is commonly used, *manumissio inter amicos*, reflects the public but not official character of informal manumission rituals.[19] The status of freedmen without Roman citizenship was regulated by the *lex Junia*, passed in the age of Augustus.[20] By this law, freedmen without citizenship acquired Latin status and hence were known as Junian Latins.[21] Junian Latin status was a legal construct within which the legal rights of the freedman as free person were protected. But the estate of the Junian Latin was treated as though it were still a *peculium*, the property of a slave.[22] The Junian Latin had no testamentary rights, so that on his death all of his property returned to his patron. Salvian described Junian Latin status most succinctly: they live as though free, die as though slaves.[23]

---

[12] Dig. 40.7, on *statu liberi*. Buckland 1908, 286–91.   [13] Buckland 1908, 537–44.
[14] Gaius, Inst. 1.38–9.   [15] Gaius, Inst. 1.17.
[16] Gaius, Inst. 1.18, 1.39; Dig. 40.2.15–6. Buckland 1908, 539.
[17] On *iteratio*, see Sirks 1983 and 1981.   [18] Gaius, Inst. 1.17–22.
[19] Gaius, Inst. 1.44. See López Barja de Quiroga 2007, 37–40; Scholl 2001; Balestri Fumagalli 1982; Albanese 1962 (overemphasizing the formal structure); Biscardi 1939; Buckland 1908, 446.
[20] Sirks 1981.   [21] Weaver 1997 and 1986.   [22] Gaius, Inst. 3.55–6.
[23] Salv. Eccl. 3.7.31 (SC 176: 264): *ut vivant scilicet quasi ingenui et moriantur ut servi.*

Salvian's pithy description of Latin status dates to the AD 440s. It has been asserted that Latin status gradually withered into obscurity in late antiquity.[24] There may well be some truth in this claim, for after Salvian little is heard of Latin status.[25] But caution is in order. Without Gaius, the *Digest*, and the corpora of inscriptions from Rome, we would know little about Junian Latins. Certainly a small number of late constitutions assume that Latin status was still a coherent and comprehensible fate.[26] Even in the age of universal citizenship, the denial of full citizen rights to Latins meant that the patron stood to inherit the entire estate of the freedman. This, indeed, was probably an important stimulus behind the enactment of the *lex Iunia*.[27] The demise of Latin status over the fifth century, then, could be partly ascribable to the decline of the western economy and the subsequent reduction of complex, commercially oriented household operations run by slaves and freedmen. And a better candidate to explain the demise of Latin status is the rise of *manumissio in ecclesia*, a new form of manumission *inter vivos* that entailed full citizen rights for the freedman.

Manumission, whatever its form, made the slave a free person. This new status meant that the slave was no longer chattel, a piece of property that could be bought and sold.[28] It did not mean that the slave was no longer obligated to his patron. As chapter 9 has already outlined, the patron retained significant claims on his freedman. Besides claims against the freedman's property (greater if the slave was a Latin, but not inconsiderable even if a citizen), the patron could expect labor and respect from his former slaves.[29] In Roman law, the freed slave owed labor in the form of *operae*, quantities of work established by contract; the amount of *operae* which could be demanded was legally limited, although great variety prevailed.[30] Slaves freed by testament, we must remember, could be subjected to more stringent conditions before they actually obtained their freedom.[31] Freedmen also owed their patrons *obsequium*, though it is important that what constituted *obsequium* was undefined.[32] Patrons could take legal action if they felt that their freedmen were ungrateful, *ingratus*. Failure to show *obsequium* was not distinct from "ingratitude."[33] The Diocletianic rescripts examined in chapter 9 reveal that conflicts between freedmen and their patrons, and their patrons' heirs, were commonplace. Patron–freedmen

---

[24] E.g. Arangio-Ruiz 1974, 272; Mitteis 1891, 379–81.   [25] Abolished by Justinian: CJ 7.6.1 (AD 531).
[26] CT 2.22.1 (AD 320): see p. 487. CT 4.12.3 (AD 320); CT 4.6.3 (AD 336), on which see chapter 11. CT 9.24.1 (AD 326); Nov. Marc. 4.1.1 (AD 454).
[27] Sirks 1981.   [28] Buckland 1908, 438. Also Samuel 1965.
[29] Andreau 1993, 183. Gaius, Inst. 3.39–76.   [30] Waldstein 1986. See chapter 9.
[31] Dig. 40.7 preserves numerous examples.   [32] Quadrato 1996.   [33] Dig. 37.14.19.

relations were a zone of structural tension, where the interface between law
and practice was inherently problematic; this fact lies behind many of the
changes to the law of manumission in late antiquity.

LATE ANTIQUE RITES: THE *ALAPA* AND *MANUMISSIO* IN ECCLESIA

The late empire witnessed the rise of new forms of manumission and the
hardening of rules governing patron–freedmen relations: new rites, fewer
rights. The imperial recognition of *manumissio in ecclesia* merits detailed
attention. But first it is worth considering another development, the significance of which is less immediately apparent. In late antiquity a slap on
the slave's face became a prominent part of manumission ceremonies. The
alapa of manumission, *rhapisma* in Greek, is abundantly attested but has
received little scholarly attention.[34] The evidence for the *alapa* congregates
in the late empire; besides a mention in the fables of Phaedrus, there is no
reference to the practice before the fourth century.[35] Then, in late antiquity, the evidence becomes abundant, in both Latin and Greek. The *alapa*
is scarcely mentioned in the corpus of Roman law, because it was not a
legally constitutive act.[36] Yet the slap became practically synonymous with
the act of manumission in the late antique sources. Ephraem the Syrian
could claim that "all slaves, when they are freed, receive the slap."[37] The
Spiritual Homilies of Pseudo-Macarius use the slap as a byword for manumission: "he was slapped like a slave being freed."[38] Gregory of Nyssa,
Pseudo-Caesarius, Sedulius, Claudian, and Isidore accepted it as a matter
of course that manumissions would include the ritual slap.[39] As Tondo
has perceptively noted, the verb "strike" in Greek became equivalent to
"manumit."[40]

The sources agree that the *alapa* was a blow delivered with the hand to the
side of the head. Claudian explicitly informs us that the slave's cheeks were

---

[34] Tondo 1967; Charvet 1953; Nisbet 1918.
[35] Phaed. Fab. 2.5 (Mueller: 26). Tondo 1967, 178. Cueva 2001, on Petronius.
[36] Buckland 1908, 451–2. Mentioned only twice in Roman law: Nov. 81 (AD 539) and CJ 8.48.6 (AD 531).
[37] Ephr. Syr. Serm. pass. Salv. 34 (Phrantzoles: 34): Πάντες μὲν οἱ οἰκέται, ὅταν ἐλευθεροῦνται, ῥάπισμα λαμβάνουσιν.
[38] Ps.-Mac. Hom. spir. 44.8 (Dörries, Klostermann, and Krüger: 295): καὶ ῥαπίσας ὡς δοῦλον ἠλευθέρωσεν.
[39] Ps.-Caes. Resp. 185 (Riedinger: 160); Gr. Nyss. Pasch. 250 (Gebhardt: 250); Sedul. Op. 5.7 (CSEL 10: 278); Claud. Quart. cons. Hon. lines 612–15 (Hall: 83); Isid. Hisp. Etym. 9.4.48 (Lindsay).
[40] Tondo 1967, 181.

"reddened."[41] John Malalas, describing the origins of the ritual, claimed the blow was given three times with the master's palm on the cheek, but he is the only source to mention multiple slaps.[42] Gregory also assumes the cheek.[43] The rise of the *alapa* seems to have displaced an older ritual in which a slave was spun around to symbolize the entry into a new state.[44] The spin is mentioned in early sources; the slap is mentioned in late sources. Only one author associates the two. Isidore claimed that *apud veteres* the slave was turned around, spun, by the slap, but he has conflated the *alapa* and the earlier practice of spinning the slave.[45] This comment has led to not a little confusion, because subsequent accounts have followed Isidore in conflating the spin and the slap.[46] The spin and the slap were clearly distinct; the spin is characteristic of the high empire, the slap of the later empire.[47]

The triumph of the *alapa* as a manumission rite was probably connected with the evolution of manumission *vindicta*, the type of formal civil manumission "per eccellenza."[48] There has been extensive modern debate over the form and nature of manumission *vindicta*, in part because the sources are oblique and contradictory.[49] One plausible reconstruction emphasizes two phases in the legal process: first the *dominus* asserted ownership and intention to manumit, then a *lictor* laid the rod, the *vindicta*, on the slave, marking the entry into freedom.[50] Regardless of the developments in the

---

[41] Claud. Quart. cons. Hon. lines 612–15 (Hall: 83): *rubuere genae*. The TLL, "Frons," 2.b.5, col. 1359, cites this passage for *frons* as *"fere i. q. caput."* *Contra* Tondo 1967, 182–3, the evidence points to the blow being administered by the master, not the consul, even in the consular manumission. His reading of Basil (at 197) is strained. Ammianus also implies that the consul, seeing the slap, *pronounced* them free (*dixerat*), and this allows a more straightforward reading of Libanius, Claudian, Gregory of Nyssa, and Malalas, too.

[42] Ioh. Mal. 7.9 (Thurn: 139–40). [43] Gr. Nyss. Pasch. 250 (Gebhardt: 250): κατὰ τῆς παρειᾶς.

[44] App. B. Civ. 4.135; Epict. Diss. 2.1.26 (Schenkl: 117); Ps.-Quint. Decl. 342 (Ritter: 350).

[45] Isid. Hisp. Etym. 9.4.48 (Lindsay). A scholion on Persius, where Isidore is repeated word for word, connects the spin with the slap. Comm. Corn. Pers. 5.75 (Clausen and Zetzel: 125). But this is not an independent source: either Isidore has copied the late antique scholion or, more likely, the medieval redactor of the scholia has borrowed from Isidore, which he does elsewhere. Zetzel 2005. The satire of Persius has nothing to say about a slap: Pers. Sat. 5.75–82 (Clausen: 24). On CJ 8.48.6 (AD 531), Tondo 1967, 175–7, who recognized that Isidore's passage was "palesemente assurda."

[46] E.g. Buckland 1908, 452.

[47] Appian says that the slave was spun by taking his hand: App. B. Civ. 4.135.

[48] Tondo 1967, 193. See too Watson 1987, 24–5; Kaser 1975, vol. II, 101, 253; Buckland 1908, 441–2, 451–9. The *alapa* was used in formal manumissions before Roman magistrates: Bas. Hom. exh. bapt. 3 (PG 31: 429); Libanius, Claudian, Cassiodorus, and Sidonius, all refer to manumission before a magistrate.

[49] Buckland 1908, 452.

[50] López Barja de Quiroga 2007, 20–6. See Wolf 1991 and Wacke 1982, 127–34, with earlier literature. Tondo 1967 and Meylan 1953. Lévy-Bruhl 1936 for a dissenting view. For the role of the *lictor*, esp. Dig. 40.2.23 (Diocletianic) and Boeth. Ad Cic. Top. 2.10 (PL 64: 1060).

classical period, in the late empire the *alapa* seems to have become the characteristic act of the *dominus*, perhaps replacing earlier rituals in which the master laid a rod on the slave to assert his ownership.[51] This accords with an important passage in Basil, which provides the clearest statement of the ritual's meaning: the blow was a symbol of the final act of violence that the slave would have to bear before he entered the state of freedom.[52] The *alapa* was thus an assertion of the master's power, and at the same time part of a rite of passage marking the transition from slavery to freedom.

The newfound prominence of the *alapa* in late antiquity is notable and is not merely an accident of the surviving evidence. Mentioned but once in the earlier periods, the *alapa* was simply presumptive among late antique authors, geographically spread from Syria to Spain. The rise of the *alapa* was a change in ritual, but it is worth considering how a new ritual could become so widespread. It is not unreasonable to suppose that the diffusion and standardization of this ritual was driven by the Roman state, which in the late empire performed ritual acts of manumission on the Kalends in provincial and imperial capitals across the empire. Libanius, Claudian, Gregory, and Sidonius explicitly mention the slap in connection with the consular manumission ceremony.[53] The diffusion of this ritual reflects the process of legal and cultural homogenization in an age of universal citizenship. If the consular manumission ceremony originated in the early fourth century, it also explains the chronological distribution of the evidence. Not unlike the steady expansion of the Kalends as an imperial holiday, the slap of manumission, performed annually before the holder of the highest honor in Roman society, gradually became synonymous with the act of manumission across the empire.[54]

It is worth noting that the *alapa* is perhaps the only form of manumission for which visual attestation survives.[55] Wiltheim, in his seventeenth-century

---

[51] López Barja de Quiroga 2007, 23–4.

[52] Bas. Hom. exh. bapt. 3 (PG 31: 429). More plausible than the theory of Nisbet 1918, that the ear is the seat of memory. Tondo 1967, 187, unconvincingly refuses to allow that the blow symbolizes the last experience of slavery. Claudian's poem also suggests that this one "happy" blow would free the slave from the lash permanently. Claud. Quart. cons. Hon. 615 (Hall: 83).

[53] Lib. Or. 12.101 (Foerster vol. 2: 44–5); Claud. Quart. cons. Hon. 612–15 (Hall: 83); Gr. Nyss. Pasch. 250 (Gebhardt: 250); Sid. Carm. 2.544–6 (Mohr: 255).

[54] Ioh. Mal. Chron. 7.9 (Thurn: 139–40), too, claims that the act was performed by governors in their provinces, which would further explain its successful diffusion. He places the gubernatorial manumission practiced in his day on the festival of the Consilia, presumably the Consualia, an August festival (rather than the Kalends) apparently still celebrated in secular form: see Roueché 1993, 6.

[55] The relief sculpture from Mariemont is probably a circus scene: esp. Wacke 1982; Ville 1963. cf. Pack 1980.

commentary, identified as a manumission the scene on the lower left panel of an ivory diptych commemorating the consulate of Anastasius in AD 517 (see figure 12.1).[56] Although most subsequent commentators have thought of the scene as a healing of the blind or a mime act, it is probably in fact a manumission.[57] It is possible to say definitively, on iconographic grounds, that the scene is not a healing of the blind.[58] A mime scene it may well be, especially given the exotic dress of the masters and the fact that mimes were a popular part of the Kalends ceremonies (which the diptychs commemorate). But even if it is a mime scene, it is likely that the characters in the play are performing a manumission. The slaps they deliver to the slaves are choreographed motion, rather than random violence, and the pose of the masters suggests a formal act.[59] In all probability, the scene is a manumission within a mime. If so, it is a quintessentially late antique image: a universal manumission ritual, within a mime act, performed as part of the consular installation, and frozen in time on an ivory diptych.

If the *alapa* had little substantive significance and has gone largely ignored, the other major change in late antique manumission rituals carried tremendous legal significance and has been the object of plentiful discussion. Under Constantine manumission in the Christian church was first recognized by the Roman state.[60] The favor shown to the Catholic church in Constantine's reform is self-evident, and many historians have inferred a relationship to Christian social doctrine: manumission in the church "trova il suo naturale terreno, la sua remota radice, nei princìpi cristiani."[61] But manumission was not liberation writ small.[62] Constantine's maneuver was not an emancipation proclamation; it was the insinuation of the Christian church into the institutional framework of slavery. Ancient Christianity was not especially concerned with forms of social liberation. The scriptural core of Christianity records how a radical apocalyptic movement quickly

---

[56] Wilthelmius 1659. This Anastasius was a relative of the emperor by the same name.
[57] Olovsdotter 2005, 49 (healing of the blind); Delbrueck 1929, 132 (parody of a healing). Webb 2008, 24–5 (mime act of obscure content); Volbach 1976, 36–7 (tragic). Leclercq 1921 (manumission).
[58] Smith 1918, 94–101, is helpful, esp. Table VI, with a comprehensive taxonomy of iconographical features of healing scenes. In the vast majority of examples, including those which are closest in date, medium, and region of production, the distinct image of Christ's fingers touching the eyes of the blind is emphasized. In most late antique representations, the blind person is also carrying a walking staff, absent in our scene. Above all, in *every* other healing of the blind, the head of the supplicant is erect or forward, not reeling backward as in the Anastasius diptych.
[59] Contrast the relief from the theater at Sabratha, Libya: Webb 2008, plate 8.
[60] Girardet 2008; Herrmann-Otto 2008; Sargenti 1986, 55–70; Herrmann 1980, 232–60; Langenfeld 1977, 24–37; Fabbrini 1965.
[61] Fabbrini 1965, 195. Caron 1983, 315; Biondi 1952–4, vol. 2, 400; Dupont 1937, 41–2; Duff 1928, 197. More prudent are Bradley 1994, 158, and Sargenti 1986, 55–6.
[62] Harrill 1995, *passim*, esp. 4.

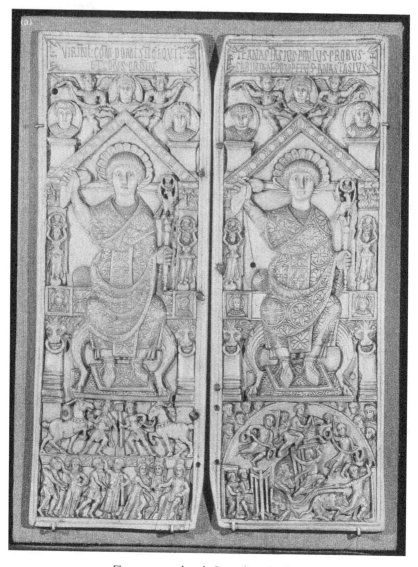

Figure 12.1a and 12.1b Ivory diptych of 517
Source: Courtesy of the Bibliothèque nationale de France

Figure 12.1 (*cont.*)

settled into Roman society.[63] The interpretation of *First Corinthians*, where Paul enjoined slaves to "use" their condition, became a debate over whether Christian slaves should seek manumission at all.[64] Emancipation simply never was and never became a goal of ancient Christianity.[65]

If Christianity promoted manumission in any new sense, it was as a part of a more general impetus to asceticism.[66] John Chrysostom, who was not afraid to support socially radical beliefs when he felt compelled, came down firmly against the independent value of manumission. He interpreted Paul's command to mean that slaves should not seek freedom.[67] He was,

---

[63] Meeks 1983.

[64] 1 Cor. 7:20–1. Patristic interpreters like Chrysostom were misreading his intent: Harrill 1995, 68–128; Corcoran 1985, 88–9.

[65] Canon 3 of the Council of Gangra condemned those who taught slaves to flee their masters in the name of piety – implying that some Christians were doing exactly that. But the language implies that these slaves were encouraged to join the ascetic movement, not resist in any political sense, and the orthodox church came down hard against slaves who became monks without their master's consent. See Grieser 2001.

[66] Garnsey 1999a, 700, and 1996, 99. E.g. Ps.-Mac. Hom. spir. 40.3 (Dörries, Klostermann, and Krüger: 276).

[67] Ioh. Chrys. In 1 Cor. 19.4–5 (PG 61: 155–7); Ioh. Chrys. Serm. in Genes. 5.84–99 (SC 433: 258–60).

however, bothered by conspicuous consumption and abhorred the showy public presence of the wealthy classes. Chrysostom would urge his listeners to own at most one or two slaves. Otherwise, he claimed in a passage that affords a glimpse into the rationalization of slave-ownership, it was no longer "philanthropy."[68] Chrysostom decided to expose the self-interest behind the rationalization:

So, if it is really out of care for them that you keep slaves, order them not to serve you. Instead, buy them, and having taught them a trade to support themselves, let them go free. When you lash them and chain them up, it is no longer a humanitarian deed. I know that I am wearisome to my listeners, but what can I do? I'm taking my stand and I won't stop saying these things, whether anything more comes of it or not.[69]

For Chrysostom, manumission was not a good deed *per se*, and it was patently undesirable as a mechanism of social change. But insofar as it coincided with asceticism, it was spiritually profitable. Chrysostom sensed he was beyond the mainstream, prodding and provoking Christian masters for fooling themselves into thinking it was humanitarian to own slaves. But ultimately, it was lavish wealth that offended him, not slavery.

The Christian church did not promote manumission, nor is manumission a pure, liberatory practice. Constantine's laws on manumission in the church cannot sustain an idealist interpretation. They belong firmly to the institutional developments of his reign. His laws on manumission in the church should be studied in the context of his laws as a whole: his other laws on slavery, on freedmen, on the church, and on testation. When considered as part of broader institutional shifts, and as a response to the social pressures of manumitting slaves, his program of ecclesiastical manumission takes on a different complexion. Constantine the liberal visionary must step aside for Constantine the patron of Catholic legitimacy and – above all – Constantine the perceptive institutional reformer.

The historian Sozomen informs us that Constantine passed three laws on manumission in the church: "Because of the strictness of the laws and many hindrances standing in the way of the master's wish to obtain the better form of freedom, which is called Roman citizenship, the emperor passed three laws resolving that all who were freed in the church with the priests

---

[68] Ioh. Chrys. In 1 Cor. 40.5 (PG 61: 353–4): οὐ φιλανθρωπίας ἕνεκεν.

[69] Ioh. Chrys. In 1 Cor. 40.5 (PG 61: 354): ἐπεί, εἰ κηδόμενος, μηδένα εἰς διακονίαν ἀπασχολήσῃς τὴν σήν, ἀλλ᾽ ἀγοράσας, καὶ τέχνας διδάξας ὥστε ἀρκεῖν ἑαυτοῖς, ἄφες ἐλευθέρους. Ὅταν δὲ μαστίζῃς, ὅταν δεσμεύῃς, οὐκέτι φιλανθρωπίας τὸ ἔργον. Καὶ οἶδα μὲν ὅτι φορτικός εἰμι τοῖς ἀκούουσιν. ἀλλὰ τί πάθω; Εἰς τοῦτο κεῖμαι, καὶ οὐ παύσομαι ταῦτα λέγων, ἄν τε γένηταί τι πλέον, ἄν τε μηδέν.

as witnesses deserved the Roman citizenship."[70] Sozomen was trained as a lawyer and was presumably informed by the *Theodosian Code*.[71] The first five books of the *Theodosian Code* have sustained particularly serious damage, and it is probable that there were originally three laws in the title CT 4.7. Only one law presently survives from this title, and another is known from the *Justinianic Code*, while a third is probably missing altogether. Because of the imperfect state of the evidence, the significance and order of the extant texts are debated.

The law CJ 1.13.1, surviving only in the *Justinianic Code*, was issued to a Protogenes and carries a date of 8 June, 316, in the manuscripts. A second law, CT 4.7.1, survives in the *Theodosian Code* as well as the *Justinianic Code*. It was issued to Osius and is securely dated to April of 321. The first problem is the relative dating of the laws. Many, including Seeck, have tried to switch their order.[72] Seeck thought that the consular dating of CJ 1.13.1, the law issued to Protogenes, should be changed from 316 (consuls Sabinus and Rufinus) to 323 (Severus and Rufinus). This would make the law issued to Osius the original and the law given to Protogenes a follow-up. Bellen added credibility to this theory by noting that the missing third law, then, could be CT 2.8.1, issued in 321, which permitted legal acts, such as emancipation and manumission, on Sundays.[73]

Some historians leave the laws in the order they stand.[74] The manuscripts say that CJ 1.13.1 was given to Protogenes. It is often assumed that this Protogenes is to be identified with a contemporary bishop of Serdica of the same name.[75] This becomes problematic, because the manuscripts date the law to "vi. id. Iun," in the year 316. But in June of 316, Licinius was in control of Serdica (assuming the battle of Cibalae was in 316). The battle at Cibalae was fought in October, and Constantine only occupied the Danubian provinces in the late fall.[76] Corcoran has "hesitantly" emended the law to read "vi k. ian."[77] Constantine can be placed in Serdica in December of 316, and this would have him issuing the law on 27 December of that year.[78] But these elaborate re-datings are probably unnecessary. Protogenes is not

---

[70] Soz. H.E. 1.9.6 (GCS 50: 21): Ὑπὸ γὰρ ἀκριβείας νόμων καὶ ἀκόντων τῶν κεκτημένων πολλῆς δυσχερείας οὔσης περὶ τὴν κτῆσιν τῆς ἀμείνονος ἐλευθερίας, ἣν πολιτείαν Ῥωμαίων καλοῦσι, τρεῖς ἔθετο νόμους ψηφισάμενος πάντας τοὺς ἐν ταῖς ἐκκλησίαις ἐλευθερουμένους ὑπὸ μάρτυσι τοῖς ἱερεῦσι πολιτείας Ῥωμαϊκῆς ἀξιοῦσθαι.

[71] Bidez, SC 306: 18–24.

[72] Herrmann 1980, 233–5; Seeck 1919, 35, 88.   [73] Bellen 1967, 319–23.

[74] Girardet 2008, 292–4; Sargenti 1986, 63–70; Langenfeld 1977, 25–31; Fabbrini 1965, 64–8.

[75] Girardet 2008, 292.   [76] Barnes 1982, 73.   [77] Corcoran 1993, 307.

[78] Barnes initially proposed the emendation, without indicating that the ides would have to be changed to Kalends to keep the law in December 316 rather than January 317. Corcoran would "hesitantly" emend the date to 27 December. See now Girardet 2008, 293–4.

an unusual name, and it is possible that the recipient is not the bishop of Serdica.[79] It is possible that the battle of Cibalae was in 314.[80] And it is even remotely possible that in June of 316, Licinius – not Constantine – issued a rescript about manumission in the church.[81] In sum, there is no insuperable objection to the year 316 as the date for CJ 1.13.1.

On purely technical grounds, the evidence does not allow a decisive conclusion about the law's date. The discussion must shift to the legal effects of each law, and the most plausible reconstruction is that the original enactment recognizing ecclesiastical manumission is lost, while the manuscript dates for the two extant laws, to the years 316 and 321, are correct. In this account, at some point before 316, Constantine recognized the validity of manumission in the church in a legal enactment which is lost. This act is paralleled by his policy of tolerance and favoritism for the Catholic church in the very first years of his reign as sole emperor of the west.[82] Legalizing Christianity meant affirming its place in the public sphere, and the approval of Christian manumission was an important part of that program. Before Constantine's recognition of *manumissio in ecclesia*, Christians, like other citizens, used "informal" mechanisms to manumit slaves.[83] Roman law acknowledged the existence of these informal means of manumission, such as *manumissio inter amicos*.[84] With *manumissio in ecclesia*, the imperial government gave its blessing to one of these informal means which had developed beyond the activity of Roman magistrates. Constantine raised this informal ceremony to the status of a state-endorsed formal procedure.

The law of 316 assumed that manumission in the church was already a recognized procedure.[85] The emperor wrote:

For some time now it has been accepted that masters may offer their slaves freedom in the Catholic church, if it is done in view of the public and with Christian priests standing as witness, in such a way that some sort of written document is brought forward in which they sign as witnesses to commemorate the deed on behalf of these parties. Thus, by you also, it is not undeserved that freedom is given or bequeathed in any agreement that any of you will wish, so long as manifest proof of your intention is apparent.[86]

---

[79] Lenski forthcoming, considers this possibility.
[80] Recently re-asserted, Girardet 2008.   [81] Corcoran 1993, on Licinian laws generally.
[82] Girardet 2008, 295; Fabbrini 1965, 80–9. More generally, Herrmann 1980, 205–390.
[83] Sargenti 1986, 58–61; Herrmann 1980, 132–49; Langenfeld 1977, 25.
[84] Scholl 2001; Balestri Fumagalli 1982; Calderone 1971.   [85] Sargenti 1986, 67–8.
[86] CJ 1.13.1: *Iam dudum placuit, ut in ecclesia catholica libertatem domini suis famulis praestare possint, si sub adspectu plebis adsistentibus christianorum antistitibus id faciant, ut propter facti memoriam vice actorum interponatur qualiscumque scriptura, in qua ipsi vice testium signent. Unde a vobis quoque ipsis non immerito dandae et relinquendae sunt libertates, quo quis vestrum pacto voluerit, dummodo vestrae voluntatis evidens appareat testimonium.*

The emperor claimed that manumission in the church had been allowed "for some time now." To be legal, the act required a witnessing public, the presence of a bishop, and a written document: minimum formal requirements to certify the performance of the manumission. The text of this law stated that clerics could manumit slaves or give them freedom in a will, though the mention of testation is possibly an interpolation of the sixth-century editors.[87]

The third law survives in the *Theodosian Code*. It was issued in 321 to Osius, the Spanish bishop and advisor to Constantine:

Anyone who, with a reverent heart, should grant deserved freedom to their slaves inside the church, shall be seen to have given it according to that legal principle by which, when all the formalities are observed, the Roman citizenship has customarily been granted. But this freedom is granted only in the case of those who shall give it under the supervision of the priests. We further concede to clerics, however, that whoever among them grants freedom to his own slaves, they shall be said to concede the full enjoyment of freedom, not only when they act in the eyes of the church and the congregation of believers, but also when they grant freedom by final legal testament or command it to be given by any words, so that on the day the will is published they achieve express freedom, without any witness or intercessor of this right.[88]

The law of 316 made no explicit distinction between formal or informal manumission. The law of 321 specified that *manumissio in ecclesia* would result in full Roman citizenship: it was equivalent to manumission before a magistrate. This power was a major innovation in legal terms, and a significant expansion that made formal manumission *inter vivos* much easier. Sozomen claimed that the reason for Constantine's recognition of manumission in the church was precisely the difficulty of obtaining full manumission with complete Roman citizenship. The law of 321 is more specific about the Roman citizenship, but Fabbrini convincingly argued that the original enactment, now lost, must have allowed this capacity, the second law, CJ 1.13.1 of 316 to Protogenes, simply assumed it, and the third law, CT 4.7.1 of 323, explicitly re-affirmed it.[89]

---

[87] Mor 1928.

[88] CT 4.7.1: *Qui religiosa mente in ecclesiae gremio servulis suis meritam concesserint libertatem, eandem eodem iure donasse videantur, quo civitas Romana sollemnitatibus decursis dari consuevit; sed hoc dumtaxat his, qui sub aspectu antistitum dederint, placuit relaxari. Clericis autem amplius concedimus, ut, cum suis famulis tribuunt libertatem, non solum in conspectu ecclesiae ac religiosi populi plenum fructum libertatis concessisse dicantur, verum etiam, cum postremo iudicio libertates dederint seu quibuscumque verbis dari praeceperint, ita ut ex die publicatae voluntatis sine aliquo iuris teste vel interprete conpetat directa libertas.*

[89] Fabbrini 1965, 56–68.

CT 4.7.1 re-stated the existing right to manumit *inter vivos* and then added a detailed description about the privileges of the clergy. Clerics were allowed to bestow freedom by testament. Moreover, this testamentary act could be accomplished "by any words." Roman law required formal language in these types of instructions, but Constantine allowed clerics to leave their commands in "any words." Constantine specified that the manumission was valid without any attestation or action by an agent. Legal wills were witnessed acts, and after the testator died, the seals of the witnesses were broken and the will was read publicly.[90] Constantine's intention was emphatic: a cleric's wish to manumit his own slave by a will was immediately and irrefutably effective. The law ensured that clerics had the privilege of leaving freedom to their slaves through a will, without any technical hindrances.

Testamentary manumission was common.[91] A will could either command the slave's freedom directly or empower an agent to perform the manumission. If a slave was granted direct freedom, it was accomplished immediately. If the testator appointed an agent to perform the manumission (*fideicommissum*), the agent would carry out one of the normal means of freeing the slave. If the manumission was performed by *fideicommissum*, the agent became the patron of the slave. Under CT 4.7.1, the slave freed in the will of a cleric obtained "*directa libertas*," freedom conferred without any intervening action of the heir. It is distinct from fideicommissary manumission, which required legal manumission to be effected at some later point by the trustee.[92] Mor argued, plausibly, that CT 4.7.1 allowed the *libertini* of clerics, freed by testament, to enjoy complete freedom without owing obligations to a patron.[93] The whole law implies, of course, that clerics like everyone else were often in no rush to manumit their slaves *inter vivos*. They recognized the benefits of holding their slaves until death.

The law of 321 did not create manumission in the church nor did it raise it to the status of formal manumission. The concern with testation, and specifically clerical testation, should be considered the main purpose of this law, and it corresponded closely to Constantine's legislative preoccupations in this period.[94] Constantine's tenure as emperor of the western empire saw a campaign to simplify important aspects of the law of property, especially with regard to the law of inheritance.[95] Constantine tried to reduce the practice of informing against claims to property or wills. His feelings about

---

[90] Champlin 1991, 5–6, 75–6.   [91] Buckland 1908, 479–532.
[92] CJ 7.2.4. Berger 1953, 438. Buckland 1908, 479–513.   [93] Mor 1928, 101.
[94] Sargenti 1986, 68–9.   [95] Evans Grubbs 1995, 112–23.

delation were sharp and simple. In the words of a Constantinian law, delation was "the single worst evil in human life."[96]

This legislative program was particularly energetic in 320 and 321. In 320 Constantine issued an *Ad Populum* edict which not only overturned the Augustan inheritance restrictions, but also vastly simplified inheritance procedures.[97] Constantine eliminated the requirement for formal, legal language in a valid will. In words that strikingly recall the language of the law on manumission given to Osius, Constantine gave testators "the free power of using any words whatsoever."[98] In 320 Constantine both created the possibility for childless men and women to create legally valid testaments disposing of their property, and he eliminated the formalist requirements of these documents. Thus the law of 321 makes sense as a re-affirmation that clerics could not only free their slaves through a will, but that they could do so without any technical language and without any further action required by agents.

Constantine took special care to protect wills that involved the church. On 3 July, 321, a constitution was posted at Rome which validated post-mortem gifts to the church. The law made Constantine's purpose clear: "there shall not be meaningless contests."[99] This law was issued within weeks, if not days, of the measure on manumission in the church. In the spring of 321, Constantine was at Sirmium. The law on manumission was given to Osius on 18 April, 321. The law permitting the church to acquire property through testaments was posted at Rome on 3 July. Naturally, time elapsed for travel from the Danube to Rome, and the law posted at Rome was given a month or two earlier.[100] The law on manumission in the church, with its emphasis on testamentary procedure, came out of the consistory at nearly the same time as the law protecting wills that left property to the church. Over these years, Constantine was aiming to curtail litigation over wills, in particular those pertaining to the church, by dropping formalist requirements.[101]

Wills were often bitterly contested. "Do you not see those who are always challenging wills in the courtrooms?"[102] Wills involving gifts to the church would be especially prone to provoke challenges from heirs

---

[96] CT 10.10.2: *unum maximum humanae vitae malum.* [97] See chapter 11.
[98] CJ 6.23.15: *quibuscumque verbis uti liberam habeant facultatem.*
[99] CT 16.2.4: *non sint cassa iudicia.*
[100] The edict given at Serdica on 31 January of 320 was posted at Rome on 1 April: Seeck 1919, 169.
[101] Barnes 1981, 50.
[102] Ast. Am. 3.8 (Datema: 32): Ἡ οὐχ ὁρᾷς τοὺς συνεχῶς ἐν τοῖς δικαστηρίοις κατὰ τῶν διαθηκῶν ἀγωνιζομένους; Champlin 1991, 82–102. See CJ 7.4.12 (AD 294); CJ 7.2.10 (AD 293); CJ 7.16.32 (AD 294); CJ 7.2.12 (AD 293).

or disinherited relations. The property of clergymen might be vulnerable, since many of them may not have had direct lineal descendants to act as heirs and since the unhindered right of childless men and women to transmit property was a recent reform of Constantine. Manumission by will was a practice fraught with uncertainty, doubly so if it involved clerics.[103] CT 4.7.1 was a comprehensive protection of a cleric's right to manumit his slaves by testament. Given the extremity of this dispensation and the thrust of Constantine's other laws in the same narrow period, the inference must be that the law issued to Osius was essentially about the procedures of clerical testation. This solution has the distinct advantage of fitting into the broader chronology of Constantine's legislative concerns and his contemporary fixation on ecclesiastical property and testation around 320–1.

One late antique document provides particular insights into the delicate situation faced by clerics who wished to free slaves in their wills. "The earliest complete Roman law will" from antiquity is, in fact, a late antique document written by a Christian bishop.[104] The will was composed by Gregory of Nazianzus.[105] During his time in Constantinople, Gregory fell ill and consequently wrote a will. Gregory knew the perils of settling an estate: his brother, Caesarius, died unexpectedly and Gregory was left to handle his property.[106] Caesarius had been a successful man, serving as court physician, and left behind a considerable amount of wealth, much of it scattered in various land-holdings. Gregory found himself quarreling with slaves, overseers, and creditors. Eventually he gave up and turned the estate over to the imperial treasury.[107] Gregory's own will was thus the document of a man experienced in the hazards of testation. And even though it is the will of an ascetic, who claimed that "all" his property had "already" been left to the church, the will reflects the challenges facing a clerical slave-owner in late antiquity.[108]

Gregory declared his will "valid and effective in every court and before every authority."[109] Gregory appointed three overseers who were to administer his property for the charitable purposes of the church:

---

[103] cf. a real case: Aug. Serm. 356 (Lambot: 134–7).
[104] Champlin 1991, 29. Now Jones 2004, 95–100.   [105] Van Dam 1995, esp. 119–26; Martroye 1924.
[106] Van Dam 1995, 122; Gallay 1943, 90.
[107] Bas. Ep. 32.1–2 (Courtonne: 74). Van Dam 1995, 122–6.
[108] *Diatheke*, lines 10–12 (Beaucamp: 30): Ἤδη ... πᾶσάν. Beaucamp, 48, believes that Gregory had already granted the revenues of his properties to the poor via the church, but not yet rendered full ownership. On the scale of his property, see Coulie 1985, 10–21, and 28.
[109] *Diatheke*, lines 8–9 (Beaucamp: 30): κυρίαν καὶ βεβαίαν ἐπὶ παντὸς δικαστηρίου καὶ πάσης ἐξουσίας. See commentary, 47–8.

Marcellus, deacon and monk, Gregorius, a deacon originally from Gregory's "household," implying he had been Gregory's slave, and Eustathius, a monk also from Gregory's household.[110] Gregory installed the deacon and monk Gregorius, a freed member of his household, as his heir.[111] Gregory named a trusted freedman as his heir, but not without a stern warning to keep the "fear of God in front of his eyes" and to maintain "all" his property for the maintenance of the poor.[112] Gregory was at the mercy of the trustworthiness *and* the competence of his freedman heir.

"All the slaves whom I freed, either of my own volition or at the command of my blessed parents, I wish all of them now to stay in freedom and their entire *peculium* to remain secure and undisturbed."[113] This clause reveals a pattern of complex, multi-generational slave-ownership. Gregory not only had slaves that he had manumitted and given a *peculium*, he had also manumitted slaves at his parents' request, presumably by *fideicommissum* or after the fulfillment of a condition – very possibly *paramonê* service for Gregory or his siblings. Gregory ordered that they remain in freedom. The confirmation of their freedom was legally superfluous but not imprudent given the social vulnerability of freedmen.

Gregory's will provided for a female relative, Russiana. He gave her funds to install herself in an estate of her choosing. He added, "I also wish that two slave-maidens whom she has selected be delivered to her, indeed that they should serve her for the rest of her life. If she is grateful to them, let her have the capacity to honor them with freedom. But if not, these too should be conveyed to the church."[114] This grant was a sort of *usufruct* in the two slave-girls, rather than *dominium*, for the slaves returned to the ownership of the church at her death. But he did explicitly grant her the capacity to manumit them, or equally not to manumit them, according to her wishes.[115] She was to have this essential tool of the slave-holder at her

---

[110] *Diatheke*, lines 13–8 (Beaucamp: 30): ἐκ τῆς οἰκίας μου.

[111] *Diatheke*, lines 19–20 (Beaucamp: 30). Beaucamp, 51, "cette formule transpose en grec les termes latins solennels . . . "

[112] *Diatheke*, lines 27–31 (Beaucamp: 32): τὸν τοῦ Θεοῦ φόβον πρὸ ὀφθαλμῶν . . . πᾶσάν μου τὴν οὐσίαν.

[113] *Diatheke*, lines 32–5 (Beaucamp: 32): Τοὺς οὖν οἰκέτας, οὓς ἠλευθέρωσα, εἴτε ἐξ ἐμῆς προαιρέσεως εἴτε ἐξ ἐντολῶν τῶν μακαρίων γονέων μου, τούτους πάντας βούλομαι καὶ νῦν ἐλευθέρους μένειν καὶ τὰ πεκούλια αὐτοῖς πάντα μένειν βεβαίως ἀνενόχλητα.

[114] *Diatheke*, lines 52–5 (Beaucamp: 34): Προστεθῆναι δὲ αὐτῇ βούλομαι καὶ δύο κόρας, ἃς ἂν αὐτὴ ἐπιλέξηται, οὕτω μέντοι ὥστε αὐτῇ παραμεῖναι τὰς κόρας, ἃς αὐτὴ ἐπιλέχηται, οὕτω μέντοι ὥστε αὐτῇ παραμεῖναι τὰς κόρας μέχρι τοῦ τῆς ζωῆς αὐτῆς χρόνου. καὶ εἰ μὲν αὐταῖς εὐχαριστήσειεν, ἐξεῖναι αὐτῇ ἐλευθερίᾳ τιμῆσαι αὐτάς · εἰ δὲ μή, καὶ αὐτὰς διενεγκεῖν τῇ αὐτῇ ἐκκλησίᾳ.

[115] cf. CJ 3.33.9 (AD 293).

disposal. Gregory was still an active slave-owner, willing to buy or transfer human property, and he assumed that an aging Christian woman would need two slave attendants. Gregory dealt with three more slaves, too. "I have already manumitted Theophilus, the slave who serves me."[116] Theophilus was a freedman bound by a *paramonê* clause. Theophilus was given five *solidi* as a legacy. His brother Eupraxius was still a slave, and he was declared free and given a legacy of five *solidi* as well.[117] Gregory freed another slave, Theodosius, his secretary, and gave him the same legacy.[118] It is impossible to say what accounted for the staggered manumission of Gregory's slaves. The variables of friendship, control, reward, and obedience were at play.

Gregory's testament is one of the most complete to survive from antiquity. It offers a still-shot of an ascetic, most of whose property was presumably already given to the church. It illustrates the complicated but precise apportionment of human property and human labor between multiple generations. It exemplifies the perils of manumission and testation. Gregory the patriarch wanted his slaves to be freed, even as he worried for their fate and the fate of the other anonymous freedmen. He knew all too well that his control over the future was only as strong as his testament. Slavery was a system of human property, and whatever his personal benevolence, Gregory's ownership of slaves implicated him in the practice, with its complications and risks, and the inescapable consequences of bartering in humans.[119]

In the laws on ecclesiastical manumission, as in documents such as Gregory's will, there is often a dark lining which reminds us of the real nature of any institution so embedded in the practice of holding humans as property. The concern over the efficacy of testamentary manumission among the clergy reiterates the secular complications of manumission. Manumission was a delicate social act, and *manumissio in ecclesia* was supremely responsive to this aspect of freeing slaves. From its inception, manumission in the church was meant to be a well-armored institutional response to the complex of social problems inherent in the practice of manumission. Diocletian's rescripts show an imperial government that was constantly mediating disputes created by the alienation of this most complicated form of property: 51 of the 185 Hermogenian rescripts involving slavery touched, in some way, on manumission. Manumission was an institutional problem. This is a primary fact, and it must be at the center of any attempt to explain *why* manumission in the church was created.

---

[116] *Diatheke*, lines 57 (Beaucamp: 34): Θεόφιλον τὸν παῖδα, τὸν παραμένοντά μοι, ἤδη ἠλευθέρωσα.
[117] *Diatheke*, lines 58–60 (Beaucamp: 34).
[118] *Diatheke*, lines 60–2 (Beaucamp: 34).   [119] *Contra* Kontoulis 1993, 281–2.

From Godefroy onward, there has been no shortage of debate about the origins of manumission in the church.[120] Godefroy suggested that it originated from temple slavery in the eastern Mediterranean. This view stresses continuity within the ideological history of sacral and Christian manumission: a broad religious impulse towards emancipation runs as a submerged current throughout the eastern provinces. Another view argues that manumission in the church was a new institution, created whole-cloth by the first Christian emperor under the influence of Christian doctrine.[121] Both of these views are problematic. The connection between sacral manumission and manumission in the Christian church was not so ethereal. Manumission in the church was part of the bustling world of "informal" social life hovering below the state's field of vision. Sargenti has been critical of the view that manumission in the church was a descendant of sacral consecration, largely because of the formal differences between consecration and manumission in the church.[122] But function was more important than form. Manumission in the Christian church derived from sacral predecessors insofar as they constituted an effective way of mediating the social tensions of manumission.[123] It was the social effectiveness of sacral manumission that made it a rough model for *manumissio in ecclesia*.

Manumissio in ecclesia was an amalgam. Like civil manumission, the result was full, legal citizenship. The capacity to create Roman citizens was a powerful statement of the Christian church's institutional legitimacy, its place in the public sphere. In this way, Constantine endorsed the church as an institution with the favor of the state, a favor which even went beyond the informal rights of temples. But like sacral manumission, *manumissio in ecclesia* was sensitive to the fragility of the manumission act and used sacred space and sacred communities to stabilize the practice. Sacral manumission was an ancestor of *manumissio in ecclesia* insofar as it was an institutionalized response to the natural dangers of manumission, a timeworn answer to the delicate re-adjustment of power between master and slave.

Constantine specified that *manumissio in ecclesia* should occur in the church and before witnesses. The specific charge that manumission be public in nature and involve communal observation is a clue that Constantine wanted the practice to be embedded in stable, ritualized forms that implicated the congregation. Constantine also required documentation. Sacral manumissions involved the deposition of manumission documents with the priests. Constantine wanted documents drawn up *propter facti*

[120] See esp. Zelnick-Abramovitz 2005, 86–98; Calderone 1971, 377–87.
[121] Fabbrini 1965.   [122] Sargenti 1986, 59–61.   [123] Bradley 1994, 158.

memoriam, but it is not as though he were interested in the abstract memorialization of the process. These documents could be used in disputes between masters and slaves. Likewise, should the patron and freedman disagree over the manumission or its conditions, the presence of witnesses reinforced the act.[124] Religious personnel – especially priests – formed a community of knowledge about the mutual obligations of patron and freedman.[125] In a predominantly oral culture, this ritualized, publicized, memorialized, and attested act was crafted to ensure its stability.[126]

Constantine explicitly mandated the presence of the priest. By late antiquity the power to conduct formal Roman manumissions had devolved down to the level of the civic magistrate, and the bestowal of this power upon the priest gave him an important privilege of public authority.[127] Sacral manumissions too had required the supervision of the priest. Moreover, it was argued in chapter 9 that the Roman governor of Macedonia authorized the priests to mediate disputes between patrons and freedmen; this would create a further parallel with manumission in the Christian church, for in a law of 318, Constantine granted bishops jurisdiction in civil cases.[128] Constantine's concession of civil jurisdiction to bishops was, in timing and conception, parallel to his concession of *manumissio in ecclesia*. Both made a quasi-magistrate out of the bishop. Moreover, the civil authority of the bishop made him ideally suited to handle disputes between patrons and freedmen, and a direct connection between the two grants is possible.[129] The *audientia episcopalis* is a window into Constantine's wider intentions for Christian manumission. He created a stable, fully functional system of manumission equipped to handle the practice in all its prolonged, confrontational reality. At the same time, it was a serious institutional endorsement of his favored religion. Constantine's creation of *manumissio in ecclesia* took advantage of his partisanship towards the Christian ecclesiastical hierarchy in order to create a socially workable means of formal manumission. The use of sacred space, ritualized performance, spiritual authority, and public witness has an obvious affinity to

---

[124] Gibson 1999, 150.

[125] Samuel 1965, 276–9; Sokolowski 1954, 176–81. Some examples from Delphi: GDI 2049, 2072, 2073, 1971.

[126] Rapp 2005, 239–42, emphasizes the notarial role. Zelnick-Abramovitz 2005, 194, shows how important publicity, records, procedure, and priests were in sacral manumissions.

[127] PS 2.25.4. CJ 7.1.4 (AD 319–23).

[128] CT 1.27.1. Confirmed and expanded in Const. Sirm. 1 (AD 333). See Rapp 2005, 242–52; Lenski 2001; Harries 1999, 191–2; Cimma 1989, esp. 69–79; Lamoreaux 1995.

[129] Church canons show that bishops mediated patron–freedmen relationships through *audientia*: see pp. 491–2.

sacral manumission, to those aspects of sacral manumission that made it effective.

By creating manumission in the church, the imperial state did not endorse or catalyze an ideological revolution in the slave system. Manumission in the church could not materially alter the framework of manumission, which remained fundamentally rooted in disciplinary practices. We should not be misled by mere words. As Chrysostom recognized, masters could think of themselves as "philanthropic," even as they exploited their slaves. With manumission in the church, the state did not promote liberation; it found a willing and able subcontractor for this arena of conflict-ridden social practice.

THE DUTIES OF FREEDMEN

Constantine's creation of manumission in the church was not his only significant reform of manumission. Constantine altered the status of freedmen in the civil law in a more sweeping fashion than any Roman emperor since Augustus. His legislation on freedmen underscores the priority of pragmatic, institutional considerations over idealistic humanitarian motives. Roman law considered disputes between patrons and freedmen a civil affair.[130] In Ulpian's commentary on the duties of a governor, he wrote, "Governors should hear complaints by patrons against freedmen and not deal with such cases superficially since, if a freedman is ungrateful, the governor should not let his behavior go unpunished."[131] Roman law was ominously vague about what constituted "ingratitude," and disputes surely arose about labor and respect.[132] Patrons could take their complaints to the governor, but the incapacity of a freedman to press charges against his former master also suggests a more brutal continuity of power and dependence.[133]

The model of the patron–freedman relationship enshrined in Roman law assumes a degree of legal culture probably uncommon in many regions and social groups. A papyrus from the late third century is highly instructive. Two sisters inherited a "slave" (δοῦλον) from their parents.[134] On the

---

[130] Waldstein 1986, 345–77.
[131] Dig. 37.14.1: *patronorum querellas adversus libertos praesides audire et non translaticie exsequi debent, cum, si ingratus libertus sit, non impune ferre eum oporteat.* Lightly adapted from Watson 1985. cf. also Dig. 1.16.9.3.
[132] Quadrato 1996, esp. 345.
[133] Dig. 37.15.5.1; Dig. 37.15.7.2; Dig. 44.44.16; Dig. 43.16.1.43; Dig. 37.15.5.10. Optimistic: Watson 1987, 39–40.
[134] P. Oxy. Hels. 26 (296).

parents' death he was to remain serving them, but he did "not wish to remain (παραμένειν) in our service," nor even "to render us the payments" which a slave pays the master.[135] The word *paramonê* is a clue that he was probably freed by the will but left in service to the daughters, who still regarded him as their "slave."[136] He would not comply, and the sisters petitioned the government official because they were "unable to bear this arrogance from a slave."[137] This is a rare, unpolished look at a patron's rather than a Roman jurist's view. The distinction between disrespect and the failure to fulfill a contractual obligation could be too fine a point.

Roman governors could apply severe penalties to delinquent freedmen: fine, exile, or corporal punishment. A noticeable omission is re-enslavement.[138] Roman patrons were not allowed to reduce their freedmen into slavery again. Tacitus reported a senatorial debate on this question in the time of Nero, in which many senators wanted to give patrons this right.[139] But the right to re-enslave was excluded from the Roman law of patronage.[140] Customs in the eastern Mediterranean, on the other hand, were diverse.[141] Manumission inscriptions could include a stipulation that if *paramonê* obligations were not met, the manumission was void: effectively, re-enslavement.[142] There are, on the other hand, inscriptions that explicitly prohibit re-enslavement. It is not possible to sort out whether Hellenic law had a foundational principle that governed patron–freedmen relations. These were contentious arrangements, and no universal standard appears to have developed.

Several problems converged in the third century to make this a flashpoint for legal conflict. The underlying diversity of Mediterranean customs clashed with Roman law. Roman civil law, moreover, was ambiguous about the substance of "ingratitude," which patrons might naturally associate with obedience and, by extension, labor. The habits of power, and the temptation to re-enslave freedmen, proved inveterate. Diocletian's legal compilations show an imperial chancery that tried to emphasize the standards of the classical law. Clearly, he faced a not inconsiderable number of these cases.[143] The classical law was a balancing act between patrons' rights

---

[135] P. Oxy. Hels. 26: οὐ βούλεται παραμένειν τῇ ἡμῶν ὑπηρεσίᾳ οὐδ' αὖ ἀποφορὰς διδόναι.
[136] On the ambiguity of freed slaves in *paramonê*, Zelnick-Abramovitz 2005, 243. See Andreau 1993, 184–5, for other freedmen called "slaves."
[137] P. Oxy. Hels. 26: μὴ φεροῦσα τὴν οἰκέτου θρασύτητα.
[138] Andreau 1993, 185; De Francisci 1927.
[139] Tac. Ann. 13.26–27 (Heubner: 286–7). Manning 1986.
[140] Fr. Dos. 5. De Francisci 1927, esp. 297–315. Though see Dig. 25.3.6.1, with Sargenti 1990, 182.
[141] De Francisci 1927, 313–14, re-enslavement the "misura normale."   [142] Mitteis 1891, 390.
[143] CJ 7.16.23 (AD 293); CJ 7.16.26 (AD 294); CJ 7.16.30 (AD 294); CJ 7.16.33 (AD 294).

and minimal protections of freedmen.[144] In an environment of universal citizenship and earnest attempts to settle legal disputes in terms of Roman rules, this intricate balance was difficult to maintain.

Constantine did what the Roman senate had declined to do in the age of Nero: he permitted the re-enslavement of freedmen. The reform was part of a large edict issued to the *praefectus urbi*, Maximus, in early 320.[145] The law was issued on 30 January, thus one day before Constantine's landmark *Ad Populum* edict, which was a major legislative package amending various aspects of the civil law. Constantine's law would have read:

... If a manumitted slave shows himself to be ungrateful to his patron and should by some arrogance or disobedience arch his neck against him or incur the guilt of a minor offense, he is to be sent back under the power and authority of his patron, if the patron can show that the freedman is ungrateful in a case brought before the governor's court or before appointed judges. And any children who will be born afterwards will be slaves, since the misdeeds of parents cannot injure those who it will be shown were born during the time while the parents enjoyed freedom. If he, having lost the Roman citizenship, will have been made a Latin, and should pass away in this status, his entire *peculium* should be claimed for the patron or the patron's children or grandchildren, who have never lost their rightful familial claim . . .[146]

The law was a complete collapse of the classical standard. The ungrateful freedman was one that lifted his neck, in arrogance (*iactantia*) or disobedience (*contumacia*).[147] A freedman was ungrateful even if he was guilty of only a "minor offense."[148] In any of these cases, the slave could be subjected again to the master's power and authority – re-enslaved. Constantine also imagined that a freedmen might be punished by a loss of citizenship,

---

[144] Treggiari 1969a, 81.

[145] The reconstruction of this legislation, and its dating, given by Sargenti is compelling: Sargenti 1990. The law included CJ 7.1.4, CJ 6.7.2, and CT 2.22.1. There are considerable problems with the protocols of these laws. CT 4.10.1 (AD 332) is an excerpt of CJ 6.7.2 and was supposedly given from Cologne, whereas Constantine was in the east. Moreover, CJ 6.7.2 was dated to 326, a notoriously problematic year for consular dating, often confused with 320. The recipient, the prefect Maximus, was no longer in office in 326. The same problem bedevils CT 2.22.1. But if all were issued on 30 January, 320, they formed a coherent edict on the punishment of freedmen.

[146] CJ 6.7.2.pr: *si manumissus ingratus circa patronum suum extiterit et quadam iactantia vel contumacia cervices adversus eum erexerit aut levis offensae contraxerit culpam, a patronis rursus sub imperia dicionemque mittatur, si in iudicio vel apud pedaneos iudices patroni querella exserta ingratum eum ostendat: filiis etiam qui postea nati fuerint servituris, quoniam illis delicta parentium non nocet, quos tunc ortos esse constiterit, dum libertate illi potirentur . . . * CT 2.22.1: *si is, qui dignitate Romanae civitatis amissa Latinus fuerit effectus, in eodem statu munere lucis excesserit, omne peculium eius a patrono vel a patroni filiis sive nepotibus, qui nequaquam ius agnationis amiserint, vindicetur . . .*

[147] *Iactantia*: see TLL 7.1 cols. 43–4. *Contumacia*: see TLL 4 cols. 796–7. cf. Digest, 49.1.28.1.

[148] "*Levis offensa*" is not common legal parlance. Only one reference in the Digest: Dig. 34.4.3.11.

which returned the offender to a lower grade in the order of freedmen, Latin status.[149] In sum, Constantine permitted several drastic penalties, up to and including loss of citizenship and re-enslavement, as legitimate punishments for ungrateful freedmen.

Constantine recognized re-enslavement, and he expanded the definition of the ungrateful freedman in such vague terms that it covered disrespect, disobedience, or "slight offenses." The law was a conspicuous victory for the rights of patrons at the expense of freedmen. But it was above all a simplification. Constantine resolved the complexity of the law by enshrining the robust authority of the patron in statute. This was not a counter-current to his recognition of manumission in the church. The new standard for the control over freedmen brought the statutory law of the Roman state into harmony with the natural balance of social power. Not only should this law quash any notion that Constantine's approach to slavery was motivated by humanitarian instincts, it actually sheds light on his broader legislative purpose: to create a functional and pragmatic legal framework for manumission that could work across an empire of citizens.

The sources after Constantine never mention the more complex penalty of reduction to Latin status. Re-enslavement, however, clearly became "the fundamental regulating norm" throughout the rest of late antiquity.[150] In the late fourth century, Ambrose used the law of patronage to create a spiritual metaphor. Ambrose told his Christians they were "redeemed" by Christ and should think of him as their manumittor. Being a "freedman" of Christ, he argued, was superior even to plain "freedom." Ambrose claimed that Christians should remember their manumittor, their "patron," by offering *obsequium*. If they failed, "because of ingratitude," their freedom might be revoked.[151] Ambrose had served as a Roman governor before becoming bishop, and his intricate knowledge of Roman law allowed him to make a spiritual point by referencing the slavish responsibilities of freedmen towards their patrons and the harsh penalties for failing to fulfill those duties.

The hard-line approach of Constantine was a bellwether of change. In the fifth century, the possibility of re-enslaving ungrateful freedmen was expanded. In 423 freedmen were forbidden to press suit against heirs of their patron, and the heirs were also granted the capacity to re-enslave ungrateful freedmen. This legal disability was created so that freedmen would not "forget" that they had been given liberty and revert to the "wickedness of

---

[149] See p. 466, on Latin status.   [150] Sargenti 1990, 196: "la fondamentale norma regolatrice."
[151] Ambr. Iac. 1.3.12 (CSEL 32.2: 12–13): *ut patrono tuo noveris legitimum obsequium deferendum, ne ab ingrato revocetur libertas.*

their servile birth."[152] The law was given from Ravenna amidst a slew of legislation on procedures for making accusations.[153] Three years later, another western law reaffirmed that freedmen could indeed be reduced to slavery if they failed to demonstrate gratitude.[154] These laws against freedmen were issued from the western court. In 447, Valentinian III repealed the ruling which allowed the patron's heirs to re-enslave freedmen. His reasoning was that heirs were using the statute to oppress freedmen on the grounds of ingratitude.[155] This shows that, a generation after their enactment, the laws were actively influencing patron–freedmen relationships. Henceforth, Valentinian declared, no heir or relative could hold the freedman liable for *obsequium* or ingratitude. He was careful to say that patrons and heirs could still avail themselves of public law to punish their freedmen, but heirs were denied the capacity to re-enslave freedmen.[156] The edict restored the Roman law to its late Constantinian form.

In the east, the right to re-enslave freedmen for ingratitude was enshrined in the Justinianic codification. It was listed as a primary example of the loss of status in the *Institutes*.[157] A *Novel* of Justinian reaffirmed that patrons had the ability to revoke the manumission if freedmen were ungrateful or failed to show *obsequium*.[158] The survival of this harsh provision into the codification of Justinian is all the more significant in light of the fact that Justinian enacted a broad program liberalizing manumission.[159] He made manumission simpler to effect and uniform in its legal consequences. He eliminated obstacles to manumission, and in general promoted freedom as a legal and political slogan during his reign. The persistence of the right to re-enslave freedmen throughout his tenure as emperor, then, only shows how deeply rooted this norm was in the patron–freedman relationship.

MANUMISSION IN THE CHURCH IN THE FIFTH CENTURY AND BEYOND

The ongoing importance of manumission in the church can be followed in a handful of documents, including a sermon of Augustine and a series of conciliar texts from late antique Gaul. This evidence is worth briefly surveying because it underscores the fact that the patron–freedman relationship, and its inherent tensions, should be in the foreground. The twenty-first sermon in the homiletic corpus of Augustine is a speech which

[152] CT 4.10.2 (AD 423): *immemores nequitiam . . . servilis ingenii.*
[153] Including CT 1.6.11, CT 2.1.12, CT 9.1.19, and CT 9.6.4.
[154] CT 4.10.3 (AD 426); cf. CJ 6.7.4 (AD 426).   [155] Nov. Val. 25 (AD 447).
[156] Nov. Val 25. De Francisci 1927, 319.   [157] Inst. 1.16.1. Melluso 2000, 30–1.
[158] Nov. 78.2 (AD 539).   [159] Melluso 2000, 59–85.

took manumission as its central metaphor. In the sort of day-to-day detail that he so often used in his homilies, Augustine gave a vivid account of ecclesiastical manumission:

> You lead your slave who is to be manumitted into the church. There is silence, your petition is read out or notice of your will is made. You say that you manumit the slave who has served you faithfully in every way. You esteem him, you honor him, you give to him the price of freedom . . . To manumit your slave, you tear up the deed of ownership over him.[160]

Though Constantine had legalized manumission in the church nearly a century before, the Catholic church in Africa apparently did not adopt the practice immediately. A canon from the council at Carthage of 401 claimed that the African church would only institute the practice under advisement from Italy.[161] The Catholic sect had not gained ascendancy in Africa until this period, and it deferred carefully to Italy on important matters.[162] It is conceivable that the church was cautious about manumitting slaves because of the social overtones of the Donatist movement.[163] The early fifth century was a moment when the church rapidly consolidated its civil functions. Interestingly, the African church did not practice ecclesiastical manumission until this later, decisive, phase of Christianization.

Augustine's vignette reveals both imperial influence and the survival of native rituals. Augustine referred to a practice in which the manumission was symbolized by the physical destruction of the slave's ownership papers.[164] It was a literal performance of the legal effect of manumission, which took the slave out of the realm of property. But this was surely a survival from a local ritual. In other parts of the empire, ownership documents were stored by temple personnel.[165] To take another example of local variation, Gregory of Nyssa imagined ecclesiastical manumission taking place on Easter, but Ephraem the Syrian assumed that the turn of the new year, at the Nativity celebration, was the season of manumission.[166] Within an envelope of imperial uniformity, native habits endured.

---

[160] Aug. Serm. 21.6 (CC 41: 281–2): *Servum tuum manu mittendum ducis in ecclesiam. Fit silentium. Recitatur libellus tuus, aut fit tui desiderii prosecutio. Dicis te servum manumittere, quod tibi in omnibus servaverit fidem. Hoc diligis, hoc honoras, hoc donas praemio libertatis . . . Ut manumittas servum tuum, frangis tabulas eius.*

[161] *Registri ecclesiae Carthaginensis exerpta*, canons 64 and 82 (CC 149: 198 and 204). On the date and transmission, see Cross 1961.

[162] Merdinger 1997, 88–110.

[163] cf. *Registri ecclesiae Carthaginensis exerpta*, canon 57 (CC 149: 195). Aug. Ep. 185.15 (CSEL 57: 14).

[164] cf. CJ 7.6.1.11 (AD 531).   [165] E.g. ISMDA nos. 51, 63.

[166] Gr. Nyss. Pasch. 249 (Gebhardt: 249). Ephr. Syr. Hymn. nat. 5, 17, and 22 (SC 459: 116, 215, and 256).

The manumission described by Augustine took place in the church, during a solemn moment, in front of the congregation. It was a formal, public act, effected before the crowd and the ecclesiastical authorities. During the scene, the master expressed the qualities of the slave that made him worthy of the manumission. Above all, the emphasis was on loyalty, the weighty word *fides* – which was the keystone of the spiritual message that Augustine proceeded to elaborate.[167] Augustine's manumission scene has been noticed by historians, but its final outcome has not received comment. Augustine imagined that the master would come to regret the act. "If the slave whom you are manumitting should not show you faith, and should not make himself worthy of your manumission by remaining faithful, and if you should discover him involved in some fraud in your household, what would you exclaim?"[168] The master would clamor, "Bad slave, you do not remain faithful to me?"[169] The master would complain vociferously, pulling down heaven with his voice, and "all who hear him say, 'he speaks truly.'"[170] Augustine's entire metaphor turns on the scenario of an ungrateful freedman and an aggrieved patron. The patron took his complaint to God and the congregation. Augustine was well aware of the tension inherent in the patron–freedmen relationship.

A series of conciliar canons from the fifth and sixth centuries addressed precisely the problem at the center of Augustine's metaphor. Since the church increasingly provided the institutional framework for manumission, it found itself mediating disputes between patrons and freedmen, enforcing the mutual rights and obligations which governed their relationship. The fifth-century church in Gaul initially showed resolve to protect freedmen against re-enslavement but, like the Roman state, it eventually succumbed to the elemental force of the patron's power, allowing re-enslavement. The church nevertheless tried to maintain strict limits on the use of this punishment and to enforce a modicum of procedural integrity.

At the *Council of Orange*, held in 441, the assembly of Gallic bishops voted to protect freedmen manumitted in the church.[171] Interestingly, the council claimed that ecclesiastical manumission freed the slave from *obsequium*, an automatic requirement in Roman law, and sternly threatened to

---

[167] cf. Bradley 1994, 163.
[168] Aug. Serm. 21.7 (CC 41: 282): *si tibi servus tuus quem manumittis fidem non exhiberet, nec se manumissione tua dignum fidem servando faceret, et eum in aliquibus in domo tua fraudibus invenires, quid clamares?*
[169] Aug. Serm. 21.7 (CC 41: 282): *male serve, fidem mihi non servas?*
[170] Aug. Serm. 21.7 (CC 41: 282): *et omnes qui audiunt: Verum dicit.*
[171] Conc. Araus., canon 6 (7) (CC 148: 79).

punish anyone who tried to re-enslave a freedman. Later canons preserved from the *Second Council of Arles*, possibly issued around 501, held that no one could revoke a manumission performed in a church in the name of ingratitude, without first confirming in the municipal records that the freedman was obligated.[172] This canon was a relapse to the harsher standard, since the church was willing to compass the re-enslavement of freedmen, but it set serious standards for proving the freedman's guilt. A council held at Agde only a few years later clarified the church's position. If any patron tried to revoke the manumission before a hearing had been held, he was to be expelled from the church.[173] This canon made it clear that, despite its intention to protect freedmen, the church would in fact provide legal redress for patrons. The church's position as mediator between patrons and freedmen remained a burden into the sixth century.[174]

The conciliar acts of late Roman Gaul are a unique window on the history of manumission in the church. They demonstrate how a non-state institution absorbed the civil function of manumission. They prove, emphatically, that the tension of the patron–freedman relationship – not the technicalities of the manumission procedure – must be in the foreground. It is no wonder that when Constantine gave the church the right to manumit slaves, he simultaneously granted bishops the right to hear civil disputes. He also recognized, from the start, that testamentary manumission and clerical wills might be especially open to contest. Most fatefully, Constantine eliminated the classical rule of irrevocable freedom and allowed the re-enslavement of freedmen. Patrons throughout late antiquity enjoyed this sharp weapon in their arsenal of power. The canons provide a record of the church as it struggled – like the Roman state before it – to find a balance between the inevitable power of the patron and the sanctity of that line between freedom and slavery, which it now governed.

CONCLUSIONS: MANUMISSION AND INSTITUTIONAL CHANGE IN LATE ANTIQUITY

The history of manumission in late antiquity traces the entire institutional revolution which characterized the period. From an obscure village goddess in third-century Macedonia, through the consuls in the midst of the roaring crowds in the imperial capital, to the earnest bishops of fifth-century Gaul, the places and actors evoked in this narrative were part of a complex

---

[172] Conc. Arel. II, canon 34 (CC 148: 121). On this collection, Mathisen 1997.
[173] Conc. Agath., canon 29 (CC 148: 206).   [174] Conc. Aurel. V, canon 7 (MGH Conc. 1: 102–3).

transformation that occurred in the late antique Mediterranean, a double movement of universalization and then fragmentation. The history of manumission in late antiquity contains all the dialectical opposites which made the period so complex and so dynamic: the central, universalizing impulse of the imperial state versus the ingrained habits of local custom; the high principles of classical jurisprudence against the inevitable realities of social power; the rise of new institutions within broader continuities of state and society; the voluble ideology of Christianity amidst the deeper endurance of material reality. Manumission was the release from slavery, but it was part and parcel of the slave system. The story of manumission in late antiquity allows us to see the changing institutional framework within which late antique men and women understood and sought to control the complex realities of status and power.

Conclusion

After the fall: Roman slavery and the end of antiquity

By the end of the sixth century, Gregory the Great, bishop of Rome, was firmly convinced that the last days were at hand. Gregory had just lived through a miserable decade. He had been installed as pope in 590, amidst terrible floods that spawned a vicious sequence of famine and plague, all harrowingly attested in the sources.[1] Plague had become endemic in the Mediterranean, flaring into crisis every decade or two.[2] Gregory was born about the time the plague first arrived. As a Roman who had lived through the advent of this disease, who had seen firsthand the seemingly endless cycle of wars between Ostrogoths, Byzantines, and Lombards, he might well have believed he was living in the end times. Gregory's Rome was, compared even to its relatively recent past, in lamentable shape, irreversibly on course to become little more than an ecclesiastical museum. Within a few decades, Rome would reach its absolute nadir, cut off from all but the most rudimentary circuits of seaborne trade. Its population was only one-tenth its late Roman size, and the city's material culture was incomparably poorer, for rich and humble alike. Rome had fallen.[3]

The author of the Biblical *Revelation*, writing at the very zenith of Roman power, had imagined that when the Eternal City was destroyed, slave merchants, who traded in the bodies and souls of men, would weep in mourning.[4] Yet the fall of Rome did not witness the end of slavery. This much is abundantly evident in Gregory the Great's letters, which show him mediating conflict between masters and slaves, managing episodes of servile violence, handling cases of asylum, and manumitting slaves, "whom nature made free, but whom the law of nations subjected to the yoke

---

[1] E.g., Lib. Pont. Pelagius II (MGH GPR: 160).   [2] See essays in Little 2007.
[3] See the archaeological literature cited in the Introduction.
[4] Rev. 18.13: καὶ σωμάτων καὶ ψυχὰς ἀνθρώπων.

of servitude."[5] Gregory was not so distant from the late Roman past we
have explored in this book. He knew and followed the slave law as it
appeared in the *Corpus iuris civilis*, Roman law in its Justinianic form.[6]
Gregory himself was the scion of an ancient senatorial family, raised like
Symmachus or Melania in a grand household on the Caelian hill. Like his
distant ancestors, Gregory can be found managing the servile labor force of
far-flung ecclesiastical estates, whose lands were concentrated, tellingly, in
the old heartlands of senatorial property. What, then, had changed between
the age of Melania and the age of Gregory?

   The letters of Gregory preserve plenty of clues that he was already living
in a transformed world. Gregory inhabited a world where religious identity
overrides civil status: the relations between Jewish owners and Christian
slaves were an intractable problem, and recalcitrant pagan slaves were to
be coerced into accepting the true faith "by lashes and tortures."[7] An even
more profound material change can be traced in his letters: the lineaments
of a new slave trade. When Gregory needed Anglian slaves, he instructed
an ecclesiastical official in Gaul to buy the slaves for him.[8] Gregory had
Gallic *solidi* he needed to spend – a revealing comment on economic
fragmentation – but it has also been suggested that the Anglian slaves
were not to be found for sale in Rome.[9] In another instance, Gregory sent
to Sardinia for slaves.[10] Other letters illuminate a trade route controlled
by Jewish merchants carrying slaves out of Marseilles, via Naples, and
apparently to eastern shores – bypassing Rome along the way.[11] In one
document Gregory sent money with an agent to Libya to ransom Italians
who were being shipped towards the southeastern Mediterranean.[12] Once
the final destiny for countless bodies and souls of men, Rome, by AD
600, was no longer even a port of call along the shadowy early medieval
commerce in slaves.

   The scattered clues in the letters of Gregory are perilously meager evidence on which to construct grand arguments about the transformation
of the late Roman slave trade. But the new itinerary of the slave trade,
glimpsed through the prism of a churchman's letters, is only one of many

[5] For slavery in the writings of Greg. Mag., see Serfass 2006. Manumission: Greg. Mag. Ep. 6.12 (CC
  140: 380): *quos ab initio natura liberos protulit et ius gentium iugo substituit servitutis.* Conflict: Greg.
  Mag. Ep. 3.1 (CC 140: 146).
[6] Serfass 2006, 88–9.
[7] Jewish/Christian issues: Greg. Mag. Ep. 3.37, 4.9, 6.30 (CC 140: 182, 225, 402). Pagan slaves: Greg.
  Mag. Ep. 9.205 (CC 140A: 764): *verberibus cruciatibusque.*
[8] Greg. Mag. Ep. 6.10 (CC 140: 378). See Serfass 2006, 88.   [9] McCormick 2001, 625.
[10] Greg. Mag. Ep. 9.124 (CC 140A: 675).   [11] Greg. Mag. Ep. 6.29, 9.105 (CC 140: 402, 657–8).
[12] Greg. Mag. Ep. 3.16 (CC 140: 163).

signs that the old structures sustaining Roman slavery had given way to a new, thoroughly medieval age. It is an age that, thanks to the archaeologist's spade, has become better known to us than once seemed imaginable. But it is a world that lies beyond the scope of this study. This book has looked at the long fourth century, and it has tried to present a synchronic, structural account of Roman slavery during the last, long phase of its existence. Inevitably, though, the claims made in these pages have consequences for the study of slavery into the centuries of the early middle ages. It is fitting, then, if we conclude by trespassing beyond the temporal boundaries of the investigation and propose an outline of what the history of slavery across the post-Roman centuries might look like.

THE END OF ROMAN SLAVERY IN THE WEST

The century and a half leading up to the age of Gregory the Great saw the installation of Germanic kingdoms on the soil of the western empire. There is extensive debate over the real nature and destructive toll of this process, but a history of slavery over the fifth and sixth centuries will have to come to terms with the extent of actual disruption in the patterns of society and economy in the post-Roman west. This much is certain: there is no shortage of evidence for slaves in the centuries after the fall of Rome.[13] The letters of Gregory the Great are not an isolated or idiosyncratic example. The most characteristic types of written evidence from this period, such as barbarian law codes and hagiography, provide ample testimony to the continuing importance of slavery. But is the image of continuity illusory or real?

If the post-Roman evidence is to undergo a re-appraisal, there are lessons from this study which might be carried into the later period. First, it is insufficient to speak baldly of "continuity" and "discontinuity." This habit is a variant of the larger tendency to describe ancient slavery in qualitative terms that do more to hinder than promote an acute critical analysis. The analysis must be specific about the extent of slave-ownership and the role of slavery in the economy. The terms may require adjustment, but to understand the changes in the slave system of the post-Roman west, it is imperative to ask the series of questions pursued in part I. Was there sub-elite slave-ownership and, if so, how extensive was it? Were slaves used as domestic laborers, business managers, textile workers, or agricultural employees? What were the structurally significant components of the slave

---

[13] Grieser 1997; Bonnassie 1991; Nehlsen 1972; Verlinden 1955–77; Bloch 1975, for overviews.

supply? How large was the exchange economy and what was the role of slave labor in the production of commodities? These questions will be even harder to answer in the fifth and sixth centuries, but at the very least they must be asked.

A history of slavery over the fifth and sixth centuries, moreover, must be situated within a plausible account of the economic history of the period, and archaeology must play a prominent part in the investigation. Not only is the textual record woefully incomplete, it is potentially misleading. Archaeology provides a continuous stream of random data to correct the lapses and distortions of the textual record.[14] Early medieval archaeology has been a particularly vibrant field over the last few decades. And if the findings which have emerged offer a correction to the bleakest accounts of gloom and doom, the material evidence in aggregate presents an image of serious economic dislocation and structural simplification in the "dark ages." The fate of slavery in the post-Roman west was determined by the overall reduction of wealth, by the loss of social complexity, by lower rates of urbanism, and by the recession of trade and forms of estate-based agriculture associated with commodity exchange.

Wickham has used the archaeological record to undermine a strongly continualist reading of late antique slavery.[15] In his interpretation, changes in the underlying structures of settlement and exchange give the lie to any notion that Roman slavery persisted into the post-Roman centuries (as some have argued, largely on the basis of the barbarian law codes). He is undoubtedly right, for the centuries *after* the fall of Rome. The shift from villa to village, from a settlement system organized around elite rural habitations to one where peasants visibly dominate the rural sector, is a surface reflection of a deeper breakdown in the circuits of ownership, production, and exchange. The change was neither sudden nor total, but the overall direction and depth of the change is documented in what is now a formidable corpus of excavation and survey evidence.

The transition from Roman to post-Roman societies in the west was not a shift from one mode of production to another (slave, feudal, or peasant). The transition was from an unusually complex society to much simpler forms of social and economic organization. The fall of the empire saw a dramatic loss of structural complexity.[16] Roman society, with its exceptional levels of commerce and urbanism, fostered an unusually complex stratification of wealth. Roman society knew a staggering, tripartite hierarchy

---

[14] See Francovich 2005.   [15] Wickham 2005a, esp. 258–302.
[16] Tainter 1990, 188, is still conceptually useful.

of wealth; not only were the rich unimaginably rich, but beneath them was a social element – modest by modern standards, exceptional by pre-modern measures – living above subsistence. In the post-Roman centuries, the decisive middle was gradually lost, and a simpler, binary division of wealth asserted itself.

The process of social simplification asserted itself at both the top and bottom of society. Post-Roman aristocracies changed as much as the lower classes. Wickham has highlighted the structural, economic importance of the change. The Roman aristocracy was unusual in being a civilian aristocracy; the upper tiers of the status hierarchy were based, quite nakedly, on wealth.[17] The Roman elite was an agro-commercial elite. There were changes already in the long fourth century – the rise of an imperial service elite (whose salaries, however, provided them with capital) and, even more fatefully, the rise of an ecclesiastical elite. After the fall of Rome, it is the civilian, commercial aspect of the aristocracy which suffered most; the military and ecclesiastical castes were pushed to the fore. This is the elite we can follow in the colorful pages of Gregory of Tours' history, with its Roman bishops clinging to a civilized past and its violent Merovingian overlords roaming the landscape. What we need to imagine, behind the new, vividly drawn social figures, is the different relation between the aristocracy and agricultural production which lies behind the story.

The fate of the lower classes in the post-Roman west is a more difficult problem. We should resist the temptation to compress all laboring dependents into a single undifferentiated mass. The idea of a centuries-long "merger" among the lower classes, leading eventually to serfdom, has occupied a place in the historiography that is neither empirically nor analytically justified. There were real chattel slaves – born, captured, or otherwise enslaved – who were owned and exploited in the post-Roman west.[18] We have posited the existence of millions of slaves in the late empire, and it would be shocking if there were not remnants of the slave population deep into the post-Roman era. What we should be looking for, though, is the overall direction of economic and institutional changes that created the conditions for chattel slavery. In other words, in the fifth and sixth centuries, we need to imagine not only changes in the status system *per se*, but in the dynamic forces which created slavery.

The enduring coherence of the late Roman status system probably separates the immediate successor kingdoms (Visigothic Spain, the Merovingian Francia, Ostrogothic and Byzantine Italy) from the societies of the

---

[17] Wickham 2005a, 154–258, esp. 158.   [18] See Rio 2006.

central middle ages. There is a crucial but elusive divide in the history of slavery somewhere in the dark depths of the seventh century. The eclipse of the imperial order in parts of the west led to a countryside that was institutionally primitive, allowing new forms of coercion and new means of extracting labor. Taxation and rents were increasingly confounded.[19] In the same way that the Latin language slowly, and largely beyond our ken, evolved into the romance tongues, the law of status lived on – fragmented, in different local dialects, without the complex grammar provided by the rule of Roman law.[20] In language as in law, we should not be misled by the occasional pronouncement which reflects a studious control over ancient models. When *servi* and *mancipia* appear in the ever-more abundant documentary sources of the eighth century and beyond, convincing work suggests that these are not slaves.[21] They belong among history's innumerable victims of more mundane forms of subjection and dependence. The use of Romanist terminology is misleading, and of course it eventually occasioned the transposition of a new word, *sclavus*, slave, to describe human beings who were actually property.

There are complementary types of data which confirm a great structural transformation in the post-Roman centuries. Gregory the Great's letters and the new vocabulary of slavery are not the only clues that the future of slavery, and the slave trade, pointed east in the early middle ages. So, too, does Henning's study of iron slave shackles, which dramatically illustrates the changing patterns of slavery in the first millennium. In the Roman and late Roman period, shackles are found in Roman cities and on Roman farms; in the post-Roman and early medieval contexts, shackles are found exclusively in the ports out of which the Carolingians shipped their human cargo.[22] These patterns are confirmed in the long-term history of slave prices, too. The Roman empire made the Mediterranean an integrated market, in which prices in the coastal regions came into equilibrium. But by the early middle ages, demand was regionalized, as reflected by the cluster of higher prices in the Levant, and it is apparent why the slave trade moved towards eastern markets (see the figure on p. 503).[23]

The successor societies of the post-Roman west, from ca. AD 450–650, inherited sizeable slave populations, and the violence of the age continually created new captives, new slaves. But the reduction in the demand for slaves was ultimately the decisive secular trend. The recession of

---

[19] Wickham 1984.   [20] Nehlsen 1972.
[21] Wickham 2005a, 286–93; Renard 2000; Davies 1996. *Contra*, Hammer 2002; Pelteret 1995; Bonnassie 1991.
[22] Henning 2008.   [23] Harper 2010; medieval data from McCormick 2001.

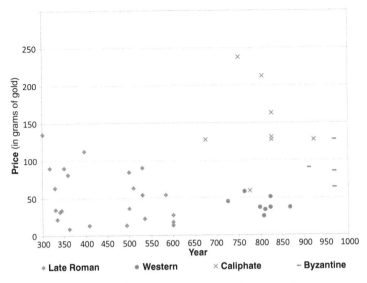

Slave prices in the late Roman empire and early middle ages

exchange-oriented production undermined the demand for higher-risk, controllable forms of estate labor.[24] The demise of the towns obliterated the premature middling element of Roman society, along with its slave-owning habits. The status system rooted in Roman civil law lost its moorings but never totally collapsed. Germanic forms of dependence surely had an impact.[25] Men and women also came to think of their identity in religious and not just civil terms.[26] The slaves in the post-Roman sources – on papal estates, in the will of Remigius, in the letters of Gregory the Great or the histories of Gregory of Tours – are slaves, and it would be unwise to deny this fact.[27] But slaves and slave-owners were increasingly exceptional, marginal. The archaeological record provides incomparable testimony to the slow recession of commercial exchange and the consequent slacking of elite control over agriculture.

Yet, these were truly post-Roman societies in a way that societies of the Carolingian era were not. This is of primary significance for the history of slavery, and for the history of labor and dependency in general. After a long arc of decline, by the seventh century the basic vocabulary of status was capable of undergoing radical change. This change was possible only because slavery had been in decline now for two centuries. The *servi*

---

[24] Wickham 2005a, 265.   [25] Lenski 2008, esp. 95–104.
[26] Fynn-Paul 2009.   [27] Banaji 2009.

of the eighth- and ninth-century polyptychs are slaves in the same way
that Charles was the Roman emperor. In this fact we should not see a
long evolution from ancient slavery to medieval feudalism. We should
recognize the use of a Roman past which had died away slowly, very slowly,
but so completely that its basic terms could be used in a way that had
nothing to do with the world of the late empire which we have been able to
explore.

THE END OF ROMAN SLAVERY IN THE EAST

The letters of Gregory the Great cast a brief sidelight on the slave trade at
the end of the sixth century. They seem to document the flow of human
chattel out of the barbarian kingdoms towards the richer markets of the east.
In Gregory's lifetime the east–west trade routes across the Mediterranean
remained open, even if the circulation of goods turned more slowly than
before. Gregory himself had traveled along those routes on an embassy to
the court at Constantinople, where he would have encountered a city vastly
more prosperous than his native Rome. The efflorescence of the eastern
Mediterranean in late antiquity is now a familiar fact, and it provides us
with a better sense of where the slaves we see in Gregory's letters were
destined. The slave trade – with its high-value, ambulatory commodities –
would remain a staple of Mediterranean commerce across the dark ages.[28]
And by the eighth and ninth centuries, western Europe had clearly become
a major exporter of human chattel into the heartland of medieval slavery,
the Islamic Caliphate. But when did the eastward drift of the slave trade
begin? What does the history of slavery in the east look like between the
division of the Roman empire and the rise of Islam?

Slavery has never played a prominent role in the social histories of
the eastern Mediterranean in the late Roman empire.[29] Yet the sources
provide considerable evidence for the intensive use of slave labor over
the long fourth century, in households and on rural estates alike. The
existence of slaves in Greek households of the Roman empire is not, of
course, totally unexpected, even if it has not received quite the sustained
attention it deserves.[30] But the presence of slaves in the countryside of the
fourth century has not been explained. In chapter 4 we argued that the
expansion of commodity production drove demand for controllable labor –
demand that outstripped the supply of wage labor. Literary, epigraphic, and

---

[28] Above all McCormick 2002 and 2001. Fynn-Paul 2009; Shaw 2008.
[29] Though see Bagnall 1993.   [30] Marinovič, Golubcova, and Šifman 1992.

papyrological evidence combine to present a consistent image of a landscape in which slave labor was instrumental in elite control over production.

There is a case to be made that the eastern slave system entered a gradual recession from the middle of the fifth century. The evidence, as always, is less certain than we would like. There is a major lacuna in the middle of the fifth century, in the papyri and even in the literary remains. And when the lights turn on again in the sixth century, slaves are suddenly much less prominent. In the papyri, they are substantially fewer.[31] In the literary evidence, they are still there, although they are not omnipresent as they were in the fourth century. There are simply fewer mentions of slaves, and there is less insistence from contemporary observers that slavery played a fundamental role in society.

The laws of Justinian represent one of the great repositories of information on sixth-century society; yet, despite the great mass of source material, contradictory images of the slave system emerge. Justinian was a radical reformer who cloaked his agenda in the language of the Roman past.[32] His amendments to the law of slavery were far-reaching, but they are exceedingly difficult to interpret as evidence for underlying realities. On the one hand, the extraordinary amount of slave law preserved in the *Corpus iuris civilis* attests a more than antiquarian interest in the institution, while the *Novellae* undoubtedly reflect a lively concern for the problem of slavery. On the other hand, we can agree with Melluso that Justinian's slave law hints at a weakened slave system.[33] Justinian abolished the *senatus consultum Claudianum*; he liberalized the rules governing the legitimation of offspring from slave-women; he abrogated the Augustan marriage and manumission restrictions. His intentions, at times, were overtly Christian, and he raised the protection of freedom to a core theme of his government. The issue of slavery pervades his legal activity, but not, after all, in a way that necessarily suggests it was a dominant social institution.[34] Slavery seems to be the passive object of Justinian's robust legislative will.

If slavery was in gradual recession in the eastern Mediterranean over the fifth and sixth centuries, the explanation for this trend is not obvious. In the west the progressive loss of economic complexity explains the direction of the slave system, but in the east the economy was healthy across the fifth century and deep into the sixth. Chapter 4 argued that part of the

---

[31] Fikhman 1997, 1974, and 1973 is at least suggestive for the fifth, sixth, and seventh centuries. (But Bagnall forthcoming and 1993 is convincing about the fourth century.)

[32] Pazdernik 2005.   [33] Melluso 2000, 230.

[34] See, for instance, the types of slaves (eunuchs, scribes, doctors) specified in the price schedule, CJ 7.7.1 (AD 530). If not conclusive, this is at least highly suggestive: Harper 2010.

explanation lies in the nature of the eastern labor market, in combination with the new fiscal policy of the Roman state. In the east, a village-based settlement system and a tradition of wage labor made slavery inherently unstable. The demographic expansion of the late Roman east made slave labor less attractive, less necessary. Moreover, the fiscal rules restricting the movement of registered laborers had acute effects in this environment. Over the late fifth century, the laws increasingly address the status of *adscripticii*, registered estate workers; by the time of Justinian their status is a major object of imperial attention.[35] We do not need to posit that slaves and *adscripticii* became indiscriminately merged, nor that serfdom was the inevitable destiny of the labor system, to admit that the fiscal regime had major effects.

Even as estate-based slavery was in decline, forms of household slavery remained relatively strong into the sixth century.[36] Demographic growth and fiscal policy did little to create substitutes for slave labor outside the agricultural sector. We should probably imagine that the non-agricultural slavery of the early Byzantine east was the most stable and enduring part of the ancient slave system. This was not an inconsiderable survival. It was an important bridge, even in the late sixth and early seventh centuries, between late Roman slavery and the establishment of Islam. The Caliphate would become the principal source of demand for slaves, but the Islamic slave system was not built on virgin soil. And slavery would continue to play a role in Byzantine households deep into the middle ages.

CHURCH AND SLAVERY IN THE MIDDLE AGES

This book has argued that the relationship between Christianity and slavery was complex and dynamic. Always at the core of the relationship, embedded in the scriptural legacy of the religion, was the church's willingness to accommodate slavery as an institution. The church accepted slavery and with it the practices of domination. But this is obvious, and should be the beginning of discussion rather than the end. In every generation the church found itself in a new position *vis-à-vis* society, and its ideas interacted with social realities in a constantly shifting framework of church, state, and society.

The time period covered by this book was a particularly dynamic and decisive phase in the history of Christianization, a period which saw the legalization of the religion under Constantine and its full-scale adoption

[35] Sirks 2008; Grey 2007a.   [36] See Rotman 2004.

as the state religion under Theodosius. The long fourth century was the age of conversion. The massive and rapid growth of the church lies in the background of the Christian authors who have been our guides. The waves of new believers, and the newfound civil authority of the church, prompted the Christian leadership to sort out many of its social attitudes at a new depth. We find men like Augustine and Chrysostom trying to explain the origins and justification of slavery in Christian terms. The long fourth century thus became an age of creative social discourse. This was an age that has left the only direct criticism of slavery as an institution from the entire ancient world.

The decisions made by the institutional church in late antiquity would prove highly influential, shaping canon law for the next millennium. The church accepted most of the practices associated with slavery. It accepted the violent underpinnings of the master's authority. As pre-Christian philosophers had done for centuries, Christian advocates promoted a discourse of polite mastery to temper the extreme use of violence, but the use of physical discipline was too deeply embedded to be the object of any radical questioning.[37] Likewise the church fully accepted the exploitation of the slave's labor. But the one area where the church charted a truly new path was in the realm of sexual reform. The Christian leadership refused to accept the fundamentally status-based sexual rules of the ancient world, and it poured considerable pastoral energy into reforming social habits.[38] The church even had some influence in public law – for instance, in the stream of rules against the coerced prostitution of slaves. There were also limits: the late Roman church did not recognize servile marriages, and the state would not alter the foundational rules of *adulterium* and *stuprum*.

A history of Christian attitudes towards slavery would have to be different still in the post-Roman centuries, east and west. In some ways the creative window opened by the age of conversion would slowly close, and the fifth and sixth centuries saw a re-accommodation between church and slavery along many of the lines set down in the fourth century. In the post-Roman centuries, moreover, religious identity and slavery begin to overlap in new and fateful ways.[39] The roots of this process, to be sure, lie in the fourth century, where we find the first laws restricting Jewish ownership of slaves.[40] But in the early middle ages, the ideology of slavery will become intertwined with religious boundaries in unprecedented and irreversible fashion. The practice of ransoming captives, moreover, became a major undertaking of the church, but at the same time re-inforced the sense of

---

[37] See chapter 5.   [38] Harper forthcoming a.   [39] Fynn-Paul 2009.   [40] De Bonfils 1993.

a Christian identity that transcended civil borders. By the eighth or ninth century, the lines which had been forming hardened, and the Mediterranean was a slaving lake divided along firmly religious boundaries.[41]

THE END OF THE PAST

Moses Finley did more than anyone to make the history of ancient slavery a respectable topic in the western academy, and one of his most enduring contributions was to suggest the idea of the "genuine slave society." Finley made it possible to recognize the structural importance of slavery outside the Marxist paradigm; his notion of a slave society was more sophisticated, more subtle, than the idea that a "slave mode of production" dominated all of antiquity. Finley's intervention must be understood as a corrective, aimed at both the mechanistic conceptions of the Marxist tradition and the arid constructions of the humanistic tradition. In this respect, Finley's notion of a slave society was successful beyond measure. Yet, today, his terms can seem outmoded: we know more about the pervasiveness of slavery in world history, and we should suspect that there were actually fewer slaves in Roman society than even Finley would have allowed. And this book, certainly, has emphasized the autonomous role of production and exchange, rather than Weber's "political capitalism," as the real mechanism of the Roman slave system. But is not the central insight of Finley's vision intact? Is it not still worth saying that the Roman empire created a genuine slave society?

The assertion that the Romans created a slave society is, ultimately, a claim to historical exceptionalism. And the more we learn about the Romans, the more such claims of exceptionalism seem defensible. Our more scientific age sees Roman exceptionalism in terms of pottery rather than poetry, in pollution deposits, coin circulation, and ceramic distributions. The Roman empire was a massive and enduring lunge towards modernity, and slavery was an elemental part of that civilization.[42] Yet the transition to modernity was a road full of contingencies, not a series of predetermined stages. To understand Roman slavery, we have to appreciate both the familiar mechanics of production and exchange, and also the unfamiliar sensuous environment of the ancient Mediterranean. Roman slavery was produced by the unique conjunctures of a first-millennium efflorescence. It emerged in a world of aggressive and frank sexuality; a world where textile production was staggeringly primitive; a world in which wine

---

[41] McCormick 2001, 733–77.   [42] See esp. Schiavone 2000, for thoughts along these lines.

was the psychotropic commodity *par excellence*; a world where identity and status were still thoroughly civic. The sum of all those particularities made Roman slavery what it was, one of the only pre-modern slave systems in which slavery pervaded every aspect of social thought and practice.

There is a deep truth behind the enduring impulse to connect the decline of slavery with the transition from antiquity to the middle ages. But the end of Roman slavery was not a vanishing act or an evolutionary mutation – it was a systems collapse. The slave society of the Romans fragmented and became a multitude of societies with slaves. This was not a superficial development. The distinction between a slave society and a society with slaves is an analytical device invented by historians, but it captures something essential about life in the Roman empire, which was in its structure and its human experience profoundly shaped by the mass-scale domination of slaves. The inhabitants of the Roman world insisted on the centrality of slavery in sexual rules, in habits of violence, in the economy of honor, in the material realm of production, in the legal order. In the mind of the preacher whose words have so often served as our guide, the world was inconceivable without slavery. The household and the city, the rich and the poor, the urban and the rural: slavery was implicated in every aspect of social life. By the late sixth or seventh century, no one was insisting that slavery was central in the production of wealth, in the construction of social honor, or in the order of public law. That is ultimately the most important, most compelling, and most human testimony to the slow passage across one of the great thresholds of civilizational change.

Appendixes

The word οἰκέτης *in late antiquity*

The word οἰκέτης is, along with δοῦλος, one of the two most common terms for slave in late antique Greek (for the early history of the word, see Gschnitzer 1976, 20–1, 71). It is effectively synonymous with δοῦλος, and authors regularly use the two as exact equivalents. The primary distinction is that δοῦλος lends itself more readily to abstract usages, whereas οἰκέτης is a highly concrete, situational term. So, for instance, δουλεία is the primary word for the abstract quality of slavery, whereas the equivalent οἰκετεία is virtually never used (for a rare example, see Josephus, *Antiquitates Judaicae*, 8.6.3). When Libanius, for example, wants to claim that slavery is a peaceful condition that allows the slave to sleep at night without the worries of a free man, he uses δουλεία for the condition, οἰκέτης for the slave who is sleeping (*Progymnasmata* 9.6.16: Οὐδὲν τοσοῦτον ἡ δουλεία. ὁ μέν γε οἰκέτης καθεύδει ῥαθύμως ταῖς τοῦ δεσπότου φροντίσι τρεφόμενος . . .). In the discussion that follows, I will try to support four claims about the word οἰκέτης in the social idiom of late antique Greek. First, the term οἰκέτης is an equivalent of δοῦλος and ἀνδράποδον. Second, οἰκέτης implies unfree legal status. Third, the οἰκέτης was a chattel slave, not a servant. Fourth, the word οἰκέτης is not equivalent to "domestic slave." After this discussion I will consider objections to the view that οἰκέτης should be exclusively indicative of slave status.

1. An οἰκέτης was identical to a δοῦλος or an ἀνδράποδον. It is not rare for an author to switch between the terms arbitrarily in a way that leaves no doubt the groups are coterminous. This is as true of δοῦλος (*Apostolic Constitutions*, 4.12: Περὶ δὲ οἰκετῶν τί ἂν εἴποιμεν πλεῖον, ἢ ὅτι καὶ ὁ δοῦλος εὔνοιαν εἰσφερέτω πρὸς τὸν δεσπότην μετὰ φόβου Θεοῦ) as of ἀνδράποδον (Themistius, *Orationes*, 1.11a: τί γὰρ ἂν ὁ τοιοῦτος διενέγκαι πλουσίου φαύλου πολλὰ ἀνδράποδα κεκτημένου, σεμνυνομένου τε καὶ αὐχοῦντος ὅτι πάντων ἄμεινον πράττει τῶν οἰκετῶν;). Sometimes the aim was simply to vary the diction (e.g. Cyril of Alexandria, *Commentarii in Joannem*, 9.721A: ὡς καὶ ἐν δούλου τάξει

κατατάττεσθαι δεῖν, οὐδὲ αὐτὴν καταφρίττοντα τὴν οἰκέτη πρέπουσαν λειτουργίαν ἀποπληροῦν, διὰ τοῦ καὶ ἀπονίζειν τῶν ἀδελφῶν τοὺς πόδας, καὶ λέντιον περιθέσθαι διὰ τὴν χρείαν. ἄθρει γὰρ ὅπως ἀνδραποδῶδες τὸ χρῆμά ἐστιν, ὅσον εἰς ἔθη φημὶ τὰ ἐν κόσμῳ καὶ τὰς ἔξωτριβάς). At other times, the versatile derivatives of δοῦλος were needed (John Chrysostom, *Sermones in Genesim*, 3.112–19: καὶ καθάπερ ἐπὶ τῶν οἰκετῶν, οἱ μὲν εὐδοκιμοῦντες φοβεροὶ τοῖς συνδούλοις εἰσίν). And insofar as δοῦλος was more abstract, οἰκέτης more concrete, the former was perhaps more likely to be used in the plural, the latter in the singular – for example, Libanius claimed that festivals brought temporary freedom to slaves (δούλοις), so that even a lazy slave (οἰκέτης) was spared a beating (*Orationes*, 9.1).

2. The οἰκέτης was unfree in a society where civil law tightly regulated the line between freedom and slavery (see part III). οἰκέτης is a status term. So, for instance, Eusebius could claim that Constantine freed anyone who, under the rule of Licinius, had illegitimately become an οἰκέτης (*De vita Constantini*, 2.34.2: καὶ οἷον αἰφνίδιον οἰκέτην ἑαυτὸν ἀντ’ ἐλευθέρου γνούς, ἐλευθερίας τῆς πρόσθεν καθ’ ἡμέτερον λαβόμενος πρόσταγμα). This is especially clear in passages which speak of the manumission of an οἰκέτης. In a homily, Asterius of Amasea spoke of the son who resented his father because the latter freed a slave (*Homilies*, 3.11: οἰκέτην ἀφῇ τῆς δουλείας) and thereby diminished the patrimony. In a late Roman joke collection, an absent-minded professor tried to console his crying slaves (25: τῶν οἰκετῶν κλαιόντων) – who were on a sinking ship with him – by informing them that they were freed in his will (ἐν διαθήκαις ἐλευθέρους ἀφῆκα)! A passage in the *Quaestiones et responsiones* of Pseudo-Caesarius refers to the slap which slaves received in the ritual of manumission (185: ῥάπη γὰρ ἐλευθεροῦσιν τοὺς οἰκέτας οἱ κύριοι ἅμα τοῦ παῖσαι τῆς δουλείας ἀπελαύνοντες). Being an οἰκέτης brought all the social and legal disadvantages of slave status, including presumptive physical abuse (Gregory of Nyssa, *Adversos eos qui castigationes aegre ferunt*, col. 313: οὐ γὰρ τύπτομέν σε ὡς οἰκέτην) and constant labor (Cyril of Jerusalem, *Catecheses ad illuminandos*, 9.7: οὐκ ἂν οἰκέτης παρὰ δεσποτῶν ἔλαβεν ἀνάπαυσιν, εἰ μὴ τὸ σκότος ἐπάναγκες ἐπῆγε προθεσμίαν). Justinian's *Novels* regularly use οἰκέτης as a synonym for δοῦλος (e.g. *Novel* 2: ἐπὶ τριετίαν ὅλην, εἴτε ἐλεύθεροι τυχὸν εἴτε δοῦλοι καθεστήκοιεν, προσκαρτερεῖν οὔπω τοῦ μοναχικοῦ σχήματος ἠξιωμένους... καὶ τοὺς εὐλαβεστάτους αὐτῶν ἡγουμένους πυνθάνεσθαί τε αὐτῶν, εἴτε ἐλεύθεροι καθεστήκοιεν εἴτε οἰκέται, καὶ πόθεν αὐτοὺς ἐπιθυμίατοῦ μονήρους εἰσῆλθε βίου). In the *Novels*, I have found

thirty-six instances of οἰκέτ- versus fifty instances of δοῦλ-, though many of the usages of the latter are forms of δουλεία and δουλεύειν. Justinian could also refer in his laws to the manumission of οἰκέται (*Novel* 1: καὶ φιδεϊκομμισσαρίοις καὶ οἰκέταις ἐλευθερίᾳ τιμηθεῖσι προσιέναι). The οἰκέτης was legally unfree and thus vulnerable to the legal disabilities inherent in slave status, including automatic torture in the extraction of legal testimony (*Novel* 1: παρρησίαν εἶναι μὴ μόνον διὰ τῆς τῶν οἰκετῶν βασάνου τὸ πρᾶγμα ζητεῖν – καὶ γὰρ δὴ καὶ τοῦτο δίδομεν κατὰ τὴν πρῴην παρ᾽ ἡμῶν εἰρημένην ἐπὶ ταῖς οἰκετικαῖς βασάνοις παρατήρησιν; Syrianus, *Commentarium in Hermogenis librum peri staseon*, 71: ἀλλὰ τοὺς οἰκέτας βασάνῳ τἀληθῆ λέγειν καταναγκάσομεν; καὶ τίς οὐκ οἶδεν ὡς ἐπίορκος εἰ καὶ ἄπιστος ἡ τῶν ἀνδραπόδων φύσις).

3. The οἰκέτης was a chattel slave, a piece of property that could be bought, sold, or otherwise transferred. A master bought the οἰκέτης on the market (John Chrysostom, *Ad illuminandos catechesis*, 2.5: καθάπερ ἡμεῖς οἰκέτας ἀγοράζοντες, αὐτοὺς τοὺς πωλουμένους πρότερον ἐρωτῶμεν, εἰ βούλονται ἡμῖν δουλεῦσαι), completed the legal formalities of sale (John Chrysostom, *Ad populum Antiochenum*, 16.2: κἂν οἰκέτας ὠνεῖσθαι), and immediately changed the slave's name (John Chrysostom, *De mutatione nominum*, 3.3: καθάπερ δεσπότης οἰκέτην πριάμενος, εἶτα βουλόμενος αὐτὸν διδάξαι τὴν δεσποτείαν, μετατίθησιν αὐτοῦ τὸ ὄνομα). Likewise, the οἰκέτης could be given away (Procopius, *De bellis*, 3.2.18: οἰκέταις τισὶ δωρεῖσθαι βούλοιτο αὐτῶν ἕκαστον). οἰκέται were included on standard lists of chattel – "farms and estates, herds and slaves" (Basil, *Homilia in martyrem Julittam*, 1: καὶ ἀγροὺς καὶ κώμας, καὶ βοσκήματα καὶ οἰκέτας). One became an οἰκέτης through birth to slave parents or capture in war. In his *Lexicon* Hesychius stated that an οἰκέτης differed from a homeborn slave in that the former also included war captives (267: διαφέρει δὲ οἰκέτης οἰκότριβος· ὁ μὲν γὰρ οἰκότριψ γονέων δοῦλος· ὁ δὲ οἰκέτης οὐ πάντως· ἀλλὰ καὶ ὁ αἰχμάλωτος· καὶ ὁ ἐν οἴκῳ ὤν). It was also possible for οἰκέται to become fugitives (Synesius, *Epistulae*, 145: οἰκέτης ἐμὸς ἐδραπέτευσεν), because their hatred towards their owners was unalterable (Firmus of Caesarea, *Epistulae*, 36: ἀκατάλλακτον μῖσος τοῖς οἰκέταις πρὸς τοὺς δεσπότας ἐστίν, οἳ τοὺς κεκτημένους ἀποδιδράσκοντες ἑτέροις δουλεύειν μᾶλλον ἢ τοῖς οἰκείοις δεσπόταις ἀνέχονται). In the words of Palladius, the relief for the fugitive slave was typically brief (Palladius, *Lausiac History*, 35: καὶ βραχεῖαν ἀναπνεύσας ὥραν, ὡς δραπετεύσας οἰκέτης δεσπότην).

4. Although οἰκέτης is sometimes translated as "servant," "domestic slave," or other terms implying a functional designation, it is important

to recognize that the term οἰκέτης does not indicate that the slave was occupied with domestic tasks (so already Bieżuńska-Małowist, 1974–7, vol. 2, 11). For instance, οἰκέται could be found busy at farm labor under the control of an overseer – or slacking off (Iamblichus, *De vita Pythagorica*, 31.197: ὡς εἶδε τόν τε ἐπίτροπον καὶ τοὺς ἄλλους οἰκέτας οὐκ εὖ τῶν περὶ τὴν γεωργίαν ἐπιμελείας πεποιημένους). Libanius could imagine that the education of young men did not leave their patrimonial estates without farm labor, since their families owned sufficient numbers of slaves (Libanius, *Declamationes*, 1.129: εἰ δ᾽ οἷς οἰκέται πολλοί, καὶ σὺ δὲ τοῦτο ὡμολόγηκας, Ἄνυτε, πλησιάζειν Σωκράτει λέγων οὐ τοὺς ταπεινοτάτους, πῶς ἄσπορον ποίει τὴν χώραν καὶ τὴν γῆν ἀπεστέρει γεωργῶν, εἰ τοῖς τοὺς ἀγροὺς κεκτημένοις καὶ τὰς περιουσίας πρὸς τῷ τῆς ψυχῆς φροντίζειν καὶ τῆς γῆς ὑπῆρχεν ἐπιμελεῖσθαι). Hesychius (5662) defined ἐργεῖται as οἱ ἐπ᾽ ἀγρὸν οἰκέται and in another context (8548) referred to οἰκέται ἀγροῖκοι. The word οἰκέτης is related to οἶκος, with its connotations of "the property, the patrimony," in the same way that οἰκοδεσπότης implies "master of the household" in a proprietary, not physical, sense of the household. An οἰκέτης is a "property-ling," if we want to catch the semantic penumbra of the word. There is no doubt that the mass of οἰκέται on the Appianus estate were performing agricultural labor (but on their status, see pp. 517–18). The term οἰκέτης simply does not have any significance for the nature of the slave's employment.

Possible objections. Having read every instance of οἰκέτης yielded by a TLG-search of the fourth through sixth centuries, I have not found any example which suggests that οἰκέται were anything other than slaves. One exception is slightly earlier, a convoluted and self-contradictory passage in that monstrosity of erudition, the *Deipnosophistae* of Athenaeus (6.266–7). In a long and aimless conversation on the history and vocabulary of slavery, several snippets of classical literature and philosophy are parsed for their insights into the language of slavery. In the crucial passage, several classical usages of the words δοῦλος and οἰκέτης are analyzed. On the one hand, a work of Chryippus, *On Similarity of Meanings*, is quoted to the effect that there is an important distinction between δοῦλος and οἰκέτης: the former are still called δοῦλοι after they are freed, whereas οἰκέτης refers to someone still in the condition of slavery. If the claim is accurate (see p. 486 for freedmen called slaves), this only proves that the term οἰκέτης was specific to someone actually in the condition of slavery. A few sentences later, Athenaeus quotes two plays of the classical period, the *Laertes* by Ion of Chios and the *Omphale*, a satyr-play of Achaeus. The former uses δοῦλος and οἰκέτης as synonyms, but the latter has a line in which someone is

said to be "rich in slaves, rich in property" (ὡς εὔδουλος, ὡς εὔοικος ἦν).
Athenaeus glosses this line with the claim "he is saying in an idiosyncratic
way that the man is good to his slaves and his servants, since there is a
common sense in which οἰκέτης is one who spends his time in the house
and may be a free man" (ἰδίως λέγων ὡς χρηστὸς ἐς τοὺς δούλους ἐστὶ
καὶ τοὺς οἰκέτας. ὅτι δὲ οἰκέτης ἐστὶν ὁ κατὰ τὴν οἰκίαν διατρίβων κἂν
ἐλεύθερος ᾖ κοινόν). Athenaeus takes the phrase "rich in slaves, rich in
property" as though it were meant to draw a distinction between δοῦλος
and οἰκέτης. Maybe Athenaeus was right that οἰκέτης could have the sense
of a house-servant or a free man, but surely it is noteworthy that the only
example he could adduce is a strained interpretation of a line of classical
poetry. Likewise, LSJ, while admitting that the two words are frequently
synonymous, gives a sense of οἰκέτης as "opp. δοῦλοι" by citing the passage
of Chrysippus and three passages of Plato's Laws (763a, 777a, 853e) which
are all unconvincing (the first is a pleonasm, the second a synonym, the
third an attempt to vary the diction: Plácido 1997).

The most problematic exceptions, by far, are the two examples of possibly
free οἰκέται who appear in third-century papyri, discussed by Rathbone
1991, 106–16. There are contemporary papyri which make it abundantly
clear that οἰκέται could be slaves (in P. Oxy. 27.2474, a man manumitted
two οἰκέται). The οἰκέται in the Heroninos archive (P. Lund IV 13, P.
Hamb. Inv. 107) appear free on the basis of onomastic criteria: both bear
the *gentilicium* Aurelius. One of these, who had a patronymic, reported a
theft; the other certified his paganism before public officials. There is no
easy way around this evidence, but we should note an interesting rescript of
the late third century preserved in the *Justinianic Code* (CJ 4.36.1, AD 293).
A slave-woman had illicitly procured her freedom by giving her *peculium*
to a third party who used it to purchase her out of slavery, without her
master knowing that he was accepting his own money for the deal! What is
most interesting is that the rescript names her as Aurelia Dionysia, "obwohl
Diokletians Kanzlei ihr ausdrücklich mitteilt, dass sie keinen Anspruch auf
die Freiheit hat" (Huchthausen 1974, 253). Moreover, across history, slaves
have often used names – including surnames – that contradicted their
status, especially when they represented themselves outside of the master's
domain (see Gutman 1976, 230–56), so this is another possible explanation.
There is also evidence that freedmen were occasionally called "slaves" (see
Andreau 1993, 184–5 and cf. P. Oxy. Hels. 26 of AD 296); perhaps the
οἰκέται in P. Lund IV 13 and P. Hamb. Inv. 107 were freedmen? None of
these suggestions sits easily with the public context of the papyri in question
(cf. Bagnall 1991, for the care with which status designations were applied

in the papyri, and in CJ 7.16.9 of AD 293 and 7.14.10 of AD 294 the links between legal status and names are recognized). The fact that some οἰκέται on the Appianus estate had wives and children is not a probative argument against slave status, especially in light of the Thera inscription (see Harper 2008), nor is the fact that they had some independent property (see Roth 2005a). The fact that οἰκέται on the Appianus estate were given rations so exiguous they would barely meet the minimal caloric requirements of a working male (in distinction to the more "highly paid" hired workers on the estate) is consistent with the inference that the οἰκέται were slaves. Rathbone shows that οἰκέται were attached to the estate for life. This at least implies some sort of dependence: Rathbone argues, not implausibly, that dire poverty and the need for fiscal patronage drove men into these sorts of low-paying, lifelong arrangements. Perhaps the use of the word οἰκέτης reflects the shadowlands of legal status at the point where brutal poverty met total dependence (see for example P. Strass. 40 of AD 569, admittedly much later, and see chapter 10 on the difficulty of classifying such relationships in Roman law). Given the overwhelming literary evidence (truly, thousands of extant examples) that οἰκέται were slaves, it is hard to think of a perfectly attractive solution to the documentary evidence of the third century.

Certainly, οἰκέτης meant "slave" and nothing else in the earlier periods of Greek history: see Foxhall 2007, 74; Pomeroy 1994, 316; Jameson 1977, 137. For the Byzantine period, see the discussion of Rotman 2004, 251: "les mots oiketês et doulos sont employés parallèlement pour designer un esclave quelconque, contrairement à pais/paidiskê – toujours domestique."

Slaves in the Codex Hermogenianus

Law (CJ)	Day	Year	Category
7.14.4	10 Jan	293	Status
6.2.9	7 Feb	293	Crime
6.8.1	18 Mar	293	Status
7.9.3	18 Mar	293	Status
7.14.5	4 Apr	293	Status
2.12.16	5 Apr	293	Agents
4.26.7	5 Apr	293	*Peculium*
3.32.12	8 Apr	293	Ownership
7.27.2	9 Apr	293	Crime
8.42.10	9 Apr	293	Inheritance
8.50.9	9 Apr	293	*Postliminium*
3.22.3	12 Apr	293	Status
4.14.6	12 Apr	293	Patron–freedmen
3.32.13	13 Apr	293	Ownership
6.2.10	13 Apr	293	Crime
7.60.2	13 Apr	293	Property
4.19.10	14 Apr	293	Status; sex
7.16.9	14 Apr	293	Status
7.16.10	14 Apr	293	Status
7.16.11	14 Apr	293	Status
7.16.12	14 Apr	293	Status; sex
4.49.7	15 Apr	293	Manumission
7.14.6	25 Apr	293	Status
6.50.13	27 Apr	293	Inheritance
7.16.13	27 Apr	293	Status; property
7.16.14	28 Apr	293	Status
2.20.4	29 Apr	293	Sex; manumission
9.41.13	29 Apr	293	Torture
7.1.2	30 Apr	293	Manumission
7.19.5	30 Apr	293	Status; property
8.44.18	30 Apr	293	Status
9.33.4	30 Apr	293	Crime

(cont.)

Law (CJ)	Day	Year	Category
7.16.15	10 May	293	Status
7.16.16	10 May	293	Status
8.50.10	13 May	293	*Postliminium*
4.6.6	14 May	293	Manumission
9.20.9	15 May	293	Crime; fugitive
4.57.6	17 May	293	Manumission
7.16.17	23 May	293	Status
6.3.12	24 May	293	Patron–freedmen; inheritance
7.14.7	17 Jun	293	Status
8.44.21	21 Jun	293	Status; property
8.44.20	26 Jun	293	Property; inheritance
5.34.7	6 Jul	293	Inheritance
7.16.18	15 Jul	293	Status
9.46.6	17 Aug	293	Torture
7.22.1	23 Aug	293	Status; fugitive
7.16.19	27 Aug	293	Status
7.16.20	27 Aug	293	Status; patron–freedmen
9.9.25	28 Aug	293	Sex
4.36.1	1 Oct	293	Manumission
3.41.3	3 Oct	293	Crime
4.26.10	3 Oct	293	*Peculium*
6.38.2	7 Oct	293	Property; inheritance
7.16.21	7 Oct	293	Status
6.2.12	15 Oct	293	Crime
6.5.1	17 Oct	293	Patron–freedmen
6.17.1	21 Oct	293	Status
4.23.2	4 Nov	293	Property
9.20.10	5 Nov	293	Crime
9.20.11	5 Nov	293	Status; crime
4.34.9	7 Nov	293	Property
7.16.22	27 Nov	293	Status
4.26.11	30 Nov	293	*Peculium*
3.33.9	1 Dec	293	Inheritance; manumission
4.19.13	1 Dec	293	Property
7.2.12	1 Dec	293	Testamentary manumission
7.2.13	1 Dec	293	Testamentary manumission
3.41.4	15 Dec	293	Crime
6.27.3	17 Dec	293	Inheritance; sex
8.50.11	18 Dec	293	*Postliminium*
9.25.1	18 Dec	293	Name
4.49.11	23 Dec	293	Manumission
6.2.14	25 Dec	293	Crime
6.5.2	25 Dec	293	Patron–freedmen
4.19.15	27 Dec	293	Status
8.15.7	27 Dec	293	Property
4.24.11	28 Dec	293	Property
8.24.2	28 Dec	293	Property

Law (CJ)	Day	Year	Category
8.50.12	28 Dec	293	*Postliminium*
7.14.8	29 Dec	293	Status; manumission
7.16.23	29 Dec	293	Patron–freedmen; inheritance
7.16.24	29 Dec	293	Status
7.19.6	30 Dec	293	Status; crime
4.26.12	20 Jan	294	*Peculium*
8.14.5	21 Jan	294	Property
8.44.24	27 Jan	294	Status; property
3.15.2	4 Feb	294	Status
5.3.10	8 Feb	294	Property
6.30.11	8 Feb	294	Inheritance; manumission
6.55.6	8 Feb	294	Sex
7.26.7	8 Feb	294	Crime
4.19.17	9 Feb	294	Status; manumission
7.16.25	9 Feb	294	Status; manumission
8.46.8	9 Feb	294	Freedmen
4.6.9	10 Feb	294	Manumission
4.51.4	11 Feb	294	Inheritance
2.36.3	13 Feb	294	Property
8.44.25	13 Feb	294	Status
8.37.8	18 Feb	294	Property
3.32.20	24 Feb	294	Property
8.27.15	1 Mar	294	Property
6.37.17	5 Mar	294	Inheritance
3.22.4	6 Mar	294	Status
4.38.6	7 Mar	294	Sex
4.38.7	7 Mar	294	Property
7.10.6	7 Mar	294	Manumission
7.14.10	7 Mar	294	Status
7.14.11	7 Mar	294	Status
7.14.9	7 Mar	294	Status; *postliminium*
7.16.26	9 Mar	294	Patron–freedmen
8.50.13	11 Mar	294	*Postliminium*
2.12.19	14 Mar	294	Agents
7.2.11	17 Mar	294	Testamentary manumission
8.50.14	17 Mar	294	*Postliminium*
3.3.2 Edict	18 Mar	294	Status/manumission
7.2.10	18 Mar	294	Testamentary manumission
3.41.5	28 Mar	294	Crime
6.59.4	30 Mar	294	Inheritance
7.16.27	30 Mar	294	Status; inheritance
7.34.2	30 Mar	294	Property
8.44.26	31 Mar	294	Property
7.45.8	3 Apr	294	Property
9.41.14	6 Apr	294	Torture

(*cont.*)

Law (CJ)	Day	Year	Category
9.41.15	9 Apr	294	Torture
7.16.28	10 Apr	294	Status
4.13.5	11 Apr	294	Property
2.4.26	13 Apr	294	Status
2.53.5	14 Apr	294	*Postliminium*
6.55.7	14 Apr	294	Freedmen
7.4.11	15 Apr	294	Testamentary manumission
7.4.12	15 Apr	294	Testamentary manumission
3.1.7	16 Apr	294	Property
6.1.2	29 Apr	294	Fugitives
9.12.4	15 Jun	294	Crime
5.16.22	1 Aug	294	Manumission
6.2.16	1 Aug	294	Crime
3.22.5	2 Aug	294	Status
6.24.10	17 Aug	294	Inheritance
1.18.8	28 Aug	294	Inheritance; manumission
9.20.12	12 Sep	294	Crime; fugitive
2.18.21	26 Sep	294	Manumission
8.50.15	27 Sep	294	*Postliminium*
8.50.16	27 Sep	294	*Postliminium*
8.55.6	27 Sep	294	Property
7.23.1	3 Oct	294	Inheritance; *peculium*
3.32.21	10 Oct	294	Ownership
7.16.29	11 Oct	294	Status; sex
7.16.30	11 Oct	294	Patron–freedmen
7.16.31	11 Oct	294	Status
8.42.19	11 Oct	294	Agency
4.10.12	17 Oct	294	Status
6.42.28	18 Oct	294	Inheritance; manumission
9.35.8	18 Oct	294	Crime
4.20.8	25 Oct	294	Crime
5.12.24	27 Oct	294	Property; sex
8.42.20	28 Oct	294	Property
4.25.5	29 Oct	294	Agents
8.50.17	30 Oct	294	*Postliminium*
7.16.32	5 Nov	294	Inheritance; manumission
7.35.6	8 Nov	294	*Postliminium*
7.16.33	10 Nov	294	Patron–freedmen
7.16.34	13 Nov	294	Status; sex
3.32.23	16 Nov	294	Ownership
4.25.6	18 Nov	294	Agents
9.35.9	26 Nov	294	Crime
7.20.2	27 Nov	294	Status
7.14.12	29 Nov	294	Status
4.19.20	2 Dec	294	Status
9.20.14	4 Dec	294	Crime

Law (CJ)	Day	Year	Category
7.16.35	5 Dec	294	Status
6.56.2	7 Dec	294	Sex; inheritance
7.14.13	7 Dec	294	Status
7.4.13	7 Dec	294	Testamentary manumission
1.18.9	8 Dec	294	Property; status dispute
4.49.14	9 Dec	294	Property
7.33.8	9 Dec	294	Inheritance
8.44.30	13 Dec	294	Property
3.32.27	15 Dec	294	Ownership
7.16.36	17 Dec	294	Status; manumission
7.16.37	17 Dec	294	Status
7.16.38	17 Dec	294	Status
6.59.9	18 Dec	294	Sex; inheritance
9.35.10	18 Dec	294	Status
6.8.2	21 Dec	294	Status
4.19.22	24 Dec	294	Status
4.48.6	25 Dec	294	Property
7.14.14	26 Dec	294	Status
7.16.39	26 Dec	294	Status
8.13.25	26 Dec	294	Property
8.13.26	27 Dec	294	Property
3.36.22	28 Dec	294	Inheritance

Bibliography

ABBREVIATIONS

AARC	*Atti dell'Accademia romanistica costantiniana* (Naples, 1975–)
ANRW	Hildegard Temporini *et al.*, eds., *Aufstieg und Niedergang der römischen Welt: Geschichte und Kultur Roms im Spiegel der neueren Forschung* (Berlin, 1972–)
CAG	*Commentaria in Aristotelem graeca* (Berlin 1882–1909)
CC	*Corpus christianorum, series latina* (Turnhout, 1953–)
CCSG	*Corpus christianorum series graeca* (Turnhout, 1977–)
CJ	*Codex Justinianus* (see p. 537)
CMG	*Corpus medicorum graecorum* (Berlin, 1908–)
CSCO	*Corpus scriptorum christianorum orientalium* (Louvain, 1903–)
CSEL	*Corpus scriptorum ecclesiasticorum latinorum* (Vienna, 1866–)
CT	*Codex Theodosianus* (see p. 537)
DACL	*Dictionnaire d'archéologie chretienne et de liturgie*, eds. F. Cabrol and H. Leclerq (Paris 1907–53)
Dig.	*Digest* (see p. 537)
GCS	*Die griechischen christlichen Schriftsteller* (Leipzig and Berlin, 1891–)
LSJ	H. G. Liddell, R. Scott, H. S. Jones, and R. McKenzie, *A Greek–English Lexicon*, 9th edn. (Oxford, 1996)
MGH AA	*Monumenta Germaniae historica, Auctores antiquissimi* (Hanover and Berlin, 1877–1919)
MGH Conc.	*Monumenta Germaniae historica, Concilia* (Hanover and Berlin, 1893–)
MGH GPR	*Monumenta Germaniae historica, Gestorum Pontificum Romanorum*, 1, ed. T. Mommsen (Berlin, 1898)
PG	*Patrologiae cursus completus . . . series graeca*, ed. J. P. Migne (Paris, 1857–86)
PIR	*Prosopographia imperii romani saeculi I, II, III*, ed. E. Klebs, H. Dessau *et al.* (Berlin and Leipzig, 1897–)
PL	*Patrologiae cursus completus . . . series . . . ecclesiae latinae*, ed. J. P. Migne (Paris, 1844–64)

PLRE   Ed. A. H. M. Jones *et al.*, *The Prosopography of the Later Roman Empire* (Cambridge, 1971–92)

PLS   *Patrologiae cursus completus. Series Latina. Supplementum*, ed. J. P. Migne (Paris 1958–74)

PO   *Patrologia orientalis*, ed. R. Graffin *et al.* (Paris, 1904–)

RE   *Paulys Realencyclopädie der classischen Altertumswissenschaft*, ed. G. Wissowa (Stuttgart, 1893–)

SC   *Sources chrétiennes* (Paris, 1941–)

SEG   *Supplementum epigraphicum graecum* (Leiden, 1923–71; Amsterdam, 1979–)

TLL   *Thesaurus linguae latinae* (Leipzig, 1900–)

PRIMARY SOURCES: TEXTS

Achilles Tatius, *Leucippe et Clitophon*, ed. J.-P. Garnaud, *Achille Tatius d'Alexandrie: Le roman de Leucippé et Clitophon* (Paris, 1991).

Adamantius Judaeus, *Physiognomica*, ed. R. Foerster, *Scriptores physiognomonici Graeci et Latini*, vol. 1. (Leipzig, 1893).

Aelian, *Epistulae rusticae*, ed. P. Leone (Milan, 1974).

Aeneas of Gaza, *Epistulae*, ed. L. Massa Positano, *Epistole²* (Naples, 1962).

Aeneas of Gaza, *Theophrastus... dialogus*, ed. M. E. Colonna (Naples, 1958).

Aetius, *Iatricorum liber*, ed. A. Olivieri, CMG 8.1 (Leipzig, 1935).

Agathias, *Historiae*, ed. R. Keydell, *Historiarum libri quinque* (Berlin, 1967).

Ambrose, *De Abraham*, ed. C. Schenkl, CSEL 32.1 (Vienna, 1897) 501–638.

Ambrose, *De apologia prophetae David*, ed. P. Hadot, *Apologie de David*, SC 239 (Paris, 1977).

Ambrose, *De excessu fratris Satyri*, ed. O. Faller, CSEL 73 (Vienna, 1955) 209–325.

Ambrose, *De fuga saeculi*, ed. C. Schenkl, CSEL 32.2 (Vienna, 1897) 163–207.

Ambrose, *De Iacob*, ed. C. Schenkl, CSEL 32.2 (Vienna, 1897) 3–70.

Ambrose, *De Ioseph*, ed. C. Schenkl, CSEL 32.2 (Vienna, 1897) 73–122.

Ambrose, *De Nabuthae*, ed. C. Schenkl, CSEL 32.2 (Vienna, 1897) 469–516.

Ambrose, *De obitu Valentiniani*, ed. O. Faller, CSEL 73 (Vienna, 1955) 327–67.

Ambrose, *De officiis ministrorum*, ed. M. Testard, CC 15 (Turnhout, 1957).

Ambrose, *De paradiso*, ed. C. Schenkl, CSEL 32.1 (Vienna, 1897) 265–336.

Ambrose, *De sacramentis*, ed. O. Faller, CSEL 73 (Vienna, 1955) 15–85.

Ambrose, *De Tobia*, ed. C. Schenkl, CSEL 32.2 (Vienna, 1897) 519–73.

Ambrose, *De virginibus*, ed. F. Gori (Milan, 1989).

Ambrose, *Epistulae*, ed. O. Faller, CSEL 82 (Vienna, 1968).

Ambrose, *Explanatio psalmorum*, ed. M. Petschenig, CSEL 64 (Vienna, 1919).

Ambrose, *Expositio evangelii secundum Lucam*, ed. M. Adriaen, CC 14 (Turnhout, 1957).

Ambrose, *Expositio psalmi* CXVIII, ed. M. Petschenig, CSEL 62 (Vienna, 1913).

Ambrosiaster, *Commentarius in Pauli epistulam ad Colossenses*, ed. H. Vogels, CSEL 81.2 (Vienna, 1969).

526   *Bibliography*

Ambrosiaster, *Commentarius in Pauli epistulam ad Galatas*, ed. H. Vogels, CSEL 81.2 (Vienna, 1966).
Ambrosiaster, *Commentarius in Pauli epistulam ad Romanos*, ed. H. Vogels, CSEL 81.1 (Vienna, 1966).
Ammianus Marcellinus, *Res gestae*, ed. W. Seyfarth, 2 vols. (Leipzig, 1978).
Anthologia Graeca, ed. H. Beckby, 4 vols. (Munich, 1957).
Anthologia Latina, eds. F. Buecheler and A. Riese, 2 vols. (Leipzig, 1894–1926).
Apophthegmata Patrum. PG 65: 72–440.
Appianus, *Historia Romana*, eds. L. Mendelssohn and P. Viereck (Leipzig, 1986).
Apuleius, *Metamorphoses*, ed. R. Helm, vol. 1 (Leipzig, 1905).
Aristaenetus, *Epistulae*, ed. O. Mazal (Stuttgart, 1971).
Aristotle, *Rhetorica*, ed. W. D. Ross (Oxford, 1964).
Arnobius, *Adversus nationes*, ed. A. Reifferscheid, CSEL 4 (Vienna, 1875).
Artemidorus, *Oneirocritica*, ed. R. Pack (Leipzig, 1983).
Asterius of Amasea, *Homiliae*, ed. C. Datema (Leiden, 1970).
Asterius of Antioch, *Commentarii in Psalmos*, ed. M. Richard, *Asterii sophistae commentariorum in Psalmos quae supersunt* (Oslo, 1956).
Pseudo-Athanasius, *De fallacia diaboli*, ed. R. P. Casey, "An Early Homily on the Devil Ascribed to Athanasius of Alexandria," *Journal of Theological Studies* 36 (1935) 4–10.
Pseudo-Athanasius, *De virginitate*, ed. D. Brakke, CSCO 593 (Louvain, 2002).
Athanasius, *Epistola ad episcopos Aegypti et Libyae*. PG 25: 537–93.
Athanasius, *Historia Arianorum*, ed. H. G. Opitz, *Athanasius Werke*, vol. 2.1 (Berlin, 1940).
Athanasius, *In illud: Qui dixerit verbum in filium*. PG 26: 648–76.
Pseudo-Athanasius, *Quaestiones ad Antiochum ducem*. PG 28: 597–700.
Pseudo-Athanasius, *Vita sanctae Syncleticae*, ed. L. Abelarga, *The Life of Saint Syncletica: Introduction, Critical Text, Commentary* (Greek) (Thessalonica, 2002).
Athenaeus, *Deipnosophistae*, ed. G. Kaibel (Leipzig, 1887–90).
Pseudo-Augustine, *De sobrietate et castitate*. PL 40: 1105–12.
Augustine, *Confessiones*, ed. L. Verheijen, CC 27 (Turnhout, 1981).
Augustine, *Contra Cresconium*, ed. M. Petschenig, CSEL 52.2 (Vienna, 1909) 325–582.
Augustine, *Contra Faustum*, ed. J. Zycha, CSEL 25.1 (Vienna, 1891) 251–797.
Augustine, *Contra Iulianum*. PL 44: 641–874.
Augustine, *Contra mendacium*, ed. J. Zycha, CSEL 41 (Vienna, 1900) 469–528.
Augustine, *De bono conjugali*, ed. J. Zycha, CSEL 41 (Vienna, 1900) 187–231.
Augustine, *De civitate Dei*, eds. B. Dombart and A. Kalb, CC 47–8 (Turnhout, 1955).
Augustine, *De cura pro mortuis gerenda*, ed. J. Zycha, CSEL 41 (Vienna, 1900) 621–660.
Augustine, *De doctrina christiana*, ed. J. Martin, CC 32 (Turnhout, 1962).
Augustine, *De libero arbitrio*, ed. W. Green, CC 29 (Turnhout, 1970) 211–321.
Augustine, *De moribus ecclesiae catholicae et Manichaeorum*. PL 32: 1309–78.

Augustine, *De nuptiis et concupiscentia*, eds. C. Urba and J. Zycha, CSEL 42 (Vienna, 1902).

Augustine, *De ordine*, ed. W. Green, CC 29 (Turnhout, 1970) 89–137.

Augustine, *De peccatorum meritis*, eds. C. Urba and J. Zycha, CSEL 60 (Vienna, 1913) 3–151.

Augustine, *De sermone Domini in monte*, ed. A. Mutzenbecher, CC 35 (Turnhout, 1967).

Augustine, *De spiritu et littera*, eds. C. Urba and J. Zycha, CSEL 60 (Vienna, 1913) 155–228.

Augustine, *De utilitate credendi*, ed. J. Zycha, CSEL 25.1 (Vienna, 1891) 1–48.

Augustine, *De utilitate ieiunii*, ed. R. van der Plaetse, CC 46 (Turnhout, 1969) 231–41.

Augustine, *Enarrationes in Psalmos* (1–32), ed. C. Weidmann, CSEL 93.1A (Vienna, 2003).

Augustine, *Enarrationes in Psalmos*, eds. E. Dekkers and J. Fraipont, CC 38–40 (Turnhout, 1956).

Augustine, *Epistulae*, ed. A. Goldbacher, CSEL 34.1–2, 44, 57, 58 (Vienna, 1895–1923).

Augustine, *Epistulae**, ed. J. Divjak, *Epistolae ex duobus codicibus nuper in lucem prolatae*, CSEL 88 (Vienna, 1981).

Augustine, *In Iohannis epistulam ad Parthos tractatus*. PL 35: 1977–2062.

Augustine, *In Iohannis evangelium tractatus*, ed. R. Willems, CC 36 (Turnhout, 1954).

Augustine, *Locutionum in heptateuchum*, ed. J. Fraipont, CC 33 (Turnhout, 1958) 381–465.

Augustine, *Quaestiones in heptateuchum*, ed. J. Fraipont, CC 33 (Turnhout, 1958) 3–377.

Augustine, *Sermones*. PL 38–9.

Augustine, *Sermones*, ed. G. Morin, *Miscellanea Agostiniana*, vol. 1 (Rome, 1930).

Augustine, *Sermones* (*1–50*), ed. C. Lambot, CC 41 (Turnhout, 1961).

Augustine, *Sermones novissimi*, ed. F. Dolbeau, *Vingt-six sermons au peuple d'Afrique* (Paris, 1996).

Augustine, *Sermones selecti duodeviginti*, ed. C. Lambot, *Stromata patristica et mediaevalia*, vol. 1 (Utrecht, 1950).

Aurelius Victor, *De Caesaribus*, ed. P. Dufraigne (Paris, 1975).

Ausonius, *The Works of Ausonius: Edited with Introduction and Commentary*, ed. R. P. H. Green (Oxford, 1991).

Barsanuphius and John, *Quaestiones et responsiones*, ed. F. Neyt, *Correspondance*, SC 426, 427, 450, 451, 468 (Paris, 1997–2002).

Pseudo-Basil, *Homilia de virginitate*, eds. D. Amand and M. C. Moons, "Une curieuse homélie grecque inédite sur la virginité adressée aux pères de famille," *Revue bénédictine* 63 (1953) 35–69.

Basil of Ancyra, *De virginitate*. PG 30: 669–809.

Basil of Caesarea, *Asceticon magnum sive Quaestiones (regulae fusius tractatae)*. PG 31: 901–1052.

Basil of Caesarea, *De jejunio.* PG 31: 164–97.

Basil of Caesarea (dub.), *Enarratio in prophetam Isaiam.* PG 30: 116–668.

Basil of Caesarea, *Epistulae*, ed. Y. Courtonne, *Lettres*, 3 vols. (Paris, 1957–66).

Basil of Caesarea, *Homilia dicta tempore famis et siccitatis.* PG 31: 304–28.

Basil of Caesarea, *Homilia exhortatoria ad sanctum baptisma.* PG 31: 424–44.

Basil of Caesarea, *Homilia in divites*, ed. Y. Courtonne, *Homélies sur la richesse, édition critique et exégétique* (Paris, 1935).

Basil of Caesarea, *Homilia in illud: Attende tibi ipsi*, ed. S. Rudberg, *L'homélie de Basile de Césarée sur le mot "Observe-toi toi-même"* (Stockholm, 1962).

Basil of Caesarea, *Homilia in illud: Destruam horrea mea*, ed. Y. Courtonne, *Homélies sur la richesse, édition critique et exégétique* (Paris, 1935).

Basil of Caesarea, *Homilia in martyrem Julittam.* PG 31: 237–61.

Basil of Caesarea, *Homiliae in Hexaemeron*, ed. S. Giet, *Homélies sur l'hexaéméron*, SC 26² (Paris, 1968).

Basil of Caesarea, *Homiliae super Psalmos.* PG 29: 209–494.

Basil of Caesarea, *Quod deus non est auctor malorum.* PG 31: 329–53.

Pseudo-Basil of Seleukia, *De vita et miraculis sanctae Theclae*, ed. G. Dagron (Brussels, 1978).

Boethius, *Commentaria in Ciceronis Topica.* PL 64: 1039–1174.

Caesar, *De bello gallico*, ed. W. Hering (Leipzig, 1987).

Pseudo-Caesarius, *Quaestiones et responsiones*, ed. R. Riedinger, *Die Erotapokriseis* (Berlin, 1989).

Caesarius of Arles, *Sermones*, ed. G. Morin, CC 103 (Turnhout, 1953).

Callinicus, *Vita Hypatii*, ed. G. Bartelink, SC 177 (Paris, 1971).

Cassiodorus, *Expositio Psalmorum*, ed. M. Adriaen, CC 98 (Turnhout, 1958).

Cassiodorus, *Variae*, ed. Å. J. Fridh, *Variarum libri XII*, CC 96 (Turnhout, 1973).

Cato, *De agricultura*, ed. R. Goujard (Paris, 1975).

Choricius of Gaza, *Orationes*, eds. R. Foerster and E. Richtsteig, *Choricii Gazaei opera* (Leipzig, 1929).

Chronica gallica, ed. T. Mommsen, MGH AA 9 (Berlin, 1892) 615–66.

Chronographus anni CCCLIV, ed. T. Mommsen, MGH AA 9 (Berlin, 1892) 13–196.

Chrysippus, *Encomium in sanctum Theodorum*, ed. A. Sigalas, *Des Chrysippos von Jerusalem Enkomion auf den heiligen Theodoros Teron* (Leipzig, 1921).

Claudian, *De quarto consulatu Honorii*, ed. J. B. Hall, *Carmina* (Leipzig, 1985).

Claudian, *In Eutropium*, ed. J. B. Hall, *Carmina* (Leipzig, 1985) 143–89.

Clement of Alexandria, *Paedagogus*, eds. C. Mondésert, C. Matray, and H.-I. Marrou, SC 70, 108, 158 (Paris, 1960–70).

Colloquium Harleianum, ed. G. Goetz, *Corpus glossariorum Latinorum*, vol. 3 (Leipzig, 1892) 635–59.

Columella, *De re rustica*, ed. V. Lundström (Uppsala, 1897–1968).

Commentum Cornuti in Persium, eds. W. Clausen and J. Zetzel (Munich, 2004).

Constitutiones apostolorum, ed. M. Metzger, SC 320, 329, 336 (Paris, 1985–7).

Corippus, *In laudem Iustini*, ed. A. Cameron (London, 1976).

Cosmas Indicopleustes, *Topographia Christiana*, ed. W. Wolska-Conus, SC 141 (Paris, 1968).

Cyril of Alexandria, *Commentarii in Joannem*, ed. P. Pusey, *Commentarii in Joannem* (Oxford, 1872).

Cyril of Alexandria, *Commentarius in Isaiam prophetam*. PG 70: 9–1449.

Cyril of Alexandria, *De adoratione et cultu in spiritu et veritate*. PG 68: 132–1125.

Cyril of Alexandria, *Epistulae paschales sive Homiliae*. PG 77: 401–981.

Cyril of Alexandria, *In epistulam 1 ad Corinthios*. PG 74: 855–914.

Cyril of Alexandria, *In epistulam ad Romanos*, ed. P. E. Pusey, 3 vols. (Oxford, 1872).

Cyril of Alexandria, *Sermon against the Eunuchs*, in George the Monk, ed. C. de Boor, *Georgi monachi chronicon*, vol. 2 (Leipzig, 1978) 651–6.

Cyril of Jerusalem, *Catecheses ad illuminandos*, eds. W. C. Reischl and J. Rupp, *Cyrilli Hierosolymorum archiepiscopi opera quae supersunt omnia*, 2 vols. (Munich, 1848–60) vol. 1, 28–320, vol. 2, 2–342.

Cyril of Jerusalem, *Procathechesis*, eds. W. C. Reischl and J. Rupp, *Cyrilli Hierosolymorum archiepiscopi opera quae supersunt omnia*, 2 vols. (Munich, 1848–60) vol. 1, 1–26.

De miraculis sancti Stephani protomartyris. PL 41: 833–54.

Diadochus, *Capita centum de perfectione*, ed. J. Rutherford, *One hundred practical texts of perception and spiritual discernment from Diadochos of Photike* (Belfast, 2000).

Didymus the Blind, *In epistulas catholicas brevis enarratio*, ed. F. Zoepfl (Münster, 1914).

Dio Chrysostom, *Orationes*, ed. J. de Arnim, 2 vols. (Berlin, 1896).

Diodorus, *Commentarii in Psalmos*, ed. J.-M. Olivier, CCSG 6 (Turnhout, 1980).

Diodorus, *Fragmenta in epistulam ad Romanos*, ed. K. Staab, *Pauluskommentare aus der griechischen Kirche aus Katenenhandschriften gesammelt* (Münster, 1933).

Diodorus Siculus, *Bibliotheca historica*, eds. P. Bertrac and Y. Vernière (Paris, 1983).

Diomedes, *Ars Grammatica*, ed. H. Keil, *Grammatici latini* 1 (Leipzig, 1870) 299–529.

Pseudo-Dionysius the Areopagite, *Epistulae*, eds. G. Heil and A. M. Ritter, *Corpus Dionysiacum* II (Berlin, 1991).

Dorotheus of Gaza, *Doctrinae diversae I–XVII*, eds. L. Regnault and J. de Préville, SC 92 (Paris, 2001).

Ennodius, *Carmina*, ed. G. Hartel, *Opera omnia*, CSEL 6 (Vienna, 1882) 507–608.

Ennodius, *Epistulae*, ed. G. Hartel, *Opera omnia* CSEL 6 (Vienna, 1882) 1–260.

Ennodius, *Opuscula*, ed. G. Hartel, *Opera omnia* CSEL 6 (Vienna, 1882) 261–419.

Ephraem the Syrian, *Hymnes sur la nativité*, eds. F. Graffin and F. Cassingena-Trévidy, SC 459 (Paris, 2001).

Ephraem the Syrian, *Sermo de passione salvatoris*, ed. K. G. Phrantzoles, Ὁσίου Ἐφραίμ τοῦ Σύρου ἔργα, vol. 7 (Thessalonica, 1998) 31–41.

Ephraem the Syrian, *Sermones paraenetici ad monachos Aegypti*, ed. K. G. Phrantzoles, Ὁσίου Ἐφραίμ τοῦ Σύρου ἔργα, vol. 3 (Thessalonica, 1990) 36–294.

Epictetus, *Epicteti Dissertationes*, ed. H. Schenkl (Leipzig, 1916).

Epiphanius, *Panarion*, ed. K. Holl, GCS 37 (Leipzig, 1933).

Epistola Severi ad omnem ecclesiam, ed. S. Bradbury, *Letter on the Conversion of the Jews* (Oxford, 1996).

Eugippius, *Vita Severini*, ed. P. Régerat, *Vie de saint Séverin*, SC 374 (Paris, 1991).

Eunapius, *Fragmenta*, ed. R. C. Blockley, *The Fragmentary Classicizing Historians of the Later Roman Empire: Eunapius, Olympiodorus, Priscus, and Malchus*, 2 vols. (Liverpool, 1981–3) vol. 2, 2–150.

Eunapius, *Vitae sophistarum*, ed. J. Giangrande (Rome, 1956).

Eusebius, *Historia ecclesiastica*, ed. G. Bardy, SC 31, 41, 55, 73 (Paris, 1952–94).

Eusebius, *Praeparatio evangelica*, ed. É. Places, SC 206, 215, 228, 262, 266, 292, 307, 338, 369 (Paris, 1974–91).

Eutropius, *Breviarium historiae Romanae*, ed. H. Dietsch (Leipzig, 1850).

Evagrius Ponticus, *Rerum monachalium rationes*. PG 40: 1252–64.

Evagrius Scholasticus, *Historia ecclesiastica*, eds. J. Bidez and L. Parmentier, *The Ecclesiastical History of Evagrius* (London, 1898).

Excerpta Valesiana, ed. J. Moreau (Leipzig, 1968).

Expositio totius mundi et gentium, ed. J. Rougé, SC 124 (Paris, 1966).

Ferrandus of Carthage, *Epistulae ad Fulgentium*, ed. J. Fraipont, CC 91 (Turnhout, 1968).

Firmicus Maternus, *Mathesis*, ed. P. Monat, 3 vols. (Paris, 1992–4).

Firmus of Caesarea, *Epistulae*, eds. M.-A. Calvet-Sebasti and P.-L. Gatier, SC 350 (Paris, 1989).

Four Desert Fathers, ed. T. Vivian (Crestwood, 2004).

Four Martyrdoms from the Pierpont Morgan Coptic Codices, eds. E. Reymond and J. Barns (Oxford, 1973).

Pseudo-Fulgentius of Ruspe, *Sermones*. PL 65: 858–954.

Gelasius, *Epistulae*, ed. A. Thiel, *Epistolae Romanorum pontificum . . .* (Hildesheim, 1868).

Geoponica, ed. H. Beckh (Leipzig, 1895).

Gerontius, *Vita Melaniae*, ed. D. Gorce, SC 90 (Paris, 1962).

Gerontius, *Vita Melaniae (L)*, ed. P. Laurence (Jerusalem, 2002).

Gregory of Nazianzus, *Ad cives Nazianzenos (Oratio 17)*. PG 35: 964–81.

Gregory of Nazianzus, *Carmina* 1.2 = *Carmina moralia*. PG 37: 521–968.

Gregory of Nazianzus, *Carmina* 2.1 = *Carmina de se ipso*. PG 37: 969–1029, 1166–1452.

Gregory of Nazianzus, *Orationes* (20–3), ed. J. Mossay, SC 270 (Paris, 1980).

Gregory of Nazianzus, *Orationes* (42–3), ed. J. Bernardi, SC 384 (Paris, 1992).

Gregory of Nyssa, *Adversus eos qui castigationes aegre ferunt*. PG 46: 308–16.

Gregory of Nyssa, *Antirrheticus adversus Apollinarium*, ed. F. Müller, *Gregorii Nysseni opera*, vol. 3.1 (Leiden, 1958).

Gregory of Nyssa, *Contra Eunomium*, ed. W. Jaeger, *Opera*, vol. 1–2 (Leiden, 1960).

Gregory of Nyssa, *Contra usurarios*, ed. E. Gebhardt, *Opera*, vol. 9 (Leiden, 1958).

Gregory of Nyssa, *De beneficentia*, ed. A. van Heck, *Opera*, vol. 9 (Leiden, 1967).

Gregory of Nyssa (sp.), *De creatione hominis*, ed. H. Hörner, *Opera*, Suppl. (Leiden, 1972).

Gregory of Nyssa, *De iis qui baptisum differunt.* PG 46: 416–32.

Gregory of Nyssa, *De virginitate*, ed. M. Aubineau, *De virginitate*, SC 119 (Paris, 1966).

Gregory of Nyssa, *De vita Moysis*, ed. J. Daniélou, SC 1² (Paris, 2000).

Gregory of Nyssa, *Epistulae*, ed. P. Maraval, SC 363 (Paris, 1990).

Gregory of Nyssa, *Epistula canonica ad Letoium*, ed. E. Mühlenberg, *Opera*, vol. 3.5 (Leiden, 2008).

Gregory of Nyssa, *In canticum canticorum*, ed. H. Langerbeck, *Opera*, vol. 6 (Leiden, 1960).

Gregory of Nyssa, *In diem luminum*, ed. E. Gebhardt, *Opera*, vol. 9 (Leiden, 1958).

Gregory of Nyssa, *In Ecclesiasten*, ed. F. Vinel, *Homélies sur l'Ecclésiaste*, SC 416 (Paris, 1996).

Gregory of Nyssa, *In illud tunc et ipse filius*, ed. J. K. Downing, *Opera*, vol. 3.2 (Leiden, 1987).

Gregory of Nyssa, *In sanctum pascha*, ed. E. Gebhardt, *Opera*, vol. 9 (Leiden, 1958).

Gregory of Nyssa, *Vita Macrinae*, ed. P. Maraval, SC 178 (Paris, 1971).

Gregory the Great, *Epistulae*, ed. D. Norberg, CC 140–140A (Turnhout, 1982).

Heliodorus, *Scholia in Dionysii Thracis, Scholia Marciana*, ed. A. Hilgard, *Grammatici Graeci*, vol. 1.3 (Leipzig, 1901).

Hephaestion, ed. D. Pingree, *Hephaestionis Thebani apotelesmaticorum libri tres*, 2 vols. (Leipzig, 1973).

Hermas, *Pastor*, ed. R. Joly, *Le pasteur*, SC 53 (Paris, 1958).

Herodotus, *Historiae*, ed. H. B. Rosén, 2 vols. (Leipzig, 1987).

Hesychius, *Lexicon*, ed. M. Schmidt, 5 vols. (Jena, 1858–68).

Hilary of Poitiers, *De trinitate*, ed. P. Smulders, CC 62A (Turnhout, 1980).

Hilary of Poitiers, *Tractatus super Psalmos*, ed. A. Zingerle, CSEL 22 (Vienna, 1891).

Historia Apollonii regis Tyri, ed. G. A. A. Kortekaas (Groningen, 1984).

Historia monachorum in Aegypto, ed. A.-J. Festugière (Brussels, 1971).

Horace, *Sermones*, eds. O. Keller and A. Holder, *Opera*, 2 vols. (Leipzig, 1899–1925) vol. 2, 1–161.

Hydatius, *Hydatii Limici chronica subdita*, ed. R. Burgess (Oxford, 1993).

Iamblichus, *De vita Pythagorica*, ed. U. Klein (Leipzig, 1937).

Isidore of Pelusium, *Epistulae*, ed. P. Évieux, *Isidore de Péluse: Lettres*. SC 422, 454 (Paris, 1997–2000).

Isidore of Seville, *Etymologiarum sive Originum*, ed. W. M. Lindsay (Oxford, 1911).

Jerome, *Ad Titum.* PL 26: 555–600.

Jerome, *Adversus Helvidium.* PL 23: 183–206.

Jerome, *Adversus Iovinianum.* PL 23: 221–352.

Jerome, *Commentarii in Esaiam*, ed. M. Adriaen, CC 73 (Turnhout, 1963).

Jerome, *Commentarius ad Ephesios.* PL 26: 439–554.

Jerome, *Commentarius in Ecclesiasten*, ed. M. Adriaen, CC 72 (Turnhout, 1959).

Jerome, *Contra Rufinum*, ed. P. Lardet, CC 79 (Turnhout, 1982).

Jerome, *Contra Vigilantium.* PL 23: 337–52.

Jerome, *Epistulae*, ed. I. Hilberg, CSEL 54–6 (Vienna, 1910–18).

Jerome, *In Zachariam*, ed. M. Adriaen, *Commentarii in prophetas minores*, CC 76A (Turnhout, 1970).

Jerome, *Vita Hilaronis*, ed. A. Bastiaensen, *Vite dei Santi*, vol. 4 (Rome, 1975) 72–142.

Jerome, *Vita Malchi*. In *Trois vies de moines*, eds. P. Leclerc and E. Morales, SC 508 (Paris, 2007).

Pseudo-Chrysostom, *In Psalmum 50*. PG 55: 565–75.

John Chrysostom, *Ad eos qui scandalizati sunt*, ed. A.-M. Malingrey, *Sur la providence de Dieu*, SC 79² (Paris, 2000).

John Chrysostom, *Ad illuminandos catechesis*. PG 49: 223–40.

John Chrysostom, *Ad populum Antiochenum*. PG 49: 15–222.

John Chrysostom, *Ad Stagirium a daemone vexatum*. PG 47: 423–94.

John Chrysostom, *Ad Stelechium de compunctione*. PG 47: 411–22.

John Chrysostom, *Ad Theodorum lapsum*, ed. J. Dumortier, SC 117 (Paris, 1966).

John Chrysostom, *Ad viduam juniorem*, eds. G. H. Ettlinger and B. Grillet, *A une jeune veuve: Sur le mariage unique*, SC 138 (Paris, 1968).

John Chrysostom, *Adversos Iudaeos*. PG 48: 843–942.

John Chrysostom, *Adversus oppugnatores vitae monasticae*. PG 47: 319–86.

John Chrysostom, *Contra eos qui subintroductas habent virgines*, ed. J. Dumortier, *Les cohabitations suspectes* (Paris, 1955).

John Chrysostom, *De decem millium talentorum*. PG 51: 17–30.

John Chrysostom, *De eleemosyna*. PG 51: 261–72.

John Chrysostom, *De Lazaro*. PG 48: 963–1054.

John Chrysostom, *De libello repudii*. PG 51: 217–26.

John Chrysostom, *De mutatione nominum*. PG 51: 113–56.

John Chrysostom, *De non iterando conjugio*, eds. B. Grillet and G. Ettlinger, SC 138 (Paris, 1968).

John Chrysostom, *De sacerdotio*, ed. A.-M. Malingrey, *Jean Chrysostome: Sur le sacerdoce*, SC 272 (Paris, 1980).

John Chrysostom, *De virginitate*, ed. B. Grillet, *La virginité*, SC 125 (Paris, 1966).

John Chrysostom, *Epistulae ad Olympiadem*, ed. A.-M. Malingrey, *Jean Chrysostome: Lettres à Olympias*, SC 13 bis (Paris, 1968).

John Chrysostom, *Expositiones in Psalmos*. PG 55: 39–498.

John Chrysostom, *Homilia habita postquam presbyter Gothus*. PG 63: 499–510.

John Chrysostom, *In acta apostolorum*. PG 60: 13–384.

John Chrysostom, *In ascensionem domini nostri Jesu Christi*. PG 50: 441–52.

John Chrysostom, *In epistulam ad Colossenses*. PG 62: 299–392.

John Chrysostom, *In epistulam 1 ad Corinthios*. PG 61: 9–382.

John Chrysostom, *In epistulam ad Ephesios*. PG 62: 9–176.

John Chrysostom, *In epistulam ad Hebraeos*. PG 63: 9–236.

John Chrysostom, *In epistulam ad Philemonem*. PG 62: 701–20.

John Chrysostom, *In epistulam ad Philippenses*. PG 62: 177–298.

John Chrysostom, *In epistulam ad Romanos*. PG 60: 391–682.

John Chrysostom, *In epistulam 1 ad Thessalonicenses*. PG 62: 391–468.

John Chrysostom, *In epistulam* ii *ad Thessalonicenses*. PG 62: 467–500.

John Chrysostom, *In epistulam* i *ad Timotheum*. PG 62: 501–600.

John Chrysostom, *In epistulam* ii *ad Timotheum*. PG 62: 599–662.

John Chrysostom, *In epistulam ad Titum*. PG 62: 663–700.

John Chrysostom, *In Genesim (homiliae 1–67)*. PG 53: 21–385. PG 54: 385–580.

John Chrysostom, *In Genesim (sermones 1–9)*, ed. L. Brottier, *Sermons sur la Genèse*, SC 433 (Paris, 1998).

John Chrysostom, *In illud: Habentes eundem spiritum*. PG 51: 271–302.

John Chrysostom, *In illud: Hoc scitote quod in novissimis diebus*. PG 56: 271–80.

John Chrysostom, *In illud: Propter fornicationes autem unusquisque suam uxorem habeat*. PG 51: 207–18.

John Chrysostom, *In illud: Salutate Priscillam et Aquilam*. PG 51: 187–208.

John Chrysostom, *In Joannem*. PG 59: 23–482.

John Chrysostom, *In Matthaeum*. PG 57: 13–472. PG 58: 471–794.

John Chrysostom, *In principium Actorum*. PG 51: 65–112.

John Chrysostom, *Non esse ad gratiam concionandum*. PG 50: 653–62.

John Chrysostom, *Quod regulares feminae viris cohabitare non debeant*, ed. J. Dumortier, *Comment observer la virginité* (Paris, 1955).

John Moschus, *Pratum spirituale*. PG 87: 2852–3112.

John Moschus, *Pratum spirituale*, ed. T. Nissen, "Unbekannte Erzählungen aus dem Pratum Spirituale," *Byzantinische Zeitschrift* 38 (1938) 354–72.

John Philoponus, *De aeternitate mundi*, ed. H. Rabe, *Ioannes Philoponus: De aeternitate mundi contra Proclum* (Leipzig, 1899).

John Philoponus, *Epitome libri diaitetes*, ed. A. Sanda, *Opuscula monophysitica* (Beirut, 1930).

John Philoponus, *In libros de generatione animalium commentaria*, ed. M. Hayduck, *Commentaria in Aristotelem Graeca*, vol. 14.3 (Berlin, 1903).

Julian, *Epistulae*, ed. J. Bidez, *L'empereur Julien: Oeuvres complètes*, vol. 1.2 (Paris, 1960).

Julian, *Misopogon*, ed. C. Lacombrade, *L'empereur Julien: Oeuvres complètes*, vol. 2.2 (Paris, 1964) 156–99.

Julian, *Orationes*, ed. G. Rochefort, *L'empereur Julien: Oeuvres complètes*, vol. 1–2 (Paris, 1932–64).

Lactantius, *De ira Dei*, ed. C. Ingremeau, SC 289 (Paris, 1982).

Lactantius, *De mortibus persecutorum*, ed. J. Creed (Oxford, 1984).

Lactantius, *Divinae institutiones*, ed. S. Brandt, CSEL 19.1 (Vienna, 1890).

Libanius, *Declamationes*, ed. R. Foerster, *Opera*, vols. 5–7 (Leipzig, 1909–13).

Libanius, *Epistulae*, ed. R. Foerster, *Opera*, vols. 10–11 (Leipzig, 1921–2).

Libanius, *Orationes*, ed. R. Foerster, *Opera*, vols. 1–4 (Leipzig, 1903–8).

Libanius, *Progymnasmata*, ed. R. Foerster, *Opera*, vol. 8 (Leipzig, 1915).

Pseudo-Macarius, *Homiliae spirituales*, ed. H. Dörries, E. Klostermann, and M. Krüger (Berlin, 1964).

Pseudo-Macarius, *Sermones*, ed. H. Berthold, *Makarios/Symeon Reden und Briefe*, 2 vols. (Berlin, 1973).

John Malalas, *Chronographia*, ed. I. Thurn (Berlin, 2000).

Mark the Deacon, *Vita Porphyrii*, eds. H. Grégoire and M.-A. Kugener, *Vie de Porphyre* (Paris, 1930).

Maximus of Turin, *Sermones*. PL 57: 529–760.

Menander, *Division of Epideictic Speeches*, eds. D. Russell and N. Wilson, *Menander Rhetor* (Oxford, 1981).

Miracles of St. Menas, ed. T. Detorakēs, *Mēnas ho megalomartys* (Herakleion, 1995).

Olympiodorus, *In Platonis Alcibiadem commentarii*, ed. L. G. Westerink, *Olympiodorus: Commentary on the First Alcibiades of Plato* (Amsterdam, 1956).

Oribasius, *Collectiones medicae*, ed. J. Raeder, *Oribasii collectionum medicarum reliquiae*, CMG 6.1.1 (Leipzig, 1928).

Orosius, *Historiarum adversus paganos libri* VII, ed. M.-P. Arnaud-Lindet (Paris, 1990–1).

Palladius, *De insitione*, ed. R. Rodgers (Leipzig, 1975).

Palladius, *Dialogus de vita sancti Joanni Chrysostomi*, eds. A.-M. Malingrey and P. Leclercq, SC 341 (Paris, 1988).

Palladius, *Historia Lausiaca*, ed. C. Butler, *The Lausiac History of Palladius*, 2 vols. (Hildesheim, 1967, orig. 1904).

Palladius, *Opus agriculturae*, ed. R. Rodgers (Leipzig, 1975).

Palladius, *Opus agriculturae*, ed. R. Martin, 2nd edn. (Paris, 2003, orig. 1976).

Palladius Medicus, *Commentarii in Hippocratis librum sextum de morbis popularibus*, ed. F. R. Dietz, *Scholia in Hippocratem et Galenum*, 2 vols. (Königsberg, 1834).

Panegyrici Latini, ed. E. Galletier, *Panégyriques latins*, 3 vols. (Paris, 1949–55).

Patria Constantinopolis, ed. T. Preger, *Scriptores originum Constantinopolitanarum* (Leipzig, 1907).

Paulinus of Nola, *Carmina*, ed. G. von Hartel, CSEL 30 (Vienna, 1894).

Paulinus of Nola, *Epistulae*, ed. G. von Hartel, CSEL 29 (Vienna, 1999).

Paulinus of Pella, *Eucharisticos*, ed. C. Moussy, SC 209 (Paris, 1974).

Periplus Maris Erythraei, ed. L. Casson (Princeton, 1989).

Persius, *Saturae*, ed. W. V. Clausen (Oxford, 1959).

Peter of Alexandria, *On Riches*, eds. B. Pearson and T. Vivian, *Two Coptic Homilies Attributed to Saint Peter of Alexandria* (Rome, 1993).

Peter Chrysologus, *Sermones*, ed. A. Olivar, CC 24B (Turnhout, 1982).

Petronius, *Satyricon*, ed. K. Mueller, *Satyricon reliquiae*, 4th edn. (Stuttgart, 1995).

Phaedrus, *Fabulae Aesopiae*, ed. L. Mueller (Leipzig, 1873).

Philo, *De Josepho*, ed. L. Cohn, *Philonis Alexandrini opera quae supersunt*, vol. 4 (Berlin, 1902) 61–118.

Philo, *De specialibus legibus*, ed. A. Mosès, *Opera*, vol. 25 (Paris, 1970).

Philo, *Quod omnis probus liber sit*, ed. L. Cohn, *Philonis Alexandrini opera quae supersunt*, vol. 6 (Berlin, 1915) 1–31.

Philogelos, ed. A. Thierfelder, *Philogelos der Lachfreund von Hierokles und Philagrios* (Munich, 1968).

Philostratus, *Vita Apollonii*, ed. C. P. Jones, 3 vols. (Cambridge, MA, 2005–6).

Pliny, *Epistulae*, ed. R. A. B. Mynors (Oxford, 1963).

Pliny the Elder, *Naturalis historia*, eds. R. König and G. Winkler (Munich, 1973–2004).

Plutarch, *De amore prolis*, ed. M. Pohlenz, *Plutarchi moralia* (Leipzig, 1929).

Procopius of Caesarea, *De bellis*, eds. J. Haury and G. Wirth, vol. 1–2 (Leipzig, repr. 2001).

Procopius of Caesarea, *Historia arcana*, eds. J. Haury and G. Wirth, vol. 3 (Leipzig, repr. 2001).

Procopius of Gaza, *Commentarii in Isaiam*. PG 87.2: 1817–2717.

Procopius of Gaza, ed. H. Diels, "Über die von Prokop beschriebene Kunstuhr von Gaza," *Abhandlungen der preussischen Akademie der Wissenschaften, philosophisch-historische Klasse* 26 (Berlin, 1917) 27–39.

Pseudacronis scholia in Horatium vetustiora, ed. O Keller, vol. 2 (Leipzig, 1904).

Querolus, sive Aulularia incerti auctoris comoedia una cum indice verborum, ed. G. Ranstrand (Göteborg, 1951).

Pseudo-Quintilian, *Declamationes minores*, ed. M. Winterbottom (New York, 1984).

Quintilian, *Institutio Oratoria*, ed. M. Winterbottom, 2 vols. (Oxford, 1970).

Rutilius Namatianus, *De reditu suo*, ed. E. Doblhofer (Heidelberg, 1972).

Salvian of Marseilles, *Ad ecclesiam*, ed. C. Halm, MGH AA 1 (Berlin, 1877) 120–68.

Salvian of Marseilles, *De gubernatione Dei*, ed. C. Halm, MGH AA 1 (Berlin, 1877) 1–108.

Scriptores Historiae Augustae, ed. H. Hohl, 3rd edn., 2 vols. (Leipzig, 1997).

Sedulius, *Paschale opus*, ed. I. Huemer, CSEL 10 (Vienna, 1885).

Seneca, *De beneficiis*, ed. E. Hermes, vol. 1 (Leipzig, 1905).

Seneca the Elder, *Controversiae*, ed. M. Winterbottom, vol. 2 (Cambridge, MA, 1974).

Severianus of Gabala, *Fragmenta in epistulam ad Romanos*, ed. K. Staab, *Pauluskommentare aus der griechischen Kirche aus Katenenhandschriften gesammelt* (Münster, 1933) 213–25.

Severianus of Gabala, *In Genesim*. PG 56: 519–22.

Severianus of Gabala, *In tribus pueris*. PG 56: 593–600.

Sidonius Apollinaris, *Epistulae*, ed. B. Krusch, MGH AA 8 (Berlin, 1887) 1–172.

Sidonius Apollinaris, *Carmina*, ed. P. Mohr (Leipzig, 1895).

Socrates, *Historia ecclesiastica*. PG 67: 34–842.

Sopater, *Diairesis Zētēmatōn*, ed. C. Walz, *Rhetores graeci*, vol. 8 (London, 1835) 2–385.

Sopater, *Eis tēn ermogenous technēn*, ed. C. Walz, *Rhetores graeci*, vol. 5 (London, 1835) 1–211.

Sozomen, *Historia ecclesiastica*, eds. J. Bidez and G. C. Hansen, GCS 50 (Berlin, 1960).

Stephanus, *Ethnica*, ed. A. Meineke (Berlin, 1849).
Sulpicius Severus, *Dialogorum libri ii*, ed. C. Halm, CSEL 1 (Vienna, 1866).
Sulpicius Severus, *Epistulae iii*, ed. C. Halm, CSEL 1 (Vienna, 1866).
Sulpicius Severus, *Vita sancti Martini Turonensis*, ed. J. Fontaine, SC 133 (Paris, 1967).
Symmachus, *Epistulae*, ed. O. Seeck, MGH AA 6.1 (Berlin, 1883) 1–278.
Symmachus, *Relationes*, ed. O. Seeck, MGH AA 6.1 (Berlin, 1883) 279–319.
Synesius, *Calvitii encomium*, ed. N. Terzaghi (Rome, 1944).
Synesius, *Catastases*, ed. N. Terzaghi (Rome, 1939).
Synesius, *Epistulae*, ed. A. Garzya, *Epistolae* (Rome, 1979).
Synesius, *De regno*, ed. N. Terzaghi (Rome, 1939).
Syrianus, *Commentarium in Hermogenis librum peri staseon*, ed. H. Rabe, *Syriani in Hermogenem commentaria*, 2 vols. (Leipzig, 1893).
Tacitus, *Annales*, ed. H. Heubner (Leipzig, 1983).
Tacitus, *Germania*, ed. E. Koestermann (Leipzig, 1949).
Talmud = Talmud Bavli: The Gemara: The Classic Vilna Edition, with an Annotated, Interpretive Elucidation, as an Aid to Talmud Study, ed. Yisroel Simcha Schorr. Schottenstein Edition (Brooklyn, 1997–).
Tertullian, *Ad uxorem*, ed. C. Munier, SC 273 (Paris, 1980).
Tertullian, *Apologeticum*, ed. E. Dekkers, *Tertulliani opera*, CC 1–2 (Turnhout, 1954) vol. 1, 77–171.
Themistius, *Orationes*, eds. G. Downey and H. Schenkl, *Themistii orationes quae supersunt*, 3 vols. (Leipzig, 1965–74).
Theodore of Mopsuestia, *In epistulam ad Corinthios*, ed. K. Staab, *Pauluskommentare aus der griechischen Kirche aus Katenenhandschriften gesammelt* (Münster, 1933) 172–96.
Theodoret of Cyrrhus, *De providentia orationes*. PG 83: 556–773.
Theodoret of Cyrrhus, *Epistulae*, ed. Y. Azéma, *Correspondance*, SC 40, 98, 111 (Paris, 1955–65).
Theodoret of Cyrrhus, *Historia ecclesiastica*, ed. L. Parmentier, GCS 5 (Berlin, 1998).
Theodoret of Cyrrhus, *Historia religiosa*, eds. P. Canivet and A. Leroy-Molinghen, *Histoire des moines de Syrie*, SC 234 (Paris, 1977).
Theodoret, *Interpretatio epistulae i ad Corinthios*, in *Interpretatio in xiv epistulas sancti Pauli*. PG 82: 36–877.
Theodoret of Cyrrhus, *Interpretatio epistulae ad Hebraeos*, in *Interpretatio in xiv epistulas sancti Pauli*. PG 82: 36–877.
Varro, *De re rustica*, ed. H. Keil (Leipzig, 1889).
Victor of Vita, *Historia persecutionis Africanae provinciae*, ed. M. Petschenig, CSEL 7 (Vienna, 1881).
Vita Aesopi, ed. B. Perry, *Aesopica*, vol. 1 (New York, 1980).
Vita Alexandri, ed. E. de Stoop, *Vie d'Alexandre l'Acémète*, PO 6.5 (Turnhout, 1911).
Zeno of Verona, *Tractatus*, ed. B. Löfstedt, CC 22 (Turnhout, 1971).
Zosimus, *Historia nova*, ed. F. Paschoud, 3 vols. (Paris, 1971–89).

PRIMARY SOURCES: LAWS

Codex Justinianus = Ed. P. Krueger, *Corpus iuris civilis*, vol. 2 (Berlin, 1915).
Codex Theodosianus = Eds. T. Mommsen and P. Krueger, *Theodosiani libri* XVI *cum constitutionibus sirmondianis*... (Berlin, 1905).
Collatio = *Mosaicarum et Romanarum legum collatio*, ed. T. Mommsen, *Collectio librorum iuris anteiustiniani*, vol. 3 (Berlin, 1890) 107–98.
Consultatio = *Consultatio veteris cuiusdam iurisconsulti*, ed. J. Baviera, *Fontes iuris romani antejustiniani²*, vol. 2 (Florence, 1968, orig. 1940) 593–613.
Digest = Eds. T. Mommsen and P. Krueger, *Corpus iuris civilis*, vol. 1 (Berlin, 1922).
Edictum de pretiis rerum venalium, ed. M. Giacchero (Genoa, 1974).
Edictum Theodorici, ed. F. Bluhme, MGH Leges 5 (Hanover, 1875) 145–79.
Fragmenta Vaticana. T. Mommsen, *Collectio librorum iuris anteiustiniani in usum scholarum*, vol. 3 (Berlin, 1890) 1–106.
Fragmentum Dositheanum, ed. G. Goetz, *Corpus Glossarium Latinorum*, vol. 3 (Leipzig, 1888) 48–56, 102–8.
Gai Institutionum Epitome, eds. E. Seckel and B. Kuebler, *Iurisprudentiae anteiustiniani reliquias⁶* (Leipzig, 1911) 395–431.
Gaius, *Institutiones*, ed. F. de Zulueta, 2 vols. (Oxford, 1946–53).
Inquisitio de theloneis Raffelstettensis, eds. A. Boretius and V. Krause, MGH Capitularia 2 (Hanover, 1897) 249–52.
Laterculus Veronensis, ed. O. Seeck (Berlin, 1876).
Lex Visigothorum, ed. K. Zeumer, MGH Leges nationum Germanicarum, 1.1 (Hanover, 1902).
Novellae Justiniani, eds. W. Kroll and R. Schöll, *Corpus iuris civilis*, vol. 3. (Berlin, 1968, orig. 1895).
Pauli sententiae, ed. J. Baviera, *Fontes iuris romani antejustiniani²*, vol. 2 (Florence, 1968, orig. 1940) 319–417.
Syro-Roman Lawbook, ed. W. Selb, *Das syrisch-römisches Rechtsbuch*, 3 vols. (Vienna, 2002).
Regulae Ulpiani, ed. J. Baviera, *Fontes iuris romani antejustiniani²*, vol. 2 (Florence, 1968, orig. 1940) 261–301.

PRIMARY SOURCES: PAPYRI AND OSTRACA

BGU 1 = *Aegyptische Urkunden aus den Königlichen Museen zu Berlin, Griechische Urkunden* (Berlin, 1895).
BGU 2 = *Aegyptische Urkunden aus den Königlichen Museen zu Berlin, Griechische Urkunden* (Berlin, 1903).
BGU 4 = *Aegyptische Urkunden aus den Königlichen Museen zu Berlin, Griechische Urkunden* (Berlin, 1912).
CPJ = Ed. V. Tcherikover, *Corpus Papyrorum Judaicarum* (Cambridge, MA, 1957–64).
CPR 6 = *Corpus Papyrorum Raineri*, ed. H. Harrauer (Vienna, 1985).

M. Chr. = Eds. L. Mitteis and U. Wilcken, *Grundzüge und Chrestomathie der Papyruskunde*, 2 vols. (Leipzig and Berlin, 1912).

R. Marichal, *Les ostraca de Bu Njem* (Tripoli, 1992).

P. Abinn. = Ed. H. I. Bell *et al.*, *The Abinnaeus Archive: Papers of a Roman Officer in the Reign of Constantius II* (Oxford, 1962).

P. Amh. 2 = Eds. B. P. Grenfell and A. S. Hunt, *The Amherst Papyri: Classical Fragments and Documents of the Ptolemaic, Roman and Byzantine Periods* (London, 1901).

P. Ammon 2 = Eds. K. Maresch and I. Andorlini, *Papyri aus den Sammlungen des Istituto Papirologico "G. Vitelli" (Università di Firenze), der Duke University, Durham, NC, und der Universität Köln* (Paderborn, 2006).

P. Athen. = Ed. G. A. Petropoulos, *Papyri Societatis Archaeologicae Atheniensis* (Athens, 1939).

P. Bad. 4 = Ed. F. Bilabel, *Veröffentlichungen aus den badischen Papyrus-Sammlungen: Griechische Papyri* (Heidelberg, 1924).

P. Bodl. = Ed. R. P. Salomons, *Papyri Bodleianae* (Amsterdam, 1996).

P. Brem. = Ed. U. Wilcken, *Die Bremer Papyri* (Berlin, 1936).

P. Brux. = Ed. G. Nachtergael, *Papyri Bruxellenses Graecae* (Brussels, 1974).

P. Cair. Isid. = Eds. A. Boak and H. C. Youtie, *The Archive of Aurelius Isidorus in the Egyptian Museum, Cairo, and the University of Michigan* (Ann Arbor, 1960).

P. Cair. Zen. IV = Ed. C. C. Edgar, *Zenon Papyri* (Cairo, 1931).

P. Charite = Ed. K. A. Worp, *Das Aurelia Charite Archiv* (Zutphen, 1981).

P. Euphr., D. Feissel, J. Gascou, and J. Teixidor, "Documents d'archives romains inédits du Moyen Euphrate (IIIe s. après J.-C.)," *Journal des Savants* (1997) 3–35.

P. Flor. 1 = Ed. G. Vitelli, *Documenti pubblici e privati dell'età romana e bizantina* (Milan, 1906).

P. Hamb. 4 = Eds. B. Kramer and D. Hagedorn, *Griechische Papyrusurkunden der Hamburger Staats- und Universitätsbibliothek* (Stuttgart and Leipzig, 1998).

P. Harr. 2 = Eds. R. A. Coles *et al.*, *The Rendel Harris Papyri of Woodbrooke College, Birmingham* (Zutphen, 1985).

P. Haun. 3 = Eds. T. Larsen and A. Bülow-Jacobsen, *Papyri Graecae Haunienses* (Bonn, 1985).

P. Herm. Rees = Ed. B. R. Rees, *Papyri from Hermopolis and Other Documents of the Byzantine Period* (London, 1964).

P. Kellis 1 = Ed. K. A. Worp, *Papyri from Kellis* (Oxford, 1995).

P. Köln 5 = Eds. M. Gronewald, K. Maresch, and W. Schäfer, *Kölner Papyri* (Opladen, 1985).

P. Lips. = Ed. L. Mitteis, *Griechische Urkunden der Papyrussammlung zu Leipzig* (Leipzig, 1906).

P. Lond. 3 = Eds. F. G. Kenyon and H. I. Bell, *Greek Papyri in the British Museum* (London, 1907).

P. Lugd. Bat. = Eds. E. Boswinkel *et al.*, *Papyrologica Lugduno-Batava* (Leiden, 1965).

P. Neph. = Eds. B. Kramer *et al.*, *Das Archiv des Nepheros und verwandte Texte* (Mainz, 1987).

P. Nessana = Ed. C. J. Kraemer, *Excavations at Nessana III: Non-Literary Papyri* (Princeton, 1958).

P. Oxy. = *The Oxyrhynchus Papyri* (London, 1898–).

P. Oxy. Hels. = Ed. H. Zilliacus *et al.*, *Fifty Oxyrhynchus Papyri* (Helsinki, 1979).

P. Petrie = Eds. J. P. Mahaffy, *The Flinders Petrie Papyri*, vol. 1 (Dublin, 1891).

P. Princeton = Ed. E. H. Kase, *Papyri in the Princeton University Collections*, vol. 2 (Baltimore, 1936).

P. Rain. Cent. = *Festschrift zum 100-jährigen Bestehen der Papyrussammlung der Österreichischen Nationalbibliothek, Papyrus Erzherzog Rainer* (Vienna, 1983).

P. Ryl. 4 = Eds. C. H. Roberts and E. G. Turner, *Catalogue of the Greek and Latin Papyri in the John Rylands Library, Manchester: Documents of the Ptolemaic, Roman and Byzantine Periods* (Manchester, 1952).

PSI 8 = *Papiri greci e latini* (Florence, 1927).

PSI 9 = *Papiri greci e latini* (Florence, 1929).

PSI 10 = *Papiri greci e latini* (Florence, 1932).

P. Sijp. = Eds. A. J. B. Sirks and K. A. Worp, *Papyri in Memory of P. J. Sijpesteijn* (Oakville, 2007).

P. Strasb. = Ed. F. Preisigke *et al.*, *Griechische Papyrus der Kaiserlichen Universitäts- und Landes-bibliothek zu Strassburg* (Leipzig, 1912–89).

P. Tebt. 2 = Eds. B. P. Grenfell, A. S. Hunt, and J. G. Smyly, *The Tebtunis Papyri* (London, 1907).

F. Preisigke, *Archiv für Papyrusforschung und Verwandte Gebiete* 3 (1906) 415–24.

SB 5 = *Sammelbuch griechischer Urkunden aus Aegypten* (Heidelberg and Wiesbaden, 1934–55).

SB 12 = *Sammelbuch griechischer Urkunden aus Aegypten* (Wiesbaden, 1976–7).

SB 18 = *Sammelbuch griechischer Urkunden aus Aegypten* (Wiesbaden, 1993).

SPP 20 = Ed. C. Wessely, *Catalogus Papyrorum Raineri. Series Graeca* (Leipzig, 1921).

P. Vindob. G 39761 = Ed. F. Hoogendijk, "Byzantinischer Sklavenkauf," *Archiv für Papyrusforschung* 42 (1996) 225–34.

PRIMARY SOURCES: INSCRIPTIONS

CIL = *Corpus Inscriptionum Latinarum* (Berlin, 1863–).

G. Dagron and D. Feissel, eds., *Inscriptions de Cilicie* (Paris, 1987).

GDI = Eds. R. Bechtel and H. Collitz, *Sammlung der griechischen Dialekt-Inschriften*, 4 vols. (Göttingen, 1884–1915).

E. Geroussi-Bendermacher, "Propriété foncière et inventaire d'esclaves: Un texte inédit de Perissa (Thera) tardo-antique," in V. Anastasiadis and P. Doukellis, eds., *Esclavage antique et discriminations socio-culturelles* (New York, 2005) 335–58.

IG 2.1 = Ed. U. Koehler, *Inscriptiones graecae* (Berlin, 1877).

IG 2.2 = Ed. U. Koehler, *Inscriptiones graecae* (Berlin, 1883).

IG 12.2 = Ed. G. Paton, *Inscriptiones graecae* (Berlin, 1899).

IG 12.3 = Ed. F. Hiller, *Inscriptiones graecae* (Berlin, 1898).
IG 14 = Ed. G. Kaibel, *Inscriptiones graecae* (Berlin, 1890).
IGLS = Eds. L. Jalabert and R. Mouterde, *Inscriptions grecques et latines de la Syrie* (Paris, 1929–).
IGRR = Ed. R. Cagnat, *Inscriptiones graecae ad res romanas pertinentes* (Paris, 1911–27).
IGSK 36.1. = Ed. F. Poljakov, *Inschriften von Tralleis und Nysa* (Bonn, 1989).
IGSK 57 = Eds. H. R. Horsley and S. Mitchell, *The Inscriptions of Central Pisidia* (Bonn, 2000).
ILS = Ed. H. Dessau, *Inscriptiones latinae selectae*, 3 vols. (Berlin, 1892–1916).
I.Magnesia = O. Kern, *Die Inschriften von Magnesia am Maeander* (Berlin, 1900).
ISMDA = P. Petsas *et al.*, *Inscriptions du sanctuaire de la mère des dieux autochtone de Leukopetra (Macedoine)* (Athens, 2000).
G. Kiourtzian, *Recueil des inscriptions grecques chrétiennes des Cyclades* (Paris, 2000).
TAM = *Tituli Asiae Minoris* (Vienna, 1901–).

PRIMARY SOURCES: CONCILIAR DOCUMENTS

Concilium Agathense, ed. C. Munier, *Concilia galliae*, CC 148 (Turnhout, 1963) 189–228.
Concilium Arausicanum, ed. C. Munier, *Concilia galliae*, CC 148 (Turnhout, 1963) 76–93.
Concilium Arelatense 11, ed. C. Munier, *Concilia galliae*, CC 148 (Turnhout, 1963) 111–30.
Concilium Aurelianense v, ed. F. Maassen, MGH Leges, Concilia aevi Merovingici (Hanover, 1883) 86–98.
Concilium Eliberritanum, ed. J. Mansi, *Sacrorum conciliorum nova amplissima collectio*, vol. 2 (Florence, 1759) 1–20.
Concilium Vasense, ed. C. Munier, *Concilia galliae*, CC 148 (Turnhout, 1963) 94–104.
Concilium Veneticum, ed. C. Munier, *Concilia galliae*, CC 148 (Turnhout, 1963) 150–8.
Registri ecclesiae Carthaginensis excerpta, ed. C. Munier, *Concilia Africae*, CC 149 (Turnhout, 1974) 173–247.

PRIMARY SOURCES: ELECTRONIC RESOURCES

Cetedoc Library of Christian Latin Texts, CLCLT-5 (Turnhout, 2002–).
Thesaurus Linguae Graecae (TLG) (Irvine, 1972–), www.tlg.irvine.edu. Online full-text database.

SECONDARY SOURCES

Albanese, B. 1962, "La struttura della *manumissio inter amicos*: contributo alla storia dell'*amicitia romana*," *Annali del seminario giuridico della Università di Palermo* 29: 5–103.
1991, "Appunti sul SC. Claudiano," *Scritti giuridici* 1, Palermo, orig. 1951, 29–39.

Alcock, S. 1993, *Graecia Capta: The Landscapes of Roman Greece*, Cambridge.

Alföldy, G. 1972, "Die Freilassung von Sklaven und die Struktur der Sklaverei in der römischen Kaiserzeit," *Rivista storica dell' Antichità* 2: 97–129.

1986, *The Social History of Rome*, trans. D. Braund and F. Pollock, Baltimore.

Allard, P. 1876, *Les esclaves chrétiens: depuis les premiers temps de l'Église jusqu'à la fin de la domination romaine en Occident*, Paris.

1907, "Une grande fortune romaine au cinquième siècle," *Revue des questions historiques* 81: 5–30.

Allen, P. and Mayer, W. 1993, "Computer and Homily: Accessing the Everyday Life of Early Christians," *Vigiliae Christianae* 47: 260–80.

Allen, R. 2009, "How Prosperous Were the Romans? Evidence from Diocletian's Price Edict (AD 301)," in *Quantifying the Roman Economy: Methods and Problems*, eds. A. Bowman and A. Wilson, Oxford, 327–45.

Alston, R. 2001, "Urban Population in Late Roman Egypt and the End of the Ancient World," in *Debating Roman Demography*, ed. W. Scheidel, Boston, 161–204.

Amouretti, M. 1986, *Le pain et l'huile dans la Grèce antique*, Paris.

Anderson, P. 1974, *Passages from Antiquity to Feudalism*, London.

Anderson, R. and Gallman, R. 1977, "Slaves as Fixed Capital: Slave Labor and Southern Economic Development," *Journal of American History* 64: 24–46.

Andreassi, M. 1999, "P. Oxy. III 413 (Moicheutria), rr. 122–4 verso," *Zeitschrift für Papyrologie und Epigraphik* 124: 17–21.

Andreau, J. 1986, "Declino e morte dei mestieri bancari nel Mediterraneo occidentale (III–IV d.C.)," in *Società romana e impero tardoantico*, vol. 1, ed. A. Giardina, Rome, 601–15, 814–18.

1993, "The Freedman," in *The Romans*, ed. A. Giardina, Chicago, 175–98.

1999, *Banking and Business in the Roman World*, trans. J. Lloyd, Cambridge.

Andreau, J. and Descat, R. 2006, *Esclave en Grèce et à Rome*, Paris.

Andreau, J. and Maucourant, J. 1999, "À propos de la 'rationalité économique' dans l'antiquité gréco-romaine," *Topoi Orient-Occident* 9: 48–102.

Andreotti, R. 1965, "L'applicazione del 'Senatus Consultum Claudianum' nel Basso impero," in *Neue Beiträge zur Geschichte der alten Welt*, vol. 2, ed. W. Welskopf, Berlin, 3–12.

Anné, L. 1941. *Les rites des fiançailles et la donation pour cause de mariage sous le Bas-Empire*, Louvain.

Arangio-Ruiz, V. 1974, "L'application du droit romain en Égypte après la constitution antoninienne," *Studi epigrafici e papirologici*, Naples, 258–94.

Archi, G. 1976, *Teodosio II e la sua codificazione*, Naples.

Arjava, A. 1988, "Divorce in Later Roman Law," *Arctos* 22: 5–21.

1996, *Women and Law in Late Antiquity*, Oxford.

1998, "Ein verschollenes Gesetz des Codex Theodosianus über uneheliche Kinder (CT 4, 6, 7a)," *Zeitschrift der Savigny-Stiftung für Rechtsgeschichte. Romanistiche Abteilung* 115: 414–18.

Arnaud, P. 2007, "Diocletian's Price Edict: The Prices of Seaborne Transport and the Average Duration of Maritime Travel," *Journal of Roman Archaeology* 20: 321–36.

Astolfi, R. 1970, *La Lex Iulia et Papia*, Padua.

1993, Review of Luchetti, *La legittimazione dei figli naturali nelle fonti tardo-imperiali e giustinianee, Studia et documenta historiae et iuris* 59: 383–99.

Atkinson, K. 1966, "The Purpose of the Manumission Laws of Augustus," *Irish Jurist* 1: 356–74.

Aubert, J.-J. 1994, *Business Managers in Ancient Rome: A Social and Economic Study of Institores, 200 B.C.–A.D. 250*, Leiden.

Aurigemma, S. 1926, *I mosaici di Zliten*, Rome.

Bagnall, R. 1991, "Freedmen and Freedwomen with Fathers?," *Journal of Juristic Papyrology* 21: 7–8.

1992, "Landholding in Late Roman Egypt: The Distribution of Wealth," *Journal of Roman Studies* 82: 128–49.

1993, "Slavery and Society in Late Roman Egypt," in *Law, Politics, and Society in the Ancient Mediterranean World*, eds. B. Halpern and D. Hobson, Sheffield, 220–40.

1996, *Egypt in Late Antiquity*, Princeton.

1997a, *The Kellis Agricultural Account Book*, Oxford.

1997b, "Missing Females in Roman Egypt," *Scripta classica Israelica* 16: 121–38.

2005, "Evidence and Models for the Economy of Roman Egypt," in *The Ancient Economy: Evidence and Models*, eds. I. Morris and J. Manning, Stanford, 187–204.

2007, "From Hermopolis to Antioch in Business Class," *Journal of Roman Archaeology* 20: 591–94.

Forthcoming, *Everyday Writing in the Graeco-Roman East*, Sather Classical Lectures, Berkeley.

Bagnall, R. and Frier, B. 1994, *The Demography of Roman Egypt*, New York.

Bagnall, R., Frier, B., and Rutherford, I. 1997, *The Census Register P. Oxy. 984: The Reverse of Pindar's Paeans*, Brussels.

Bagnall, R. and Worp, K. 1978, *The Chronological Systems of Byzantine Egypt*, Zutphen.

1980, "Papyrus Documentation in Egypt from Constantine to Justinian," in *Miscellanea papyrologica*, ed. R. Pintaudi, Florence, 13–23.

Bagnall, R. *et al.* 1987, *Consuls of the Later Roman Empire*, Atlanta.

Balard, M. 1968, "Remarques sur les esclaves à Gênes dans la seconde moitié du XIIIᵉ siècle," *Mélanges d'archéologie et d'histoire* 80: 627–80.

Balestri Fumagalli, M. 1982, "Nuove riflessioni sulla '*manumissio inter amicos*,'" in *Studi in onore di Arnaldo Biscardi*, Milan, 117–69.

Balmelle, C. 2001, *Les demeures aristocratiques d'Aquitaine: société et culture de l'antiquité tardive dans le sud-ouest de la Gaule*, Bordeaux.

Balty, J. 1982, "*Paedagogiani*-pages, de Rome à Byzance," in *Rayonnement grec: hommages à Charles Delvoye*, eds. L. Hadermann-Misguich and G. Raepsaet, Brussels, 299–312.

Banaji, J. 1977, "Modes of Production in a Materialist Conception of History," *Capital and Class* 2: 1–44.

1992, "Historical Arguments for a 'Logic of Deployment' in 'Precapitalist' Agriculture," *Journal of Historical Sociology* 5: 379–91.

1997, "Lavoratori liberi e residenza coatta: il colonato romano in prospettiva storica," in *Terre, proprietari, e contadini*, ed. E. Lo Cascio, Rome, 253–80.

2001, *Agrarian Change in Late Antiquity: Gold, Labour, and Aristocratic Dominance*, Oxford.

2009, "Aristocracies, Peasantries and the Framing of the Early Middle Ages," *Journal of Agrarian Change* 9: 59–91.

Bang, P. 2008, *The Roman Bazaar: A Comparative Study of Trade and Markets in a Tributary Empire*, Cambridge.

Barnes, T. D. 1981, *Constantine and Eusebius*, Cambridge, MA.

1982, *The New Empire of Diocletian and Constantine*, Cambridge, MA.

Barnish, S. J. B. 1985, "The Wealth of Julius Argentarius: Late Antique Banking and the Mediterranean Economy," *Byzantion* 55: 5–38.

Barone Adesi, G. 1990, "'Servi fugitivi in ecclesia': Indirizzi cristiani e legislazione imperiale," *AARC* 8: 695–741.

Barton, C. 2001, *Roman Honor: The Fire in the Bones*, Berkeley.

Barzel, Y. 1997, *Economic Analysis of Property Rights*, 2nd edn., New York.

Bassanelli Sommariva, G. 1988, "Brevi considerazioni su CTh. 9, 7, 1," *AARC* 7: 309–23.

2003, "L'uso delle rubriche da parte dei commissari teodosiani," *AARC* 14: 197–239.

Batcheller, J. 2001, "Goat-hair Textiles from Karanis, Egypt," in *The Roman Textile Industry and Its Influence*, eds. P. Rogers *et al.*, Oxford, 38–47.

Bavant, B. 1989, "Cadre de vie et habitat urbain en Italie centrale byzantine (VIe-VIIIe siècles)," *Mélanges de l'École française de Rome, Moyen Âge* 101: 465–532.

Beaucamp, J. 1989. "L'Égypte byzantine: biens des parents, biens du couple?", in *Eherecht und Familiengut in Antike und Mittelalter*, ed. D. Simon, Munich, 61–76.

1990–2, *Le statut de la femme a Byzance*, 2 vols., Paris.

Becker, G. 1965, "A Theory of the Allocation of Time,"*Economic Journal* 75: 493–517.

1981, *A Treatise on the Family*, Cambridge, MA.

Bellen, H. 1967, Review of Fabbrini, *La manumissio in ecclesia*, Tijdschrift voor rechtsgeschiedenis 35: 319–23.

1971, *Studien zur Sklavenflucht im römischen Kaiserreich*, Wiesbaden.

Bellen, H. and Heinen, H. 2003, *Bibliographie zur antiken Sklaverei*, 2 vols., Stuttgart.

Beloch, J. 1886, *Die Bevölkerung der griechisch-römischen Welt*, Leipzig.

Berger, A. 1953, *Encyclopedic Dictionary of Roman Law*, Philadelphia.

Berlin, I. 1998, *Many Thousands Gone: The First Two Centuries of Slavery in North America*, Cambridge, MA.

Berlin, I. and Morgan, P., eds. 1991, *The Slaves' Economy: Independent Production by Slaves in the Americas*, London.

1993, *Cultivation and Culture: Labor and the Shaping of Slave Life in the Americas*, Charlottesville.

Bernardi, J. 1968, *La prédication des pères cappadociens: le prédicateur et son auditoire*, Paris.

Berrouard, M.-F. 1985, "Un tournant dans la vie de l'église d'Afrique: les deux missions d'Alypius en Italie à la lumière de lettres 10*, 15*, 16*, 22*, 23*A de St. Augustin," *Revue des études augustiniennes et patristiques* 31: 46–70.

Betzig, L. 1992a, "Roman Monogamy," *Ethology and Sociobiology* 13: 351–83.

1992b, "Roman Polygyny," *Ethology and Sociobiology* 13: 309–49.

Bianchini, M. 1979, *Caso concreto e "lex generalis": per lo studio della tecnica e della politica normativa da Costantino a Teodosio II*, Milan.

1984, "Sul regime delle unioni fra libere e *adscripticii* nella legislazione giustinianea," in *Studi in onore di Cesare Sanfilippo* v, Milan, 59–123.

Bieżuńska-Małowist, I. 1974–7, *L'esclavage dans l'Égypte*, 2 vols., Wrocław.

1978, "La vie familiale des esclaves," *Index* 8: 140–3.

Biondi, B. 1952–4, *Il diritto romano cristiano*, 3 vols., Milan.

Biot, E. 1840, *De l'abolition de l'esclavage ancien en occident . . .*, Paris.

Biscardi, A. 1939, *Manumissio per mensam e affrancazioni pretorie*, Florence.

Blassingame, J. 1972, *The Slave Community: Plantation Life in the Antebellum South*, New York.

Blazquez, J. 1978, "Problemas económicos y sociales en la vida de Melania, la Joven, y en la *Historia Lausiaca* de Palladio," *Memorias de historia antigua* 2: 103–23.

Bloch, M. 1975, "Comment et pourquoi finit l'esclavage antique?," *Annales. Histoire, Sciences Sociales* 2: 161–70, orig. 1947.

Bloomer, W. M. 1997, "Schooling in Persona: Imagination and Subordination in Roman Education," *Classical Antiquity* 16: 57–78.

Bodel, J. 2005, "*Caveat emptor*: Towards a Study of Roman Slave Traders," *Journal of Roman Archaeology* 18: 181–95.

Forthcoming, "Slave Labor and Roman Society," in *The Cambridge World History of Slavery, Volume 1: The Ancient Mediterranean World*, eds. K. Bradley and P. Cartledge, Cambridge.

Boese, W. E. 1973, "A Study of the Slave Trade and the Sources of Slaves in the Roman Republic and the Early Roman Empire," Diss., University of Washington.

Bömer, F. 1960, *Untersuchungen über die Religion der Sklaven in Griechenland und Rom, II: Die sogenannte sakrale Freilassung in Griechenland und die (δοῦλοι) ἱεροί*, Wiesbaden.

Bonfante, P. 1925, *Corso di diritto romano*, vol. 1, Rome.

Bonnassie, P. 1991, *From Slavery to Feudalism in South-western Europe*, New York.

Bonner, S. 1977, *Education in Ancient Rome*, London.

Booth, A. 1979, "The Schooling of Slaves in First-Century Rome," *Transactions of the American Philological Association* 109: 11–19.

Boswell, J. 1988, *The Kindness of Strangers: The Abandonment of Children in Western Europe from Late Antiquity to the Renaissance*, New York.

Boulvert, G. 1984, "L'État du principat et la fin de l'esclavage antique," in *Studi in onore di Cesare Sanfilippo*, Milan, 125–43.

Boulvert, G. and Morabito, M. 1982, "Le droit de l'esclavage sous le Haut-Empire," *ANRW* 2.14: 98–182.

Bouraselis, K. 1989, *Theia Dōrea*, Athens.

Bowden, W., Lavan, L., and Machado, C., eds. 2004, *Recent Research on the Late Antique Countryside*, Boston.

Bowes, K. 2006, "Out of Pirenne's Shadow? Late Antique San Vincenzo Reconsidered," in *Between Text and Territory: Survey and Excavations in the Terra of San Vincenzo al Volturno*, eds. K. Bowes *et al.*, London, 287–305.

Bowman, A. 1985, "Landholding in the Hermopolite Nome in the Fourth Century A.D.," *Journal of Roman Studies* 75: 137–63.

2000, "Urbanization in Roman Egypt," in *Romanization and the City: Creation, Transformations, and Failures*, ed. E. Fentress, Portsmouth, 173–88.

Bowman, A. and Wilson, A., eds. 2009, *Quantifying the Roman Economy: Methods and Problems*, Oxford.

Braconi, P. 1995, "Il 'Calcidico' di Lepcis Magna era un mercato di schiavi?," *Journal of Roman Archaeology* 18: 213–19.

Bradley, K. R. 1978, "The Age at Time of Sale of Female Slaves," *Arethusa* 11: 243–52.

1987a, "On the Roman Slave Supply and Slave Breeding," in *Classical Slavery*, ed. M. Finley, London, 42–64.

1987b, *Slaves and Masters in the Roman Empire: A Study in Social Control*, New York.

1989, *Slavery and Rebellion in the Roman World, 140 B.C.–70 B.C.*, Bloomington.

1991, "The Social Role of the Nurse in the Roman World," in *Discovering the Roman Family: Studies in Roman Social History*, ed. K. R. Bradley, New York, 13–36.

1994, *Slavery and Society at Rome*, Cambridge.

2000a, "Animalizing the Slave: The Truth of Fiction," *Journal of Roman Studies* 90: 110–25.

2000b, "Prostitution, the Law of Rome, and Social Policy," *Journal of Roman Archaeology* 13: 468–75.

2004, "On Captives under the Principate," *Phoenix* 58: 298–318.

Brakke, D. 2001, "Ethiopian Demons: Male Sexuality, the Black-Skinned Other, and the Monastic Self," *Journal of the History of Sexuality* 10: 501–35.

Bransbourg, G. 2008, "Fiscalité impériale et finances municipales au IVe siècle," *Antiquité tardive* 16: 255–96.

Braund, D. and Tsetskhladze, G. 1989, "The Export of Slaves from Colchis," *Classical Quarterly* 39: 114–25.

Brockmeyer, N. 1979, *Antike Sklaverei*, Darmstadt.

Brogiolo, G. 1996a, "Conclusioni," in *La fine delle ville romane: trasformazioni nelle campagne tra tarda antichità e alto medioevo*, ed. G. Brogiolo, Mantua, 107–10.

1996b, *La fine delle ville romane: trasformazioni nelle campagne tra tarda antichità e alto medioevo*, Mantua.

2005, "Risultati e prospettive della ricerca archeologica sulle campagne altomedievali italiane," in *Dopo la fine delle ville: le campagne dal VI al IX secolo: Gavi, 8–10 maggio 2004*, eds. G. Brogiolo *et al.*, Mantua, 7–16.

Brogiolo, G. and Chavarría Arnau, A. 2005, *Aristocrazie e campagne nell'Occidente da Costantino a Carlo Magno*, Florence.

Brogiolo, G., Chavarría Arnau, A., and Valenti, M., eds. 2005, *Dopo la fine delle ville: le campagne dal VI al IX secolo: Gavi, 8–10 maggio 2004*, Mantua.

Brogiolo, G., Gauthier, N., and Christie, N., eds. 2000, *Towns and Their Territories between Late Antiquity and the Early Middle Ages*, Leiden.

Brogiolo, G. and Ward-Perkins, B., eds. 1999, *The Idea and Ideal of the Town between Late Antiquity and the Early Middle Ages*, Leiden.

Brown, C. and Morgan, P., eds. 2006, *Arming Slaves: From Classical Times to the Modern Age*, New Haven.

Brown, P. 1971, *The World of Late Antiquity: From Marcus Aurelius to Muhammad*, London.

   1974, "*Mohammed and Charlemagne* by Henri Pirenne," *Daedalus* 103: 25–33.

   1988, *The Body and Society: Men, Women, and Sexual Renunciation in Early Christianity*, New York.

   1992, *Power and Persuasion in Late Antiquity: Towards a Christian Empire*, Madison.

   2002, *Poverty and Leadership in the Later Roman Empire*, Hanover.

Brunt, P. 1971, *Italian Manpower, 225 BC–AD 14*, Oxford.

Buckland, W. W. 1908, *The Roman Law of Slavery: The Condition of the Slave in Private Law from Augustus to Justinian*, Cambridge.

Budak, N. 2000, "Slavery in Late Medieval Dalmatia–Croatia: Labour, Legal Status, Integration," *Mélanges de l'École française de Rome, Moyen Âge* 112: 745–60.

Bush, M. 1996, "Serfdom in Medieval and Modern Europe: A Comparison," in *Serfdom and Slavery: Studies in Legal Bondage*, ed. M. Bush, London, 199–224.

Cabanes, P. 1974, "Les inscriptions du théâtre de Bouthrotos," in *Actes du colloque 1972 sur l'esclavage*, Paris, 105–209.

Calderini, A. 1908, *La manomissione e la condizione dei liberti in Grecia*, Milan.

Calderini, S. 1946, "Ricerche sull'industria e il commercio dei tessuti in Egitto," *Aegyptus* 26: 13–83.

Calderone, S. 1971, "Intorno ai problemi della manumissio in ecclesia," in *Studi in onore di Giuseppe Grosso*, vol. 4, Turin, 377–97.

Cambiano, G. 1987, "Aristotle and the Anonymous Opponents of Slavery," in *Classical Slavery*, ed. M. Finley, London, 28–52.

Cameron, Alan. and Long, J. 1993, *Barbarians and Politics at the Court of Arcadius*, Berkeley.

Cameron, Archibald. 1939a, "ΘΡΕΠΤΟΣ and Related Terms in the Inscriptions of Asia Minor," in *Anatolian Studies Presented to W. H. Buckler*, eds. W. M. Calder and J. Keil, Manchester, 27–62.

   1939b, "Inscriptions Relating to Sacral Manumission and Confession," *Harvard Theological Review* 32: 143–79.

Cameron, Averil. 1970, *Agathias*, Oxford.

   ed. 1976, *Corippus, In laudem Iustini*, London.

Campbell, G., Miers, S., and Miller, J. 2005, "Women in Western Systems of Slavery: Introduction," *Slavery & Abolition* 26: 161–79.

2006, "Children in European Systems of Slavery: Introduction," *Slavery & Abolition* 27: 163–82.

Cannata, C. 1962, *'Possessio" "Possessor" "Possidere" nelle fonti giuridiche del basso impero romano*, Milan.

Cantarella, E. 1991, "Homicides of Honor: The Development of Italian Adultery Law over Two Millennia," in *The Family in Italy: From Antiquity to the Present*, eds. D. Kertzer and R. Saller, New Haven, 229–44.

1996, "Famiglia, proprietà e schiavitù nel mondo antico," in *Storia dell'economia mondiale 1: Permanenze e mutamenti dall'antichità al medioevo*, ed. V. Castronovo, Rome, 117–32.

Capogrossi Colognesi, L. 1986, "Grandi proprietari, contadini e coloni nell'Italia romana (I–III d.C.)," in *Società romana e impero tardoantico*, vol. 1, ed. A. Giardina, Bari, 325–65, 703–23.

1997, "The Limits of the Ancient City and the Evolution of the Medieval City in the Thought of Max Weber," in *Roman Urbanism: Beyond the Consumer City*, ed. H. Parkins, London, 27–37.

Carandini, A. 1979, *L'anatomia della scimmia: la formazione economica della società prima del capitale: con un commento alle Forme che precedono la produzione capitalistica dai Grundrisse di Marx*, Turin.

1981, "Sviluppo e crisi delle manifatture rurali e urbane," in *Società romana e produzione schiavistica*, vol. 2, eds. A. Giardina and A. Schiavone, Rome, 249–60.

1983, "Columella's Vineyard and the Rationality of the Roman Economy," *Opus* 2: 177–204.

1986, *Settefinestre: una villa schiavistica nell'Etruria romana*, 3 vols., ed. A. Carandini, Modena.

1988, *Schiavi in Italia: gli strumenti pensanti dei Romani fra tarda Repubblica e medio Impero*, Rome.

1989a, "L'economia italica fra tarda Repubblica e medio Impero considerata dal punto di vista di una merce: il vino," in *Amphores romaines et histoire économique: dix ans de recherché*, Rome, 505–21.

1989b, "Villa romana e la piantagione schiavistica," in *Storia di Roma*, vol. 4, eds. E. Gabba and A. Schiavone, Turin, 101–200.

Carcaterra, A. 1990, "La schiavitù nel IV secolo. 'Spinte' e 'stimoli' cristiani delle leggi a favore degli schiavi,"*AARC* 8: 147–79.

Cardascia, G. 1950, "L'apparition dans le droit des classes d'*honestiores* et d'*humiliores*," *Revue historique de droit français et étranger* 28: 305–37, 461–85.

Carlsen, J. 1991, "*Magister pecoris*: The Nomenclature and Qualifications of the Chief Herdsman in Roman Pasturage," *Analecta Romana Instituti Danici* 20: 59–65.

1995, *Vilici and Roman Estate Managers until* AD *284*, Rome.

2002, "Estate Managers in Ancient Greek Agriculture," in *Ancient History Matters: Studies Presented to Jens Erik Skydsgaard on His Seventieth Birthday*, eds. K. Ascani *et al.*, Rome, 117–26.

Caron, P. 1983, "L'influenza cristiana sulla legislazione imperiale romana in materia di schiavitù," in *Studi in onore di Arnaldo Biscardi* 4, 311–23.

Carr, K. 1999, "Women's Work: Spinning and Weaving in the Greek Home," in *Archéologie des textiles des origines au ve siècle*, ed. M. Feugère, Montagnac, 163–6.

Carrié, J.-M. 1982, "Le 'colonat du Bas-empire': un mythe historiographique?," *Opus* 1: 351–70.

1983, "Un roman des origines: les généalogies du 'colonat du Bas-empire,'" *Opus* 2: 205–51.

1994, "Dioclétien et la fiscalité," *Antiquité tardive* 2: 33–64.

2005, "Une rationalité quand même," *Topoi orient-occident* 12: 293–303.

Cartledge, P. 1985, "Rebels and Sambos in Classical Greece: A Comparative View," in *Crux: Essays Presented to G. E. M. De Ste. Croix on His 75th Birthday*, eds. P. A. Cartledge and F. D. Harvey, London, 16–46.

2001, "The Political Economy of Greek Slavery," in *Money, Labour and Land: Approaches to the Economies of Ancient Greece*, eds. P. Cartledge, E. Cohen, and L. Foxhall, London, 156–66.

Casana, J. 2004, "The Archaeological Landscape of Late Roman Antioch," in *Culture and Society in Later Roman Antioch*, eds. I. Sandwell and J. Huskinson, Oxford, 102–25.

Cenderelli, A. 1965, *Ricerche sul* Codex Hermogenianus, Milan.

Cervellera, M. A. 1982, "Omosessualità e ideologia schiavistica in Petronio," *Index* 11: 221–34.

Češka, J. 1964, "Brachte der Dominat das Ende der sklavischen Unfreiheit?," *Sborník prací Filosofické fakulty brněnské university: E, Řada archeologicko-klasická* 9: 113–17.

Champlin, E. 1991, *Final Judgments: Duty and Emotion in Roman Wills, 200 BC–AD 250*, Berkeley.

Charvet, L. 1953, "Alapa," *Studia et documenta historiae et iuris* 19: 334–9.

Chastagnol, A. 1976, "Remarques sur les sénateurs orientaux dans le IVe siècle," *Acta antiqua Academiae Scientiarum Hungaricae* 24: 341–56.

1986, "La législation sur les biens des villes au IVe siècle à la lumière d'une inscription d'Éphèse," AARC 6, Perugia, 77–104.

1988, "La fin de l'ordre équestre: réflexions sur la prosopographie des derniers chevaliers romains," *Mélanges de l'École française de Rome. Moyen Âge* 100: 199–206.

Chavarría Arnau, A. 2004, "Interpreting the Transformation of Late Roman Villas: The Case of *Hispania*," in *Landscapes of Change: Rural Evolutions in Late Antiquity and the Early Middle Ages*, ed. N. Christie, Burlington, 67–102.

2007, *El final de las "villae" en "Hispania" (siglos IV–VII)*, Turnhout.

Chavarría, A. and Lewit, T. 2004, "Archaeological Research on the Late Antique Countryside: A Bibliographic Essay," in *Recent Research on the Late Antique Countryside*, eds. W. Bowden, L. Lavan, and C. Machado, Boston, 3–51.

Christie, N. 2004, "Landscapes of Change in Late Antiquity and the Early Middle Ages: Themes, Directions, and Problems," in *Landscapes of Change: Rural*

Evolutions in Late Antiquity and the Early Middle Ages, ed. N. Christie, Burlington, 1–37.

2006, *From Constantine to Charlemagne: An Archaeology of Italy*, AD *300–800*, Burlington.

Ciccotti, E. 1899, *Il tramonto della schiavitù nel mondo antico*, Turin.

Cimma, M. R. 1989, *L'Episcopalis audientia nelle costitutzioni imperiali da Costantino a Giustiniano*, Turin.

Citti, V. 1997, "Πόρνη καὶ δούλη: una coppia nominale in Lisia," in *Schiavi e dipendenti nell'ambito dell'* "oikos" *e della* "familia," eds. M. Moggi and G. Cordiano, Pisa, 91–6.

Clark, E. 1984, *The Life of Melania the Younger: Introduction, Translation, Commentary*, New York.

1991, "Sex, Shame, and Rhetoric: En-Gendering Early Christian Ethics," *Journal of the American Academy of Religion* 59: 221–45.

1999, *Reading Renunciation: Asceticism and Scripture in Early Christianity*, Princeton.

Clark, G. 2007, *A Farewell to Alms: A Brief Economic History of the World*, Princeton.

Clark, P. 1998, "Women, Slaves, and the Hierarchies of Domestic Violence: The Family of St. Augustine," in *Women and Slaves in Greco-Roman Culture: Differential Equations*, eds. S. Joshel and S. Murnaghan, London, 109–29.

Cloke, G. 1995, *"This Female Man of God": Women and Spiritual Power in the Patristic Age*, AD *350–450*, London.

Cohen, D. 1991a, *Law, Sexuality, and Society: The Enforcement of Morals in Classical Athens*, Cambridge.

1991b, "The Augustan Law on Adultery: The Social and Cultural Context," in *The Family in Italy*, eds. D. Kertzer and R. Saller, New Haven, 109–26.

Cole Libby, D. and Paiva, C. 2000, "Manumission Practices in a Late Eighteenth-Century Brazilian Slave Parish: São José d'El Rey in 1795," *Slavery & Abolition* 21: 96–127.

Coleman, K. 1990, "Fatal Charades: Roman Executions Staged as Mythological Enactments," *Journal of Roman Studies* 80: 44–73.

Cooper, K. 1996, *The Virgin and the Bride: Idealized Womanhood in Late Antiquity*, Cambridge, MA.

2007a, *The Fall of the Roman Household*, Cambridge.

2007b, "Closely-Watched Households: Visibility, Exposure and Private Power in the Roman *domus*," *Past & Present* 197: 3–33.

Corbier, M. 1981, "Proprietà e gestione della terra: grande proprietà fondiaria ed economia contadina," in *Società romana e produzione schiavistica*, vol. 1, eds. A. Giardina and A. Schiavone, Rome, 427–44.

2001, "Child Exposure and Abandonment," in *Childhood, Class, and Kin in the Roman World*, ed. S. Dixon, London, 52–73.

Corcoran, G. 1985, *Saint Augustine on Slavery*, Rome.

Corcoran, S. 1993, "Hidden from History: The Legislation of Licinius," in *The Theodosian Code*, eds. J. Harries and I. Wood, Ithaca, 97–119.

2000, *The Empire of the Tetrarchs: Imperial Pronouncements and Government,* AD *284–324,* rev. edn., Oxford.

2003, "The Donation and Will of Vincent of Huesca: Latin Text and English Translation," *Antiquité tardive* 11: 215–21.

2004, "The Publication of Law in the Era of the Tetrarchs – Diocletian, Galerius, Gregorius, and Hermogenian," in *Diokletian und die Tetrarchie. Aspekte einer Zeitenwende,* eds. A. Demandt, A. Goltz, and H. Schlange-Schöningen, Berlin, 56–73.

2006, "The Tetrarchy: Policy and Image as Reflected in Imperial Announcements," in *Die Tetrarchie: ein neues Regierungssystem und seine mediale Präsentation,* eds. D. Boschung and W. Eck, Wiesbaden, 31–62.

Coriat, J.-P. 1985, "La technique du rescrit à la fin du principat," *Studia et documenta historiae et iuris* 51: 319–48.

Corsini, C. 1976, "Materiali per lo studio della famiglia in Toscana nei secoli XVII–XIX: gli esposti," *Quaderni storici* 33: 998–1052.

Costambeys, M. 2009, "Settlement, Taxation and the Condition of the Peasantry in Post-Roman Central Italy," *Journal of Agrarian Change* 9: 92–119.

Cotton, H. 1993, "The Guardianship of Jesus Son of Babatha: Roman and Local Law in the Province of Arabia," *Journal of Roman Studies* 83: 94–113.

Coulie, B. 1985, *Les richesses dans l'œuvre de saint Grégoire de Nazianze: étude littéraire et historique,* Louvain.

Cracco Ruggini, L. 1961, *Economia e società nell' "Italia annonaria," rapporti fra agricoltura e commercio dal* IV *al* VI *secolo d. C.,* Milan.

Cribiore, R. 2001, *Gymnastics of the Mind: Greek Education in Hellenistic and Roman Egypt,* Princeton.

2007, *The School of Libanius in Late Antique Antioch,* Princeton.

Crone, P. 1987, *Roman, Provincial, and Islamic Law: The Origins of the Islamic Patronate,* New York.

Crook, J. 1967a, *Law and Life of Rome,* London.

1967b, "Gaius, Institutes, 1.84–86," *Classical Review* 17: 7–8.

Cross, F. L. 1961, "History and Fiction in the African Canons," *Journal of Theological Studies* 12: 227–47.

Cueva, E. 2001, "Petronius *Satyrica* 38.6–11: *Alapa* Revisited," *Classical Philology* 96: 68–76.

Cunningham, M. and Allen, P., eds. 1998, *Preacher and Audience: Studies in Early Christian and Byzantine Homiletics,* Leiden.

Dagron, G. 1974, *Naissance d'une capitale: Constantinople et ses institutions de 330 à 451,* Paris.

1984, *Constantinople imaginaire: Études sur le recueil des* Patria, Paris.

Dal Lago, E. and Katsari, C. 2008, "Ideal Models of Slave Management in the Roman World and in the Ante-bellum American South," in *Slave Systems: Ancient and Modern,* eds. E. Dal Lago and C. Katsari, Cambridge, 187–213.

Dalla, D. 1987, *Ubi Venus Mutatur: Omosessualità e diritto nel mondo romano,* Milan.

1988, "Aspetti della patria potestà e dei rapporti tra genitori e figli nell'epoca postclassica," *AARC* 7: 89–109.

Danielou, J. 1955, "Chronologie des sermons de Grégoire de Nysse," *Revue des sciences religieuses* 29: 346–72.

Dar, S. 1986, *Landscape and Pattern: An Archaeological Survey of Samaria 800 B.C.E.–636 C.E.*, Oxford.

Dark, K. 1996, "Proto-industrialisation and the End of the Roman Economy," in *External Contacts and the Economy of Late Roman Britain and Post-Roman Britain*, ed. K. Dark, Woodbridge, 1–21.

2004, "The Late Antique Landscape of Britain, AD 300–700," in *Landscapes of Change: Rural Evolutions in Late Antiquity and the Early Middle Ages*, ed. N. Christie, Burlington, 279–99.

D'Arms, J. H. 1981, *Commerce and Social Standing in Ancient Rome*, Cambridge, MA.

Daudet, P. 1941, *L'établissement de la compétence de l'Église en matière de divorce & de consanguinité, France, xème–xiième siècles*, Paris.

Dauphin, C. 1998, *La Palestine byzantine: peuplement et populations*, Oxford.

Davies, W. 1996, "On Servile Status in the Early Middle Ages," in *Serfdom and Slavery: Studies in Legal Bondage*, ed. M. Bush, London, 225–46.

Davis, D. B. 1966, *The Problem of Slavery in Western Culture*, Ithaca.

2006, *Inhuman Bondage: The Rise and Fall of Slavery in the New World*, Oxford.

De Bonfils, G. 1993, *Gli schiavi degli ebrei nella legislazione del IV secolo: storia di un divieto*, Bari.

1995, "L'obbligo di vendere lo schiavo cristiano alla chiesa e la clausola del *competens pretium*," *AARC* 10: 503–18.

De Bruyn, T. 1999, "Flogging a Son: The Emergence of the *Pater Flagellans* in Latin Christian Discourse," *Journal of Early Christian Studies* 7: 249–90.

de Callataÿ, F. 2005, "The Graeco-Roman Economy in the Super-long Run: Lead, Copper, and Shipwrecks," *Journal of Roman Archaeology* 18: 361–72.

De Filipi, M. 1997, *Fragmenta Vaticana: storia di un testo normativo*, Bari.

De Francisci, P. 1927, "La *revocatio in servitutem*," in *Mélanges de droit romain dédiés à Georges Cornil*, Ghent, 295–323.

de Ligt, L. 1993, *Fairs and Markets in the Roman Empire: Economic and Social Aspects of Periodic Trade in a Pre-industrial Society*, Amsterdam.

De Martino, F. 1988a, "Nuove considerazioni sul passaggio dall'antichità al medioevo," in *Alte Geschichte und Wissenschaftsgeschichte: Festschrift für Karl Christ zum 65. Geburtstag*, Darmstadt, 309–24.

1988b, *Uomini e terre in Occidente: tra tardo antico e medioevo*, Naples.

1993a, "Sull' alimentazione degli schiavi," *La parola del passato: rivista di studi antichi* 48: 401–27.

1993b, "Il colonato fra economia e diritto," in *Storia di Roma, 3.1: L'età tardoantica: crisi e trasformazione*, ed. A. Schiavone, Turin, 789–822.

De Neeve, P. W. 1984a, *Private Farm-tenancy in Roman Italy during the Late Republic and the Early Principate*, Amsterdam.

1984b, *Peasants in Peril: Location and Economy in Italy in the Second Century B.C.*, Amsterdam.

De Ste. Croix, G. E. M. 1981, *The Class Struggle in the Ancient Greek World*, Ithaca.

de Vos, M. 2000, *Rus Africum: terra, acqua, olio nell'Africa settentrionale: scavo e ricognizione nei dintorni di Dougga*, Trento.

Decker, M. 2001, "Food for an Empire: Wine and Oil Production in North Syria," in *Economy and Exchange in the East Mediterranean during Late Antiquity*, eds. S. Kingsley and M. Decker, Oxford, 69–86.

Delaney, C. 1987, "Seeds of Honor, Fields of Shame," in *Honor and Shame and the Unity of the Mediterranean*, ed. D. Gilmore, Washington, DC, 35–48.

Delbrueck, R. 1929, *Die Consulardiptychen und verwandte Denkmäler*, Leipzig.

Delmaire, R. 1989, *Largesses sacrées et res privata: l'aerarium impérial et son administration du IVe au VIe siècle*, Rome.

Demandt, A. 1998, *Geschichte der Spätantike: das römische Reich von Diocletian bis Justinian, 284–565 n. Chr*, Munich.

Deming, W. 1995, *Paul on Marriage and Celibacy: The Hellenistic Background of I Corinthians 7*, Cambridge.

Dennis, T. 1982, "The Relationship between Gregory of Nyssa's Attack on Slavery in his Fourth Homily on Ecclesiastes and his Treatise *De Hominis Opificio*," *Studia Patristica* 17: 1065–72.

Di Porto, A. 1984, *Impresa collettiva e schiavo "manager" in Roma antica (II sec. a.C.–II sec. d.C.)*, Milan.

Dietz, S. *et al.* 1995, *Africa Proconsularis: Regional Studies in the Segermes Valley of Northern Tunesia*, Århus.

Dionisotti, A. C. 1982, "From Ausonius' Schooldays? A Schoolbook and Its Relatives," *Journal of Roman Studies* 72: 83–125.

Diptee, A. 2006, "African Children in the British Slave Trade during the Late Eighteenth Century," *Slavery & Abolition* 27: 183–96.

Dixon, S. 1992, *The Roman Family*, Baltimore.

2003, "Sex and the Married Woman in Ancient Rome," in *Early Christian Families in Context*, eds. D. Balch and C. Osiek, Grand Rapids, 111–29.

Dockès, P. 1979, *La libération médiévale*, Paris.

Dopsch, A. 1918–20, *Wirtschaftliche und soziale grundlagen der europäischen kulturentwicklung, aus der zeit von Caesar bis auf Karl den Grossen*, Vienna.

D'Oriano, R. and Riccardi, E. 2004, "Les épaves d'Olbie," in *Barbares en Méditerranée de la Rome tardive au début de l'Islam*, ed. S. Kingsley, London, 89–95.

Dossey, L. 2008, "Wife Beating and Manliness in Late Antiquity," *Past & Present* 199: 3–40.

Downey, G. 1961, *A History of Antioch in Syria: From Seleucus to the Arab Conquest*, Princeton.

Drago, A. T. 2007, *Aristeneto: Lettere d'amore*, Lecce.

Drake, H. A., ed. 2006, *Violence in Late Antiquity: Perceptions and Practices*, Burlington.

Drinkwater, J. 1989, "Patronage in Roman Gaul and the Problem of the Bagau-
dae," in *Patronage in Ancient Society*, ed. A. Wallace-Hadrill, London, 189–
203.

2001, "The Gallo-Roman Woollen Industry and the Great Debate: The Igel
Column Revisited," in *Economies beyond Agriculture in the Classical World*,
eds. D. Mattingly and J. Salmon, New York, 297–308.

DuBois, P. 2003, *Slaves and Other Objects*, Chicago.

Duby, G. 1978, *Medieval Marriage: Two Models from Twelfth-century France*,
Baltimore.

Ducloux, A. 1994, *Ad ecclesiam confugere: naissance du droit d'asile dans les églises
(IVe–milieu du Ve s.)*, Paris.

Duff, A. 1928, *Freedmen in the Early Roman Empire*, Oxford.

Dumont, J.-Ch. 1999, "La villa esclavagiste?," *Topoi orient-occident* 9: 113–25.

Dunbabin, K. 1978, *The Mosaics of Roman North Africa: Studies in Iconography and
Patronage*, Oxford.

2003a, "The Waiting Servant in Later Roman Art," *American Journal of Philology*
124: 443–68.

2003b, *The Roman Banquet: Images of Conviviality*, Cambridge.

Duncan-Jones, R. 1974, *The Roman Economy: Quantitative Studies*, Cambridge.

1982, *The Economy of the Roman Empire: Quantitative Studies*[2], Cambridge, orig.
1974.

1986, Review of *Colonus: Private Farm-Tenancy in Roman Italy during the Repub-
lic and the Early Principate* by P. W. De Neeve; Servus Quasi Colonus:
Forme non Tradizionali di Organizzazione del Lavoro nella Società Romana
by G. Giliberti; *Agriculture and Agricultural Practice in Roman Law* by
R. J. Buck; *Die Kolonen in Italien und den Westlichen Provinzen des Römischen
Reiches: Eine Untersuchung der Literarischen, Juristischen, und Epigraphischen
Quellen vom 2. Jahrhundert v.u.z. bis zu den Severern* by K.-P. Johne, J. Köhn,
V. Weber, *Journal of Roman Studies* 76: 295–7.

1990, *Structure and Scale in the Roman Economy*, Cambridge.

Dunn, A. 2004, "Continuity and Change in the Macedonian Countryside, from
Gallienus to Justinian," in *Recent Research on the Late Antique Countryside*,
eds. W. Bowden, L. Lavan, and C. Machado, Boston, 535–86.

Dupont, C. 1937, *Les constitutions de Constantin et le droit privé au début du IVe
siècle: les personnes*, Lille.

Durliat, J. 1990, *De la ville antique à la ville byzantine: le problème des subsistances*,
Rome.

Dyson, S. 1981, "Some Reflections on the Archaeology of Southern Etruria,"
Journal of Field Archaeology 8: 79–83.

Eibach, D. 1980, *Untersuchungen zum spätantiken Kolonat in der kaiserlichen Gesetzgebung: unter besonderer Berücksichtigung der Terminologie*, Cologne.

Elm, S. 1994, *Virgins of God: The Making of Asceticism in Late Antiquity*, Oxford.

1996, "'Pierced by Bronze Needles': Anti-Montanist Charges of Ritual Stigma-
tization in their Fourth-Century Context," *Journal of Early Christian Studies*
4: 409–39.

2004, "Marking the Self in Late Antiquity: Inscriptions, Baptism, and the Conversion of Mimes," in *Stigmata: Poetiken der Körperinschrift*, eds. B. Menke and B. Vinken, Munich, 47–68.

Epstein, S. 1999, "A Late Medieval Lawyer Confronts Slavery: The Cases of Bartolomeo de Bosco," *Slavery & Abolition* 20: 49–68.

Erdkamp, P. 1999, "Agriculture, Underemployment, and the Cost of Rural Labour in the Roman World," *Classical Quarterly* 49: 556–72.

2001, "Beyond the Limits of the 'Consumer City'. A Model of the Urban and Rural Economy in the Roman World," *Historia* 50: 332–56.

2002, "'A Starving Mob Has No Respect': Urban Markets and Food Riots in the Roman World, 100 B.C.–400 A.D.," in *The Transformation of Economic Life under the Roman Empire*, eds. L. de Blois and J. Rich, Amsterdam, 93–115.

Erim, K. and Reynolds, J. 1969, "A Letter of Gordian III from Aphrodisias in Caria," *Journal of Roman Studies* 59: 56–8.

Evans Grubbs, J. 1993, "'Marriage More Shameful than Adultery': Slave–Mistress Relationships, 'Mixed Marriages,' and Late Roman Law," *Phoenix* 47: 125–54.

1995, *Law and Family in Late Antiquity: The Emperor Constantine's Marriage Legislation*, Oxford.

2000, "The Slave Who Avenged Her Master's Death: *Codex Justinianus* 1.19.1 and 7.13.1," *Ancient History Bulletin* 14: 81–8.

2005, "Parent–Child Conflict in the Roman Family: The Evidence of the Code of Justinian," in *The Roman Family in the Empire: Rome, Italy, and Beyond*, ed. M. George, Oxford, 93–128.

2007, "Marrying and Its Documentation in Later Roman Law," in *To Have and To Hold: Marrying and Its Documentation in Western Christendom, 400–1600*, eds. P. Reynolds and J. Witte, Cambridge, 43–94.

2009a, "Marriage and Family Relationships in the Late Roman West," in *A Companion to Late Antiquity*, ed. P. Rousseau, Malden, 201–19.

2009b, "Church, State, and Children: Christian and Imperial Attitudes Toward Infant Exposure in Late Antiquity," in *The Power of Religion in Late Antiquity*, eds. A. Cain and N. Lenski, Burlington, 119–31.

Fabbrini, F. 1965, *La manumissio in ecclesia*, Milan.

Fabre, G. 1981, *Libertus: recherches sur les rapports patron-affranchi à la fin de la République romaine*, Rome.

Fagan, G. 1999, "Interpreting the Evidence: Did Slaves Bathe at the Baths?," in *Roman Baths and Bathing*, eds. D. E. Johnston and J. DeLaine, Portsmouth, 25–34.

Fairchilds, S. 1983, *Domestic Enemies: Servants and their Masters in Old Regime France*, Baltimore.

Faust, D. 1982, *James Henry Hammond and the Old South: A Design for Mastery*, Baton Rouge.

Feissel, D. 1995, "Les constitutions des tétrarques connues par l'épigraphie: inventaire et notes critiques," *Antiquité tardive* 3: 33–53.

Fejfer, H. and Mathiesen, H. 1992, "Ayios Kononas. A Late Roman/Early Byzantine Site in the Akamas," in *Acta Cypria: Acts of an International Congress on Cypriote Archaeology held in Göteborg on 22–24 August 1991*, vol. 2, ed. P. Åström, Göteborg, 67–83.

Fellmeth, U. 2002, *"Eine wohlhabende Stadt sei nahe . . . " Die Standortfaktoren in der römischen Agrarökonomie im Zusammenhang mit den Verkehrs- und Raumordnungsstrukturen im römischen Italien*, St. Katharinen.

Fenoaltea, S. 1984, "Slavery and Supervision in Comparative Perspective," *Journal of Economic History* 44: 635–68.

Fentress, E. 2005, "On the Block: *Catastae, chalcidica,* and *cryptae* in Early Imperial Italy," *Journal of Roman Archaeology* 18: 220–34.

2008, "Spinning a Model: Female Slaves in Roman Villas," *Journal of Roman Archaeology* 21: 419–22.

Fentress, E., Goodson, C., and Maiuro, M. 2009, "Excavations at Villa Magna 2009," *Journal of Fasti Online* 169: www.fastionline.org/docs/FOLDER-it-2009–169.pdf.

Ferdi, S. 2005, *Corpus des mosaïques de Cherchel*, Paris.

Ferri, R. 2008, "Il latino dei *Colloquia scholica*," in *Aspetti della scuola nel mondo Romano: Atti del Convegno (Pisa, 5–6 dicembre 2006)*, eds. F. Bellandi and R. Ferri, Amsterdam, 111–77.

Fikhman, I. F. 1973, "Sklaven und Sklavenarbeit im spätrömischen Oxyrhynchus," *Jahrbuch für Wirtschaftsgeschichte* 2: 149–206.

1974, "Slaves in Byzantine Oxyrhynchus," in *Akten des XIII Internationalen Papyrologenkongresses*, Munich, 117–24.

1995, "Aspects économiques de la dépendance individuelle dans l'Égypte romaine et tardive," in *Esclavage et dépendance dans l'historiographie soviétique récente*, eds. M. M. Mactoux and E. Geny, Paris, 156–84.

1997, Review of R. Bagnall, *Reading Papyri, Writing Ancient History, Scripta classica Israelica* 16: 279–85.

2006, *Wirtschaft und Gesellschaft im spätantiken Ägypten: Kleine Schriften*, Stuttgart.

Fildes, V. 1988, "Wet Nursing in Antiquity c. 300 BC–c. 700 AD," in *Wet Nursing: A History from Antiquity to the Present*, ed. V. Fildes, Oxford, 1–25.

Findlay, R. 1975, "Slavery, Incentives, and Manumission: A Theoretical Model," *Journal of Political Economy* 83: 922–33.

1989, *The "Triangular Trade" and the Atlantic Economy of the Eighteenth Century: A Simple General-Equilibrium Model*, Princeton.

Finley, M. 1962, "The Black Sea and Danubian Regions and the Slave Trade in Antiquity," *Klio* 40: 51–9.

1968, "Slavery," *International Encyclopedia of the Social Sciences*, vol. 14: 307–13.

1998, *Ancient Slavery and Modern Ideology*[2], Princeton, orig. 1980.

1999, *The Ancient Economy*[2] (updated edn., orig. 1973), Berkeley.

Firpo, G. 1991, "Il problema servile tra Costantino e Giustiniano. Pensiero cristiano e legislazione imperiale," in *L'impero romano-cristiano*, ed. M. Sordi, Rome, 95–119.

Fisher, N. R. E. 1993, *Slavery in Classical Greece*, London.

Fitzgerald, W. 2000, *Slavery and the Roman Literary Imagination*, Cambridge.

Fitzmyer, J. 2008, *First Corinthians: A New Translation with Introduction and Commentary*, New Haven.

Flemming, R. 1999, "*Quae corpore quaestum facit*: The Sexual Economy of Female Prostitution in the Roman Empire," *Journal of Roman Studies* 89: 38–61.

Flory, M. 1978, "Family in *Familia*: Kinship and Community in Slavery," *American Journal of Ancient History* 3: 78–95.

Fogel, R. W. 1989, *Without Consent or Contract: The Rise and Fall of American Slavery*, New York.

Fogel, R. W. and Engerman, S. 1974, *Time on the Cross: The Economics of American Negro Slavery*, Boston.

Follett, R. 2003, "Heat, Sex, and Sugar: Pregnancy and Childbearing in the Slave Quarters," *Journal of Family History* 28: 510–39.

Forbes, C. 1955, "The Education and Training of Slaves in Antiquity," *Transactions of the American Philological Association* 86: 321–60.

Foss, C. 1994, "The Lycian Coast in the Byzantine Age," *Dumbarton Oaks Papers* 48: 1–52.

1997, "Syria in Transition: An Archaeological Perspective," *Dumbarton Oaks Papers* 51: 189–269.

Fossati Vanzetti, M. B. 1983, "Vendita ed esposizione degli infanti da Costantino a Giustiniano," *Studia et documenta historiae et iuris* 49: 179–224.

Foucault, M. 1986, *The Care of the Self: The History of Sexuality*, vol. 3, trans. R. Hurley, New York.

Fountoulakis, A. 2007, "Punishing the Lecherous Slave: Desire and Power in Herondas 5," in *Fear of Slaves, Fear of Enslavement in the Ancient Mediterranean... GIREA, Rethymnon, 4–7 novembre 2004*, ed. A. Serghidou, Besançon, 251–64.

Foxhall, L. 1990, "The Dependent Tenant: Land, Leasing, and Labour in Italy and Greece," *Journal of Roman Studies* 80: 97–114.

2007, *Olive Cultivation in Ancient Greece: Seeking the Ancient Economy*, Oxford.

Fraginals, M. M., Klein, H., and Engerman, S. 1983, "The Level and Structure of Slave Prices on Cuban Plantations in the Mid-Nineteenth Century: Some Comparative Perspectives," *American Historical Review* 88: 1201–18.

Frakes, R. 2001, *Contra potentium iniurias: The Defensor Civitatis and Late Roman Justice*, Munich.

Franciosi, G. 1961, *Il processo di libertà in diritto romano*, Naples.

Francovich, R. 2005, "Conclusioni," in *Dopo la fine delle ville: le campagne dal VI al IX secolo: Gavi, 8–10 maggio 2004*, ed. G. Brogiolo, Mantua, 349–51.

Francovich, R. and Hodges, R. 2003, *Villa to Village: The Transformation of the Roman Countryside in Italy*, London.

Fraser, P. 1972, "Notes on Two Rhodian Institutions," *Annual of the British School at Athens* 67: 113–24.

Frayn, J. 1984, *Sheep-rearing and the Wool Trade in Italy during the Roman Period*, Liverpool.

Frend, W. 1993, "Fathers and Slaves: St. Augustine and Some Eastern Contemporaries," *Antiquitas* 1435: 59–69.

Frézouls, E. 1980, "La vie rurale au Bas-Empire d'après l'oeuvre de Palladius," *Ktéma* 5: 193–210.

Friedl, R. 1996, *Der Konkubinat im kaiserzeitlichen Rom: von Augustus bis Septimius Severus*, Stuttgart.

Frier, B. 2000, "Demography," in *The Cambridge Ancient History²*, eds. A. K. Bowman *et al.*, vol. 11, Cambridge, 787–816.

Frier, B. and Kehoe, D. 2007, "Law and Economic Institutions," in *The Cambridge Economic History of the Greco-Roman World*, eds. W. Scheidel, I. Morris, and R. Saller, Cambridge, 113–43.

Friesen, S. 2004, "Poverty in Pauline Studies: Beyond the So-Called New Consensus," *Journal for the Study of the New Testament* 26: 323–61.

2008, "Injustice or God's Will? Early Christian Explanations of Poverty," in *Wealth and Poverty in Early Church and Society*, ed. S. Holman, Grand Rapids, 17–36.

Frost, F. 1977, "Phourkari. A Villa Complex in the Argolid (Greece)," *International Journal of Nautical Archaeology* 6: 233–8.

Frost, P. 1991, "Attitudes towards Blacks in the Early Christian Era," *Second Century* 8: 1–11.

Fynn-Paul, J. 2009, "Empire, Monotheism, and Slavery in the Greater Mediterranean Region from Antiquity to the Early Modern Era," *Past & Present* 205: 3–40.

Gabba, E. 1988, "La pastorizia nell'età tardo-imperiale in Italia," in *Pastoral Economies in Classical Antiquity*, ed. C. R. Whittaker, Cambridge, 134–42.

Gaca, K. 2003, *The Making of Fornication: Eros, Ethics, and Political Reform in Greek Philosophy and Early Christianity*, Berkeley.

Gallant, T. 1991, *Risk and Survival in Ancient Greece: Reconstructing the Rural Domestic Economy*, Stanford.

Gallay, P. 1943, *La vie de Saint Grégoire de Nazianze*, Paris.

Gamauf, R. 2007, "Cum aliter nulla domus tuta esse possit . . . : Fear of Slaves and Roman Law," in *Fear of Slaves, Fear of Enslavement in the Ancient Mediterranean . . . GIREA, Rethymnon, 4–7 novembre 2004*, ed. A. Serghidou, Besançon, 145–64.

Gardner, J. 1986, "Proofs of Status in the Roman World," *Bulletin of the Institute of Classical Studies* 33: 1–14.

1989, "The Adoption of Roman Freedmen," *Phoenix* 43: 236–57.

1991, "The Purpose of the *Lex Fufia Caninia*," *Échos du monde classique* 10: 21–39.

Garlan, Y. 1988, *Slavery in Ancient Greece*, trans. J. Lloyd, rev. and exp. edn., Ithaca.

Garnsey, P. 1970, *Social Status and Legal Privilege in the Roman Empire*, Oxford.

1972, "Review of *Studien zur Sklavenflucht im römischen Kaiserreich*, by H. Bellen," *Phoenix* 26: 206–7.

1981, "Independent Freedmen and the Economy of Roman Italy," *Klio* 63: 359–71.

ed. 1988a, *Non-Slave Labour in the Graeco-Roman World*, Cambridge.

1988b, *Famine and Food Supply in the Graeco-Roman World: Responses to Risk and Crisis*, Cambridge.

1988c, "Mountain Economies in Southern Europe: Thoughts on the Early History, Continuity, and Individuality of Mediterranean Upland Pastoralism," in *Pastoral Economies in Classical Antiquity*, ed. C. R. Whittaker, Cambridge, 196–209.

1996, *Ideas of Slavery from Aristotle to Augustine*, Cambridge.

1997, "Sons, Slaves, and Christians," in *The Roman Family in Italy: Status, Sentiment, Space*, eds. B. Rawson and P. Weaver, Oxford, 101–21.

1998a, "Slavery as Institution and Metaphor in the New Sermons (with special reference to Dolbeau 2 and 21)," in *Augustin Prédicateur (395–411): actes du Colloque International de Chantilly (5–7 septembre 1996)*, ed. G. Madec, Paris, 471–9.

1998b, *Cities, Peasants, and Food in Classical Antiquity: Essays in Social and Economic History*, Cambridge.

1999a, "Slaves," in *Late Antiquity: A Guide to the Postclassical World*, eds. G. W. Bowersock, P. Brown, and O. Grabar, Cambridge, MA, 699–700.

1999b, "Retour sur *Non-Slave Labour*: À propos du choix des travailleurs agricoles dans le monde antique," in *Le travail: recherches historiques*, eds. J. Annequin *et al.*, Besançon, 101–14.

2000, "Introduction: The Hellenistic and Roman Periods," in *The Cambridge History of Greek and Roman Political Thought*, eds. C. Rowe and M. Schofield, Cambridge, 401–14.

2004, "Roman Citizenship and Roman Law in the Late Empire," in *Approaching Late Antiquity: The Transformation from Early to Late Empire*, eds. S. Swain and M. Edwards, Oxford, 133–55.

Garnsey, P. and Woolf, G. 1989, "Patronage of the Rural Poor in the Roman World," in *Patronage in Ancient Society*, ed. A. Wallace-Hadrill, London, 153–70.

Garrido-Hory, M. 1981a, "La vision du dépendant chex Martial à travers les relations sexuelles," *Index* 10: 298–314.

1981b, *Martial et l'esclavage*, Paris.

1996, "Les esclaves africains dans la poésie réaliste," in *L'Africa romana: Atti del XII Convegno di Studio Olbia, 12–15 dicembre 1996*, eds. M. Khanoussi, P. Ruggeri, and C. Vismara, Olbia, 921–35.

Gascou, J. 1985, "Les grands domaines, la cité et l'état en Égypte byzantine," *Travaux et mémoires* 9:1–90.

Gaudemet, J. 1958, *L'Église dans l'empire romain: IVe–Ve siècles*, Paris.

1980, *Sociétés et mariage*, Strasbourg.

1992, "La Constitution 'ad populum' du 31 Janvier 320," in *Droit et société aux derniers siècles de l'Empire romain*, Naples, 3–22.

Gavitt, P. 1994, "'Perche non avea chi la ghovernasse.' Cultural Values, Family Resources, and Abandonment in the Florence of Lorenzo de' Medici, 1467–85," in *Poor Women and Children in the European Past*, eds. J. Henderson and R. Wall, London, 65–93.

Gebbia, C. 1987, "*Pueros vel vendere vel locare*. Schiavitú e realtà africana nelle nuove lettere di S. Agostino," in *L'Africa romana, Atti del* IV *convegno di studio Sassari*, ed. A. Mastino, Sassari, 215–27.

Genovese, E. 1974, *Roll, Jordan, Roll: The World the Slaves Made*, New York.

1979, *From Rebellion to Revolution: Afro-American Slave Revolts in the Making of the Modern World*, Baton Rouge.

George, M. 2003, "Images of Black Slaves in the Roman Empire," *Syllecta classica* 14: 161–85.

Geroussi-Bendermacher, E. 2005, "Propriété foncière et inventaire d'esclaves: Un texte inédit de Perissa (Thera) tardo-antique," in *Esclavage antique et discriminations socio-culturelles*, eds. V. Anastasiadis and P. Doukellis, New York, 335–58.

Geyer, P. 1924, "Lais," *RE* 12.1: cols. 513–16.

Giardina, A. 1986, "Palladio, il latifondo italico, e l'occultamento della società rurale," in *Società romana e impero tardoantico*, vol. 1, ed. A. Giardina, Rome, 31–6.

1988, "Carità eversiva," *Studi storici: rivista trimestrale dell' Istituto Gramsci* 29: 127–42.

1997a, "Gli schiavi, i coloni, e i problemi di una transizione," in *Terre, proprietari, e contadini*, ed. E. Lo Cascio, Rome, 311–23.

1997b, "L'Italia, il modo di produzione schiavistico, e i tempi di una crisi," in *L'Italia romana: storie di un'identità incompiuta*, Rome, 233–64.

1997c, "Esplosione di tardo-antico," *Studi storici: rivista trimestrale dell' Istituto Gramsci* 40: 157–80.

2007, "The Transition to Late Antiquity," in *The Cambridge Economic History of the Greco-Roman World*, eds. W. Scheidel, I. Morris, and R. Saller, Cambridge, 743–68.

Gibson, E. 1999, *The Jewish Manumission Inscriptions of the Bosporus Kingdom*, Tübingen.

Gibson, S., Kingsley, S., and Clark, J. 1999, "Town and Country in the Southern Carmel: Report on the Landscape Archaeology Project at Dor," *Levant* 31: 71–121.

Giddens, A. 1984, *The Constitution of Society: Outline of the Theory of Structuration*, Berkeley.

Giliberti, G. 1981, Servus quasi colonus: *forme non tradizionali di organizzazione del lavoro nella società romana*, Naples.

1999, *Servi della terra: ricerche per una storia del colonato*, Turin.

Gillam, J. 1965, "Dura Rosters and the Constitutio Antoniniana," *Historia* 14: 74–92.

Gilly-Elway, H. 2000, "Soziale Aspekte frühislamischer Sklaverei," *Der Islam* 77: 116–68.

Gilmore, D., ed. 1987a, *Honor and Shame and the Unity of the Mediterranean*, Washington, DC.

1987b, "Introduction: The Shame of Dishonor," in *Honor and Shame and the Unity of the Mediterranean*, ed. D. Gilmore, Washington, DC, 2–21.

Gioffré, D. 1971, *Il mercato degli schiavi a Genova nel secolo* xv, Genoa.

Giordiano, A. 1980, "S. Agostino e la schiavitù," *Rivista rosminiana di filosofia e di cultura* 74: 392–412.

Giovannini, M. 1987, "Female Chastity Codes in the Circum-Mediterranean: Comparative Perspectives," in *Honor and Shame and the Unity of the Mediterranean*, ed. D. Gilmore, Washington, DC, 61–74.

Girardet, K. 2008, "Vom Sonnen-Tag zum Sonntag. Der *dies solis* in Gesetzgebung und Politik Konstantins d. Gr," *Zeitschrift für antikes Christentum* 11: 279–310.

Glancy, J. 1998, "Obstacles to Slaves' Participation in the Corinthian Church," *Journal of Biblical Literature* 117: 481–501.

2002, *Slavery in Early Christianity*, Oxford.

Gleason, M. 1995, *Making Men: Sophists and Self-Presentation in Ancient Rome*, Princeton.

Glotz, G. 1877, "Expositio," in *Dictionnaire des antiquités grecques et romaines*, vol. 2, eds. C. Daremberg and E. Saglio, Paris, 930–9.

Goitein, S. D. 1967–93, *A Mediterranean Society: The Jewish Communities of the Arab World as Portrayed in the Documents of the Cairo Genizah*, 6 vols., Berkeley.

Goldenberg, D. 2003, *The Curse of Ham: Race and Slavery in Early Judaism, Christianity, and Islam*, Princeton.

Goldhill, S. 1995, *Foucault's Virginity: Ancient Erotic Fiction and the History of Sexuality*, Cambridge.

Goldsmith, R. W. 1984, "An Estimate of the Size and Structure of the National Product of the Early Roman Empire," *Review of Income and Wealth* 30: 263–88.

Goldstone, J. 2002, "Efflorescences and Economic Growth in World History: Rethinking the 'Rise of the West' and the Industrial Revolution," *Journal of World History* 13: 323–89.

Göll, H. 1859, "Über den Processus consularis der Kaiserzeit," *Philologus* 14: 586–612.

Gonzalez, A. 2002, "Provenance des esclaves au Haut-Empire: *Pax romana* et approvisionnement," in *Routes et marchés d'esclaves, 26e colloque du GIREA*, ed. M. Garrido-Hory, Paris, 65–82.

González, J. 1986, "The *Lex Irnitana*: A New Copy of the Flavian Municipal Law," *Journal of Roman Studies* 76: 147–243.

Goody, J. 1976, *Production and Reproduction: A Comparative Study of the Domestic Domain*, Cambridge.

1980, "Slavery in Time and Space," in *Asian and African Systems of Slavery*, ed. J. Watson, Oxford, 16–42.

1990, *The Oriental, the Ancient, and the Primitive: Systems of Marriage and the Family in the Pre-Industrial Societies of Eurasia*, Cambridge.

2004, *Capitalism and Modernity: The Great Debate*, Cambridge.

Gould, V. M. 1997, "'The House that Was Never a Home': Slave Family and Household Organization in New Orleans, 1820–50," *Slavery & Abolition* 18: 90–103.

Grantham, G. 1999, "Contra Ricardo: On the Macroeconomics of Pre-industrial Economies," *European Review of Economic History* 2: 199–232.

Greene, E. 1998, *The Erotics of Domination: Male Desire and the Mistress in Latin Love Poetry*, Baltimore.

Greene, K. 2008, "Learning to Consume: Consumption and Consumerism in the Roman Empire," *Journal of Roman Archaeology* 21: 64–82.

Grey, C. 2007a, "Contextualizing *Colonatus*: The *Origo* of the Late Roman Empire," *Journal of Roman Studies* 97: 155–75.

2007b, "Revisiting the 'Problem' of *agri deserti* in the Late Roman Empire," *Journal of Roman Archaeology* 20: 362–76.

2008, "Two Young Lovers: An Abduction Marriage and its Consequences in Fifth-Century Gaul," *Classical Quarterly* 58: 286–302.

Forthcoming, "Slavery in the Late Roman World," in *The Cambridge World History of Slavery, Volume 1: The Ancient Mediterranean World*, eds. K. Bradley and P. Cartledge, Cambridge, 482–509.

Grieser, H. 1997, *Sklaverei im spätantiken und frühmittelalterlichen Gallien (5.-7. Jh.): das Zeugnis der christlichen Quellen*, Stuttgart.

2001, "Asketische Bewegungen in Kleinasien im 4. Jahrhundert und ihre Haltung zur Sklaverei," in *Fünfzig Jahre Forschungen zur antiken Sklaverei an der Mainzer Akademie*, eds. H. Bellen and H. Heinen, Stuttgart, 381–400.

Grodzynski, D. 1984, "Tortures mortelles et catégories sociales. Les *summa supplicia* dans le droit romain aux IIIe et IVe s.," in *Du châtiment dans la cité: supplices corporels et peine de mort dans le monde antique*, Rome, 397–403.

Gschnitzer, F. 1976, *Studien zur griechischen Terminologie der Sklaverei*, vol. 2, Wiesbaden.

Gsell, S. 1932, "Esclaves ruraux dans l'Afrique romaine," *Mélanges Gustave Glotz*, Paris, 397–415.

Günther, R. 1984, *Vom Untergang Westroms zum Reich der Merowinger: zur Entstehung des Feudalismus in Europa*, Berlin.

Gustafson, W. 1997, "*Inscripta in Fronte*: Penal Tattooing in Late Antiquity," *Classical Antiquity* 16: 79–105.

Gutman, H. 1975, *Slavery and the Numbers Game: A Critique of "Time on the Cross,"* Chicago.

1976, *The Black Family in Slavery and Freedom, 1750–1925*, New York.

Guyot, P. 1980, *Eunuchen als Sklaven und Freigelassene in der griechisch-römischen Antike*, Stuttgart.

Hahn, I. 1961, "Freie Arbeit und Sklavenarbeit in der spätantiken Stadt," *Annales Universitatis scientiarum Budapestinensis, Sectio Historica* 3: 23–39.

1976, "Sklaven und Sklavenfrage im politischen Denken der Spätantike," *Klio* 58: 459–70.

Hallett, J. and Skinner, M., eds. 1997, *Roman Sexualities*, Princeton.

Halperin, D. 1990, *One Hundred Years of Homosexuality: And Other Essays on Greek Love*, New York.

Halperin, D., Winkler, J., and Zeitlin, F., eds. 1990, *Before Sexuality: The Construction of Erotic Experience in the Ancient Greek World*, Princeton.

Hammer, C. 2002, *A Large-Scale Slave Society of the Early Middle Ages: Slaves and Their Families in Early Medieval Bavaria*, Burlington.

Handley, E. W., Austin, C. F. L., and Horváth, L. 2007, "New Readings in the Fragment of Hyperides' *Against Timandros* from the Archimedes Palimpsest," *Zeitschrift für Papyrologie und Epigraphik* 162: 1–4.

Hanes, C. 1996, "Turnover Cost and the Distribution of Slave Labor in Anglo-America," *Journal of Economic History* 56: 307–29.

Hardy, E. 1931, *The Large Estates of Byzantine Egypt*, New York.

Harper, K. 2008, "The Greek Census Inscriptions of Late Antiquity," *Journal of Roman Studies* 98: 83–119.

2010, "Slave Prices in Late Antiquity (and in the Very Long Term)," *Historia: Zeitschrift für alte Geschichte* 59: 206–38.

Forthcoming a, "Marriage and Family," in *The Oxford Handbook of Late Antiquity*, ed. S. Johnson, Oxford.

Forthcoming b, "The *Senatus consultum Claudianum* in the *Codex Theodosianus*: Social History and Legal Texts," *Classical Quarterly* 60.

Forthcoming c, "The End of Roman Slavery and the Idea of Transition," in *Actes du colloque international du Groupe International de Recherches sur l'Esclavage dans l'Antiquité*, ed. A. Pinzone.

Forthcoming d, "Predigtliteratur," *Handwörterbuch der antiken Sklaverei*, eds. H. Heinen *et al.*, forthcoming.

Forthcoming e, "*PORNEIA*: The Making of a Christian Sexual Norm," *Journal of Biblical Literature*.

Harries, J. 1988, "The Roman Imperial Quaestor from Constantine to Theodosius II," *Journal of Roman Studies* 78: 148–72.

1999, *Law and Empire in Late Antiquity*, Cambridge.

Harries, J. and Wood, I., eds. 1993, *The Theodosian Code*, Ithaca.

Harrill, J. A. 1995, *The Manumission of Slaves in Early Christianity*, Tübingen.

1999, "The Vice of Slave Dealers in Greco-Roman Society: The Use of a Topos in 1 Timothy 1:10," *Journal of Biblical Literature* 118: 97–122.

Harris, W. V. 1980, "Towards a Study of the Roman Slave Trade," in *The Seaborne Commerce of Ancient Rome* (MAAR 36), eds. J. H. D'Arms and E. C. Kopff, Rome, 117–40.

1988, "On the Applicability of the Concept of Class in Roman History," in *Forms of Control and Subordination in Antiquity*, eds. T. Yuge and M. Doi, Tokyo, 598–610.

1993, "Between Archaic and Modern," in *The Inscribed Economy: Production and Distribution in the Roman Empire in the Light of* "instrumentum domesticum," ed. W. V. Harris, Ann Arbor, 11–29.

1994, "Child-exposure in the Roman Empire," *Journal of Roman Studies* 84: 1–22.

1999, "Demography, Geography, and the Sources of Roman Slaves," *Journal of Roman Studies* 89: 62–75.

ed. 2005, *The Spread of Christianity in the First Four Centuries*, Leiden.

ed. 2008, *The Monetary Systems of the Greeks and Romans*, Oxford.

Härtel, G. 1975, "Die Widerspiegelung des Untergangs der antiken Sklavenhalterordnung anhand des *Codex Theodosianus* und des *Codex Justinianus*," *Živa Antika* 25: 226–40.

Hasegawa, K. 2005, *The Familia Urbana during the Early Empire: A Study of the Columbaria Inscriptions*, Oxford.

Hatzopoulos, M. B. 2004, "La société provinciale de Macédoine sous l'empire à la lumière des inscriptions du sanctuaire de Leukopétra," in *L'hellénisme d'époque romaine: nouveaux documents, nouvelles approches*, ed. S. Follet, Paris, 45–53.

Heath, M. 2004, *Menander: A Rhetor in Context*, Oxford.

Heather, P. 1998, "Senators and Senates," in *The Cambridge Ancient History*[2], vol. 13, eds. A. Cameron and P. Garnsey, Cambridge, 184–210.

2005, *The Fall of the Roman Empire*, London.

Held, W. 1971, "Der römische Kolonat am Ende des 2. und zu Beginn des 3. Jh.," *Altertum* 17: 174–8.

Hendy, M. 1985, *Studies in the Byzantine Monetary Economy, c. 300–1450*, Cambridge.

Henning, J. 2008, "Strong Rulers – Weak Economy? Rome, the Carolingians, and the Archaeology of Slavery in the First Millennium," in *The Long Morning of Medieval Europe: New Directions in Early Medieval Studies*, Aldershot, 33–53.

Herlihy, D. 1985, *Medieval Households*, Cambridge, MA.

1995. "Biology and History: The Triumph of Monogamy," *Journal of Interdisciplinary History* 25: 571–83.

Hermansen, G. 1978, "The Population of Imperial Rome: The Regionaries," *Historia* 27: 129–68.

Hernæs, P. and Iversen, T., eds. 2002, *Slavery across Time and Space: Studies in Slavery in Medieval Europe and Africa*, Trondheim.

Herrmann, E. 1980, *Ecclesia in Re publica: die Entwicklung der Kirche von pseudostaatlicher zu staatlich inkorporierter Existenz*, Frankfurt.

Herrmann-Otto, E. 1994, *Ex ancilla natus: Untersuchungen zu den "hausgeborenen" Sklaven und Sklavinnen im Westen des römischen Kaiserreiches*, Stuttgart.

1999, "*Causae liberales*," *Index* 27: 141–59.

2002, "Modes d'acquisition des esclaves dans l'Empire romain. Aspects juridiques et socio-économiques," in *Routes et marchés d'esclaves, 26e colloque du GIREA*, ed. M. Garrido-Hory, Paris, 113–26.

2008, "Konstantin, die Sklaven, und die Kirche," in *Antike Lebenswelten: Konstanz – Wandel – Wirkungsmacht, Festschrift für Ingomar Weiler zum 70. Geburtstag*, eds. P. Mauritsch *et al.*, Wiesbaden, 354–66.

Heucke, C. 1994, *Circus und Hippodrome als politischer Raum*, Hildesheim.

Hezser, C. 2003, "The Impact of Household Slaves on the Jewish Family in Roman Palestine," *Journal for the Study of Judaism in the Persian, Hellenistic and Roman Period* 34: 375–424.

2005, *Jewish Slavery in Antiquity*, Oxford.

Hickey, T. 2007, "Aristocratic Landholding and the Economy of Byzantine Egypt," in *Egypt in the Byzantine World, 300–700*, ed. R. Bagnall, Cambridge, 288–308.

2008, "An Inconvenient Truth? *P.Oxy.* 18.2196 verso, the Apion Estate, and *fiscalité* in the Late Antique Oxyrhynchite," *The Bulletin of the American Society of Papyrologists* 45: 87–100.

Higginbotham, L. and Kopytoff, B. 1989, "Property First, Humanity Second: The Recognition of the Slave's Human Nature in Virginia Civil Law," *Ohio State Law Journal* 50: 511–40.

Higman, B. W. 2001, "The Invention of Slave Society," in *Slavery, Freedom, and Gender: The Dynamics of Caribbean Society*, ed. B. Moore, Kingston, 57–75.

Hill, E. 1995, *Works of Saint Augustine: A Translation for the 21st Century: Sermons*, vol. 10, Brooklyn.

Hirschfeld, Y. 1997, "Farms and Villages in Byzantine Palestine," *Dumbarton Oaks Papers* 51: 33–71.

2001, "Habitat," in *Interpreting Late Antiquity: Essays on the Postclassical World*, eds. G. W. Bowersock, P. Brown, and O. Grabar, Cambridge, MA, 258–72.

Hirter, H. 1960, "Die Soziologie der antiken Prostitution im Lichte des heidnischen und christlichen Schrifttums," *Jahrbuch für Antike und Christentum* 3: 70–111.

His, R. 1896, *Die Domänen der römischen Kaiserzeit*, Leipzig.

Hitchner, B. 1990, "The Kasserine Archaeological Survey, 1987," *Antiquités africaines* 26: 231–60.

1994, "Image and Reality: The Changing Face of Pastoralism in the Tunisian High Steppe," in *Landuse in the Roman Empire*, ed. J. Carlsen, Rome, 27–43.

2005, "'The Advantages of Wealth and Luxury': The Case for Economic Growth in the Roman Empire," in *The Ancient Economy: Evidence and Models*, eds. J. G. Manning and I. Morris, Stanford, 207–22.

Hobsbawm, E. 1964, "Introduction," to K. Marx, *Pre-Capitalist Economic Formations*, London, 9–65.

Hodkinson, S. 1988, "Animal Husbandry in the Greek Polis," in *Pastoral Economies in Classical Antiquity*, ed. C. R. Whittaker, Cambridge, 35–74.

Hoetink, H. R. 1959, "Autour du 'Sénatus-Consulte Claudien,'" in *Mélanges Lévy-Bruhl*, Paris, 153–62.

Holman, S. 2001, *The Hungry Are Dying: Beggars and Bishops in Roman Cappadocia*, New York.

ed. 2008, *Wealth and Poverty in Early Church and Society*, Grand Rapids.

Honoré, T. 1994, *Emperors and Lawyers²*, Oxford.

1998, *Law in the Crisis of Empire: The Theodosian Dynasty and its Quaestors*, Oxford.

2004, "Roman Law AD 200–400: From Cosmopolis to Rechtstaat?," in *Approaching Late Antiquity: The Transformation from Early to Late Empire*, eds. S. Swain and M. Edwards, Oxford, 109–32.

Hopkins, K. 1978, *Conquerors and Slaves*, New York.

1980, "Taxes and Trade in the Roman Empire (200 B.C.–400 A.D)," *Journal of Roman Studies* 70: 101–25.

1993, "Novel Evidence for Roman Slavery," *Past & Present* 138: 3–27.

2000, "Rent, Taxes, Trade, and the City of Rome," in *Mercati permanenti e mercati periodici nel mondo romano: Atti degli Incontri capresi di storia dell'economia antica (Capri 13–15 ottobre 1997)*, ed. E. Lo Cascio, Bari, 253–67.

Hopkins, M. K. 1961, "Social Mobility in the Later Roman Empire: The Evidence of Ausonius," *Classical Quarterly* 11: 239–49.

Horden, P. and Purcell, N. 2000, *The Corrupting Sea: A Study of Mediterranean History*, Oxford.

Horsley, H. R. and Mitchell, S. 2000: *see* IGSK 57.

Huchthausen, L. 1974, "Kaiserliche Rechtsauskünfte an Sklaven und in ihrer Freiheit angefochtene Personen aus dem Codex Iustinianus," *Wissenschaftliche Zeitschrift der Wilhelm-Pieck-Universität Rostock* 23: 251–7.

1976, "Zum Problem der 'Freiheitsbegünstigung' (*favor libertatis*) im römischen Recht," *Philologus* 120: 47–72.

Humbert, M. 1983, "Enfants à louer ou à vendre: Augustin et l'autorité parentale (Ep. 10* et 24*)," in *Les Lettres de Saint Augustin découvertes par Johannes Divjak: communications présentées au colloque des 20 et 21 Septembre 1982*, ed. J. Divjak, Paris, 189–203.

Humfress, C. 2006, "Civil Law and Social Life," in *The Cambridge Companion to the Age of Constantine*, ed. N. Lenski, Cambridge, 205–25.

Hunt, P. 1999, *Slaves, Warfare and Ideology in the Greek Historians*, Cambridge.

Hunwick, J. 1992, "Black Africans in the Mediterranean World: Introduction to a Neglected Aspect of the African Diaspora," in *The Human Commodity: Perspectives on the Trans-Saharan Slave Trade*, ed. E. Savage, London, 5–38.

Ilan, T. 1996, *Jewish Women in Greco-Roman Palestine*, Tübingen.

Imbert, J. 1949, "Réflexions sur le christianisme et l'esclavage en droit romain," *Revue internationale des droits de l'antiquité* 2: 445–76.

Inscoe, J. 1995, "Mountain Masters as Confederate Opportunists: The Profitablity of Slavery in Western North Carolina, 1861–5," *Slavery & Abolition* 16: 85–100.

Jacobs, A. and Krawiec, R. 2003, "Father Knows Best? Christian Families in the Age of Asceticism," *Journal of Early Christian Studies* 11: 257–63.

Jacoby, D. 1961, "La population de Constantinople à la époque byzantine: un problème de démographie urbaine," *Byzantion* 31: 81–110.

Jaeger, W. 1974, *Die Sklaverei bei Johannes Chrysostomus*, Diss., University of Kiel.

Jameson, M. 1977, "Agriculture and Slavery in Classical Athens," *Classical Journal* 73: 122–45.

Jameson, M. *et al.* 1994, *A Greek Countryside: The Southern Argolid from Prehistory to the Present Day*, Stanford.

Jensen, J. 1978, "Does Porneia Mean Fornication? A Critique of Bruce Malina," *Novum Testamentum* 20: 161–84.

Johnson, S. 2006, *The Life and Miracles of Thekla: A Literary Study*, Washington, DC.

Johnson, W. 1999, *Soul by Soul: Life inside the Antebellum Slave Market*, Cambridge, MA.

Jolowicz, H. F. 1932, *Historical Introduction to the Study of Roman Law*, Cambridge.

Jones, A. H. M. 1940, *The Greek City: From Alexander to Justinian*, Oxford.
1949, "The Roman Civil Service (Clerical and Sub-clerical Grades)," *Journal of Roman Studies* 39: 38–55.
1953, "Census Records of the Later Roman Empire," *Journal of Roman Studies* 43: 49–64.
1956, "Slavery in the Ancient World," *Economic History Review* 9: 185–99.
1960, "The Cloth Industry under the Roman Empire," *Economic History Review* 13: 183–92.
1964, *The Later Roman Empire, 284–602: A Social, Economic, and Administrative Survey*, Oxford.
Jones, C. P. 1987, "Stigma: Tattooing and Branding in Graeco-Roman Antiquity," *Journal of Roman Studies* 77: 139–55.
1993, "Greek Drama in the Roman Empire," in *Theater and Society in the Classical World*, ed. R. Scodel, Ann Arbor, 39–52.
2004, "A Roman Will in Cappadocia," *Epigraphica Anatolica* 37: 95–100.
2005, "Culture in the Careers of Eastern Senators," in *Senatores populi Romani: Realität und mediale Präsentation einer Führungsschicht*, eds. W. Eck and M. Heil, Stuttgart, 263–70.
2008, "Hyperides and the Sale of Slave Families," *Zeitschrift für Papyrologie und Epigraphik* 164: 19–20.
Jongman, W. 1988, *The Economy and Society of Pompeii*, Amsterdam.
2000a, "Wool and the Textile Industry of Roman Italy: A Working Hypothesis," in *Mercati permanenti e mercati periodici nel mondo romano: Atti degli Incontri capresi di storia dell'economia antica (Capri 13–15 ottobre 1997)*, ed. E. Lo Cascio, Bari, 187–97.
2000b, "Hunger and Power: Theories, Models, and Methods in Roman Economic History," in *Interdependence of Institutions and Private Entrepreneurs*, ed. A. Bongenaar, Leiden, 259–84.
2003, "Slavery and the Growth of Rome. The Transformation of Italy in the Second and First Centuries BCE," in *Rome the Cosmopolis*, eds. C. Edwards and G. Woolf, Cambridge, 100–22.
2006, "The Rise and Fall of the Roman Economy: Population, Rents, and Entitlements," in *Ancient Economies, Modern Methodologies: Archaeology, Comparative History, Models, and Institutions*, eds. P. Bang, M. Ikeguchi, and H. Ziche, Bari, 237–54.
Jonkers, E. J. 1933–4, "De l'influence du christianisme sur la législation relative à l'esclavage dans l'antiquité," *Mnemosyne* 1: 241–80.
Joshel, S. 1986, "Nurturing the Master's Child: Slavery and the Roman Child-Nurse," *Signs* 12: 3–22.
1992, *Work, Identity, and Legal Status at Rome: A Study of the Occupational Inscriptions*, Norman.
Joshel, S. and Murnaghan, S. 1998, "Introduction: Differential Equations," in *Women and Slaves in Greco-Roman Culture: Differential Equations*, eds. S. Joshel and S. Murnaghan, London, 1–21.
Juglar, L. 1894, *Du rôle des ésclaves et des affranchis dans le commerce*, Paris, repr. 1972, Rome.

Kahane, H. and Kahane, R. 1962, "Notes on the Linguistic History of *Sclavus*," in *Studi in onore di Ettore Lo Gatto e Giovanni Maver*, Florence, 345–60.

Karabélias, E. 1990, "Rapports juridiques entre concubins dans le droit romain tardif (donations, *actio furti*, successions)," *AARC* 8: 439–53.

Karagiorgou, O. 2001, "LR2: A Container for the Military *annona* on the Danubian Border," in *Economy and Exchange in the East Mediterranean during Late Antiquity*, eds. S. Kingsley and M. Decker, Oxford, 129–66.

Karasch, M. 1987, *Slave Life in Rio de Janeiro, 1808–1850*, Princeton.

Kaser, M. 1938, "Die Geschichte der Patronatsgewalt über Freigelassene," *Zeitschrift der Savigny-Stiftung für Rechtsgeschichte. Romanistiche Abteilung* 58: 88–135.

   1971, *Das römische Privatrecht I: Das altrömische, das vorklassische und klassische Recht*, Munich.

   1975, *Das römische Privatrecht II: Die nachklassische Entwicklung*, Munich.

   1996, *Das Römische Zivilprozessrecht*, Munich.

Kaster, R. 1988, *Guardians of Language: The Grammarian and Society in Late Antiquity*, Berkeley.

   1997, "The Shame of the Romans," *Transactions of the American Philological Association* 127: 1–19.

   2005, *Emotion, Restraint, and Community in Ancient Rome*, New York.

Keenan, J. 1989, "Roman Criminal Law in a Berlin Papyrus Codex," *Archiv für Papyrusforschung und verwandte Gebiete* 35: 15–23.

Kehoe, D. 1992, *Management and Investment on Estates in Roman Egypt during the Early Empire*, Bonn.

   1997, *Investment, Profit, and Tenancy: The Jurists and the Roman Agrarian Economy*, Ann Arbor.

   2007, *Law and Rural Economy in the Roman Empire*, Ann Arbor.

Kelly, C. 2004, *Ruling the Later Roman Empire*, Cambridge, MA.

Kingsley, S. 2001, "The Economic Impact of the Palestinian Wine Trade in Late Antiquity," in *Economy and Exchange in the East Mediterranean during Late Antiquity*, eds. S. Kingsley and M. Decker, Oxford, 44–68.

   2002, *A Sixth-century AD Shipwreck off the Carmel Coast, Israel: Dor D and Holy Land Wine Trade*, Oxford.

Kingsley, S. and Decker, M., eds. 2001, *Economy and Exchange in the East Mediterranean during Late Antiquity*, Oxford.

Kinzig, W. 1990, *In Search of Asterius: Studies on the Authorship of the Homilies on the Psalms*, Göttingen.

   1997, "The Greek Christian Writers," in *Handbook of Classical Rhetoric in the Hellenistic Period, 330 B.C.–A.D. 400*, ed. S. Porter, Leiden, 633–70.

Kirchhoff, R. 1994, *Die Sünde gegen den eigenen Leib: Studien zu pornē und porneia in 1 Kor 6, 12–20 und dem sozio-kulturellen Kontext der paulinischen Adressaten*, Göttingen.

Kirschenbaum, A. 1987, *Sons, Slaves, and Freedmen in Roman Commerce*, Washington, DC.

Klein, R. 1988, *Die Sklaverei in der Sicht der Bischöfe Ambrosius und Augustinus*, Stuttgart.

1999, "Zum Verhältnis von Herren und Sklaven in der Spätantike," in *Roma versa per aevum: Ausgewählte Schriften zur heidnischen und christlichen Spätantike*, New York, 356–93.

2000, *Die Haltung der kappadokischen Bischöfe Basilius von Caesarea, Gregor von Nazianz, und Gregor von Nyssa zur Sklaverei*, Stuttgart.

2001, "Der Kirchenvater Hieronymus und die Sklaverei. Ein Einblick," in *Fünfzig Jahre Forschungen zur antiken Sklaverei an der Mainzer Akademie, 1950–2000: Miscellanea zum Jubiläum*, eds. H. Bellen and H. Heinen, Stuttgart, 401–25.

Klingenberg, G. 2005, *Corpus der römischen Rechtsquellen zur antiken Sklaverei (CRRS)*, vol. 10: *Juristische speziell definierte Sklavengruppen*. 6. Servus fugitivus, Stuttgart.

Kolendo, J. 1980, *L'agricoltura nell'Italia romana: tecniche agrarie e progresso economico dalla tarda repubblica al principato*, Rome.

1981, "L'esclavage et la vie sexuelle des hommes libres à Rome," *Index* 10: 288–97.

Konstan, D. 1994a, *Sexual Symmetry: Love in the Ancient Novel and Related Genres*, Princeton.

1994b, "*Apollonius, King of Tyre* and the Greek Novel," in *The Search for the Ancient Novel*, ed. J. Tatum, Baltimore, 173–82.

Kontoulis, G. 1993, *Zum Problem der Sklaverei (ΔΟΥΛΕΙΑ) bei den Kappadokischen Kirchenvatern und Johannes Chrysostomus*, Bonn.

Koons, K. and Hofstra, W., eds. 2000, *After the Backcountry: Rural Life in the Great Valley of Virginia 1800–1900*, Knoxville.

Koptev, A. V. 1995, "Législation romaine des IVe et Ve siècles sur les mariages d'esclaves et de colons," in *Esclavage et dépendance dans l'historiographie soviétique récente*, eds. M. M. Mactoux and E. Geny, Paris, 127–55.

Kortekaas, G. A. A. 2007, *Commentary on the* Historia Apollonii Regis Tyri, Leiden.

Kron, G. 2000, "Roman Ley-farming," *Journal of Roman Archaeology* 13: 277–87.

2005, "Sustainable Roman Intensive Mixed Farming Methods: Water Conservation and Erosion Control," *Caesarodunum* 39: 285–308.

Kudlien, F. 1986, "*Empticius servus*: Bemerkungen zum antiken Sklavenmarkt," *Historia* 35: 240–56.

1991, *Sklaven-Mentalität im Spiegel antiker Wahrsagerei*, Stuttgart.

Kuefler, M. 2001, *The Manly Eunuch: Masculinity, Gender Ambiguity, and Christian Ideology in Late Antiquity*, Chicago.

Kulikowski, M. 2004, *Late Roman Spain and its Cities*, Baltimore.

Küppers, J. 1979, "Zum 'Querolus' (p. 17.7–22 R) und seiner Datierung," *Philologus* 123: 303–23.

1989, "Die spätantike Prosakomödie 'Querolus sive Aulularia' und das Problem ihrer Vorlagen," *Philologus* 133: 82–103.

Kurfess, A. 1953, "Ad Ausonium," *Gymnasium* 60: 262–3.

Kuziščin, V. 1979, "Le caractère de la main d'œuvre dans un domaine du IVe siècle d'après le traité de Palladius," in *Actes du colloque sur l'esclavage*, Warsaw, 239–55.

Laes, C. 2008, "Child Slaves at Work in Roman Antiquity," *Ancient Society* 38: 235–83.

Laiou, A. ed. 1993, *Consent and Coercion to Sex and Marriage in Ancient and Medieval Societies*, Washington, DC.

Lambertini, R. 1987, "Due rescritti in tema di '*venditiones filiorum*,'" *Labeo* 33: 186–92.

Lambot, C. 1969, "Le sermon CCXXIV de S. Augustin et ses recensions interpolées," *Revue bénédictine* 79: 193–205.

Lamoreaux, J. 1995, "Episcopal Courts in Late Antiquity," *Journal of Early Christian Studies* 3: 143–67.

Lanfranchi, F. 1938, *Il diritto nei retori romani*, Milan.

Langenfeld, H. 1977, *Christianisierungspolitik und Sklavengesetzgebung der römischen Kaiser von Konstantin bis Theodosius II*, Bonn.

Laniado, A. 2002, *Recherches sur les notables municipaux dans l'Empire proto-byzantin*, Paris.

Latte, K. 1920, *Heiliges Recht: Untersuchungen zur Geschichte der sakralen Rechts-formen in Griechenland*, Tübingen.

Lavan, L., ed. 2001, *Recent Research in Late-Antique Urbanism*, Portsmouth.

Leclerc, P. and Morales, E., eds. 2007, *Jérôme, Trois vies de moines*, SC 508, Paris.

Leclercq, H. 1921, "Diptyques," *DACL* 4: cols. 1045–1170.

Lefort, J. 2002, "The Rural Economy, Seventh–Twelfth Centuries," in *The Economic History of Byzantium: From the Seventh through the Fifteenth Century*, ed. A. Laiou, Washington, DC, 231–310.

Lendon, J. 1997, *Empire of Honour: The Art of Government in the Roman World*, Oxford.

Lenski, N. 1996, Review of P. Rousseau, *Basil of Caesarea*, *Bryn Mawr Classical Review* 7: 438–44.

1999, "Assimilation and Revolt in the Territory of Isauria, from the 1st Century BC to the 6th Century AD," *Journal of the Economic and Social History of the Orient* 42: 413–65.

2001, "Evidence for the *Audientia episcopalis* in the New Letters of Augustine," in *Law, Society, and Authority in Late Antiquity*, ed. R. Mathisen, Oxford, 83–97.

2006a, "*Servi Publici* in the Late Antique City," in *Die Stadt in der Spätantike*, eds. J.-U. Krause and C. Witschel, Stuttgart, 335–57.

ed. 2006b, *The Cambridge Companion to the Age of Constantine*, Cambridge.

2006c, "The Reign of Constantine," in *The Cambridge Companion to the Age of Constantine*, ed. N. Lenski, Cambridge, 59–90.

2008, "Captivity, Slavery, and Cultural Exchange between Rome and the Germans from the First to the Seventh Century CE," in *Invisible Citizens: Captives and their Consequences*, ed. C. Cameron, Salt Lake City, 80–109.

2009, "Schiavi armati e la formazione di eserciti privati nel mondo tardoantico," in *Ordine e Disordine nel mondo greco e romano*, ed. G. P. Urso, Pisa, 145–75.

2010, Review of Y. Rotman, *Byzantine Slavery in the Mediterranean World*, *Bryn Mawr Classical Review*, 2010.05.14.

Forthcoming, "Constantine and Slavery: *Libertas* and the Fusion of Roman and Christian Values," *AARC* 15.

Lenz, K. 2001, "Late Roman Rural Settlement in the Southern Part of the Province *Germania Secunda* in Comparison with Other Regions of the Roman Rhineland," in *Les campagnes de la Gaule à la fin de l'Antiquité: actes du colloque, Montpellier, 11–14 mars 1998*, eds. P. Ouzoulias *et al.*, Antibes, 113–46.

Leone, A. and Mattingly, D. 2004, "Vandal, Byzantine, and Arab Rural Landscapes in North Africa," in *Landscapes of Change: Rural Evolutions in Late Antiquity and the Early Middle Ages*, ed. N. Christie, Burlington, 135–62.

Leonhard, R. 1899, "Cautio," *RE* 3.2: cols. 1814–19.

Leontsini, S. 1989, *Die Prostitution im frühen Byzanz*, Vienna.

Lepelley, C. 1981a, *Les cités de l'Afrique romaine au bas-empire*, Paris.

    1981b, "La crise de l'Afrique romaine au début du ve siècle, d'après les lettres nouvellement découvertes de saint Augustin," *Comptes rendus. Académie des inscriptions et belles-lettres* 125: 445–63.

    1983, "Liberté, colonat, et esclavage d'après la Lettre 24*: la jurisdiction épiscopale 'de liberali causa,'" in *Les Lettres de Saint Augustin découvertes par Johannes Divjak: communications présentées au colloque des 20 et 21 Septembre 1982*, ed. J. Divjak, Paris, 329–42.

    1986, "Fine dell'ordine equestre: le tappe dell'unificazione della classe dirigente romana nel IV secolo," in *Società romana e impero tardoantico*, vol. 1, ed. A. Giardina, Rome, 227–44, 664–7.

    1996, "Vers la fin du 'privilège de liberté': l'amoindrissement de l'autonomie des cités à l'aube du bas-empire," in *"Splendissimia civitas." Études d'histoire romaine en hommage à François Jacques*, eds. A. Chastagnol, E. Demougin, and C. Lepelley, Paris, 207–20.

Lepore, J. 2005, *New York Burning: Liberty, Slavery, and Conspiracy in Eighteenth-Century Manhattan*, New York.

Letourneur, M.-J. 2002, "La circulation des messagers chez Jérôme," in *Routes et marchés d'esclaves, 26e colloque du GIREA*, ed. M. Garrido-Hory, Paris, 127–37.

Leveau, P. 1984, *Caesarea de Maurétanie: une ville romaine et ses campagnes*, Rome.

Levy, E. 1945, *Pauli Sententiae: A Palingenesia of the Opening Titles as a Specimen of Research in West Roman Vulgar Law*, Ithaca.

    1951, *West Roman Vulgar Law: The Law of Property*, Philadelphia.

Lévy-Bruhl, H. 1936, "L'affranchissement par la vindicte," in *Studi in onore di Salvatore Riccobono nel XL anno del suo insegnamento*, vol. 3, Palermo, 1–19.

Lewis, B. 1990, *Race and Slavery in the Middle East*, Oxford.

Lewit, T. 1991, *Agricultural Production in the Roman Economy*, Oxford.

    2004, *Villas, Farms, and the Late Roman Rural Economy: Third to Fifth Centuries AD*, Oxford.

Leyerle, B. 2001, *Theatrical Shows and Ascetic Lives: John Chrysostom's Attack on Spiritual Marriage*, Berkeley.

Liebeschuetz, J. H. W. G. 1972, *Antioch: City and Imperial Administration in the Later Roman Empire*, Oxford.

2001, "The Uses and Abuses of the Concept of 'Decline' in Later Roman History," in *Recent Research in Late-Antique Urbanism*, ed. L. Lavan, Portsmouth, 233–8.

Liebs, D. 1987, *Die Jurisprudenz im spätantiken Italien*, Berlin.

1993, *Römische Jurisprudenz in Afrika: mit Studien zu den pseudopaulinischen Sentenzen*, Berlin.

2008a, "Die Rolle der Paulussentenzen bei der Ermittlung des römischen Rechts," in *Hermeneutik der Quellentexte des römischen Rechts*, ed. M. Avenarius, Baden-Baden, 157–75.

2008b, "Roman Vulgar Law in Late Antiquity," in *Aspects of Law in Late Antiquity: Dedicated to A. M. Honoré on the Occasion of the Sixtieth Year of His Teaching in Oxford*, ed. A. J. B. Sirks, Oxford, 35–53.

Lintott, A. 2002, "Freedmen and Slaves in the Light of Legal Documents from First-century A.D. Campania," *Classical Quarterly* 52: 555–65.

Little, L., ed. 2007, *Plague and the End of Antiquity: The Pandemic of 541–750*, Cambridge.

Lo Cascio, E., ed. 1997, *Terre, proprietari e contadini dell'impero romano: dall'affitto agrario al colonato tardoantico*, Rome.

ed. 2000, *Mercati permanenti e mercati periodici nel mondo romano: Atti degli Incontri capresi di storia dell'economia antica (Capri 13–15 ottobre 1997)*, Bari.

2001, "La population," *Pallas* 55: 179–98.

2002, "Considerazioni sul numero degli schiavi e sulle loro fonti di approvvigionamento in età imperiale," in *Études de démographie du monde gréco-romain*, ed. W. Suder, Wrocław, 51–65.

2006, "The Role of the State in the Roman Economy: Making Use of the New Institutional Economics," in *Ancient Economies, Modern Methodologies: Archaeology, Comparative History, Models, and Institutions*, eds. P. Bang, M. Ikeguchi, and H. Ziche, Bari, 215–34.

2009, *Crescita e declino: Studi di storia dell'economia romana*, Rome.

Loenertz, R.-J. 1958, "Observations sur quelques lettres d'Énée de Gaza," *Historisches Jahrbuch* 77: 438–43.

Long, J. 1996, *Claudian's In Eutropium, or, How, When, and Why to Slander a Eunuch*, Chapel Hill.

López, C. and Pérez, D. 2000, "Mujeres esclavas en la Antigüedad: Producción y reproducción en las unidades domésticas," *Arenal* 7: 5–40.

López Barja de Quiroga, P. 2007, *Historia de la manumisión en Roma: de los orígenes a los Severos*, Madrid.

Los, A. 1995, "La condition sociale des affranchis privés au 1er siècle après J.-C.," *Annales: Histoire, sciences sociales* 50: 1011–43.

Loseby, S. T. 2007, "The Ceramic Data and the Transformation of the Roman World," in *LRCW 2: Late Roman Coarse Wares, Cooking Wares and Amphorae in the Mediterranean: Archaeology and Archaeometry*, eds. M. Bonifay and J.-C. Tréglia, Oxford, 1–14.

Lovejoy, P. 2003, *Transformations in Slavery: A History of Slavery in Africa²*, Cambridge, orig. 1983.

Lovejoy, P. and Richardson, D. 1995, "Competing Markets for Male and Female Slaves: Prices in the Interior of West Africa, 1780–1850," *International Journal of African Historical Studies*, 28: 261–93.

Lovén, L. 1998a, "*Lanam fecit*: Woolworking and Female Virtue," in *Aspects of Women in Antiquity: Proceedings of the First Nordic Symposium on Women's Lives in Antiquity*, Göteborg, 85–95.

1998b, "Male and Female Professions in the Textile Production of Roman Italy," in *Textiles in European Archaeology: Report from the 6th NESAT Symposium*, eds. L. Jørgensen and C. Rinaldo, Göteborg, 73–8.

Luchetti, G. 1990, *La legittimazione dei figli naturali nelle fonti tardo imperiali e giustinianee*, Milan.

Lunn-Rockliffe, S. 2006, "A Pragmatic Approach to Poverty and Riches: Ambrosiaster's *quaestio* 124*," in *Poverty in the Roman World*, eds. M. Atkins and R. Osborne, Cambridge, 115–29.

Lutz, C. 1947, *Musonius Rufus: "The Roman Socrates,"* New Haven.

MacCormack, S. 1981, *Art and Ceremony in Late Antiquity*, Berkeley.

MacDonald, K. 1990, "Mechanisms of Sexual Egalitarianism in Western Europe," *Ethology and Sociobiology* 11: 195–238.

MacMullen, R. 1964, "Social Mobility and the Theodosian Code," *Journal of Roman Studies* 54: 49–53.

1984, *Christianizing the Roman Empire (A.D. 100–400)*, New Haven.

1986a, "What Difference Did Christianity Make?," *Historia* 35: 322–43.

1986b, "Judicial Savagery in the Roman Empire," *Chiron* 16: 147–66.

1987, "Late Roman Slavery," *Historia* 36: 359–82.

1989, "The Preacher and His Audience (AD 350–400)," *Journal of Theological Studies* 40: 503–11.

1990, *Changes in the Roman Empire: Essays in the Ordinary*, Princeton.

Maddison, A. 2007, *Contours of the World Economy, 1–2030 AD: Essays in Macroeconomic History*, Oxford.

Magness, J. 2003, *The Archaeology of the Early Islamic Settlement in Palestine*, Winona Lake.

Malineau, V. 2005, "L'apport de l'*Apologie des mimes* de Chorikios de Gaza à la connaissance du théâtre du VIe siècle," in *Gaza dans l'Antiquité tardive*, ed. C. Saliou, Salerno, 149–69.

Mañaricua, E. 1940, *El matrimonio de los esclavos: estudio histórico jurídico hasta la fijación de la disciplina en el derecho canónico*, Rome.

Manca Masciadri, M. and Montevecchi, O. 1982, "Contratti di baliatico e vendite fiduciarie a Tebtynis," *Aegyptus* 62: 148–61.

Manfredini, A. 1988, "Costantino la '*tabernaria*' il vino," *AARC* 7: 325–41.

Mango, C. 1985, *La développement urbain de Constantinople (IVe–VIIe siècles)*, Paris.

Manning, C. 1986, "*Actio ingrati*," *Studia et documenta historiae et iuris* 52: 61–72.

Maraval, P. 1970, "L'èglise du ɪve siècle et l'esclavage," *Studia Moralia* 8: 319–46.

Marazzi, F. 2004, "La valle del Tevere nella tarda antichità: inquadramento dei problemi archeologici," in *Bridging the Tiber: Approaches to Regional Archaeology in the Middle Tiber Valley*, ed. H. Patterson, London, 103–9.

Marcone, A. 1988, *Il colonato tardoantico nella storiografia moderna (da Fustel de Coulanges ai nostri giorni)*, Como.

Marichal, R. 1992, *see* Papyri and ostraca.

Marinovič, L. P., Golubcova, E. S., and Šifman, I. 1992, *Die Sklaverei in den östlichen Provinzen des römischen Reiches im 1.–3. Jahrhundert*, Stuttgart.

Markus, R. 1990, *The End of Ancient Christianity*, Cambridge.

Martin, D. 1990, *Slavery as Salvation: The Metaphor of Slavery in Pauline Christianity*, New Haven.

  2003, "Slave Families and Slaves in Families," in *Early Christian Families in Context*, eds. D. Balch and C. Osiek, Grand Rapids, 207–30.

Martini, R. 1988, "Sulla vendita dei neonati nella legislazione Costantiniana," *AARC* 7: 423–32.

Martroye, F. 1924, "Le testament de Saint Grégoire de Nazianze," *Mémoires de la Société nationale des Antiquaires de France* 76: 219–63.

Mary, M. 1954, "Slavery in the Writings of St. Augustine," *Classical Journal* 49: 363–8.

Marzano, A. 2007, *Roman Villas in Central Italy: A Social and Economic History*, Leiden.

Masi Doria, C. 1993, Civitas operae obsequium: *tre studi sulla condizione giuridica dei liberti*, Naples.

Mason, H. 1974, *Greek Terms for Roman Institutions: A Lexicon and Analysis*, Toronto.

Mathisen, R. 1997, "The 'Second Council of Arles' and the Spirit of Compilation and Codification in Late Roman Gaul," *Journal of Early Christian Studies* 5, 511–54.

  2006, "Peregrini, Barbari, and Cives Romani: Concepts of Citizenship and the Legal Identity of Barbarians in the Later Roman Empire," *American Historical Review* 111: 1011–40.

Matthews, J. 2000, *Laying Down the Law: A Study of the Theodosian Code*, New Haven.

  2001, "Interpreting the *Interpretationes* of the *Breviarium*," in *Law, Society, and Authority in Late Antiquity*, ed. R. Mathisen, Oxford, 11–32.

  2006, *The Journey of Theophanes: Travel, Business, and Daily Life in the Roman East*, New Haven.

Mattingly, D. 1994, *Tripolitania*, Ann Arbor.

  2003, *The Archaeology of the Fazzān*, Tripoli.

Mattingly, D. and Hitchner, B. 1995, "Roman Africa: An Archaeological Review," *Journal of Roman Studies* 85: 165–213.

Maxwell, J. 2006, *Christianization and Communication in Late Antiquity: John Chrysostom and His Congregation in Antioch*, Cambridge.

Mayer, W. 1997, "The Dynamics of Liturgical Space: Aspects of the Interaction between John Chrysostom and His Audiences," *Ephemerides Liturgicae* III: 104–15.

2000, "Who Came to Hear John Chrysostom Preach?: Recovering a Late Fourth-Century Preacher's Audience," *Ephemerides theologicae Lovanienses* 76: 73–87.

2005, *The Homilies of St. John Chrysostom – Provenance: Reshaping the Foundations*, Rome.

2006, "Poverty and Society in the World of John Chrysostom," in *Social and Political Life in Late Antiquity*, eds. W. Bowden, A. Gutteridge, and C. Machado, Leiden, 465–84.

2008, "Homiletics," in *The Oxford Handbook of Early Christian Studies*, eds. S. Ashbrook Harvey and D. Hunter, Oxford: 565–83.

Mayer-Maly, T. 1958, "Das Notverkaufsrecht des Hausvaters," *Zeitschrift der Savigny-Stiftung für Rechtsgeschichte. Romanistiche Abteilung* 75: 116–55.

Mayerson, P. 1978, "Anti-Black Sentiment in the 'Vitae Patrum,'" *Harvard Theological Review* 71: 304–11.

1985, "The Wine and Vineyards of Gaza in the Byzantine Period," *Bulletin of the American Schools of Oriental Research* 257: 75–80.

Maza, S. 1983, *Servants and Masters in Eighteenth-Century France: The Uses of Loyalty*, Princeton.

Mazza, M. 1975, "Prefazione," to E. Shtaerman and M. Trofimova, *La schiavitù nell'Italia imperiale*, Rome, V–XLIV.

1977, "Introduzione," re-edn. of E. Ciccotti, *Il tramonto della schiavitù nel mondo antico*, Rome, V–LXVI.

1986, *La fatica dell'uomo: schiavi e liberi nel mondo romano*, Catania.

Mazzarino, S. 1966, *The End of the Ancient World*, trans. G. Holmes, London 1966, orig. 1959.

McBride, T. 1976, *The Domestic Revolution: The Modernization of Household Service in England and France, 1820–1920*, New York.

McCail, R. 1971, "The Erotic and Ascetic Poetry of Agathias Scholasticus," *Byzantion* 41: 205–67.

McCambley, C. 1991, "Against Those Who Practice Usury by Gregory of Nyssa," *Greek Orthodox Theological Review* 36: 287–302.

McCarthy, K. 2000, *Slaves, Masters, and the Art of Authority in Plautine Comedy*, Princeton.

McClure, L. 2003, *Courtesans at Table: Gender and Greek Literary Culture in Athenaeus*, New York.

McCormick, M. 1985, "Analyzing Imperial Ceremonies," *Jahrbuch des Österreichischen Byzantinistik* 35: 1–20.

1987, *Eternal Victory: Triumphal Rulership in Late Antiquity, Byzantium, and the Early Medieval West*, Cambridge.

1998, "Bateaux de vie, bateaux de mort. Maladie, commerce, transports annonaires et le passage économique du Bas-Empire au moyen âge," in *Morfologie sociali e culturali in Europa fra tarda antichità e alto medioevo*, Spoleto, 35–118.

2001, *Origins of the European Economy: Communications and Commerce* A.D. *300–900*, Cambridge.

2002, "New Light on the 'Dark Ages': How the Slave Trade Fuelled the Carolingian Economy," *Past & Present* 177: 17–54.

Forthcoming, "Movements and Markets in the First Millennium: Information, Containers and Shipwrecks," Dumbarton Oaks Symposium, 2008, Trade and Markets in Byzantium.

McGinn, T. 1991, "Concubinage and the *Lex Iulia* on Adultery," *Transactions of the American Philological Association* 121: 335–75.

1997, "The Legal Definition of Prostitute in Late Antiquity," *Memoirs of the American Academy in Rome* 42: 73–116.

1998, *Prostitution, Sexuality, and the Law*, New York.

1999, "The Social Policy of the Emperor Constantine in *Codex Theodosianus* 4.6.3," *Tijdschrift voor rechtsgeschiedenis* 67: 57–73.

2004, *The Economy of Prostitution in the Roman World: A Study of Social History and the Brothel*, Ann Arbor.

McGuire, M. R. P. 1927, *S. Ambrosii De Nabuthae: A Commentary, with an Introduction and Translation*, Washington, DC.

McKeown, N. 2007, *The Invention of Ancient Slavery?*, London.

Mee, C. and Forbes, H. 1997, *A Rough and Rocky Place: The Landscape and Settlement History of the Methana Peninsula, Greece: Results of the Methana Survey Project Sponsored by the British School of Athens and the University of Liverpool*, Liverpool.

Meeks, W. 1983, *The First Urban Christians: The Social World of the Apostle Paul*, New Haven.

Melluso, M. 2000, *La schiavitù nell'età giustinianea: disciplina giuridica e rilevanza sociale*, Paris.

2002, "Alcune testimonianze in tema di mercati di schiavi nel tardo antico," in *Routes et marchés d'esclaves, 26e colloque du GIREA*, ed. M. Garrido-Hory, Paris, 345–70.

Memmer, M. 1991, "*Ad servitutem aut ad lupanar* . . . Ein Beitrag zur Rechtsstellung von Findelkindern nach römischen Recht – unter besonderer Berücksichtigung von §§ 77, 98 *Sententiae Syriacae*," *Zeitschrift der Savigny-Stiftung für Rechtsgeschichte. Romanistiche Abteilung* 108: 21–93.

Mercogliano, F. 1997, *Tituli ex corpore Ulpiani: Storia di un testo*, Naples.

Merdinger, J. 1997, *Rome and the African Church in the Time of Augustine*, New Haven.

Meslin, M. 1970, *La fête des kalendes de janvier dans l'empire romain*, Brussels.

Metzger, E. 2000, "The Case of Petronia Justa," *Revue internationale des droits de l'antiquité* 47: 151–65.

Meyer, E. 1924, "Die Sklaverei im Altertum," in *Kleine Schriften*, vol. 1, Halle, 1924, 169–212, orig. 1898.

Meyer, E. 2002, Review of *Inscriptions du sanctuaire de la mère des dieux autochtone de Leukopetra (Macédoine)*, *American Journal of Philology* 123: 136–40.

2004, *Legitimacy and Law in the Roman World: Tabulae in Roman Belief and Practice*, Cambridge.

Meyer, P. 1895, *Der römische Konkubinat nach den Rechtsquellen und den Inschriften*, Leipzig.

Meylan, P. 1953, "L'individualité de la 'manumissio vindicta,'" in *Studi in onore di Vincenzo Arangio-Ruiz nel* XLV *anno del suo insegnamento*, vol. 4, Naples, 469–84.

Miers, S. and Kopytoff, I. 1977, "African 'Slavery' as an Institution of Marginality," in *Slavery in Africa: Historical and Anthropological Perspectives*, eds. S. Miers and I. Kopytoff, Madison, 3–81.

Millar, F. 1999, "The Greek East and Roman Law: The Dossier of M. Cn. Licinius Rufinus," *Journal of Roman Studies* 89: 90–108.

Minor, C. 2000, "Reclassifying the Bacaudae: Some Reasons for Caution," *Ancient World* 31: 74–95.

Mitteis, L. 1891, *Reichsrecht und Volksrecht in den östlichen Provinzen des römischen Kaiserreichs: Mit Beiträgen zur Kenntniss des griechischen Rechts und der spätrömischen Rechtsentwicklung*, Leipzig.

Modrzejewski, J. 1970, "La règle de droit dans l'Égypte romaine," in *Proceedings of the* XIIth *International Congress of Papyrology*, Toronto, 317–77.

1974, "A propos de la tutelle dative des femmes dans l'Égypte romaine," *Akten des* XIII *Internationalen Papyrologenkongresses*, eds. E. Kiessling and H.-A. Rupprecht, Munich, 263–92.

1982, "Ménandre de Laodicée et l'Édit de Caracalla," in *Symposion 1977: Vorträge zur griechischen und hellenistischen Rechtsgeschichte*, eds. J. Modrzejewski and D. Liebs, Cologne, 335–63.

1988, "'La loi des Égyptiens': le droit grec dans l'Égypte romaine," *Proceedings of the* XVIII *International Congress of Papyrology*, vol. 2, ed. B. Mandilaras, Athens, 383–99.

Molina, B. 1972, "Does Porneia Mean Fornication?," *Novum Testamentum* 14: 10–17.

Mommsen, T. 1905, "Bürgerlicher und peregrinischer Freiheitsschutz im römischen Staat," in *Gesammelte Schriften*, vol. 3, Berlin, 1–20.

Mor, C. 1928, "La 'Manumissio in Ecclesia,'" *Rivista di storia del diritto italiano* 1: 80–150.

Morabito, M. 1981, *Les réalités de l'esclavage d'après le Digeste*, Paris.

1986, "Droit romain et realités sociales de la sexualité servile," *Dialogues d'histoire ancienne* 12: 371–86.

Morales, H. 2004, *Vision and Narrative in Achilles Tatius' Leucippe and Clitophon*, Cambridge.

Morel, J.-P. 2007, "Early Rome and Italy," in *The Cambridge Economic History of the Greco-Roman World*, eds. W. Scheidel, I. Morris, and R. Saller, Cambridge, 487–510.

Morgan, P. 1988, "Task and Gang Systems: The Organization of Labor on New World Plantations," in *Work and Labor in Early America*, ed. S. Innes, Chapel Hill, 189–220.

Moriarty, R. 1993, "Human Owners, Human Slaves: Gregory of Nyssa, *Hom. Eccl. 4*," in *Papers Presented at the Eleventh International Conference on Patristic Studies Held in Oxford, 1991*, vol. 4, Louvain, 62–9.

Morley, N. 1996, *Metropolis and Hinterland: The City of Rome and the Italian Economy, 200 B.C.–200 A.D.*, Cambridge.

2006, "Narrative Economy," in *Ancient Economies, Modern Methodologies: Archaeology, Comparative History, Models, and Institutions*, eds. P. Bang, M. Ikeguchi, and H. Ziche, Bari, 27–47.

2007a, "The Early Roman Empire: Distribution," in *The Cambridge Economic History of the Greco-Roman World*, eds. W. Scheidel, I. Morris, and R. Saller, Cambridge, 570–91.

2007b, *Trade in Classical Antiquity*, Cambridge.

Morris, C. 1998, "The Articulation of Two Worlds: The Master–Slave Relationship Reconsidered," *Journal of American History* 85: 982–1007.

Morris, I. 2002, "Hard Surfaces," in *Money, Labour, and Land: Approaches to the Economies of Ancient Greece*, eds. P. Cartledge, E. Cohen, and L. Foxhall, London, 8–43.

2005, "Archaeology, Standards of Living, and Greek Economic History," in *The Ancient Economy: Evidence and Models*, eds. J. G. Manning and I. Morris, Stanford, 91–126.

Morris, I. and Manning, J. G. 2005, "Introduction," in *The Ancient Economy: Evidence and Models*, eds. J. G. Manning and I. Morris, Stanford, 1–44.

Morris, T. 1996, *Southern Slavery and the Law, 1619–1860*, Chapel Hill.

Morrison, C. and Sodini, J.-P. 2002, "The Sixth-Century Economy," in *The Economic History of Byzantium from the Seventh through the Fifteenth Centuries*, ed. A. Laiou, Washington, DC, 171–220.

Motomura, R. 1988, "The Practice of Exposing Infants and its Effects on the Development of Slavery in the Ancient World," in *Forms of Control and Subordination in Antiquity*, eds. T. Yuge and M. Doi, Leiden, 410–15.

Murga, J. L. 1982, "Una extraña aplicación del senadoconsulto Claudiano en el Codigo de Teodosio," *Studi Sanfilippo* 1, Milan, 415–41.

Murga Gener, J. L. 1981, "Una nueva versión del contubernio Claudiano en el Codex Teodosiano," *Revue internationale des droits de l'antiquité* 28: 163–87.

Nagle, D. B. 2006, *The Household as the Foundation of Aristotle's Polis*, New York.

Naragon, M. 1994, "Communities in Motion: Drapetomania, Work and the Development of African–American Slave Cultures," *Slavery & Abolition* 15: 63–87.

Nardi, D. 1978, "Il *ius vendendi* del *pater familias* nella legislazione di Costantino," *Atti dell'Accademia di Scienze Morali e Politiche di Napoli* 89: 53–99.

1984, "Ancora sul '*ius vendendi*' del '*pater familias*' nella legislazione di Costantino," in *Sodalitas: Scritti in onore di Antonio Guarino*, vol. 5, Naples, 2287–2308.

Nathan, G. 2000, *The Family in Late Antiquity: The Rise of Christianity and the Endurance of Tradition*, London.

Navarra, M. 1988, "Testi costantiniani in materiale di filiazione naturale," *AARC* 7: 459–75.

1990, "A proposito delle unioni tra libere e schiavi nella legislazione costantiniana," *AARC* 8: 427–37.

Nehlsen, H. 1972, *Sklavenrecht zwischen Antike und Mittelalter: germanisches und römisches Recht in den germanischen Rechtsaufzeichnungen*, Göttingen.

Neri, V. 1998, *I marginali nell'occidente tardoantico*, Bari.

Nettis, A. 2000, "Padroni, sesso e schiavi," *Index* 28: 156–72.

Neusner, J. 1982, *The Talmud of the Land of Israel: A Preliminary Translation and Explanation*, vol. 33, Abodah Zarah, Chicago.

Nichols, J. 1988, "On the Standard Size of the *Ordo Decurionum*," *Zeitschrift der Savigny-Stiftung für Rechtsgeschichte. Romanistiche Abteilung* 105: 712–19.

Niederwimmer, K. 1975, *Askese und Mysterium: über Ehe, Ehescheidung und Eheverzicht in den Anfängen des christlichen Glaubens*, Göttingen.

Nisbet, R. 1918, "The *Festuca* and *Alapa* of Manumission," *Journal of Roman Studies* 8: 1–14.

Norman, A. 2000, *Antioch as a Centre of Hellenic Culture as Observed by Libanius*, Liverpool.

Nörr, D. 1969, "Bemerkungen zur sakralen Freilassung in der späten Prinzipatszeit," in *Studi in onore di Edoardo Volterra*, vol. 2, Milan, 619–45.

Nussbaum, M. and Sihvola, H., eds. 2002, *The Sleep of Reason: Erotic Experience and Sexual Ethics in Ancient Greece and Rome*, Chicago.

Oakes, J. 1990, *Slavery and Freedom: An Interpretation of the Old South*, New York.

Oates, J. 1969, "A Rhodian Auction Sale of a Slave Girl," *Journal of Egyptian Archaeology* 55: 191–210.

Olivar, A. 1991, *La predicación cristiana antigua*, Barcelona.

Oliver, J. H. 1952, "The Eleusinian Endowment," *Hesperia* 21: 381–99.

Olovsdotter, C. 2005, *The Consular Image: An Iconological Study of the Consular Diptychs*, Oxford.

Omitowoju, R. 2002, *Rape and the Politics of Consent in Classical Athens*, Cambridge.

Origo, I. 1955, "The Domestic Enemy: The Eastern Slaves in Tuscany in the Fourteenth and Fifteenth Centuries," *Speculum* 30: 321–66.

Osborne, R. 1995, "The Economics and Politics of Slavery at Athens," in *The Greek World*, ed. A. Powell, London, 27–43.

2006, "Introduction: Roman Poverty in Context," in *Poverty in the Roman World*, eds. M. Atkins and R. Osborne, Cambridge, 1–20.

Osiek, C. 2003, "Female Slaves, Porneia, and the Limits of Obedience," in *Early Christian Families in Context*, eds. D. Balch and C. Osiek, Grand Rapids, 255–74.

Osman, G. 2005, "Foreign Slaves in Mecca and Medina in the Formative Islamic Period," *Islam and Christian–Muslim Relations* 16: 345–59.

Pack, E. 1980, "Manumissio in circo? Zum sog. Freilassungsrelief in Mariemont," in *Studien zur antiken Sozialgeschichte: Festschrift F. Vittinghoff*, ed. W. Eck, Cologne, 179–95.

Panella, C. 1981, "La distribuzione e i mercati," in *Società romana e produzione schiavistica, vol. 2: merci, mercati e scambi nel Mediterraneo*, eds. A. Giardina and A. Schiavone, Rome, 55–80.

1986, "Le merci: produzioni, itinerari, e destini," in *Società romana e impero tardoantico, vol. 3: le merci e gli insedimenti*, ed. A. Giardina, Rome, 431–59.

1989, "Le anfore italiche del II secolo," in *Amphores romaines et histoire économique: dix ans de recherché*, Rome, 138–79.

1993, "Merci e scambi nel Mediterraneo in età tardoantica," in *Storia di Roma, vol. 3 – L'età tardoantica 2: I luoghi e le culture*, eds. A. Carandini, L. Cracco Ruggini, and A. Giardina, Turin, 613–97.

Paquette, R. 2000, "The Drivers Shall Lead Them: Image and Reality in Slave Resistance," in *Slavery, Secession, and Southern History*, eds. R. Paquette and L. Ferleger, Charlottesville, 31–58.

Parker, A. J. 1992, *Ancient Shipwrecks of the Mediterranean and Roman Provinces*, Oxford.

Parker, H. 1997, "The Teratogenic Grid," in *Roman Sexualities*, eds. J. Hallett and M. Skinner, Princeton, 47–65.

2007, "Free Women and Male Slaves, or Mandingo Meets the Roman Empire," in *Fear of Slaves, Fear of Enslavement in the Ancient Mediterranean . . . GIREA, Rethymnon, 4–7 novembre 2004*, ed. A. Serghidou, Besançon, 281–98.

Parkins, H., ed. 1997, *Roman Urbanism: Beyond the Consumer City*, London.

Parra, E. J. *et al.* 2001, "Ancestral Proportions and Admixture Dynamics in Geographically Defined African Americans Living in South Carolina," *American Journal of Physical Anthropology* 114: 18–29.

Paton, D. 1996, "Decency, Dependence and the Lash: Gender and the British Debate over Slave Emancipation, 1830–34," *Slavery & Abolition* 17: 163–84.

Patterson, H. and Rovelli, A. 2004, "Ceramics and Coins in the Middle Tiber Valley from the Fifth to the Tenth Centuries AD," in *Bridging the Tiber: Approaches to Regional Archaeology in the Middle Tiber Valley*, ed. H. Patterson, London, 269–85.

Patterson, O. 1982, *Slavery and Social Death: A Comparative Study*, Cambridge, MA.

2008, "Slavery, Gender, and Work in the Pre-Modern World and Early Greece: A Cross-Cultural Analysis," in *Slave Systems: Ancient and Modern*, eds. E. Dal Lago and C. Katsari, Cambridge, 32–69.

Pazdernik, C. 2005, "Justinianic Ideology and the Power of the Past," in *The Cambridge Companion to the Age of Justinian*, ed. M. Maas, Cambridge, 185–212.

Peachin, M. 1996, *Iudex Vice Caesaris: Deputy Emperors and the Administration of Justice during the Principate*, Stuttgart.

2007, "A Petition to a Centurion from the NYU Papyrus Collection and the Question of Informal Adjudication Performed by Soldiers," in *Papyri in*

Memory of P. J. Sijpesteijn, eds. A. J. B. Sirks and K. A. Worp, Oakville, 79–97.

Pelteret, D. 1995, *Slavery in Early Mediaeval England: From the Reign of Alfred until the Twelfth Century*, Woodbridge.

Percival, J. 1976, *The Roman Villa: An Historical Introduction*, Berkeley.

Peristiany, J. 1966, *Honour and Shame: The Values of Mediterranean Society*, Chicago.

Pétré-Grenouilleau, O. 2004, *Les traites négrières: essai d'histoire globale*, Paris.

Petsas, P. *et al.* 2000, *see under* Inscriptions.

Pharr, C. 1952, *The Theodosian Code and Novels, and the Sirmondian Constitutions*, Princeton.

Phillips, W. D. 1985, *Slavery from Roman Times to the Early Transatlantic Trade*, Minneapolis.

Pierce, R. H. 1995, "A Sale of an Alodian Slave Girl: Reexamination of Papyrus Strassburg Inv. 1404," *Symbolae Osloense* 70: 148–65.

Pieri, D. 2005, *Le commerce du vin oriental à l'époque byzantine, ve–viie siècles: le témoignage des amphores en Gaule*, Beirut.

Pirenne, H. 1937, *Mahomet et Charlemagne*, Paris.

Pitt-Rivers, J. 1977, *The Fate of Shechem: or, The Politics of Sex: Essays in the Anthropology of the Mediterranean*, Cambridge.

Plácido, D. 1997, "Los 'oikétai,' entre la dependencia personal y la producción," in *Schiavi e dipendenti nell'ambito dell' "oikos" e della "familia,"* eds. M. Moggi and G. Cordiano, Pisa, 105–16.

Pleket, W. 1990, "Wirtschaft und Gesellschaft des Imperium Romanum," in *Handbuch der europäischen Wirtschafts- und Sozialgeschichte, Bd. 1, Europäische Wirtschafts- und Sozialgeschichte in der römischen Kaiserzeit*, ed. F. Vittinghoff, Stuttgart, 25–160.

Pólay, E. 1969, "Die Sklavenehe im antiken Rom," *Altertum* 15: 83–91.

Pollak, R. 1985, "A Transaction Cost Approach to Families and Households," *Journal of Economic Literature* 23: 581–608.

Pomeroy, S. 1986, "Copronyms and the Exposure of Infants in Egypt," in *Studies in Roman Law in Memory of A. Arthur Schiller*, eds. R. Bagnall and W. Harris, Leiden, 147–62.

   1994, *Xenophon Oeconomicus: A Social and Historical Commentary*, Oxford.

Potter, D. 2004, *The Roman Empire at Bay: AD 180–395*, New York.

Potter, T. 1979, *The Changing Landscape of South Etruria*, London.

Purcell, N. 1985, "Wine and Wealth in Ancient Italy," *Journal of Roman Studies* 75: 1–19.

   1995, "The Roman *villa* and the Landscape of Production," in *Urban Society in Roman Italy*, eds. T. J. Cornell and K. Lomas, London, 151–79.

   1999, "The Populace of Rome in Late Antiquity: Problems of Classification and Historical Description," in *The Transformations of Urbs Roma in Late Antiquity*, eds. W. Harris *et al.*, Portsmouth, 135–61.

Quadrato, R. 1996, "*Beneficium manumissionis* e *obsequium*," *Index* 24: 341–53.

Ragib, Y. 2002, *Actes de vente d'esclaves et d'animaux d'Égypte mediévale*, 2 vols., Cairo.

Ramin, J. and Veyne, P. 1981, "Droit romain et société: les hommes libres qui passent pour esclaves et l'esclavage volontaire," *Historia* 30: 472–97.

Rapp, C. 2005, *Holy Bishops in Late Antiquity: The Nature of Christian Leadership in an Age of Transition*, Berkeley.

Rathbone, D. 1981, "The Development of Agriculture in the 'Ager Cosanus' during the Roman Republic: Problems of Evidence and Interpretation," *Journal of Roman Studies* 71: 10–23.

1983, "The Slave Mode of Production in Italy": Review of *Società romana e produzione schiavistica*, eds. A. Giardina and A. Schiavone, *Journal of Roman Studies* 73: 160–8.

1991, *Economic Rationalism and Rural Society in Third-century* A.D. *Egypt: The Heroninos Archive and the Appianus Estate*, New York.

2000, Review of D. Kehoe, *Investment, Profit, and Tenancy: The Jurists and the Roman Agrarian Economy*, *Classical Review* 50: 652–3.

2003, "The Financing of Maritime Commerce in the Roman Empire, I–II AD," in *Credito e moneta nel mondo romano*, ed. E. Lo Cascio, Bari, 197–229.

2005, "Economic Rationalism and the Heroninos Archive," *Topoi Orient–Occident* 12: 261–9.

2008, "Poor Peasants and Silent Sherds," in *People, Land, and Politics: Demographic Developments and the Transformation of Roman Italy, 300 BC–AD 14*, eds. L. de Ligt and S. Northwood, Leiden, 305–32.

Rautman, M. 2000, "The Busy Countryside of Late Roman Cyprus," *Report of the Department of Antiquities, Cyprus*, 317–31.

Rawson, B. 1974, "Roman Concubinage and Other *de facto* Marriages," *Transactions of the American Philological Association* 104: 279–305.

ed. 1991, *Marriage, Divorce, and Children in Ancient Rome*, Oxford.

Rawson, B. and Weaver, P., eds. 1997, *The Roman Family in Italy: Status, Sentiment, Space*, Oxford.

Rebenich, S. 2002, *Jerome*, New York.

Reeve, M. D. 1976, "Tricipitinus' Son," *Zeitschrift für Papyrologie und Epigraphik* 22: 21–31.

Renard, E. 2000, "Les *mancipia* carolingiens étaient-ils des esclaves? Les données du polyptique de Montier-en-Der dans le contexte documentaire du IXème siècle," in *Les moines du Der*, eds. P. Corbet, J. Lusse, and G. Viard, Langres, 179–209.

Reynolds, P. 2005, "Levantine Amphorae from Cilicia to Gaza: A Typology and Analysis of Regional Production Trends from the 1st to 7th centuries," in *LRCW 1: Late Roman Coarse Wares, Cooking Wares and Amphorae in the Mediterranean: Archaeology and Archaeometry*, ed. J. Esparraguera, Oxford, 563–611.

Reynolds, P. 1994, *Marriage in the Western Church: The Christianization of Marriage during the Patristic and Early Medieval Periods*, Leiden.

Rich, J., ed. 1992, *The City in Late Antiquity*, New York.

Richlin, A. 1992, *The Garden of Priapus: Sexuality and Aggression in Roman Humor*, rev. edn., Oxford.

Ricl, M. 1993, "Consécration d'esclaves en Macédoine sous l'empire," *Ziva Antika* 43: 129–44.

1995, "Les katagraphai du santuaire d'Apollon Lairbénos," *Arkeoloji Dergisi* 3: 167–95.

2001, "Donations of Slaves and Freeborn Children to Deities in Roman Macedonia and Phrygia. A Reconsideration," *Tyche* 16: 127–60.

Rilinger, R. 1988, *Humiliores-Honestiores: zu einer sozialen Dichotomie im Strafrecht der römischen Kaiserzeit*, Munich.

Ringrose, K. 2003, *The Perfect Servant: Eunuchs and the Social Construction of Gender in Byzantium*, Chicago.

Rio, A. 2006, "Freedom and Unfreedom in Early Medieval Francia: The Evidence of the Legal Formulae," *Past & Present* 193: 7–40.

Ripoll, G. and Arce, J. 2000, "The Transformation and End of Roman *villae* in the West (Fourth–Seventh Centuries): Problems and Perspectives," in *Towns and Their Territories between Late Antiquity and the Early Middle Ages*, eds. G. Brogiolo, N. Gauthier, and N. Christie, Leiden, 63–114.

Rizzelli, G. 1987, "'Stuprum' e 'adulterium' nella cultura Augustea e la 'lex Iulia de adulteriis' (Pap. 1 *adult*. D. 48,5,6,1 e Mod. 9 *diff*. D. 50,16,101 pr.)," *Bullettino dell' Istituto di Diritto Romano* 29: 355–88.

1988, "In margine a Paul. Sent. 2, 26, 11," *Bullettino dell' Istituto di Diritto Romano* 30: 733–43.

Robinson, O. 2000, "Roman Criminal Law: Rhetoric and Reality. Some Forms of Rhetoric in the *Theodosian Code*," in *Au-delà des frontières: Mélanges de droit romain offerts à Witold Wołodkiewicz*, eds. M. Zabłocka *et al.*, vol. 2, Warsaw, 765–85.

Robleda, O. 1976, *Il diritto degli schiavi nell'antica Roma*, Rome.

Rochette, B. 2008, "L'enseignement du latin comme L² dans la *Pars Orientis* de l'Empire romain: les *Hermeneumata Pseudodositheana*," in *Aspetti della scuola nel mondo Romano: Atti del Convegno (Pisa, 5–6 dicembre 2006)*, eds. F. Bellandi and R. Ferri, Amsterdam, 81–109.

Romano, D. 1996, *Housecraft and Statecraft: Domestic Service in Renaissance Venice, 1400–1600*, Baltimore.

Rosafio, P. 1994, "Slaves and *Coloni* in the Villa System," in *Landuse in the Roman Empire*, ed. J. Carlsen, Rome, 145–58.

Rosenfeld, B.-Z. and Menirav, J. 2005, *Markets and Marketing in Roman Palestine*, Leiden.

Rossiter, J. J. 1989, "Roman Villas of the Greek East and the Villa in Gregory of Nyssa *Ep*. 20," *Journal of Roman Archaeology* 2: 101–10.

Rostovtzeff, M. 1926, *The Social and Economic History of the Roman Empire*, Oxford.

Roth, U. 2002, "Food Rations in Cato's *De agri cultura* and Female Slave Labour," *Ostraka* 11: 195–213.

2005a, "To Have and To Be: Food, Status, and the *Peculium* of Agricultural Slaves," *Journal of Roman Archaeology* 18: 278–92.

2005b, "No More Slave Gangs: Varro, *De re rustica* 1.2.20–1," *Classical Quarterly* 55: 310–15.

2007, *Thinking Tools: Agricultural Slavery between Evidence and Models*, London.

2008, "Cicero, a Legal Dispute, and a *terminus ante quem* for the Large-scale Exploitation of Female Slaves in Roman Italy," *Index* 36: 575–84.

Rotman, Y. 2000, "Formes de la non-liberté dans la campagne byzantine aux VIIe–XIe siècles," *Mélanges de l'École française de Rome. Moyen Âge* 112: 499–510.

2004, *Les esclaves et l'esclavage: de la Méditerranée antique à la Méditerranée médiévale, VIe–XIe siècles*, Paris.

Roueché, C. 1993, *Performers and Partisans at Aphrodisias in the Roman and Late Byzantine Periods*, London.

1995, "*Aurarii* in the Auditoria," *Zeitschrift für Papyrologie und Epigraphik* 105: 37–50.

2002, "Images of Performance: New Evidence from Ephesus," in *Greek and Roman Actors: Aspects of an Ancient Profession*, eds. P. Easterling and E. Hall, Cambridge, 254–81.

Rougé, J. 1983, "Escroquerie et brigandage en Afrique romaine au temps de saint Augustin (*Ep.* 8* et 10*)," in *Les Lettres de Saint Augustin découvertes par Johannes Divjak: communications présentées au colloque des 20 et 21 septembre 1982*, ed. J. Divjak, Paris, 177–88.

Rousseau, P. 1994, *Basil of Caesarea*, Berkeley.

Rousselle, A. 1988, *Porneia: On Desire and the Body in Antiquity*, trans. F. Pheasant, Oxford, orig. 1983.

1989, "Personal Status and Sexual Practice in the Roman Empire," in *Zone 5: Fragments for a History of the Human Body*, New York, 300–33.

Rowlandson, J. 1996, *Landowners and Tenants in Roman Egypt: The Social Relations of Agriculture in the Oxyrhynchite Nome*, Oxford.

1999, "Agricultural Tenancy and Village Society in Roman Egypt," in *Agriculture in Egypt: From Pharaonic to Modern Times*, eds. A. Bowman and E. Rogan, Oxford, 138–58.

Russell, D. 1983, *Greek Declamation*, Cambridge.

Russell, D. and Wilson, N. 1981, *see* Primary Sources, Menander.

Russi, A. 1986, "I pastori e l'esposizione degli infanti nella tarda legislazione imperiale e nei documenti epigrafici," *Mélanges de l'École française de Rome. Antiquité* 98: 855–72.

Sachot, M. 1994, "Homilie," *Reallexikon für Antike und Christentum* 16: 148–75.

Safrai, Z. 1994, *The Economy of Roman Palestine*, London.

Saller, R. 1984, "*Familia, Domus*, and Roman Conceptions of the Family," *Phoenix* 38: 336–55.

1987a, "Men's Age at Marriage and its Consequences in the Roman Family," *Classical Philology* 82: 21–34.

1987b, "Slavery in the Roman Family," *Slavery & Abolition* 8: 65–87.

1994, *Patriarchy, Property, and Death in the Roman Family*, Cambridge.
2003, "Women, Slaves, and the Economy of the Roman Household," in *Early Christian Families in Context*, eds. D. Balch and C. Osiek, Grand Rapids, 185–204.
2005, "Framing the Debate Over Growth in the Ancient Economy," in *The Ancient Economy: Evidence and Models*, eds. J. G. Manning and I. Morris, Stanford, 223–38.
2007a, "Household and Gender," in *The Cambridge Economic History of the Greco-Roman World*, eds. W. Scheidel, I. Morris, and R. Saller, Cambridge, 87–112.
2007b, "Trade and Models of the Economy," *Journal of Roman Archaeology* 20: 493–4.
Saller, R. and Shaw, B. 1984, "Tombstones and Roman Family Relations in the Principate: Civilians, Soldiers and Slaves," *Journal of Roman Studies* 74: 124–56.
Salway, B. 2010, "*Mancipium rusticum sive urbanum*: The Slave Chapter of Diocletian's Edict on Maximum Prices," in *By the Sweat of Your Brow: Roman Slavery in its Socio-economic Setting*, ed. U. Roth, London, 1–20.
Salzman, M. 2002, *The Making of a Christian Aristocracy: Social and Religious Change in the Western Roman Empire*, Cambridge, MA.
Samson, R. 1989, "Rural Slavery, Inscriptions, Archaeology and Marx: A Response to Ramsay MacMullen's 'Late Roman Slavery'," *Historia* 38: 99–110.
Samuel, A. E. 1965, "The Role of *Paramone* Clauses in Ancient Documents," *Journal of Juristic Papyrology* 15: 221–311.
Sánchez León, J. 1996, *Las Bagaudas, rebeldes, demonios, mártires: revueltas campesinas en Galia e Hispania durante el Bajo Imperio*, Jaén.
Sargenti, M. 1938, *Il diritto privato nella legislazione di Costantino: persone e famiglia*, Milan.
1981, "Il matrimonio nella legislazione di Valentiniano e Teodosio," *AARC* 4: 239–57.
1986, "Il diritto privato nella legislazione di Costantino," in *Studi sul diritto del tardo impero*, Padua, 1–109.
1990, "Costantino e la condizione del liberto ingrato nelle costituzioni tardo imperiali," *AARC* 8: 181–97.
Sargenti, M. and Siola, R. B. B. 1991, *Normativa imperiale e diritto romano negli scritti di S. Ambrogio*, Milan.
Sarikakis, Th. 1977, *Rōmaioi archontes tēs eparchias Makedonia*, vol. 2, Thessalonika.
Sarnowski, T. 1978, *Les représentations de villas sur les mosaïques africaines tardives*, Warsaw.
Sarris, P. 2004, "The Origins of the Manorial Economy: New Insights from Late Antiquity," *English Historical Review* 119: 279–311.
2006, *Economy and Society in the Age of Justinian*, Cambridge.
Sasse, C. 1958, *Die Constitutio Antoniniana*, Wiesbaden.
Satlow, M. 2001, *Jewish Marriage in Antiquity*, Princeton.

Schaps, D. 1976, "A Disputed Slave in Boeotia," *Zeitschrift für Papyrologie und Epigraphik* 20: 63–4.

Scheidel, W. 1993, "Slavery and the Shackled Mind: On Fortune-telling and Slave Mentality in the Graeco-Roman World," *Ancient History Bulletin* 7: 107–14.

1994a, "Columellas privates *ius liberorum*: Literatur, Recht, Demographie. Einige Probleme," *Latomus* 53: 513–27.

1994b, "Grain Cultivation in the Villa Economy of Roman Italy," in *Landuse in the Roman Empire*, ed. J. Carlsen, Rome, 159–66.

1994c, *Grundpacht und Lohnarbeit in der Landwirtschaft des römischen Italien*, Frankfurt.

1995–6a, "The Most Silent Women of Greece and Rome: Rural Labour and Women's Life in the Ancient World," *Greece and Rome* 42: 202–17 and 43: 1–10.

1996b, "Reflections on the Differential Valuation of Slaves in Diocletian's Price Edict and in the United States," *Münstersche Beiträge zur antiken Handelsgeschichte* 15: 67–79.

1996c, "Finances, Figures, and Fiction," *Classical Quarterly* 46: 222–38.

1997, "Quantifying the Sources of Slaves in the Early Roman Empire," *Journal of Roman Studies* 87: 156–69.

1999, "The Slave Population of Roman Italy: Speculation and Constraints," *Topoi Orient–Occident* 9: 129–44.

2000, "Slaves of the Soil," *Journal of Roman Archaeology* 13: 727–32.

2001a, "Progress and Problems in Roman Demography," in *Debating Roman Demography*, ed. W. Scheidel, Boston, 1–81.

2001b, "Roman Age Structure: Evidence and Models," *Journal of Roman Studies* 91: 1–26.

2005a, "Human Mobility in Roman Italy, II: The Slave Population," *Journal of Roman Studies* 95: 64–79.

2005b, "Real Slave Prices and the Relative Cost of Slave Labor in the Greco-Roman World," *Ancient Society* 35: 1–17.

2007, "Demography," in *The Cambridge Economic History of the Greco-Roman World*, eds. W. Scheidel, I. Morris, and R. Saller, Cambridge, 38–86.

2008, "The Comparative Economics of Slavery in the Greco-Roman World," in *Slave Systems: Ancient and Modern*, eds. E. Dal Lago and C. Katsari, Cambridge, 105–26.

2009a, "Sex and Empire: A Darwinian Perspective," in *The Dynamics of Ancient Empires: State Power from Assyria to Byzantium*, eds. I. Morris and W. Scheidel, Oxford, 255–324.

2009b, "In Search of Roman Economic Growth," *Journal of Roman Archaeology* 22: 46–70.

Forthcoming, "The Roman Slave Supply," in *The Cambridge World History of Slavery, 1: The Ancient Mediterranean World*, eds. K. Bradley and P. Cartledge, Cambridge.

Scheidel, W. and Friesen, S. 2009, "The Size of the Economy and the Distribution of Income in the Roman Empire," *Journal of Roman Studies* 99: 61–91.

Scheidel, W., Morris, I., and Saller, R., eds. 2007, *The Cambridge Economic History of the Greco-Roman World*, Cambridge.

Schiavone, A. 2000, *The End of the Past*, trans. M. Schneider, Cambridge, MA.

Schlinkert, D. 1994, "Der Hofeunuch in der Spätantike: Ein Gefährlicher Aussenseiter?," *Hermes* 122: 342–59.

Scholl, R. 2001, "'Freilassung unter Freunden' im römischen Ägypten," in *Fünfzig Jahre Forschungen zur antiken Sklaverei an der Mainzer Akademie, 1950–2000: Miscellanea zum Jubiläum*, eds. H. Bellen and H. Heinen, Stuttgart, 159–69.

Scholten, H. 1995, *Der Eunuch in Kaisernähe: zur politischen und sozialen Bedeutung des "praepositus sacri cubiculi" im 4. und 5. Jahrhundert n. Chr.*, Frankfurt.

Schönbauer, E. 1931, "Reichsrecht gegen Volksrecht? Studien über die Bedeutung der Constitutio Antoniniana für die römische Rechtsentwicklung," *Zeitschrift der Savigny-Stiftung für Rechtsgeschichte. Romanistiche Abteilung* 51: 277–335.

Schulz, F. 1942, "Roman Registers of Birth and Birth Certificates," *Journal of Roman Studies* 32: 78–91.

Schulze, H. 1998, *Ammen und Pädagogen: Sklavinnen und Sklaven als Erzieher in der antiken Kunst und Gesellschaft*, Mainz.

Schumacher, L. 2001, *Sklaverei in der Antike: Alltag und Schicksal der Unfreien*, Munich.

Scott, E. 1993, *A Gazetteer of Roman Villas in Britain*, Leicester.

Scott, S. 2004, "Elites, Exhibitionism, and the Society of the Late Roman Villa," in *Landscapes of Change: Rural Evolutions in Late Antiquity and the Early Middle Ages*, ed. N. Christie, Burlington, 39–65.

Seeck, O. 1919, *Regesten der Kaiser und Päpste für die Jahre 311 bis 476 n. Chr.: Vorarbeit zu einer Prosopographie der christlichen Kaiserzeit*, Stuttgart.

Serfass, A. 2006, "Slavery and Pope Gregory the Great," *Journal of Early Christian Studies* 14: 77–103.

Serrao, F. 2000, "Impresa, mercato, diritto," in *Mercati permanenti e mercati periodici nel mondo romano*, ed. E. Lo Cascio, Bari, 31–67.

Seyfarth, W. 1963, *Soziale Fragen der spätrömischen Kaiserzeit im Spiegel des Theodosianus*, Berlin.

Sfameni, C. 2004, "Residential Villas in Late Antiquity: Continuity and Change," in *Recent Research on the Late Antique Countryside*, eds. W. Bowden, L. Lavan, and C. Machado, Boston, 335–75.

Shanzer, D. 2002, "*Avulsa a Latere Meo*: Augustine's Spare Rib: Confessions 6.15.25," *Journal of Roman Studies* 92: 157–76.

Shaw, B. 1984, "Bandits in the Roman Empire," *Past & Present* 105: 3–52.

1987a, "The Family in Late Antiquity: The Experience of Augustine," *Past & Present* 115: 3–51.

1987b, "The Age of Roman Girls at Marriage: Some Reconsiderations," *Journal of Roman Studies* 77: 30–46.

1995, "Autonomy and Tribute: Mountain and Plain in Mauretania Tingitana," in *Rulers, Nomads, and Christians in Roman North Africa*, section 8, Brookfield, 66–89.

1996, "Body/Power/Identity: Passions of the Martyrs," *Journal of Early Christian Studies* 4: 269–312.

1998, "'A Wolf by the Ears': M. I. Finley's *Ancient Slavery and Modern Ideology* in Historical Context," Foreword to Finley, *Ancient Slavery and Modern Ideology*², Princeton, 3–74.

2000, "Rebels and Outsiders," in *The Cambridge Ancient History*², vol. II, eds. A. Bowman, P. Garnsey, and D. Rathbone, Cambridge, 361–403.

2001a, *Spartacus and the Slave Wars: A Brief History with Documents*, Boston.

2001b, "Raising and Killing Children: Two Roman Myths," *Mnemosyne* 54: 31–77.

2002, "'With Whom I Lived': Measuring Roman Marriage," *Ancient Society* 32: 195–242.

2008, "After Rome: Transformations of the Early Mediterranean World," *New Left Review* 51: 89–114.

Sherwin White, A. N. 1973, *The Roman Citizenship*², Oxford.

Shtaerman, E. 1964, *Die Krise der Sklavenhalterordnung im Westen des römischen Reiches*, Berlin.

1984, "Die Krise der Sklavenwirtschaft in römischen Kaiserreich," in *Actes du VIIe Congrès de la Fédération Internationale des Associations d'Études Classiques*, Budapest, 47–54.

Shtaerman, E. and Trofimova, M. 1975, *La schiavitù nell'Italia imperiale*, Rome.

Sicari, A. 1991, *Prostituzione e tutela giuridica della schiava: un problema di politica legislativa nell'impero romano*, Bari.

Silver, M. 2007, "Roman Economic Growth and Living Standards: Perceptions versus Evidence," *Ancient Society* 37: 191–252.

Simon, D. 1977, *Konstantinisches Kaiserrecht: Studien anhand der Reskriptenpraxis und des Schenkungsrechts*, Frankfurt.

Sirks, A. J. B. 1981, "Informal Manumission and the Lex Junia," *Revue internationale des droits de l'antiquité* 28: 247–76.

1983, "The *lex Junia* and the Effects of Informal Manumission and Iteration," *Revue internationale des droits de l'antiquité* 30: 211–92.

1991, *Food for Rome: The Legal Structure of the Transportation and Processing of Supplies for the Imperial Distributions in Rome and Constantinople*, Amsterdam.

1994, "Ad senatus consultum Claudianum," *Zeitschrift der Savigny-Stiftung für Rechtsgeschichte. Romanistiche Abteilung* III: 436–7.

2005, "Der Zweck des Senatus Consultum Claudianum von 52 n. Chr.," *Zeitschrift der Savigny-Stiftung für Rechtsgeschichte. Romanistiche Abteilung* 122: 138–49.

2007, *The Theodosian Code: A Study*, Friedrichsdorf.

2008, "The Colonate in Justinian's Reign," *Journal of Roman Studies* 98: 120–43.

Sittl, C. 1890, *Die Gebärden Griechen und Römer*, Leipzig.

Sivan, H. 1993, *Ausonius of Bordeaux: Genesis of a Gallic Aristocracy*, London.

Skinner, M. 2005, *Sexuality in Greek and Roman Culture*, Malden.

Slootjes, D. 2006, *The Governor and His Subjects in the Later Roman Empire*, Boston.

Smadja, E. 1999, "L'affranchissement des femmes esclaves à Rome," in *Femmes-esclaves: modèles d'interprétation anthropologique, économique, juridique*, eds. F. Merola and A. Marino, Naples, 355–68.

Smail, D. 2003, *The Consumption of Justice: Emotions, Publicity, and Legal Culture in Marseille, 1264–1423*, Ithaca.

Smith, E. B. 1918, *Early Christian Iconography and a School of Ivory Carvers in Provence*, Princeton.

Snowden, F. 1970, *Blacks in Antiquity: Ethiopians in the Greco-Roman Experience*, Cambridge, MA.

Sodini, J.-P. 1993, "La contribution de l'archéologie à la connaissance du monde byzantin (IVe-VIIe siècles)," *Dumbarton Oaks Papers* 47: 139–84.

et al. 1980, "Dèhés (Syrie du Nord), campagnes I–III (1976–1978): recherches sur l'habitat rural," *Syria* 57: 1–304.

Sokolowski, F. 1954, "The Real Meaning of Sacral Manumission," *Harvard Theological Review* 47: 173–81.

Solazzi, S. 1972, "Il rispetto per la famiglia dello schiavo," in *Scritti di diritto romano*, vol. 6, Naples, 576–81.

Soler, E. 2004, "Les acteurs d'Antioche et les excès de la cité au IVe siècle ap. J-C.," in *Le status de l'acteur dans l'Antiquité grecque et romaine*, eds., C. Hugoniot, F. Hurlet, and S. Milanezi, Tours, 251–72.

Solin, H. 1996, *Die stadtrömischen Sklavennamen: ein Namenbuch*, 3 vols., Stuttgart.

Söllner, A. 2000, *Corpus der römischen Rechtsquellen zur antiken Sklaverei* (CRRS), vol. 9: *Irrtümlich als Sklaven gehaltene freie Menschen und Sklaven in unsicheren Eigentumsverhältnissen*. Homines liberi et servi alieni bona fide servientes, Stuttgart.

Solow, B. 1985, "Caribbean Slavery and British Growth," *Journal of Development Economics* 17: 99–115.

Soraci, R. 1983, "La legislazione di Costantino sulla schiavitù: Ettore Ciccotti e il dibattito storiografico moderno," *Quaderni catanesi di studi classici e medievali* 5: 57–77.

Sotgiu, G. 1973–4, "Un collare di schiavo rinvenuto in Sardegna," *Archeologia classica* 25–6: 688–97.

Spira, A. and Klock, C., eds. 1981, *The Easter Sermons of Gregory of Nyssa: Translation and Commentary. Proceedings of the Fourth International Colloquium on Gregory of Nyssa, Cambridge, England, 11–15 September, 1978*, Cambridge.

Spurr, M. 1986, *Arable Cultivation in Roman Italy, c. 200 B.C.–c. A.D. 100*, London.

Štaerman *see* Shtaerman

Steckel, R. 1982, "The Fertility of American Slaves," *Research in Economic History* 7: 239–86.

Steinwater, A. 1916, "Iudex," *RE* 9.2: cols. 2464–73.

Stevenson, W. 1995, "The Rise of Eunuchs in Greco-Roman Antiquity," *Journal of the History of Sexuality* 5: 495–511.

Stone, D. 2005, *Decision-making in Medieval Agriculture*, Oxford.

Straus, J. 1988, "L'esclavage dans l'Égypte romaine," *ANRW* 2.10.1: 841–911.

2004, *L'achat et la vente des esclaves dans l'Égypte romaine*, Munich.

Stuard, S. M. 1983, "Urban Domestic Slavery in Medieval Ragusa," *Journal of Medieval History* 9: 155–71.

Stuiber, A. 1978, "Konstantinische und christliche Beurteilung der Sklaventötung," *Jahrbuch für Antike und Christentum* 21: 65–73.

Stumpp, B. 1998, *Prostitution in der römischen Antike*, Berlin.

Sutch, R. 1975, "The Breeding of Slaves for Sale and the Westward Expansion of Slavery, 1850–1860," in *Race and Slavery in the Western Hemisphere: Quantitative Studies*, eds. S. Engerman and E. Genovese, Princeton, 173–210.

Sweet, J. 2002, "Manumission in Rio de Janeiro, 1749–54: An African Perspective," *Slavery & Abolition* 23: 54–70.

Syme, R. 1960, "Bastards in the Roman Aristocracy," *Proceedings of the American Philosophical Society* 104: 323–7.

Szidat, J. 1985, "Zum Sklavenhandel in der Spätantike (Aug. epist. 10*)," *Historia* 34: 360–71.

Tacoma, L. 2006, *Fragile Hierarchies: The Urban Elites of Third Century Roman Egypt*, Leiden.

Tadman, M. 2000, "The Demographic Cost of Sugar: Debates on Slave Societies and Natural Increase in the Americas," *American Historical Review* 105: 1534–75.

Tainter, J. 1990, *The Collapse of Complex Societies*, Cambridge.

Tataki, A. B. 1988, *Ancient Beroea: Prosopography and Society*, Athens.

Tate, G. 1992, *Les campagnes de la Syrie du Nord du IIe au VIIe siècle: un exemple d'expansion démographique et économique dans les campagnes à la fin de l'antiquité*, Paris.

Tate, J. 2008a, "Christianity and the Legal Status of Abandoned Children in the Later Roman Empire," *Journal of Law and Religion* 24: 123–41.

2008b, "Inheritance Rights of Nonmarital Children in Late Roman Law," *Roman Legal Tradition* 4: 1–36.

2008c, "Codification of Late Roman Inheritance Law: Fideicommissa and the Theodosian Code," *Tijdschrift voor rechtsgeschiedenis* 76: 237–48.

Taubenschlag, R. 1930, "Geschichte der Rezeption des römischen Privatrechts in Aegypten," *Studi in onore di Pietro Bonfante nel XL anno d'insegnamento*, Milan, 369–440.

1944, *The Law of Greco-Roman Egypt in the Light of the Papyri*, New York.

Tchalenko, G. 1953–8, *Villages antiques de la Syrie du nord: le massif du Bélus à l'époque romaine*, 3 vols., Paris.

Tchernia, A. 1986, *Le vin de l'Italie romaine*, Rome.

2006, "La crise de l'Italie impériale et la concurrence des provinces," *Cahiers du centre de recherches historiques* 37: 137–56.

Teall, J. 1971, "The Byzantine Agricultural Tradition," *Dumbarton Oaks Papers* 25: 33–59.

Teitler, H. C. 1985, *Notarii and Exceptores: An Inquiry into Role and Significance of Shorthand Writers in the Imperial and Ecclesiastical Bureaucracy of the Roman Empire (from the Early Principate to circa 450 A.D.)*, Utrecht.

Tellegen Couperus, O. 1982, "Manumission of Slaves and Collusion in Diocl. C. 7,2,12,2," *Studi in onore di Arnaldo Biscardi*, vol. 5, Milan, 207–15.

Temin, P. 2001, "A Market Economy in the Early Roman Empire," *Journal of Roman Studies* 91: 169–81.

2004, "The Labor Market of the Early Roman Empire," *Journal of Interdisciplinary History* 34: 513–38.

2005, "Estimating the GDP of the Early Roman Empire," in *Innovazione tecnica e progresso economico nel mondo romano*, ed. E. Lo Cascio, Rome, 31–54.

Thébert, Y. 1993, "The Slave," in *The Romans*, ed. A. Giardina, Chicago, 138–74.

Thomas, P. J. 1984, "Concubinitas in Roman Law," in *Huldigingsbundel Paul van Warmelo*, Pretoria, 230–6.

Thompson, E. A. 1952, "Peasant Revolts in Late Roman Gaul and Spain," *Past & Present* 2: 11–23.

Thompson, F. Hugh. 1993, "Iron Age and Roman Slave-Shackles," *Archaeological Journal* 150: 58–168.

2003, *The Archaeology of Greek and Roman Slavery*, London.

Thompson, L. 1969, *Africa in Classical Antiquity: Nine Studies*, Ibadan.

1989, *Romans and Blacks*, Norman.

Thonemann, P. 2007, "Estates and the Land in Late Roman Asia Minor," *Chiron* 37: 435–78.

Thurmond, D. L. 1994, "Some Roman Slave Collars in CIL," *Athenaeum* 82 (72): 459–93.

Toman, J. T. 2005, "The Gang System and Comparative Advantage," *Explorations in Economic History* 42: 310–23.

Tondo, G. 1967, *Aspetti simbolici e magici nella struttura giuridica della manumissio vindicta*, Milan.

Toubert, P. 1998, "L'institution du mariage chrétien, de l'antiquité tardive à l'an mil," in *Morfologie sociali e culturali in Europa fra tarda antichità e alto medioevo: 3–9 aprile 1997*, Spoleto, 503–53.

Tougher, S. 1997, "Byzantine Eunuchs: An Overview," in *Women, Men, and Eunuchs: Gender in Byzantium*, ed. L. James, London, 168–84.

2002, "In or Out? Origins of Court Eunuchs," in *Eunuchs in Antiquity and Beyond*, ed. S. Tougher, London, 143–59.

Treggiari, S. 1969a, *Roman Freedmen during the Late Republic*, Oxford.

1969b, "The Freedmen of Cicero," *Greece and Rome* 16: 195–204.

1975a, "Jobs in the Household of Livia," *Papers of the British School of Rome* 43: 48–77.

1975b, "Family Life among the Staff of the Volusii," *Transactions of the American Philological Association* 105: 393–401.

1979a, "Questions on Women Domestics in the Roman West," in *Schiavitù, manomissione e classi dipendenti nel mondo antico*, ed. M. Capozza, Rome, 185–201.

1979b, "Lower Class Women in the Roman Economy," *Florilegium* 1: 65–86.

1981, "Concubinae," *Papers of the British School of Rome* 49: 59–81.

1991, *Roman Marriage: Iusti Coniuges from the Time of Cicero to the Time of Ulpian*, Oxford.

Tucker, R. 1978, *The Marx-Engels Reader²*, New York.

Turley, D. 2000, *Slavery*, Oxford.

Turpin, W. 1987, "The Purpose of the Roman Law Codes," *Zeitschrift der Savigny-Stiftung für Rechtsgeschichte. Romanistiche Abteilung* 104: 620–30.

1991, "Imperial Subscriptions and the Administration of Justice," *Journal of Roman Studies* 81: 101–18.

1999, "*Formula, cognitio*, and Proceedings *extra ordinem*," *Revue internationale des droits de l'antiquité* 46: 499–574.

Uggeri, G. 1998, "L'urbanistica di Antiochia sull'Oronte," *Rivista di topografia antica* 8: 179–222.

Urbainczyk, T. 2008, *Slave Revolts in Antiquity*, Berkeley.

Uthemann, K.-H. 1998, "Forms of Communication in the Homilies of Severian of Gabala: A Contribution to the Reception of the Diatribe as a Method of Exposition," in *Preacher and Audience: Studies in Early Christian and Byzantine Homiletics*, eds. M. Cunningham and P. Allen, Leiden, 139–77.

Valenti, M. 2004, *L'insediamento altomedievale nelle campagne toscane: paesaggi, popolamento e villaggi tra VI e X secolo*, Florence.

2005, "La formazione dell'insediamento altomedievale in Toscana. Dallo spessore dei numeri alla costruzione dei modelli," in *Dopo la fine delle ville: le campagne dal VI al IX secolo. Gavi, 8–10 maggio 2004*, ed. G. Brogiolo, Mantua, 193–219.

Van Dam, R. 1995, "Self-Representation in the Will of Gregory of Nazianzus," *Journal of Theological Studies* 46: 118–48.

van de Wiel, C. 1978, "La légitimation par mariage subséquent, de Constantin à Justinien. Sa réception sporadique dans le droit byzantin," *Revue internationale des droits de l'antiquité* 25: 307–50.

Van Der Meer, F. 1978, *Augustine the Bishop: The Life and Work of a Father of the Church*, trans. B. Battershaw and G. Lamb, London, orig. 1947.

Van der Wal, N. 1981, "*Edictum* und *lex generalis*: Form und Inhalt der Kaisergesetze im spätrömischen Reich," *Revue internationale des droits de l'antiquité* 28: 277–313.

Van Minnen, P. 1986, "The Volume of the Oxyrhynchite Textile Trade," *Münstersche Beiträge zur antiken Handelsgeschichte* 5: 88–95.

Van Ossel, P. 1992, *Établissements ruraux de l'antiquité tardive dans le nord de la Gaule*, Paris.

1997, "Structure, évolution et statut des habitats ruraux au Bas-Empire en Île-de-France," in *L'époque romaine tardive en Île-de-France: les campagnes de*

Bibliography

l'Île-de-France de Constantin à Clovis, eds. P. Ouzoulias and P. Van Ossel, Paris, 94–119.

Van Ossel, P. and Ouzoulias, P. 2000, "Rural Settlement Economy in Northern Gaul in the Late Empire: An Overview and Assessment," *Journal of Roman Archaeology* 13: 133–60.

Vanhaverbeke, H. and Waelkens, M. 2003, *The Chora of Sagalassos: The Evolution of the Settlement Pattern from Prehistoric until Recent Times*, Turnhout.

Vera, D. 1983, "Strutture agrarie e strutture patrimoniali nella tarda antichità: l'aristocrazia romana fra agricoltura e commercio," *Opus* 2: 489–533.

1986a, "Forme e funzioni della rendita fondiaria nella tarda antichità," in *Società romana e impero tardoantico*, vol. 1, ed. A. Giardina, Rome, 367–477.

1986b, "Simmaco e le sue proprietà: struttura e funzionamento di un patrimonio aristocratico del quarto secolo d.C.," in *Colloque Genevois sur Symmaque*, Paris, 231–70.

1989, "Del servus al servus quasi colonus: Una altra transició?," *L'Avenç* 131: 32–7.

1995, "Dalla villa perfecta alla villa di Palladio: sulle trasformazioni del sistema agrario in Italia fra principato e dominato," *Athenaeum* 83: 189–211, 331–56.

1998, "Le forme del lavoro rurale: aspetti della trasformazione dell'Europa romana fra tarda antichità e alto medioevo," in *Morfologie sociali e culturali fra tarda antichità e alto medioevo (Spoleto 3–9 aprile 1997)*, Spoleto, 293–342.

1999, "I silenzi di Palladio e l'Italia: osservazioni sull'ultimo agronomo romano," *Antiquité tardive* 7: 283–97.

2002, "Res pecuariae imperiali e concili municipali nell' Apulia tardoantica," in *Ancient History Matters: Studies Presented to Jens Erik Skydsgaard on His Seventieth Birthday*, eds. K. Ascani *et al.*, Rome, 245–57.

2007, "Essere 'schiavi della terra' nell'Italia tardoantica: le razionalitá di una dipendenza," *Studia historica* 25: 489–505.

Verhulst, A. 1966, "La genèse du régime domanial classique en France au haut moyen âge," in *Agricoltura e mondo rurale in Occidente nell'alto medioevo*, Spoleto, 135–60.

Verlinden, C. 1943, "L'origine de *sclavus = esclave*," *Archivum latinitatis medii aevi* 17: 97–128.

1955–77, *L'esclavage dans l'Europe médiévale*, 2 vols., Bruges.

Veyne, P. 1961, "Vie de Trimalchion," *Annales. Économies, Sociétés, Civilisations* 2: 213–47.

1981, "Le dossier des esclaves-colons romains," *Revue historique* 265: 3–25.

1987, "The Roman Empire," in *A History of Private Life*, vol. 1, ed. P. Veyne, Cambridge, MA, orig. 1985, 6–234.

Vicari, F. 2001, *Produzione e commercio dei tessuti nell'Occidente romano*, Oxford.

Ville, G. 1963, "Le relief R 14 (26) de Mariemont ne figure pas un affranchissement par la vindicte mais une scène de cirque," *Latomus* 22: 14–30.

Volbach, W. 1976, *Elfenbeinarbeiten der Spätantike und des frühen Mittelalters*, 3rd edn., Mainz.

Volpe, G. 1996, *Contadini, pastori e mercanti nell'Apulia tardoantica*, Bari.

Volterra, E. 1937, "L'efficacia delle costituzioni imperiali emanate per le provincie e l'istituto dell'expositio," in *Studi di storia e diritto in onore di Enrico Besta*, vol. 1, Milan, 447–77.

Voss, E. 1982, *Recht und Rhetorik in den Kaisergesetzen der Spätantike: eine Untersuchung zum nachklassischen Kauf- und Übereignungsrecht*, Frankfurt.

Voss, W. 1985, "Der Grundsatz der 'ärgeren Hand' bei Sklaven, Kolonen, und Hörigen," in *Römisches Recht in der europäischen Tradition*, eds. O. Behrends *et al.*, Ebelsbach, 117–84.

Vuolanto, V. 2003, "Selling a Freeborn Child: Rhetoric and Social Realities in the Late Roman World," *Ancient Society* 33: 169–207.

Wacke, A. 1982, "Das relief-fragment nr. 26 aus Mariemont: Zirkus-szene oder *manumissio vindicta*? Prolegomena zu einer antiken Rechtsarchäologie," in *Studi in onore di Arnaldo Biscardi*, Milan, 117–45.

Waldstein, W. 1986, *Operae Libertorum: Untersuchungen zur Dienstpflicht freigelassener Sklaven*, Stuttgart.

1990, "Schiavitù e cristianesimo da Costantino a Teodosio II," *AARC* 8: 123–45.

Wallace-Hadrill, A. 1991, "Houses and Households: Sampling Pompeii and Herculaneum," in *Marriage, Divorce, and Children in Ancient Rome*, ed. B. Rawson, Oxford, 191–227.

Wallon, H. 1847, *Histoire de l'esclavage dans l'antiquité*, 3 vols., Paris.

Walsh, L. 1985, "Land, Landlord, and Leaseholder: Estate Management and Tenant Fortunes in Southern Maryland, 1642–1820," *Agricultural History* 59: 373–96.

Walters, J. 1997, "Invading the Roman Body: Manliness and Impenetrability in Roman Thought," in *Roman Sexualities*, eds. J. Hallett and M. Skinner, Princeton, 29–43.

Ward-Perkins, B. 2005, *The Fall of Rome and the End of Civilization*, New York.

Waring, M. 1988, *Counting for Nothing: What Men Value and What Women are Worth*, Wellington.

Watson, A. 1973, "Private Law in the Rescripts of Carus, Carinus, and Numerianus," *Tijdschrift voor rechtsgeschiedenis* 41: 19–34.

1974, "The Rescripts of the Emperor Probus (276–282 A.D.)," *Tulane Law Review* 48: 1122–8.

ed. 1985, *The Digest of Justinian*, 4 vols., with English trans., Philadelphia.

1987, *Roman Slave Law*, Baltimore.

1991, "A Slave's Marriage: Dowry or Deposit," *Journal of Legal History* 12: 132–9.

Watson, J. 1980a, "Slavery as an Institution: Open and Closed Systems," in *Asian and African Systems of Slavery*, ed. J. Watson, Oxford, 1–15.

1980b, "Transactions in People: The Chinese Market in Slaves, Servants, and Heirs," in *Asian and African Systems of Slavery*, ed. J. Watson, Oxford, 223–50.

Weaver, P. R. C. 1964, "Gaius 1.84 and the S.C. Claudianum," *Classical Review* 78: 137–9.

1972, *Familia Caesaris: A Social Study of the Emperor's Freedmen and Slaves*, Cambridge.

1986, "The Status of Children in Mixed Marriages," in *The Family in Ancient Rome*, ed. B. Rawson, Ithaca, 145–69.

1997, "Children of Junian Latins," in *The Roman Family in Italy: Status, Sentiment, Space*, eds. B. Rawson and P. Weaver, Oxford, 55–72.

Webb, R. 2002, "Female Performers in Late Antiquity," in *Greek and Roman Actors: Aspects of an Ancient Profession*, eds. P. Easterling and E. Hall, Cambridge, 282–303.

2008, *Demons and Dancers: Performance in Late Antiquity*, Cambridge, MA.

Weber, M. 1896, "Die sozialen Gründe des Untergangs der antiken Kultur," in *Die Wahrheit* 6: 57–77; repr. and trans. R. I. Frank, *The Agrarian Sociology of Ancient Civilizations*, London, 387–411.

Webster, J. 2005, "Archaeologies of Slavery and Servitude: Bringing 'New World' Perspectives to Roman Britain," *Journal of Roman Archaeology* 18: 161–79.

2008, "Less Beloved: Roman Archaeology, Slavery and the Failure to Compare," *Archaeological Dialogues* 15: 103–23.

Weiler, I. 2001, "Eine Sklavin wird frei: zur Rolle des Geschlechts bei der Freilassung," in *Fünfzig Jahre Forschungen zur antiken Sklaverei an der Mainzer Akademie, 1950–2000: Miscellanea zum Jubiläum*, eds. H. Bellen and H. Heinen, Stuttgart, 113–32.

2003, *Die Beendigung des Sklavenstatus im Altertum: ein Beitrag zur vergleichenden Sozialgeschichte*, Stuttgart.

Weiß, A. 2004, *Sklave der Stadt: Untersuchungen zur öffentlichen Sklaverei in den Städten des römischen Reiches*, Stuttgart.

Weiss, E. 1921, "Kinderaussetzung," *RE* 11.1: cols. 463–72.

Welborn, L. L. 2005, *Paul, the Fool of Christ: A Study of 1 Corinthians 1–4 in the Comic-philosophic Tradition*, London.

Welwei, K.-W. 2000, *Sub corona vendere: quellenkritische Studien zu Kriegsgefangenschaft und Sklaverei im Rom bis zum Ende des Hannibalkrieges*, Stuttgart.

Westermann, W. 1948, "The *Paramone* as General Service Contract," *Journal of Juristic Papyrology* 2: 9–50.

1955, *The Slave Systems of Greek and Roman Antiquity*, Philadelphia.

White, D., Burton, M., and Brudner, L. 1977, "Entailment Theory and Method: A Cross-Cultural Analysis of the Sexual Division of Labor," *Behavior Science Research* 12: 1–24.

Whittaker, C. R. 1987, "Circe's Pigs: From Slavery to Serfdom in the Later Roman World," in *Classical Slavery*, ed. M. Finley, London, 88–122.

1988, ed. *Pastoral Economies in Classical Antiquity*, Cambridge.

Whittaker, C. R. and Garnsey, P. 1998, "Rural Life in the Later Roman Empire," in *Cambridge Ancient History*[2], vol. 13: *The Late Empire, A.D. 337–425*, eds. A. Cameron and P. Garnsey, Cambridge, 277–311.

Whittaker, C. R. and Grabar, O. 1999, "Slaves," in *Late Antiquity: A Guide to the Postclassical World*, eds. G. W. Bowersock, P. Brown, and O. Grabar, Cambridge, MA, 698–9.

Whittow, M. 1990, "Ruling the Late Roman and Early Byzantine City: A Continuous History," *Past & Present* 129: 3–29.

2009, "Early Medieval Byzantium and the End of the Ancient World," *Journal of Agrarian Change* 9: 143–53.

Wickham, C. 1984, "The Other Transition: From the Ancient World to Feudalism," *Past & Present* 103: 3–36.

1988, "Marx, Sherlock Holmes, and Late Roman Commerce," *Journal of Roman Studies* 78: 183–93.

2005a, *Framing the Early Middle Ages: Europe and the Mediterranean, 400–800*, Oxford.

2005b, "Conclusioni," in *Dopo la fine delle ville: le campagne dal VI al IX secolo. Gavi, 8–10 maggio 2004*, ed. G. Brogiolo, Mantua, 351–7.

Wieacker, F. 1955, *Vulgarismus und Klassizismus im Recht der Spätantike*, Heidelberg.

Wiedemann, T. 1981, *Greek and Roman Slavery*, Baltimore.

1985, "The Regularity of Manumission at Rome," *Classical Quarterly* 35: 162–75.

Wieling, H. 1990, "Die Gesetzgebung Constantins zur Erwerbsfähigkeit der Konkubinenkinder," *AARC* 8: 455–71.

1999, *Corpus der römischen Rechtsquellen zur antiken Sklaverei, vol. 1: Die Begründung des Sklavenstatus nach Ius Gentium und Ius Civile*, Stuttgart.

Wiemken, H. 1972, *Der griechische Mimus: Dokumente zur Geschichte des antiken Volkstheaters*, Bremen.

Wiesner, M. 1986, *Working Women in Renaissance Germany*, New Brunswick.

Wilcken, U. 1920, "Zu den Kaiserreskripten," *Hermes* 55: 1–42.

Wild, J. P. 1970, *Textile Manufacture in the Northern Roman Provinces*, Cambridge.

1994, "Tunic No. 4219: An Archaeological and Historical Perspective," *Riggisberger Berichte* 2: 9–36.

1999, "Textile Manufacture: A Rural Craft?," in *Artisanat et productions artisanales en milieu rural dans les provinces du nord-ouest de l'Empire romain*, ed. M. Polfer, Montagnac, 29–37.

2002, "The Textile Industries of Roman Britain," *Britannia* 22: 1–42.

2003, "The Eastern Mediterranean, 323 BC–AD 350," in *The Cambridge History of Western Textiles*, vol. 1, ed. D. Jenkins, Cambridge, 102–17.

Williams, C. 2010, *Roman Homosexuality*, 2nd edn., Oxford.

Williams, M. 2005, "The Jewish Family in Judaea from Pompey to Hadrian – The Limits of Romanization," in *The Roman Family in the Empire: Rome, Italy, and Beyond*, ed. M. George, Oxford, 159–82.

Williams, W. 1974, "The Libellus Procedure and the Severan Papyri," *Journal of Roman Studies* 64: 86–103.

1980, "The Publication of Imperial Subscripts," *Zeitschrift für Papyrologie und Epigraphik* 40: 283–94.

Willvonseder, R. 1983, "xxv annorum operae," *Zeitschrift der Savigny-Stiftung für Rechtsgeschichte. Romanistiche Abteilung* 100: 533–41.

Wilson, A. 2001a, "Water-mills at Amida: Ammianus Marcellinus 18.8.11," *Classical Quarterly* 51: 231–6.

2001b, "Timgad and Textile Production," in *Economies beyond Agriculture in the Classical World*, eds. D. Mattingly and J. Salmon, New York, 271–96.

2002, "Machines, Power and the Ancient Economy," *Journal of Roman Studies* 92: 1–32.

2003, "The Archaeology of the Roman *fullonica*," *Journal of Roman Archaeology* 16: 442–6.

2004a, "Archaeological Evidence for Textile Production and Dyeing in Roman North Africa," in Purpureae vestes: *Actas del I Symposium Internacional sobre Textiles y Tintes del Mediterráneo en época romana*, Valencia, 155–64.

2004b, "Tuscan Landscapes: Surveying the Albegna Valley," *Journal of Roman Archaeology* 17: 569–76.

Wilson, R. 1990, *Sicily under the Roman Empire: The Archaeology of a Roman Province, 36 BC–AD 535*, Warminster.

2008, "*Vivere in villa*: Rural Residences of the Roman Rich in Italy," *Journal of Roman Archaeology* 21: 479–88.

Wilthelmius, A. 1659, *Diptychon Leodiense ex consulari factum episcopale, et in illud commentarius*, Liège.

Winkler, J. 1990, *The Constraints of Desire: The Anthropology of Sex and Gender in Ancient Greece*, New York.

Wipszycka, E. 1965, *L'industrie textile dans l'Égypte romaine*, Warsaw.

Wolf, J. G. 1991, "Die *manumissio vindicta* und der Freiheitsprozeß: ein Rekonstruktionsversuch," in *Libertas: Grundrechtliche und rechtsstaatliche Gewährungen in Antike und Gegenwart*, eds. O. Behrends and M. Diesselhorst, Ebelsbach, 61–96.

Wolff, H. J. 1945, "The Background of the Post-Classical Legislation on Illegitimacy," *Seminar* 3: 21–45.

1950, "Doctrinal Trends in Postclassical Roman Marriage Law," *Zeitschrift der Savigny-Stiftung für Rechtsgeschichte. Romanistiche Abteilung* 67: 261–319.

Wood, E. 1983, "Agricultural Slavery in Classical Athens," *American Journal of Ancient History* 8: 1–47.

Wood, N. 1988, *Cicero's Social and Political Thought*, Berkeley.

Woolf, G. 2006, "Writing Poverty in Rome," in *Poverty in the Roman World*, eds. M. Atkins and R. Osborne, Cambridge, 83–99.

Wright, G. 1978, *The Political Economy of the Cotton South: Households, Markets, and Wealth in the Nineteenth Century*, New York.

2006, *Slavery and American Economic Development*, Baton Rouge.

Wyatt-Brown, B. 1986, *Honor and Violence in the Old South*, New York.

Young, N. 1990, "The Figure of the Paidagōgos in Art and Literature," *Biblical Archaeologist* 53: 80–6.

Yuge, T. 1982, "Die Gesetze im *Codex Theodosianus* über die eheliche Bindung von freien Frauen mit Sklaven," *Klio* 64: 145–50.

Zachos, G. 2007, "The Interference of the City in the Elateian Manumissions," in *Fear of Slaves, Fear of Enslavement in the Ancient Mediterranean... GIREA, Rethymnon, 4–7 novembre 2004*, ed. A. Serghidou, Besançon, 115–24.

Zelnick-Abramovitz, R. 2005, *Not Wholly Free: The Concept of Manumission and the Status of Manumitted Slaves in the Ancient Greek World*, Boston.

Zetzel, J. 2005, *Marginal Scholarship and Textual Deviance: The Commentarium Cornuti and the Early Scholia on Persius*, London.

Zoz de Biasio, M. G. 1983, "Nota minima sulla tutela dei nuclei familiari servili," in *Studi in onore di Arnaldo Biscardi*, vol. 4, Milan, 537–44.

Zucker, L. 1933, *De Tobia: A Commentary, with an Introduction and Translation*, Washington, DC.

Zuckerman, C. 1998, "Two Reforms of the 370s: Recruiting Soldiers and Senators in the Divided Empire," *Byzantion* 56: 79–139.

Index

cooks, 46, 108, 124, 233, 310, 333
Cooper, Kate, 329
Corinth, 47, 176, 254, 312
Cosmas Indicopleustes, 138
  on Ethiopian slaves, 90
cotton, 63, 64, 71, 77, 225
couriers, 125–7
craftsmen, 64, 121, 160, 177, 196, 220, 225,
    245
  in Palladius, 189
  on Melania's estate, 194
Cremna, 372
Crete, 96, 259, 260
cuckoldry, 204, 255, 335, 336
curial order, 40, 45, 47, 55, 124, 165, 184, 450,
    456, 458
  crisis of, 45, 459
  eastern, 163
curse of Ham, 90, 213
Cyrene, 291
Cyril of Alexandria, 19
  on eunuchs, 339
  on trade in free children, 81
  on wealthy households, 46

Danube river, 85, 277, 380, 475, 479
debt, 155, 193, 268, 309, 333, 404, 414
  bondage, 149
  slaves as collateral on, 268, 382, 394, 405
declamations, 298, 337
defensor civitatis, 53
Delos, 97
Delphi, 374
  manumission records, 244
Dio Chrysostom
  on self-sale, 79
Diocletian, 10, 368, 378–90, 437
  and aristocracy, 450, 456
  classicism of, 363, 398, 403, 406, 423
  on illicit enslavement, 399, 405
  on patron–freedmen relations, 486
  on torture, 383
  on transmission of status, 385
  Price Edict, 61, 77, 128
  rescripts, 359, 364, 369, 397, 409, 450, 467,
    482
diptychs, ivory, 353, 470–1
disease, 71, 74, 297, 497
dispensatores, 125
domestic slavery
  and supervision, 223
  economics of, 101–3
  skilled labor, 112–28
  textile production, 128–35
  unskilled labor, 103–12

domestic sphere
  as female domain, 329
Domitian, 396
Donatism, 183, 195, 278, 490
Dopsch, Alfons, 11
Dossey, Leslie, 232
Duncan-Jones, Richard, 167

Easter
  manumission on, 463, 490
egregii, 450
Egypt, 5, 11, 15, 25, 35, 57, 84, 88, 90, 96, 97, 98,
    100, 107, 135, 139, 150, 172, 199, 244, 245,
    264, 291, 357
  agricultural slavery, 171–6
  availability of documentary evidence, 163
  Byzantine estates, 179
  child sale, 80
  endurance of land leasing, 165
  household slavery, 53–5
  imperial, 58
  population density, 151, 157, 158
  rates of manumission, 244
  tenurial patterns, 164
eleutherai, 174, 282, 291, 306
Engels, Friedrich, 7
Ennodius
  on wine production, 182
enslavement, 27, 78–83, 364, 391–423
entrepreneurs, slaves as, 127
Ephraem the Syrian
  on *alapa*, 468
  on manumission, 490
Epiphanius, 308
epistolography, 126, 267
epitropoi, 121, 122–3
equestrian order, 40, 45, 55, 388, 444, 450, 454,
    456
Essenes, 345
Ethiopians, 88–91, 96
Etruria
  wine industry, 191
eunuchs, 44, 98, 106, 337–40, 437, 505
  as sexual objects, 296
Eutropius, 98, 339, 354
Evans Grubbs, Judith, 426, 427, 432, 439
Expositio totius mundi, 14, 86, 97
eye contact, 332

Fabbrini, Fabrizio, 477
familia Caesaris, 72, 437
familiae rusticae, 41
familiae urbanae, 41, 70, 160
fear, 35, 37, 208, 211, 219, 226, 228, 230, 234,
    235–6, 253, 256, 327, 331, 341, 342

CPSIA information can be obtained
at www.ICGtesting.com
Printed in the USA
LVHW041818270721
693845LV00015B/928